Handbook of Social
Psychophysiology

Wiley PSYCHOPHYSIOLOGY *Handbooks*

Series Editor: Anthony J. Gale
University of Southampton

Handbook of Clinical Psychophysiology:
Edited by Graham Turpin

Handbook of Social Psychophysiology:
Edited by Hugh Wagner and Antony Manstead

Handbook of Social Psychophysiology

Edited by

Hugh Wagner and Antony Manstead

University of Manchester

WILEY

Chichester · New York · Brisbane · Toronto · Singapore

157
W7

Library of Congress Cataloging-in-Publication Data

Handbook of Social Psychophysiology/edited by
   Hugh Wagner and Antony Manstead.
        p.   cm.—(Wiley handbooks of psychophysiology)
     Bibliography: p.
     Includes index.
     ISBN 0 471 91156 9
     1. Emotions—Physiological aspects.   2. Psychobiology.
   I. Wagner, Hugh L.   II. Manstead, A. S. R.   III. Series.
   QP401.B56 1989
   152.4—dc19

                                                    88–20733
                                                        CIP

British Library Cataloguing in Publication Data

Handbook of social psychophysiology.—(Wiley handbooks of psychophysiology).
   1. Man. Emotions. Psychophysiological aspects
   I. Wagner, Hugh   II. Manstead, Antony
   152.4

   ISBN 0 471 91156 9

Phototypesetting by Thomson Press (India) Limited, New Delhi
Printed and bound in Great Britain by Bath Press Ltd, Bath

Handbook of Social Psychophysiology

Contents

Handbook of Social Psychophysiology

List of Contributors

Dennis Barnes, *Department of Psychiatry, University of Texas Southwestern Medical Center, Dallas, Texas, USA.*

Andrew Baum, *Department of Medical Psychology, Uniformed Services University of the Health Sciences, Bethesda, Maryland, USA.*

Ross Buck, *Department of Communication Sciences, University of Connecticut, Storrs, Connecticut, USA.*

Brad J. Bushman, *Department of Psychology, University of Missouri, Columbia, Missouri, USA.*

John T. Cacioppo, *Department of Psychology, Ohio State University, Columbus, Ohio, USA.*

Margaret S. Clark, *Department of Psychology, Carnegie Mellon University, Pittsburgh, Pennsylvania, USA.*

Laura M. Davidson, *Department of Medical Psychology, Uniformed Services University of the Health Sciences, Bethesda, Maryland, USA.*

Paul Ekman, *Human Interaction Laboratory, University of California, San Francisco, California, USA.*

Sherri L. Frederick, *Department of Psychology, University of Oregon, Eugene, Oregon, USA.*

Robert J. Gatchel, *Department of Psychiatry, University of Texas Southwestern Medical Center, Dallas, Texas, USA.*

Russell G. Geen, *Department of Psychology, University of Missouri, Columbia, Missouri, USA.*

Lisa R. Herrick, *Department of Psychology, Catholic University of America, Washington, DC, USA.*

Clifford I. Notarius, *Department of Psychology, Catholic University of America, Washington, DC, USA.*

Jaak Panksepp, *Department of Psychology, Bowling Green State University, Bowling Green, Ohio, USA.*

Kathryn Popp, *Department of Medical Psychology, Uniformed Services University of the Health Sciences, Bethesda, Maryland, USA.*

David L. Rosenhan, *Department of Psychology, Stanford University, Stanford, California, USA.*

Peter Salovey, *Department of Psychology, Yale University, New Haven, Connecticut, USA.*

Klaus R. Scherer, *Department of Psychology, University of Geneva, Geneva, Switzerland.*

Louis G. Tassinary, *Department of Psychology, University of Iowa, Iowa City, Iowa, USA.*

Don M. Tucker, *Department of Psychology, University of Oregon, Eugene, Oregon, USA.*

Hugh Wagner, *Department of Psychology, University of Manchester, Manchester, UK.*

Carol Silvia Weisse, *Department of Medical Psychology, Uniformed Services University of the Health Sciences, Bethesda, Maryland, USA.*

Gail M. Williamson, *Department of Psychology, Carnegie Mellon University, Pittsburgh, Pennsylvania, USA.*

Dolf Zillmann, *Institute for Communication Research, Indiana University, Bloomington, Indiana, USA.*

Series Editor's Foreword

Psychophysiology is still an emerging discipline even though its key journal *Psychophysiology*, published by the Society for Psychophysiological Research, is now in its 25th year. The very complexity of the subject matter of psychophysiology makes theory building particularly hazardous. Even where a theory has sound formal properties, the move to empirical data is rarely straightforward. The inclusion of variables which are easy to justify from a theoretical point of view in no way guarantees that the outcome of an experiment will be easy to interpret, will relate to previous data, or will settle theoretical issues once and for all. Typically, some of the data tell one story, while the remainder offer a puzzle. Psychophysiology, still in its intellectual infancy, suffers from the imperative of being too ambitious.

Psychophysiology seeks to integrate data along a bio-social continuum. It therefore has to tackle several major issues, drawing upon a number of separate, even disparate, approaches or sub-disciplines. Genetic predisposition is recognised as a source of variance both for general characteristics and for individual variations. Inherent biological characteristics are expressed in terms of the biochemistry of the nervous system and its functional organisation. Yet these too are seen to be open to the influence of ontogeny and learning.

The measurement of biological variables has been a major concern in psychophysiology and the development of the minicomputer and then the microcomputer has revolutionised the acquisition and analysis of data. In this sphere, that of measurement, several psychophysiologists have made their mark; one consequence is that there are certain minimal acceptable standards for measurement and for reporting results. Regrettably, many papers in psychophysiological journals still report data which fail to satisfy some of the basic properties of adequate measurement.

While the burden of experimentation and measurement has fallen on the assessment of central and autonomic nervous system variables, psychophysiologists recognise the need to integrate such data with data describing behavior, performance and subjective state. Without reference to observable behavior and subjective experience psychophysiology remains a physiological and not a psychological discipline. It is the measurement of both behavior and experiential state, as well as non-invasive assessment of physiological change, which marks off psychophysiology from its parent discipline, physiological psychology. Yet measurement in these non-physiological domains creates major problems for a systematic scientist to tackle, even when they are taken separately. The notion that the psychophysiologist seeks to *integrate* data derived from such disparate domains of description marks off psychophysiology from most other disciplines of psychology. It imposes a tremendous intellectual burden on the researcher and, of course, upon the theorist.

Given that psychophysiologists employ human subjects as their experimental material, the issues of consciousness, self-regulation and self-control must also be handled. As Porges, Ackles and Truax (1983) point out, there are multiple logical relations between the domains of physiology, behavior, experience and subjective report, and each logical relation, in its turn, creates special difficulties for experimental design, measurement, and the interpretation of data. Gale (1988) has addressed some of the key conceptual and practical issues in psychophysiological research, including a critical evaluation of the ubiquitous and over-utilised concept of arousal and an appraisal of which variables are best suited to which problems.

The *Handbook of Social Psychophysiology* presents a beautiful illustration of both the hazards and the promise of psychophysiology. The editors have chosen to focus on the issues surrounding emotion, its expression, and its interactional and regulatory relationships with social process. The traditional concerns with emotional processes have recently been revived and this vigorous and developing field of research has also led to a resurgence of interest in fundamental psychophysiological problems (Wagner, 1988). In the present volume Hugh Wagner and Antony Manstead have brought together leading authorities in the fields of the biological basis of emotion, the overt expression of emotion and arousal, the influence on physiology of social context, and the integration of physiological response with social interaction. They sample mood states, arousal, aggression and the biological correlates of attitude and prosocial behaviors.

While each of these areas of social psychophysiology sustains a research community in its own right, it is clear that there are implications for all psychophysiological experimental situations. For the psychophysiology experiment is itself a social event, in which subject and experimenter expectations, passing moods and deeper emotions are an inevitable consequence of the world of the laboratory. Emotion is on the hidden agenda of all psychophysiological research. Thus the issues addressed in this volume have twin relevance for both psychophysiological theorising about emotion and psychophysiological research in general.

Other volumes in the Series address overlapping concerns in different spheres of theory and application. Volume 2, edited by Graham Turpin, focuses on the fast growing field of clinical psychophysiology and will be of relevance both to basic researchers as well as clinical practitioners. Volume 3, edited by Richard Shepherd, explores the psychophysiology of human eating and nutritional behavior and will introduce psychophysiologists to new concerns, for the field of human eating has yet to attract the research interest which it clearly deserves. Volume 4, edited by myself and Michael Eysenck, reviews the long-established field of the psychophysiological study of individual differences in personality and intelligence. Finally, Volume 5, edited by Richard Jennings and Michael G. H. Coles, explores central and autonomic nervous system correlates of cognitive processes in a radical fashion, by focusing on processes rather than response systems.

In inviting world authorities in their fields to contribute to the *Wiley Psychophysiology Handbooks* Series we have encouraged them to offer state-of-the-art reviews. We hope that these well-referenced and timely papers will stand as essential sources for both students and advanced researchers. We have focused on depth of approach rather than breadth; thus even within a Series it has been impossible to address all the key issues in each area of concern and the reader should treat the Series as an essential complement to other major volumes (for example, Coles, Donchin and Porges, 1986).

It is clear that psychophysiology raises more questions than answers, but would science be fun if everything were clear-cut? One advantage of uncertainty is that new discoveries are that much sweeter.

ANTHONY GALE

University of Southampton, October 1988

REFERENCES

Coles, M. G. H., Donchin, E., and Porges, S. W. (1986) *Psychophysiology: Systems, Processes, and Applications*. New York: Guilford.
Gale, A. (1988) The psychophysiological context. In: A. Gale, and B. Christie (Eds) *Psychophysiology and the Electronic Workplace*, Chichester: Wiley.
Porges, S. W., Ackles, P. A., and Truax, S. R. (1983) Psychophysiological measurement: methodological constraints. In: A. Gale, and J. A. Edwards (Eds) *Physiological Correlates of Human Behaviour. Volume 1. Basic Issues*. London: Academic Press.
Wagner, H. L. (ed). (1988) *Social Psychophysiology and Emotion: Theory and clinical applications*. Chichester: Wiley.

Preface

There is a long tradition of theory and research on emotions and social processes conducted implicitly or explicitly within a biological framework. This is more obvious in the case of emotions, where a number of long-standing theoretical disputes have centred on issues that are the province of biological psychology. For example, the James–Cannon 'debate' involved (and still involves) the key issues of peripheral versus central processes in the generation of emotions, and of specific physiological states versus general arousal as the substrate of different emotions. Emotions are, most would agree, essentially characterized by experiential factors, yet almost all theorists have recognized their 'biological' nature. This recognition has taken a number of forms. Some have been concerned, as noted above, with the nature of the anatomical structures and/or physiological mechanisms mediating emotional experience and behavior, or with the physiological or endocrinal response to emotional stimuli; others with the phylogenetic origins and the adaptive functions of the emotions; and still others with the innateness of certain 'fundamental' emotions. Another interest has been in the communication of emotions in humans and in other species. Of course, these areas of interest are not mutually exclusive.

The eight chapters in the first three parts of this volume demonstrate this wide range of approaches and problems in the biological psychology of emotions, and each of the issues mentioned above is discussed in at least one chapter. The eight chapters represent key areas in which essentially biological approaches to emotions are of current theoretical importance.

Emotions and social processes are intimately related, since emotions are a central feature of social interaction. Although the contribution of biological psychology to social behaviour may not be readily apparent, it is nevertheless pervasive. The most important contributions are conceptual: concepts of arousal have been used as theoretical constructs in almost every area of social psychology, often with little detailed consideration of the nature of the concept. Less frequently, but increasingly, researchers have turned to psychophysiological techniques in the investigation of social phenomena, or to broader biological contexts in their explanations. The seven chapters in the last two parts of this volume present the current state of research and thinking in those areas of social psychology in which psychophysiological constructs or methods are already prominent, or are likely to play a role in contributing to knowledge.

Our aim has been to produce a volume providing an up-to-date survey of research and thinking in these interrelated areas. This volume is intended to serve as an important research and teaching resource for professionals, postgraduates, and advanced undergraduates in the fields of physiological psychology, psychophysiology, and social psychology. There are many people whom we should thank for helping us to complete this enterprise. We are grateful to Tony Gale, the Series Editor, for inviting us to edit this volume, and to Michael Coombs and Wendy Hudlass at John Wiley for their support at various stages of the project. Above all, however, we would like to thank the chapter authors. The task of producing this book has not been quite as problem-free as we would have liked, but that was not the fault of those whose chapters appear here. We are grateful to them for agreeing to contribute, for being responsive to feedback, and for their patience as the final stages of the book were completed.

HUGH WAGNER, ANTONY MANSTEAD

Manchester, April 1988

PART 1

CENTRAL PROCESSES IN EMOTIONS

Introduction

No matter what one's view of the origins of emotional experience and behaviour, it is clear that the brain must play a central role. It seems sensible, therefore, to start our exploration of the biological psychology of emotions with a consideration of the role of the brain in emotion. In the two chapters in this part of the book we consider the role of the brain from two directions—the predominantly animal-subject approach to subcortical mechanisms in emotion, and the predominantly human-subject approach to cortical processes.

Panksepp (Chapter 1, *The neurobiology of emotions: of animal brains and human feelings*) concentrates on the subcortical mechanisms of emotion. Using a variety of research methods, considerable progress has been made in delineating these circuits and describing the role they play in the control of basic emotional behaviour and experience. The relevance to the understanding of human emotions of the investigation of these neural circuits in other species is based largely on the genetic heritage shared by humans and other mammals. The complexities of human feelings result from the linguistic and cognitive subtleties enabled by greater brain growth. This greater cortical mass appears to provide little by way of additional mechanisms specifically for the elaboration of the basic emotions. Panksepp argues that the influence of the subcortical mechanisms on the information processing of the cortex is greater than the control of the cognitive areas of the cortex over the underlying basic emotion circuits.

Panksepp provides a brief summary of the lines of evidence that support the recognition of five emotive command circuits, corresponding roughly to *foraging–expectancy*, *anger–rage*, *fear–anxiety*, *separation distress–panic*, and *social play–joy*. It is clear that new neuroscience methodologies will lead to a rapid expansion in our understanding of these circuits, and Panksepp signposts some of the likely directions this expansion will take. He also offers some suggestions about the implications of these circuits for an understanding of human emotions and psychiatric conditions, and finishes with speculations about the extent to which neuroscience will ever have much to say about human emotions such as love.

Panksepp's concentration on subcortical mechanisms is complemented by a review of cortical functions in emotions by Tucker and Frederick (Chapter 2, *Emotion and brain lateralization*). While Panksepp asserts that he finds little or no evidence for lateral specialization in subcortical systems, Tucker and Frederick's central task is to demonstrate that the left and right cerebral hemispheres have different roles in the expression, recognition, and experience of emotions. Evidence for this specialization comes from a variety of sources, including laboratory studies on intact humans and studies of patients with various brain lesions. A major controversy in this area concerns the interpretation of lesion evidence. The more widely accepted view is that a lesion in one hemisphere reveals the function or emotional orientation of the intact hemisphere. Tucker and Frederick, in contrast, argue that a lesion may disinhibit the emotional orientation of the damaged hemisphere, and they point to evidence that supports this interpretation.

Another feature of Tucker and Frederick's chapter is their stress on the importance of other cerebral axes in the control of hemispheric specialization and of emotional behaviour. In particular, they review evidence that demonstrates the importance of the anterior–posterior axis, and argue that the complexity of the effects of lesions reflects the complexity of the interactions between the hemispheres, with activation of specific cortical areas being modulated by the frontal lobes via thalamic structures. In this they find evidence for lateralization at the subcortical level, in contrast to Panksepp's conclusion. They also point to another axis that shows specialization, namely the dorsal and ventral pathways that link the sensory areas of the cortex to the limbic system. The functional roles of these two pathways in visual perception, relating to peripheral/spatial perception and object recognition respectively, seem to be paralleled by their roles in emotion. These different roles might relate to the cognitive specializations of the right and left hemispheres, roughly syncretic versus analytic, which forms the basis of emotional specialization.

Chapter 1

The Neurobiology of Emotions: Of Animal Brains and Human Feelings

Jaak Panksepp

Bowling Green State University

ABSTRACT

Recent evidence is summarized concerning the neurobiological nature of brain systems for the elaboration of the primary emotions, which include the foraging–expectancy system, the anger–rage system, the fear–anxiety system, the separation-distress–panic system, and social-play circuitry. The rough outlines of the neuroanatomies and neurochemistries of these systems have been established, and they appear to be the primal substrates from which human affective experiences are generated.

AN HISTORICAL OVERVIEW

The perspective of ancient scholars was that emotions emerge from the body while reason emanates from the brain. The James–Lange theory extended that idea by suggesting that the reasoning brain elaborates emotions via reafferent feedback from peripheral physiological changes which arise from highly aroused behavior patterns. Both viewpoints have proved to be largely incorrect. Modern analysis indicates that emotionality emerges from neural circuits of the visceral brain, which are modulated to some extent by peripheral somatic and autonomic feedbacks (e.g. see Mancia and Zanchetti, 1981; Parkinson, 1985). However,

Handbook of Social Psychophysiology, Edited by H. Wagner and A. Manstead,
© 1989 John Wiley & Sons Ltd

modern neuroscience has also revealed a complex peripheral enteric nervous system (Gershon, 1981) which guides the intrinsic movement of the viscera (whose vast chemistries are widely represented in emotional areas of the brain), leading to many avenues of cross-talk between brain circuits which control affect and viscera. At present, however, we do not know to what extent visceral feelings during emotional states arise directly from sensory inputs from the gut or from intrinsic activities of visceral 'homunculi' in the brain.

While there is no clear evidence that emotionality is caused by peripheral physiological changes, an essential role for brain circuits seems definitive, especially of primitive ventromedial limbic areas of the brain (MacLean, 1973, 1985; Panksepp, 1982, 1985). Both somatic and visceral areas of the brain funnel and blend information through the third layer of MacLean's 'triune' brain—the 'reptilian' basal ganglia—to yield coordinated patterns of motor outflow (Figure 1.1). The dichotomy between visceral and somatic nervous tissue is no mere metaphor, but a distinction affirmed by abundant behavioral, neurophysiological, and neurochemical data (e.g. Figure 1.2). Had the visceral/emotional nervous system been known at the turn of the century, the James—Lange theory may never have been proposed. Rather, the prevailing view may have been that

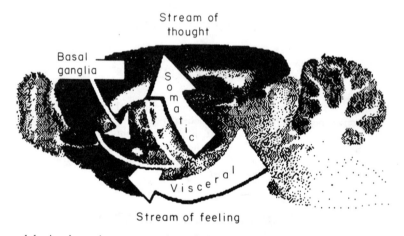

Stream of
thought

Basal
ganglia

Somatic

Visceral

Stream of feeling

Figure 1.1. A schematic representation of visceral and somatic nervous systems on a digitized glutamate receptor map of the rat brain. The dorsal-somatic brain (thalamic–neocortical axis) collects information about the outside world while the ventral-visceral brain (hypothalamic–limbic axis) collects information about the internal world and contains a series of distinct neural systems to elaborate the basic emotions. Both of these systems converge on sensory–motor control programs of basal ganglia to generate behavior in which both somatic and visceral processes are blended. The selection of a glutamate receptor map for this depiction was premised on the fact that this system presently constitutes the best candidate as a primary substrate of memory (as theorized by Lynch and Baudry, 1984).

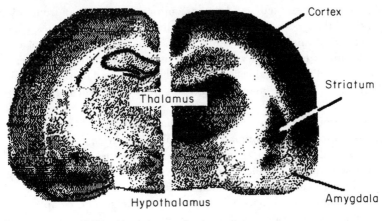

Figure 1.2. Two computer digitized coronal views of the rat brain which highlight a major biochemical distinction between somatic and visceral brains. On the left, a hemisection is stained for cell bodies, and the darkness of the various brain areas represents overall cell densities. On the right, the same brain processed for ^{14}C-2-deoxy-D-glucose autoradiography, and the darkness is related to overall amount of metabolic processing which is related largely to total amounts of neural activity. Clearly, the thalamic–neocortical axis contains no more cells than the hypothalamic–limbic axis, but overall neuronal firing is much higher. There are many other anatomical, physiological, and biochemical distinctions between visceral and somatic nervous systems which clearly indicate that the dichotomy between the 'thinking' and 'feeling' parts of the brain is fundamental and not just a poetic metaphor.

affective states can be instigated by various sensory and perceptual inputs to subcortical emotive circuits, including those arising from certain higher brain processes (explaining how cognitions come to evoke affective experiences).

ON THE PSYCHOBIOLOGICAL STUDY OF EMOTIONS

Basic emotions will eventually be understood as concrete circuit entities in the brain, having distinct anatomies and neurochemistries. Hence, a general definition of 'emotion' must be based, in part, on the characteristics of the underlying brain circuits. For instance, primary emotive circuits may share many common features (e.g. they may be constituted of long-axoned, trans-diencephalic, sensory–motor command systems that bring behavior, autonomic/hormonal processes, and dynamic subjective feeling states into rapid coherence). Our experimental work is based on the assumption that primary emotive circuits are essentially similar in all mammals (Panksepp, 1982), and that human emotional complexities arise more from non-emotive cortical potentials which generate linguistic/cognitive subtleties and diverse cultural histories than from any major differences in the types of brain circuits which mediate affective states. Hence, the psychobiological analysis of the animal brain may effectively reveal the basic nature of human emotionality, permitting us to sift the biologically permanent from the culturally changeable facets of emotionality—and thereby help distinguish the universals of the mammalian brain from the particulars of individual species.

And why should one believe that the animal brain can tell us such a great deal about the basic nature of human emotionality? In brief, the nucleus of every mammalian cell, whether of man or mouse, contains the same amount of DNA. Comparable numbers of proteins are expressed from this massively shared genetic heritage in all mammals. The higher primates and the cetacians are not exceptional among mammals, with respect to their genetic complexity. Their mental uniqueness arises not from any intrinsic complexity of their genetic libraries, but rather from their relatively unrestrained higher-brain growth, which could have been instigated via modest changes in regulatory genes which control the speed and degree of cortical expansion. To the best of our knowledge, the vestment of cortical complexity in highly cerebrated species provides little new circuitry for the elaboration of basic emotional tendencies (although it surely contributes new special-purpose perceptual and cognitive processes for the accessing, as well as inhibition, of emotional circuits).

In short, it presently seems that the basic emotions are constituted of primitive, genetically prewired circuit entities of the visceral brain (and related somatic areas such as the dorsomedial thalamus)—circuits which appear to influence information processing in higher cognitive areas of the cortex. By comparison, those higher cognitive areas have only modest control over the underlying emotive circuits, although the ability of cognitive processes to instigate everyday feelings cannot be denied. In computer parlance, emotive circuits may be similar to the operating system/read-only-memory (ROM) functions which govern information processing within random access memory (RAM space). Through such a conception, the biological and cognitive perspectives to emotions can be blended into a coherent whole. In my estimation, the key to a general solution to the puzzle of primary-process emotionality is the specification of how the emotional ROMs are organized in the brain.

My aim for the rest of this chapter is to provide an update on selected recent developments in understanding brain systems that mediate the basic emotions of anger (rage), anxiety (fear), hope (expectancy), sorrow (panic) and play (joy). I will not reiterate materials I have reviewed elsewhere (Panksepp, 1981a, b, 1982, 1985, 1986a, b, 1988), nor will I cover the extensive neurological work recently summarized in the *Biological Foundations of Emotion*, edited by Plutchik and Kellerman (1986). Although emotive ROMs impose executive coordination over a variety of brain and bodily processes, because of space limitations and coverage elsewhere in this volume, I will not cover peripheral physiological, hormonal, and behavioral changes, but will focus on central mechanisms.

EXECUTIVE EMOTIVE CIRCUITS OF THE BRAIN

There is presently adequate evidence for the existence of four or five emotive command circuits in the brain. Since the semantic labeling of such circuits with affective terms is surely problematic, I usually refer to them with multiple labels. They are: (1) the foraging–expectancy–curiosity–investigatory system, (2) the anger–rage circuit, (3) the anxiety–fear circuit, (4) the separation–distress–sorrow–anguish–panic network, and presently I would also include (5) social-play circuitry as a primal emotive system. Play circuitry may be a major source of joy in the brain and a primal force in the development of courage, social dominance, and sociosexual competence. I do not include other common human feelings which appear in modern 'human' taxonomies—such as acceptance, disgust, contempt, shame, and surprise—in the primal list for two reasons: (1) There is as yet no evidence that those processes are mediated by the types of executive systems envisaged herein, and (2) if those affects are included as basic emotions, it is not clear how the vast array of other human feelings (e.g. guilt, envy, jealousy, lust, hunger, thirst, cold, pain, boredom, frustration, etc.) can be logically excluded. In short, the concept of basic emotion is best restricted to those genetically ordained brain systems which appear to be constructed on a command system design.

NEUROANATOMIES AND NEUROCHEMISTRIES

The neuroanatomy and neurochemistry of no emotive system has yet been resolved definitively, although existing evidence is summarized in Table 1.1. Our ignorance is understandable, for powerful neuroscience methodologies by which the biological issues could be detailed have become available only recently. Simple techniques for antereograde and retrograde tracing of circuits (with autoradiography of radioactive amino acids and high-resolution histofluorochemical procedures, respectively) and neurochemical and functional characterization of systems with metabolic imaging (e.g. see Figure 1.2) and immunocytochemistry (Figure 1.3) are now generally available. Accordingly, the next few decades could yield a revolution in the visualization of emotive circuits, especially at the neurochemical level (e.g. that depicted in Figure 1.3). However, functional ideas will remain hard to test directly unless ways are developed to manipulate the individual circuits, such as the neurotoxins which exist for selective destruction of the 'classic' neurochemical systems of the brain (Jonsson, 1980). Ways to manipulate the new peptide systems remain coarse at present, but promising immunological probes are on the horizon (Panksepp, 1986c).

It is unlikely that any basic emotion is organized simply around a *single* command transmitter, but each system is likely to have key ones. Preliminary results indicate that powerful affective changes can be elicited by administration of several peptides into the brain. For instance, central administration of both corticotropin releasing factor (CRF) and growth-hormone–release-hormone

Table 1.1. Major brain areas involved in the instigation of the primary emotions, and putative major transmitters which facilitate each emotion. Each system is also modulated by nonspecific excitatory and inhibitory transmitters such as norepinephrine, serotonin, and GABA (not indicated). Acetylcholine seems to participate in a positive and probably specific way in each of the primary emotions. Because of space limitations, I have not attempted to fully document the suggestions made herein, but many pertinent references can be obtained from my past reviews cited at the end of this chapter.

Emotive system	Putative brain areas involved	Proposed excitatory neurotransmitters
Expectation	Ventral tegmental area	Dopamine
	Lateral hypothalamus	Neurotensin
	Basal forebrain	Acetylcholine
	Frontal cortex	Opioids
Anger–rage	Central gray	Acetylcholine
	Medial hypothalamus	Glutamate
	Medial amygdala	
Anxiety–fear	Central gray	Acetylcholine
	Ventro-lateral hypothalmus	Glutamate
	Central amygdala nucleus	Diazepam Binding
	Lateral temporal lobe	Inhibitor (DBI)
Grief–panic	Dorsal mesencephalon	Acetylcholine
	Dorsomedial thalamus	Glutamate
	Bed nucleus of stria terminalis	Corticotropin release
	Ventral septal/preoptic area	factor (CRF)
	Anterior cingulate area	ACTH/MSH peptides
Play–joy	Ventral tegmental area	Dopamine
	Parafascicular area	Opioids
	Parietal cortex	Acetylcholine

(GH-RH) produce prolonged, excited locomotion in rats (Britton, Koob, Rivier, and Vale, 1982; Tannenbaum, 1984). From our own recent work, to be described later, CRF appears to be a command transmitter in the separation distress–panic system. It is tempting to speculate that all basic emotions have command peptides within their executive structures, but pertinent behavioral data remain scarce. However, one general principle (of some aesthetic appeal), is that the central functions of neuropeptides are typically congruent with their known peripheral functions (Panksepp, 1986c). That could be a source of many fruitful hypotheses. For example, on the basis of the epidermal camouflage functions of melanocyte stimulating hormone (MSH), one might predict that alpha-MSH in the brain mediates cautious, hiding, and defensive types of psychobehavioral tendencies. Highly specific peptide coding of neurobehavioral processes, including emotions, may well exist, and new findings may lead to credible peptide 'phrenologies' in the near future.

While the cornucopia of peptides being revealed in the brain will provide vast

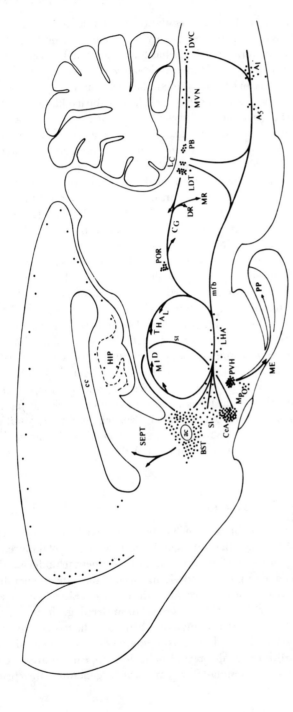

Figure 1.3. A saggital depiction of corticotropin releasing factor-(CRF-) containing neural systems in the rat brain according to Swanson, Sawchenko, Rivier, and Vale (1983). For anatomical designations, consult the original article. Dots indicate cell bodies; while major fiber systems are indicated by solid lines. Not only does this system represent the type of trajectory which has the necessary characteristics to be a core sensory/motor command system for the emotions (as suggested previously; e.g., Figure 3 in Panksepp, 1982), but CRF circuitry almost perfectly overlaps areas of the brain from which separation-like distress-vocalizations can be elicited with localized electrical stimulation. This figure has been reprinted with the permission of the first author and the publisher (Karger, Basel).

new possibilities for understanding the regulation of emotionality (as well as related autonomic and cognitive processes), many of the older neurochemistries of the brain, from which behavioral specificity has long been sought, seem only to have nonspecific effects on behavior and emotionality (Panksepp, 1986c). For instance, the possibility was once entertained that serotonin may specifically mediate anxiety, but this concept has been demolished by the likelihood that high serotonin activity in brain generally reduces all behaviors: data once taken as evidence for serotonin mediation of anxiety (i.e. that the amine could intensify punished behavior) turned out to reflect a mere increase in general behavioral inhibition (see Soubrié, 1986, and accompanying commentaries). Indeed, electrical stimulation of serotonin neurons of the dorsal raphe suppresses fear-like escape induced by stimulation of either dorsal central gray or medial hypothalamus (Schmitt, Sandner, Colpaert and DeWitte, 1983). Thus, the heightened activity of raphe neurons in animals which are confronted by fearful situations (Walletschek and Raab, 1982) may simply reflect auto-regulatory serotonergic processes which help maintain neural homeostasis during emotional stress.

Likewise, norepinephrine activity from the locus coeruleus has been viewed as a potential key to understanding anxiety (Redmond and Huang, 1979), but the more likely possibility is that the attention provoking effects of this system (Foote, Bloom, and Aston-Jones, 1983) only intensify fearful behaviors when the animal is already in an anxiety provoking situation. At best, this system participates in nonspecific aspects of stress. Certainly elimination of this system does not reduce separation anxiety, nor does it eliminate the ability of drugs such as clonidine and morphine to reduce separation distress (Rossi, Sahley, and Panksepp, 1983). Likewise, electrical stimulation of the locus coeruleus in humans yields 'no anxiety or other mental discomfort or disturbance' (Libet, Feinstein, and Gleason, 1986). Although many key neural issues remain to be addressed empirically, the next five sections summarize selected recent work on each of the primal emotive systems outlined above.

The Foraging–Expectancy System

Detailed evidence concerning this system has been reviewed previously (Panksepp, 1981a, 1986a). We assume that much of the vast storehouse of data related to self-stimulation along the medial forebrain bundle is pertinent to understanding this system, and it is assumed that the underlying circuits mediate a generalized aspect of appetitive behavior. For instance, all of the diverse positively motivated behaviors exhibited by animals (e.g. thermoregulation, feeding, drinking, salt-appetite, hoarding, predation, sexuality, maternal behavior, shelter-seeking) seem to be effected, to a substantial extent, by a common emotive brain circuit. The command impulse for all these goal-directed behaviors appears to arise from a shared foraging–expectancy command system which generates the primal tendency for an animal to move from where it is to where it must be to acquire materials needed for survival (Panksepp, 1971, 1981a, 1982, 1986a). It is generally believed that the study of this system is very pertinent to understanding subjective states such as pleasure and joy, but relatively little with regard to analysis of such internal states can be achieved in animals.

One straightforward behavioral assay for activity in this emotive system (at least in rats) is the generation of sniffing by electrical stimulation of the lateral hypothalamus. Such sniffing can be evoked even under anesthesia, and can serve as an accurate predictor of subsequent self-stimulation tendencies. Current thresholds for evocation of sniffing and self-stimultion are highly correlated (approx. 0.90) (Rossi and Panksepp, 1983), and the data also suggested that sniffing is the more 'basic' function of this system since it is routinely obtained at lower current thresholds than self-stimulation at the same site.

While there is a great deal of evidence that a key ingredient in self-stimulation foraging exploratory/curiosity behaviors is brain dopamine activity (see Wise (1982), and accompanying commentaries), the rate of electrically elicited sniffing is not reduced markedly by dopamine receptor blockade, although spontaneous exploratory sniffing can be markedly attenuated by neuroleptics. Pharmacological manipulation of transmitter systems has in no case yet been found to reduce robustly the rate of electrically evoked sniffing. Accordingly, the command structure for foraging–expectancy, though constituted partially of mesolimbic dopamine activity, includes transmitters which remain to be identified.

Although ventral tegmental dopamine cells appear to be at the heart of the foraging–expectancy system, it is noteworthy how many other transmitters, especially peptides, converge on this area (Palkovits and Brownstein, 1985). Dopamine interactions with cholecystokinin, enkephalin, neurotensin, substance P, and substance K have recently been reviewed (Kalivas, 1985), and the various discrete motivations may access this generalized emotive system via these various synaptic chemistries.

In humans, a psychological correlate of activity in this emotional system is considered to be anticipatory eagerness, an insistent curiosity, and highly engaged interest in, and desire for, positive goal-directed activities. The system is envisioned to mediate the heightened feeling of expectation and anticipation when positive rewards and incentives are available in a situation. The system helps elaborate plans and associated memories, and excessive activity within this circuit seems to yield acute schizophrenic symptoms. Self-stimulation along this system presently appears to be a fine animal model for acute schizophrenia, although it has not been widely used in that way. From a psychophysiological perspective, the autonomic correlates of this emotion, as well as the other primary emotions, may be best determined by direct electrical and chemical stimulation of the underlying command systems (although circuit proximities will pose many interpretive problems).

The Anger–Rage System

The anger–rage circuit has been well characterized with retrograde and antereograde neural mapping, as well as via metabolic imaging techniques (Fuchs, Edinger, and Siegel, 1985a, b; Watson, Troiano, Poulakos, Weiner, Block and Siegel, 1983); the main results are summarized in Table 1.1. Quiet-biting attack and rage circuits are modulated by separate mesencephalic controls; predatory attack is promoted by activation of the lateral tegmentum, while affective defense is promoted by activation of medial zones (Shaikh, Brutus, Siegel, and Siegel, 1985). Parenthetically, within the present theoretical context, feline 'quiet-biting' predatory attack is considered to be largely a species-typical expression of a cat's foraging–expectancy circuit. Another problem in evaluating results in the field of 'stimulus-bound' aggression is that brain stimulation commonly elicits a 'defensive' form of aggression which may be largely a consequence of mixed activation of nearby rage and fear command systems. The two systems appear to interdigitate throughout the neuroaxis.

With respect to neurochemical influences, recent work continues to affirm the importance of ACh in organizing the rage response, with agonists like carbachol facilitating (Brudzynski, Kielczykowska, and Romaniuk, 1982), and muscarinic antagonists reducing rage/defense (Baker, Hosko, Rutt, and McGrath, 1960; Romaniuk, Brudzynski, and Gronska, 1973). Affective attack, provoked by electrical stimulation of the hypothalamus, is also reduced, perhaps nonspecifically, with alcohol (Johansson, Huhtala, and Kaakso, 1984). Selective reductions may be achieved with new drugs, such as DU27716, whose neurochemical effects remain ambiguous (van der Poel, Olivier, Mos, Kruk, Meelis, and vanAken, 1982). Recent pharmacological data in the area of aggression is thoroughly summarized in a recent volume (Olivier, Mos, and Brain, 1987), and hence, will not be detailed here.

The Fear–Anxiety System

Although there is a vast amount of literature on anxiety (e.g. Tuma and Maser, 1985), no consensus yet exists concerning the nature of the underlying neurological circuits (see Gray, 1982). The position of a few investigators is that the diencephalic fear/flight circuits are the basic substrates. The anatomy of this system has recently been analyzed using modern anatomical techniques (Fuchs and Siegel, 1984). It is represented in anterior hypothalamic, medial preoptic regions and dorsomedial hypothalamus, with strong rostal connections to bed nucleus of stria terminalis and amygdala, and descending connections to the centrum medianum–parafascicular complex, down through the dorsal part of midbrain central gray. Brain stimulation studies have further clarified interactions in this fear circuit. Central gray fear sites can be driven from hypothalamic sites (Sandner, Schmitt, and Karli, 1982), and lesions downstream (e.g. in central gray) reduce the aversiveness of stimulation upstream (Sandner, Schmitt, and Karli, 1985). As might be anticipated from straightforward psychological considerations, the intensity of such negative affective states is ameliorated by activation of positive expectancy systems in ventral tegmentum and lateral hypothalamus (Schmitt and Karli, 1984; Moreau, Schmitt, and Karli, 1986).

Alcohol, the time-honored anti-anxiety agent, reduces fear partially by actions on circuitry in the central gray (Bovier, Broekkamp, and Lloyd, 1984), and a potential mechanism of action has been revealed by the discovery of drugs which can prevent the behavioral effects of alcohol through GABA receptor coupled chloride channel control (Suzdak, Glowa, Crawley, Schwartz, Skolnick, and Paul, 1986). Benzodiazepines also reduce anxiety by facilitation of GABA activity (Tallman and Gallager, 1985). The ability of benzodiazepines to reduce hypothalamic fear responses has been known for some time (Olds, Hogberg, and Olds, 1964; Panksepp, Gandelman, and Trowill, 1970), and similar actions have now been confirmed within downstream representations of the fear system in the central gray (Bovier, Broekkamp, and Lloyd, 1982; Brandao, de Aguiar, and Graeff, 1982; Moriyama, Ichimaru, and Gomita, 1984; Schenberg and Graeff, 1978). Blockade of GABA receptors and GABA synthesis in both central gray and medial hypothalamus intensifies fear (Brandao, de Aguiar, and Graeff, 1982; Brandao, DiScala, Bouchet, and Schmitt, 1986), providing further support for GABA-convergent anti-anxiety mechanisms in the brain.

Still, it should be noted that GABA may be a generalized inhibitor for all emotive activities. GABA is present throughout the brain (Mugnani and Oertel, 1985) and seems to exert broad inhibitory effects on practically all behaviors. Why placement of GABA agonists into the brain can promote certain forms of aggression (DePaulis and Vergnes, 1985) appears puzzling; but, such effects could be due to facilitation of the neural underpinnings of excessive confidence (e.g. reduced fear).

Morphine also reduces the aversive intensity of central gray stimulation (Jenck, Schmitt, and Karli, 1983; Moreau, Schmitt, and Karli, 1985; Schenk, Williams, Coupal, and Shizgal, 1980) while naloxone intensifies it (Sasson and Kornetsky, 1983). Whether benzodiazepine/GABA and morphine act on the same aversive substrates in the central gray must await further research.

A notable recent discovery is the provisional identification of a peptide which competes with benzodiazepine binding sites [i.e. diazepam binding inhibitor (DBI)], which may be a central trigger for fear (Ferrero, Guidotti, Conti-Tronconi, and Costa, 1984). It is also noteworthy that centrally administered curare and carbachol can precipitate intense flight (Brudzynski, Gronska, and Romaniuk, 1973; Buccafusco and Brezenoff, 1980; Panksepp *et al.*, 1983) suggesting a key function for curariform and or nicotinic ACh receptors in the genesis of fear. Considering the role of this transmitter in rage, behavioral specificity could be achieved if anger is mediated by muscarinic synapses while fear is elaborated via other ACh receptors. Excitatory amino acids applied to the above circuits also trigger behavioral indicants of apparent fear, including explosive flight and freezing (Bandler, DePaulis and Vergnes, 1985).

Telencephalic elaboration of anxiety emerges largely from the amygdala and surrounding temporal lobes tissue. The central nucleus of the amygdala appears essential for fear elaboration (e.g. Bolhuis, Fitzgerald, Dijk, and Koolhass, 1984; Hitchcock and Davis, 1986; Jellestad, Markowska, Bakke, and Walther, 1986; Riolobos, 1986), and it may be the gateway for the long-axoned descending command circuit for fear (Hopkins and Holstege, 1978).

To what extent the fear–flight circuits of the brain actually mediate conditional fear responses such as freezing remains to be clarified. It is possible that such conditional responses could be sustained without the ongoing operation of flight circuitry. This issue is highlighted by one novel approach to mapping fear in the brain by measurement of local brain-evoked responses to danger cues (Irisawa and Iwasaki, 1986). While hypothalamic and dorsomedial thalamic areas respond rapidly to danger, the central gray does not, suggesting the functions of that area are below the level of psychic awareness—a conclusion which is difficult to reconcile with the fact that stimulation near the central gray can provoke very frightening subjective feelings in humans (e.g. Amano *et al.* 1979). Irisawa and Iwasaki's (1986) analysis suggests that the perception of fear may be initiated in the frontal lobes, a finding that seems at odds with the fact that medial prefrontal damage powerfully reduces fearfulness in rats (Holson, 1986). Clearly, more work on both the unconditional and conditional aspects of brain control of fear is needed for definitive conclusions.

The Separation-Distress–Panic System for Social Affect

The localization of this system has been guided by identification of brain areas which mediate separation induced distress vocalizations (DVs) (for summary, see Table 1.1). Endogenous opioids were the first neurochemical controls in this circuit to be identified. The prediction that opioid activity would quell activity in separation distress circuits was based on a straightforward analogy between social and narcotic dependence. This analogy harbored a homology,and highlights how psychological and neural perspectives can be theoretically blended. The evidence for this idea is summarized elsewhere (Panksepp, Herman, Vilberg, Bishop, and DeEskinazi, 1980; Panksepp, 1981b, c, 1986; Panksepp, Siviy, and Normansell, 1985). Details regarding the subcortical vocalization machinery of the vertebrate brain have also been summarized recently (Newman, 1988; Panksepp, Herman, Bishop, Normansell, and Crepeau, 1988). The CRF system of the brain (Figure 1.3), in addition to being the potential mediator of generalized stress (Swanson, Sawchenko, Rivier, and Vale, 1983), may also specifically trigger separation-distress–panic responses. CRF, centrally applied to the fourth ventricle region, yields a robust activation of crying in domestic chicks, and is especially powerful in reducing the comforting effects of other chicks as well as the test animals' own mirrored reflections (Panksepp, Crepeau, and Clynes 1987). CRF-treated animals also actively seek a central position in the flock as if needing more security.

The distribution of the CRF system (Figure 1.3) nicely highlights the type of neural trajectories which has previously been envisaged for emotive command systems (e.g. Panksepp, 1982, Figure 1.3). However, other 'executive chemistries' will surely be involved in the overall circuit design. Additional candidates have emerged from our attempts to identify central neurochemical manipulations which activate distress vocalizations. While most neuropharmaceuticals have little effect on the response, the few that increase it (such as opioid, serotonin, and muscarinic acetylcholine receptor antagonists) do so via modulatory, as opposed to 'command', influences (Panksepp, Meeker, and Bean, 1980; Panksepp, Bean, Bishop, Vilberg, and Sahley, 1980). However, two types of drugs placed intraventricularly do drive vocalizations: curariform agents activate concurrent fixed-action patterns of fear (vigorous flight with repetitive head scanning) and panic (separation type DVs). Similar patterns of emotional agitation can be evoked with drugs that activate glutamate receptors of the kainate variety (for review, see Panksepp, Herman, Bishop, Nomansell, and Crepeau 1988). These data suggest that glutamic acid (via a kainate receptor) and acetylcholine (operating perhaps through a distinct type of curariform receptor) may be important excitatory influences within the command circuitry for separation distress–panic. We think this brain system constitutes the primary process neural substrates for human sadness, sorrow, and grief. We believe that the further study of this system may shed light on a variety of psychiatric conditions including autism (Panksepp and Sahley, 1987), panic attacks, obsessive–compulsive disorders, social phobias, shyness, and post-traumatic stress disorders.

The Social-Play (Joy?) Circuit

The psychobiological analysis of play was non-existent a decade ago. Now, because of the willingness of psychobiological investigators to pursue more subtle intervening processes in the nervous system, we have some sketchy ideas of how ludic processes are elaborated in the brain (for reviews see Meaney, Stewart, and Beatty, 1985; Panksepp, Siviy, and Normansell, 1984; Thor and Holloway, 1984). As for all other emotive systems, the executive command structure for play is subcortically organized (Murphey, MacLean, and Hamilton, 1981; Normansell and Panksepp, 1984). A great number of pharmacological manipulations can modify play (for review, see Panksepp, Normansell, Cox, Crepeau, and Sacks, 1987), but most effects may be rather meaningless, merely indicating the many nonspecific ways one can disrupt highly coordinated behaviors. The pharmacological data do suggest, however, that brain opioid, dopamine and acetylcholine systems may specifically facilitate play (Panksepp, Siviy, and Nomansell, 1984; Panksepp, Crepeau, and Clynes, 1987). Conversely, all drugs which precipitate negative emotions and moods probably disrupt play. To highlight this, in our first attempt to modify central neurochemistries directly in a play study, we observed that intracranial CRF (injected into the third ventricle region in doses of 0.2 μg and above) eliminated the social play of rats (Panksepp, Crepeau, and Clynes, 1987).

The approximate location of neural circuits for play must presently be estimated from lesion data. Play circuitry is controlled powerfully by somatosensory systems (Siviy and Panksepp, 1987a), and the executive circuits for play appear to pass through nonspecific mesencephalic and diencephalic projection areas for somatosensory circuits, namely the parafascicular and posterior thalamic areas (Siviy and Panksepp, 1985, 1987b). Although such estimates are coarse, when the neural circuitries have been worked out in detail, they may well highlight the brain sources for much of human joy.

HIGHER-BRAIN SYSTEMS AND FEELING STATES

If emotional systems were as vital for the survival and well-being of animals during early mammalian evolution as is commonly believed, then it is likely that higher-brain evolution was severely constrained by the dictates of those systems. Indeed, many higher-brain mechanisms may have evolved to provide subtle perceptual control over emotional processes. Various decision-making mechanisms for modulating activities in subcortical emotional command circuitry may exist in more recently evolved cortical areas. For instance, the temporal lobe is one brain area where perceptions instigate emotional tendencies, especially anger and fear (for six diverse reviews of relevant work see the chapters by MacLean; Rolls; Frank and Ervin; Kling; Aggleton and Mishkin; and Fonberg; in Plutchik and Kellerman, 1986).

Although we know little at the cortical level with respect to specific emotions, the psychosurgery literature from the middle part of this century suggests that each of the primal emotions has specialized paleocortical areas which mediate higher decision-making processes related to emotionality (for a review, see Panksepp, 1985). Estimates of where these higher emotional 'centers of gravity' may be concentrated are summarized in Figure 1.4, and include anterior cingulate areas for control of social emotions, frontal cortical and basal forebrain areas for elaboration of positive expectancies, lateral temporal and central amygdal regions for elaboration of fear, and medial temporal and amygdala regions for elaboration of anger–rage. To round out the picture, superior temporal and mid-parietal regions, because of their somatosensory-auditory/body-image functions, are postulated as higher repositories for elaboration of play–joy processes. These brain areas may, with accruing life experiences of each animal, serve functions similar to programmable read-only-memories (PROMs) of modern special purpose computers. Such higher levels of emotional processing may provide the subtle textures to human emotional feelings which have evolved from the more basic command

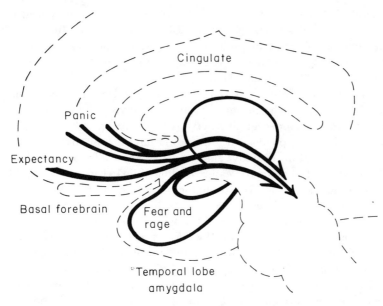

Figure 1.4. A schematic diagram of the approximate higher brain areas which elaborate the basic emotions. Each basic emotive command system appears to have higher 'spheres of influence' which probably help instigate the perceptual aspects of the various emotions as well as intrinsic second-order emotive processes related to specific cognitive/affective strategies which are promoted by each type of emotion. The rationale for localizing the systems in this manner are summarized more fully in Panksepp (1985, 1986).

circuits. For instance, various social emotions related to loss of companionship and support—such as grieving, shame, guilt, and jealousy—may be controlled by median limbic cortex which is coextensive with the anterior cingulate area (i.e. the higher representations of the 'panic' system). See MacLean (1985) and Panksepp (1986c) for further discussion of these issues.

And how do the other, more subtle, human emotions emerge from brain activities. Where is love to be found in this tangled skein (Liebowitz, 1985)? Will neuroscience ever have much of substance to say about that? Is it an opioid addiction, a powerful stimulant, a reducer of grieving, activity within a joy–play circuit, a flow of activity through all the dynamically interactive emotive circuits of the brain . . . a cortical construct based on certain cognitive decisions? We do not yet know, but in our theorizing we should take everyday observations as well as folk-tales, passed down through generations, as important sources of idea. To be 'broken-hearted' after the severance of love may not be a mere metaphor, but a reflection of powerful tides of neural influence through the cardio-visceral projection areas of the emotional brain. It is only through the empirical evaluation of such theoretical notions that substantive knowledge of basic emotional processes can emerge. For instance, the loss of a loved one can apparently lead to life-threatening ventricular arrythmias (Reich, DeSilva, Lown, and Murawski, 1981), and the analysis of the relationships between brain, emotions, immunity, and health is beginning to yield major insights into the sources of many illnesses (for a recent review, see Melnechuk, 1988).

Conversely, insight into the governance of psychological processes may be promoted if we acknowledge the intrinsic power of the visceral–emotional nervous system over the somatic–cognitive nervous system (Figure 1.1). Human tendencies to think and ponder may be powerfully channeled by activities of emotional circuits. Many cognitive abilities may reflect evolutionary elaborations which were guided by emotive demands, leading ultimately to a variety of higher-order operating systems that constitute the more subtle human sentiments.

Finally, I would share a few thoughts regarding the topic of the next chapter. Hemispheric specialization (Figure 1.5) probably operates more on the higher-order perceptual/communicative and PROM side of emotions than on genetically ordained affective/fixed-action pattern/autonomic ROM impulses which, at least from my personal research, appear to be quite symmetrically organized subcortically: in several tests with right vs left decortications we have observed no differences in the social play of rats nor in the courting vocalization of male guinea-pigs. Likewise, in our hands, right vs left hemispherectomy has not differentially modified separation-induced distress vocalizations of domestic chicks (Panksepp, unpublished data). Although our attempts to find emotional

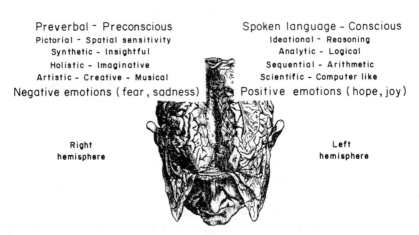

Preverbal – Preconscious
Pictorial – Spatial sensitivity
Synthetic – Insightful
Holistic – Imaginative
Artistic – Creative – Musical
Negative emotions (fear, sadness)

Spoken language – Conscious
Ideational – Reasoning
Analytic – Logical
Sequential – Arithmetic
Scientific – Computer like
Positive emotions (hope, joy)

Right
hemisphere

Left
hemisphere

Figure 1.5. A summary of hemispheric functions in the governance of emotionality and other functions, as depicted in an illustration from *De Fabrica* (1543) by Andreas Vesalius which reveals the corpus callosum joining the two hemispheres. Although in humans it is much easier to analyze the role of the cerebral hemispheres in governance of emotionality than it is to analyze the role of the subcortical areas, it should be remembered that the main psychic 'energies' for the various emotions emerge from the hidden ventral-visceral brain rather than from the more accessible dorsal-somatic brain (see also Figures 1.1 and 1.2).

lateralization effects following massive ablations of each of the cerebral hemispheres has not been successful, there is abundant evidence for the lateralization of a variety of behavioral functions in animals (Denenberg, 1983; Glick, 1985), as well as for very basic functions such as neuroendocrine controls (Gerendai, 1984) and sympathetic inputs to the heart during emotional arousal (Lane and Schwartz, 1987). Clearly, more work on the subcortical issues is indicated.

Although there are a variety of mechanisms which could explain cerebral laterality of emotionality (see Chapter 2), we may never know the evolutionary pressures which led to such specializations. One intriguing idea is that it may have been guided by an important preexisting biological laterality, perhaps the fact that the heart is positioned in the left side of the body. If there was a selective survival advantage to defending the left (cardiac) side of the body more than the right, then the right hemisphere may have become a specialist in defensive perceptual attitudes (for fear and panic). The defensiveness of the right cerebral hemisphere may have encouraged the right hand to emerge as the more likely manipulator of the world (for hunting, gathering, and attack). If language evolved for symbolic representation of the outside world, it should have come to be coordinated with right hand functions, and hence, the left hemisphere could have become the natural home for linguistic functions. Further, since outwardly directed activities such as foraging, hunting, and play are positive life-supporting activities, their expressions should have been accompanied by positive mood states, providing a natural disposition for positive emotionality to sprout more abundantly in the left hemisphere. Although such distal evolutionary explanations must remain in the realm of camp-fire stories, they may encourage the search for hemispheric neural asymmetries in higher emotive circuits of the human brain (e.g. Figure 1.4). At present, though, anatomical, neurochemical, and functional characterization of the subcortical emotive systems in the brains of 'lower' mammals remains the more workable task in the area.

REFERENCES

Amano, K., Notani, M., Iseki, H., Kawabatake, H., Tanikawa, T., Kawamura, H., and Kitamura, K. (1979) Homovanillic acid concentrations of the third venticular CSF before and after electrical stimulation of the periventricular gray in humans. In E. R. Hitchcock, H. T. Ballantine, Jr and B. A. Meyerson (Eds) *Modern Concepts in Psychiatric Surgery*. Amsterdam: Elsevier.

Baker, W. W., Hosko, M. J., Rutt, W. J., and McGrath, J. R. (1960) Tremorine-induced rage and its antagonism by atropine. *Proceedings of the Society for Experimental Biology and Medicine*, **104**, 214–17.

Bandler, R., DePaulis, A., and Vergnes, M. (1985) Identification of midbrain neurones mediating defensive behaviour in the rat by microinjections of excitatory amino acids. *Behavioral Brain Research*, **15**, 107–19.

Bolhuis, J. J., Fitzgerald, R. E., Dijk, D. J., and Koolhaas, J. M. (1984) The corticomedial amygdala and learing in an agonistic situation in the rat. *Physiology and Behavior*, **32**, 575–9.

Bovier, Ph., Broekkamp, C. L., and Lloyd, K. G. (1982) Ethyl alcohol on escape from electrical periaqueductal gray stimulation in rats. *Pharmacology, Biochemistry and Behavior,* **21**, 353–6.

Bovier, Ph., Broekkamp, C. L. E., and Lloyd, K. G. (1984) Enhancing GABAergic transmission reverses the aversive state in rats induced by electrical stimulation of the periaqueductal grey region. *Brain Research,* **248**, 313–20.

Brandao, M. L., de Aguiar, J. C., and Graeff, F. G. (1982). GABA mediation of the anti-aversive action of minor tranquilizers. *Pharmacology, Biochemistry and Behavior,* **16**, 397–402.

Brandao, M. L., DiScala, G., Bouchet, M. J., and Schmitt, P. (1986). Escape behavior produced by the blockade of glutamic acid decarboxylase (GAD) in the mesencephalic central gray or medial hypothalamus. *Pharmacology, Biochemistry and Behavior,* **24**, 497–501.

Britton, D. R., Koob, G. F., Rivier, J., and Vale, W. (1982) Intraventricular corticotropin-releasing factor enhances behavioral effects of noverly. *Life Sciences,* **31**, 133–9.

Brudzynski, S., Gronska, J., and Romaniuk, A. (1973) Studies on localization of defensive reactions in the hypothalamus of cats by the method of chemostimulation. *Acta Physiologica Polonica,* **24**, 631–41.

Brudzynski, S. M., Kielczykowska, E., and Romaniuk, A. (1982) The effects of external stimuli on the emotional-aversive response evoked by intrahypothalamic carbachol injections. *Behavioural Brain Research,* **4**, 33–43.

Buccafusco, J. J., and Brezenoff, H. E. (1980) Opposing influences on behavior mediated by muscarinic and nicotinin receptors in the rat posterior hypothalamic nucleus. *Psychopharmacology,* **67**, 249–54.

Denenberg, V. H. (1983) Animal studies of laterality. In K. M. Heilman and P. Satz (Eds) *Neuropsychology of Human Emotion.* New York: Guilford Press.

DePaulis, A., and Vergnes, M. (1985) Elicitation of conspecific attack of defense in the male rat by intraventricular injections of a GABA agonist or antagonist. *Physiology and Behavior,* **35**, 447–53.

Ferrero, P., Guidotti, A., Conti-Tronconi, B., and Costa, E. (1984) A brain octade-caneuropeptide generated by tryptic digestion of DBI (diazepam binding inhibitor) functions as a proconflict ligand of benzodiazepine recognition sites. *Neuropharmacology,* **227**, 1359–62.

Foote, S., Bloom, S., and Aston-Jones, G. (1983) Nucleus locus ceruleus: new evidence of anatomical and physiological specificity. *Physiological Reviews,* **63**, 744–914.

Fuchs, S. A. G., Edinger, H. M., and Siegel, A. (1985a) The organization of the hypothalamic pathways mediating affective defense behavior in the cat. *Brain Research,* **330**, 77–92.

Fuchs, S. A. G., Edinger, H. M., and Siegel, A. (1985b) The role of the anterior hypothalamus in affective defense behavior elicited from the ventromedial hypothalamus of the cat. *Brain Research,* **330**, 93–107.

Fuchs, S. A. G., and Siegel, A. (1984) Neural pathways mediating hypothalamically elicited flight behavior in the cat. *Brain Research,* **306**, 263–81.

Gerendai, I. (1984) Lateralization of neuroendocrine control. In N. Geshwind and A. M. Glaburda (Eds) *Cerebral Dominance: The Biological Foundations.* Cambridge, MA, Harvard University Press.

Gershon, M. D. (1981) The enteric nervous system. *Annual Review of Neuroscience,* **4**, 227–72.

Glick, S. D. (Ed.) (1985) *Cerebral Lateralization in Nonhuman Species.* New York: Academic Press.

Gray, J. A. (1982) Multiple book review of *The Neuropsychology of Anxiety: An enquiry into the functions of the septo-hippocampal system. The Behavioral and Brain Sciences,* **5**, 469–534.

Hitchcock, J., and Davis, M. (1986) Lesions of the amygdala, but not of the cerebellum or red nucleus, block conditioned fear as measured with the potentiated startle paradigm. *Behavioral Neuroscience*, **100**, 11–22.

Holson, R. R. (1986) Mesial prefrontal cortical lesions and timidity in rats. I. Reactivity to aversive stimuli. *Physiology and Behavior*, **37**, 221–30.

Hopkins, D. A., and Holstege, G. (1978) Amygdaloid projections to the mesencephalon, pon and medulla oblongata in the rat. *Experimental Brain Research*, **32**, 529–47.

Irisawa, N., and Iwasaki, T. (1986) Aversive-CS-specific alterations of evoked potentials in limbic and related areas of rats. *Physiology and Behavior*, **37**, 61–7.

Jellestad, F. K., Markowska, A., Bakke, H. K., and Walther, B. (1986) Behavioral effects after ibotenic acid, 6-OHDA and electrolytic lesions in the central amygdala nucleus of the rat. *Physiology and Behavior*, **37**, 855–862.

Jenck, F., Schmitt, P., and Karli, P. (1983) Morphine applied to the mesencephalic central gray suppresses brain stimulation induced escape. *Pharmacology, Biochemistry and Behavior*, **19**, 301–8.

Johansson, G., Huhtala, A., and Kaakso, M.-L. (1984) Effects of ethyl alcohol on hypothalamic affective defense in the cat. *Pharmacology, Biochemistry and Behavior*, **20**, 841–4.

Jonsson, G. (1980) Chemical neurotoxins as denervation tools in neurobiology. *Annual Review of Neuroscience*, **3**, 169–87.

Kalivas, P. W. (1985) Interactions between neuropeptides and dopamine neurons in the ventromedial mesencephalon. *Neuroscience and Biobehavioral Reviews*, **9**, 573–87.

Lane, R. D., and Schwartz, G. E. (1987) Induction of lateralized sympathetic input to the heart by the CNS during emotional arousal: a possible neurophysiologic trigger of sudden cardiac death. *Psychosomatic Medicine*, **49**, 274–84.

Libet, B., Feinstein, B., and Gleason, C. A. (1986) Stimulation of locus coeruleus in man, via chronically implanted electrodes. *Neuroscience Abstracts*, **12**, 1162.

Liebowitz, M. R. (1985) *The Chemistry of Love*. Boston: Little, Brown.

Lynch, G., and Baudry, M. (1984) The biochemistry of memory: a new and specific hypothesis. *Science*, **224**, 1057–63.

MacLean, P. D. (1973) *A Triune Concept of the Brain and Behavior*. Toronto: University of Toronto Press.

MacLean, P. D. (1985) Brain evolution relating to family, play and the separation call. *Archives of General Psychiatry*, **42**, 405–17.

Mancia, G., and Zanchetti, A. (1981) Hypothalamic control of autonomic functions. In P. J. Morgane and J. Panksepp (Eds) *Handbook of the Hypothalamus: Vol. 3, Part B. Behavioral Studies of the Hypothalamus*. New York: Dekker.

Meaney, M., Stewart, J., and Beatty, W. W. (1985) Sex differences in social play: The socialization of sex roles. In J. S. Rosenblatt, C. Beer, M.-C. Busnel, and P. J. B. Slater (Eds) *Advances in the Study of Behavior*. New York: Academic Press.

Melnechuk, T. (1988) Emotions, brain, immunity, and health: a review. In M. Clynes and J. Panksepp (Eds) *Emotions and Psychopathology*. New York: Plenum Press.

Moreau, J.-L., Schmitt, P., and Karli, P. (1985) Morphine applied to the ventral tegmentum differentially affects centrally and peripherally induced aversive effects. *Pharmacology, Biochemistry and Behavior*, **23**, 931–6.

Moreau, J.-L., Schmitt, P., and Karli, P. (1986) Ventral tegmental stimulation modulates centrally induced escape responding. *Physiology and Behavior*, **36**, 9–15.

Moriyama, M., Ichimaru, Y., and Gomita, Y. (1984) Behavioral suppression using intracranial reward and punishment: effects of benzodiazepines. *Pharmacology, Biochemistry and Behavior*, **21**, 773–8.

Mugnaini, E., and Oertel, W. H. (1985) An atlas of the distribution of GABAergic neurons and terminals in the rat CNS as revealed by GAD immunohistochemistry. In A. Bjorklund and T. Hokfeld (Eds) *Handbook of Chemical Neuroanatomy. Vol. 4: GABA and*

Neuropeptides in the CNS, Part 1. Amsterdam: Elsevier.

Murphey, M. R., MacLean, P. D. and Hamilton, S. C. (1981) Species-typical behavior of hamsters deprived from birth of the neocortex. *Science*, **213**, 459–61.

Newman, J. D. (Ed) (1988) *Physiological Controls of Mammalian Vocalization.* New York: Plenum Press.

Normansell, L. and Panksepp, J. (1984) Play in decortical rats. *Neuroscience Abstracts*, **10**, 612.

Olds, M. E., Hogberg, D. and Olds, J. (1964) Tranquilizer action on thalamic and midbrain escape behavior. *American Journal of Physiology*, **206**, 515–20.

Olivier, B., Mos, J., and Brain, P. (Eds) (1987) *Ethopharmacology of Agonistic Behavior in Animals and Humans.* Dordrecht: Nijhoff.

Palkovits, M. and Brownstein, M. J. (1985) Distribution of neuropeptides in the central nervous system using biochemical micromethods. In A. Bjorklund and T. Hokfelt (Eds) *Handbook of Chemical Neuroanatomy. Vol. 4: GABA and neuropeptides in the CNS, Part I.* Amsterdam: Elsevier.

Panksepp, J. (1971) Aggression elicited by electrical stimulation of the hypothalamus in the albino rat. *Physiology and Behavior*, **6**, 321–9.

Panksepp, J. (1981a) Hypothalamic integration of behavior: Rewards, punishments and related psychological processes. In P. J. Morgane and J. Panksepp (Eds) *Handbook of the Hypothalamus*, New York, Marcel Dekker, pp. 289–431.

Panksepp, J. (1981b) Brain opioids—a neurochemical substrate for narcotic and social dependence. In S. J. Cooper (Ed) *Theory in Psychopharmacology, Vol. 1,* London: Academic Press, pp. 149–175.

Panksepp, J. (1982) Toward a general psychobiological theory of emotions. *The Behavioral and Brain Sciences*, **5**, 407–68.

Panksepp, J. (1985) Mood changes. In P. J. Vinken, G. W. Bruyn, and H. L. Klawans (Eds), *Handbook of Clinical Neurology*, Revised series, Vol. 1(45), pp. 272–285. Amsterdam: Elsevier.

Panksepp, J. (1986a) The anatomy of emotions. In R. Plutchik and H. Kellerman (Eds) *Emotions: Theory, Research and Experience, Vol. 3. Biological Foundations of Emotions*, pp. 91–124. New York: Academic Press.

Panksepp, J. (1986b) The psychobiology of prosocial behaviors: separation distress, play and altruism. In C. Zahn-Waxler, E. M. Cummings, and R. Iannotti (Eds) *Altruism and Aggression: Biological and Social Origins*, pp. 19–57. Cambridge: Cambridge University Press.

Panksepp, J. (1986c) The neurochemistry of behavior. *Annual Review of Psychology*, **37**, 77–107.

Panksepp, J. (1988) The psychobiology of emotions: the animal side of human feelings. *Experimental Brain Research*, In press.

Panksepp, J., Bean, N. J., Bishop, P., Vilberg, T., and Sahely, T. L. (1980) Opioid blockade and social comfort in chicks. *Pharmacology, Biochemistry and Behavior*, **13**, 673–83.

Panksepp, J., Crepeau, L. and Clynes, M. (1987) Effects of CRF on separation distress and juvenile play. *Neuroscience Abstracts*, **13**, 1320.

Panksepp, J., Gandelman, R., and Trowill, J. (1970) Modulation of hypothalamic self-stimulation and escape behavior by chlordiazepoxide. *Physiology and Behavior*, **5**, 965–9.

Panksepp, J., Herman, B. H., Bishop, P., Normansell, L., and Crepeau, L. (1988) Neural and neurochemical control of separation distress. In J. D. Newman (Ed.) *The Physiological Control of Mammalian Vocalization.* New York: Plenum Press.

Panksepp, J., Herman, B. H., Vilberg, T., Bishop, P. and DeEskinazi, F. G. (1980) Endogenous opioids and social behavior. *Neuroscience and Biobehavioral Reviews*, **4**, 473–87.

Panksepp, J., Meeker, R., and Bean, N. J. (1980) The neurochemical control of crying. *Pharmacology, Biochemistry and Behavior*, **12**, 437–43.

Panksepp, J., Normansell, L., Siviy, S., Buchanan, A., Zolovick, A., Rossi, J., and Conner, R. (1983) A cholinergic command circuit for separation distress? *Neuroscience Abstracts*, **9**, 979.

Panksepp, J., Normansell, L., Cox, J. F., Crepeau, L. J., and Sacks, D. S. (1987) Psychopharmacology of social play. In B. Olivier, J. Mos, and P. Brain (Eds) *Ethopharmacology of Agonistic Behavior in Animals and Humans*. Dordrecht: Nijhoff.

Panksepp, J., and Sahley, T. (1987) Possible brain opioid involvement in disrupted social intent and language development in autism. In E. Schopler and G. Mesibov (Eds) *Neurobiological Issues in Autism*. New York: Plenum Press.

Panksepp, J., Siviy, S., and Normansell, L. (1984) The psychobiology of play: theoretical and methodological perspectives. *Neuroscience and Biobehavioral Reviews*, **8**, 465–92.

Panksepp, J., Siviy, S., and Normansell, L. (1985) Brain opioids and social emotions. In M. Reite and T. Fields (Eds) *The Psychobiology of Attachment and Separation*. New York: Academic Press.

Parkinson, B. (1985) Emotional effects of false autonomic feedback. *Psychological Bulletin*, **98**, 471–94.

Plutchik, R. and Kellerman, H. (1986) *Emotion: Theory, Research, and Experience, Vol. 3: Biological Foundations of Emotions*. New York: Academic Press.

Redmond, D. E. Jr and Huang, Y. H. (1979) New evidence for a locus coeruleus–norepinephrine connection with anxiety. *Life Science*, **25**, 2149–62.

Reich, P., DeSilva, R., Lown, B., and Murawski, J. (1981) Acute psychological disturbances preceding life-threatening venticular arrythmias. *Journal of the American Medical Association*, **246**, 233–5.

Riolobos, A. S. (1986) Differential effect of chemical lesion and electrocoagulation of the central amygdaloid nucleus on active avoidance responses. *Physiology and Behavior*, **36**, 441–4.

Romaniuk, A., Brudzynski, S., and Gronska, J. (1973) The effect of chemical blockade of hypothalamic cholinergic system on defensive reactions in cats. *Acta Physiologica Polonica*, **24**, 809–16.

Rossi, J., III and Panksepp, J. (1983) The relationship between electrically elicited sniffing and self-stimulation in the rat. *Neuroscience Abstracts*, **9**, 564.

Rossi, J., Sahley, T. L., and Panksepp, J. (1983) The role of brain norepinephrine in clonidine suppression of isolation-induced distress in the domestic chick. *Psychopharmacology*, **79**, 338–42.

Sandner, G., Schmitt, P., and Karli, P. (1982) Effect of medial hypothalamic stimulation inducing both escape and approach on unit activity in rat mesencephalon. *Physiology and Behavior*, **29**, 269–74.

Sandner, G., Schmitt, P., and Karli, P. (1985) Effects of hypothalamic lesions on central gray stimulation induced escape behavior and on withdrawal reactions in the rat. *Physiology and Behavior*, **34**, 291–7.

Sasson, S., and Kornetsky, C. (1983) Naloxone lowers brain-stimulation escape thresholds. *Pharmacology, Biochemistry and Behavior*, **18**, 231–3.

Schenberg, L. C. and Graeff, F. G. (1978) Role of the periaqueductal gray substance in the antianxiety action of benzodiazepines. *Pharmacology, Biochemistry and Behavior*, **9**, 287–95.

Schenk, S., Williams, T., Coupal, A. and Shizgal, P. (1980) A comparison between the effects of morphine on the rewarding and aversive properties of lateral hypothalamic and central gray stimulation. *Physiological Psychology*, **3**, 372–8.

Schmitt, P., and Karli, P. (1984) Interactions between aversive and rewarding effects of hypothalamic stimulations. *Physiology and Behavior*, **32**, 617–27.

Schmitt, P., Sandner, G., Colpaert, F. C. and DeWitte, P. (1983) Effects of dorsal raphe stimulation on escape induced by medial hypothalamic or central gray stimulation. *Behavioral Brain Research*, **8**, 289–307.

Shaikh, M. B., Brutus, M., Siegel, H. E. and Siegel, A. (1985) Topographically organized midbrain modulation of predatory and defensive aggression in the cat. *Brain Research*, **336**, 308–12.

Siviy, S. M., and Panksepp, J. (1985) Dorsomedial diencephalic involvement in the juvenile play of rat. *Behavioral Neuroscience*, **99**, 1103–13.

Siviy, S. M., and Panksepp, J. (1987a) Juvenile play in the rat: thalamic and brain stem involvement. *Physiology and Behavior*, **41**, 103–14.

Siviy, S. M., and Panksepp, J. (1987b) Sensory modulation of juvenile play in rats. *Developmental Psychobiology*, **20**, 39–55.

Soubrié, P. (1986) Reconciling the role of central serotonin neurons in human and animal behavior. *Behavioral and Brain Sciences*, **9**, 319–63.

Suzdak, P. D., Glowa, J. R., Crawley, J. N., Schwartz, R. D., Skolnick, P., and Paul, S. M. (1986) A selective imidazobenzodiazepine antagonist of ethanol in the rat. *Science*, **234**, 1243–7.

Swanson, L. W., Sawchenko, P. E., Rivier, J., and Vale, W. W. (1983) Organization of ovine corticotropin-releasing factor immunoreactive cells and fivers in the rat brain: an immunohistochemical study. *Neuroendocrinology*, **36**, 165–86.

Tallman, J. F., and Gallager, D. W. (1985) The GABA-ergic system: a locus of benzodiazepine action. *Annual Review of Neuroscience*, **8**, 21–44.

Tannenbaum, G. S. (1984) Growth hormone-releasing factor: Direct effects on growth hormone, glucose, and behavior via the brain. *Science*, **226**, 1270–7.

Thor, D. H., and Holloway, W. R. (1984) Social play in juvenile rats: a decade of methodological and experimental research. *Neuroscience and Biobehavioral Reviews*, **8**, 455–64.

Tuma, A. H., and Maser, J. D. (Eds) (1985) *Anxiety and the Anxiety Disorders*. Hillsdale, NJ: Erlbaum.

van der Poel, A. M., Olivier, B., Mos, J., Kruk, M. R., Meelis, W., and vanAken, J. H. M. (1982) Anti-aggressive effect of a new phenylpiperazine compound (DU27716) on hypothalamically induced behavioural activities. *Pharmacology, Biochemistry and Behavior*, **17**, 147–53.

Walletschek, H., and Raab, A. (1982) Spontaneous activity of dorsal raphe neurons during defensive and offensive encounters in the tree-shrew. *Physiology and Behavior*, **28**, 697–705.

Watson, R. E., Troiano, R., Poulakos, J., Weiner, S., Block, C. H., and Siegel, A. (1983) A [14C]2-deoxyglucose analysis of the functional neural pathways of the limbic forebrain in the rat. I. The amygdala. *Brain Research Reviews*, **5**, 1–44.

Wise, R. A. (1982) Neuroleptics and operant behavior: the anhedonia hypothesis. *The Brain and Behavioral Sciences*, **5**, 39–87.

Chapter 2

Emotion and Brain Lateralization

Don M. Tucker and Sherri L. Frederick
University of Oregon

ABSTRACT

Neuropsychological research on emotion has shown that hemispheric specialization for cognitive functions extends into the emotional domain. Many aspects of everyday emotional behavior, including expression and understanding of emotion through nonverbal channels, appear to be the specialty of the right hemisphere of right-handers. Other evidence, from studies of brain lesions, psychopathology, and normal emotion, suggests that both hemispheres play roles, possibly opposite ones, in regulating emotional balance. Although there are several controversies in this literature over how to interpret the evidence, this evidence shows clearly that it will soon be possible to base a science of emotion not only on introspective phenomena and autonomic measures, but on a complex set of brain processes.

The study of how the two cerebral hemispheres differ in function is a relatively new area of investigation. Even within this young research domain, interest in the cerebral lateralization of emotion is the infant, born in the wake of its cognitive counterparts. In many ways, the trend in neuropsychology has paralleled the course followed by cognitive psychology, beginning with an emphasis on purely cognitive, rational, 'top-down' determinants of behavior to a more recent recognition of the effects emotions can have on experience and behavior. In research on hemispheric specialization, several lines of evidence suggest that

Handbook of Social Psychophysiology, Edited by H. Wagner and A. Manstead,
© 1989 John Wiley & Sons Ltd

neither cognition nor emotion can be understood as entirely separate from one another.

The literature relevant to the lateralization of emotion is extensive, diverse, and rapidly growing. To cover each line of evidence in this space, our review must be somewhat superficial and selective, and we will refer to reviews of specific topics for more thorough accounts of findings and methodologies. We only cite selectively the findings on hemispheric dysfunction in psychopathology, which are complex and highly relevant for an understanding of normal emotion (see Flor–Henry and Gruzelier, 1983; Gruzelier, 1983; Silberman and Weingartner, 1986; Tucker, 1981; Walker and McGuire, 1982 for reviews). Our purpose is threefold: (1) to introduce the reader to the issues and major findings in this literature, (2) to consider concepts of hemispheric function that are consistent with the several lines of evidence, and (3) to begin to explore what the implications of this neuro-psychological evidence might be for psychological theories of human emotion. The issues in the literature are complex, both in terms of neural mechanisms and in terms of what is meant by 'emotion.' There is substantial controversy over how to interpret each hemisphere's contribution to emotional functioning. Yet we think it will become clear that however these controversies are resolved, there will be important implications for scientific psychology.

We begin with evidence that important aspects of human emotional communication draw on the cognitive processing of the right hemisphere. Much of this evidence can be interpreted from a cognitive perspective, considering how each hemisphere's cognitive skills provide unique ways of dealing with emotional information. This line of evidence is fairly straightforward and uncontroversial in the neuropsychological literature, yet it has rather provocative implications when it is applied to questions of how emotion interacts with cognition in the context of social behavior and naturalistic judgments.

Other, more controversial, evidence suggests a different perspective, from which each hemisphere's cognitive processes are controlled by a different emotional orientation. The first clue to lateralized emotional orientations came from studies of brain lesions: lesions to the left hemisphere were found to be more likely to produce a depressive–catastrophic response, whereas those to the right hemisphere were often followed by denial and inappropriate optimism (Gainotti, 1972). A reasonable interpretation of these effects would be that the patient's response would reflect the emotional orientation of the undamaged hemisphere (Sackeim, Greenberg, Weiman, Gur, Hungerbuhler, and Geschwind, 1982). Thoughout the literature, investigators who have been impressed with this interpretation have gathered evidence in support of a positive emotional orientation for the left hemisphere, versus a more negative one for the right. Other interpretations of the lesion evidence are possible, however, and we will emphasize evidence that supports the less popular interpretation that lesions may disinhibit the lesioned hemisphere's characteristic emotional orientation (Tucker, 1981).

The interpretation of the lesion evidence is a pivotal theoretical point in the hemispheric specialization literature, influencing the approach researchers have taken to understanding both normal emotion and psychopathology. We will consider several factors that are relevant to determining how a lesion influences emotional orientation, including the involvement of frontal structures, the thalamic control of regional cortical activation, and neurotransmitter-specific midbrain mechanisms for controlling general neural arousal and activation. A remarkable discovery has been that there is a lateral asymmetry in the anatomy and function of these basic control mechanisms. Furthermore, there have been important recent advances in understanding limbic mechanisms that are integral to both memory processes and emotional behavior. Several findings of hemispheric asymmetry in temporal–limbic systems suggest that an appreciation of hemispheric emotional orientations will be essential in clarifying the adaptive features of the limbic control of memory and cognition in the human brain.

These several questions of neural self-regulation mechanisms lead beyond the lateral dimension of brain organization to questions of functional differentiation on the anterior–posterior and dorsal–ventral dimensions. Indeed, we will review theoretical accounts that suggest that lateralization for emotion or cognition can only be understood in the context of these more fundamental dimensions. The theoretical issues thus run to rather complex considerations of brain systems. One of the attractive features of early research on hemispheric specialization was that each hemisphere was easily seen as a psychological unit—a subdivision of the mind. It may seem more difficult to attribute psychological properties to the subcortical mechanisms that have become critical to understanding lateral specialization for emotion. Yet we will conclude our review by suggesting that the model of neural mechanisms that promises to emerge from neuropsychological research in the next few years will provide an integrated account of cortical and subcortical mechanisms of emotion, and that it will have clear psychological implications, not only for theories of emotion, but for understanding the adaptive mechanisms that regulate memory and cognition.

RIGHT HEMISPHERE SPECIALIZATION FOR EMOTIONAL COMMUNICATION

Interest in lateral asymmetry of function arose initially from the discoveries of Broca and Wernicke that damage to certain areas of the left cerebral hemisphere impaired the ability to either express (anterior damage) or understand (posterior damage) language while right hemisphere damage did not appear to result in any such deficits. It is an indication of how integral language was to early concepts of the mind that with its verbal skills the left hemisphere was seen as the 'dominant' hemisphere.

In time it was recognized that the right hemisphere had its own specialized functions and, indeed, was not a spare tire. The right hemisphere proved to be superior to the left in performing spatial tasks (Nebes, 1978) and contributes importantly to such tasks as music perception and the perception of environmental sounds (see Bradshaw and Nettleton, 1981, for a review). The most instructive evidence has shown that lateral specialization is best described not in terms of specific mental functions, but in terms of a specialized approach to processing information in each hemisphere.

An important initial observation was that when asked to copy line drawings, left-lesioned patients showed a lack of detail in their drawings, although the general shape of the drawing was correct. Right-lesioned patients, on the other hand, produced drawings with detail but gross errors in overall form (Hecaen, 1962). From careful observations of each hemisphere's problem-solving approach in the behavior of commisurotomy or split-brain patients, Levy (1969) proposed the general formulation that the left hemisphere excels in analytic perception and cognition, whereas the right hemisphere is skilled in the synthetic or holistic apprehension of information. This characterization of lateral specialization in terms of cognitive structure, although at times controversial, has been an important organizing principle for interpretations of hemispheric congnitive processes. A related formulation has described the left hemisphere as more important when cognitive operations are serial or sequential, whereas the right hemisphere is more important when several operations are maintained in parallel (Bradshaw and Nettleton, 1981; Cohen, 1973).

As researchers explored various aspects of brain lateralization, one interesting finding was that emotional information, such as in a facial expression or tone of voice, seemed to show particularly strong right hemisphere lateralization. This was initially recognized in studies of comprehension rather than expression of emotion, perhaps because comprehension skill is easier to assess, and perhaps because in brain-lesioned patients, a deficit in emotional expressiveness could be mistaken for a lack of emotionality.

UNDERSTANDING AND EXPRESSING EMOTION IN TONE OF VOICE

In the 1940s, Monrad–Krohn (1963) introduced the term 'prosody' to describe the emotional intonation of speech. He observed that not only is it impaired with certain forms of brain damage, it may be exaggerated in psychiatric disorders such as mania. Researchers using dichotic listening methods to assess hemispheric contribution to speech perception observed a left ear (right hemisphere) superiority for perceiving intonation (Blumstein and Cooper, 1974; Haggard and Parkinson, 1971). Carmon and Nachson (1973) found this left ear effect for identifying crying, shrieking, and laughing. That it is specifically emotional intonation that is important to the right hemisphere's contribution to speech perception was shown in research using intonation to indicate phrase structure; under these conditions normals show a right ear (left hemisphere) advantage for interpreting the intonation (Zurif and Mendelsohn, 1972). Other researchers confirmed a right hemisphere superiority for recognition of emotional intonation, using not only dichotic listening methods (Beaton, 1979; Bryden, Ley, and Sugarman, 1982) but even monaural presentation of the spoken sentences (Safer and Leventhal, 1977). Safer and Leventhal found that when sentences were presented to the left ear, subjects were more likely to be influenced by the speaker's tone of voice than the verbal content of the sentences.

Systematic observations of patients with unilateral brain lesions confirmed the right hemisphere's role in the perception of prosody. Heilman, Scholes, and Watson (1975) pointed out that at the turn of the century Hughlings Jackson observed that aphasics who could not use propositional language may show substantial sparing of emotional speech. Heilman *et al.* had left- and right-lesioned patients listen to emotionally intoned sentences, then point to a drawing of the face that matched the emotion. Right-lesioned patients were more impaired in identifying the emotional expression. A similar emotional comprehension deficit following right hemisphere damage was observed by Tucker, Watson, and Heilman (1976). Schlanger, Schlanger, and Gerstman (1976), however, found both left- and right-lesioned patients were impaired in recognizing emotional sentences. Heilman, Bowers, Speedie, and Coslett (1984) also found that both left- and right-hemisphere-damaged patients performed more poorly than normals in emotional recognition, although right-lesioned patients were significantly more impaired than their left-lesioned counterparts. These findings suggest that, although the specifically emotional aspects of prosodic interpretation are more right-lateralized, the left hemisphere may contribute to aspects of prosody that serve a linguistic function.

In addition to its role in prosodic comprehension, there is also evidence that the right hemisphere is important to prosodic expression. Ross and Mesulam (1979) have suggested that the prosodic language functions of the right hemisphere may be organized in a manner similar to that of the left hemisphere, such that damage to the right homologue of Broca's area may cause impairments in prosodic expression while damage to the area of the right hemisphere corresponding to Wernicke's area may disturb prosodic receptive functions. In contrast to the hyperprosody which Monrad–Krohn (1963) observed in mania, Kent and Rosenbek (1982) found that right-brain-damaged patients may speak in a monotone. Borod, Koff, Perlman–Lorch, and Nicholas (in press) compared the emotional expressiveness of right- and left-brain-damaged patients and found that, while left-damaged patients were impaired in their utilization of speech in response to emotion eliciting stimuli, right-damaged subjects showed a decreased use of facial and intonational channels in expressing emotion. Interestingly, Buck and Duffy (1980) report that, in contrast to right-damaged patients who show only marginal sending accuracy in emotional expression, when left-damaged patients viewed emotional slides they were rated as more expressive than both right-damaged and control subjects. Buck and Duffy consider the possibility that the left hemisphere may normally afford some inhibitory control over the right hemisphere's expressiveness.

ASYMMETRY IN FACIAL EXPRESSIONS OF EMOTION

A particularly productive line of research has examined asymmetries in facial expressions of emotion. This work has stimulated enough interest to allow replication of the major findings and clarification of several methodological issues. Reviews of the mechanisms controlling emotional facial expressions have clarified the multiple levels of neural systems involved (Rinn, 1984; Sackeim and Gur, 1982). And recent findings point to intriguing developmental changes in the asymmetry of facial displays that may provide clues to early mechanisms of emotional lateralization.

The initial observation seems to have been provided by Campbell (1978), who found that when asked to pose for photographs of facial stimuli, the subjects showed a larger smile on the left side of the face. Sackeim, Gur, and Saucy (1978)· used split-half composite photographs (formed from half of a photograph combined with its mirror image to make a whole face) of actors displaying emotional facial movements. Naive judges rated the left-face composites as more intense. Borod and Caron (1980) examined the asymmetry of facial displays as subjects imagined themselves in various emotional states; for both positive and negative states the expressions were more intense on the left side of the face.

One initial question with these results was whether the facial asymmetry applied only to posed, and not spontaneous, emotional expressions. Ekman, Hager, and Friesen (1981) presented evidence of a lack of asymmetry in spontaneous emotional expressions scored with their systematic facial muscle coding system. Moscovitch and Olds (1982) observed facial expressions during restaurant conversations, and found that these were more intense on the left face. But Ekman *et al.* (1981) argued that these expressions were not truly emotional but may have been part of the linguistic communication. Borod, Koff, and White (1983) examined facial asymmetry surreptitiously as subjects examined emotionally positive or negative slides, and as the subjects posed emotional expressions: both were more intense on the left side of the face. Dopson, Beckwith, Tucker, and Bullard–Bates (1984) also examined facial expressions surreptitiously as subjects underwent mood induction through recalling positive or negative personal experiences. For both these spontaneous facial expressions, and for posed expressions requested of the subjects after the mood induction experiment, the split-half photographs showed greater intensity on the left face.

Another question has been whether positive and negative emotions show different patterns of facial asymmetry. This was suggested as a trend in the data of Sackeim *et al.* (1978) and supported by an EMG study of facial expressions by Schwartz, Ahern, and Brown (1979). Borod, Koff, and Back (1986) reviewed this issue in their own research and in other studies in the literature. Most of the studies they found had examined posed expressions. Of these, none showed a greater right-face intensity for positive emotions, but the greater left-face intensity was in several cases stronger for negative emotions. In their study of spontaneous expressions, Borod *et al.* (1983) found greater left-sided intensity for negative emotions for males and females, but greater left-sided intensity for positive emotions only for males. Although they did not have enough male subjects to analyze for sex differences, Dopson *et al.* (1984) found greater left-face intensity for spontaneous expressions as subjects recalled both positive and negative emotional experiences.

The greater intensity of emotional expressions on the left side of the face thus seems to hold for spontaneous as well as posed expressions. This question of deliberateness versus spontaneity is an interesting one for understanding the neuropsychology of emotion. As several authors have pointed out (Ekman *et al.*, 1981; Rinn, 1984), voluntary expressions are thought to be cortically mediated, while spontaneous expressions are mediated through extrapyramidal pathways (although Sackeim and Gur, 1982, emphasize that simple distinctions between these pathways may not be possible). Monrad–Krohn (1924) observed that following a cortical lesion a patient may be unable to carry out voluntary movements with the side of the face contralateral to the lesion, but spontaneous emotional expressions may be symmetrical or even exaggerated contralaterally.

It has generally been assumed that a left-face intensity effect occurs because of greater facilitation of emotional expression by the right hemisphere. Although this fits with the several other lines of evidence on right hemisphere emotional functions, it is not the only possible interpretation. The consideration of the differential influences of voluntary cortical versus spontaneous subcortical influences on facial expression raises the question of whether the asymmetry of facial expressions observed in normals could be explained solely by a greater inhibition of the right face by the left hemisphere (Dopson *et al.*, 1984). An inhibitory role for the left hemisphere in regulating emotion has been suggested in the context of brain injury (Buck and Duffy, 1980), psychiatric disorders (Flor–Henry, 1983), and normal emotion (Shearer and Tucker, 1981; Tucker and Newman, 1981). Rinn (1984) raised this possibility in his review of facial asymmetry, and questioned whether an inhibitory influence from the left hemisphere may operate more strongly in negative emotion, thus enhancing the observed facial asymmetry for negative emotion.

The issue of cortical inhibition of subcortical contributions of facial expression has also been raised by the intriguing finding that for infants the expression of emotion may be more intense on the right side of the face. In researching adult perception of infants' emotional expressions, Best (1986) found an unexpected asymmetry in the rated intensity of split-half composites of infants' faces: the right side of the face was rated as more expressive. This effect seemed particularly strong for positive emotions. This finding was confirmed in a study of a sample of infants whose response to emotion-producing stimuli was examined at three periods during the first year of life (Rothbart, Taylor, and Tucker, in press). Ratings of facial asymmetry for facial displays of emotion were made from videotapes, with appropriate controls for the observer's left-field perceptual bias: these showed a significantly greater right-face expressiveness across all three age periods. A developmental trend in emotional responses was observed across these periods, with decreasing distress and greater pleasure. Yet there was no interaction of facial laterality with emotional valence in these data: the right-face expressiveness was observed for both pleasure and distress.

Best (1986) suggested that earlier maturation of the right hemisphere, which has been suggested by electrophysiological and other evidence (Whitaker, 1978; Tucker, 1986), could be one explanation of the infants' right-face intensity. The general model of neural development involves cortical maturation providing inhibitory control over subcortical responsiveness (Brodal, 1969); early maturation of the right hemisphere would provide earlier cortical inhibition of the left face, and thus greater expressiveness on the right side. Rothbart *et al.* adopt Best's interpretation for their own findings as well, but point out that if this is correct, the process of emotional development would entail a remarkable lateral reversal, through which the right hemisphere's initial lead in cortical inhibition of subcortical responsiveness would be transformed into a relative facilitation in the more mature brain. Could it be that its early maturation leads to a close integration of the right hemisphere's cortical function with limbic and brainstem mechanisms?

ASYMMETRIES IN PERCEIVING FACIALLY EXPRESSED EMOTION

Understanding facially expressed emotion has also been shown to require the right hemisphere's perceptual skills, although some authors have suggested that each hemisphere is specialized for emotions of differing valence. In work with brain damaged patients, Etcoff (1984) found right-damaged patients to be significantly impaired in their ability to differentiate facial emotions. Similarly, Borod *et al.* (1986) found patients with right lateralized damage to be less accurate than left-damaged and normal control subjects in perceiving negative and neutral emotion, although the groups did not differ in their perception of positive emotion.

Campbell (1978) found a preferential right hemisphere involvement in emotion with normal subjects. She used chimeric stimuli in which half-smiling/half-neutral faces were presented to be rated for intensity of expression. Campbell found that faces in which the smiling side was flashed to the left visual field (and thus seen by the right hemisphere) were rated as more intense than when the smile was seen in the right visual field. Heller and Levy (1981) found similar results, but these held only for right-handed subjects.

Dimond, Farrington and Johnson (1976) fitted subjects with custom contact lenses which allowed them to present whole movies to only one visual field. Using a Tom and Jerry cartoon, a travelogue, and a film of surgery, they asked subjects to rate the films on a variety of dimensions and found that films presented to the left visual field were rated as more unpleasant and horrific than when presented to the right visual field. Right-visual-field ratings did not differ from control ratings. While Dimond *et al.* suggest that their results indicate that the right hemisphere has a negative view of the world, their findings could also be seen as consistent with the idea that the left hemisphere plays an inhibitory role in emotion.

Reuter–Lorenz, Givis, and Moscovitch (1983) also suggested a right-hemisphere-negative and left-hemisphere-positive specialization based on their findings of faster reaction times for same–different judgements for sad faces in the left visual field and for happy faces in the right visual field. However, they noted that these differences may be due to the fact that happy faces may be identified on the basis of a single feature (i.e. a smiling mouth), facilitating an analytic strategy, whereas sad faces require a more holistic attention to the entire face.

Using six different emotions, Natale, Gur, and Gur (1983) found that all expressions but happiness were judged as more negative when presented to the right hemisphere. Since the majority of emotions used in this study were in fact negative, it is difficult to say whether these results support the proposal of a right-hemisphere-negative bias or whether the right hemisphere perceives emotion more intensely. In another experiment, where subjects were asked to judge what emotion predominated in tachistoscopically presented chimeric faces, Natale *et al.* did not find a right-hemisphere-negative bias but did find a left hemisphere bias for positive judgements. It is of interest to note that both studies finding a left hemisphere positive bias have involved decision tasks rather than identification or rating tasks, and an important methodological issue is whether this effect could be due to the easier single-feature discriminability of happy faces.

Ley and Bryden (1979) found that emotion recognition for both positive and negative emotion was significantly more accurate for stimuli projected to the left visual field. Saxby and Bryden (1985) obtained similar results with children as early as the first grade. Best (1986) found right hemisphere presentation to increase the intensity ratings of both positive and negative facial expressions, although this effect was larger for negative emotion (crying).

One concern in this literature has been that results suggesting right hemisphere specialization for emotion perception could be confounded by a more general right hemisphere specialization for face perception. However, Etcoff (1984) and Ley and Bryden (1979) analyzed their data for both face and emotion perception and found performance on these aspects to be uncorrelated. Suberi and McKeever (1977) found that, while subjects showed a left visual half-field advantage for recognizing memorized faces, this asymmetry was enhanced for memorizing emotional versus neutral faces.

ASYMMETRIC SEXUAL AROUSAL

This question of whether the right hemisphere has closer relations to limbic controls than the left has been raised in several of the reviews of the neuropsychology of emotion (Borod *et al.*, 1986; Buck, 1985; Tucker, 1981). One relevant set of findings points to right-lateralization of neural mechanisms of sexual arousal. Given the importance of temporal cortical structures to the limbic system, and the role of the septal region of the limbic system in sexual arousal, it is not surprising that temporal lobe epilepsy is associated with sexual dysfunctions. This literature is reviewed by Flor-Henry (1980). In many cases of temporal lobe epilepsy, the patients become hyposexual, although hypersexuality is occasionaly observed after abrupt cessation of seizures, either postictally or after unilateral temporal lobectomy. Flor-Henry reviews several remarkable case histories of epileptics with disturbed sexual behavior. In some cases the epileptics were plagued with unsatiable urges, in other cases they showed bizarre deviations, and in all cases of orgasmic auras where lateralization was indicated, the focus was in the right hemisphere.

Flor-Henry (1980) points to suggestions that the right hemisphere is particularly involved in REM sleep, which is accompanied by genital signs of sexual arousal. He cites reports of tricyclic antidepressant overdoses, which are followed by both REM rebound and unpleasant erotic stimulation. Consistent with the evidence of right hemisphere involvement in affective disorders (Flor-Henry, 1983), Flor-Henry emphasizes the hypersexuality shown by manics and the hyposexuality of depressives.

Cohen, Rosen, and Goldstein (1976) had subjects masturbate to orgasm in the laboratory. They found that during orgasm there was a marked increase in theta activity in the EEG over right central regions. Cohen, Rosen, and Goldstein (1985) provided further EEG evidence of right hemisphere involvement in sexual arousal, and showed that this may differentiate normal from sexually dysfunctional males. Findings consistent with Flor-Henry's account of a link between sexual arousal, dreaming, and the right hemisphere was gathered by Rosen, Goldstein, Scoles, and Lazarus (in press), who observed that right-lateralized EEG changes were associated with both nocturnal penile tumescence and with REM stages. The relation between tumescence and right hemisphere EEG appeared to increase over the course of the night. Rosen *et al.* cited evidence that nocturnal penile tumescence can be inhibited by anxiety, both from the previous day and from current dreams. However, they found no relation between daytime emotional state, or sexual experience, and nocturnal penile tumescence in their sample.

Tucker and Dawson (1984) also examined EEG lateralization during sexual arousal. They asked method actors to use their expertise in achieving emotional states to become either depressed or sexually aroused as EEG data were collected. Analysis of alpha desynchronization showed relatively greater activation of posterior right hemisphere regions than corresponding left hemisphere regions during sexual arousal. In the contrast condition of depression, alpha increased generally, but particularly over the right hemisphere, indicating decreased activity level on that side of the brain. Analysis of measures of coherence among the EEG channels showed an interesting parallel to the Cohen *et al.* (1976) findings on orgasm: as they became aroused the actors showed an increase in theta coherence among right hemisphere channels.

Coslett and Heilman (1986) reported that, for males, sexual dysfunction is more common after right hemisphere stroke than it is after left hemisphere stroke. Ratings of change in libido from patient interviews showed a significant decline after right hemisphere stroke but not after left hemisphere stroke. Since denial of problems is more common after right than left lesions, it is unlikely that response bias could account for these results. Both spouse reports of sexual function and patient reports of decreased frequency of intercourse showed that 9 of 12 right-hemisphere-stroke patients suffered from sexual dysfunction, compared with 4 of 14 left-hemisphere-stroke patients.

UNDERSTANDING COMPLEX EMOTIONAL STIMULI

The research that has used experimental methods to examine specific aspects of nonverbal emotional communication, such as tone of voice or facial display, has the advantage of relating hemispheric contributions to specific cognitive and perceptual skills. Some of the most interesting indications of right hemisphere contributions to emotion have come, however, from studies that have examined the effects of unilateral lesions with more complex stimulus materials, such as stories. Wechsler (1973) found that both right- and left-lesioned patients had difficulty with remembering emotionally toned stories. Right-lesioned patients gave responses that were particularly idiosyncratic and self-referential. Cicone, Wapner, and Gardner (1980) examined effects of brain lesions on recognition of emotional faces, drawings that had emotional or nonemotional content, and written phrases that may have portrayed emotion. They observed that the right-lesioned patients often gave confabulatory responses. Gardner, Ling, Flamm and Silverman (1975) presented cartoons to brain-injured patients and found the left-lesioned patients had difficulty with reading captions, as might be expected, but were relatively unimpaired in appreciating the humor. Right-lesioned patients, on the other hand, either laughed indiscriminately throughout the test or not at all, confabulated, and made impossible inferences. Bihrle, Brownell, Powelson, and Gardner (1986) had left- and right-lesioned patients choose the punchline to a cartoon or a story. The right-lesioned patients showed an impaired appreciation of the coherence of the punchline with the story theme, and often chose a non-sequitur ending. Left-hemisphere-damaged patients chose the semantically coherent ending, even when this was not surprising, and thus not funny. These results are consistent with other evidence that the right hemisphere, even though it has limited verbal skills, is important for integrating contextual information in a story (Delis, Wapner, Gardner, and Moses, 1983).

EMOTION AND SYNCRETIC COGNITION

To go beyond localizing aspects of emotional behavior in the right hemisphere, and to work towards an explanation of neuropsychological mechanisms of emotion, it becomes necessary to consider the theoretical implications of emotional lateralization. The most solid ground seems to be hemispheric cognitive functions. Are there qualities of the right hemisphere's cognitive processes that are particularly important to emotion? Safer and Leventhal (1977) suggested that emotion requires the integration of various sources of information, visceral as well as sensory, and the right hemisphere's holistic skills may be particularly suited to this task. Tucker (1981) developed this theme by consideration of Werner's (1957) developmental psychology. Werner described the child's cognition as 'syncretic,' in which various sources of information—visceral, postural, sensory, and mnemonic—are fused in an undifferentiated experiential matrix. This preverbal form of mental function is not unlike Freud's (1953) primary process cognition. Both Werner and Freud considered this kind of preverbal cognition to be integral to adult mental function, even though it retains primitive psychological features.

Drawing on this reasoning, Buck (1985) proposed that the most direct read-out of emotional systems to cognitive processes occurs through syncretic cognition. Buck suggested that syncretic cognition is integral to the more subtle and complex emotional processes. Whereas more elementary emotional mechanisms operate fairly directly on behavior, through reflexes or homeostatic loops, Buck proposes that in more complex emotions an important function of the emotion is to inform the cognitive system, and the right hemisphere's syncretic representation may provide the vehicle for this. More recently, Folkman and Lazarus (1986) have suggested that syncretic cognition may provide a fast and direct form of cognitive appraisal, through which experiential events are translated into emotional states. In the recent debate in the psychological literature over whether emotions spring directly from sensation or must be produced by cognitive appraisal (Lazarus, 1982), the question seems to have become not only at what level of neural mechanism do we agree that an emotion has occurred, but how primitive appraisal mechanisms might operate. An appreciation of right hemisphere cognitive operations offers new ways of thinking about such elementary, preverbal appraisals.

In speculating further on the right hemisphere's cognitive handling of emotion, Tucker (1986) emphasized that the term 'syncretic' describes the right hemisphere's cognitive structure; there also seem to be hemispheric differences in cognitive content and process. Whereas the content of left hemisphere represent-ations are in their fundamental form verbal, in which an internal code is substituted for sensory experience, the mental representations in the right hemisphere are analogical, a continuous and direct mirroring of the qualities of sensation. This difference in representational form may have important implic-ations for how lateralized cognitions access the person's emotional processes. A verbal communication is mediated through code transformations, through which the receiver must reconstruct the semantics of the message. An analogical communication reflects the sender's affective state in a more continuous, fluid, and direct fashion. A certain tone of voice seems to mirror the speaker's internal emotional workings. And the perception of that intonation, because it involves an analogical representation of the communication, may more directly modulate the receiver's own emotional dynamics.

Hemispheric differences in cognitive process have also been described in the cognitive laterality literature, wherein the left hemisphere is more skilled at sequential or serial operations, and the right is better at parallel processing (Bradshaw and Nettleton, 1981; Cohen, 1973). Through representing multiple mental operations in parallel, the right hemisphere's processing of emotional experience may allocate memory resources more broadly than does the sequential, focused cognition of the left hemisphere. As a result, these parallel processes may operate more on the fringes of working memory, exerting control on experience but perhaps being less accessible to conscious awareness.

It may not be just theories of emotion that can be viewed from a neuropsychological perspective, but current concepts of social cognition and decision-making in a naturalistic context. Although academic notions of decision-making in psychology, social policy, and economics have emphasized rational cognitive operations, descriptive studies of how people think shows that while people are capable of rational operations, most judgements are highly influenced by what is 'available' in current memory at the time (Kahneman, Slovic, and Tversky, 1982). In turn, experiments manipulating the cognitive availability of information have found that a major factor is the 'vividness' of the information. Pallid statistics fade in the face of a vivid example. Is this not a description of right hemisphere representational features? Is it relevant that the right hemisphere's representational mode appears particularly entwined with emotional experience?

Understanding the right hemisphere would seem to provide new ways of specifying what is meant by primitive cognition. Yet the evidence of the importance of the right hemisphere to text comprehension (Delis *et al.*, 1983) should also be instructive. Abstracting and comprehending the 'gist' from complex information, even verbal information, seems to require an intact right hemisphere. Findings such as this emphasize the importance of primitive, preverbal, forms of conceptualization, not only for emotional meaning, but for any complex process of knowledge.

LATERALIZATION FOR POSITIVE AND NEGATIVE EMOTIONS

UNILATERAL LESIONS

When a patient is emotionally distressed after suffering a brain lesion, this reaction can be seen as a normal response to the loss of function caused by the lesion. A tendency for depressive–catastrophic responses to occur more frequently after left hemisphere lesions was observed by Goldstein (1952) in his classic psychological studies of lesioned patients. For many years this was attributed to the greater importance of left than right hemisphere cognitive functions (Dikman and Reitan, 1974).

However, as early as Babinski, neurologists observed that the attentional neglect for the left body side that occurred with right hemisphere lesions may be accompanied by a striking indifference to problems of living (Denny–Brown, Meyer, and Horenstein, 1952). Although the emotional effects of brain lesions were not given the same importance, nor assessed with the same rigor, as cognitive and perceptual effects, the descriptions of left and right hemisphere syndromes in the neurological literature commented on these emotional features. Hecaen (1962), for example, described that in his series of patients, catastrophic responses most often followed left hemisphere damage, whereas indifference reactions followed right damage. A turning point in the literature was the systematic study of emotional effects of unilateral lesions by Gainotti (1972). Gainotti reported that while emotional responses were not observed in all patients, there was a significantly greater incidence of negative emotional responses after left hemisphere insult, whereas patients with right hemisphere damage were more often indifferent or even inappropriately jovial.

HEMISPHERE SEDATION

Another influential set of findings came from observation of patients in whom one hemisphere had been sedated, through unilateral carotid injection of a barbiturate, to determine speech lateralization prior to neurosurgery. Terzian and Cecotto reported that after the left hemisphere had been sedated the patients showed a depressive emotional response, whereas after right hemisphere sedation they appeared euphoric (Terzian, 1964). Although Milner (1967) did not observe emotional responses in her patient series, this may have been due to the larger barbiturate dose used in her setting (see also Kolb and Milner, 1981). Further studies by Italian researchers reported that although there were clear individual differences in the patients' responses, the emotional responses were generally in line with those described by Terzian and Cecotto (Perria, Rosadini, and Rossi, 1961; Rossi and Rosadini, 1967). After left hemisphere sedation the patients were markedly pessimistic about themselves and their life circumstances; after right hemisphere sedation they would respond with optimism and laughter.

INTERPRETING THE VALENCE EVIDENCE

Although many neuropsychologists doubted the validity or importance of these suggestions of differing emotional orientations of the two hemispheres, others became intrigued with the implications. The initial interpretive question seemed to be why the brain would have one side emotionally positive and the other side negative. Kinsbourne (1978) offered an interesting speculation. He suggested that the left hemisphere's skill in sequential motor control may afford it a particular role in approach behavior. Approach behavior may require a finer control of motor functions than does withdrawal, which may be regulated by the more global motor organization of the right hemisphere. This interpretation has proved influential in the neuropsychological literature. It was based on the assumption that after sedation or damage to a hemisphere, the resulting emotional behavior reflected the intrinsic orientation of the intact hemisphere. The assumption that damage to a region of the brain decreases the functions of that region is perhaps the most straightforward tenet of modern localizationist neuropsychology. Yet there have been some suggestions that damage to a hemisphere can result in an exaggeration of its functioning.

Hughlings Jackson (Taylor, 1958) emphasized the hierarchic nature of brain organization, in both phylogenetic and ontogenetic progressions, and he proposed that damage to higher centers may release more primitive mechanisms from inhibitory control. The disappearance of primitive, vestigial reflexes with cortical maturation during early development, and the reappearance of these reflexes with cortical damage, are consistent with Jackson's model. The exaggeration of spontaneous facial expressions contralateral to a cortical lesion suggested to Monrad–Krohn (1924) that such lesions may disinhibit subcortical emotional processes.

Using the Rorschach inkblot test to study the perceptual abilities of unilaterally lesioned patients, Hall, Hall, and Lavoie (1968) observed that some characteristics of the patients' behavior seemed to reflect a pathological exaggeration of the behavior of the lesioned hemisphere. The right-lesioned patients, even though their form perception was particularly poor, seemed to respond strongly to the color, shading, and texture of the inkblot. The left-lesioned patients, with intact right hemispheres, gave more typical form responses, yet they seemed particularly unable to construct alternative spatial organizations and thus were strikingly unimaginative. In reviewing these findings, Tucker (1981) pointed out that the emotional orientations in the descriptions of these patients seemed consistent with those observed in the Italian studies: the right-lesioned patients were fluent, expansive, and uncritical of their responses, while the left-lesioned patients seem to have been constricted and self-critical. Tucker proposed that in emotional behavior, the primary effects of a unilateral lesion may be to disinhibit the more primitive emotional functioning of the lesioned hemisphere.

The unilateral sedation evidence supports this interpretation. It might be concluded that during inactivation of one hemisphere the emotional response would reflect a release or disinhibition of the other hemisphere. Thus, the depressive response after left hemisphere sedation would indicate that the right hemisphere has a bias toward negative emotion. However, in these studies the emotional responses did not occur when the hemisphere was actually sedated, but only as it was recovering and the EEG had returned to an activated state. Furthermore, Rossi and Rosadini (1967) point out that the typical emotional responses could be observed after barbiturate doses that were too low to produce the motor impairment or speech loss that indicate actual sedation of the injected hemisphere. These features of the unilateral sedation evidence thus indicate that the observed emotional response does not reflect the normal tendency of the unsedated hemisphere—which would be expected to be apparent during the sedation phase—but rather some degradation of the functioning of the injected hemisphere, leading to an exaggeration of its emotional tone during the recovery phase.

Sackeim and his associates searched for the kind of evidence that might answer the question of which hemisphere produces which emotional valence (Sackeim *et al.*, 1982). In their review of case reports of pathological laughing or crying in the neurological literature, they observed a pattern that was consistent with the earlier lesion and sedation findings: uncontrolled laughing outbursts were more frequent following right hemisphere damage, whereas pathological crying was more common after left hemisphere insult. Although confirming that there is some lateralization of emotional valence, these findings did not determine whether the lesion disinhibited the emotion of the lesioned hemisphere or the intact one. Examining the emotional features of behavior in case reports of hemispherectomy, Sackeim *et al.* found that most of the cases were right hemispherectomy, as might be expected. The most typical emotional orientation of these patients was positive. Because the entire right cortex had been removed, they could conclude that the emotional response did not involve a disinhibition of any right cortical regions.

But it could have reflected a disinhibition of subcortical emotional response. To address this issue, Sackeim *et al.* conducted a third review, this time of cases in which laughing or crying was observed during epileptic seizures. Citing evidence that seizures reflect increased physiological functioning of brain tissue, Sackeim *et al.* reasoned that the findings in these cases could settle the direction of lateralization. There were few cases of ictal crying. The reports of laughing outbursts during seizures involved twice as many left- as right-sided foci, leading Sackeim *et al.* to affirm the contralateral release interpretation, indicating that the positive emotional responses observed in several kinds of brain dysfunction reflect the normal orientation of the left hemisphere, whereas the negative emotional responses reflect the inherent orientation of the right hemisphere.

TEMPORAL LOBE EPILEPSY

Other kinds of seizure data also support lateralization for positive and negative emotional orientations. Deglin and Nikolaenko (1975) used unilateral ECT with psychiatric patients and found that left hemisphere ECT worsened mood, whereas right hemisphere ECT produced euphoric responses. These emotional effects were not observed during the seizures, but reflected the patient's emotional state at a later point in time. Thus, these findings parallel the unilateral lesion observations. However, Strauss, Wada, and Kosaka (1983) did not find laterality differences when they observed the facial expressions of epileptic patients as seizures were chemically-induced in the left or right hemisphere. Strauss (1986) does describe differing emotional responses that she and her associates observed in the postictal state in a woman who had right and left temporal lobe seizures on differing occasions: following left hemisphere seizures she appeared agitated and depressed, whereas following right hemisphere seizures she appeared euphoric.

Emotional and personality changes may occur over a period of several years as a result of the seizures of temporal lobe epilepsy. Bear and Fedio (1977) contrasted the self-reports and observer reports of patients with right or left temporal foci. The test items distinguishing the right and left groups showed the left-focus group to manifest an 'ideative' bias, showing a concern with the significance of philosophical and religious issues. The right-focus group showed an 'emotive' bias, endorsing items with more emotional content. Considering the differing roles of the left and right hemispheres in intellectual versus emotional processes, Bear and Fedio (1977) hypothesized that the epileptic disorder resulted in a 'functional hyperconnection' of limbic mechanisms with cortical processes, such that for the left-focus group the left hemisphere's intellectual functioning became invested with great importance, whereas for the right-temporal group it was the right hemisphere's emotional processes that were charged with significance.

By contrasting the patients' self-ratings with ratings made by observers, Bear and Fedio (1977) found markedly differing self-report biases for the two patient groups. The left-temporal group appeared to emphasize their negative characteristics; the right-temporal group denied problems and emphasized positive traits.

In the context of long-standing controversies in the literature on personality changes in epilepsy, the provocative findigns reported by Bear and Fedio have not gone unchallenged (cf. Mungas, 1982). However, the pattern of self-report differences between left- and right-focus group has received additional support from more recent studies. Strauss, Risser, and Jones (1982) studied fear experiences in temporal lobe epileptics. Ictal fear (during seizures) was equally common with left and right foci. Reports of interictal fear showed more concern with sexual and social situations for the left-temporal-focus group. For males, the right focus group reported less fear overall than the left focus group. This finding could reflect less fear for the right focus group, or it could reflect a positive self-report bias. Brandt, Seidman, and Kohl (1985) used the Bear and Fedio scales with left- and right-temporal-lobe epileptics and found the left-focus patients to report greater degrees of several negative traits, including obsessionalism, viscosity, and humorlessness, while the right-focus group's report of these characteristics did not differ from normals.

Reviewing these findings and other recent studies, Fedio (1986) emphasizes the importance of self-report biases in questionnaire research with temporal lobe epileptics. He describes a more recent study of patients with temporal lobe removals to control epilepsy (Fedio and Martin, 1983). Although the patients were less disturbed than those in the Bear and Fedio (1977) sample, the laterality findings were similar for both the self-report bias and ideative–emotive differences. The left-focus patients were more self-critical and were more ruminative and religious. The right-focus patients were self-enhancing and they displayed a greater degree of emotionality.

SECONDARY MANIA WITH THALAMIC LESIONS

In interpreting the effects of unilateral lesions, or unilateral epileptic foci, a critical issue is the relation between cortical functions and subcortical control structures. Some particularly interesting cases have been described in whom manic behavior appeared following a thalamic cerebral infarction (Cummings and Mendez, 1984). The involvement of the thalamus in these lesions was inferred from the loss of pain and temperature sensitivity; in both cases the dense sensory loss was on the left, implicating the right thalamus. Both patients showed the left unilateral neglect that is often observed with right hemisphere lesions. In both cases, the patients' symptoms would have indicated clinical mania if not accompanied by neurologic signs. Both patients became euphoric, with pressured speech, high behavioral activity, and decreased need for sleep. One patient became hypersexual, reporting sexual arousal for the first time in a year, and visited a prostitute. The other became grandiose, inviting the hospital staff to kiss his feet. Reviewing other cases of secondary mania in the literature, Cummings and Mendez found that the lesions often involved diencephalic structures, and were often bilateral. Of the predominantly unilateral cases, however, ten were on the right compared with two on the left.

Silberman and Weingartner's (1986) review of the lateralization and emotion literature found these observations of secondary mania to refute the interpretation that the emotional valence effects of unilateral lesions represents a disinhibition of ipsilateral subcortical processes. In these cases the lesion was subcortical, and yet it was still a right-sided lesion that resulted in a more positive emotional response. However, the role of thalamic structures in mediating hemispheric activity is complex, involving a high degree of inhibitory control (Yingling and Skinner, 1977). The nuclei of the thalamus serve as relays for sensory projections to the cortex, and they provide important controls on the electrophysiological activation of cortical regions. Surrounding the specific thalamic nuclei is a spherical sheet of neurons, the nucleus reticularis thalamus, that inhibits thalamic traffic to, and activation of, the cortex. This inhibitory function is itself inhibited by projections from the brainstem reticular formation, supporting the brainstem's global activation function. In contrast, a frontal cortical mediothalamic system provides excitatory control over the nucleus reticularis, thus inhibiting cortical activity. Remarkably, this frontal inhibition appears to draw on the topographic organization of the nucleus reticularis and its thalamic inhibitory control, thus achieving a finely differentiated inhibitory tuning of regional cortical activation (Yingling and Skinner, 1977).

ARGUMENTS FOR THE IPSILATERAL EMOTIONAL RELEASE INTERPRETATION

Because inhibition is thus integral to thalamic control of brain activity, we suggest that the secondary mania following thalamic lesions could be interpreted as reflecting a degraded exaggeration of the right hemisphere's normal affective functioning. The hypersexuality shown by one of the patients would be consistent with exaggerated right hemisphere activity. Given the evidence of right hemisphere mediation of sexual arousal and behavior (Coslett and Heilman, 1986; Flor–Henry, 1980), the fact that hypersexuality is often characteristic of manics, and hyposexuality of depressives, may indicate that elation in an intact brain is associated with exaggerated right hemisphere contributions to behavior.

The interpretation of the diverse findings on hemispheric emotional valence requires a careful consideration of both the neurophysiological and the psychological evidence. Although it is still poorly understood how various brain lesions or sedation influence the mechanisms regulating brain activity, we suggest that there is as much neurophysiological evidence for the ipsilateral release interpretation as for the contralateral release notion, and perhaps more. The fact that the emotional responses after hemispheric sedation were not observed during actual sedation is strong evidence against the contralateral release notion.

As Sackeim *et al.* (1982) have described, the clearest support for the left-positive, right-negative interpretation comes from the ictal laughing findings (which were more frequent with left hemisphere seizures). Although it might seem that the violent neural activity during a seizure could exaggerate the hemisphere's emotional response, this is not the only possible interpretation. The fact that anencephalic infants show fairly normal facial expressions of emotion indicates that primitive emotional displays can be organized in the brainstem (Buck, 1988). Brainstem disinhibition is also indicated in the emotional displays of pseudobulbar palsy (Rinn, 1984). An alternative interpretation of the ictal laughing data is that a seizure involving cortical and limbic structures may disinhibit hypothalamic and brainstem mechanisms of emotional response. Furthermore, if unilateral seizures necessarily exaggerate a hemisphere's emotional function, we would have expected to see positive and negative facial expressions of emotion as unilateral seizures were induced by Strauss *et al.* (1983); these were not found.

Considering the psychological aspects of the evidence on hemispheric valence, we think the evidence for ipsilateral disinhibition is convincing. In many of the studies, the emotional changes were integrated with cognitive changes, and in several cases the cognitive changes indicated exaggeration of the damaged hemisphere. Although not indicating lateralization, it is instructive that the emotional orientations created by unilateral sedation were accompanied by complex cognitive operations: the patients appraised their life circumstances in catastrophic or optimistic terms. In the case of the changes in perceptual style observed by Hall *et al.* (1968), aspects of the damaged hemisphere's cognitive functioning appeared exaggerated. The right-lesioned patients, for example, showed greater flexibility in visuospatial constructions, suggesting exaggerated right hemisphere functioning, even though the percepts they produced were inappropriate and poorly organized. As they adopted this expansive perceptual style, their emotional tone was characteristically uncritical.

The studies of left- and right-temporal-lobe epileptics alone showed exaggerations of the impaired hemisphere's contributions to both cognitive and emotional style. McIntyre, Pritchard, and Lombroso (1976) found that whereas right-temporal-lobe epileptics were impulsive in responding to the matching familiar figures test, the left-temporal group was more inhibited or reflective. These differences seem consistent with the expansive versus constricted styles characterized by Hall *et al.* (1968). The Bear and Fedio (1977) findings provide the clearest indications of exaggerated cognitive functioning from the impaired hemisphere, and the characteristic emotional bias of these patients paralleled that in the lesion studies. The left-focus group showed ideative ruminations, intellectualizations, and a self-critical bias; the right-focus group showed exaggerated emotionality and a self-enhancing bias.

The confluence of these cognitive characteristics with these emotional orientations is familiar in the clinical personality literature. The obsessive–compulsive style involves restricted emotionality and a pessimistic tone, as well as ruminative intellectualization; the hysteric style involves not only exaggerated emotionality but 'la belle indifference' and 'Polyannaish' optimism (Shapiro, 1965). Levy (1982) pointed out a similar parallel between hemispheric cognitive characteristics and the introversion–extraversion dimension of personality. She suggests that the pessimistic affective tone of the introvert reflects the involvement of greater left and less right hemisphere contribution, while the sunny disposition of the impulsive extravert reflects exaggerated right hemisphere function. In studying individual differences in hemispheric activation, Levy, Heller, Banich, and Burton (1983) separated subjects into those who showed a strong right visual field advantage on a verbal task (apparent left hemisphere activation) versus those who showed a weak right field effect (apparent right hemisphere activation). In rating their own performance, neither group was biased in rating their right field visual performance, but in rating left field (right hemisphere) performance, the subjects who showed characteristic left hemisphere activation were self-critical; those showing right hemisphere activation were self-enhancing. Swenson and Tucker (1983) related a questionnaire measure of hemispheric cognitive style to a self-report measure of emotion. In two samples of university students, those endorsing a right hemisphere cognitive style reported a more positive emotional orientation and scored higher on a measure of self-report bias than did those endorsing a left hemisphere cognitive style.

FRONTAL LOBE ASYMMETRIES AND INTRAHEMISPHERIC CONTROL

Although there are advantages to the construct of a 'hemisphere' as a unit of the brain and mind, we have seen that an appreciation of intrahemispheric mechanisms becomes essential to understanding the relation between cortical and subcortical control mechanisms. Recent evidence has shown that even when considering cortical functions, it is essential to differentiate between the roles of anterior and posterior cortical systems to characterize adequately emotional functioning. Involvement of the frontal lobes has been found to be a pivotal factor both in studies of emitonal effects of brain lesions and in EEG studies of emotional states in normals.

The anterior–posterior axis was implicated in emotional specialization as clinicians observed differing emotional outlooks of aphasics with anterior or posterior damage (Benson, 1973; Benson and Geschwind, 1975). Whereas the aphasics with more anterior damage appeared frustrated and depressed at their expressive language deficit, those with posterior damage seemed to show a more positive orientation. The fluent but ungrammatical, and often nonsensical, speech produced by the posterior-lesioned aphasics suggested that with the loss of certain posterior left hemisphere regions there may be a loss of critical verbal self-monitoring (Tucker, 1986).

Some clinical observations suggested that the anterior–posterior axis is critical to right hemisphere emotional functioning as well. Luria (1973) noted that the syndrome of personality disinhibition that often follows frontal lesions may be more common following right frontal damage. More recently, the development of computerized tomographic methods has improved lesion localization sufficiently that studies of emotional effects of brain damage can examine involvement of specific structures. Working with stroke victims, Robinson and his associates have reported an important set of findings that suggest that the emotional responses often observed after unilateral lesions seem to occur only when the frontal lobe of the hemisphere is involved.

Robinson and Szetela (1981) assessed the degree of depression reported by left-hemisphere-stroke patients, using interviewer rating and self-report methods. They found that frontal lobe involvement appeared to be the critical factor; the closer the lesion was to the frontal pole of the left hemisphere the greater the patient's depression. Robinson, Kubos, Rao, and Price (1984) examined both right- and left-lesioned patients and replicated their earlier result: for the left hemisphere, the closer the lesion was to the frontal pole the greater the depression.

However, for the right-lesioned patients an opposite trend was observed, with less depression correlating with greater proximity of the lesion to the frontal pole. The right-lesioned patients were described as inappropriately cheerful and apathetic. In a study of emotional responses in right-lesioned patients, Finset (1982) also observed intrahemispheric effects, with a depressive response found only with right posterior lesions, and indifference observed only for patients with right anterior involvement. In further studies, Robinson and associates have determined that even with bilateral lesions, the critical factor in producing depression appears to be damage to the left frontal lobe (Lipsey, Robinson, Pearlson, Rao, and Price, 1983).

Kolb and Milner (1981) examined the effects of brain lesions on facial expressions of emotion. Frontal lesions markedly decreased facial expressivity. Although Kolb and Milner concluded that right and left frontal lesions did not differ in emotional effects, their data on facial expressions observed during neuropsychological testing show a substantial reduction in smiling for the left-frontal-lesion patients when compared with right-frontal patients who did not differ from patients with posterior lesions.

FRONTAL EEG FINDINGS IN NORMAL EMOTION

Davidson, Schwartz, Saron, Bennett, and Goleman (1979) had subjects indicate whether their emotional reaction to a videotaped stimulus was positive or negative. They found that frontal lobe EEG changes were the best indicators of reported emotional state: when subjects indicated more-positive emotion there was greater EEG activation (desynchrony of alpha) over the left than over the right frontal region, and a reversal of this asymmetry during more-positive emotional responses. Davidson *et al.* interpreted their findings as consistent with the left-hemisphere-positive right-hemisphere-negative model, and as further specifying the importance of frontal regions in each hemisphere's emotional response.

Tucker, Stenslie, Roth, and Shearer (1981) also examined EEG asymmetry during emotional states, and observed that of four recording sites in each hemisphere, only data from the frontal electrodes differentiated between the conditions. In this experiment, depressed and euphoric moods were hypnotically induced in university students. In previous research, Tucker *et al.* had observed that students reporting depression also reported poor visual imagery. When a depressed mood was induced in an unselected sample of students, it resulted in an asymmetry of performance on an auditory task; when depressed the students showed a bias to report tones as sounding louder in the right than in the left ear. Because this could reflect increased left or decreased right hemisphere activation during depression, Tucker *et al.* (1981) repeated the study while recording EEG data. During the euphoria induction there were no significant asymmetries. During the depression condition the EEG indicated increased activation (alpha desynchrony) over the right frontal lobe.

A related observation has been reported with rCBF methods by Mathew, Wilson, and Daniel (1985). Normal men were given an injection of a benzodiazepine that produced relaxation and euphoria; the drug produced a reduction in blood flow that was particularly marked for the right frontal lobe.

Although their frontal lobe EEG data were similar to those of Davidson *et al.* (1979), the interpretation Tucker *et al.* advanced for those data differed. Citing evidence of impaired right hemisphere performance in psychiatric depressives (Flor–Henry, 1983; Goldstein, Filskov, Weaver, and Ives, 1977) and their own finding of a right-ear auditory attentional bias, Tucker *et al.* proposed that a neuropsychological mechanism of depression may be an inhibitory influence from the right frontal region, acting to decrease posterior right hemisphere cognitive processing.

Thus, it seems that both normal emotional states and the emotional effects of hemispheric lesions may depend on frontal activity. Yet the interpretation of which hemisphere tends toward which emotional orientation depends on whether the frontal lobe activity is associated with an increase or decrease in the hemisphere's functioning. That the personality 'disinhibition syndrome' is seen with frontal lesions (Hecaen, 1964; Luria, 1973) is consistent with an inhibitory role for frontal cortex. Electrophysiological studies in animals have shown that stimulation of frontal cortex may inhibit the event-related potential to auditory stimuli recorded in the posterior regions of the ipsilateral hemisphere (Alexander, Newman, and Symmes, 1976). Studies in humans have shown frontal lesioned patients to have abnormally large event-related potentials to unattended stimuli recorded over the hemisphere posterior to the lesion (Knight, Hillyard, Woods, and Neville, 1981), as if the frontal-thalamic gating mechanism (Yingling and Skinner, 1977) were impaired. These findings show that a frontal inhibitory influence operates in auditory perception. Thus, the shift in auditory judgements that Tucker *et al.* (1981) observed during a depressed mood may have resulted directly from an inhibitory influence from the right frontal region acting on right temporal auditory mechanisms.

In more recent research, Tucker and Dawson (1984) had method actors create the emotional states of sexual arousal and depression. Although sexual arousal was associated with increased activation (alpha desynchrony) of the posterior right hemisphere (as well as increased theta coherence), and depression was associated with decreased posterior right hemisphere activation as hypothesized, not significant frontal lobe changes were observed. Ahern and Schwartz (1985) did find differential frontal activation as female subjects were asked questions with emotional content. Questions that elicited fear showed greater activation (alpha desynchronization) in the right frontal region, whereas those eliciting both happiness and sadness were associated with relatively greater left frontal activation.

Davidson and his associates have observed frontal lobe asymmetries in several experiments. Their research has shown the importance of individual differences, it has addressed the question of the relation between frontal activity and posterior hemisphere function, and it has pointed to possibilities for understanding hemispheric contributions to social interaction in the first years of life. Davidson (1984) reports unpublished research, with Bennett and Saron, in which subjects were asked to generate personal associations to emotional and neutral words. EEG asymmetry recorded from frontal, but not parietal, regions was related to subjects' ratings of the words; subjects rating them more positively showed greater activation of the left frontal lobe. Schaffer, Davidson, and Saron (1983) used scores on the Beck Depression Inventory to select university students who reported substantial depression. In the resting EEG, the depressed subjects showed significantly greater right frontal activation than did control subjects. Citing evidence that in a number of experiments in his laboratory the asymmetry of frontal EEG was in an opposite direction from that in the parietal EEG, Davidson (1984) proposes that there may be a reciprocal inhibition between frontal and parietal regions, such that poor right hemisphere cognitive functions are observed at the same time as activation of right frontal regions.

Fox and Davidson (1984) questioned whether the elementary emotional responses of disgust and interest in neonates would be associated with differential hemispheric function. These emotions were created by introducing a sucrose solution or a citric acid solution into the infant's mouth. In addition to the frontal and parietal EEGs, the infants' facial responses to the tastes were videotaped to validate the induction of the intended responses. Interpreting EEG power broadly in the 3–12 Hz band for the infants, Fox and Davidson observed relatively greater left frontal activation in the sucrose versus the citric acid condition, whereas no significant differences were observed for the parietal region. Davidson and Fox (1982) recorded the EEG from infants viewing a videotape of a woman displaying a happy or a sad expression. The frontal ratios again discriminated between conditions, with the direction indicating relatively greater left than right frontal activation in the happy condition compared with relative symmetry of the frontal EEG in the sad condition.

In recent studies, Fox and Davidson have provided additional evidence that asymmetries of frontal lobe function are important to both specific emotional states and individual differences in the first years of life. Davidson and Fox (1987) examined 10-month-old infants and observed that facial expressions of joy that included activity of the orbicularis (eye squint) muscle occurred in response to seeing the mother approach, whereas smiles without orbicularis activity occurred in response to the approach of a stranger. The orbicularis or 'felt' smile was associated with left frontal activation in the EEG while the unfelt smile upon stranger approach was associated with right frontal activation. In these same infants, facial expressions of anger and sadness in the absence of crying were associated with left frontal activation but the same expressions during crying were associated with right frontal activation. Davidson and Fox found that individual differences in the frontal EEG of 10-month-old infants recorded at the beginning of the experiment predicted later response to separation: those who cried in response to maternal separation showed greater right frontal EEG activation during the baseline period.

The problems of interpreting the functional significance of EEG asymmetries are even greater in work with infants than in that with adult subjects. Replication is required in other laboratories, and the infants' pattern of frontal lobe changes during specific emotional states is more complex than described by a left-hemisphere-positive, right-hemisphere-negative model of frontal lobe function. Yet these findings are clearly provocative. They suggest that a better understanding of hemispheric roles in emotion could clarify basic neural mechanisms that mediate the child's response to the challenges of socialization.

EMOTIONAL ASYMMETRIES IN RATS

Although our emphasis in this chapter is on the human literature, it is important to point out that, contrary to the traditional assumption that only human brains are lateralized, studies with rats are providing an important animal model of emotional aspects of hemispheric specialization. Lesioning the rat's left or right hemisphere, Denenberg (1981) found that rats with an intact right hemisphere were more 'emotional' on two measures: they were more likely to remember a taste aversion and more likely to engage in mouse-killing than rats with left hemisphere lesions. Importantly, these lateralization effects were found only for those rats handled during early development. Rats that were not handled showed no lateralization effects. The implication of these results is that right hemisphere lateralization for emotional processes may be dependent on the quality of early experience even in rats.

In another measure of 'emotionality,' the rats' level of activity in an open-field situation, Denenberg and his associates again found differential effects of right and left hemisphere lesions, but this time the rats with right hemisphere lesions appeared more emotional, i.e. they were more active. This increased activity level after right hemisphere lesions has also been reported by Robinson (1979), who also found decreased levels of the neurotransmitters norepinephrine and dopamine after right but not left hemisphere lesions. Denenberg's (1981) interpretation of the increase in activity after right hemisphere lesions was that the lesion releases the left hemisphere from callosal inhibition. Davidson (1984) interpreted the rats' increased behavioral activity as representing increased approach behavior mediated by the left hemisphere. However, the role of callosal inhibition has been challenged by the findings of Dewberry, Lipsey, Saad, Moran, and Robinson (1986) who showed that even after callosal sections in infancy, rats later showed hyperactivity after right but not left cortical lesions.

Pearlson and Robinson (1981) lesioned the frontal pole of each hemisphere in rats and found right but not left frontal lesions led to increased behavioral activity and decreased norepinephrine levels in the locus coeruleus and in the cortex bilaterally. In addition to suggesting that neurotransmitter pathways may be inherently asymmetric, these findings suggest that it is right frontal damage specifically which increases behavioral activity and, by inference, emotionality. Crowne, Richardson, and Dawson (1987) recently found that right but not left parietal lesions *decrease* behavioral activity in the open field. Importantly, they also found that sectioning the corpus callosum soon after birth did not reverse this lesion effect, as would be predicted if the effect of the lesion was to release the contralateral hemisphere from reciprocal inhibition. Indeed, the group with the callosal section and right parietal lesion showed a substantially greater decrease in open-field activity than the other groups.

Although psychological theories of emotion emphasize experiential and cognitive factors, we must accept that the rat's phenomenology is limited. The implication of the rat data is that there are lateral asymmetries in basic mechanisms of behavioral control in the vertebrate brain. When the hemispheres are found to contribute differently to human emotion, we might conclude that the difference has to do with higher cognitive functions that are lateralized in the cotex, such as the different roles of language or nonverbal cognition in emotional experience. But the animal evidence points to a more fundamental asymmetry of behavioral control mechanisms.

THEORETICAL PERSPECTIVES ON BRAIN LATERALIZATION

Several findings thus show that it is essential to consider the differential roles of anterior and posterior systems within a hemisphere. Although it has gone out of vogue, for many years the anterior–posterior dimension was the primary focus of research on brain function in emotion and personality (Meyer, 1966). Drawing on his extensive observations in primate work, Pribram's (1981) account of neuropsychological systems in emotion places a major emphasis on the functional differentiation between frontal and parietal association cortex.

Integrating concepts of hemispheric specialization with other models of brain systems will be essential if we are to move from speculations about which emotion is in which hemisphere to an explanation of the adaptive mechanisms of brain function. Some recent theoretical work has suggested that an adequate understanding of lateral specialization—for emotion or cognition—will require an appreciation of how hemispheric specialization has emerged from more fundamental dimensions of neural organization.

REFORMULATING THE APPROACH–AVOIDANCE MODEL

As described above, Kinsbourne's implication of the left hemisphere in approach behavior, and the right in avoidance, has been an important heuristic model for many investigators. Kinsbourne and Bemporad (1984) considered how lateral specialization may interact with functional differentiation in the front–back dimension in the control of emotion. They point to Pribram's (1981) characterization of the regulatory functions of frontal cortex, in contrast to the perceptual representation functions of posterior cortex. The affective counterpart of this distinction was suggested by the clinical observations of Denny–Brown, who found that frontal damage produces an imbalance toward parietal control, leading to a reactivity to the immediate context, whereas parietal damage and exaggerated frontal control may lead to avoidance reactions (Denny–Brown *et al.*, 1952). Thus, the approach–avoidance distinction was originally formulated along the front–back rather than the left–right axis.

Kinsbourne and Bemporad (1984) consider the specific roles that anterior and posterior cortex may have within the functionally differentiated hemispheres. They propose that the right hemisphere's emotional functions are particularly important to interrupting ongoing behavior and leading the person to orient to the interrupting event. The left hemisphere's emotional functions have more to do with action control than emotional control, and are important to motivated action particularly. In their review 'of the lateralization and emotion literature, Kinsbourne and Bemporad suggest that it is anterior regions of the left and right hemispheres that are more involved in positive and negative emotions, respectively. They suggest that much of the evidence implicating the right hemisphere for both positive and negative emotions can be seen to involve the more passive, input qualities of right posterior regions, whereas the left hemisphere's involvement is more important for action-oriented functions of planning and overt responding.

SELF-REGULATION THROUGH ACTIVATION AND AROUSAL

Tucker and Williamson (1984) began with the evidence that not only does each hemisphere's cognitive functions provide a differing way of handling emotional arousal—the greater elaboration of effect by the right hemisphere's syncretic cognition, the greater control provided by the left hemisphere's more sequential and analytic cognition—there also seems to be a dependence of each hemisphere's cognition on a unique form of emotional arousal. The evidence is perhaps the clearest for the relation of right hemisphere cognitive function to the person's mood level. In both psychiatric patients and normals, depression appears to be associated with impaired right hemisphere function (Flor-Henry, 1983; Goldstein *et al.*, 1977; Schaffer *et al.*, 1983; Tucker *et al.*, 1981), and an elevation in mood appears to enhance right hemisphere function (Kronfol, Hansher, Digre and Waziri, 1978; Kushnir, Gordons and Heifetz, 1980). This link between right hemisphere cognitive function and mood level seems to suggest some kind of adaptive self-regulation. For the left hemisphere, the dynamic variation in function with changes in emotional arousal are perhaps less clear, but the parallel between the left hemisphere overactivation of schizophrenics (Gur, 1978; 1985) and that observed in trait anxious normals (Tucker, Antes, Stenslie, and Barnhardt, 1978; Tyler and Tucker, 1982) is intriguing. Does anxiety serve as an arousal mechanism that preferentially engages the functioning of the left hemisphere?

To consider these issues, Tucker and Williamson (1984) examined the literature on the mechanisms regulating brain activity. They found an important theoretical distinction drawn by Pribram and McGuinness (1975), between a tonic activation system supporting motor readiness and a phasic arousal system supporting perceptual responsivity. Examining the literature on the neurotransmitter pathways that serve as integral mechanisms for these control systems, Tucker and Williamson found that, contrary to the conventional assumption that the reticular activating system turns the brain on or off in a simple quantitative fashion, each major neurotransmitter system seems to produce qualitative changes in brain function and behavior. When pharmacologically overstimulated, the dopaminergic pathways important to motor readiness do not simply increase motor behavior; they lead to repetitive and stereotyped actions. Tucker and Williamson proposed that this represents a *redundancy bias* that is the control mode of the tonic motor activation system. They speculated further that the left hemisphere has evolved to capitalize on this control mode, and that its contributions to higher psychological functions, such as focal attention and analytic cognition, still require the more primitive neural control mechanism of the redundancy bias.

Another major neurotransmitter system, the norepinephrine pathway, also appears to be integral to regulating brain activity, yet with a qualitatively different control bias. It appears to increase the rate at which the brain habituates to constant stimulation. This is an opposite cybernetic mode from a redundancy bias; it may support the phasic arousal system. Tucker and Williamson theorize that this *habituation bias* causes the brain to orient to novelty, and thus to maintain a broad range of unique information in working memory. They propose that the expansive attentional mode thus created may be the primitive substrate of the right hemisphere's holistic cognitive and perceptual skills.

Although this theorizing required gross oversimplifications of the complex evidence on neurotransmitter mechanisms, it does suggest how it might be possible to reason from neurophysiological control processes to psychological ones. There is increasing evidence that neurotransmitter pathways are lateralized in their anatomy and function (Glick, Ross, and Hough, 1982; Myslobodsky and Weiner, 1976; reviewed by Tucker and Williamson, 1984). And the control exerted by neurotransmitter pathways is clearly relevant to the question of emotional arousal. The dopamine pathways are thought to be functionally exaggerated in schizophrenia (Matthysse, 1977); the redundancy bias of the tonic activation system provides an interesting theoretical mechanism to explain the deficits of left hemisphere overactivation in this disorder. In more adaptive instances, the effects of this control mode may be observed in the focused attention (Easterbrook, 1959) and restricted associations (Spence, 1958) of normal anxiety. The affective disorders are thought to reflect abnormalities of the norepinephrine and serotonin pathways (Schildkraut, 1965). If it is the case that an elated mood entails an enhancement of the habituation bias of the phasic arousal system, it may be possible to understand the adaptive control of attention by the mood system that when exaggerated, as in mania, can lead to rapid shifts of attention, stimulus-seeking, and expansive thinking.

This model thus proposes that the hemispheres' higher cognitive functions emerge from more primitive control mechanisms: mechanisms that have the inherent emotional qualities of anxiety and mood. Furthermore, the more fundamental dimension of brain organization for the tonic activation and phasic arousal systems is not left–right but front–back: Motor readiness supporting anterior systems, perceptual responsivity supporting the posterior brain (Pribram, 1981; Pribram and McGuinness, 1975). Tucker (1987) speculates that hemispheric specialization may have evolved to capitalize on the cybernetics of tonic activation and phasic arousal. By allowing posterior, as well as anterior, left hemisphere regions to draw on the redundancy bias, left hemisphere specialization may have brought a tighter and more sequentially organized control to the perceptual operations of the posterior brain. This may have allowed the routinized decoding of speech. Similarly, it may be that anterior, as well as posterior, regions of the right hemisphere have evolved to elaborate on the cybernetic advantages of control by phasic arousal, thus leading to a particularly important role for right frontal regions in regulating affective processes.

DORSAL AND VENTRAL ROUTES INTO LIMBIC STRUCTURES

Research on visual memory in primates by Mishkin and his associates (Aggleton and Mishkin, 1986; Bachevalier and Mishkin, 1984; Malamut, Saunders, and Mishkin, 1984) has delineated the functional roles of two separate pathways that proceed from sensory areas to the limbic system. A ventral pathway from occipital cortex to temporal cortex appears specialized for what might be called object recognition—identification of objects by multiple attributes independent of their location in the visual field. This pathway is particularly important for foveal visual perception. Bear (1983) suggests that this pathway is important for learning the adaptive significance of objects. The dorsal pathway proceeds from primary visual cortex to the inferior parietal lobule, which has extensive interconnections with the cingulate cortex of the limbic system. Playing a major role in spatial perception, the dorsal pathway appears to coordinate peripheral visual data particularly. Bear suggests that it is important to emotional surveillance.

Bear (1983) points out the frontal extensions of these anatomical pathways. The ventral pathways extends to orbital frontal cortex, which is interconnected with the rostral temporal lobe. The frontal projection of the dorsal system is to dorsolateral frontal cortex, which has extensive connections with cingulate and other dorsal limbic structures. Bear proposes that the functional differentiation between these ventral and dorsal systems could help explain the differing emotional deficits produced by lesions to orbital versus dorsolateral frontal cortex. Dorsolateral frontal lesions may produce apathy and neglect phenomena; this may be associated with a defect in the emotional surveillance function of the dorsal pathway. Orbital lesions may produce personality disinhibition and impulsivity; Bear suggests these deficits may represent the loss of learned restraints mediated by the ventral limbic system.

Drawing from Geschwind's (1965) emphasis on the importance of transcortical connections in the human brain, Bear speculates that left hemisphere specialization may have entailed cross-model cortical connections that are not mediated through limbic structures. This may support left hemisphere cognitive processes, particularly involving the dorsal pathway, that are not tightly directed by more primitive directives from the limbic system. On the other hand, the retention of substantial interconnection with the limbic system in the human right hemisphere may explain the emotional importance of right hemisphere perception and cognition. Although affording it 'distance' from limbic structures, this arrangement does not leave the left hemisphere entirely unemotional. Bear points to the intellectualized cognitive style of the left temporal lobe epileptics as reflecting the infusion of verbal and intellectual material with affective significance, perhaps through hyperconnection of ventral limbic structures with left cortical regions. Similarly, the emotional cognitive style of right temporal lobe epileptics is seen as an exaggerated link between limbic and cortical processes in the right hemisphere.

The work on these visual memory pathways suggests a major functional differentiation in information processing systems in the primate brain; Bear's speculations provide intriguing suggestions for how to understand the adaptive features of these unique cortico-limbic mechanisms, and how to understand the differential involvement of these mechanisms with emotional lateralization. Although he is certainly correct in considering how hemispheric specialization has involved both the dorsal and ventral pathways in each hemisphere, there are also striking parallels between cognitive functions of the ventral and dorsal systems and the cognitive specializations of the left and right hemispheres, respectively. The ventral pathway's integration of stimulus attributes to create object constancy and its handling of foveal vision would seem essential to support the left hemisphere's verbal representations, analytic cognition, and focal attention. The dorsal pathway's role in spatial localization and its emphasis on peripheral vision would seem integral to the right hemisphere's visuospatial competence and holistic attention. Data in support of this parallel have been provided in event-related potential research by Harter, Aine, and Schroeder (1982). When instructions required attention to the conjunction of attributes of a stimulus, the potentials apparently reflecting perceptual processing were larger over the left hemisphere; when instructions required attention to the spatial localization of the stimulus, the potentials were larger over the right hemisphere.

The clinical neuropsychological evidence shows that without intact limbic structures the cortex is incapable of memory (Damasio, 1986; Squires, 1986). The reasonable inference is that the limbic regulation of memory is carried out according to the perceived adaptive value of the information processed by cortical systems. The clarification of the differing functional roles of the dorsal and ventral pathways into the limbic system—and the role of these pathways in hemispheric specialization—would seem to hold the promise of important insights into the adaptive control of memory and cognition.

IMPLICATIONS FOR PSYCHOLOGICAL THEORIES OF EMOTION

Although our goal has been to review the evidence on the roles of the left and right hemispheres in emotion, we have found that these roles cannot be understood without considering complex neurophysiological issues. As questions of the interactions among brain systems become more specific, and as neural imaging technologies become more sophisticated, it seems clear that psychophysiological research on emotion must develop a more articulate model of neurophysiological control systems.

But how are these neurophysiological systems relevant to emotional experience? Psychological theories of emotion have always been tested on the proving grounds of introspection. Since James (1884) wondered whether his emotional experience led or lagged his visceral response, psychologists have created theories of emotion to fit the subjective vantage point. Anyone can test the facial theory of emotion by making a face and seeing how it feels. Each of us can reflect on the phenomenological significance of an adrenalin surge. But what subjective meaning can there be to the activation of the right frontal lobe? To the inhibition of thalamic activating mechanisms by the frontal cortical mediothalamic pathway?

PHENOMENOLOGY OF BRAIN

The challenge for neuropsychological approaches to emotion will be to account for psychological as well as neurophysiological complexity. We suggest that the neurophysiological evidence provides a rich source of new perspectives on the varieties of mental experience. Current psychological theories of emotion *are* based on physiological mechanisms—facial movements or visceral tingling—but these are the mechanisms of a nineteenth-century physiology. Psychological theories have not taken advantage of the increasing scientific appreciation of the functional neurophysiology of emotion. Biological approaches to psychopathology do draw from modern neuroscience. Yet too often they attempt to reason directly from a disordered neurochemical mechanism to symptoms of a diagnostic category with no consideration of the intervening psychological processes.

We suggest that many of the brain mechanisms we have touched on in this review must be relevant not only to emotional behavior, but also to qualities of emotional experience. At the most elementary level we find the brain's activity regulated by neurotransmitter-specific pathways. The rush of elation as the cocaine user potentiates noradrenergic release points to a direct influence of neurochemistry on subjective experience. It is becoming increasingly apparent how neurochemical modulation is important to normal, as well as abnormal, mental function. Panksepp (1981) finds that small doses of opiates can still the young animal's cry for its mother. Neurochemical influences seem to shape the most fundamental experiences of social attachment.

We have seen the integral role of limbic structures in emotion. Because these are structures we share with primitive mammals, and because they are demonstrably important to sexual and aggressive behavior, they have been thought to be important only to primitive urges. Yet the increasing evidence that the cortex cannot retain experience without limbic involvement suggests that these structures are essential to higher cognitive processes. More directly relevant to questions of phenomenology is the evidence from recent human limbic stimulation studies (Gloor, Olivier, Quesney, Andermann, and Horowitz, 1982). In epileptic patients with chronic deep electrodes, Gloor *et al.* observed that when stimulation was accompanied by a conscious experience—involving an emotion, a hallucination, and/or a distorted sense of familiarity—the brain activity invariably involved limbic structures. Cortical involvement was neither necessary nor sufficient for a conscious event, but limbic activity was both. The remarkable conclusion suggested by these observations is that the limbic system provides the capacity to integrate neural activity across time—a capacity that is required not only for working memory, but also for conscious awareness.

Thus, from the neurophysiological perspective, it is not only a question of how we can become cognizant of emotional mechanisms of the brain, but also of how emotional mechanisms support consciousness. Are there affective qualities inherent to the operation of the other controls on attention and arousal that we have found to be important to a neuropsychology of emotion? The right parietal region is implicated not only in the comprehension of emotional communication (Ross and Mesulam, 1979), but also in basic processes of regulating arousal (Heilman and Van De Able, 1979) and orienting attention (Posner, Friedrich, Walker, and Rafal, 1983). Mesulam (1981) describes connections of parietal cortex to cingulate regions of the dorsal limbic system, where single unit activity is observed only if the perceived object has adaptive significance for the organism. Is it this limbic connection that adds the subjective experience of significance to perception?

For other mechanisms, particularly those involving inhibitory control, the implications for emotional experience are perhaps less clear. But just as there can be perceptual immediacy to shadows or silence, neural inhibitory processes may make themselves felt in experience. As a frontal lobe modulates thalamocortical traffic, and thereby differentiates the patterning of cortical activation, is there not also a corresponding differentiation of the pattern of experience?

UNDERSTANDING HEMISPHERIC SPECIALIZATION

For each of these neurophysiological mechanisms, we find a qualitative difference in the way the mechanisms operate in the left and right hemispheres. The elementary controls exerted by neurotransmitter pathways seem to influence on hemisphere more than the other. When temporal lobe epilepsy exaggerates the connection of limbic structures with cortex, we find markedly different syndromes on the right and the left. Considering either lesions or EEG activity, the left and right frontal lobes often seem to show opposite roles in emotional states. In our review, we have emphasized the neurophysiological mechanisms that must be considered in interpreting hemispheric specialization for emotion. In this final section, we will also consider psychological concepts that can guide our interpretation of hemispheric contributions.

The findings on emotional communication show fairly consistently that the right hemisphere's role is particularly important. Here we can understand the importance of hemispheric specialization for cognition: the right hemisphere's analogical representation and its capacity for holistic integration of perceptual information seem to be essential for conveying and interpreting emotion. Although it is important to appreciate the verbal communication of emotion (Strauss, 1986), the left hemisphere's verbal representation and its more structured and propositional organization of information appear to operate at a greater distance from one's internal affective dynamics.

The observations of emotional effects of brain lesions now seem to indicate strongly that there is some differentiation of emotional valence between the hemispheres. We have emphasized a novel interpretation of this evidence: in many cases the abnormal emotional response seems to reflect an exaggeration of the injured hemisphere's characteristic orientation. Just as Hall *et al.* (1968) found that a hemispheric lesion could result in a degraded overinvolvement of the lesioned hemisphere in perceptual processing, we suggest that much of the evidence on positive and negative emotional reactions following brain lesions reflects a disinhibition of the damaged hemisphere's normal emotional tone. Most important is the confluence of exaggerated cognitive features and affective features shown by Bear and Fedio's (1977) temporal lobe epileptics: the left-focus patients' intellectual ruminations were accompanied by self-critical affective orientation; the right-focus patients' emotionality was accompanied by self-enhancing denial.

We suggest this interpretation of the lesion evidence is more consistent with the evidence of hemispheric function in psychopathology and personality than the left-positive-emotion, right-negative-emotion interpretation. Certainly, when we find exaggerated left hemisphere function in schizophrenia or obsessive–compulsive disorder we do not find an excess of positive emotion. However, even in the direction we have interpreted it, a simple positive–negative model of emotional lateralization does not really fit the psychopathology nor the personality evidence. Rather, consistent with Levy's interpretations (Levy, 1982), it seems that the positive–negative dimension of emotional valence depends most closely on the right hemisphere's level of function. This is the dimension of mood level, varying from depression to elation. The left hemisphere's characteristic affect is also important. It seems to be an anxious vigilance, the affective manifestation of the tonic activation system that supports the left hemisphere's role in motor organization. Although perhaps not as 'emotional' as the right hemisphere, the left hemisphere does seem to have a characteristic affective orientation, and this may be important to the catastrophic response seen with anterior (Disinhibiting) left hemisphere lesions, and to the vigilant anxiety seen in certain forms of schizophrenia or personality disorders.

Tucker and Williamson (1984) theorized that the right hemisphere's cognitive functions emerged to elaborate on the more primitive control mechanisms of the phasic perceptual arousal system. As it modulates attention by applying a habituation bias, this control system determines the person's subjective position on the depression–elation dimension. Consistent with the notion that the right hemisphere's cognition is particularly important to perceptual responsiveness (Jackson, 1879; Kinsbourne and Bemporad, 1984), in an elated mood the person's attention is extraverted, responsive to both social stimuli and internal urges. The manic is hyperprosodic, hypersexual, and socially extraverted; the depressive is low on each count. The manic's ideation not only shows abrupt transitions reflecting the habituation bias of the phasic arousal system, it is also holistic and expansive, with remote associations primed and accessible to current working memory (Andreasen and Powers, 1975; Shaw, Mann, Stokes, and Manevitz, 1986).

Accompanying the global and impressionistic cognitive style of the hysteric personality we also find exaggerated prosody, a concern with sexuality, and social extraversion. The characteristic 'Pollyannaish' optimism of this style reflects a reliance on an elevated mood, although the propensity for panic disorders and mood lability suggest that not all aspects of a right hemisphere style of self-control are positive. The hysteric's 'belle indifference' is a remarkable parallel to the anosognosia or denial of illness associated with right hemisphere lesions, even to the extent of including left-sided conversion disorders (Galin, Diamond, and Braff, 1977) to parallel the left unilateral neglect seen with right hemisphere lesions (Heilman, 1979).

The right hemisphere seems to mediate something like a primary process mode of orienting to the social environment (Galin, 1974; Fedio, 1986), a mode which is integral to hedonic tone, and which is socially extraverted. This is not just an animalistic id, however, because it also seems to involve self-enhancing cognitive operations that psychoanalytic theory would ascribe to the ego.

We suggest that the exaggerations of right hemisphere contributions in disordered personalities can provide a general outline of its functional characteristics in the normal brain. To rely on the right hemisphere's processing is to have experience represented in analog form. Mental representations closely mirror environmental events and internal bodily processes. This is a phenomenologically rich mode of perception, perhaps not just because it is concrete, but because emotional dynamics are so easily touched by the perceptual process. The holistic nature of representation causes experience to fuse many undifferentiated influences. In a strongly extraverted orientation, the syncretic fusion of experience merges self and context. In this mode of functioning, emotion is only loosely controlled. Once elicited, fear can become panic.

Although potentially aversive, the right hemisphere's cognitive functions seem to be strongly engaged in states of elation. The self-enhancing cognitive operations seen in cases of right hemisphere exaggeration suggest that certain self-evaluative mechanisms and the capacity to self-regulate on the depression–elation dimension involve right hemisphere operations. Although exaggerated in narcissistic, hysteric, or psychopathic personalities, these self-enhancing cognitive mechanisms may be essential for normal or even optimal personality functioning.

Although in normal personality we would expect a high degree of integration of left and right hemisphere modes, in persons such as schizophrenics and obsessives who show exaggerated left hemisphere functioning we often find anhedonia— suggesting that the right hemisphere's contribution to hedonic tone has been somehow thwarted. Along with the stereotypes of thought and action that seem to follow from their chronic anxiety, obsessives and schizophrenics are socially introverted. The exaggerated dopaminergic function brought on by chronic stimulant abuse is particularly informative: the neurophysiological changes seem to produce both hypervigilance and social introversion which combine to create a paranoid psychosis. Although the left hemisphere's psychological orientation may have important features in common with secondary process cognition (Galin, 1974, 1977), it is certainly not affectless. It seems to support mechanisms of self-criticism that psychoanalytic theory might ascribe to the superego. Do the left hemisphere's language mechanisms serve to internalize the results of the socialization process?

It may be easiest to appreciate left hemisphere contributions to normal emotional phenomenology by considering the control offered by its cognitive representations. To frame meaning in verbal, propositional form creates 'objectivity.' Propositions—unlike the more ephemeral and dynamic analogical representations of the right hemisphere—have a tenacity in working memory, allowing the relation between premise and conclusion to be considered. Yet the redundancy bias of the motor control system that allows this tenacity in working memory also has essential adaptive roles—such as in anxiety or hostility. When these emotional states exert their controls on attention, there is a certain fixity to experience. An insult demands rumination.

If this model of hemispheric affective–cognitive mechanisms is correct, it suggests some interesting implications not only for psychological theories of emotion, but also for the phenomenology of attention and cognition. There appear to be certain emotional orientations that are required to modulate effectively the hemispheres' specialized cognitive capacities. To allow the right hemisphere's analogical representation to achieve an optimal mirroring of experience seems to require a receptive attentional mode, a certain extraversion, which is closely linked to mood level. To prime the extent of internal representations required to condition working memory for holistic thinking may require an adequate degree of elation. On the other hand, to structure more actively one's cognitive processes, ordering the implications of ideas logically from one to the next, it may be necessary to draw on the affective control mechanisms that seem to regulate the left hemisphere's cognitive operations. Analytic thinking may not be possible without focused attention, and the redundancy bias that affords the requisite constancy to working memory may only be engaged as an effect of frontal, limbic, and basal ganglia systems whose evolution has been guided by the more primitive tasks of maintaining motor readiness under states of vigilance and hostility.

CONCLUSION

Research on hemispheric specialization for emotion has opened up a rich vein of evidence that should be mined by neurophysiological and psychological theoreticians alike. At the neurophysiological level, the research questions must be addressed to more specific levels of analysis than a 'hemisphere.' Neurochemical systems, cortical–limbic interactions, and dorsal–ventral and anterior–posterior dimensions of cortical organization must be considered. In turn, the full story of each of these levels of analysis seems to require a full account of the implications of lateral specialization. The two frontal lobes, for example, are not created equal. In psychological terms, there are several levels of functioning that must be considered, from elementary kinds of emotional arousal and activation to differing forms of conceptual structure. For psychological theories of emotion, the study of hemispheric specialization offers new opportunities to consider the continuity from elementary emotional mechanisms to the most complex processes of experience and behavior.

REFERENCES

Aggleton, J. P., and Mishkin, M. (1986) The amygdala: sensory gateway to the emotions. In R. Plutchik and H. Kellerman (Eds), *Emotion: Theory, Research and Experience*, Vol. 3, pp. 281–99. New York: Academic Press.

Ahern, G. L., and Schwartz, G. E. (1985) Differential lateralization for positive and negative emotion in the human brain: EEG spectral analysis. *Neuropsychologia*, **23**, 745–55.

Alexander, G. E., Newman, J. D., and Symmes, D. (1976) Convergence of prefrontal and acoustic inputs upon neurons in the superior temporal gyrus of the awake squirrel monkey. *Brain Research*, **116**, 334–8.

Andreasen, N. J. C., and Powers, P. S. (1975) Creativity and psychosis: an examination of conceptual styles. *Archives of General Psychiatry*, **32**, 70–3.

Bachevalier, J., and Mishkin, M. (1984) An early and a late developing system for learning and retention in infant monkeys. *Behavioral Neuroscience*, **98**, 770–8.

Bear, D. M. (1983) Hemispheric specialization and the neurology of emotion. *Archives of Neurology*, **40**, 195–202.

Bear, D. M., and Fedio, P. (1977) Quantitative analysis of interictal behavior in temporal lobe epilepsy. *Archives of Neurology*, **34**, 454–67.

Beaton, A. A. (1979) Hemispheric emotional asymmetry in a dichotic listening task. *Acta Psychologica*, **43**, 103–9.

Benson, D. F. (1973) Psychiatric aspects of aphasia. *British Journal of Psychiatry*, **123**, 555–66.

Benson, D. F., and Geschwind, N. (1985) The aphasias and related disturbances. In A. B. Baker and L. D. Baker (Eds), *Clinical Neurology*. New York: Harper & Row.

Best, C. T. (1986) Hemispheric asymmetries if the perception and expression of infant facial emotions. Paper presented at the meeting of the International Neuropsychological Society, Denver, CO, February.

Bihrle, A. M., Brownell, H. H., Powelson, J. A., and Gardner, H. (1986) Comprehension of humorous and non-humorous materials by left and right brain-damaged patients. *Brain and Cognition*, **5**, 399–411.

Blumstein, S., and Cooper, W. E. (1974) Hemispheric processing of intonation contours. *Cortex*, **10**, 146–158.

Borod, J. C., and Caron, H. S. (1980) Facedness and emotion related to lateral dominance, sex and expression type. *Neuropsychologia*, **18**, 237–41.

Borod, J. C., Koff, E., and Buck, R. (1986) The neuropsychology of facial expression: data from normal and brain-damaged adults. In P. Blanck, R. Buck, and R. Rosenthal (Eds), *Nonverbal Communication in the Clinical Context*. University Park, PA: Penn State Press.

Borod, J. C., Koff, E., Perlman–Lorch, M., and Nicholas, M. (1986) The expression and perception of facial emotion in patients with focal brain damage. *Neuropsychologia*, **24**, 169–80.

Borod, J. C., Koff, E., and White, B. (1983) Facial asymmetry in posed and spontaneous expressions of emotion. *Brain and Cognition*, **2**, 165–75.

Bradshaw, J. L., and Nettleton, N. C. (1981) The nature of hemispheric specialization in man. *Behavioral and Brain Sciences*, **4**, 51–91.

Brandt, J., Seidman, L. J., and Kohl, D. (1985) Personality characteristics of epileptic patients: a controlled study of generalized and temporal lobe cases. *Journal of Clinical and Experimental Neuropsychology*, **7**, 25–38.

Brodal, A. (1969) *Neurological Anatomy: In Relation to Clinical Medicine*. New York: Oxford University Press.

Bryden, M. P., Ley, R. G., and Sugarman, J. H. (1982) A left-ear advantage for identifying the emotional quality of tonal sequences. *Neuropsychologia*, **20**, 83–87.

Buck, R. (1988) *Human Motivation and Emotion*. New York: John Wiley.

Buck, R. (1985) Prime theory: an integrated view of motivation and emotion. *Psychological Review*, **92**, 389–413.

Buck, R., and Duffy, J. (1980) Nonverbal communication of affect in brain-damaged patients. *Cortex*, **16**, 351–62.

Campbell, R. (1978) Asymmetries in interpreting and expressing a posed facial expression. *Cortex*, **14**, 327–42.

Carmon, A., and Nachson, I. (1973) Ear asymmetry in perception of emotional nonverbal stimuli. *Acta Psychologica*, **37**, 351–7.

Cicone, M., Wapner, W., and Gardner, H. (1980) Sensitivity to emotional expressions and situations in organic patients. *Cortex*, **16**, 145–58.

Cohen, A. S., Rosen, R. C., and Goldstein, L. (1985) EEG hemispheric asymmetry during sexual arousal: psychophysiological patterns in responsive, unresponsive and dysfunctional males. *Journal of Abnormal Psychology*, **94**, 580–90.

Cohen, G. (1973) Hemispheric differences in serial versus parallel processing. *Journal of Experimental Psychology*, **97**, 349–56.

Cohen, H. D., Rosen, R. C., and Goldstein, L. (1976) Electroencephalographic laterality changes during human sexual orgasm. *Archives of Sexual Behavior*, **5**(3), 189–99.

Coslett, H. B., and Heilman, K. M. (1986) Male sexual function: Impairment after right hemisphere stroke. *Archives of neurology*, **43**, 1036–9.

Crowne, D. P., Richardson, C. M., and Dawson, K. A. (1987) Lateralization of emotionality in right parietal cortex of the rat. *Behavioral Neuroscience*, **101**, 134–8.

Cummings, J. L., and Mendez, M. F. (1984). Secondary mania with focal cerebrovascular lesions. *American Journal of Psychiatry*, **141**, 1084–7.

Damasio, A. R. (1986) Anatomical substrates of memory processes. Invited lecture, EPIC VIII, Stanford, CA, 1986.

Davidson, R. J. (1984) Affect, cognition and hemispheric specialization. In C. E. Izard, J. Kagan, and R. Zajonc (Eds), *Emotion, Cognition and Behaviour*. New York: Cambridge University Press.

Davidson, R. J., and Fox, N. A. (1982) Asymmetrical brain activity discriminates between positive and negative affective stimuli in human infants. *Science*, **218**, 1235–7.

Davidson, R. J., and Fox, N. A. (1987) Frontal brain asymmetry predicts infants' response to maternal separation. Manuscript submitted for publication.

Davidson, R. J. Schwartz, G. E., Saron, C., Bennett, J., and Goleman, D. J. (1979) Frontal versus parietal EEG asymmetry during positive and negative affect. *Psychophysiology* (abstract), **16**, 202–3.

Deglin, V. L., and Nikolaenko, N. N. (1975) Role of the dominant hemisphere in the regulation of emotional states. *Human Physiology*, **1**, 394.

Delis, D. C., Wapner, W., Gardner, H., and Moses, J. A. (1983) The contribution of the right hemisphere to the organization of paragraphs. *Cortex*, **19**, 43–50.

Denenberg, V. H. (1981) Hemispheric laterality in animals and then effects of early experience. *Behavioral and Brain Sciences*, **4**, 1–49.

Denny–Brown, D., Meyer, J. W. and Horenstein, S. (1952) The significance of perceptual rivalry resulting from parietal lesions. *Brain*, **75**(4) 433–71.

Dewberry, R. G., Lipsey, J. R., Saad, K., Moran, T. H., and Robinson, R. G. (1986) Lateralized response to cortical injury in the rat: interhemispheric interaction. *Behavioral Neuroscience*, **100**, 556–562.

Dikmen, S., and Reitan, R. M. (1974) Minnesota Multiphasic Personality Inventory correlates of dysphasic language disturbances. *Journal of Abnormal Psychology*, **83**, 675–679.

Dimond, S. J., Farrington, L., and Johnson, P. (1976) Differing emotional response from right and left hemispheres. *Nature*, **261**, 690–2.

Dopson, W. G., Beckwith, B. E., Tucker, D. M., and Bullard–Bates, P. C. (1984) Asymmetry of facial expression in spontaneous emotion. *Cortex*, **20**, 243–52.

Easterbrook, J. A. (1959) The effect of emotion on cue utilization and the organization of behavior. *Psychological Review*, **66**, 183–201.

Ekman, P. Hager, J. C., and Friesen, W. V. (1981) The asymmetry of emotional and deliberate facial actions. *Psychophysiology*, **18**, 101–6.

Etcoff, N. L. (1984) Selective attention to facial identity and facial emotion. *Neuropsychologia*, **22**, 281–95.

Fedio, P. (1986) Behavioral characteristics of patients with temporal lobe epilepsy. *Psychiatric Clinics of North America*, **9**, 267–81.

Fedio, P., and Martin, A. (1983). Ideative-emotive behavioral characteristics of patients following left or right temporal lobectomy. *Epilepsia*, **24**, 117–30.

Finset, A. (1982) Depressive behavior, outburst of crying and emotional indifference in left hemiplegics. Paper presented at the Second Annual Symposium of Models and Techniques of Cognitive Rehabilitation, pp. 1–18.

Flor-Henry, P. (1969) Psychosis and temporal lobe epilepsy: a controlled investigation. *Epilepsia*, **10**, 363–95.

Flor-Henry, P. (1980) Cerebral aspects of the orgasmic response: normal and deviational. In R. Forlec and W. Pasini (Eds), *Medical Sexology*, pp. 256–62. Elsevier: Amsterdam.

Flor-Henry, P., and Gruzelier, J. (Eds) (1983) *Laterality and Psychopathology*, Vol. II. Amsterdam: Elsevier.

Folkman, S., and Lazarus, R. S. (1986) Coping and emotion. Paper presented at the symposium, Psychological and Biological Processes in the Development of Emotion, University of Chicago, September, 1986.

Fox, N. A., and Davidson, R. J. (1984) EEG asymmetry in response to sour tastes in newborn infants. *Neuropsychologia*, **24**, 417–22.

Freeman, R. L., Galaburda, A. M., Cabal, R. D., and Geschwind, N. (1985) The neurology of depression. *Archives of Neurology*, **42**, 289–91.

Freud, S. (1953) An outline of psychoanalysis. In *Standard Edition*, Vol. 23. London: Hogarth Press. (First German Edition, 1940.)

Gainotti, G. (1972) Studies on the functional organization of the minor hemisphere. *International Journal of Mental Health*, **1**(3), 78–82.

Galin, D. (1974) Implications for psychiatry of left and right cerebral specialization: a neurophysiological context for unconscious processes. *Archives of General Psychiatry*, **31**, 572–83.

Galin, D. (1977) Lateral specialization and psychiatric issues: speculations on development and the evolution of consciousness. In *Conference on the Evolution and Lateralization of the Brain. Annals of the New York Academy of Sciences*, **299**, 399–411.

Galin, D., Diamond, R., and Braff, D. (1977) Lateralization of conversion symptoms: more frequent on the left. *American Journal of Psychiatry*, **134**, 578–80.

Gardner, H., Ling, P. K., Flamm, L. and Silverman, J. (1975). Comprehension and appreciation of humorous material following brain damage. *Brain*, **98**, 399–412.

Geschwind, N. (1965) Disconnection syndromes in animals and man. *Brain*, **88**, 237–294.

Glick, S. D., Ross, D. A., and Hough, L. B. (1982) Lateral asymmetry of neurotransmitters in human brain. *Brain Research*, **234**, 53–63.

Gloor, P., Olivier, A., Quesney, L. F., Andermann, F., and Horowitz, S. (1982) The role of the limbic system in experiential phenomena of temporal lobe epilepsy. *Annals of Neurology*, **12**, 129–144.

Goldstein, K. (1952) The effect of brain damage on the personality. *Psychiatry*, **15**, 245–260.

Goldstein, S. G., Filskov, S. B., Weaver, L. A. and Ives, J. (1977) Neuropsychological effects of electroconvulsive therapy. *Journal of Clinical Psychology*, **33**, 798–806.

Gruzelier, J. H. (1983) A critical assessment and integration of lateral asymmetries in schizophrenia. In M. Myslobodsky (Ed.), *Hemisyndromes: Psychobiology, Neurology and Psychiatry*, pp. 265–326. New York: Academic Press.

Gur, R. E. (1978). Left hemisphere dysfunction and left hemisphere overactivation in schizophrenia. *Journal of Abnormal Psychology*, **87**, 226–38.

Gur, R. E. (1985). Positron emission tomography in psychiatric disorders. *Psychiatric Annals*, **15**, 268–71.

Haggard, M. P., and Parkinson, A. M. (1971) Stimulus and task factors as determinants of ear advantages. *Quarterly Journal of Experimental Psychology*, **23**, 168–177.

Hall, M. M., Hall, G. C., and Lavoie, P. (1968) Ideation in patients with unilateral or bilateral midline brain lesions. *Journal of Abnormal Psychology*, **73**, 526–31.

Harter, M. R., Aine, C., and Schroeder, C. (1982) Hemispheric differences in neural processing of stimulus location and type: effects of selective attention on visual evoked potentials. *Neuropsychologia*, **20**, 421–38.

Hecaen, H. (1962) Clinical symptomatology in right and left hemisphere lesions. In V. B.

Mountcastle (Ed.) *Interhemispheric Relations and Cerebral Dominance.* Baltimore, MD: Johns Hopkins Press.

Hecaen, H. (1964) Mental symptoms associated with tumors of the frontal lobe. In J. M. Warren and K. Akert (Eds), *The Frontal Granular Cortex and Behavior.* New York: McGraw-Hill.

Heilman, K. M. (1979) Neglect and related disorders. In K. M. Heilman and E. Valenstein (Eds), *Clinical Neuropsychology.* New York: Oxford University Press.

Heilman, K. M., Bowers, D., Speedie, L., and Coslett, H. B. (1984). Comprehension of affective and non-affective prosody. *Neurology,* **34**, 917–30.

Heilman, K. M., Scholes, R., and Watson, R. T. (1975) Auditory affective agnosia: disturbed comprehension of affective speech. *Journal of Neurology, Neurosurgery, and Psychiatry,* **38**, 69–72.

Heilman, K. M., and Van Den Abell, T. (1979) Right hemisphere dominance for mediating cerebral activation. *Neuropsychologia,* **17**,

Heller, W., and Levy, J. (1981) Perception and expression of emotion in right-handers and left-handers. *Neuropsychologia,* **19**, 263–72.

Jackson, J. H. (1879) On affections of speech from diseases of the brain. *Brain,* **2**, 203–22.

James, W. (1884) What is emotion? *Mind,* **4**, 118–204.

Kahneman, D., Slovic, P., and Tversky, A. (1982) Judgment under uncertainty: Heuristics and biases. Cambridge: Cambridge University Press.

Kent, R. D., and Rosenbek, J. C. (1982) Prosodic disturbance and neurologic lesion. *Brain and Language,* **15**, 259–291.

Kinsbourne, M. (1978) The biological determinants of functional bisymmetry and asymmetry. In M. Kinsbourne (Ed.), *Asymmetrical Functions of the Brain,* pp. 3–13, New York: Cambridge University Press.

Kinsbourne, M., and Bemporad, B. (1984) Lateralization of emotion: a model and the evidence. In N. Fox and R. J. Davidson (Eds), *The Psychobiology of Affective Development.* Hillsdale, NJ: Erlbaum.

Knight, R. T., Hillyard, S. A., Woods, D. L. and Neville, H. J. (1981) The effects of frontal cortex lesions on event-related potentials during auditory selective attention. *Electroencephalography and Clinical Neurophysiology,* **52**, 571–82.

Kolb, B., and Milner, B. (1981) Observations on spontaneous facial expression after focal cerebral excisions and after intracorotid injection of sodium amytal. *Neuropsychologia,* **19**, 505–14.

Kronfol, Z., Hamsher, K., Digre, K., and Waziri, R. (1978). Depression and hemisphere functions: changes associated with unilateral ECT. *British Journal of Psychiatry,* **132**, 560–567.

Kushnir, M. Gordon, H., and Heifetz, A. (1980) Cognitive asymmetries in bipolar and unipolar depressed patients. Paper presented to the International Neuropsychological Society, San Francisco, February, 1980.

Lazarus, R. (1982) Thoughts on the relations between emotion and cognition. *American Psychologist,* **37**(9), 1019–24.

Levy, J. (1969) Possible basis for the evolution of lateral specialization of the human brain. *Nature,* **224**, 614–15.

Levy, J. (1982) Individual difference in cerebral hemisphere asymmetry: theoretical issues and experimental considerations. In J. Hellidge (Ed.), *Cerebral Hemisphere Asymmetry: Method, Theory and Application.* New York: Praeger Scientific.

Levy, J., Heller, W., Banich, M. T., and Burton, L. A. (1983) Are variations among right-handed individuals in perceptual asymmetries caused by characteristic arousal differences between hemispheres? *Journal of Experimental Psychology: Human Perception and Performance,* **9**, 329–58.

Ley, R. G., and Bryden, M. P. (1979) Hemispheric differences in processing emotions and faces. *Brain and Language*, **7**, 127–38.

Lipsey, J. R., Robinson, R. G., Pearlson, G. D., Rao, K., and Price, T. R. (1983) Mood change following bi-lateral hemisphere brain injury. *British Journal of Psychiatry*, **143**, 266–273.

Luria, A. R. (1973) *The Working Brain;* An Introduction to Neuropsychology. New York: Basic Books.

Malamut, B. L., Saunders, R. C., and Mishkin, M. (1984) Monkeys with combined amygdalo-hippocampal lesions succeed in object discrimination learning despite 24-hour intertrial intervals. *Behavioral Neuroscience*, **8**, 759–69.

Mathew, R. J., Wilson, W. H., and Daniel, D. G. (1985) The effect of nonsedating doses of diazepam on regional cerebral blood flow. *Biological Psychiatry*, **20**, 1109–16.

Matthysse, S. (1977). Dopamine and selective attention. *Advances in Biochemical Psychopharmacology*, **16**, 667–9.

McIntyre, M., Pritchard, P. B., and Lombroso, C. T. (1976) Left and right temporal lobe epileptics: a controlled investigation of some psychological differences. *Epilepsia*, **17**, 377–386.

Mesulam, M. M. (1981) A cortical network for directed attention and unilateral neglect. *Annals of Neurology*, **10**, 309–25.

Meyer, V. (1966) Psychological effects of brain damage. In H. J. Eysenck (Ed.), *Handbook of Abnormal Psychology*. New York: Basic Books.

Milner, B. (1967) Discussion of the paper: Experimental analysis of cerebral dominance in man. In C. H. Millikan and F. L. Darley (Eds), *Brain Mechanisms Underlying Speech and Language*. New York: Grune & Stratton.

Monrad–Krohn, G. H. (1924) On the dissociation of voluntary and emotional innervation in facial paresis of central origin. *Brain*, **47**, 22–35.

Monrad–Krohn, G. H. (1963) The third element of speech: prosody and its disorders. In L. Halpern (Ed.), *Problems of Dynamic Neurology*. New York: Grune & Stratton.

Moscovitch, M., and Olds, J. (1982) Asymmetries in spontaneous facial expressions and their possible relation to hemispheric specialization. *Neuropsychologia*, **20**, 71–81.

Mungas, D. (1982) Interictal behavior abnormality in temporal lobe epilepsy: a specific syndrone or nonspecific psychopathology? *Archives of General Psychiatry*, **39**, 108–111.

Myslobodsky, M. S. and Weiner, M. (1976) Pharmacologic implications of hemispheric asymmetry. *Life Sciences*, **19**, 1467–1478.

Natale, M., Gur, R. E., and Gur, R. C. (1983) Hemispheric asymmetries in processing emotional expressions. *Neuropsychologia*, **21**, 555–65.

Nebes, R. D. (1978) Direct examination of cognitive function in the left and right hemispheres. In M. Kinsbourne (Ed.), *Asymmetrical Function of the Brain*, pp. 99–140. Cambridge: Cambridge University Press.

Panksepp, J. (1981) Brain opiods: a neurochemical substrate for narcotic and social dependence. In S. Cooper (Ed.), *Theory in Psychopharmacology*, Vol. 1. New York: Academic Press.

Pearlson, G. D., and Robinson, R. G. (1981) Suction lesions of the frontal cerebral cortex in the rat induce asymmetrical behavioral and catecholaminergic responses. *Brain Research*, **218**, 233–42.

Perria, L., Rosadini, G., and Rossi, G. F. (1961) Determination of side of cerebral dominance with amobabital. *Archives of Neurology*, **4**, 173–81.

Posner, M. I., Friedrich, F. J., Walker, J., and Rafal, R. (1983) Neural control of the direction of covert visual orienting. Paper presented at the Meetings of the Psychonomic Society, November, 1983.

Pribram, K. H. (1981) Emotions. In S. K. Filskov and T. J. Boll (Eds), *Handbook of Clinical Neuropsychology*, pp. 102–34. New York: Wiley-Interscience.

Pribram, K. H., and McGuinness, D. (1975) Arousal, activation, and effort in the control of attention. *Psychological Review*, **82**, 116–49.

Reuter–Lorenz, P. A., Givis, R. P., and Moscovitch, M. (1983) Hemispheric specialization and the perception of emotion: evidence from right-handers and from inverted and non-inverted left handers. *Neuropsychologia*, **21**, 687–92.

Rinn, W. E. (1984) The neuropsychology of facial expression: a review of the neurological and psychological mechanisms for producing facial expressions. *Psychological Bulletin*, **95**, 52–77.

Robinson, R. G. (1979) Differential behavioral and biochemical effects of right and left hemispheric cerebral infarction in the rat. *Science*, **205**, 707–10.

Robinson, R. G., Kubos, K. L., Rao, K., and Price, T. R. (1984) Mood disorders in stroke patients: importance of location of lesion. *Brain*, **107**, 81–93.

Robinson, R. G., and Szetela, B. (1981) Mood change following left hemispheric brain injury. *Annals of Neurology*, **9**, 447–53.

Rosen, R. C., Goldstein, L., Scoles, V., and Lazarus, C. (in press) Psychophysiological correlates of nocturnal penile tumescence (NPT) in normal males. *Psychosomatic Medicine*,

Ross, E., and Mesulam, M. M. (1979) Dominant language functions of the right hemisphere? Prosody and emotional gesturing. *Archives of Neurology*, **36**, 144–8.

Rossi, G. F. and Rosadini, G. (1967) Experimental analysis of cerebral dominance in man. In C. H. Millikan and F. L. Darley (Eds), *Brain Mechanisms Underlying Speech and Language*. New York: Grune & Stratton.

Rothbart, M. K., Taylor, S., and Tucker, D. M. (in press) Right-sided asymmetries in infant emotional expression, *Neuropsychologia*.

Sackeim, H. A., Greenberg, M. S., Weiman, A. L., Gur, R. C., Hungerbuhler, J. P., and Geschwind, M. (1982) Hemispheric asymmetry in the expression of positive and negative emotions: neurologic evidence. *Archives of Neurology*, **39**, 210–18.

Sackeim, H. A., and Gur, R. C. (1982) Facial asymmetry and the communication of emotion. In J. T. Cacioppo and R. E. Petty (Eds), *Social Psychophysiology*. New York: Guilford Press.

Sackeim, H. A., Gur, R. C., and Saucy, M. C. (1978) Emotions are expressed more intensely on the left side of the face. *Science*, **202**, 434–6.

Safer, M. A., and Leventhal, H. (1977) Ear differences in evaluating emotional tone of voice and verbal content. *Journal of Experimental Psychology: Human Perception and Performance*, **3**, 75–82.

Saxby, L., and Bryden, M. P. (1985) Left visual-field advantage in children for processing visual emotional stimuli. *Developmental Psychology*, **21**, 253–61.

Schaffer, C. E., Davidson, R. J., and Saron, C. (1983) Frontal and parietal electroencephalogram asymmetry in depressed and nondepressed subjects. *Biological Psychiatry*, **18**, 753–62.

Schildkraut, J. (1965) The catecholamine hypothesis of affective disorders: a review of supporting evidence. *American Journal of Psychiatry*, **122**, 509–22.

Schlanger, B. B., Schlanger, P., and Gerstman, L. J. (1976) The perception of emotionally toned sentences by right hemisphere damaged and aphasic subjects. *Brain and Language*, **3**, 396–403.

Schwartz, G. E., Davidson, R. J., and Maer, F. (1975) Right hemisphere lateralization for emotion in the human brain: interactions with cognition. *Science*, **190**, 286–288.

Shapiro, D. (1965) *Neurotic Styles*. New York: Basic Books.

Shaw, E. D., Mann, J. J., Stokes, P. E., and Manevitz, Z. (1986) Effects of lithium carbonate on associative productivity and idiosyncracy in bipolar outpatients. *American Journal of Psychiatry*, **143**, 1166–9.

Shearer, S. L., and Tucker, D. M. (1981) Differential cognitive contributions of the cerebral hemispheres in the modulation of emotional arousal. *Cognitive Therapy and Research*, **5**, 85–93.

Silberman, E. K., and Weingartner, H. (1986) Hemispheric lateralization of functions related to emotion. *Brain and Cognition*, **5**, 322–53.

Spence, K. W. (1958) A theory of emotionally based drive (D) and its relation to performance in simple learning situations. *American Psychologist*, **13**, 131–141.

Squires, L. R. (1986) Mechanisms of memory. *Science*, **232**, 1612–19.

Strauss, E. (1983) Perception of emotional words. *Neuropsychologia*, **21**, 99–103.

Strauss, E. (1986) Cerebral representation of emotion. In P. Blanck, R. Buck, and R. Rosenthal (Eds), *Nonverbal Communication in the Clinical Context*, pp. 176–95. University Park, PA: Pennsylvania State Press.

Strauss, E., Risser, A., and Jones, M. W. (1982) Fear responses in patients with epilepsy. *Archives of Neurology*, **39**, 626–30.

Strauss, E., Wada, J., and Kosaka, B. (1983) Spontaneous facial expressions occurring at onset of focal seizure activity. *Archives of Neurology*, **40**, 545–7.

Suberi, M., and McKeever, W. F. (1977) Differential right hemispheric memory storage of emotional and non-emotional faces. *Neuropsychologia*, **15**, 757–68.

Swenson, R. A., and Tucker, D. M. (1983) Lateralized cognitive style and self-description. *International Journal of Neuroscience*, **21**, 91–100.

Terzian, H. (1964) Behavioral and EEG effects of intracarotid sodium amytal injection. *Acta Neurochirgia*, **12**, 230–239.

Tucker, D. M. (1981) Lateral brain function, emotion, and conceptualization. *Psychological Bulletin*, **89**, 19–46.

Tucker, D. M. (1986) Neural control of emotional communication. In P. Blanck, R. Buck and R. Rosenthal (Eds), *Nonverbal Communication in the Clinical Context*. Cambridge: Cambridge University Press.

Tucker, D. M. (1987) Hemisphere specialization: a mechanism for unifying anterior and posterior brain regions. In D. Ottoson (Ed.), *The Dual Brain: Specialization and Unification of the Cerebral Hemispheres*. Stockholm: Wenner–Gren Foundation.

Tucker, D. M., Antes, J. R., Stenslie, C. E., and Barnhardt, T. N. (1978) Anxiety and lateral cerebral function. *Journal of Abnormal Psychology*, **87**, 380–3.

Tucker, D. M., and Dawson, S. L. (1984) Asymmetric EEG power and coherence as method actors generated emotions. *Biological Psychology*, **19**, 63–75.

Tucker, D. M., and Newman, J. P. (1981) Verbal versus imaginal cognitive stratagies in the inhibition of emotional arousal. *Cognitive Therapy and Research*, **5**, 197–202.

Tucker, D. M., Roth, R. S., Arneson, B. A., and Buckingham, V. (1977) Right hemispheric activation during stress. *Neuropsychologia*, **15**, 697–700.

Tucker, D. M., Stenslie, C. E., Roth, R. S., and Shearer, S. (1981) Right frontal lobe activation and right hemisphere performance decrement during a depressed mood. *Archives of General Psychiatry*, **38**, 169–74.

Tucker, D. M., Watson, R. G., and Heilman, K. M. (1976) Affective discrimination and evocation in patients with right parietal disease. *Neurology*, **26**, 354.

Tucker, D. M., and Williamson, P. A. (1984) Asymmetric neural control systems in human self-regulation. *Psychological Review*, **91**, 185–215.

Tyler, S. K., and Tucker, D. M. (1982) Anxiety and perceptual structure: individual differences in neuropsychological function. *Journal of Abnormal Psychology*, **91**, 210–20.

Walker, E. and McGuire, M. (1982) Intra- and inter-hemispheric information processing in schizophrenia. *Psychological Bulletin*, **29**, 701–25.

Wechsler, A. F. (1973) The effect of organic brain disease on recall of emotionally charged versus neutral narrative texts. *Neurology*, **23**, 130–5.

Werner, H. (1957) *The Comparative Psychology of Mental Development*. New York: Harper.

Whitaker, H. A. (1978) Is the right leftover? Commentary on Corballis & Morgan, 'On the biological basis of human laterality.' *Behavioral and Brain Sciences*, **1**.

Yingling, C. D., and Skinner, J. E. (1977) Gating of thalamic input to cerebral cortex by nucleus reticularis thalami. In J. E. Desmedt (Ed.), *Attention, Voluntary Contraction, and Event-related Potentials. Progress in Clinical Neurophysiology*, Vol. 1, pp. 70–96. Basel: Karger.

Zurif, E. B., and Mendelsohn, M. (1972) Hemispheric specialization for the perception of speech sounds: the influence of intonation and structure. *Perception and Psychophysics*, **11**, 329–32.

PART 2

PERIPHERAL PROCESSES IN EMOTIONS

Introduction

There has been almost universal agreement that emotions involve hormonal and peripheral physiological changes. Beyond this, the nature and role of these changes have been the basis of much dispute. One of the chief differences has concerned whether they are the *cause* (or one of the causes) of the emotional response or one of the *components* or *consequences* of emotional response. The second major difference among conceptions of the role of physiological arousal in emotion, cutting across the issue of cause and effect, is the issue of the *physiological specificity* of emotions. There are, and have been, theorists who take extreme views on this, arguing that different emotions all have the same underlying physiological state, usually sympathetic arousal. Others argue that different emotions are accompanied by specific physiological patterns.

The first two chapters in this part of the book address the second of these theoretical issues, and the authors agree that we are not in a position to draw conclusions about the direction of causality in the relationships between physiological and endocrine changes and emotion. Wagner (Chapter 3, *The peripheral physiological differentiation of emotions*) concentrates on a series of studies commencing in the 1950s that attempted to demonstrate, mostly using laboratory manipulations of various kinds, that different emotions are associated with different patterns of peripheral physiological activity. Despite the difficulties of conducting research on this topic, a fairly consistent picture emerges for two emotions, whereby fear is associated with increased heart rate and systolic and diastolic blood pressure, and anger with a greater increase in diastolic blood pressure and muscle action potentials. Differences for other emotions are much less consistent. The anger–fear differences are confirmed by studies of the excretion of catecholamines during various naturally occurring events or laboratory manipulations. Although the investigators have not always interpreted their own results in this way, it is argued that anger is shown to be associated with greater secretion of norepinephrine than epinephrine, and fear with greater secretion of epinephrine.

It is argued that the physiological differences between emotions represent functional patterns to deal with different demands of environmental circumstances, and that these might be organised by subcortical circuits of the type described by Panksepp in Chapter 1. Finally, it is argued that the implications of differential patterns for illness are more important than the simple demonstration of such patterns.

Popp and Baum (Chapter 4, *Hormones and emotions: affective correlates of endocrine activity*) concentrate on research relating activity in a number of endocrine systems to emotions and emotional behaviour. They summarize work with both humans and other species that relates anxiety- and fear-related behaviour to increased corticosteroid production. Their review also suggests a relationship between these types of behaviour and catecholamines. In contrast to the conclusion reached by Wagner in Chapter 3, some evidence suggests a greater role for norepinephrine than for epinephrine. Central catecholamines are also shown to increase during anxiety, a result that can be related to the subcortical circuits discussed by Panksepp in Chapter 1. Aggressive behaviour has been found to be related to testosterone levels, and this effect is modulated by oestrogen administration in female mice. The effect of androgens can also be mediated by pheromone production, as is demonstrated by studies of the effect of the urine of mice with specific behavioural or endocrine characteristics on aggressive behaviour of conspecifics. The level of insulin is also positively related to aggressive behaviour.

There is some evidence linking depression to levels of gonadal hormones in women, but much better evidence for a link between thyroid hormones and the depression–mania dimension, and for increased cortisol secretion in depression. Finally, the role of endogenous opioids in elation is discussed. Popp and Baum conclude by emphasizing that they do not regard endocrine changes as the causes of emotion. The study of endocrine changes is not aimed at revealing the causes of emotions, but at a better understanding of the nature of emotional experience.

Gatchel and Barnes (Chapter 5, *Physiological self-control and emotion*) accept the differentiability of the physiological components of emotion, and briefly discuss the role of physiological changes as one of the subsystems of the overall emotional response. However, their main purpose is to consider the evidence that directly changing these physiological components of an emotion will change the emotion. This is important not only theoretically, but also because it suggests the possibility that physiological self-control will have health benefits. They concentrate on the modification of anxiety, partly because of its clear therapeutic implications and partly because this is where most of the evidence originates. The major method that has been used in such investigations is the use of biofeedback. Gatchel and Barnes update earlier reviews and conclude that the data suggest that biofeedback of any of a variety of physiological parameters is not especially effective (compared with other treatment methods) in the reduction of anxiety.

Moreover, as Gatchel and Barnes go on to discuss, the anxiety reduction that does result from biofeedback might be attributable to other factors such as the strong placebo effect that undoubtedly accompanies biofeedback. Another problem is that changing one aspect of an emotional response need not produce a change in the entire emotional pattern. Perhaps the most important issue here, however, concerns the role of perceived control in the reduction of anxiety. Certainly, the importance of perceived control in the reduction of the impact of stressful events has been demonstrated. Finally, Gatchel and Barnes consider the relation between perceived control and the placebo effect, and suggest that placebo drugs might function by giving patients the perception of control over their symptoms.

Chapter 3

The Peripheral Physiological Differentiation of Emotions

Hugh Wagner
University of Manchester

ABSTRACT

Two bodies of literature directly relating to the issue of the physiological differentiability of emotions are reviewed. Contrary to the views of a number of authors, it is concluded that data from studies of physiological parameters and of catecholamine excretion during states of anger and fear firmly demonstrate the relationship suggested by Ax in 1953, that anger is associated with excretion of epinephrine (E) and norepinephrine (NE), and fear with the excretion of E. Differentiation of other emotions is not well established. The theoretical and health implications of these findings are discussed.

One of the major debates between theories of emotion has been the issue of the *physiological specificity* of emotions. There are, and have been, theorists who take extreme views on this, on the one hand arguing that different emotions all have the same underlying physiological state, usually sympathetic arousal (the activation theorists, e.g. Duffy, 1972; Schachter, 1964; Zillmann, 1983). On the other hand are those theorists who argue that different emotions are accompanied by specific physiological patterns (e.g. Arnold, 1960; Izard, 1977; James, 1884). In this chapter I shall consider the evidence that bears directly on this issue of the specificity of the peripheral physiological changes accompanying emotions.

Handbook of Social Psychophysiology, Edited by H. Wagner and A. Manstead,
© 1989 John Wiley & Sons Ltd

METHODOLOGICAL ISSUES

Each of us is presumably aware of at least some degree of specificity in our physiological responses to emotions. A number of physiological changes produce interoceptively mediated sensations. For example, we feel nausea in disgust and fear, we get 'butterflies' when nervous, a 'lump in the throat' when sad, and our faces may become hot when we are embarrassed. Specific changes may also be perceived by way of exteroceptors. For instance, we may become aware of our hearts pounding when we are afraid, hear the blood rushing in our ears when angry, and feel perspiration on our palms when afraid. There are also changes that are externally visible, including a number of facial cutaneous vascular changes: blushing with embarrassment, blanching with fear, and going 'purple' with rage. From such experiences [and others that James (1884) might have called 'coarser examples'] it might seem that physiological specificity of emotions is undeniable. Why, then, have so many theorists resisted adopting such a view?

Despite the examples given above, there are relatively few studies clearly demonstrating physiological specificity. Stemmler (1984) has claimed that those who refer to this type of study tend to ignore the 'larger number' in which no evidence for physiological specificity has been found. However, we need to be cautious before concluding that a majority verdict in favour of nonspecificity must carry the day. There are several reasons why studies might fail to demonstrate any physiological specificity that does exist, and we need to look at these before considering the evidence for specificity. Indeed, many of the studies that appear to fail to demonstrate specificity have not been designed or conducted in such a way as to be capable of demonstrating the physiological differentiability of emotions.

In order to look for physiological specificity in emotions it is, of course, first necessary not only to produce emotions, but also to produce different and relatively pure emotions. None of these is a task to be taken lightly, and failure at any of these levels will render useless any resultant failure to differentiate emotional conditions physiologically. This is true of some studies cited by Stemmler (1984) as failing to demonstrate specificity. For example, Oken, Heath, Shipman, Goldstein, Grinker, and Fisch (1966) compared responses to an anxiety-provoking stimulus with those to white noise which produced 'little, if any, affective response to the sound' (p. 628). Chessick, Bassan, and Shattan (1966) were able to produce different physiological patterns for three states but argued 'We are convinced that it is impossible to experimentally produce anger, anxiety, or pain in any "pure" form. For example, in our experiment it turned out that the anger situation produced a higher or at least equal subjective anxiety report than the anxiety situation' (p. 164).

Ney and Gale (1988) have discussed such difficulties in the generation of emotional states in the laboratory, and have suggested that the only sure way to induce real emotions is to use real situations, such as conversations. People react to (and interact with) the environment differently, so that the same emotional stimulus or experimental manipulation will not have the same meaning for each individual, and will not arouse the same emotion (or be part of the same emotion) for each individual. For this reason it is essential to define the occurrence and nature of emotions during this type of experiment by the statements or behaviour of the subjects. This usually means relying on self-reports, and the status of these has been quite widely debated (e.g. Levenson, 1988). Nevertheless, the most characteristic (perhaps definitive) feature of emotion is its experiential quality, and it is clear that this can only be indicated by self-report.

Even if the experimenter is able to produce different and relatively pure emotions in the laboratory, and is able to identify what they are, in order to demonstrate specificity the appropriate physiological systems must be observed. Choice of parameters seems often to have been determined on the basis of availability or convenience rather than on indications such as the perceptible differences mentioned above or the possible functional nature of physiological changes in emotion. Furthermore, the specific physiological changes characteristic of different emotions are likely to be *patterns*, which might differ in subtle ways, rather than simple gross differences in one or two parameters. If this is so, precise, multivariate techniques will be required to differentiate them (Fahrenberg, 1986; Stemmler, 1984).

Perhaps the greatest difficulty facing the experimenter attempting to demonstrate physiological specificity is what Lacey, Bateman, and Van Lehn (1953) called *autonomic response specificity*: the tendency of individuals to respond maximally with the same physiological parameter regardless of the stressor. This *individual* specificity does not logically exclude *stimulus* specificity (e.g. emotional differentiation), but the likelihood that any stimulus specificity has to be superimposed on (or modified by) individual specificity must make the demonstration of specific patterns of physiological change in different emotions much more difficult. In essence, the simple assumption that emotion *A* will produce physiological pattern *A'*, and emotion *B* will produce pattern *B'* ignores the fact that emotion is an *interaction* between the individual and the environment. Individual differences will arise not only because individuals interpret the same stimulus conditions differently, but also because they have different characteristic responses. Fahrenberg (1986) called this *motivation* specificity, and reviewed a series of studies comparing the different types of specificity, though not explicitly from an emotion perspective. He estimated that, with stimulus conditions ranging from comic slides and music to isometric exercise and blood taking, individual specificity accounts for 28–40% of the variance of physiological measures, motivational specificity for 17–21%, and stimulus specificity for only 5–19%.

Despite these difficulties, a number of formal or informal studies have been made of autonomic specificity, and the balance of the evidence is clearly in favour of specificity. We concentrate here on studies which have aimed at direct demonstrations of specificity, that is by comparing two or more emotional states.

ANGER AND FEAR

AUTONOMICALLY MEDIATED CHANGES IN ANGER AND FEAR

Some of the earliest evidence comes from quite informal observations of bodily changes during emotion. The most famous of these were made by Wolf and Wolff (1947) on the patient Tom, who had a large gastric fistula that permitted the observation of his gastric mucosa. Wolf and Wolff reported that when Tom was alarmed, and experiencing fear, there was an acute blanching of the mucosa accompanied by lessened secretion. During sadness or self-reproach there was a more prolonged and less severe lowering of vascularity and secretion. When Tom was feeling resentment, hostility or anger his gastric mucosa became reddened and engorged, and secretion increased.

Wolff (1950) subsequently described a number of observations of changes in mucous membranes, smooth muscle, heart, circulation, renal haemodynamics, and skeletal muscles, made under conditions of anxiety, resentment, anger, fear, and frustration, some of which support the initial results with Tom. The observations on Tom were confirmed with another patient by Engel, Reichsman, and Segal (1956).

Following these early observations, experimental work concentrated on the question of the physiological differentiability of anger and fear. The first reported attempt to demonstrate formally in the laboratory that emotions are associated with specific physiological states was that of Ax (1953). He recorded nine physiological functions in 43 subjects. During a session in which they were instructed simply to relax on a bed and listen to their preferred music, two manipulations to induce fear and anger were introduced; 22 subjects receiving the fear manipulation first. The fear manipulation involved the subject receiving small electric shocks, followed by the threat of dangerous equipment malfunction. The anger manipulation involved the subject being abused and roughly handled by the polygraph operator.

For each of 14 derived physiological variables the maximal rises and falls during the stimulus period and the following 2 minutes were noted as deviations from the levels just before stimulation. Anger was associated with greater increases in diastolic blood pressure (DBP), number of skin conductance responses (SCRs), and electromyogram (EMG), together with a larger drop in minimum heart rate (HR). Fear was accompanied by greater increases in skin conductance level (SCL), number of muscle tension peaks, and respiration rate (RR). Ax concluded that his data demonstrated that fear and anger are associated with different physiological patterns, and that these are powerful enough to overcome individual response stereotypy. Some features of the fear and anger patterns suggested to Ax that the former is like the pattern produced by E injection, while the Latter was like the response to a combination of E and NE.

Schachter (1957) reported a study carried out in the same laboratory as Ax's study. The procedures were similar to those of Ax, with the addition of painful stimulation, the cold pressor test, and the physiological measures were the same as those used by Ax, although the same derived scores were not always used.

Schachter rated each subject's pattern of response on a 5-point scale, ranging from $+2$ (indicating a marked NE-like response) to -2 (indicating a marked E-like response). Each of these was defined by the occurrence of a particular combination of cardiovascular changes. The mean scores on this scale were *pain*: $+0.9$, *fear*: -1.1, and *anger*: -0.1. The conclusion that these show, respectively, moderate NE, E, and mixed effects for the three conditions must be moderated by high variances for these scores, especially for anger. While 31 of 47 subjects had NE-like patterns for pain, and 35 of 48 subjects showed an E-like response to fear stimulation, in anger, 19 subjects showed NE responses, 22 E responses, and only seven actually showed a mixed effect. In terms of particular parameters, Schachter's findings directly support Ax's for EMG, SCL, and RR, but not for DBP, although his derived measure of peripheral resistance (mean BP divided by cardiac output index) increased in anger and decreased in fear, which is a not inconsistent result. A greater increase in mean HR for fear is also consistent with Ax's more complicated description of HR changes.

It seems likely that, for at least some subjects, some degree of fear will carry over into the anger condition which always followed it; if the equipment has malfunctioned once, why not twice? It is possible that the negative scores shown by those who were rated high on anger reflected a degree of residual fear. It is possible that subjects who were most afraid in the fear condition would also be most angry subsequently, and might also have more residual fear.

Funkenstein, King, and Drolette (1954, 1957) subjected 69 students to stress-inducing laboratory tasks, after which they were interviewed concerning their feelings and reactions. The investigators subsequently scored recordings of the interviews for emotional feelings. Subjects were divided into seven groups, including one consisting of those who expressed only, or mostly, anxiety, one of those who expressed anger directed at the experimenter ('anger-out'), and one of those who were angry at themselves ('anger-in'). Before and during the stress period, systolic blood pressure (SBP) and DBP, HR, and ballistocardiograph (BCG) parameters were recorded. Of greatest concern here are the findings that anger-out subjects had lower SBP increase and lower HR increase than anxiety subjects, and decreases (rather than increases) in BCG parameters relating to cardiac stroke volume and output. Anger-in (which Funkenstein *et al.* suggested occurs in depressed patients) differed from anxiety only in showing smaller cardiac output increase, while anger-out differed from anger-in in the same respects as it did from anxiety, except that there was no SBP difference.

The relationship of the anxiety and anger-out results to E and NE is confirmed by unpublished findings of Funkenstein that are referred to by Funkenstein *et al.* (1957), which showed that E infusion produced increases in HR and the BCG parameters used in the earlier study, while after NE infusion a pattern similar to the anger-out pattern was produced.

Funkenstein and his co-workers also investigated the action of a parasympathomimetic agent, methacholine (mecholyl), on hypertension in psychotic patients and normal persons. Hypertension is usually due either to increased cardiac output or, more frequently, to increased peripheral resistance (from vasoconstriction), and a parasympathomimetic drug should reduce both of these effects, and hence should always lower BP. However, Funkenstein (1956) found that the patients could be divided into two groups on the basis of the effect methacholine had on their BP; one group showed a profound and sustained decrease in BP, while the other showed only a small and brief decrease. Psychiatric assessments of the predominant emotional characteristics of the patients revealed that almost all of those showing the first, profound, effect of methacholine on BP were judged to be expressing depression or anxiety, while almost all of those showing the smaller effect were judged to be expressing interpersonal anger. The explanation for these differences appeared to be related, once again, to the actions of E and NE. When the mechanism of blood pressure control was through cardiac output, it seemed to be controlled by E, whereas NE acts to increase blood pressure by increasing peripheral vasoconstriction. Methacholine has a greater and more sustained effect on the E-produced increased cardiac output than on the NE-produced vasoconstriction. Hence, it seems that patients showing depression and anxiety ('anger-in' in Funkenstein's terminology) have an E-related hypertension, while those showing anger ('anger-out') have an NE-related hypertension. This is the same relationship as that suggested by Ax and by Schachter. Funkenstein *et al.* (1957) have confirmed these relationships by examining the characteristic responses to frustration or stress (anger or anxiety/depression) of a student sample.

Oken (1960) compared HR with SBP and DBP changes in psychiatric patients during interviews designed to produce anxiety or anger. Because the intended affective change was not always the most pronounced, as judged from self-report or behavioural indices, the physiological changes were correlated with anxiety and anger ratings for each of the ten subjects. Anger ratings correlated significantly with both DBP and SBP, and nonsignificantly with HR. Anxiety ratings correlated significantly with only DBP. None of the anger correlations was significantly greater than the corresponding anxiety correlation. These findings seem to contradict those of the earlier researchers discussed above, with anger showing a high degree of relation to SBP as well as to DBP. However, Oken argued that his data are not directly contradictory, since the correlational method used was not entirely compatible with the patterning procedure of Ax and of Schachter. Furthermore, he pointed to procedural differences such as the more indirect method of inducing emotions he used, and the necessity for his subjects to respond overtly during the procedure.

A further feature of Oken's study helps to resolve this issue. Subjects were divided into those who expressed their anger and those who suppressed it. *Expressers* had low DBP and high SBP, while *suppressors*, conversely, had high DBP and low SBP. Ax's and Schachter's subjects might well have tended to suppress their anger in their laboratory situation, and some of the observations cited by Ax do suggest this. The differentiation in these studies between individuals who express anger and those who suppress it is an important one, to which I shall return.

A contrary view of the circulatory changes during the emotions of fear and anger was given by Harris, Schoenfeld, Gwynne, Weissler, and Warren (1964). They used cardiac catheterization and serial blood chemistry to examine '20 episodes of intense, lifelike fear and anger induced by hypnosis in 9 subjects'. Similar haemodynamic changes were observed in both types of state: increased cardiac output, HR, and mean BP, and decreased stroke volume and peripheral resistance. Respiration rate more than doubled. The authors concluded that fear and anger produce identical haemodynamic responses. These authors' choice of mean BP rather than SBP and DBP separately might in part account for their failure to find differences.

Following the tentative proposal by Ax (1953) that the physiological pattern of fear corresponded to the action of E, while that of anger was similar to the combined action of E and NE, Chessick *et al.* (1966) conducted a study to compare the effects of infusions of these substances with the effects of manipulations intended to produce anxiety, anger, and pain. The experimental manipulations all took place in one session, in the order: anxiety (produced by leaving the infusion equipment in the subject's view after telling him to expect the insertion of the intravenous needle); the three drug conditions (E, NE, or placebo); pain (a 'not-too-sharp' needle jabbed into the finger); and anger (drinking as much water as possible through a tube with repeated badgering by the experimenters). Subjective responses were assessed by self-ratings for anxiety and the ratings of two observers for anger and pain.

The anxiety manipulation caused significant increases in both SBP and DBP, HR, and BCG amplitude, while the anger manipulation was associated with an increase in SBP, significantly larger increases in DBP and HR, and decreases in axillary temperature and neck EMG. These results partially confirm the earlier findings, although differences for HR are not as clear. However, there was no direct relationship between the responses to the affective conditions and those to the catecholamine infusions. The authors concluded that 'attributing the effects of pain, anger, or anxiety to the action of epinephrine or norepinephrine represents a gross oversimplification' (p. 164).

Roberts and Weerts (1982) reported the results of an investigation into the psychophysiology of fear and anger, using a somewhat different methodology, which attempted to overcome the difficulties inherent in presenting a hetero-geneous group of subjects with standard stimulus situations and hoping that they would all respond similarly. These authors selected 16 subjects on the basis of their self-ratings of fear and anger imagery. Each subject was asked to imagine six scenes—high and low fear, high and low anger, and two neutral—while HR and DBP and SBP were monitored. The results were that while all three physiological parameters increased more for high intensity than for low intensity emotional images, DBP showed a significantly larger increase for high anger than for high fear scenes. The findings for BP thus confirm those of Ax (1953) and Schachter (1957), although the expected greater HR increase for fear was not shown by these subjects. Roberts and Weerts argued, however, that an incidental finding—i.e. that HR increase correlated negatively with rated anger in anger scenes—is consistent with the earlier findings.

Schwartz, Weinberger, and Singer (1981) used a similar technique, in which subjects imagined a scene from their own past which produced one of anger, fear, happiness, or sadness. To investigate further whether the physiological changes in these emotions differ from the SNS activation of exercise, after imagining each scene for 2 minutes the subjects exercised by stepping up and down while they 'nonverbally (facially and posturally) expressed the feelings appropriate to the imagined situations' (p. 347). SBP and DBP and HR were measured during imagery and exercise for the four emotions and for control and relaxation conditions. The results during imagery partly confirmed earlier work. DBP showed a greater rise for anger than for fear, as did mean arterial pressure, which showed similar changes for fear, happiness, sadness, and control. SBP did not differentiate between the four emotions, although it was significantly raised in all, compared with the control and relaxation conditions. This was also true of HR, although anger and fear showed greater HR increases than did happiness, with sadness falling in between.

Exercise removed the differential effect of emotion condition on DBP, with each condition showing a small decrease (interpreted as a consequence of peripheral vasodilatation in response to the demands of exercise). SBP, on the other hand, now differentiated emotions, showing the largest increases during fear and anger, then happiness, with sadness no higher than during control and relaxation conditions. Heart rate showed the highest increases during anger, then fear and happiness, then control, then sadness and relaxation. Since the postural expression of emotions in which subjects were asked to engage included rate of exercise, and since subjects stepped faster in fear, anger, and happiness conditions than in the others, some of the observed differences might be explained by this factor.

Ekman, Levenson, and Friesen (1983) used a similar imagery method, and in addition used a novel method based on the assumption that facial expression is an important component of emotion. They looked at six emotions: fear, anger, surprise, disgust, sadness, and happiness. In order to avoid complications caused by frustration and embarrassment their subjects were 12 professional actors and four scientists who study the face, each of whom performed two tasks. The first ('directed facial action') involved following directions (after training) to contract particular facial muscles, which produced the expression of individual emotions without the subject actually being instructed to produce an emotional expression. There were also two non-emotional expressions to act as a control for movement. In the second task ('relived emotion') subjects were asked to 'relive' a past emotional experience. The first task lasted for 10 seconds, the second for 30 seconds. Physiological data (HR, left and right finger temperature, SRL, and forearm EMG) were only used in task 1 if videotapes showed that the instructed actions had been made, or in task 2 if the subjects rated their emotional experience at, or greater than, the midpoint of a nine-point rating scale and no other emotion was rated as highly. This helped to ensure that the emotional experience was relatively 'pure'.

Significant differences in autonomic functions were observed between the emotional conditions; that these were not secondary to somatic changes was indicated by the lack of differences on the forearm EMG measure. In the facial action task, anger was differentiated from fear and sadness by higher skin temperature changes, and in the relived emotions task, sadness differed from fear, anger, and disgust by a greater fall in SRL (disgust showing an increase). On both tasks, anger and fear were differentiated from happiness by having significantly higher HR, and anger was associated with greater increases in skin temperature than was happiness. These results again differentiate anger from fear, although here the difference is that anger has larger skin temperature increases. This is not inconsistent with the earlier findings of more peripheral vasoconstriction in anger that in fear, since that refers to (noradrenergic) constriction of blood vessel in the muscles, whereas increased finger temperature reflects dilatation of blood vessels in the skin (release from adrenergic activity).

Stemmler (1984) compared the responses of 34 physiological parameters (CNS, autonomic, and skeletal) to experimental conditions designed to arouse fear (a plunge into darkness during the reading of Poe's *Fall of the House of Usher*), anger (subjects attempted insoluble anagrams following rudely delivered instructions, and had to shout 'I don't know' with increasing intensity owing to an ostensible failure of the sound system in the laboratory), and joy (the approach of the end of the session, positively toned instructions, and the promise of greater than expected payment for participation). The results showed that 14 physiological parameters individually differentiated between the three conditions, partially replicating earlier results. Fear produced decreased muscle tone, low SCL, and increased vasoconstriction, and anger was accompanied by increased muscle tone vasodilatation, and increased frontalis tension. Joy was not associated with any pronounced characteristics, but had decreased frontalis activity and increased hand temperature. Discriminant analysis appeared to confirm that the three emotional situations were associated with different physiological patterns, and also differed from non-emotional stages of the experiment, although anger and happiness were not significantly different from one another. However, one weakness of this analysis is that Stemmler included all measures on all subjects, despite the fact that up to 65% of the subjects failed to report the 'appropriate' emotion.

Another feature of Stemmler's experiment is that, in order to avoid confounding the emotional experience with the demands of the induction procedure, the emotional differentiation was attemped for measurement periods immediately following the attempted induction of each emotion. This raises two problems. It is likely that the emotional and physiological effects of the manipulation will decrease in intensity, or even change in nature, after the end of induction, thereby lessening the apparent differentiability of the states. Secondly, this procedure reduces the ecological validity of the experiment. The situational determinants of an emotional state, their perception by the individual, and the individual's cognitive and behavioural attempts to respond to situational demands are all integral parts of the emotional experience. If the physiological changes in emotion are of any functional significance, then they must be evaluated in the context of the full emotional situation. Stemmler interpreted his data as failing to show emotion-specific patterns, but rather specific person–situation transactions. However, emotions *are* just such transactions.

James, Yee, Harshfield, Blank, and Pickering (1986) used ambulatory monitoring to record the SBP and DBP of 90 borderline hypertensives every 15 minutes over a 24-hour period, while the subjects went about their normal daily life. Each time a reading was made while the subjects were awake they recorded what they were doing and whether they felt happy, angry, or anxious. Both SBP and DBP were significantly higher in anxiety and anger than in happiness, while DBP was higher (but not significantly so) in anger than in anxiety.

This result is typical of much work relating anger to cardiovascular function in general, and hypertension in particular (see Diamond, 1982; Rosenman, 1985). Frequently, it is suppressed anger that is implicated in hypertension. Dimsdale Pierce, Schoenfeld, Brown, Zusman, and Graham (1986), for example, found that SBP in a large sample of men and women was significantly higher in those who described their responses to anger-provoking situations as suppressed. Most of this research does not examine differential emotions. In one study that did, Schneider, Egan, Johnson, Drobny, and Julius (1986) used psychometric evaluations of anxiety and anger with two groups of hypertensives, one whose mean BP returned to normal when they returned home from the clinic, and the other whose BP remained elevated. The high-home-BP group reported greater anger, which they tended not to express, than the low-home-BP group. The two groups did not differ in anxiety. However, anxiety has been found to be related to BP, albeit not as frequently as has anger. Whitehead, Blackwell, DeSilva, and Robinson(1977), for example, had hypertensive patients record their own BP four times each day, and rate themselves on scales of anger and anxiety. They found anxiety to be related to BP more strongly than was anger. Further discussion of the relationship between anger and cardiovascular disorders can be found in the volume edited by Chesney and Rosenman (1985).

The research I have reviewed in this section has used a variety of means of inducing emotions and a variety of physiological measures. Despite this, certain consistencies have emerged, most clearly the differentiation between anger and fear in terms of their cardiovascular patterns.

CATECHOLAMINE EXCRETION IN ANGER AND FEAR

There is a considerable body of evidence based on the estimation of E and NE excretion to support the conclusions reached about fear and anger in the previous section. Much of this evidence is less direct, relying not on the experimental manipulation of subjects' emotional state but on assumptions of, or clinical assessment of, that state. One of the earliest of these studies was undertaken by Elmadjian, Hope, and Lamson (1957), who assayed the amounts of these catecholamines in the urine of normal subjects, sportsmen, and psychiatric patients, under a variety of conditions. A group of 20 professional ice hockey players (a game involving high levels of aggression) gave urine samples before and after participating in a game. Norepinephrine levels increased to nearly six times, while E increased less than three times, the pre-game level; two players who did not participate showed the same increase in E but only a small increase in NE. The goal tender showed nearly three times the pre-game E and NE levels, while the coach had doubled E and unchanged NE excretion.

A consistent result was obtained from studies of neuropsychiatric patients undergoing an interview before about 20 medical staff, the outcome of which determined the patient's future. Catecholamine excretion after this presumably anxiety-provoking interview was compared with excretion at the same time on a control day. Epinephrine excretion was nearly doubled while NE remained the same. Normal subjects awaiting insulin tolerance and methacholine tests showed no change in excretion of either catecholamine if they were familiar with the procedure, but elevated excretion of NE or of NE *and* E if it was unfamiliar and they were anxious. Finally, a group of ten psychotic patients who had been rated on hostility and motor activity were examined. Patients with active and hostile patterns of behaviour had higher NE excretion, and some also had elevated E excretion.

Elmadjian *et al.* concluded that these results support the view that increased NE excretion, with or without increased excretion of E, accompanies 'active, aggressive emotional displays' (for example the participating hockey players), while a 'tense, anxious but passive display' (in the non-participant hockey players and the coach, for instance) accompanied increased E alone. However, it is noticeable that there are numerous exceptions in these groups of subjects (like the subjects anxiously awaiting tests), and this, coupled with the uncertainty of the determinations of emotional state in these cases, should lead us to be cautious in accepting this conclusion without other supporting evidence.

During investigations of cardiovascular response to gravitational stress Cohen and Silverman (1959) made some observations that are relevant here. In a few subjects they induced, or assessed, anger before a centrifuge test, and were able to compare their catecholamine excretion with that in tests in which anger had not been induced, or with that of subjects who showed primarily fear. Angry subjects showed increased NE excretion, usually in conjunction with somewhat increased

E excretion, while predominantly anxious subjects usually showed raised E levels alone. These results, then, support Elmadjian *et al.*'s conclusion, and the assumptions about the roles of E and NE made by those who studied ANS changes.

Further work by this research group investigated the catecholamine excretion levels of individuals who, rather than being induced into different emotional states by circumstances, were categorized as having aggressive or anxious *traits*. Cohen, Silverman, Waddell, and Zuidema (1961), for example, used a number of projective tests to elicit aggressive or anxious responses in ulcer patients and control subjects. Subjects classified as aggressive by the Focused Thematic Test (a modification of the TAT) had a higher proportion of NE in the excreted catecholamines than did those with non-aggressive, anxious traits. Results in accordance with this generalization were also obtained in other research by this group.

However, data from Frankenhaeuser's laboratory apparently fail to support these results. Bloom, von Euler, and Frankenhaeuser (1963), studying physiological responses during parachute jumps and other activities in trainee paratroopers, found no reliable relation between catecholamine excretion and self- or other-rated personality traits, although, as they themselves pointed out, the small number of subjects undermines the importance of this result. Although the personality findings failed to support the catecholamine and emotion relationship, other results from this study are consistent with the earlier findings. In what might be expected to be predominantly anxiety-provoking activities, E excretion consistently increased more than NE excretion. However, Frankenhaeuser, Mellis, Bjorkvall, Rissler, and Patkai (1968) found no difference in the relative rates of E and NE excretion in persons judged to have predominantly aggressive or anxious personalities.

In contrast, Fine and Sweeney (1968) measured catecholamine excretion rates over 24-hour periods during which 27 subjects were exposed to 'minimally and moderately "stressful"' conditions (timed test completion and cold stress). The tests completed included projective and questionnaire measures of aggressiveness and anxiety–neuroticism. Their results showed that subjects rated above median aggressiveness on the TAT excreted more NE than those below the median; E excretion rates did not differ between these two groups. However, it should be noted that the correlation between NE excretion rate and trait aggression was low.

Frankenhaeuser (1978, 1984) took issue with the notion that E and NE are associated with fear and anger, respectively. Rather than being associated with one or other emotion, she claimed that more recent studies suggested that *both* catecholamines may be excreted in a variety of emotions, particularly when these involve uncertainty and lack of control, but that the threshold for NE release in response to psychosocial stimulation is much higher than that for E release. This statement is, however, quite clearly inconsistent with some of the results of Elmadjian *et al.* (1957) and Cohen and Silverman (1959), as well as with the ANS data considered in the previous section. Frankenhaeuser's argument leads to the prediction that whenever NE excretion is increased E excretion must also be increased, since the threshold for the latter is lower and both are nonspecific. This is clearly not the case in many of the studies already reviewed, nor in many that we shall examine subsequently.

Frankenhaeuser attempted to support her hypothesis by reference to a series of experiments conducted either in her laboratory or in that of Levi. Frankenhaeuser and Kaareby (1962) found no relationship between catecholamine excretion and 'extrapunitive' and 'intropunitive' reactions as defined by a sentence-completion task and self-ratings. This was primarily a study of the effects of the CNS depressant *meprobamate* on catecholamine excretion during stress. The stressors used all involved tasks that could not be completed, often in conjunction with criticism, and so might be expected to cause anger. Both E *and* NE showed marked increases during the stress periods. Furthermore, while meprobamate did not produce a significant reduction in E excretion, it did produce a significant and profound reduction in NE excretion. Both extra- and intropunitive reactions increased under stress in the placebo group but not in the meprobamate group. These observations are consistent with the view that NE excretion accompanies anger as part of the emotional response to these stressors, and the notion that anger and NE are reduced by meprobamate.

Levi (1965) showed a group of female subjects, on successive days, four feature films that were intended to arouse feelings of 'equanimity', amusement, aggressiveness, and fright. Catecholamine excretion was measured before, during, and after each film. Epinephrine and NE excretion followed the same pattern in each film, with increases in E for all films apart from the scenic one (the 'equanimity' condition), but a significantly greater increase in NE excretion for the horror film than for the aggressive film, which is not the pattern one would expect, since subjects rated themselves as 'predominantly' experiencing the intended emotion for each film. This looks, at first sight, to be powerful evidence against the E–fear, NE–anger link. However, Kemper (1978) has critically analysed this study, arguing that the dramatic force of films depends on the production of multiple emotions. In particular, each of Levi's film stimuli, including the comedy, would have involved uncertainty and uncontrollability before the denouement. This is why each film produced an increase in E excretion, despite apparent differences in predominant mood.

A later experiment from this laboratory does provide support for the NE–anger relation, although the authors, Carlson, Levi, and Oro (1972), do not themselves subscribe to this interpretation. In this study of 'stress', subjects had to conduct a very difficult sorting task against a background of loud noise, a bright light, time pressure, and criticism. It seems likely that such treatment, especially the last part, would induce anger in subjects, but unfortunately the investigators only asked subjects to rate the 'pressingness' and 'unpleasantness' of the experience. If anger was induced, we would expect an increase in NE, which is just what did occur.

Kemper (1978) also critically examined experiments cited by Frankenhaeuser

(1978), from her own laboratory, as evidence against the specificity theory. Frankenhaeuser and Rissler (1970) conducted a four-session experiment; in the first three sessions male subjects were exposed to electric shocks, the fourth session being a relaxation control condition. Over the first three sessions the subject's ability to avoid the shocks increased from no control in Session 1 to the avoidance of most shocks by rapid response in Session 3. Urinary excretion of E and NE during each session was measured. Epinephrine excretion decreased across sessions as, Frankenhaeuser argued, the degree of control varied from helplessness to ability to master the disturbing influences. Norepinephrine excretion, in contrast, did not diminish across the sessions. Kemper argued that, like Carlson *et al.* (1972), Frankenhaeuser and Rissler failed to recognize the potential for the production of anger in their experimental set-up. Specifically, subjects had been told that they would be able to gain control over the receipt of shocks, yet were unable to avoid more than 60% of them. This situation, Kemper argued, would be likely to elicit and maintain anger even if fear is reduced. Thus, the data support the specificity hypothesis.

Another study cited by Frankenhaeuser (1978, 1984) in support of her anti-specificity view is that of Pátkai (1971). Subjects undertook four tasks designed to produce either positive or negative affective states. The pleasant tasks were playing bingo (with small winnings but no stakes) and 'inactivity'. In the unpleasant conditions subjects watched films of surgical procedures or performed tedious pencil-and-paper tests. Epinephrine excretion was greatest during bingo, then tests, films, and inactivity, in that order. Subjective estimates of pleasantness partially coincided with this order, except that inactivity was judged to be as pleasant as the tests. Norepinephrine excretion did not differ between tasks. Frankenhaeuser argued that these results show that E excretion is here associated with pleasantness, not with fear. However, if this were so, inactivity should have been associated with a higher level of E excretion. Furthermore, it will be recalled that her general hypothesis is that E and NE excretion are associated with uncertainty and lack of control rather than with fear. The order of tasks presented above in relation to E excretion is exactly the order in which uncertainty would decrease. The lack of a corresponding variation in NE excretion might simply reflect a generally fairly low level of uncertainty. From the point of view of the specificity hypothesis we would not expect increased NE excretion since the conditions of the experiment should not provoke anger.

The main problem with this series of studies in relation to the physiological differentiation of emotions is the failure of the investigators to appreciate the likely emotional outcomes of their manipulations, or adequately to assess their subjects' emotional state. (It should, of course, be noted that emotional differentiation has not been the primary aim of this research). This, coupled with variations in the interpretation of the expected response of NE under experimental conditions, has led to the erroneous conclusion that the specificity notion is incompatible with the data.

One study in which there was better estimation of subjective state was that of Frankenhaeuser, Nordheden, Myrsten, and Post (1971). Subjects were 'overstimulated' (by a complex sensorimotor task), 'understimulated' (by a vigilance task), or given medium stimulation (reading magazines), each for 3 hours. Both E and NE excretion were higher in under- and overstimulation than in the medium condition, although during understimulation E remained level and NE excretion fell. During overstimulation, on the other hand, the excretion of both catecholamines rose, E remaining high, and NE falling a little towards the end of the period. The change in E excretion over time closely followed increasing ratings of unpleasantness (interpreted to the subjects as like the experience in a dentist's waiting room) and of irritation during overstimulation, but matched these less closely during understimulation (subjective reactions were not reported for medium stimulation). Norepinephrine excretion followed quite closely ratings of irritation and concentration during overstimulation, but not, again, during understimulation. Thus, there is evidence here for specificity, with catecholamine excretion changing more or less in parallel with emotional state during overstimulation. Why this should not also be so during understimulation is not clear.

OTHER EMOTIONS

AUTONOMICALLY MEDIATED CHANGES

In an earlier section we noted certain results for physiological changes in emotions other than anger and fear. Schwartz *et al.* (1981) compared sadness and happiness. In the imagery-alone condition sadness showed higher HR increases than happiness, although smaller increases than anger or fear. In the exercise condition, sadness did not produce changes in HR or SBP, although both increased in happiness, Ekman *et al.* (1983) also compared sadness and happiness, together with disgust and surprise. In their directed facial action task, sadness was associated with a higher HR than the other three, and differed from anger by a lower hand temperature. In the relived emotions task, sadness differed from fear, anger, and disgust with a greater fall in SRL. Stemmler (1984) found joy to be associated with increased hand temperature but with no other distinct autonomic characteristics.

Two other studies have compared sadness and other emotions. Sternbach (1962) compared the responses of a group of ten 8-year-old children to those sequences of the motion picture *Bambi* that each child thought were the saddest, scariest, nicest (happiest), and funniest. Six physiological functions were recorded: skin resistance level (SRL), gastric motility, RR, HR, eyeblink rate, and finger pulse volume (FPV). Only the sad and nice/happy scenes showed significant changes. During the sad scenes there was a near-significant increase in SRL, and a marked decrease in blink rate. Nice/happy scenes were distinguished by a slowing of gastric motility in most of the children. The former pattern was interpreted as one of inhibition of the sympathetic nervous system (SNS), as palmar sweat glands have only SNS innervation, and the less-frequent blinking was attributed to increased lacrimation. It should be noted, however, that it is now known that lacrimation is chiefly a parasympathetic nervous system (PNS) response. The decrease in rate of gastric activity during the nice/happy scenes suggested vagal (PNS) inhibition (although it could reflect SNS excitation). Other variables, such as HR, which might have been expected to reflect such patterns, failed to do so reliably. This failure to find clear patterns was attributed to the lack of a sufficient range of autonomic variables and, in view of the importance of BP in other research, this seems likely. There are also methodological difficulties inherent in asking young children at the end of an hour-long film to recall the four scenes with the greatest emotional content, and with the use of the period immediately preceding each scene as a 'baseline', regardless of its content.

Averill (1969) attempted to differentiate sadness and mirth by means of physiological measures. Eighteen male students watched three films. One, concerning the life and assassination of J. F. Kennedy, was intended to induce sadness and grief. The second was a selection from Mack Sennett films and was intended to produce mirth. As a control condition a travel film was used. SBP and DBP, HR, face and finger temperature, FPV, SCL and SCR rate, and RR were measured. Measures during the last 6 minutes of each film were compared with baseline measures. Sadness and mirth films were distinguished by the higher SBP and DBP of the former, which also produced a smaller maximal HR increase and less respiratory irregularity. The sadness film was, furthermore, distinguished from the control film by higher increases in both BP measures, increased SCR rate, smaller SCL, and smaller decreases in FPV. The mirth film differed from the control in higher SCR rate and SRR, higher RR, and more respiratory irregularity.

Averill concluded that sadness may be accompanied by increased SNS activity, which contrasts with Sternbach's findings concerning sadness with children. However, it may be that the choice of film for the sadness condition aroused emotions other than sadness; anger, for instance. Averill was alert to this possibility and had his subjects complete adjectival rating scales after viewing the film. The results showed that subjects in the sadness condition not only rated themselves as sadder than those in the mirth condition, but also as angrier, more interested, and more excited. Schwartz et al. (1981) have pointed out that the pattern during the Kennedy stimulus was rather like that of anger that we have seen above, with larger increases in DBP than mean BP. There are few consistencies in these results. The increased SRL/decreased SCL found for sadness by Sternbach and by Averill conflicts with the greater decrease in SRL found for the same emotion by Ekman et al.

THE BIOLOGICAL BASIS OF EMOTIONS

The weight of the evidence reviewed in the preceding sections of this chapter supports the notion that, while it might be difficult to demonstrate empirically, at least some emotions are differentiated with respect to peripheral physiological and endocrine changes. This is particularly evident in the cases of anger and fear. The main issue that remains concerns the significance of these specific patterns.

Given that the body has the capability of responding differentially in preparation for the different demands that are made on it (see Wagner, 1988), it makes perfect adaptive sense for it to do so. The pattern of fear is that which Cannon (1929) described as the changes which accompany both fear and rage. He argued that they need to be the same since the requirements of the body are the same in situations that arouse these two emotions. That is, the changes are 'favorable to supreme muscular exertion' (p. 206): diversion of blood to the muscles from the viscera, increased HR and stroke volume, with consequential increase in SBP and DBP, mobilization of glycogen, and related changes. The fact that a different pattern has now been established for anger, including muscular vasoconstriction, as opposed to dilatation, and larger HR increases with greater DBP increases, suggests that a different function is served. Schwartz *et al.* (1981) argued that vasoconstriction and increased DBP are associated with increased isometric muscle strength and vigilance, and provide protection against acute haemorrhage. Each of these would be useful during aggressive behaviour associated with anger, rather than during flight from a fearful stimulus. They cite evidence that such differential patterns occur in the same animals faced with a presumably frightening or an angering animal. Ax's (1953) finding of increased muscle tension in anger (reflecting an isometric, strength response) and more frequent muscle action potentials in fear (suggesting an isotonic, active response) is consistent with this interpretation.

Henry (1986) has summarized experimental work with animals that demonstrates that other species also show different physiological and behavioural response patterns for fight and flight. He argues that these different patterns are organized by different centres in the limbic system. If the situation is perceived as a threat that might be overcome, the experienced emotion is anger, and the central nucleus of the amygdala organizes a behavioural pattern of fighting and persistent effort, accompanied by a greater increase of NE secretion than of E, and by increased BP, HR, and secretion of other hormones such as testosterone and renin. This pattern can be characterized as a sympathetic–adrenal medullary one. When threat is perceived as insurmountable but escapable (therefore involving uncontrollability), the experienced emotion is fear and this is accompanied by escape or avoidance behaviour together with an increase in ACTH and cortisol secretion, a consequential greater increase in secretion of E than of NE, and smaller increases in HR and BP. This is a pituitary–adrenal cortical pattern.

Differentiation of other emotions physiologically is much less well established, although there is evidence that sadness is associated with relatively lower DBP, with increased cardiac output, inhibition of gastrointestinal activity, and perhaps decreases in SRL.

Henry (1986) had adduced evidence for central mechanisms underlying other emotions. Thus, a threat that can be neither overcome nor escaped leads to defeat or depression, accompanied behaviourally by subordination, and physiologically by a decrease in HR and in testosterone secretion and increases in cortisol and ACTH secretion. This pattern, Henry argued, is organized in the hippocampal septum. Averill (1969) offered a functional interpretation of grief, resulting from the loss of a significant relationship, in ensuring group cohesiveness in species where social living is necessary for survival. Separation from the group, or from a specific member of the group, is a stressful event both psychologically and physiologically. The initial, shock, stage of grief is likely to be characterized by the same changes as occur in any acutely stressful circumstances and, behaviourally and psychologically, it is accompanied by striving for the lost person. The subsequent, despair, stage of grief (corresponding, perhaps, to the sadness studied in the laboratory investigations outlined here) is accompanied by passivity.

Two other patterns described follow the perception of support in the environment, and correspond to what Henry calls 'serenity' (relaxation, grooming) and elation (control, bonding). While the evidence supporting these is less strong, the former seems to be organized in the amygdala, and is accompanied by decreased BP, HR, and both E and NE secretion. The latter is marked by decreased ACTH and cortisol secretion, but by increased testosterone secretion.

Thus, it seems that the understanding of differential physiological patterning in emotions is of significance for coping with different demands of different environmental circumstances. These patterns are organized by subcortical structures such as those described by Henry (1986) and Panksepp (Chapter 1 of this volume).

ILLNESS AND THE PHYSIOLOGICAL DIFFERENTIABILITY OF EMOTIONS

The question of the physiological differentiability of emotions is, as I pointed out at the beginning of this chapter, of some historical importance in the theory of emotion. More important, however, are the health implications of such distinctions. I have already drawn attention to the role played by anger, particularly suppressed anger, in the aetiology of hypertension. The recognition of this role represents a move away from investigations of the effects of some general or global 'stress' on the behaviour and health of the individual, a tradition that stems largely from the work of Selye (1946). The move is towards a greater consideration of the *individual's* response to a situation, of whether a situation constitutes a stressor for the individual, of the specific meaning of a situation for the individual, and of the individual's specific response to the situation.

This approach should not be confused with another strand in psychosomatic research—that of specificity theory, which is usually traced back to the work of Alexander (1950). Alexander's theory stated that the repression of specific emotions resulted in dysfunction of specific organs which, in the presence of other causal factors, would lead to disease. As Lipowski (1984) has pointed out, this theory became discredited, largely because of its simplistic, linear-causal approach to pathogenesis. The recognition of individual differences in interaction with the environment is not, of course, new. For example, the 'Type A behaviour pattern' was described nearly 30 years ago (Friedman and Rosenman, 1959). What has taken longer to be accepted, as I have tried to demonstrate in this chapter, is that different environmental demands lead to different physiological responses, and that these may, in interaction with individual characteristics, be a major determinant of pathology.

There are many other examples of links between illness and emotions that suggest or reflect specificity. Greer and Morris (1975) showed that women who were subsequently diagnosed as having breast cancer showed greater suppressed anger and more extreme expressed anger than those with a benign disease. On a 3-year follow-up of women treated for breast cancer Greer, Morris, and Pettingale (1979) found that those who showed denial or a fighting spirit had a better survival rate than those who responded with stoical acceptance or feelings of helplessness or hopelessness. In a prospective study, Shekelle *et al.* (1981) showed that depression was related to a doubled rate of cancer mortality over a 17-year period. Appel, Holroyd, and Gorkin (1983) have suggested that anger expression might be an adaptive response in cancer patients if it counteracts maladaptive hopelessness and depression.

Stein (1986) has argued that psychosomatic medicine needs to reconsider the issue of specificity. Specificity is a property of many biological systems, and the interaction of emotional, CNS, neurotransmitter, endocrine, and immune systems, in particular, must be studied if we are to understand the role of psychological factors in disease. This, then, must be the way forward. The laboratory demonstration of physiological differences between emotions should have served its purpose. What is now needed is systematic study of the interactions between the various systems in the search for underlying mechanisms.

REFERENCES

Alexander, D. F. (1950) *Psychosomatic Medicine*. New York: Norton.

Appel, M. A., Holroyd, K. A., and Gorkin, L. (1983) Anger and the etiology and progression of physical illness. In L. Temoshok, C. Van Dyke, and L. S. Zegans (Eds), *Emotions in Health and Illness: Theoretical and Research Foundations*, pp. 73–87. New York: Grune and Stratton.

Arnold, M. B. (1960) *Emotion and Personality*, New York: Columbia University Press.

Averill, J. R. (1969) Autonomic response patterns during sadness and mirth. *Psychophysiology*, **5**, 399–414.

Ax, A. F. (1953) The physiological differentiation between fear and in humans. *Psychosomatic Medicine*, **15**, 433–42.

Bloom, G., von Euler, U. S., and Frankenhaeuser, M. (1963) Catecholamine excretion and personality traits in paratroop trainees. *Acta Physiologica Scandinavica*, **58**, 77–89.

Cannon, W. B. (1929) *Bodily Changes in Pain, Hunger, Fear, and Rage*, New York: Ronald.

Carlson, L. A., Levi, L. and Oro, L. (1972) Stressor-induced changes in plasma lipids and urinary excretion of catecholamines and their modification by nicotinic acid. In L. Levi (Ed.), *Stress and Distress in Response to Psychosocial Stimuli. Acta Medica Scandinavica*, Supplementum 528. Stockholm: Almquist & Wicksell.

Chesney, M. A., and Rosenman, R. H. (1985) *Anger and Hostility in Cardiovascular and Behavioral Disorders*. Washington: Hemisphere.

Chessick, R. D., Bassan, M., and Shattan, S. (1966) A comparison of the effect of infused catecholamines and certain affect states. *American Journal of Psychiatry*, **123**, 156–65.

Cohen, S. I. and Silverman, A. J. (1959) Psychophysiological investigations of vascular response variability. *Journal of Psychosomatic Research*, **3**, 185–210.

Cohen, S. I., Silverman, A. J., Waddell, W., and Zuidema, G. D. (1961) Urinary catecholamine levels, gastric secretion and specific psychological factors in ulcer and non-ulcer patients. *Journal of Psychosomatic Research*, **5**, 90–115.

Diamond, E. (1982) The role of anger and hostility in essential hypertension and coronary heart disease. *Psychological Bulletin*, **92**, 410–33.

Dimsdale, J. E., Pierce, C., Schoenfeld, D., Brown, A., Zusman, R., and Graham, R. (1986) Suppressed anger and blood pressure: the effects of race, sex, social class, obesity, and age, *Psychosomatic Medicine*, **48**, 430–6.

Duffy, E. (1972) Activation. In N. S. Greenfield and R. A. Sternbach (Eds), *Handbook of Psychophysiology*, pp. 577–622. New York: Rinehart & Winston.

Ekman, P., Levenson, R. W., and Friesen, W. V. (1983) Autonomic nervous system activity distinguishes among emotions. *Science*, **221**, 1208–10.

Elmadjian, F. J., Hope, M., and Lamson, E. T. (1957) Excretion of E and NE in various emotional states. *Journal of Clinical Endocrinology*, **17**, 608–20.

Engel, G. M., Reichsman, F., and Segal, M. L. (1956) A study of an infant with a gastric fistular. I. Behavior and the rate of total hydrochloric acid secretion. *Psychosomatic Medicine*, **18**, 374–98.

Fahrenberg, J. (1968) Psychophysiological individuality: a pattern analytic approach to personality research and psychosomatic medicine. *Advances in Behaviour Research and Therapy*, **8**, 43–100.

Fine, B. J., and Sweeney, D. R. (1968) Personality traits, and situational factors, and catecholamine excretion. *Journal of Experimental Research in Personality*, **3**, 15–27.

Frankenhaeuser, M. (1978) *Psychoneuroendocrine Sex Differences in Adaptation to the Psychosocial Environment*. New York: Academic Press.

Frankenhaeuser, M. (1984) Psychoneuroendocrine approaches to the study of stressful person–environment transactions. In H. Selye (Ed.), *Selye's Guide to Stress Research*, pp 46–70. New York: Van Nostrand Reinhold.

Frankenhaeuser, M., and Kaareby, S. (1962) Effects of meprobamate on catecholamine excretion during mental stress. *Perceptual and Motor Skills*, **15**, 571–7.

Frankenhaeuser, M., Mellis, I., Bjorkvall, C., Rissler, A., and Pátkai, P. (1968) Catecholamine excretion as related to cognitive and emotional reaction patterns. *Psychosomatic Medicine*, **30**, 109–20.

Frankenhaeuser, M., Nordheden, B., Myrsten, A. L., and Post, B. (1971) Psychophysiological reactions to understimulation and overstimulation. *Acta Psychologia*, **35**, 298–308.

Frankenhaeuser, M., and Rissler, A. (1970) Effects of punishment on catecholamine release and efficiency of performance. *Psychopharmacologia*, **17**, 378–90.

Friedman, M., and Rosenman, R. H. (1959) Association of specific overt behavior pattern with blood and cardiovascular findings. *Journal of the American Medical Association*, **169**, 1286–96.

Funkenstein, D. H. (1956) Nor-E-like and E-like substances in relation to human behavior. *Journal of Nervous and Mental Diseases*, **124**, 58–68.

Funkenstein, D. H., King, S. H., and Drolette, M. (1954) The direction of anger during a laboratory stress-inducing situation. *Psychosomatic Medicine*, **16**, 404–13.

Funkenstein, D. H., King, S. H., and Drolette, M. (1957) *Mastery of Stress*. Cambridge, Ma: Harvard University Press.

Greer, S. and Morris, T. (1975) Psychological attributes of women who develop breast cancer: a controlled study. *Journal of Psychosomatic Research*, **19**, 147–53.

Greer, S., Morris, T., and Pettingale, K. W. (1979) Psychological response to breast cancer: effect on outcome, *Lancet*, **2**, 785–7.

Harris, W. S., Schoenfeld, C. D., Gwynne, P. H., Weissler, A. M., and Warren, J. V. (1964) Circulatory and humoral responses to fear and anger. *Journal of Laboratory and Clinical Medicine*, **64**, 867 (abstract).

Henry, J. P. (1986) Neuroendocrine response patterns. In R. Plutchik and H. Kellerman (Eds), *Emotion: Theory, Research, and Experience. Vol. 3. Biological Foundations of Emotion*, pp. 37–60. New York: Academic Press.

Izard, C. E. (1977) *Human Emotions*, New York: Plenum Press.

James, G. D., Yee, L. S., Harshfield, G. A., Blanke, S. G., and Pickering, T. (1986) The influence of happiness, anger, and anxiety on the blood pressure of borderline hypertensives. *Psychosomatic Medicine*, **48**, 502–8.

James, W. (1884) What is an emotion? *Mind*, **9**, 188–204.

Kemper, T. D. (1978) *A Social Interactional Theory of Emotions*. New York: John Wiley.

Lacey, J. I., Bateman, D. E. and Van Lehn, R. (1953) Autonomic response specificity: an experimental study. *Psychosomatic Medicine*, **15**, 8–21.

Levenson, R. W. (1988) Emotion and the autonomic nervous system: a prospectus for research on autonomic specificity. In H. L. Wagner (Ed.), *Social Psychophysiology and Emotion: Theory and Clinical Applications*, pp. 17–42. Chichester: John Wiley.

Levi, L. (1965) The urinary output of adrenalin and noradrenalin during pleasant and unpleasant emotional states. *Psychosomatic Medicine*, **27**, 80–5.

Lipowski, Z. J. (1984) What does the work 'psychosomatic' really mean? A historical and semantic inquiry. *Psychosomatic Medicine*, **46**, 153–71.

Ney, T., and Gale, A. (1988) A critique of laboratory studies of emotion with particular reference to psychophysiological aspects. In H. L. Wagner (Ed.), *Social Psychophysiology and Emotion: Theory and Clinical Applications*, pp. 65–83. Chichester: John Wiley.

Oken, D. (1960) An experimental study of suppressed anger and blood pressure. *Archives of General Psychology*, **2**, 441–56.

Oken, D., Heath, H., Shipman, W., Goldstein, I., Grinker, R. R. and Fisch, J. (1966) The specificity of response to stressful stimuli. *Archives of General Psychiatry*, **15**, 624–34.

Pátkai, P. (1971) Catecholamine excretion in pleasant and unpleasant situations. *Acta Psychologica*, **35**, 352–63.

Roberts, R. J. and Weerts, T. C. (1982) Cardiovascular responding during anger and fear imagery. *Psychological Reports*, **50**, 219–30.

Rosenman, R. H. (1985) Health consequences of anger and implications for treatment. In M. A. Chesney and R. H. Rosenman (Eds), *Anger and Hostility in Cardiovascular and Behavioral Disorders*, pp. 103–25. Washington: Hemisphere.

Schachter, J. (1957) Pain, fear, and anger in hypertensives and normotensives: a psychophysiological study. *Psychosomatic Medicine*, **19**, 17–29.

Schachter, S. (1964) The interaction of cognitive and physiological determinants of emotional state. *Advances in Experimental Social Psychology*, **1**, 49–80.

Schneider, R. H., Egan, B. M., Johnson, E. H., Drobny, H., and Julius, S. (1986) Anger and anxiety in borderline hypertension. *Psychosomatic Medicine*, **48**, 242–8.

Schwartz, G. E., Weinberger, D. A., and Singer, J. A. (1981) Cardiovascular differentiation of happiness, sadness, anger and fear following imagery and exercise. *Psychosomatic Medicine*, **43**, 343–64.

Selye, H. (1946) The general adaptation syndrome and the diseases of adaptation. *Journal of Clinical Endocrinology*, **6**, 117–96.

Shekelle, R. B., Raynor, W. J., Ostfeld, A. M., Garron, D. C., Bieliauskas, L. A., Liu, S. C., Maliza, C., and Paul, O. (1981) Psychological depression and 17-year risk of death from cancer. *Psychosomatic Medicine*, **43**, 117–25.

Stein, M. (1986) A reconsideration of specificity in psychosomatic medicine: from olfaction to the lymphocyte. *Psychosomatic Medicine*, **48**, 3–22.

Stemmler, G. (1984) *Psychophysiologische Emotionsmuster*. Frankfurt: Lang.

Sternbach, R. A. (1962) Assessing differential autonomic patterns in emotions. *Journal of Psychosomatic Research*, **6**, 87–91.

Wagner, H. L. (1988) The theory and application of social psychophysiology. In H. L. Wagner (Ed.), *Social Psychophysiology and Emotion: Theory and Clinical Applications*, pp. 1–15. Chichester: John Wiley.

Whitehead, W. E., Blackwell., B., DeSilva, H., and Robinson, A. (1977) Anxiety and anger in hypertension. *Journal of Psychosomatic Research*, **21**, 383–9.

Wolf, S., and Wolff, H. G. (1947) *Human Gastric Function*. New York: Oxford University Press.

Wolff, H. G. (1950) Life situations, emotions, and bodily disease. In M. L. Reymert (Ed.), *Feelings and Emotions: The Mooseheart Symposium*, pp. 284–324. New York: McGraw-Hill.

Zillmann, D. (1983) Transfer of excitation in emotional behavior. In J. T. Cacioppo and R. E. Petty (Eds), *Social Psychophysiology: A Sourcebook*, pp. 215–40. New York: Guildford.

Chapter 4

Hormones and Emotions: Affective Correlates of Endocrine Activity

Kathryn Popp and Andrew Baum
Uniformed Services University of the Health Sciences

ABSTRACT

Endocrine activity is a crucial element in the experience and expression of emotion, but the mechanisms by which emotions are caused are not clear. It is fairly well established that a number of hormones covary with different emotions, but it is more difficult to determine which are causal and which are secondary to the experienced affect. Regardless of the causal sequences that are ultimately identified, the ways in which emotions and endocrine function are linked provide important insights into the nature of emotion and the relationships between mind and body. Though study of hormonal aspects of emotion is limited by methodological and conceptual issues, a number of studies of anxiety, depression, and hostility have been reported that provide a basis for considering the role of endocrine changes in affect.

The notion of a general relationship between endocrine activity and emotional state has been around for many years, but the specifics of this assumption are often arguable and rarely clear. The issue of causality has been a persistent theme in research and theorizing about physiological correlates of emotions. Regardless of

This work was supported by NSF Grant BNS 8317997 to the second author. The opinions or assertions contained herein are the private ones of the authors and are not to be construed as official or reflecting the views of the Department of Defense or the Uniformed Services University of the Health Sciences.

whether hormonal changes give rise to, or are caused by, experienced emotion, identification of correlates of emotional states has value. As Mandler (1975) has suggested, knowledge of hormonal changes associated with different emotional states can provide 'clean and lawful generalizations' and afford researchers useful insight into differences between various moods (p. 9). Granting that cognitive factors and social psychological variables are important in determining emotional experience, this chapter will focus on research studying endocrine factors as a cause of behavior thought to reflect emotion, and as a correlate of extreme emotional states.

Experiments with humans may manipulate emotional state or hormonal levels to study their interrelationships but this is often difficult to accomplish. As a result, much of our knowledge is derived from correlations between emotions and endocrine patterns among people experiencing severe emotions or emotional dysfunction. This poses problems for interpretation of findings, as a number of variables covary with extreme experience, and generalization to more 'normal' manifestations of an emotional state may be risky. Moreover, acute induction of emotions may be accompanied by hormonal activity that is different from that associated with naturally-occurring for longer-lasting affect. Intensity of emotional experience may well influence hormonal patterns as well.

These problems have led to the use of animal models of emotion in which endocrine variables or emotion induction can be manipulated precisely. Generalization of such studies to human experience may be an issue, and in animal studies of affect one does not have access to emotional experience, so behavioral analogues are used to infer emotional state. This is also problematic as in many cases one can imagine alternative accounts for observed behavior. Nevertheless, animal studies have provided important information about emotion–endocrine relationships and are complementary to the predominant methods of studying these issues in humans.

The range of emotions that has been considered is limited, further hindering interpretation of general models of emotional experience. Anxiety and depression have been studied, and aggressiveness has been examined as a means of studying endocrine correlates of anger or hostility. Research on stress has identified a number of endocrine changes that occur in the face of threat, demand, harm, or challenge, but the range of positive emotions—security, happiness, hope, warmth, and the like—has received little attention in psychophysiological studies. In this chapter, we will consider research relating endocrine markers to anxiety, aggression, and depression.

Studies of relationships between emotions and hormones can be divided into three general approaches: those that manipulate hormone levels, those that vary emotional states, and those that correlate the two variables. These approaches can be divided further into chronic and acute categories. Studies in the chronic category tend to use subjects with some long-term dysfunction along an emotional or an endocrine dimension. Thus, people with affective disorders such as depression might be studied, and associations between emotional state and hormonal activity investigated. Acute studies tend to use subjects that are 'normal' and rely on laboratory manipulations of emotions or hormonal levels to generate differences in one or both. As the human body is known to be capable of various physiological adaptations (such as increased rate of drug metabolism with chronic administration of barbiturates) when faced with a chronic need for these adaptations, the acute versus chronic distinction may be important. For this reason, the rest of the chapter will be organized into sections on different emotional states which will be subdivided according to the endocrine systems studied in relation to the particular emotion. These sections will be organized according to the types of approaches of the studies, including the chronic versus acute distinction.

ANXIETY

Theories derived from work by James (1884) and Lange (1885) suggest that physiological changes cause emotional experiences with specific biological precursors. Early studies found that fear-inducing situations resulted in physiological responses reflecting 'epinephrine' effects, while anger-provocation resulted in different physiological patterns (Ax, 1953). Later studies did not provide clear evidence of physiological determinism, indicating that emotions could not easily be distinguished by patterns of adrenal medullary or adrenocorticol response (Brown and Heninger, 1975; Levi, 1965). Research concerning anxiety and its relationship to various hormonal patterns has continued in the face of this contradictory evidence, particularly with the catecholamines and adrenocortical hormones, but has also expanded to consider changes in other hormones and responses at the level of hormone receptors.

CORTICOSTEROIDS

Evidence supports the general conclusion that anxiety is associated with increases in corticosteroids (cortisol levels in humans, corticosterone in rodents) (e.g. Gold and van Buskirk, 1976; Leshner, 1978). More recently, studies have examined possible mechanisms and causal links in the relationship between anxiety and adrenocortical hormones. Two studies that manipulated acute anxiety and measured cortisol response have also considered developmental issues, and interaction and modulation of this relationship by other hormones. A study by Tennes, Downey, and Vernadakis (1977) looked at urinary cortisol excretion rates in infants experiencing separation anxiety. No overall changes in cortisol levels were seen on days characterized by anxiety, measured by observation of behaviors such as crying. However, infants who responded to the separation with agitation did show increases in cortisol levels, while infants who responded by withdrawing did not show this change in cortisol levels. These differences were probably not due to general activity levels: an additional test day with play stimulation designed to produce pleasant excitement in the infants did not result in increased cortisol levels. Thus, corticosteroid response may distinguish between some types of emotional responding, at least at an early age.

Another study considered the effects of menstrual cycle phase on cortisol responses to a stressful interview. Although a previous study had found that cortisol reactivity was higher during the premenstrual phase than at midcycle (Marinari, Leshner, and Doyle, 1976), this study did not find any difference between responsivity during midcycle and menstrual phases (Abplanalp, Livingston, Rose, and Sandwisch, 1977). Cortisol levels were higher for women who reported higher levels of anxiety, however, supporting the notion of a general link between cortisol and anxiety. In contrast, two studies that manipulated anxiety in a more chronic context, by flooding in phobic patients, found either no elevation in plasma cortisol levels during flooding (Curtis, Buxton, Lippman, Nesse, and Wright, 1976), or elevations of cortisol in some of the patients but not in others (Curtis, Nesse, Buxton, and Lippman, 1978).

One interpretation of these findings is that there is a weak relationship between anxiety and adrenocortical response; but there are other reasons for inconsistent findings. For example, in studies using flooding to generate anxiety, subjects were willing to endure flooding and might differ in many ways, including cortisol response, from people who are unwilling to experience flooding. In support of this, in the first study anxiety did not produce an elevation in cortisol levels, and all subjects were treated for their phobias within two hours of flooding (Curtis *et al.*, 1976). In the second study, some subjects did have elevated cortisol levels in response to anxiety, and more than two hours were required to treat their phobias. Since subjects were patients with phobias and not 'normal' subjects, duration of anxiety may have systematically affected response. Cortisol response was measured by change in individual subjects' levels across sessions. Self-report of anxiety was not uncommon during the control sessions, and some subjects reported being concerned about confrontation with the phobic stimulus during the control sessions (Curtis *et al.*, 1978). Therefore the anxiety and cortisol levels may have been raised for all of the sessions, not just during the flooding. Further studies that include normal subjects and more conceptually-driven, systematic assessments would be useful in determining whether the relative lack of response is due to the chronic nature of phobias, or to methodological problems of dealing with phobic patients.

Release of corticosteroids such as cortisol is the end stage of a multitiered process that includes pituitary stimulation of the adrenal glands by secretion of adrenocorticotrophic hormone (ACTH). As a result, there are more endocrine responses during anxiety than simple changes in cortisol levels. One series of studies relating anxiety and ACTH was done using a social interaction test of anxiety in male rats. Changes in lighting and/or unfamiliarity with the test area decrease social interaction without decreasing motor activity, and this is interpreted as anxiety. Increased levels of ACTH have also been associated with reduction in social interaction without change in motor activity (File and Vellucci, 1978). As this effect was maximal 3 minutes post-injection and had disappeared after 30 minutes, File and Vellucci hypothesized that the reduced social interaction was due to ACTH and not the release of corticosterone following the increase in ACTH.

This hypothesis was supported by two later studies. Adrenalectomy led to a decrease in social interaction which returned to normal levels upon administration of corticosterone (File, Vellucci, and Wendlandt, 1979). In addition, ACTH 4–10 produced the same decrease in social interaction without a change in motor activity (File, 1979). Since ACTH 4–10 does not have steroid-releasing properties, it is unlikely that the decrease in social interaction found with ACTH was due to the release of corticosterone.

Studies of fear-mediated behavior are also consistent with the results of studies of ACTH, corticosterone, and social interaction. Administration of ACTH decreases extinction rates for active and passive avoidance tasks (DeWied, 1969; Levine and Jones, 1965). Adrenalectomy, again lowering corticosteroid levels and increasing ACTH, reduced the rate of extinction of avoidance responses (Silva, 1974; Weiss, McEven, Silva, and Kalkut, 1969). Thus, ACTH appears to increase fear-mediated behavior. In addition, administration of corticosteroid to hypophysectomized rats (i.e. raising corticosteroid levels independently of ACTH levels) inhibited fear responding (Weiss, McEwen, Silva, and Kalkut, 1969). Corticostroids may actually have an anxiolytic effect on fear-mediated behavior, either directly or by virtue of their reduction of ACTH levels.

Effects of ACTH on social interaction were counteracted by chronic (5-day) chlordiazepoxide pretreatment and acute ethanol administration (File and Vellucci, 1978). One hypothesized mechanism for ACTH-induced anxiety is serotonin (5-HT) turnover in the brain. File and Vellucci (1978) assessed 5-HT turnover rate in response to chlordiazepoxide and ACTH by determining the ratio of 5-HIAA (a metabolite of serotonin concentration to 5-HT concentration in the brain. Chronic chlordiazepoxide treatment led to a decreased 5-HIAA:5-HT ratio in the midbrain, hypothalamus, and cerebral cortex. Acute administration of ethanol also led to decrease in this ratio in the midbrain and hypothalamus. In contrast, ACTH administration resulted in an increased 5-HIAA:5-HT ratio in the midbrain and hypothalamus. Further evidence for the involvement of serotonergic neurotransmission in anxiety comes from the efficacy of clomipramine and fluroxamine, 5-HT re-uptake inhibitors, in treating anxiety disorders (Westenberg, den Boer, and Kahn, 1987).

The finding that both increases and decreases in corticosteroid are associated with anxiety suggests that ACTH may be the primary factor in this relationship (Leshner, 1978). Whether this is due to changes in muscle tension, sensitivity to aversive stimulation, or to modification of neural responses and brain function (e.g. Gibbs, Sechzer, Smith, Conners, and Weiss, 1973; Leshner, 1978; Strand, Stoboy, and Cayer, 1974) is not clear and requires further study.

CATECHOLAMINES

Studies of catecholamine response during anxiety have not provided clear evidence of a relationship between them. Use of substances that block synthesis of epinephrine and norepinephrine does appear to affect fear-mediated behaviors, while adrenal demedullation, removing epinephrine from the system, has not shown these effects as clearly (Silva, 1973). This suggests a greater role for norepinephrine (DiGiusto, 1972). Patients with panic attacks have higher levels of epinephrine and norepinephrine (Nesse, Cameron, Curtis, McCann, and Huber-Smith, 1984). The administration of yohimbine, an α_2 antagonist, results in symptoms of anxiety (Charney, Heninger, and Breier, 1984), as do administration of epinephrine and norepinephrine (Guttmacher, Murphy, and Insel, 1983). Research using injections of catecholamines, however, have yielded contradictory results, some finding increases in fear-mediated responding while others report no effects of exogenous catecholamines (e.g. Latane and Schachter, 1962; Leventhal and Killackey, 1968; Stewart and Brookshire, 1968). Recently, research interest has shifted to the use of catecholamine levels as physiological indicators of anxiety level in conjunction with self-report measures of acute anxiety, and to attempts to discover physiological mechanisms of anxiety disorders by studying changes in adrenergic receptor function.

Studies of receptor binding by adrenergic agonists have reported findings that suggest a relationship between anxiety and catecholamines. Cameron, Smith, Hollingsworth, Nesse, and Curtis (1984) found that the number of platelet binding sites for tritiated clonidine (a drug that stimulates α_2 adrenergic receptors) in subjects with panic attacks was lower than in depressed patients, but the same as in normal subjects. When receptor binding was measured with tritiated yohimbine, binding was lower in subjects with panic anxiety than in either depressed or normal subjects. Treatment of the two patient groups with imipramine led to symptomatic improvement and decreased α_2 receptor binding. Decreased receptor binding was hypothesized to be related to the increased catecholamine levels due to treatment. The decrease in binding sites due to treatment was positively correlated with symptom improvement, although pretreatment binding did not correlate with symptom severity for either group. Physiological changes associated with imipramine treatment, such as reduction in the number of binding sites, appear to be related to the reduction of anxiety. However, the role of relatively low numbers of binding sites in anxiety remains unclear. These results suggest that adrenergic receptors are involved in anxiety, and are consistent with the results of other studies that support the hypothesized relationship between catecholamines and anxiety. Both central and peripheral catecholamines have been found to increase with anxiety, and elevated locus ceruleus activity leads to signs of anxiety in animals, while decreased activity has the opposite effect (Redmond and Huang, 1979; Uhde, Boulinger, Siever, DuPont, and Post, 1982). The locus ceruleus is one of two major groups of noradrenergic cells in the brain with primary responsibility for regulating orientation to internal and external events. Unexpected environmental events, for example, are associated with increased activity in the locus ceruleus. α_2 adrenergic receptor antagonists are associated with increases in locus ceruleus activity and increased signs of anxiety, while α_2 agonists reduce locus ceruleus activity and signs of anxiety (Redmond and Huang, 1979; Uhde *et al.*, 1982). These results are consistent with the hypothesis that presynaptic α_2 adrenergic receptors function as autoregulators, inhibiting the release of neurotransmitters by the presynaptic neuron when neurotransmitter level at the synapse is high.

Recent evidence also suggests a role for benzodiazepine receptors in anxiety. Administration of β-carboline-3-carboxylic acid produces behavioral and physiological signs of anxiety in both human and animal subjects (Crawley, Ninan, Picker, Chronsos, Skolnick, and Paul, 1985; Dorow, Horowski, Paschelke, Amin, and Braestrup, 1983). Blockade of benzodiazepine receptors by administering an anxiolytic benzodiazepine such as diazepam (e.g. Valium) eliminates these effects. Research has also suggested that administration of β-carboline can produce a helpless-like response similar to learned helplessness and depression (Drugan, Maier, Skolnicks, Paul, and Crawley, 1985) and that blockade of benzodiazepine receptors blocks this effect. On the one hand, these findings suggest a higher, cortical, seat of emotional experience and/or response that may 'dictate' to the hypothalamus and give rise to endocrine correlates of that experience. It is possible, however, that these findings reflect other processes, and further research is clearly warranted.

AGGRESSION

Most studies of aggression or hostility as a function of endocrine activity are either correlational human studies or animal studies of the effects of chronic administration of various hormones on aggressive behavior. The few human studies that manipulate hormone levels and consider their effects on aggressive behavior generally involve attempts to treat aggressive behavior that has been a problem. Most of these studies have used male subjects and androgens. One possible explanation for this emphasis is that males of most species behave more aggressively than females, and this difference in level of aggression appears at puberty when testosterone levels increase dramatically.

ANDROGENS

Correlational studies of aggression and testosterone levels in human subjects suggest that the two are related. Persky, Smith, and Basu (1971) found that plasma levels of testosterone were correlated with a measure of aggression from the Buss–Durkee Hostility Inventory for a group of men between 17 and 28 years of age, but no relationship was found for men between the ages of 30 and 66. A study by Kreuz and Rose (1972) provided mixed results. They assigned members of a young criminal population to either a high aggression or a low aggression group based on the number of times each had been in solitary confinement, which was related to fighting behavior. They found no differences in testosterone levels between the two groups, and no relationship between scores on the Buss–Durkee Hostility Inventory and fighting behavior or testosterone levels. In support of the relationship between testosterone and aggression, they found that testosterone levels were related to committing violent or aggressive offenses as adolescents. The incidence of these offenses was not related to fighting behavior in prison. It is possible that some aspects of the prison environment alter aggressive behavior, since aggression outside the prison was related to testosterone levels. Alternatively, it is possible that the 'base rate' of aggressive acts in prison is uniformly high, masking possible relationships.

Other attempts to determine the relationship between androgens and aggression have manipulated the hormones and looked at resulting levels of aggression. Several human studies have considered the effects of castration on aggressive behavior. Generally, sexually-based aggression and, to some extent, other forms of aggression are markedly reduced by castration (Bremer, 1959; Hawke, 1950). Hawke found that administration of large doses of testosterone to men who had been castrated to control their aggressive behavior led to a return of aggressive behavior. Also, antiandrogens (steroids which block the effects of natural androgens) tend to reduce aggression in men (Laschet, 1973).

Most animal studies that manipulate androgens to determine hormonal effects on aggressive behavior use castration or ovariectomy and administration of specific androgens. Castration leads to a reduction of aggressive behavior in many species (Kurischko and Oettel, 1977), and administration of some androgens can restore levels of aggression (Christie and Barfield, 1979; Kurischko and Oettel, 1977; Selmanoff, Abreu, Goldman, and Ginsburg, 1977), although which androgens restore aggressive behavior may depend on the species, or even the strain (Selmanoff et al., 1977).

Gender influences response to androgen administration. Adkins and Schlesinger (1979) found that both testosterone propionate (TP) and dihydrotestosterone propionate (DHTP) activated aggressive behavior in gonadectomized female lizards, as well as in males. Ovariectomized adult guinea-pigs also responded to both TP and DHTP with an increase in aggression, although the response to DHTP was less than to TP (Goldfoot, 1979). A general conclusion drawn from studies of gonadectomized females is that females will become more aggressive if relatively high levels of androgen are administered, although some levels used result in blood levels of androgens that are still within the range of blood levels of androgens found among males of the same species (Barkley and Goldman, 1977).

Previous exposure to testosterone, even as an adult, increases later sensitivity to testosterone in females.

Androgens have also been used to explain higher levels of aggression toward the young among crowded or group-housed mice. Gray, Whitsett, and Ziesenis (1978) found that group-housed female mice were more aggressive toward the young than were isolated mice, and that ovariectomy eliminated this effect. The administration of TP, but not estrogen or progesterone, increased levels of aggression in these animals. Based on these results, the investigators hypothesized that the increase in aggression in group-housed females was due to heightened secretion of ovarian androgens.

Studies of developmental aspects of androgens and aggression typically take one of two approaches. The first approach involves a single administration of one or more androgens shortly after birth, and measuring aggressive behavior or sensitivity of aggressive behavior to androgens when the animals reach maturity. Payne (1977) found that administration of 300 mg of either TP or androstenedione to male hamsters on the day after birth was associated with increases in the level of aggressiveness displayed by the hamsters as adults. Testosterone and dihydrotestosterone did not have this effect. In another study, Giammanco and La Guardia (1979) administered TP to female rats two days after birth and found that 24% of the androgenized females killed mice, compared with a control level of 11% at 160 days of age.

A second type of developmental study involves castration of male animals at different points in their life cycle, and looking at the effects of androgen administration on aggressive behavior. Castration either before or after puberty reduces pup-killing behavior in male rats, and administration of TP restores the level of killing (Rosenberg, 1974). Barkley and Goldman (1977) found that castration at any age reduced aggressive behavior, and that testosterone replacement increased the aggressive behavior of castrated males. In general, exposure to androgens from birth to puberty is not essential for aggressive behavior to occur, but early exposure appears to increase sensitivity to androgen in adults.

Androgens can also affect aggressive behavior in a more indirect manner, via effects on pheromone production. These chemical substances affect the behavior or physiological processes of other animals, acting as sex attractants, alarm signals, and releasers of certain behavior patterns. Aggressive behavior of adult male animals toward other adult male conspecifics is generally higher than toward female conspecifics or young members of the species. This differential aggressive behavior is at least partially mediated by urinary odors. Mugford and Nowell (1970) applied the urine of mice of different sex, endocrine, and dominance status to castrated mice, and looked at the level of attack behavior in an intact male mouse when the two mice encountered each other. Castrated mice swabbed with water elicited low levels of aggressive behavior from the intact mouse. Treatment with urine from submissive male mice elicited somewhat higher levels of aggression, and treatment with urine from dominant mice elicited higher levels of aggression. In contrast, swabbing a castrated mouse with urine from an adult female mouse prevented attack. Similarly, Taylor (1982) found that swabbing adult mice with urine from juvenile mice reduced attack from aggressive male mice, and swabbing juvenile mice with urine from adult males increased attack from aggressive males.

Testosterone may control the production of the aggression-eliciting pheromones, since castrated males are attacked less by intact male mice than are sham-operated controls, and also less than are castrated mice treated with testosterone (Lee and Brake, 1972). Also, both ovariectomized and intact female mice treated with testosterone are attacked more by males than are controls. The hormone(s) controlling the production of pheromones that are responsible for inhibiting aggression towards females have not been determined. Estrogen can be ruled out because when urine from ovariectomized female mice that were treated with estrogen is applied to other mice there is increased aggression from males (Mugford and Nowell, 1971).

ESTROGENS

Estrogen has been found to affect levels of aggression in several strains of adult male mice (Brain and Poole, 1975; Edwards and Burge, 1971), but estradiol benzoate has had no effect on levels of aggression in male mice (Luttge, 1972). Antiestrogen components tend to block testosterone-induced aggression (Clark and Nowell, 1979). Estrogen administration to adult female mice generally does not increase levels of aggression. However, when either estradiol benzoate or TP was administered at birth, adult female mice responded with higher levels of aggression when estradiol benzoate was administered. Responsiveness to estradiol benzoate was not altered if hormone administration occurred later than 12 days after birth (Simon and Gandelman, 1978).

The differential responsiveness to various androgens and the antagonism of these effects by antiestrogens have been used as evidence for what is referred to as the 'aromatization hypothesis.' This hypothesis specifies that the aggression-inducing properties of androgens occur as a result of the aromatization of androgenic compounds, which results in estrogenic compounds. The hypothesis had received mixed support. Christie and Barfield (1979) found that testosterone and androstenodione (compounds which can be aromatized and which undergo a specific type of reduction) were effective in restoring aggressive behavior in castrated male rats, but 19-hydroxytestosterone, which is also aromatizable, was not effective. Although aromatization of androgen is a plausible pathway for aggression-causing effects of androgens, it is not the only one involved. A study by Simon and Whalen (1986) reported that when adult gonadectomized male mice treated with androgens or estrogens were exposed to olfactory bulbectomized male mice, aggressive behavior was restored among some strains. Simon and Whalen concluded that there were at least two mechanisms for the increased aggressive behavior in response to steroids, and that which mechanisms played the primary role depended on genetic characteristics.

INSULIN

Interest in the relationship between insulin levels and aggression grew out of earlier research on hypoglycemia and aggression. Bolton (1973) hypothesized that high levels of social conflict and hostility in Qolla Indians could be explained by the degree of hypoglycemia experienced. He found a significant relationship between the aggression ranking provided by peers, and glucose levels during a glucose tolerance test (GTT). Hypoglycemia has also been associated with violence (Bovill, 1973). Virkkunen (1986) found more-rapid increases in insulin secretion during a GTT among individuals with a diagnosed intermittent explosive disorder than in normal subjects. There was also a tendency toward reactive hypoglycemia in subjects with diagnoses of violent antisocial personality and subjects with diagnoses of intermittent explosive disorder. Virkkunen (1982) also found higher levels of insulin secretion in some violent offenders with antisocial personalities.

One explanation for the association of hypoglycemia and aggression was that reduced availability of glucose to the brain resulted in less efficient extraction of oxygen from the blood and a consequent decrease in neural functioning. This reduction in function was hypothesized to occur in neural inhibiting and result in hyperaggressiveness (Virkunen, Horobin, Jenkins, and Manku, 1987). A more recent hypothesis suggests that aggression may be associated with low levels of serotonin, and that there is a relationship between serotonin levels and insulin levels (Virkkunen, 1983). Aggression and suicide are associated with low CSF levels of 5-HIAA, a metabolite of serotonin (Brown *et al.*, 1982; Brown, Goodwin, Ballenger, Goyer, and Major, 1979). In addition, PGE (a metabolite of dihomogamma linolenic acid, DGLA), increased brain serotonin (Debnath, Bhattacharya, Sanyal, Poddar, and Ghosh, 1978). Subjects with intermittent explosive disorder have high DGLA levels, and the number of violent crimes and suicide attempts is associated with high DGLA levels (Virkkunen *et al.*, 1987).

Intracellular pancreatic β cell serotonin inhibits insulin release (Pulido, Bencosme, Bold, and Bold, 1978). In addition, administration of serotonin antagonists increase insulin response to glucose (Pontiroli, Viberti, Tognetti, and Pozza, 1975). These findings support the hypothesis of an inverse relationship between insulin and serotonin; however, more research is needed to delineate the mechanism behind the association between hypoglycemia and aggression.

DEPRESSION

Biochemical theories of depression generally focus on catecholaminergic and/or serotonergic functioning. These hypotheses resulted from early findings that reserpine, a drug which reduces levels of catecholamines and serotonin, often leads to depressive symptoms, and findings that effective antidepressant medication increased catecholaminergic and serotonergic functioning (McNeal and Cimbolic, 1986). Generally, antidepressants increase neuronal functioning in one of two ways and are classified according to their mechanism of action. Tricyclic antidepressants increase neuronal functioning by blocking amine uptake at the synapse, resulting in higher levels of catecholamines and serotonin at the synapse. The second class of antidepressants includes MAO inhibitors, which block the monoamine oxidase breakdown of catecholamines and also result in higher levels at the synapse.

Because there is no neurotransmitter that has been implicated in all observed instances of depression, biochemical theories began to consider ratios of some neurotransmitters to other neurotransmitters or hormones. One hypothesis that received experimental support was that depression resulted from a combination of low catecholamine levels and high acetylcholine levels—an imbalance between sympathetic and parasympathetic activation (Janowsky, El-Yousef, Davis, and Sekerke, 1972). Current theories view depression as a problem of dysregulation of a particular neurotransmitter system (Siever and Davis, 1984). Evidence from studies of α- and β-adrenergic receptors in normal and depressed people supports the relationship between depression and altered receptor function. Lymphocyte β_2 receptors are down-regulated in depressed individuals (Pandey, Janicak, and Davis, 1985), and physiological responses mediated by α_2 adrenergic receptors are blunted in depressed individuals (Charney, Heninger, and Sternberg, 1982; Siever *et al.*, 1984a). Recent extensions of biochemical theories have also involved cortisol, thyroid, and steroid hormones. Many of these theories and studies attempt to relate endocrine functioning and depression through catecholaminergic and serotonergic mechanisms.

GONADAL HORMONES

Evidence supporting the hypothesized relationship between sex steroids and changes in mood comes from studies of emotional changes during periods of large hormonal fluctuations in women, such as during premenstrual and postpartum periods, pregnancy, and initiation of oral contraceptive use. Premenstrual dysphoria has been reported by many women (Abramowitz, Baker, and Fleischer, 1982); however actual premenstrual mood ratings and behavior have not always reflected these reported changes in affect (Tonks, 1968). It is also possible that actual changes in affect at this time only occur in those predisposed to depression. In support of this hypothesis Halbreich and Endicott (1982) found that 62% of women who have experienced at least one major disturbance report premenstrual dysphoria, while only 14% of women who have never had a major depressive episode reported dysphoria.

Affective changes during the postpartum period seem more clearly substantiated than do premenstrual changes. Perhaps the greater changes in hormone levels during the postpartum period override differences in sensitivity to changes in hormones that lead to depression. The dysphoria following delivery occurs frequently enough to be considered a normal response (Yalom, Lunde, Moos, and Hamburg, 1968). However, the specific hormonal mechanism for this change in affect has not yet been determined.

THYROID HORMONES

Several lines of research suggest that thyroid function may be involved in affective disorders. Hypothyroid patients show reduced motor activity and other behaviors that resemble those of depressed patients. Conversely, hyperthyroid patients are similar to manic patients. Depressed patients also tend to have altered hypothalamic–pituitary–thyroid axis function. Some depressed patients tend to have relatively low plasma levels of thyroid hormones (Wilson, Prange, McClane, Rabon, and Lipton, 1970). Reduced thyroid stimulating hormone (TSH) responses to thyrotropin releasing hormone (TRH) administration also have been reported (Loosen and Prange, 1982; Peabody, Whiteford, Warner, Faull, Barchas, and Berger, 1987). High levels of cortisol often found in depressed patients are capable of blunting the TSH response (Otsuki, Dakoda, and Baba, 1973). However, these two abnormalities do not appear to be closely related in depressed patients (Kirkegaard and Carrol, 1980; Peabody *et al.*, 1987).

Thyroid hormones have been used with tricyclic antidepressants (TCAs) in treating depressed patients. The addition of triiodothyronine (T_3), one of the thyroid hormones, to tricyclic treatment regimens increased the efficacy of the drug, possibly by altering the sensitivity of adrenergic receptors (Prange, Wilson, Knox, Rabon, and Lipton, 1969). TRH also enhanced the efficacy of imipramine (Prange, Wilson, Knox, McClare, and Lipton, 1970). The use of T_3 in combination with TCAs also induced a mood elevation in some patients who did not respond to the antidepressant medication alone (Goodwin, Prange, Post, Muscettola, and Lipton, 1982). It is possible that the synergistic effects of the drug combination are due to changes in imipramine metabolites and blood levels. However, the hypothesis does not seem likely because it has been found that the administration of T_3 does not alter blood levels of impiramine, desmethylimipramine (a metabolite), or the ratio of the two (Garbutt *et al.*, 1979).

Other evidence for thyroid hormone influence on affective state comes from studies of receptor function. Both T_3 and T_4 (thyroxine) administration increase dihydroalprenolol (DHA) binding to beta-adrenergic receptors (Mason, Bondy, Nemeroff, Walker, and Bange, 1987). These findings are consistent with the up-regulation of beta-adrenergic receptors following T_4 administration. Relatively smaller doses of either T_3 or T_4 down-regulated the noradrenergic cyclic AMP generating system. Because of the differences in dosage of drugs in animal models that result in the same behavioral effects found in humans, it is difficult to determine whether the increased efficacy of TCAs and T_3 in treating depression follows down-regulation or up-regulation of β-adrenergic receptors. Mason *et al.* (1987) also reported an increased number of $5HT_2$ receptors following T_3 and T_4 administration.

CORTISOL

Studies of depressed patients indicate that they generally show increased plasma levels of cortisol (de Villiers, *et al.*, 1987), and exhibit increased daily urinary secretion of cortisol (Sachar, Hellman, Roffwarg, Halpern, Fukushima, and Gallagher, 1973; Carroll, Curtis, Davies, Mendels, and Shugarman, 1976). Cortisol levels in depressed individuals also tend to be unresponsive to dexamethasone suppression (Kalin, Rish, Janowsky, and Murphy, 1981; Siever, Unde, Jimerson, Past, Lake, and Murphy, 1984b; Kalin and Dawson, 1986). Dexamethasone is a synthetic corticoid that results in sharp reduction of glucocorticoid secretion among normal subjects. Depressed nonsuppressors have greater increases in stimulated $ACTH_{[1-24]}$ cortisol secretion than depressed suppressors and nondepressed suppresors (Kalin *et al.*, 1987). Depressed patients also have a blunted release of ACTH in response to corticotropin releasing hormone (CRH), but do not have a blunted cortisol response (Gold *et al.*, 1984).

Studies of cortisol levels during mania tend to show lower levels than during depression (Carroll, 1979), although some investigators have reported elevated cortisol levels during mania (Cookson, Silverstone, Williams, and Basser, 1985). Joyce, Donald, and Elder (1987) studied cortisol levels in four rapid-cycling bipolar affective disorder patients over several affective episodes. Three of the patients had higher cortisol levels during depressive episodes than during other mood phases. In addition, changes in cortisol levels preceded depressive affect by a period of approximatley 72 hours. Cortisol levels during mania were variable, but tended to be lower than during depression in two of the four patients.

Research concerning the relationship between cortisol and depression has also included studies of glucocorticoids and monoamine synthesis and release. Cortisol increases cerebral cortical synthesis and uptake of DA (Carpenter, Strauss, and Bunney, 1972; Melmon, 1981). It also increases the synthesis of serotonin (Martin, Reichlin, and Brown, 1977). Urinary excretion of metabolites of NE and DA (MOPEG and HVA) also increases following adrenalectomy (Caesar, Collins, and Sandler, 1970). There is a fair amount of evidence for a relationship between monoamines (NE and DA) and glucocorticoids, but the causal direction of this relationship is still in question.

ENDOGENOUS OPIOIDS

A relationship between endogenous and exogenous opiates and affective disorders has also been hypothesized. Opiate substances function as hormones and neurotransmitters, as well as producing analgesia. They are classified in categories based on their subjective effects in humans. The first category consists of opiate agonists which resemble morphine and result in euphoria and analgesia. The second category consists of opiate agonist antagonists. These chemicals generally cause analgesia and euphoria at low doses, and sedation and psychotomimetic effects at high doses. The third group consists of opiate antagonists which block the effects of both agonists and agonist–antagonists.

Two types of endogenous opiates exist. The first type consists of enkephalins which can be found in the brain but not in the pituitary gland. The second type consists of endorphins, of which there are at least four types. All of the endorphins (α, β, γ, and δ) are found in the pituitary gland, and the α- and β-endorphins are also found in the brain. The effects of the four endorphins differ, possibly as a result of differential stimulation of three types of receptors.

α-endorphins seem to be related to analgesia and euphoria, and stimulate μ-receptors, β-endorphins stimulate κ-receptors and produce sedation and analgesia and δ-endorphins stimulate ρ-receptors and produce psychosis (Goldstein, 1978; Guillemin, 1977; Hughes and Kosterlitz, 1977; Snyder, 1977).

Since opiate agonists, such as morphine, produce euphoria, they have been used as a model for mania. However, when subjects were pretreated with lithium and then given morphine (Jasinski, Nutt, Haertzen, Griffith, and Bunney, 1977), the lithium failed to block the euphoric effects of morphine. It is still possible that opiate euphoria and mania affect mood via a common mechanism, but operate at different points in the sequence of events involved in the mechanism (Mansky and Deveines, 1984).

The opiate antagonist naloxone has been administered to mania patients and has resulted in a reduction of manic symptoms in some studies, but not in others; Vartanian, Pickar, and Bunney, (1982). Mansky and Deveines (1984) have hypothesized that low activity of endogenous opiates, especially at the receptor, may be associated with depression. Increasing activity of endogenous opiates may lead to a euthymic state, and further increases may result in mania.

Running or jogging has been used in treating depressed individuals, (Griest, Klein, Eischens, Faris, Gurman, and Morgan, 1979). One hypothesis concerning the antidepressive effect of exercise focuses on the fact that it causes increases in endorphins. Exercise increases plasma levels of β-endorphins and β-lipotropin and training increases this response to exercise. Because exercise increases the β-lipotropin response and β-lipotropin is a precursor for α-endorphin as well as β-endorphin, it is possible that exercise increases α-endorphins and modifies depression.

CONCLUSIONS

In this chapter, we have largely sidestepped the issue of whether emotional changes cause endocrine changes, or if the opposite is the case. To some extent, this is due to inconclusive evidence, but it was also determined by the belief that this is not the crucial issue in studying the psychophysiology of emotions.

Study of the hormonal bases, or correlates, of emotion is not sufficient for a good understanding of emotions. Marañon's (1924) study in which subjects who had been injected with epinephrine could only report 'cold' emotions despite feeling aroused is pertinent here. Subjects reported 'as if' emotions as they became aroused—in the absence of emotion-inducing stimuli, they said they felt as if they were fearful and so on. These findings are consistent with a later study in which epinephrine was administered in the presence or absence of stimuli that could induce emotions. Clearer evidence of emotional experience was found when arousal was paired with provocative stimuli (Cantril, 1934). Hormonal changes, at least in the case of sympathetic arousal, are not sufficient to produce affect.

Some of the research discussed in this chapter suggests that ACTH may be a critical differentiating factor in emotional states. We have considered evidence of ACTH mediation of observed relationships between depression and corticosteroids and have reviewed studies indicating that ACTH may be important in anxiety and fear as well. That ACTH and sympathetic arousal are parts of different pathways of endocrine response is significant, but the fact that ACTH is associated with several different emotional states reemphasizes the insufficient nature of these hormonal changes in determining mood.

Endocrine changes are not the causes of emotion. While they may be important aspects of one's experience in emotion-inducing situations, they are often peripheral events that occur at the behest of central nervous system activity. Ultimately, neuropeptides and cortical direction of hypothalamic activity will be identified as causes of endocrine changes associated with these emotions. The value of studying endocrine–emotion associations, then, is not to answer questions about whether one change precedes or causes another but to understand better the nature of emotional experience and to classify and predict changes at several levels of analysis.

REFERENCES

Abplanalp, J. M., Livingston, L., Rose, R. M., and Sandwisch, D. (1977) Cortisol and growth hormone responses to psychological stress during the menstrual cycle. *Psychosomatic Medicine*, **39**, 158–77.

Abramowitz, E., Baker, A., and Fleischer, S. (1982) Onset of psychiatric crisis and the menstrual cycle. *American Journal of Psychiatry*, **139**, 475–8.

Adkins, E., and Schlesinger, L. (1979) Androgens and the social behavior of male and female lizards (*Anolio carolinensis*). *Hormones and Behavior*, **13**, 139–52.

Ax, A. F. (1953) The physiological differentiation between fear and anger in humans. *Psychosomatic Medicine*, **14**, 433–42.

Barkley, M., and Goldman, B. (1977) Testosterone-induced aggression in adult female mice. *Hormones and Behavior*, **9**, 76–84.

Bolton, D. (1973) Aggression and hypoglycemia among the Qolla: a study in psychological anthropology. *Ethnology*, **12**, 227–57.

Bovill, D. (1973) A case of functional hypoglycemia—a medicolegal problem. *British Journal of Psychiatry*, **123**, 353–358.

Brain, P., and Poole, A., (1975) Influences of estradiol benzoate given alone or in conjunction with dihydrotestosterone on isolation-induced fighting behaviour in castrated TO strain mice. *Journal of Endocrinology*, **65**, 37–8.

Bremer, J. (1959) *Asexualization*. New York: Macmillan.

Brown, G., Ebert, M., Goyer, P., Jimerson, D., Klein, W., Bunney, W., and Goodwin, F. (1982) Aggression, suicide, and serotonin: relationships to CSF amine metabolites. *American Journal of Psychiatry*, **139**, 741–6.

Brown, G., Goodwin, F., Ballenger, J., Goyer, P., and Major, L. (1979) Aggression in humans correlates with cerebrospinal fluid amine metabolites. *Psychiatry Research*, **1**, 131–9.

Brown, W., and Heninger, G. (1975) Cortisol, growth hormone, free fatty acids and experimentally evoked affective arousal. *American Journal of Psychiatry*, **132**, 1172–6.

Caesar, P., Collins, G., and Sandler, M. (1970) Catecholamine metabolism and monoamine oxidase activity in adrenalectomized rats. *Biochemical Pharmacology*, **19**, 921–6.

Cameron, O., Smith, C., Hollingsworth, P., Nesse, R., and Curtis, G. (1984) Platelet α_2-adrenergic receptor binding and plasma catecholamines. *Archives of General Psychiatry*, **41**, 1144–8.

Cantril, H. (1934) The social psychology of everyday life. *Psychological Bulletin*, **31**. 297–330.

Carpenter, W., Strauss, J., and Bunney, W., Jr. (1972) They psychobiology of cortisol metabolism: clinical and theoretical implications. In R. Shader (Ed.), *Psychiatric Complications of Medical Drugs*. New York: Raven Press.

Carroll, B. (1979) Neuroendocrine function in mania. In B. Shopsu (Ed.), *Manic Illness*. New York: Raven Press.

Carroll, B., Curtis, G., Davies, B., Mendels, J., and Sugarman, A. (1976) Urinary free cortisol excretion in depression. *Psychological Medicine*, **6**, 43–50.

Charney, D., Heninger, G., and Brier, A. (1984) Noradrenergic function in panic anxiety. *Archives of General Psychiatry*, **91**, 751–63.

Charney, D., Heninger, G., and Sternberg, D. (1982) Adrenergic receptor sensitivity in depression: effects of clonidine in depressed patients and healthy controls. *Archives of General Psychiatry*, **39**, 200–94.

Christie, M., and Barfield, R. (1979) Effects of aromatizable androgens on aggressive behaviour among rats (rattue norvegicus). *Journal of Endocrinology*, **83**, 17–26.

Clark, C. and Nowell, N. (1979) The effect of antiestrogen CI-628 on androgen-induced aggressive behavior in castrated male mice. *Hormones and Behavior*, **12**, 205–10.

Cookson, J., Silverstone, T., Williams, S., and Besser, G. (1985) Plasma cortisol levels in mania: associated with clinical ratings and changes during treatment with haloperidol. *British Journal of Psychiatry*, **146**, 498–502.

Crawley, J., Ninan, D., Pickar, G., Chronsos, M., Skolnick, P., and Paul, S. (1985) Pharmacological antagonism of β-carboline-induced anxiety in rhesus monkeys. *Journal of Neuroscience*, **5**, 477.

Curtis, G., Buxton, M., Lippman, D., Nesse, R., and Wright, J. (1976) 'Flooding in vivo' during the circadian phase of minimal cortisol secretion: anxiety and therapeutic success without adrenal cortical activation. *Biological Psychiatry*, **11**, 101–7.

Curtis, G., Nesse, R., Buxton, M., and Lippman, D. (1978) Anxiety and plasma cortisol at the crest of the circadian cycle: reappraisal of a classical hypothesis. *Psychosomatic Medicine*, **40**, 368–78.

Debnath, P., Bhattacharya, S., Sanyal, A., Poddar, M., and Ghosh, J. (1978) Prostaglandins: effects of prostaglandin E$_1$ on brain stomach and intestinal serotonin in man. *Biochemistry and Pharmacology*, **27**, 130–2.

DeWied, D. (1969) Effects of peptide hormones on behavior. In W. F. Ganong and L. Martini (Eds), pp. 97–140. *Frontiers in Neuroendocrinology*. New York: Oxford University Press.

DiGiusto, E. (1972) Adrenaline or peripheral noradrenaline depletion and passive avoidance in the rat. *Physiology and Behavior*, **8**, 1059–62.

Dorow, R., Horowski, R., Paschelke, G., Amin, M., and Braestrup, C. (1983) Severe anxiety induced by FG 7142, a β-carboline ligand for benzodiazepine receptors, *Lancet*, **2**, 98–9.

Drugan, R., Maier, S., Skolnick, P., Paul, S., and Crawley, J. (1985) An anxiogenic benzodiazepine receptor ligand induces learned helplessness. *European Journal of Pharmacology*, **113**, 453–7.

Edwards, D., and Burge, K. (1971) Estrogenic arousal of aggressive behavior and masculine sexual behavior in male and female mice. *Hormones and Behavior*, **2**, 239–45.

File, S. (1979) Effects of ACTH$_{4-10}$ in the social interaction test of anxiety. *Brain Research*, **171**, 157–60.

File, S., and Vellucci, S. (1978) Studies on the role of ACTH and of 5-HT in anxiety, using an animal model. *Journal of Pharmacy and Pharmacology*, **30**, 105–10.

File, S., Vellucci, S., and Wendlandt, S. (1979) Corticosterone—an anxiogenic or an anxiolytic agent? *Journal of Pharmacy and Pharmacology*, **31**, 300–5.

Garbutt, J., Malekpour, B., Brunswick, O., Johnalagadda, M., Jolliff, L., Podolak, R., Wilson, I., and Prange, A. (1979) Effects of triiodothyronine on drug levels and cardiac function in depressed patients treated with imipramine. *American Journal of Psychiatry*, **136**, 980–2.

Giammanco, S., and La Guardia, M. (1979) The influence of sex, of castration in new-born males and of androgen treatment in new-born females on the mouse-killing behaviour of the rat. *Archives Internationales de Physiologie et de Biochimie*, **87**, 943–7.

Gibbs, J., Sechzer, J., Smith, G., Conners, R., and Weiss, J. (1973) Behavioral responsiveness of adrenolectomized, hypophysectomized and intact rats to electric shock. *Journal of Comparative and Physiological Psychology*, **82**, 165–9.

Gold, P., and Buskirk, R. van. (1976) Enhancement and impairment of memory processes with post-trial injections of adrenocorticotrophic hormones. *Behavioral Biology*, **16**, 387–400.

Gold, P., Chrousos, G., Kellner, C., Post, R., Roy, A., Augerinos, P., Schulte, H., Oldfield, E., and Loriauz, D. 1984 Psychiatric implications of basic and clinical studies with corticotropin-releasing factor. *American Journal of Psychiatry*, **141**, 619–27.

Goldfoot, D. (1979) Sex-specific, behavior-specific actions of dihydrotestosterone: activation of aggression, but not mounting in ovariectomized guinea pigs. *Hormones and Behavior*, **13**, 241–255.

Goldstein, A. (1978) Opiate receptors and opiod peptides: a ten-year overview. In M. Lipton, A. DiMascia, and K. Killam, (Eds), *Pharmacology: A Generation of Progress*. New York: Raven Press.

Goodwin, F., Prange, A., Jr, Post, R., Muscettola, G., and Lipton, M. (1982) Potentiation of antidepressant effects by L-triiodothyronine in tricyclic nonresponders. *American Journal of Psychiatry*, **139**, 34–8.

Gray, L., Whitsett, J., Ziesenis, J., (1978) Hormonal regulation of aggression toward juveniles in female house mice. *Hormones and Behavior*, **11**, 310–22.

Griest, J., Klein, M., Eischens, R., Faris, J., Gurman, A., and Morgan, W. (1979) Running as a treatment for depression. *Comprehensive Psychiatry*, **20**, 41–54.

Guillemin, R., (1977) Brain peptides that act like opiates. *New England Journal of Medicine*, **296**, 226–8.

Guttmacher, L., Murphy, D., and Insel, T. (1983) Pharmacologic models of anxiety. *Comprehensive Psychiatry*, **24**, 312–26.

Halbreich, V., and Endicott, J. (1982) Future directions in the study of premenstrual changes. *Psychopharmacology Bulletin*, **18**, 109–12.

Hawke, C. (1950) Castration and sex crimes. *American Journal of Mental Deficiency*, **55**, 220–6.

Hughes, J., and Kosterlitz, S. (1977) The enkephalins: endogenous peptides with opiate receptor agonist activity. In E. Usdin, D. Hamburg, and G. Burchas, (Eds) *Neuroregulators and Psychiatric Disorders*. Oxford: Oxford University Press.

James, W. (1884) What is an emotion? *Mind*; **9**, 188–205.

Janowsky, D., El-Yousef, M., Davis, K., and Sekerke, H. (1972) A cholinergic-adrenergic hypothesis of mania and depression. *Lancet*, **2**, 632–5.

Jasinski, D., Nutt, J., Haertzen, C., Griffith, J., and Bunney, W. (1977) Lithium: effects on subjective functioning and morphine-induced euphoria. *Science*, **195**, 582–4.

Joyce, P., Donald, R., and Elder, P. (1987) Individual differences in plasma cortisol changes during mania and depression. *Journal of Affective Disorders*, **12**, 1–5.

Kalin, N., and Dawson, G. (1986) Neuroendocrine dysfunction in depression: hypothalamic-anterior pituitary systems. *Trends in Neuroscience*, **9**, 261–6.

Kalin, N., Dawson, G., Tariot, P., Shelton, S., Barksdale, C., Weiler, S., and Thienemann, M. (1987) Function of the adrenal cortex in patients with major depression. Psychiatry Research, **22**, 117–25.

Kalin, N., Rish, S., Janowsky, D., and Murphy, D. (1981) Use of the dexamethasone suppression test in clinical psychiatry. *Journal of Clinical Psychopharmacology*, **1**, 64–9.

Kirkegaard, C., and Carrol, B. (1980) Dissociation of TSH and adrenocortical disturbance in endogenous depression. *Psychiatry Research*, **3**, 253–64.

Kreutz, L. and Rose, R. (1972) Assessment of aggressive behavior and plasma testosterone in a young criminal population. *Psychosomatic Medicine*, **34**. 321–32.

Kurischko, A., and Oettel, M. (1977) Androgen-dependent fighting behavior in male mice. *Endokrinologie*, **70**, 1–5.

Lange, C. G. (1885) *Om Sindsbevaegelser*, cited in G. Mandler (1975) The search for emotion. In L. Levi (Ed.), *Emotions: Their Parameters and Measurement*, New York: pp. 1–15. Raven Press.

Laschet, U. (1973) Antiandrogen in the treatment of sex offenders: mode of action and therapeutic outcome. In I. Zubin, and J. Money (Eds), *Contemporary Sexual Behavior: Critical Issues in the 1970s*. Baltimore: Johns Hopkins University Press.

Latane, B., and Schachter, S. (1962) Adrenalin and avoidance learning. *Journal of Comparative and Physiological Psychology*, **55**, 369–72.

Lee, C., and Brake, S. (1972) Reaction of male mouse fighters to male castrates treated with testosterone propionate or oil. *Psychonomic Science*, **27**, 287–8.

Leshner, A. (1978) *An Introduction to Behavioral Endocrinology*. New York: Oxford University Press.

Leventhal, G., and Killackey, H. (1968) Adrenalin stimulation and preference for familiar stimuli. *Journal of Comparative and Physiological Psychology*, **65**, 152–5.

Levi, L. (1965) The urinary output of adrenalin and noradrenalin during pleasant and unpleasant emotional states. *Psychosomatic Medicine*, **27**, 80–5.

Levine, S., and Jones, L. (1965) Adrenocorticotrophic hormone (ACTH) and passive avoidance learning. *Journal of Comparative and Physiological Psychology*, **59**, 357–60.

Loosen, P., and Prange, A., Jr (1982) Serum thyrotropin response to thyrotropin-releasing hormone in psychiatric patients: a review. *American Journal of Psychiatry*, **139**, 405–16.

Luttge, W. (1972) Activation and inhibition of isolation-induced intermale fighting behavior in castrate CD-1 mice treated with steroidal hormones. *Hormones and Behavior*, **3**, 71–81.

Mandler, G. (1975) The search for emotion. In L. Levi (Ed.), *Emotions: Their Parameters and Measurement*, pp. 1–15. New York: Raven Press.

Mansky, P., and Deveines, D. (1984) Major psychiatric illness related to endogenous and exogenous opiates. In *Psychiatric Medicine Update: Massachusetts General Hospital Reviews*. New York: Elsevier.

Marañon, G. (1924) Contribution à l'etude de l'action emotive de l'adrenaline. *Revue Francaise Endocrinologie*, **2**, 301–25.

Marinari, K., Leshner, A., and Doyle, M. (1976) Menstrual cycle status and adrenocortical reactivity to psychological stress. *Psychoneuroendocrinology*, **1**, 213–18.

Martin, J., Reichlin, S., and Brown, G. (1977) *Clinical Neuroendocrinology*. Philadelphia: F. A. Davis.

Mason, G., Bondy, S., Nemeroff, C., Walker, C., and Bange, A., Jr (1987) The effects of thyroid state on beta-adrenergic and serotonergic receptors in rat brain. *Psychoneuroendocrinology*, **12**, 261–70.

McNeal, E. and Cimbolic, P. (1986) Antidepressants and biochemical theories of depression. *Psychological Bulletin*, **90**, 361–74.

Melmon, K. (1981) The endocrinologic function of selected autocoids: Catecholamines, acetylcholine, serotonin, and histamine. In R. Williams, (Ed.), *Textbook of Endocrinology*, pp. 515–88. Philadelphia: W. B. Saunders.

Mugford, R., and Nowell, N. (1970) Pheromones and their effect on aggression in mice. *Nature*, **226**, 967–8.

Mugford, R., and Nowell, N. (1971) Endocrine control over production and activity of the anti-aggression pheromone from female mice. *Journal of Endocrinology*, **49**, 225–32.

Nesse, R., Cameron, O., Curtis, G., McCann, D., and Huber-Smith, M. (1984) Adrenergic function in patients with panic anxiety. *Archives of General Psychiatry*, **41**, 771–6.

Otsuki, M., Dakoda, M., and Baba, S. (1973) Influence of glucocorticoids on TRH induced TSH response in man. *Journal of Clinical Endocrinology and Metabolism*, **36**, 95–102.

Pandey, G., Janicak, P., and Davis, J. (1985) Studies of beta-adrenergic receptors in leukocytes of patients with affective illness and effects of antidepressant drugs. *Psychopharmacology Bulletin*, **21**, 603–9.

Payne, A. (1977) Changes in aggressive and sexual responsiveness of male golden hamsters after neonatal androgen administration. *Journal of Endocrinology*, **73**, 331–7.

Peabody, C., Whiteford, H., Warner, D., Faull, K., Barchas, J., and Berger, P. (1987) TRH stimulation test and depression. *Psychiatry Research*, **22**, 21–8.

Persky, H., Smith, K., and Basu, G. (1971) Relation of psychologic measures of aggression and hostility to testosterone production in man. *Psychosomatic Medicine*, **33**, 265–77.

Pontiroli, A., Viberti, G., Tognetti, A., and Pozza, G. (1975) Effect of metergoline, a powerful and long-acting antiserotonergic agent, on insulin secretion in normal subjects and in patients with chemical diabetes. *Diabetologia*, **11**, 165–7.

Prange, A., Jr, Wilson, I., Knox, A., McClane, T., and Lipton, M. (1970) Enhancement of imipramine by thyroid stimulating hormone: clinical and theoretical implications. *American Journal of Psychiatry*, **127**, 191–9.

Prange, A., Jr, Wilson, I., Rabon, M., and Lipton, M. (1969). Enhancement of imipramine antidepressant activity by thyroid hormone. *American Journal of Psychiatry*, **126**, 457–69.

Pulido, O., Bencosme, S., Bold, M., and Bold, A. (1978) Intracellular pancreatic cell serotonin and the dynamics of insulin release. *Diabetologia*, **15**, 197–204.

Redmond, D., and Huang, Y. (1979) New evidence for a locus coeruleus-norepinephrine connection with anxiety. *Life Sciences*, **25**, 2140–62.

Rosenberg, K. (1974) Effects of pre- and post-pubretal castration and testosterone on pup-killing behavior in the male rat. *Physiology and Behavior*, **13**, 159–61.

Sachar, E., Hellman, L., Roffwarg, H., Halpern, E., Fukushima, D., and Gallagher, T. (1973) Disrupted 24-hour patterns of cortisol secretion in psychotic depression. *Archives of General Psychiatry.* **28**, 19–24.

Selmanoff, M., Abreu, E., Goldman, B., and Ginsburg, B. (1977) Manipulation of aggressive behavior in adult DBA/2/Bg and C57B1/10/Bg male mice implanted with testosterone in silastic tubing. *Hormones and Behavior*, **8**, 377–90.

Siever, L., and Davis, K. (1984) Dysregulation of the noradrenergic system in depression. *Psychopharmacology Bulletin*, **20**, 500–4.

Siever, L., Uhde, T., Jimerson, D., Lake, C., Silberman, E., Post, R., and Murphy, D. (1984a) Differential inhibitory responses to clonidine in 25 depressed patients and 25 normal control subjects. *American Journal of Psychiatry*, **141**, 733–41.

Siever, L., Uhde, T., Jimerson, D., Post, R., Lake, C., and Murphy, D. (1984b) Plasma cortisol responses to clonidine in depressed patients and controls: evidence for a possible alteration in noradrenergic–neuroendocrine relationships. *Archives of General Psychiatry*, **41**, 63–8.

Silva, M. (1973) Estimation of a passive avoidance response in adrenalectomized and demedullated rats. *Behavioral Biology* **9**, 553–62.

Silva, M. (1974) Effects of adrenal demedullation and adrenolectomy on an active avoidance response of rats. *Physiological Psychology*, **2**, 171–4.

Simon, N., and Gandelman, R. (1978) The estrogenic arousal of aggressive behavior in female mice. *Hormones and Behavior*, **10**, 118–27.

Simon, N., and Whalen, R. (1986) Hormonal regulation of aggression: evidence for a relationship among genotype, receptor binding, and behavioral sensitivity to androgen and estrogen. *Aggressive Behavior*, **12**, 255–66.

Snyder, S. (1977) Opiate receptors in the brain. *New England Journal of Medicine*, **296**, 266–71.

Stewart, C., and Brookshire, K. (1968) Effect of epinephrine on acquisition of conditioned fear. *Physiology and Behavior*, **3**, 601–4.

Srand, F., Stoboy, H., and Cayer, A. (1974) A possible direct action of ACTH on nerve and muscle. *Neuroendocrinology*, **13**, 1–20.

Taylor, G. (1982) Urinary odors and size protect juvenile laboratory mice from adult male attack. *Developmental Psychobiology*, **15**, 171–86.

Tennes, K., Downey, K.,and Vernadakis, A. (1977) Urinary cortisol excretion rates and anxiety in normal 1-year-old infants. *Psychosomatic Medicine*, **39**, 178–87.

Tonks, C. (1968) Premenstrual tension. *British Journal of Hospital Medicine*, **7**, 383–7.

Uhde, T., Boulinger, J., Siever, L., DuPont, R., and Post, R. (1982) Animal models of anxiety: implications for research in humans. *Psychopharmacology Bulletin*, **18**, 47–52.

Vartanian, F., Pickar, D., and Bunney, W. (1982) Short term naloxone administration in schizophrenic and manic patients. *Archives of General Psychiatry*, **39**, 313–19.

de Villiers, A., Russell, V., Carstens, M., Aalbers, C., Gagiano, C., Chalton, D., and Toljaard, J. (1987) Noradrenergic function and hypothalamic–pituitary adrenal axis activity in primary unipolar major depressive disorder. *Psychiatry Research*, **22**, 127–40.

Virkkunen, M. (1982) Reactive hypoglycemic tendency among habitually violent offenders: a further study by means of the glucose tolerance test. *Neuropsychobiology*, **8**, 35–40.

Virkkunen, M. (1983) Serum cholesterol levels in homicidal offenders. *Neuropsychobiology*, **10**, 65–9.

Virkkunen, M. (1986) Insulin secretion during the glucose tolerance test among habitually violent and impulsive offenders. *Aggressive Behavior*, **12**, 303–10.

Virkkunen, M., Horrobin, D., Jenkins, D., and Manku, M. (1987) Plasma phospholipid essential fatty acids and prostaglandins in alcoholic, habitually violent, and impulsive offenders. *Biological Psychiatry*, **22**, 1087–96.

Weiss, J., McEwen, B., Silva, M., and Kalkut, M. (1969) Pituitary–adrenal influences on fear responding. *Science*, **163**, 197–9.

Westenberg, H., den Boer, J., and Kahn, R. (1987) Psychopharmacology of anxiety disorders: on the role of serotonin in the treatment of anxiety states and phobic disorders. *Psychopharmacology Bulletin*, **23**, 145–9.

Wilson, J., Prange, A., Jr, McClane, T., Rabon, A., and Lipton, M. (1970) Thyroid enhancement of imipramine in non-retarded depression. *New England Journal of Medicine*, **282**, 1063–1067.

Yalom, I., Lunde, D., Moos, R., and Hamburg, D. (1968) Post-partum blues syndrome. *Archives of General Psychiatry*, **18**, 16–27.

Chapter 5

Physiological Self-Control and Emotion

Robert J. Gatchel and Dennis Barnes
University of Texas Southwestern Medical Center at Dallas

ABSTRACT

There is accumulating evidence of the importance of emotions in illness, mediated by the physiological changes that accompany emotions. This suggests that there might be health benefits to be derived from the self-control of these physiological processes. This chapter reviews some of the theories concerning the role of physiological changes in emotion and their effects on health, and the most recent research on the control of anxiety and anxiety-related conditions through biofeedback. The limitations of this approach are discussed in terms of the interconnectedness of the three expressive components of emotion and the role of cognitive factors, such as perceived control, in mediating these effects.

Emotion has been the focus of scientific inquiry for a century, yet often research results have been equivocal, and many questions remain unanswered. The last 50 years have seen considerable research aimed at identifying a link between emotion and physiological dysfunction and disease. Indeed, the field of psychosomatic medicine grew in importance with demonstrations that a change in emotional state will be accompanied by a change in physiological responding, and that a change in physiological functioning will frequently be accompanied by alternations in emotion. It is now generally agreed that emotions play a significant role

Handbook of Social Psychophysiology, Edited by H. Wagner and A. Manstead,

in health and illness, but delineating specific cause–effect relationships in this area has proved elusive.

In spite of the paucity of specific answers in this area, much attention has been given to the possible health benefits of physiological self-control. The possibility that emotion may be related to disease, and that voluntary emotional control may have significant health benefits, has given considerable impetus to research involving emotion, its physiological concomitants, and the possibility of altering emotional experience through psychophysiological intervention. The present chapter briefly reviews the early research on the physiological concomitants of emotion, and explores the more recent research involving physiological self-control and the alteration of affective experience.

PSYCHOPHYSIOLOGICAL THEORIES OF EMOTION

In their recent review, Fridlund, Ekman, and Oster (1986) noted that the early physiological theories of emotion were dominated by two distinct traditions. James (1884) was the principal proponent of the 'peripheralist' position, advocating that an individual's subjective experience of emotion was determined by specific patterns of autonomic nervous system arousal. A stimulus object was encountered, specific patterning of the peripheral musculature and autonomic nervous system occurred, and the result was the perception of a particular emotional experience within the individual. In contrast, Cannon (1929) conceptualized emotion from a 'centralist' perspective. His contention was that autonomic nervous system arousal was undifferentiated, and that the specific emotional experience of the individual was the result of cognitive processing of this general physiological pattern of arousal. A stimulus was perceived, and cognitive processing and physiological arousal occurred concurrently, resulting in a specific emotional valence.

These two theoretical traditions spawned a flurry of research activity which yielded primarily inconclusive and equivocal results. The excellent review by Fridlund *et al.* [1986] summarizes this research and points out that these two early theoretical traditions are now of only historical interest. The prominence of theories advocating general arousal patterns (Schachter and Singer, 1962; Selye, 1976) undoubtedly slowed the search for specific physiological response patterns corresponding to distinct emotional states. However, recent research efforts have promoted a renewed focus on this search for specificity of physiological correlates of emotion.

Examining the physiological components of distinct emotional states represents, at the very least, a complex task. Included under the wide-ranging rubric of physiological arousal are central nervous system activity, autonomic nervous system activity, and skeletal muscular responses. Relatedly, the wide range of potential individual differences in responses within these systems demands attention. For example, Tyrer (1973) has proposed a *cognitive–physiological interaction model,* and theorizes that, in some people, some emotion may be considered morbid if the somatic arousal is too intense to be explained by the cognitive cues. It is at this time, Tyrer believes, that the person turns to his or her body for an explanation of the feelings that are not understood. These people put more emphasis on somatic arousal, its intensity and its interpretation, and have been labeled 'somatosthenic' by Tyrer (1982) in later work. Other people are more likely to explain autonomic arousal as due to psychological causes and will search for a cognitive explanation of arousal. If the arousal cannot be sufficiently explained to the person experiencing it, that arousal, now negatively tinged, may become what we call anxiety (Tyrer, 1973; Tyrer, 1982). Tyrer (1982) thus emphasizes the interaction of physiological arousal and cognitive processes.

Izard (1977) has expanded upon the perspective of an interaction of physiological and cognitive factors with his *theory of differential emotions.* He believes that there are ten fundamental emotions which interact with each other, and with other biological processes, to produce primary motivation in humans. He stresses the importance of three components of emotion: 'the neural activity of the brain and somatic nervous system, striate muscle or facial–postural expression and face–brain feedback, and subjective experience' (Izard, 1977, p. 59). Izard draws from Tomkins's (1962, 1963) work on affect, and acknowledges a theoretical debt to him.

Izard's work has been successfully followed up by others (e.g. Ekman, Friesen, and Ellsworth, 1972; Ekman, Levenson, and Friesen, 1983), confirming the presence of fundamental emotions whose patterns of expression are consistent across cultures. For example, Ekman *et al.* (1983) reported differences in five physiological measures across six different affective states in a study employing actors and scientists trained in facial observation. They concluded that autonomic nervous system activity distinguished between four negative emotions, and generally distinguished positive from negative affect. They further reported similar heart rate activity for anger and fear conditions, yet they identified two distinct peripheral vascular patterns for these two different affective states.

Facial electromyography (EMG) is also beginning to be widely used to substantiate the presence of differential physiological response patterns across various affective conditions. In a recent study, Cacioppo, Petty, Losch, and Kim (1986) reported that facial EMG differentiated between valence and intensity of positive and negative affective stimuli in 28 female experimental subjects. These distinctions were evident even when visual examinations of subjects' reponses revealed no overt emotional expression.

In an earlier experiment, also evaluating facial EMG, Fridlund, Schwartz, and Fowler (1984) utilized a multivariate pattern classification system to distinguish successfully physiological response patterns of four experimentally induced affective states (happiness, sadness, anger, and fear). They reported computer pattern recognition of self-reported affect based upon psychophysiological response patterns, and reported clear EMG distinctions between positive and negative affective states. Fridlund, Hatfield, Cottom, and Fowler (1986) subsequently found little evidence in support of a general tension factor which could account for these EMG results. They reported higher EMG activity levels in high self-report anxious subjects than in low self-report anxious subjects when exposed to an experimentally-induced anxiety condition.

Finally, it should be noted that Schwartz (1983) has advocated that the study of emotion is best facilitated through a *systems perspective* and that the early difficulty in identifying specific physiological correlates of emotional states may have been due to the failure to consider patterns of emotional experience rather than singular affective states. Schwartz draws from the James–Lange theory that emphasized the reactivity of the viscera in producing patterns of somatic responses, from Izard's theory of the patterning of emotional responses, and from Schachter's and Singer's two-factor theory of emotion which includes the concept of arousal combined with cognitive labeling (Cannon, 1929; James and Lange, 1922; Schachter and Singer, 1962; Schwartz, 1982; Schwartz and Weinberger, 1980; Weinberger, Schwartz, and Davidson, 1979). Schwartz and colleagues become interested in measuring *patterns* of emotions after discovering, by serendipity, that reliable patterns could be elicited. They developed the HASAFAD, a self-report rating scale, to measure these patterns by adapting Izard's (1972) Differential Emotions Scale. Schwartz and colleagues found consistent emotional patterning in different emotional situations that could be differentiated by cardiovascular measures, facial muscle patterns, and by HASAFAD self-report (Schwartz, 1982; Schwartz and Weinberger, 1980). Schwartz and colleagues hypothesized that a person with large discrepancies or *disregulation* between the three response systems, in response to anxiety or stress, should be more prone to stress-related disease. Schwartz and colleagues also emphasize the importance of personality differences in understanding these relationships better. Some work on disregulation theory has highlighted this importance (Pennebaker and Hoover, 1986; Schwartz, 1983).

The above studies are representative of research which has successfully identified distinct physiological concomitants of various emotional states. The fact that there appear to be unique psychophysiological patterns associated with different emotional states has many clinical implications for the assessment and treatment of emotional dysfunction. The interested reader is referred to Fridlund, Ekman, and Oster (1986) or Wagner (Chapter 3, this volume) for a more complete review of research on emotion and psychophysiological patterns.

BIOFEEDBACK AND THE MODIFICATION OF EMOTION

The identification of possible specific physiological correlates of various emotions paves the way for exploration into how the experience of emotion may be affected by altering its specific physiological components. Biofeedback has become a principal instrument and methodology of study in this area among clinical practitioners and many psychophysiological researchers. In its broadest sense, the history of biofeedback may be traced back several centuries, encompassing a wide variety of self-control and voluntary regulation techniques in the East and West (Norris, 1986a). The use of biofeedback as an alternative therapeutic regimen for a variety of psychophysiological disorders is roughly 20 years old. Early work in this area demonstrated operant-type conditioning of autonomic nervous system activity (Miller, 1969), and the manipulation of alpha brain wave activity (Kamiya, 1968). The clinical usage of biofeedback has expanded dramatically during its brief history, and now includes voluntary training of numerous physiological response patterns through a variety of modalities.

Simply stated, biofeedback may be thought of as providing an individual with an objective reading of some particular physiological activity. This information is transmitted back to the individual as feedback through various sensory modalities, usually auditory or visual. Learning represents the utilization of the feedback to bring the targeted physiological activity under a greater degree of voluntary control. For the interested reader, Cassel (1985) provides a review of various forms of biofeedback currently used and offers suggestions for which specific modalities are best suited for certain treatment needs. Currently EMG biofeedback is most widely used; Fridlund and Cacioppo (1986) provide an excellent review of guidelines to be followed in its use.

The rapid proliferation of the use of biofeedback has not occurred without some major criticism. Roberts (1985) states forcefully that there is little, if any, direct correlation between biofeedback research and its current clinical practice. He cites the inability of researches to replicate several important early findings, and an apparent willingness of clinicians using biofeedback to overlook negative research results, as major factors contributing to what he describes as the current dismal state of affairs in biofeedback research. Other, less severe, criticisms (e.g., Wittmeyer and Abraham, 1985) have questioned the efficacy of biofeedback as a singular treatment modality, and link its putative effectiveness to its inclusion within a broader-based multimodal treatment emphasis.

Indeed, claims of the clinical efficacy and widespread healing potential of biofeedback were undoubtedly overstated in its early years of prominence. Since that time, much research has focused on possible placebo effects associated with biofeedback treatment. Numerous authors (Shapiro, 1973; Walsh, 1974; Russell, 1974) have expressed concern that impressive early results achieved in biofeedback studies may have been strongly influenced by placebo factors. In fact, at an early point in its history, Stroebel and Glueck (1973) referred to biofeedback as the 'ultimate placebo,' and warned that biofeedback's placebo effect may be more important than its active component. More recently, Gatchel (1979, 1982, 1988) has clearly demonstrated the important role of placebo factors in the reduction of fear and anxiety through biofeedback treatment programs. How this relates to the phenomenon of perceived control will be discussed later in this chapter.

The above-mentioned criticisms of clinical uses of biofeedback have, in turn, generated strong responses. Many (Green and Shellenberger, 1986; White and Tursky, 1986; McGovern, 1986; Norris, 1986b) have disputed Roberts's conclusions that clinical biofeedback practice bears little relationship to systematic research findings, and that biofeedback has not been sufficiently demonstrated to be an effective treatment regimen for anything. Indeed, the clinical use of biofeedback continues to proliferate and appears to be at an all-time high (Norris, 1986a). In her presidential address to the Biofeedback Society of America, Norris (1986a) asserted that the general postulate that any process amenable to consistent measurement and feedback can be brought under a degree of voluntary control has been substantiated.

This heated debate will likely continue in the years to come because of the strong advocates of biofeedback. There is certainly strong support for both sides of the controversy. It is hoped that this will stimulate additional empirical research to isolate more successfully the active therapeutic ingredients of this technology. Regardless of the outcome of this debate, however, biofeedback will continue to have widespread implications for the experimental study of physiological self-control processes and emotional experience. Recent advances in research focusing upon control, and the illusion of control, and its relationship to health and illness, has gained prominence. Moreover, the ever-increasing awareness of stress-related illnesses has also placed a premium on the potential health benefits of physiological self-control.

Given that the earlier reviewed research identified distinct physiological patterns of arousal associated with specific emotions, and taking into account the widespread availability and use of biofeedback paradigms to alter these physiological arousal states, important fundamental questions remain unanswered. Can a subjective affective experience be significantly altered simply by manipulating or modifying is concomitant physiological component? Are the increases in voluntary self-control that are achieved through biofeedback in laboratory or clinical conditions transferrable to the everyday life situations of individuals? The remainder of this chapter focuses upon these empirical questions.

BIOFEEDBACK AND THE MODIFICATION
OF ANXIETY

Of all the emotional states, anxiety has received the greatest amount of research on the use of biofeedback for its modification. Attempts to reduce anxiety through biofeedback training represents the most researched and clinically-practiced effort to bring the specific physiological correlates of an emotional state under voluntary control. Numerous biofeedback treatment protocols have been established and evaluated, with the primary goal being the reduction of the physiological substrate of anxiety. It is, therefore, worthwhile to review this research as a first step in addressing the question of whether physiological self-control can have an important impact on emotion.

In reviewing the relevant literature in this area, it is first necessary to comment upon exactly what is meant by a construct such as anxiety. As reported earlier, an emotion such as anxiety may well represent a specific patterning of underlying fundamental affective states rather than being a single fundamental emotion itself. This is an important theoretical issue which will require a great deal of future investigation. At a more general level of definition, anxiety represents an inferred construct which accounts for some form of observable behavior. It is best defined operationally as a combination of three expressive systems: (1) self-report; (2) physiological response; and (3) overt motor behavior. A notable difficulty in the study of an emotion such as anxiety is the frequent lack of a precise correlation between the three behavioral components mentioned above. Moreover, within each component, there are various indices that may not correlate well with one another. Anxiety is best studied by examining all of these components and the possible interaction between them. This, obviously, can be a very complex and difficult task.

The remainder of this chapter will focus primarily upon physiological indices of anxiety that reflect heightened autonomic nervous system activity. Although this is admittedly an overly narrow view of a basically complex, multi-behavioral emotional state, its major goal will be to evaluate whether the direct modification of one of the components—the physiological component—can have any impact on an emotion such as anxiety. There are numerous studies that have addressed this basic issue, whereas a core of research literature has not yet been generated addressing the more complex assessment issue of the modification of the multibehavioral components of a patterned emotional state.

Gatchel (1979, 1982, 1988) has previously reviewed the clinical efficacy of biofeedback treatment for anxiety reduction. Each of these previous reviews pointed out a lack of sufficient data to support the unique clinical effectiveness of biofeedback in this area. Specific results documenting the relative superiority of biofeedback treatment over less expensive and more easily administered treatment alternatives, such as muscle relaxation training and meditation exercises, were not apparent. The current review updates developing research in this area, and conclusions are then offered regarding the current status of the efficacy of physiological self-control via biofeedback and the modification of anxiety.

ANXIETY MODIFICATION IN NORMAL SUBJECTS

McKinney, Gatchel, Brantley and Harrington (1980) conducted a study in which normal subjects were administered 16 biofeedback sessions, during which they were trained to increase and decrease their heart rates. Before and immediately following each biofeedback training session, state anxiety was evaluated in these subjects by use of the Spielberger State–Trait Anxiety Inventory. Results indicated that heart-rate slowing performance was associated with a significant decrease in state anxiety; heart-rate speeding performance was associated with an increase in state anxiety.

These results were similar to earlier findings reported by Hatch and Gatchel (1979), in which a heart-rate speeding task was associated with an increase in perceived state anxiety, but were not as strong as those found in this earlier research. It was suggested that this may have been due simply to the weaker heart-rate speeding performance effects found in the McKinney *et al.* (1980) study, which, in turn, diminished the impact on the experiential state.

Regardless of the possible reasons for this lessened effect, the results of both studies clearly demonstrated the direct bidirectional modification of self-report anxiety by manipulation of the heart-rate component of outcome activity. This research itself was in direct response to the great amount of interest that was generated by the potential application of biofeedback techniques in the modification of stress-related disorders. As noted earlier, it was thought that it might prove to be a practical method of reducing aversive emotional responding through inhibition of physiological components of the stress response. The autonomic component of behavior, in particular, has long been viewed as important in the experience of anxiety, and has been used in the operational definition of anxiety and as a target behavior in its treatment by techniques such as systematic desensitization. Indeed, Mowrer (1947) had viewed the acquisition of a fear response as a result of classical conditioning directly mediated by the autonomic nervous system. However, in spite of its assumed importance, the direct investigation of this component had been, surprisingly, almost totally ignored until the recent biofeedback-related research. In terms of addressing the issue of the comparable effectiveness of less expensive and more easily administered treatment alternatives to biofeedback, Cuthbert, Kristeller, Hodes, and Lang (1981) conducted a series of studies in this area. They evaluated a number of alternative training strategies in order to determine whether such procedures would be as effective as heart rate biofeedback in producing cardiac deceleration and in reducing other indices of arousal. One strategy they evaluated was the *Relaxation Response*, which is a meditation exercise developed by Wallace and Benson (1972) and found to reduce significantly sympathetic arousal. Results clearly indicated that the heart rate biofeedback procedure was not more effective than the relaxation-response strategy for reducing psychophysiological arousal in normal subjects. Thus, biofeedback is not unique in its ability to produce self-control of physiological activity. As a whole, however, such methods appear to be effective in reducing physiological activity and simultaneously impacting on the emotional state of the individual.

ANXIETY MODIFICATION IN SUBJECTS WITH ANXIETY-RELATED PROBLEMS

Results from the reviews of studies utilizing biofeedback modalities in anxiety reduction (Gatchel, 1978, 1982, 1988) have generally indicated that there are relatively few extant studies whose design permits the analysis of the specific contributions of biofeedback techniques employed. Frequently, in this clinical evaluation research, the biofeedback procedures employed were embedded within a larger relaxation paradigm, and the degree to which *each component* constituted an active treatment modality was blurred. This has resulted, in part, in statements in the literature that biofeedback is an effective adjunctive treatment for anxiety reduction, but fares poorly when used as the sole treatment procedure (Gatchel, 1982, 1988; Wittmeyer and Abraham, 1985; Tobin 1985). Nevertheless, the issue of whether the results are directly biofeedback-produced, or produced by general relaxation effects, should not detract from the basic findings that a decrease in physiological arousal *per se* is accompanied by a concomitant decrease in self-reported anxiety.

Since the time of the last review by Gatchel (1988), a few additional studies have appeared in the scientific literature that address the issue of the effectiveness of biofeedback in reducing anxiety. For sake of completeness, we will briefly review these studies, before providing some summary statements concerning this issue. This will also provide the reader with a sample of the type of clinical biofeedback research conducted in this area.

Burke, Hickling, Alfanso, and Blanchard (1985) evaluated the usage of biofeedback-assisted relaxation techniques with four male rheumatoid arthritis patients. Three of four patients reported less daily pain after treatment and demonstrated significant pre- and post-treatment differences on a self-report anxiety measure. This biofeedback-assisted relaxation, though, served as an adjunctive therapy regimen to ongoing medical treatment with these patients. Thus, the degree to which it represented an active treatment component in those subjects demonstrating improvement remains unknown.

Blanchard, Andrasik, Applebaum, Evans, Myers, and Barron (1986) also evaluated the effects of both thermal and EMG biofeedback, as well as relaxation training, on three types of headache patients (tension, migraine, and mixed). All patients received similar treatment and were compared with a no-treatment group of similar patients who were instructed only to keep diaries of their headache symptoms. These investigators reported an interesting result. Treatment resulted in decreases in pre- and post-assessment of trait anxiety, regardless of whether the treatment was effective for headache symptoms. Treated patients also reported significantly less trait anxiety at post-treatment assessment than did control patients. They concluded that reduced anxiety levels may represent a positive psychological side-effect of biofeedback and relaxation treatment. Again, the specific design used prevents analysis of the relative contributions of the biofeedback procedures employed. However, it seems that a reduction of physiological arousal contributed significantly to the change in emotion.

In another study, Bradley (1985) examined the effects of cognitive–behavioral therapy (thermal biofeedback training and group therapy), social support group therapy, and no-treatment control in rheumatoid arthritis patients. Subjects were randomly assigned to each condition, which served as an adjunct to ongoing medical treatment for their condition. Subjects in each of the two active treatment conditions exhibited similar reductions in trait anxiety from pre- to post-treatment assessment. The treatment condition including thermal biofeedback was superior to no treatment in anxiety reduction, but demonstrated no advantage in this area over the social support group therapy condition. Furthermore, the inclusion of the biofeedback component within the cognitive–behavioral group-therapy condition prevents specific analysis of its relative contribution.

Farnill (1985) compared the relative effectiveness of EMG biofeedback and hypnosis in the treatment of computer-related anxiety in undergraduate college females. Subjects were assessed with the State–Trait Anxiety Inventory and asked to rate their own anxiety levels while interacting with the computer. Both treatment groups successfully reduced high levels of computer anxiety; however, no significant differences between the two groups were noted.

Finally Bush, Ditto, and Feuerstein (1985) compared EMG biofeedback, placebo control, and no treatment control in 66 chronic low back pain patients. All subjects were assessed psychologically, including the State–Trait Anxiety Inventory, at pre-treatment, post-treatment, and three-month follow-up. All subjects reported significant decreases in anxiety level at post-treatment follow-up; however, no significant differences among the three groups were observed. The investigators concluded that EMG biofeedback demonstrated no specific anxiety reduction effects in relation to the two control conditions. This was one of the very few studies reporting no specific relationship between change in physiological arousal and self-reported affect. This, however, may have been due to the type of complex behavior evaluated—chronic pain.

It can generally be concluded that various biofeedback modalities have demonstrated some degree of effectiveness in anxiety reduction in some patients. However, these findings appear to be mitigated somewhat by the strong role of placebo factors previously identified as present in many biofeedback studies. Furthermore, the current literature fails to support the conclusion that biofeedback is superior to other less expensive and often more easily administered anxiety reduction treatments (e.g. muscle relaxation training). Again, however, this should not be viewed as discounting the significant effect that individually-produced physiological modification has on emotion.

Some notable caveats regarding research in this area highlighted in past reviews (Gatchel, 1978, 1982, 1988) should also be reiterated here. One involves the previously mentioned distinction between state and trait anxiety. Relatively limited, short-term biofeedback is likely to have minimal, if any, effects upon long-term trait anxiety. However, effects upon state anxiety appear more plausible, as biofeedback training may provide the individual with a self-control skill that could be readily utilized to cope with transitory situational stressors. These distinctions are too often overlooked in research methodology, no doubt contributing to the inability of biofeedback measures to live up to their somewhat grandiose early billing.

Secondly, there appears to be little systematic research regarding individual differences in response to biofeedback treatment. This is in spite of well-documented individual differences in physiological responding (Lacey, 1967). It appears essential for future research in this area to take into account individual difference in psychophysiological response patterns in order best to determine the target physiological behavior to be focused upon in the biofeedback treatment. In order to produce the most effective treatment, biofeedback needs to be tailored to the individual being treated. Too often, this process of tailoring has been ignored in clinical biofeedback research in favor of what seems to be blind pursuit of specific biofeedback modalities that will ultimately prove to be effective for all individuals. Not only is such a discovery extremely unlikely, but its pursuit may obscure the systematic development of more appropriate treatment models and research paradigms that take into account differences in patterning across different emotions, as well as unique individual differences in such patterning.

Relatedly, as we highlighted earlier in this chapter, a construct such as emotion is best defined operationally as a combination of three expressive systems: self-report, physiological, and overt motor behavior. It has been found that these three systems often demonstrate low concordance and do not necessarily change in a synchronous manner with treatment (e.g. Rachman and Hodgsen, 1974). Thus, for example, general physiological arousal is in no sense totally pathognomonic of an emotion such as clinical anxiety. Such general physiological arousal is a component of many other emotions, such as anger, joy, sexual activity, as well as many other states not necessarily associated with a diagnosis of anxiety. Specific physiological patterns may occur within this general arousal state that can differentiate between these emotions. However, a demonstration of a reduction in physiological activity and patterning may not automatically indicate that a particular emotional state is being modified in some unique manner in *all* individuals.

For some individuals, the physiological component in the overall cognitive–overt motor–physiological system that is associated with a particular emotion may be small and, therefore, may not play a vital role in characterizing or changing that emotional state; one of the other behavioral system components may play a more dominant role. For others, it may constitute a major component, and therefore play an essential role. In neither case, however, would modifying this one behavioral component completely change the *entire* emotional fabric of the response. It would only, perhaps, affect certain fibers and thus the shading or quality of the overall fabric. Thus, subjects developing physiological self-control leading to a decrease in sympathetic arousal may well note some decrease in an emotion such as anxiety; however, it would not *totally* modify or eliminate this affective behavior. Only if all the fibers of the fabric, i.e. all of the behavioral components of the emotion, were changed, would a totally changed fabric or emotional state result.

Investigators should, therefore, not consider that changing an individual's physiology will automatically lead to a change in the *entire* fabric of an emotion. It may affect the shading or quality of the emotion to various degrees, but only with the comprehensive modification of all the components of the affective behavior will complete change occur.

Finally, biofeedback is certainly not the only tool utilized in physiological self-control efforts as it relates to affective experience. Various forms of hypnosis and meditation have likewise increased in popularity dramatically. Unfortunately, their rise to popularity and their often grandiose claims of effectiveness also appear to be without systematic empirical support much of the time. Properly designed studies employing appropriate controls are necessary in these areas so that responsible conclusions may be drawn regarding their potential utility in self-control efforts.

So, what can be said of physiological self-control and emotion? One safe conclusion appears to be that there will likely be no reduction in the popular appeal of potential self-control techniques in the foreseeable future. Public health awareness is ever increasing and the established links between stress and various affective states and illness seem to assure further attention in this area. The possibility of altering affective experience through physiological self-control techniques remains an intriguing area with numerous potential positive applications.

THE ROLE OF PERCEIVED CONTROL IN THE MODIFICATION OF EMOTION

Up until this point, we have discussed the issue of whether direct control of physiological responding can have a significant impact on modifying emotion. There is one other major mechanism by which self-control of physiology may affect certain emotions—through a cognitive process such as perceived personal control. Gatchel (1980) has reviewed evidence indicating that individuals react differently to emotionally stressful events that they perceive to be personally controllable, relative to those perceived to be not in their control. The dimension of perceived controllability/uncontrollability of an emotional stressor has been shown to affect significantly self-report, overt motor, and physiological components of behavior.

There have also been studies demonstrating that these stress-reducing effects can be produced merely be creating the belief in subjects that they can control the amount of stress, even though they actually cannot. The first widely cited study that experimentally manipulated the perception of effective control over a stressor where there actually was none, was conducted by Geer, Davison, and Gatchel (1970). There were two parts to the experiment. In the first part, all subjects were instructed to press a microswitch at the onset of a 6-second, painful electric shock, so that their reaction time could be measured. Following 10 such trials, half the subjects (perceived-control group) were told that by decreasing their reaction times during the second part of the experiment, which would also consist of 10 trails, they could reduce shock duration by half. These subjects were thus led to believe that they could actually exert control during the next 10 trials. All subjects, however, regardless of group assignment or reaction-time, received 3-second shocks on all 10 trials during this second part of the experiment. Thus, the actual amount of aversive stimulation was held constant across the two groups. A major finding of this study was that the no-perceived-control subjects had a significantly greater frequency of spontaneous skin conductance fluctuations during the second half of the study than did the perceived-control subjects. These results indicate that the perception of effective control, even if not veridical, can significantly decrease the electrodermal component of autonomic arousal produced by an aversive situation. Thus, there is little doubt that the perception of control, whether veridical or not, can significantly reduce the impact of emotionally stressful events. We will briefly review some of this research in the context of perceived control of physiological responses.

An experiment by Gatchel, Hatch, Watson, Smith, and Gaas (1977) compared the relative effectiveness of heart rate biofeedback, false heart rate biofeedback, muscle relaxation, and combined heart rate biofeedback/muscle relaxation training in reducing anxiety in speech-anxious subjects. Subjects in the false-biofeedback placebo group were led to believe that they were successfully learning to decrease heart rate voluntarily, which would later serve as an effective means of alleviating anxiety. Results of this study indicated that all four experimental groups showed a decrease in the self-report component of public-speaking anxiety as the result of the treatment they received. There were no significant differences between the four groups. The fact that the false-biofeedback placebo group demonstrated as much improvement as the active treatment group indicates the powerful impact of a false-biofeedback placebo condition.

Although there were no significant differences found between groups for the self-report measure of anxiety, an evaluation of the physiological indices yielded some interestingly different findings. Results indicated that the three active treatment groups showed significantly smaller heart rate and skin conductance level increases during the post-treatment assessment of anxiety in comparison to the false-biofeedback group. Again, these results demonstrate how the three major components of behavior are not always highly correlated with one another.

In a subsequent study, Gatchel, Hatch, Maynard, Turns, and Taunton-

Blackwood (1979) compared three groups: a combined muscle relaxation/ biofeedback group, which was found to produce the greatest reduction in physiological responding in the earlier Gatchel *et al.* (1977) study, a false-biofeedback group, which produced a clinically significant reduction in speech anxiety in the earlier study, and a systematic desensitization group. Results of this study indicated that, again, the false-biofeedback placebo group demonstrated as much reduction in self-reported speech anxiety as the two active treatment groups. Physiologically, it did not demonstrate as much reduction. One month later, when subjects were again tested for speech anxiety in a different speaking situation (in a larger room with an audience of six individuals, rather than the smaller room with an audience of two observers used in the earlier speech evaluation), the self-report improvement was maintained in all groups, including the false-biofeedback group. Thus, the improvement effects do not appear to be illusory or short-lived. Indeed, in an earlier study, Paul (1967) reported maintenance of gains over 2 years for treatment groups in his therapy-evaluation study, including an 'attention-placebo' group. In the Paul study, however, the 'attention-placebo' group did not improve as much as the desensitization group. In our study, though, the false-biofeedback group did improve as much as the active treatment groups. The perception by this group that they had active control over an anxiety-competing response—heart rate deceleration—appears to have influenced significantly their self-report of anxiety.

PERCEIVED CONTROL AND THE PLACEBO EFFECT

This research clearly demonstrates the important impact that the placebo effect has in biofeedback techniques directed at eliminating anxiety. The placebo effect itself was originally shown to be an important factor in medical research when it was found that inert chemical drugs, which had no direct effect upon physical events underlying various medical disorders, were often found to produce symptom reduction. An extensive literature on the placebo effect in medicine undeniably demonstrates that a patient's belief that a prescribed medication is active, even if it is in fact chemically inert, often leads to significant symptom reduction (Honigfeld, 1964; Shapiro, 1971). Indeed, as Shapiro (1959) noted: 'The history of medical treatment until relatively recently is the history of the placebo effect' [p. 303]. Even response to a chemically active drug depends to some degree on a belief in the drug's action and faith in the doctor prescribing it.

The placebo effect has also been found to be an active ingredient in psychotherapy (e.g. Wilkens, 1973), especially when anxiety is being treated. As Shapiro (1971) indicates, the effect appears to be a 'multidetermined pheno-menon' that is not yet completely understood. One important psychological factor contributing to the placebo effect that has been shown to affect the outcome of psychotherapy is generalized expectancy of improvement (Wilkens, 1973). This factor has also been implicated to be important in analogue therapy research (Borkovec, 1973).

How does perceived control relate to the placebo effect? Merely the expectancy or belief that a treatment is going to be therapeutic and effective, that it is going to provide a means of coping with a stressful symptom or array of symptoms, will often lead to that very state of affairs—symptom reduction. People suffering from a significant amount of anxiety often feel at the mercy of this aversive emotional state, with no effective means of alleviating or personally controlling it. One of the chief attractions of tranquilizers, besides the reduction of the physiological components of anxiety, is that they allow the individual the comforting perception that he or she now has a means of actively controlling the anxiety—by ingesting a drug.

This dimension of perceived controllability has been suggested by Seligman (1975) to be an active ingredient in systematic desensitization, which is a very effective form of behavior therapy used in the treatment of anxiety. For example, muscle relaxation, which is a major component of systematic desensitization, works best when it is presented as a voluntary and active process, leading individuals to believe they can actively control anxiety. In one study, Goldfried and Trier (1974) demonstrated the effectiveness of muscular relaxation training in reducing anxiety when presented as an active self-control coping skill. This self-control concept has been reviewed as an important component in behavior therapy techniques (e.g. Goldfried and Merbaum, 1973; Mahoney, 1976). Goldfried and Trier found that subjects who were given relaxation training presented as an active coping skill over which they exerted personal control demonstrated a significantly greater reduction in anxiety than subjects who were given identical training presented as an 'automatic' procedure for passively reducing anxiety.

Of course, the concept of personal control is not the entire reason why systematic desensitization, relaxation, and biofeedback work. Indeed, the techniques are still effective when relaxation is passively induced. There is little doubt, however, that the cognitive factor of controllability plays a significant role in the anxiety-reduction process. Bandura (1977) has also proposed the importance of *self-efficacy* in the treatment of maladaptive emotional behavior. Thus, direct control of physiology may not only affect the physiological component, but may also simultaneously affect the other components (e.g. the cognitive component). Again, this reinforces the importance of a full assessment of the affective response in any treatment modification attempt.

REFERENCES

Bandura, A. (1977) Self-efficacy: toward a unifying theory of behavioral change. *Psychological Review*, **84**, 191–215.
Blanchard, E. B., Andrasik, F., Applebaum, K. A., Evans, D. D., Myers, P., and Barron,

K. D. (1986) Three studies of the psychologic changes in chronic headache patients associated with biofeedback and relaxation therapies. *Psychosomatic Medicine*, **48**, 73–83.

Borkovec, T. D. (1973) The role of expectancy and physiological feedback in fear reduction: a review with special reference to subject characteristics. *Behavior Therapy*, **4**, 491–505.

Bradley, L. (1985) Effects of cognitive–behavioral therapy on pain behavior of rheumatoid arthritis (RA) patients: preliminary outcomes. *Scandinavian Journal of Behaviour Therapy*, **14**, 51–64.

Burke, E. J., Hickling, E. J., Alfonso, M. P., and Blanchard, E. B. (1985) The adjunctive use of biofeedback and relaxation in the treatment of severe rheumatoid arthritis: a preliminary investigation. *Clinical Biofeedback and Health: An International Journal*, **8**, 28–36.

Bush, C., Ditto, B., and Feuerstein, M. (1985) A controlled evaluation of paraspinal EMG biofeedback in the treatment of low back pain. *Health Psychology*, **4**, 307–21.

Cacioppo, J. T., Petty, R. E., Losch, M. E., and Kim, H. S. (1986) Electromyographic activity over facial muscle regions can differentiate the valence and intensity of affective reactions. *Journal of Personality and Social psychology*, **50**, 260–8.

Cannon, W. B. (1929) *Bodily Changes in Pain, Hunger, Fear, and Rage* (2nd edn). New York: Appleton.

Cassel, R. (1985) Biofeedback for developing self-control of tension and stress in one's hierarchy of psychological states. *Psychology: A Quarterly Journal of Human Behavior*, **22**(2), 50–7.

Cuthbert, B., Kristeller, J., Hodes, R., and Lang, P. J. (1981) Strategies of arousal control: biofeedback, meditation, and motivation. *Journal of Experimental Psychology: General*, **110**, 181–92.

Ekman, P., Friesen, W. V., and Ellsworth, P. C. (1972) *Emotion in the Human Face*. Elmsford, NY: Pergamon Press.

Ekman, P., Levenson, R., and Friesen, W. V. (1983) Autonomic nervous system activity distinguishes among emotions. *Science*, **221**, 1203–10.

Farnill, D. (1985) A comparison of hypnosis and computer-assisted biofeedback in computer-anxiety reduction. *Australian Journal of Clinical and Experimental Hypnosis*, **13**, 31–5.

Fridlund, A. J., and Cacioppo, J. T. (1986). Guidelines for human electromyographic research. *Psychophysiology*, **23**, 571–86.

Fridlund, A. J., Ekman, P., and Oster, H. (1986) Facial expressions of emotions. In A. Seigman and S. Feldstein (Eds). *Nonverbal behavior and Communication*, pp. 143–223. Hillsdale, NJ: Erlbaum.

Fridlund, A. J., Hatfield, M. E., Cottom, G. L., and Fowler, S. C. (1986) Anxiety and striate-muscle activation: evidence from electromyographic pattern analysis. *Psychophysiology*, **17**, 47–55.

Fridlund, A. J., Schwartz, G. E., and Fowler, S. C. (1984) Pattern recognition of self-reported emotional state from multiple-site facility EMG activity during affective imagery. *Psychophysiology*, **21**, 622–37.

Gatchel, R. J. (1979) Biofeedback and the modification of fear and anxiety. In R. J. Gatchel and K. P. Price (Eds), *Clinical Applications: Appraisal and Status*. Elmsford, NY: Pergamon Press.

Gatchel, R. J. (1980) Perceived control: A review and evaluation of therapeutic implications. In A. Baum and J. E. Singer (Eds), *Advances in Environmental Psychology: Applications of Personal Control*. Hillsdale, NJ: Erlbaum.

Gatchel, R. J. (1982) EMG biofeedback in anxiety reduction. In L. White and B. Turksy (Eds), *Clinical Biofeedback: Efficacy and Mechanisms*. New York: Guilford.

Gatchel, R. J. (1988) Clinical effectiveness of biofeedback in reducing anxiety. In H. Wagner (Ed.) *Social Psychophysiology and Emotion: Theory and Clinical Applications*, pp. 197–210. Chichester John Wiley.

Gatchel, R. J., Hatch, J., Maynard, A., Turns, R., and Taunton-Blackwood, A. (1979) Comparative effectiveness of biofeedback, false-biofeedback and systematic desensitization in reducing speech anxiety: short- and long-term results. *Journal of Consulting and Clinical Psychology*, **47**, 620–2.

Gatchel, R. J., Hatch, J. P., Watson, P. J., Smith, D., and Gaas, E. (1977) Comparative effectiveness of voluntary heart-rate control and muscular relaxation as active coping skills for reducing speech anxiety. *Journal of Consulting and Clinical Psychology*, **45**, 1093–1100.

Geer, J. H., Davison, G. C., and Gatchel, R. J. (1970) Reduction of stress in humans through non-veridical perceived control of aversive stimulation. *Journal of Personality and Social Psychology*, **16**, 731–8.

Goldfried, M. R., and Merbaum, M. (Eds) (1973) *Behavior Change Through Self-Control*. New York: Holt, Rinehart, & Winston.

Goldfried, M. R., and Trier, C. S. (1974) Effectiveness of relaxation as an active coping skill. *Journal of Abnormal Psychology*, **83**, 348–55.

Green, J. A., and Shellenberger, R. D. (1986) Biofeedback research and the ghost in the box: a reply to Roberts. *American Psychologist*, **9**, 1003–4.

Hatch, J. P., and Gatchel, R. J. (1979) Development of physiological response patterns concomitant with the learning of voluntary heart rate control. *Journal of Comparative and Physiological Psychology*, **93**, 306–13.

Honigfield, G. (1964) Non-specific factor in treatment. I. Review of placebo reactions and placebo reactors. *Diseases of the Nervous System*, **25**, 145–56.

Izard, C. E. (1972) *Patterns of Emotions*, New York: Academic Press.

Izard, C. E. (1977) *Human Emotions*. New York: Plenum Press.

James, W. (1884). What is an emotion? *Mind*, **9**, 188–204.

James, W., and Lange, C. G. (1922) *The Emotions*. Baltimore: Williams & Wilkins.

Kamiya, J. (1968) Operant control of EEG alpha rhythm and some of its reported effects upon consciousness. In C. Tart (Ed.), *Altered States of Consciousness*, pp. 519–29. New York: John Wiley.

Lacey, J. I. (1967) Somatic response patterns and stress: some revisions of activation theory. In M. H. Appley and R. Trumbull (Eds), *Psychological Stress*. New York: McGraw-Hill.

McGovern, H. (1986) Comment on Robert's criticism of biofeedback. *American Psychologist*, **9**, 1007.

McKinney, M. E., Gatchel, R. J., Brantley, D., and Harrington, R. (1980) The impact of biofeedback-manipulated physiological change on emotional state. *Basic and Applied Social Psychology*, **1**, 15–21.

Mahoney, M. J. (1976) *Cognition and Behavior Modification*. Cambridge, MA: Ballinger.

Miller, N. E. (1969) Learning of visceral and glandular responses. *Science*, **163**, 434–45.

Mowrer, O. H. (1947) On the dual nature of learning: a re-interpretation of 'conditioning' and 'problem-solving.' *Harvard Educational Review*, **17**, 102–48.

Norris, P. (1986a) Biofeedback, voluntary control and human potential. *Biofeedback and Self-Regulation*, **11**, 1–20.

Norris, P. (1986b). On the status of biofeedback and clinical practice. *American psychologist*, **9**, 1009–10.

Paul, G. L. (1967) Insight versus desensitization in psychotherapy two years after termination. *Journal of Consulting Psychology*, **31**, 333–348.

Pennebaker, J. W., and Hoover, C. W. (1986) Inhibition and cognition: toward an understanding of trauma and disease In R. J. Davidson, G. E. Schwartz, and D. Shapiro

(Eds), *Consciousness and Self-Regulation*, Vol. 4, pp. 107–36. New York: Plenum Press.

Rachman, S., and Hodgson, R. I. (1974) Synchrony and desynchrony in fear and avoidance. *Behaviour Research and Therapy*, **12**, 311–18.

Roberts, A. (1985) Biofeedback research, training and clinical roles. *American Psychologist*, **40**, 938–41.

Russell, E. W. (1974) The power of behavior control: a critique of behavior modification methods. *Journal of Clinical Psychology*, **30**, 111–36.

Schachter, S. and Singer, J. E. (1962) Cognitive, social and physiological determinants of emotional state. *Psychological Review*, **69**, 379–99.

Schwartz, G. E. (1982) Physiological patterning and emotion: implications for the self-regulation of emotion. In K. R. Blankstein and J. Polivy (Eds) *Self-Control and Self-Modification of Emotional Behavior*. New York: Plenum Press.

Schwartz, G. E. (1983) Disregulation theory and disease: applications to the repression/cerebral disconnection/cardiovascular disorder hypothesis. *International Review of Applied Psychology*, **32**, 95–118.

Schwartz, G. E. and Weinberger, D. A. (1980) Patterns of emotional responses to affective situations: relations among happiness, sadness, anger, fear, depression, and anxiety. *Motivation and Emotion*, **4**, 175–91.

Seligman, M. E. P. (1975) *Helplessness*. San Francisco: W. H. Freeman.

Selye, H. (1976) *The Stress of Life*. New York: McGraw-Hill.

Shapiro, D. (1973) Preface. In D. Shapiro, T. X. Barber, L. V. DiCara, J. Kamiya, N. Miller, and J. Stoyva (Eds), *Biofeedback and Self-Control*. Chicago: Aldine.

Shapiro, A. K. (1959) The placebo effect in the history of medical treatment–implications for psychiatry. *American Journal of Psychiatry*, **116**, 298–304.

Shapiro, A. K. (1971) Placebo effects in medicine, psychotherapy, and psychoanalysis. In A. E. Bergen and S. L. Garfield (Eds), *Handbook of Psychotherapy and Behavior Change*. New York: John Wiley.

Storebel, C. F. and Glueck, B. C. (1973) Biofeedback treatment in medicine and psychiatry: and ultimate placebo? *Seminars in Psychiatry*, **5**, 379–93.

Tobin, D. J. (1985) Relaxation training: guidelines for the biofeedback clinician. *Clinical Biofeedback and Health: An International Journal*, **8**, 45–51.

Tomkins, S. S. (1962) *Affect, Imagery, Consciousness*. Vol. 1. *The Positive Affects*. New York: Springer.

Tomkins, S. S. (1963) *Affect, Imagery Consciousness*. Vol. 2. *The Negative Effects*. New York: Springer.

Tyrer, P. J. The relevance of bodily feelings in emotion. *Lancet*, **1**, 915–16.

Tyrer, P. J. (1982) The concept of somatic anxiety (letter). *British Journal of Psychiatry*, **140**, 325.

Wallace, R. K., and Benson, H. (1972) The physiology of meditation. *Scientific American*, **226**, 85–90.

Walsh, D. (1974) Interactive effects of biofeedback and instructional set on subjective state. *Psychophysiology*, **11**, 428–35.

Weinberger, D. A., Schwartz, G. E., and Davidson, R. J. (1979) Low anxious, high anxious, and repressive coping styles: psychometric patterns and behavioral and physiological response to stress. *Journal of Abnormal Psychology*, **88**, 368–80.

White, L., and Tursky, B. (1986) Commentary on Roberts. *American Psychologist*, **9**, 1005–6.

Wilkens, W. (1973) Expectancy and therapeutic gain: an impirical and conceptual critique. *Journal of Consulting and Clinical Psychology*, **40**, 69–77.

Wittmeyer, I., and Abraham, D. (1985) A call for a new protocol in clinical biofeedback: the integration of upper torso EMG training into a behavior change program. *Clinical Biofeedback and Health: An International Journal*, **8**, 109–118.

PART 3

THE BIOLOGICAL CONTEXT OF EXPRESSIVE BEHAVIOUR

Introduction

Expressive behaviour has been given a number of different roles in relation to emotion, for example as one of the components of the overall emotional response, as the source (via self-perception or a 'hard-wired' mechanism) of emotional feeling, or as a means of communication about intentions or inner states. The three chapters in this part of the book reflect this interest in emotional expression and each, in a different way, relates expressive behaviour to evolutionary processes.

In Chapter 6 (*The argument and evidence about universals in facial expressions of emotion*) Ekman examines the proposition that the facial expression of a number of emotions can be demonstrated to be universal, and that this universality shows that these expressions are innate and have evolved through natural selection. He argues that the alternative view, that facial expressions are specific to each culture, is based on conceptual misunderstandings (such as the confusion of conversational signals and emotional expressions), and on the misinterpretation of flawed research. Some of this confusion has arisen because of the failure to distinguish between different types of smile, which would not all be expected to be universal. A more recent series of studies has demonstrated that at least six emotions show universality of expression, in the sense that people in different cultures produce the same posed and spontaneous expressions, and also interpret expressions as being the same emotions. Ekman goes on to discuss alternative explanations for the origin of these universal emotional expressions. The more obvious route for their evolution is through the process of ritualization, in which a behaviour that originally had a biological or instrumental function becomes modified to serve as a signal communicating information related to the original function. A different view is that species-constant learning leads to the universal modification and adoption of a behaviour for communication purposes. Ekman discusses the difficulty of distinguishing these explanations empirically, and argues that research on emotional expression should not be constrained by a narrow interpretation of the information they convey.

Scherer (Chapter 7, *Vocal correlates of emotional arousal and affective disturbance*) reviews the nature of measures of vocal expression that may be used as indicators of emotion. He discusses a number of methodological issues, including the advantages that might be gained from using these measures rather than more traditional psychophysiological methods. It is also important to consider what he calls 'pull-effects' (originating in factors outside the organism) on vocal production, as well as the 'push-effects' of physiological changes. He describes replicated findings that demonstrate regularities in the relationship between acoustic features such as fundamental frequency and intensity on the one hand, and emotions and stress on the other. This work includes laboratory studies and studies of persons with emotional disturbance. The relationships described are referred to a model of the neurophysiological structures that influence voice production through the autonomic and somatic nervous systems. Scherer points out that most of the research has been correlational, and describes a theoretical model of the effects of emotion on voice production. This model describes the possible functional significance of changes in the various subsystems of emotion (physiological responses, expression, motivational tendencies, and feelings). These functional proposals are based on evolutionary considerations, and allow Scherer to produce detailed predictions of the effects of emotions on voice production.

In Chapter 8 (*Subjective, expressive, and peripheral bodily components of emotion*) Buck presents aspects of his theory of emotion that trace each of the three components of emotion to their earliest phylogenetic origins. Emotion is essentially a 'read-out' of motivational potential through the three pathways of peripheral bodily change, expressive behaviours, and syncretic cognition. Buck describes his view of the relationships between cognition, emotion, and motivation, in which cognition has evolved because it provides a selective advantage in terms of greater sensitivity and flexibility to internal as well as external events. Cognitions of internal information are recognized in more complex animals as emotional feelings. An important peripheral contribution to emotional experience, Buck argues, comes neither from the face nor from autonomic changes, but rather by way of the immune system, whose cells produce a range of hormones, and which can cross the blood–brain barrier. These properties of the immune system have significant implications for understanding the effects of emotion on health. Expressive behaviour is important as part of a 'social biofeedback' process, by which people are educated to understand their own feelings and the demands society places on appropriate emotional feelings and displays. Emotional experience is a direct read-out, and is not secondary to visceral changes or expression. Buck relates subjective experience to direct perception, and discusses neuropsychological and other evidence supporting this. Finally, a model of the appraisal process is described which involves both cortical and subcortical structures; this is incorporated into Buck's general model of emotion.

CHAPTER 6

The Argument and Evidence about Universals in Facial Expressions of Emotion

Paul Ekman

University of California, San Francisco

ABSTRACT

Theory and evidence support the conclusion that there are some universals in facial expressions of emotion. New findings on different forms of smiling are reviewed, arguments about the origin of expressions are considered, and a proposal is put forward about the type of information provided by a facial expression of emotion.

Are facial expressions of emotion the same for all people? When someone is angry, for example, will we see the same movements appear regardless of that person's race, culture, social class, age, or sex? Is it true that we can understand a foreigner's facial expressions of emotion if we observe his or her facial expressions, that we need no special facial language school, tutoring us as to what these expressions mean in each culture? Are gestures universal too? And if facial expressions of emotion are universal is that the result of evolution?

In this chapter I shall summarize the evidence which allows answers to some of

Paul Ekman's work is supported by Research Scientist Award MH 06092 from the National Institute of Mental Health.

Handbook of Social Psychophysiology, Edited by H. Wagner and A. Manstead,
© 1989 John Wiley & Sons Ltd

these questions. I will review more than 75 years of research on this topic. Much of what is covered I have reviewed before [I draw most heavily on my and Oster's earlier review chapter on facial expression (Ekman and Oster, 1979), an earlier review (Ekman, 1973), and the most recent article on this topic (Ekman *et al.*, 1987)]. However, some of the evidence and interpretations that I present here is new, and some of the evidence has just been published or is still in press.

After a brief historical introduction I will summarize the views and evidence of those who argued that facial expressions are socially learned and culturally variable. Then the evidence for universality will be described, including new findings on how the judgement of emotional intensity manifests both universals and cultural differences. A special section will review very recent research on different forms of smiling. Theoretical arguments about the origins of facial expression and the issue of what type of information is signaled by a facial expression of emotion will be discussed.

Before beginning, a few words about the terms of discourse. Nearly 20 years ago in a review of research on facial expression Ekman, Friesen and Ellsworth (1972) chose to avoid

> The phrase 'facial expressions of emotion,' since it implies that some inner state is being manifest or shown externally, or that the behavior is intended to transmit information. Instead we have used the more awkward phrase 'face and emotion' or 'facial behavior'. (p. 3)

The alternative term 'display' is even more theoretically loaded with a particular view about the origin and function of facial activity. I have reverted to 'facial expression' because it is a more felicitous phrase than 'facial behavior' or 'face and emotion.' In doing so I have not changed my earlier rejection of the theoretical views this term might imply to some. To be explicit, facial expressions of emotion are, in my view (Ekman, 1977), as central to emotion as are the physiological changes or subjective feelings, and thus it would be mistaken to view one as the expression of the other. Also, while people do make facial expressions deliberately to transmit information, most facial expressions of emotion occur, I believe, without such deliberation. That is not to deny their importance as social signals, in either their development or current function.

HISTORICAL INTRODUCTION

More than a century ago Charles Darwin published his work on *The Expression of the Emotions in Man and Animals* (1872). It was published 13 years after his revolutionary *On the Origin of Species* (1859). Darwin claimed that we cannot understand human emotional expression without understanding the expressions of animals, for, he argued, our emotional expressions are in large part determined by our evolution. His expression book was a best-seller in its time. On the day of its publication 5267 copies were sold, more than most academic monographs today sell in their entire life in print.

Amazingly, Darwin's book had very little influence, up until 20 years ago. I have (Ekman, 1973) suggested five factors that may explain why Darwin's work on expression was ignored for so long. first, he used anthropomorphic terms, which particularly offended those students of animal behavior who are unwilling to say that animals have emotions. Second, Darwin used a great deal of anecdotal, rather than systematic, data. (We should note, however, that he was exemplary in his use of multiple data sources—observations of infants, animals, the mentally ill, and the blind. And, Darwin was the first to use a systematic method for gathering cross-cultural observations of expressions, the most commonly used method employed today.) The third reason why Darwin's work on expression was rejected was his emphasis on the innate basis of at least some emotional expressions. This did not fit the emphasis on behaviorism in psychology and on relativism in anthropology. A fourth factor was Darwin's adoption of Lamarck's theory that learned characteristics could be inherited. Finally, Darwin's emphasis on the deductive method lessened his impact on present-day ethologists who are committed to an inductive approach.

Empirical research on facial expressions of emotion has been quite episodic in the century following Darwin's expression book. Between 1920 and 1940 this topic drew the attention of many well-known psychologists: Allport, Boring, Goodenough, Guilford, Hunt, Klineberg, Landis, Munn, Titchner, and Woodworth. Interestingly, their work on expression was a minor digression in their own careers; none focused on it for long. (Goldstein, 1983, presents an interesting historical analysis of why few scientists focused for long on facial expression). The knowledge accumulated during this period was meagre. In the opinion of influential reviewers (Bruner and Tagiuri, 1954; Hunt, 1941; Tagiuri, 1968), there were no consistent answers to questions about the accuracy of information provided by facial expressions, their universality and possible innateness. During the next 20 years there were comparatively few studies of facial expression, with the exception of Schlosberg's reports (Schlosberg, 1941, 1952, 1954) that categorical judgements of emotion could be ordered in terms of underlying dimensions.

A number of recent trends have contributed to the resurgence of interest in facial expression in the last 20 years. Tomkins (1962, 1963) provided a theoretical rationale for studying the face as a means of learning about personality and emotion. He also showed that observers could obtain very high agreement in judging emotion if the facial expressions were carefully selected to show what he believes are the innate facial affects (Tomkins and McCarter, 1964). Tomkins greatly influenced both myself and Izard, helping each of us to plan our initial cross-cultural studies of facial expression. The resulting evidence of universality in facial expression rekindled interest in this topic in psychology and anthropology.

The evidence for universals in facial expression not only fit with Tomkins's theory, but also with the newly emerging interest in applying ethological methods and concepts to human behavior. Interested in the biological bases of behavior, human ethologists welcomed evidence of commonalities in social behavior across cultures. Human ethologists provided the first detailed 'catalogs' describing naturally occurring facial behavior (Blurton Jones, 1972; Brannigan and Humphries, 1972; Grant, 1969; McGrew, 1972). In the last decade, developmental psychologists investigating attachment, mother–infant interaction, and the development of emotion, have also begun to study facial expression.

Interest in facial expression also benefited from the popularity of research on nonverbal communication in the 1970s. While most of the research done under this rubric focused on hand and body movement, gaze direction, or posture, some studies included a few facial measures or used a judgement approach to assess the face.

Very recently, psychophysiologists interested in emotion have become interested in facial expression. Davidson, Ekman, Saron, Senulis, and Friesen (1988) for example, utilized the incidence of facial expression to dictate sampling points to examine EEG activity during positive and negative emotions. Ekman, Levenson, and Friesen (1983) found that voluntarily performing certain facial expressions generated emotion-specific autonomic nervous system activity.

A last factor responsible for the growing volume of research on facial expression is the development of systematic methods for measuring facial behavior. Ekman and Friesen's (1976, 1978) FACS provided the first objective, comprehensive, technique for describing facial movement in muscular terms. Izard afterwards (1979) developed an approach for describing the occurrence of selected facial behaviors that he proposed are relevant to emotion. There has also been progress in utilizing electromyography to measure facial activity (Fridlund and Cacioppo, 1986). [See Ekman (1982) for an analysis of 14 methods of measuring facial behavior.]

A number of recent reviews have covered the literature on facial expression. Ekman *et al.* (1972) reanalyzed many of the experiments conducted from 1914 to 1970. They found, contrary to Bruner and Taguiri's (1954) assessment, that the data yielded consistent, positive, answers to fundamental questions about the language used to describe facial expression, the influence of context on judgements of facial expression, the accuracy of judgements, and similarities across cultures. For other reviews of facial expression see: Charlesworth and Kreutzer (1973) on infants and children; Chevalier–Skolnikoff (1973) and Redican (1975, 1982) on nonhuman primates; Ekman (1973) on cross-cultural comparisons; Izard (1977) on theories of emotion; Ekman and Oster (1979) for a review of the research from 1969 to 1979, and Fridlund, Ekman, and Oster (1987) for an expansion and update of that review.

THE CULTURE-SPECIFIC VIEWPOINT

THEORISTS

Three theorists were extremely influential in anthropology and psychology for a number of decades, arguing that the information signaled by facial expressions is specific to each culture. None provided much evidence, but their views merit consideration for historical reasons and also to elucidate theoretical issues which they ignored but which are relevant to understanding the phenomenon.

'What is shown on the face is written there by culture.' Klineberg says he never made that statement although it was attributed to him. However, he did argue, in a more tentative way, for that view. Commenting on an anthropologist's account of how people arriving in a village wore a fierce look rather than a smile, Klineberg said:

> Not only may joy be expressed without a smile, but in addition the smile may be used in a variety of situations... a smile may mean contempt, incredulity, affection... [quoting from Lafacadio Hearn's observation of the Japanese] Samurai women were required, like the women of Sparta, to show signs of joy on hearing that their husbands or sons had fallen in battle.   (Klineberg, 1940, pp. 194–5)

Birdwhistell, an anthropologist with training in linguistics, dance, and dance notation, was another influential advocate of this view. He claimed that facial expressions are part of what he termed *kinesics*, which can be best viewed as another language, with the same type of units and organization as spoken language.

> Early in my research on human body motion, influenced by Darwin... and by my own preoccupation with human universals, I attempted to study the human smile... Not only did I find that a number of my subjects 'smiled' when they were subjected to what seemed to be a positive environment but some 'smiled' in an aversive one... [Birdwhistell, 1970, pp. 29–30].

> ... this search for universals was culture bound... There are probably no universal symbols of emotional state.... We can expect them [emotional expressions] to be learned and patterned according to the particular structure of particular societies. [p. 126].

Klineberg and Birdwhistell's observations highlight both a methodological and a conceptual problem. Let us consider first the methodological problem, which is due to the use of imprecise behavioral description. The term *smile* unfortunately covers too many different facial expressions. Ekman and Friesen (1976) distinguished dozens of such smiling expressions, which involve the deployment of different sets of muscle actions. Each of these smiles differs in appearance, although in each the lip corners are drawn upwards. The evidence I will describe later about smiling shows that when different forms of smiling are distinguished, they are found to occur in quite different circumstances. Two forms of smiling occur in other than pleasant situations, another occurs when politeness is called for, and another when enjoyment is experienced.

It is confusing to call these all *smiling*, implying that they are a singular, unified category of behavior. When these different lip-corner-up appearances are treated by the observer as one entity, then, it will appear, as it did to Klineberg and Birdwhistell, that the smile has no common meaning. It is only by understanding the anatomy of facial action, by experience in the close description of facial behavior, that such errors in describing facial behavior can be avoided. The problem is especially acute when observations are made in real time without the opportunity to review the behavior repeatedly and in slow-motion, and when the observations are made by a single observer, so there is no possibility of checking on inter-observer reliability. The use of other imprecise terms, such as frown, grimace, scowl, also encourages observers to miss what may be important distinctions.

The conceptual problem raised by Klineberg and Birdwistell is their failure to consider the possibility that differences in observed facial expression may be due to culturally imposed attempts to manage universal expressions. They treated facial expression as if it is a totally involuntary system, not capable of being voluntarily controlled. Ekman and Friesen (1969) coined the phrase *display rules* to refer to such norms about who can show which emotion to whom, and when. People learn to interfere, they proposed, with facial expressions of emotion. The observation that Klineberg cites of the fierce look during a greeting, could, from this vantage point, be due to a display rule to mask the appearance of happiness. Similarly, the smiling appearance of the grieving Samurai women could be a display rule to cover any sadness or distress with the appearance of polite smiling.

It would be quite damaging to the conclusion that there are universal expressions of emotion if there were clear evidence that when people are in an negative affect situation, experiencing pain, sadness, disgust, fear, or anger, they show an expression in which the lip corners go up, *only if* the following other explanations can be ruled out: (1) the subject who shows this smiling countenance does not believe that negative feelings must be masked with a simulated, deliberate, smile; (2) the smile is not a comment added by the subject to signal that the negative experienced can be endured (a grin-and-bear-it smile, or what Ekman and Friesen called a 'miserable smile'); (3) the smile incorporates the features which Ekman and Friesen have found to occur when enjoyment is experienced (see description below), as distinct from polite or masking smiles. There is no such evidence.

LaBarre made his major argument against universality nine years after Klineberg. He failed to distinguish facial expressions of emotion from gestures, as seen in his statement 'there is no "natural" language of emotional gesture' (LaBarre, 1947, p. 55). The distinction between gesture and emotional expression is not an easy one, but it is necessary, since gestures are socially learned and culturally variable, while there is strong evidence that facial expressions of emotion are not. Ekman and Friesen (1969) subdivide gestures into what they termed *illustrators*, movements which punctuate or help to illustrate simultaneous speech, and *emblems*, a term first suggested by Efron (1941/1972), which refers to movements which have a direct verbal translation, a dictionary definition known to all members of a culture or subculture.

Any message can be conveyed by an emblem, including factual information, commands, attitudes, and (here is the complication) feelings. The last of these I have called *referential* expressions, expressions which refer to emotions, performed in a way which signals that the emotion is not felt when the expression is made. The message conveyed by an emotional expression is, by definition, a feeling of the moment, providing information about likely antecedent events, consequent events, etc. In Ekman (1979) I give a more complete explanation of the differences between referential and emotional expressions.

It would take us too far afield to discuss thoroughly the differences between emblems, illustrators, and conversational regulators [which collectively Ekman (1979) called conversational signals] as compared with emotional expressions. It is sufficient to draw attention to the fact that every facial movement is *not* an emotional expression. While many conversational signals involve the hands, some do involve the face. Facial action is not dedicated solely to emotional expression. Brow raising, brow lowering, and a number of different types of actions which pull the lip corners up are among the most common conversational signals. LaBarre failed clearly to make these distinctions. Darwin also was not completely consistent in this regard. Darwin was primarily concerned with emotional expressions, which he considered innately determined, and thereby universal. While he mentioned a few emblems that he considered universal, he acknowledged that most were culture specific. While LaBarre focused primarily on emblems he included some emotional expressions and referential expressions.

EVIDENCE

There have been five empirical studies undertaken specifically to prove that facial expressions are either partly or totally culture specific. (Karl Heider also conducted such a study on the Dani of New Guinea, but we will consider it later as it was done to challenge work in New Guinea by Ekman and Friesen.) Dickey and Knower (1941) compared the judgements of facial expressions made by Mexican and American school children. Vinacke (1949) and Vinacke and Fong (1955) showed candid photographs to Caucasians, Chinese, and Japanese students at the University of Hawaii. Triandis and Lambert (1958) showed photographs of a professional actress to college students in the USA, Athens, and the village of Skafera in Greece. Cuceloglu (1970) used moon-like drawings to represent the face, which he showed to college students in the USA, Japan, and Turkey. Winkelmayer, Exline, Gottheil, and Paredes (1971) showed silent motion picture films of both normal and schizophrenic women to college students in the USA, Britain, and Mexico.

All five of these studies were undertaken to demonstrate that facial expressions are culture specific, and yet they found evidence of universals. Four of them also found evidence of cultural differences, but the nature of the differences found does not contradict the notion of universals in facial expressions of emotion. Each study had major flaws in the research design. Most gave little thought to the necessity to sample systematically the facial expressions they studied. Rather than selecting expressions according to either an *a priori* theory or a representative database, they took what was conveniently available.

EVIDENCE OF UNIVERSALS

Three research methods have been used in studies which obtained evidence of universals in facial expressions. (1) Poses of emotion have been elicited. (2) Spontaneous expressions have been compared in two or more cultures. (3) The most frequent type of research has been to compare the judgements of emotions made by observers in different cultures who view the same set of facial expressions.

ELICITING POSES   *Unresalib ~ Imal*

Ekman and Friesen (1971) asked members of one culture to show how their face would look if they were the person in each of a number of different emotional contexts (e.g. 'you feel sad because your child died', 'you are angry and about to fight,' etc.). They interpreted their findings as strongly supporting the possibility of universality, since observers in another culture did far better than chance in identifying which emotional contexts the posed expressions were intended to portray. This finding had unusual import because the persons displaying the expressions were members of a visually isolated New Guinea culture (the South Fore). The ability of Americans to understand these New Guinean expressions could not be attributed to prior contact between these groups nor to both having learned their expressions from mass media models.

Three problems limit these findings. First, there has been only one such study. It has not been repeated in another preliterate, visually isolated culture, nor for that matter in a literate, non-Western or Western culture. Second, not all the six emotions portrayed were accurately recognized. While anger, disgust, happiness, and sadness were distinguished from each other and from fear and surprise, the American observers could not distinguish the New Guineans' portrayals of fear and surprise. Third, the facial expressions were posed and Mead (1975) argued that establishing that posed expressions are universal need not imply that spontaneous facial expressions of emotion are universal. I (Ekman, 1977, pp. 68–70) replied to Mead that I could see no reason why people could readily interpret such posed facial expressions and readily pose them other than the likelihood that they had seen those facial expressions and experienced them in actual social life. The best answer to Mead would, of course, be from evidence on spontaneous expressions, which the next type of investigation did provide.

COMPARING SPONTANEOUS EXPRESSIONS IN DIFFERENT CULTURES

Ekman and Friesen compared spontaneous facial expressions shown by Japanese and American college students. They selected Japan as the comparison culture because of the popular notion of the inscrutability of the Oriental. They hoped to show that this was due to display rules about masking negative affect in the presence of an authority. Subjects in Tokyo and in California came into a laboratory and watched both a travelogue and stress inducing films while measurements were taken of their skin resistance and heart rate. The videotapes taken with a hidden camera unknown to the subject were later measured by persons who did not know which film was seen when the facial expressions occurred. Better than 0.90 correlation was found in the particular facial movements shown by the Japanese and by the Americans (Ekman, 1972). Virtually the same repertoire of facial movements occurred at the same points in time.

Later in the same experiment, a scientist dressed in a white coat entered the room and sat with the subject while he or she watched a stress film. Now Ekman and Friesen expected that display rules for managing facial expression in the presence of an authority figure should be operative, more so in Japan than in the USA. Measurements of the facial behavior showed that the facial movements were no longer the same. The Japanese looked more polite, showed more lip corners up (social smiling) than did the Americans (Friesen, 1972). Examining these videotapes in slow-motion revealed the actual sequencing in which a smiling movement would be superimposed over the muscular action of disgust or fear. This was the first study to show how cultural differences in the management of facial expressions (display rules) can mask universal facial expressions.

Two problems, however, limit the findings from this study. Again it is but a single study; no one has yet attempted to replicate it. The second limitation is that the mutilation films elicited only a few emotions (disgust and fear) not allowing determination of whether the full range of spontaneous emotional expressions are universal. The next type of research met these two criticisms, studying many emotions, with many replications.

COMPARING JUDGEMENTS OF EMOTION MADE BY OBSERVERS FROM DIFFERENT CULTURES

Typically, the people in each culture are shown still photographs of facial expressions, and asked to select a single emotion word or category from a list of words or categories. Very high agreement was found in the specific emotions attributed to facial expressions across five literate cultures (Ekman, 1972; Ekman, Sorenson, and Friesen, 1969), in another such study, across nine literate cultures (Izard, 1971), and in another study of a non-Western literate culture (Boucher, 1973). The strength of this evidence is its many replications. Unlike the first two kinds of research, this type of study has been repeated in many cultures, by different investigators, using different photographs of facial expression.

These studies have provided consistent evidence for the common recognition of at least six emotions (happiness, anger, fear, sadness, surprise, and disgust). Izard reported agreement also for shame and interest, but it is questionable whether it was facial expression or head position which was the clue for recognizing these emotions. There have been no other cross-cultural studies of the facial expressions of shame and interest. Ekman and Friesen (1986) have reported agreement across ten Western and non-Western literate cultures in the identification of a specific expression for contempt. Although there is some argument about this, (Izard and Haynes, 1988, and reply by Ekman and Friesen, 1988, in press; also Ricci Bitti, personal communication, 1986), Ekman and Heider (1988, in press) have again replicated the recognition of contempt in a non-Western culture.

Six questions can be raised about such judgement studies in which the same set of faces is shown to observers in different cultures. First, argument can be made that establishing agreement across cultures about the recognition of emotion across cultures does not prove that the expression of emotion is the same across these cultures. This objection seems highly implausible. The recognition of emotion is not a matter which is taught formally, but presuambly is learned by observing the expressions which actually do occur. (Some have suggested that the recognition of emotion is innate, but whether it is innate or learned, is not relevant to this particular point.) If the expression of anger involved a slack jaw and raised brows in culture A, and lowered brow and pressed lips in culture B, then those cultures should disagree in their judgements of emotion when viewing photographs of these two different expressions. But in fact that is not what occurs. Cultures agree in their attributions of anger, and other emotions.

A second objection is that the observers in all these studies were responding to posed, not spontaneous, expressions. The answer provided at the start of this section on universality to Mead's qualms about posed behavior apply here as well. It would seem quite far-fetched to propose that there are two unrelated sets of facial expressions, a posed set which for some reason is the same across cultures, and a spontaneous set which is culture specific. Furthermore, the posed expressions are similar in form to the expressions found in the cross-cultural studies of spontaneous expressions. Although such comparisons between spontaneous and posed behavior can only be made for disgust, fear, and happiness (since other emotions have not been elicited in cross-cultural studies of spontaneous expression), there is no reason to expect such similarity would not be found for other emotions. Within Western cultures such similarities between posed and spontaneous expressions have also been established for anger, surprise, and sadness.

Another answer to this question about whether universality is established if the expressions judged are posed, comes from another study that also found universality when the observers saw spontaneous facial behavior (Ekman, 1972). The expressions of the Japanese and American subjects in the study described above, in which subjects had watched body mutilation and neutral films, were shown to Japanese and American observers. These observers were asked to judge whether each person's expressions occurred in reaction to a stressful or a neutral film. The judgements made by the Japanese and American observers were highly correlated and did not differ as a function of whether they were interpreting the expressions of their own or the other culture.

A third objection is that all the people who were studied had shared visual contact. Perhaps they all learned to recognize emotional expressions, or even to make those expressions, by observing the same models in cinema, television, and photographs. This criticism is met by a judgement study in a visually isolated, preliterate New Guinea culture, the South Fore (Ekman and Friesen, 1971). (These were the same subjects whose poses of emotion were described at the beginning of this section on the evidence of universality.) The subjects had seen no movies, television or photographs. They spoke neither English nor Pidgin. They had never worked for a Caucasian or lived in a government settlement. Nearly 10% of the members of this culture were studied. For anger, happiness, sadness, disgust, and surprise (except in distinction from fear) the faces identified with each emotion were the same as in literate cultures. Karl Heider and Eleanor Rosch were skeptical of these findings, believing that facial expressions are culture specific. In 1970, on a field trip to West Irian, they repeated this study with the Dani, a more remote culture than the South Fore. They obtained a near perfect replication of Ekman and Friesen's results (reported in Ekman, 1972).

The fourth criticism of the judgement studies is that the judgement tasks which they employed might have concealed cultural differences in the perception of secondary, blended emotions. Many students of emotion have noted that facial expressions may contain more than one message (Ekman and Friesen, 1969; Izard, 1971; Plutchik, 1962; Tomkins, 1963). The two emotions in a blend may be of similar strength, or one emotion may be primary, much more salient than the other, secondary, emotion. In prior cross-cultural studies the investigators presumed that the expressions they showed displayed a single emotion rather than a blend, and therefore did not provide those who observed the expressions the opportunity to choose more than one emotion for each expression. Without such data, however, it is not possible to ascertain whether an expression conveys a single emotion or a blend, and if there is blend, whether cultures agree in their judgement of the secondary emotion. Prior evidence of cross-cultural agreement in the judgement of expressions might be limited just to the primary message and may not apply to the secondary, blended, emotions.

A recent study by Ekman *et al.* (1987) remedied this problem. In this study, members of ten literate Western and non-Western cultures were shown a set of Caucasian facial expressions. Instead of being limited to selecting one emotion term or category for each expression, the observers were allowed to indicate the presence of multiple emotions, and the relative intensity of each emotion. There was very high agreement across cultures about the secondary, blended, emotion signaled by an expression.

The fifth question is whether there is universality, not just about which emotion is signaled by an expression, but also about the intensity of the perceived emotion. Only two cross-cultural studies (Ekman, 1972; Saha, 1973) obtained intensity judgements, and no differences were found. But not many cultures were examined in either study. Ekman *et al.* (1987) addressed this question as well. They found cross-cultural agreement about the relative strength of expressions of the same emotion. With few exceptions, the ten cultures they examined agreed about which of two different expressions of the same emotion was most intense.

Ekman *et al.* (1987) also uncovered evidence of cultural differences in the absolute intensity level attributed to an expression. The Asian cultures (Hong Kong, Japan, Sumatra) attributed less-intense emotions to expressions than did the non-Asian cultures. Since all the expressions shown had been of Caucasian faces, it was not possible to know whether this might be due to a reluctance by the Asians to attribute strong emotions to a person who they could tell was a foreigner. To examine this issue Matsumoto and Ekman (1988) showed expressions of both Japanese and Americans to subjects in both countries. Regardless of the culture or sex of the person they were judging, the Japanese judged the emotions to be less intense than did the Americans. Work now in progress is investigating whether the Japanese judge personal characteristics other than emotion to be less intense than do Americans.

Although no one study, nor just one of the three kinds of research, would be conclusive, collectively they provide an enormous body of consistent evidence for the universality of at least some facial expressions of emotions. One could maintain that not every culture in the world has been studied, and therefore universality is not established. Such a conservative interpretation of the literature (Fridlund, 1988, in press) is probably a bit far-fetched. Although not every culture has been studied, many have. The cultures studied have been non-Western as well as Western; non-literate as well as literate. Not just one investigator has been involved, but many investigators working independently. Not just those who were attempting to find evidence of universality have found such evidence, but so too have those who were attempting to challenge it.

While the evidence is strong for fear, anger, disgust, sadness, surprise, and happiness, there is still question about contempt, shame, and interest. Also, there are no data about how many expressions for each emotion are universal. Nor is it known how often these universal expressions of emotion are seen in ordinary social life. Furthermore, little has yet been documented about cultural differences in facial expression, except for the single study on display rules discussed earlier and the recent evidence about differences in the judgement of emotional intensity.

NEW FINDINGS ON SMILES

Although these are not cross-cultural studies, I report them here because they are quite new, they have not been reviewed before, and they show the value of precise descriptions of facial behavior, in this case distinguishing among different forms of smiling. As described earlier, in the section on culture-specific theorists, the failure to use such precise descriptions by those who advocated a culture-specific view of expression may have been responsible for their confusion about the universality of facial expressions.

All of these studies explored a distinction between voluntary and involuntary smiling behavior. What Ekman and Friesen (1982) have termed a *enjoyment smile* includes all smiles in which the person actually experiences, and presumably would usually report, a positive emotion. (They originally called these *felt smiles*, but because that phrase could imply that the crucial issue is whether the person actually is aware of the smile itself, I think it is better to call them *enjoyment smiles*.) These positive emotions include pleasure from visual, auditory, gustatory, kinesthetic, or tactile stimulation; amusement and delight; contentment and satisfaction; beatific experiences; relief from pain, pressure, or tension; and enjoyment of another person. They proposed that these enjoyment smiles would differ in morphology and timing from more deliberate smiles such as the social, polite, or masking smile.

Their ideas about morphology were based on the writings of the French anatomist Duchenne (1862), and their own studies of voluntary facial actions. Duchenne's classic functional anatomy of facial expression was cited by Darwin (1872), but otherwise is not well known in the English-speaking world because it was never translated, and the original French volume has been out of print for many years. I quote from an English translation of Duchenne which is soon to be published.

> The emotion of frank joy is expressed on the face by the combined contraction of the zygomaticus major muscle and the orbicularis oculi. The first obeys the will but that the second is only put in play by the sweet emotions of the soul; the . . . fake joy, the deceitful laugh, cannot provoke the contraction of this latter muscle. . . . The muscle around the eye does not obey the will; it is only brought into play by a true feeling, by an agreeable emotion. Its inertia, in smiling, unmasks a false friend. (1862; 1989)

Quite consistent with Duchenne's forecast, Ekman, Roper, and Hager (1980) found that most people are unable to contract voluntarily the orbicularis oculi muscle. This action thus would not be available, in most people, for recruitment into any of the voluntary smiles.

Based on these findings and Duchenne's observations, Ekman and Friesen, proposed that the common morphological elements in the facial expressions of all such positive experiences are the action of two muscles: the zygomatic major muscle pulling the lip corners upwards towards the cheek bones; and, the outer portion of orbicularis oculi which raises the cheek and gathers the skin inwards from around the eye socket. In honor of Duchenne I propose that a smile incorporating both of these muscles be called a *Duchenne smile*.

Seven studies have obtained evidence for distinguishing this from other forms of smiling. Ekman, Friesen, and Ancoli (1980) found that Duchenne smiles occurred more often than three other types of smiling when people watched pleasant films; and only Duchenne smiles correlated with the subjective report of happiness. Ekman, Friesen, and O'Sullivan (1988) found that Duchenne smiles occurred more often when people were actually enjoying themselves, as compared with when people feigned smiling to conceal negative emotions. Fox and Davidson (1988) found that in 10-month-old infants Duchenne smiles occurred more often in response to the mother's approach, while other types of smiles occurred more often in response to the approach of a stranger; and only Duchenne smiles were associated with the left frontal EEG activation, the pattern of cerebral activity repeatedly found in positive affect. Matsumoto (1986) found that depressed patients showed more Duchenne smiles in their discharge interviews than they did in their admission interviews, but there was no difference in the rate of other kind of smiling.

The possibility that these differences among types of smiling may be universal is suggested by the findings from the next three studies, all of which were conducted in Europe. Steiner (1986) found that Duchenne smiles but not other types of smiles increased over the course of psychotherapy in patients who were judged to have improved. Ruch (1987) found that Duchenne smiles were sensitive to the amount of humor felt by German adults when responding to jokes or cartoons. Schneider (1987) found that in young children Duchenne smiles distinguished whether they had succeeded or failed in a game.

Ekman and Friesen (1982) also proposed that enjoyment smiles would differ from other smiles in the amount of time it takes for the smile to appear, how long it remained on the face before fading, and in the time required for the smile to disappear. Two studies have shown the utility of these measures of timing, which are, however, much more costly to make than the measurement of which muscles are recruited. Bugental (1986) found that women showed more enjoyment smiles with responsive children than with unresponsive children. Weiss, Blum, and Gleberman (1987) found enjoyment smiles occurred more often during post-hypnotically induced positive affect than in deliberately posed positive affect.

Collectively, these studies show that smiles should no longer be considered a single category of behavior. They can be usefully distinguished by measuring different facets of the smile. Cross-cultural studies of the different forms of smiling need to be done. It also remains to be determined how many different smiles may provide different social signals, have different functions in social interaction, and relate to different aspects of subjective experience and concomitant physiology. [See Ekman (1985) for a description of 18 different types of smiling.]

THE ORIGIN OF FACIAL EXPRESSIONS OF EMOTION

Why are particular facial muscles activated in particular emotions? For example, why are the brows raised in surprise, and lowered in anger, rather than vice versa? The findings of universal facial expressions of emotion has been taken as evidence that these expressions are innate, prewired, specialized signals that have evolved through natural selection (Darwin, 1872; Eibl-Eibesfeldt, 1972; Redican, 1975,

1982; Tomkins, 1962). From this viewpoint, the facial actions seen in emotional expressions originally served some purely biological or instrumental function in our progenitors. In addition, these actions conveyed information to others about an individual's possible future behavior, or what might have happened to elicit the action. Because this (at first) communicative value was also adaptive, the facial actions were maintained in the repertoire even if the original function was lost, or the actions were modified as a result of natural selection, to enhance their efficacy as signals. Ethologists use the term *ritualization* to describe the process by which a behavior is modified through genetic evolution to enhance its efficacy as a signal.

There is an alternative explanation to ritualization, one which stresses the current adaptive value of the expression, emphasizing ontogenetic development rather than genetic evolution. Learning experiences common to all members of a species have been invoked to explain the origin of facial expressions of emotion (Allport, 1924; Peiper, 1963).

I will argue that both explanations—ritualization and species-constant learning—have merit. Each may explain the origin of different facial expressions of emotion. Contrasting these two explanations can usefully highlight the type of research needed to enable one to choose between them. To illustrate the difference between these explanations let us consider the origin of just two facial actions, the brow raise and the brow lower.

All those who have written about the origin of brow raising have noted that this action increases the visual input, by increasing the superior visual field. The benefit of this action depends upon how deeply set the eyes are in the bony socket, the prominence of the brow raise, and how well-endowed with hair the eyebrows are. A number of other functions of brow raising have been suggested which are not supported by current knowledge of the neuroanatomy of vision. (These are discussed in Ekman, 1979.)

Brow lowering acts as a sunshade, decreasing the light coming in from the superior visual field. Brow lowering also helps to protect the eyeball from blows and also may enhance focal illumination by diminishing background light (Redican, 1982). A number of other functions of brow lowering have been suggested which have no known basis. (These are discussed in Ekman, 1979.)

Since brow lowering and brow raising have opposite effects on vision, these effects can be used to explain their role in emotional expression. Presumably brow raise occurs in surprise expressions rather than brow lowering because raising increases visual input. Similarly, brow lowering, it could be argued, occurs in anger and sadness expressions because this action decreases glare, and protects the eyeball from blows. Thus, the selection of brow raise and brow lower from their respective signals could have been the product of learning rather than genetic evolution (ritualization). Two problems weaken the ritualization explanation.

First, ritualization presumes that selection of actions for their role as signals occurred through phylogenetic evolution. Yet the evidence that in other primates brow raises occur in surprising contexts and brow lowering in antagonistic encounters is ambiguous (Chevalier–Skolnikoff, 1973; Redican, 1982). The lack of evidence of homologous eyebrow actions in non-human primates does not rule out an evolutionary account of the role of these actions in emotional expression, although the presence of such actions would be supportive.

Second, implicit in the ritualization explanation is the idea that their function as signals is innate and cannot be explained on the basis of some purely biological function in present-day *Homo sapiens*, either in adults or children. Yet those brow actions continue to serve an adaptive function for contemporary humans. Ontogeny may play more of a role than phylogeny in shaping these actions in emotional signals. The genes may determine only how the equipment works (brow raise increases the visual field). The signal value of such an action and its association with emotion (surprise) may depend primarily upon early experience, experience common to all members of the species who have functioning visual apparatus. Such reasoning would go as follows:

> Infants encounter unexpected events in which they would raise their brows to see what is happening above them. (One could even argue that the unexpected is more likely to be above than below an infant.) Over time, perhaps abetted by the signal value of the movement, brow raising and surprise would become associated. In the strictest version of this explanation, the infant would have to learn, presumably by trial and error, that brow raising increases his visual field. Alternatively, that might be given, and what he learns is to make this movement when trying to see what has unexpectedly happened. To grant even more to biology, the infant could be born equipped to raise his brows when visually scanning unexpected sudden visual events. What he needs to learn is to generalize this response to any unexpected event, regardless of whether it is visual. (Ekman, 1977, p. 66)

I do not mean to suggest that this type of species-constant learning is the correct explanation, only that it is just as plausible as an explanation based on ritualization. There is no clear evidential basis for making a choice. The origin of brow raises in surprise could be resolved by developmental data. If blind infants do not show brow raising to sudden unexpected sounds or touches, then at least we could assume that the brow raise is not wired in for surprise, nor for scanning if the eyes are not operative. Unfortunately the relevant data are equivocal (Charlesworth, 1970; Eibi-Eibesfeldt, 1972; Lersch, 1932, 1971; Goodenough, 1932; Peiper, 1963). No one has yet done a detailed descriptive study of the repertoire of facial behavior in the first year of life, for either blind or sighted infants.

Although the evidence is not as good as it could be if better research methods were employed, there is, nevertheless, evidence that the facial expressions of monkeys, apes, and humans are homologous for fear, anger, happiness, and perhaps sadness (reviewed by Redican, 1982). In summarizing a much more detailed discussion of these issues, I wrote that I think it is likely:

> that evolution played a major role in emotional expression. This must be the case for some facial actions in some facial expressions of emotion. But which ones, and on

what basis is not known. ... The problem with accepting ritualization as the explanation of the origin of facial expressions of emotion is that it forecloses investigations of issues which should be explored, it leads away from rather than toward research which needs to be done. Competing explanations should be considered and ambiguities emphasized to motivate the research which is needed. (Ekman, 1979, pp. 201–2)

WHAT INFORMATION IS PROVIDED BY FACIAL EXPRESSIONS OF EMOTION?

There is no evidence about precisely what type of information is conveyed when, during an on-going social interaction, one person sees a facial expression of emotion on another person's face. There are not even data on how noticeable facial expressions actually are when they occur as briefly as they usually do, competing with other sources of information (voice, speech content, body movement, etc.) during interactions.

The fact that in an experiment people agree in selecting an emotion term for a face does not mean that people engaged in social interaction usually respond to faces in those terms; although it must happen sometimes, at least in many cultures. The experience of having someone say to you, 'you look afraid', or 'are you afraid?' is not unknown. People may also respond to seeing an expression by noting the antecedent event rather than utilizing an emotion term. For example, instead of 'you're sad' one person might say to another, 'you look like you lost all your money in the stock market crash.' In one of the experiments reviewed earlier (Ekman and Friesen, 1971), observers had no difficulty in linking a face to an antecedent event such as, 'show me the person whose child has died.' People might also respond to a face in terms of the unobservable activities which they infer accompany that expression. 'Your heart must be pounding,' would be an example of noting a known physiological accompaniment of anger expressions. 'You must be remembering something terrible,' would be a comment on a cognitive process associated with an emotion.

Emotion terms can be thought of as a kind of shorthand, an abbreviated way to refer to a package of events and processes which comprise the phenomenon. Each emotion term, I believe, refers to a different set of organized, integrated, processes. They include the antecedent events which set off these processes, the appraisal activity brought to bear upon those antecedent events, the physiological and motor responses, the memories, thoughts, images, and information processing, and the mobilization of efforts to cope with the source of emotion. All or any of these may be implied when someone says 'he looks angry.'

It is not sensible, in my view, to suggest that 'It is probably truer for a man to say "I would like to hit you" than for him to say "I am angry"' (Andrew, 1963, p. 5). Neither is more true. 'I am angry' is a more abstract statement; a shorthand which could refer to the wish to hit, or what provoked that wish, or the sensation of feeling hot, or any other part of what makes up anger. It is much more convenient, if less precise, to use the single emotion term, than to list the sequence of processes that term encompasses. When someone uses the shorthand emotion term we cannot know which facet of emotion is being referred to unless we ask or observe.

The fact that we do not know which facet does not mean that we have no information when someone uses an emotion term. Compare a few of the differences in the information implied when someone says 'I am angry' versus 'I am disgusted.' In anger the antecedent event is more likely to be a provocation, an interference with an ongoing activity, or a threat. In disgust the antecedent event is more likely to be something distasteful, literally or figuratively. In terms of likely actions, these are movement forward, and attempts to strike in anger, as compared with a movement away or to the side, to block further input in disgust; a louder, harsher voice in anger, as compared with a more retching sound in disgust. In anger there is heart rate acceleration and warm skin temperature; there is heart rate deceleration in disgust.

I believe it is obfuscating to claim (Andrew, 1963; Fridlund, 1988; Smith, 1985) that facial expressions signal information only, or more truly, about intentions or social actions. It would be just as misleading to maintain that expressions signal information only about physiological changes or associated memories. These are not mutually exclusive, they are different aspects of the same phenomenon.

The reification, *a priori*, of but one type of information as the only real signal conveyed by a facial expression, also has the unfortunate consequence of attempting to create a division between ethologists looking at displays and psychologists studying emotional expression. Even more regrettable, it leads us away from the interesting empirical questions which should be addressed. We need to learn about which type of information is derived from a facial expression by whom, when, and in what specific types of social, cultural settings.

REFERENCES

Allport, F. H. (1924) *Social Psychology*. Boston: Houghton-Mifflin.

Andrew, R. J. (1963) Evolution of facial expression. *Science*, **141**, 1034–41.

Birdwhistell, R. L. (1970) *Kinetics and Context*. Philadelphia, PA: University of Pennsylvania Press.

Blurton Jones, N. G. (1972) Non-verbal communication in children. In R. A. Hinde (Ed.), *Nonverbal Communication*, pp. 271–96. Cambridge: Cambrdige University Press.

Boucher, J. D. (1973) Facial behavior and the perception of emotion: studies of Malays and Temuan Orang Asli. Paper presented at the Conference on Psychology Related Disciplines, Kuala Lumpur.

Brannigan, C. R., and Humphries, D. A. (1972) Human nonverbal behavior, a means of communication. In N. G. Blurton Jones (Ed.), *Ethological Studies of Child Behavior*. Cambridge: Cambridge University Press.

Bruner, J. S., and Tagiuri, R. (1954) The perception of people. In G. Lindzey (Ed.), *Handbook of Social Psychology*, Vol. 2, pp. 634–54. Reading, MA: Addison Wesley.

Bugental, D. B. (1986) Unmasking the 'polite smile': situational and personal determinants of managed affect in adult–child interaction. *Personality and Social Psychology Bulletin*, **12**, 7–16.

Charlesworth, W. R. (1970) *Surprise Reactions in Congenitally Blind and Sighted Children* (Progress Report). Washington, DC: National Institute of Mental Health.

Charlesworth, W. R., and Kreutzer, M. A. (1973) Facial expression of infants and children. In P. Ekman (Ed.), *Darwin and Facial Expression*, pp. 91–168. New York: Academic Press.

Chevalier-Skolnikoff, S. (1973) Facial expression of emotion in nonhuman primates. In P. Ekman (Ed.), *Darwin and Facial Expression*, pp. 11–83. New York: Academic Press.

Cuceloglu, D. M. (1970) Perception of facial expressions in three cultures. *Ergonomics*, **13** (1), 93–100.

Darwin, C. (1859) *On the Origin of Species by means of Natural Selection*. London: Murray.

Darwin, C. (1872) *The Expression of the Emotions in Man and Animals*. New York: Philosophical Library.

Davidson, R. J., Ekman, P., Saron, C., Senulis, J., and Friesen, W. V. (1988) Emotional expression and brain physiology I: Approach/withdrawal and cerebral asymmetry.

Dickey, R. V., and Knower, R. H. (1941) A note on some ethnological differences in recognition of simulated expressions of the emotions. *American Journal of Sociology*, **47**, 190–3.

Duchenne, B. (1862) *Mechanisme de la physionomie humaine ou analyse electrophysiologigue de l'expression des passions*. Paris: Bailliere.

Efron, D. (1972) *Gesture, Race and Culture*. The Hague: Mouton. (Originally published 1941, *Gesture and Environment*.)

Eibl-Eibesfeldt, I. (1972) Similarities and differences between cultures in expressive movements. In R. A. Hinde (Ed.), *Nonverbal Communication*, pp. 297–312. Cambridge: Cambridge University Press.

Ekman, P. (1972) Universals and cultural differences in facial expressions of emotion. In J. Cole (Ed.), *Nebraska Symposium on Motivation, 1971*, pp. 207–283. Lincoln, NE: University of Nebraska Press.

Ekman, P. (1973) Cross-cultural studies of facial expressions. In P. Ekman (Ed.), *Darwin and Facial Expression*. pp. 169–229. New York: Academic Press.

Ekman, P. (1977) Biological and cultural contributions to body and facial movement. In J. Blacking (Ed.), *The Anthropology of the Body*. pp. 34–84. London: Academic Press.

Ekman, P. (1979) About brows: emotional and conversational signals. In M. von Cranach, K. Foppa, W. Lepenies, and D. Ploog (Eds), *Human Ethology*, pp. 169–248. Cambridge: Cambridge University Press.

Ekman, P. (1982) Methods for measuring facial action. In K. Scherer and P. Ekman (Eds), *Handbook of Methods in Nonverbal Behavior Research*, pp. 45–90. New York: Cambridge University Press.

Ekman, P. (1984) Expression and the nature of emotion. In K. Scherer and P. Ekman (Eds), *Approaches to Emotion*, pp. 319–44. Hillsdale, NJ: Erlbaum.

Ekman, P. (1985) *Telling Lies*. New York: Norton.

Ekman, P., and Friesen, W. V. (1969) The repertoire of nonverbal behavior: categories, origins, usage, and coding. *Semiotica*, **1**, 49–98.

Ekman, P., and Friesen, W. V. (1971) Constants across cultures in the face and emotion. *Journal of Personality and Social Psychology*, **17**, 124–9.

Ekman, P., and Friesen, W. V. (1976) Measuring facial movement. *Journal of Environmental Psychology and Nonverbal Behavior*, **1**, 56–75.

Ekman, P., and Friesen, W. V. (1978) *The Facial Action Coding System*. Palo Alto, CA: Consulting Psychologists Press.

Ekman, P., and Friesen, W. V. (1982) Felt, false, and miserable smiles. *Journal of Nonverbal Behavior*, **6**, 238–252.

Ekman, P., and Friesen, W. V. (1986) A new pan cultural expression of emotion. *Motivation and Emotion*, **10**, 159–168.

Ekman, P., and Friesen, W. V. (1988) Who knows what about contempt: a reply to Izard and Haynes. *Motivation and Emotion*, **12**, 17–22.

Ekman, P., Friesen, W. V., and Ancoli, S. (1980) Facial signs of emotional experience. *Journal of Personality and Social Psychology*, **39**, 1125–34.

Ekman, P., Friesen, W. V., and Ellsworth, P. (1972) *Emotion in the Human Face: Guidelines for Research and an Integration of Findings*, New York: Pergamon Press. 2nd ed., *Emotion in the Human Face* (1982) New York: Cambridge University Press.

Ekman, P., Friesen, W. V., and O'Sullivan, M. (1988). Smiles when lying. *Journal of Personality and Social Psychology*, **54**, 414–20.

Ekman, P., Friesen, W. V., O'Sullivan, M., Chan, A., Diacoyanni-Tarlatzis, I., Heider, K., Krause, R., LeCompte, W. A., Pitcairn, T., Ricci-Bitti, P. E., Scherer, K. R., Tomita, M., and Tzavaras, A., (1987) Universals and cultural differences in the judgements of facial expressions of emotion. *Journal of Personality and Social Psychology*, **53**, 712–17.

Ekman, P., and Heider, K. (1988) The universality of a contempt expression: a replication. *Motivation and Emotion*, **12**, 303–8.

Ekman, P., Levenson, R. W., and Friesen, W. V. (1983) Emotions differ in autonomic nervous system activity. *Science*, **221**, 1208–10.

Ekman, P., and Oster, H. (1979) Facial expressions of emotion. *Annual Review of Psychology*, **30**, 527–54.

Ekman, P., Roper, G., and Hager, J. C. (1980) Deliberate facial movement. *Child Development*, **51**, 886–91.

Ekman, P., Sorenson, E. R., and Friesen, W. V. (1969) Pan-cultural elements in facial displays of emotions. *Science*, **164**, 86–88.

Fox, N. A., and Davidson, R. J. (1988, in press) *Patterns of Brain Electrical Activity During Facial Signs of Emotion in 10-Month-Old Infants. Developmental Psychology*, **24**, 230–6.

Fridlund, A. J. (1988, in press) What can asymmetry and laterality in facial EMG tell us about the face and brain? *International Journal of Neuroscience*, **39**, 53–69.

Fridlund, A. J., and Cacioppo, J. T. (1986) Guidelines for human electromyographic research. *Psychophysiology*, **23**, 567–89.

Fridlund, A. J., Ekman, P., and Oster, H. (1987) Facial expressions of emotion. In A. Siegman and S. Feldstein (Eds), *Nonverbal Behavior and Communication*, pp. 143–224. Hillsdale, NJ: Erlbaum.

Friesen, W. V. (1972) Cultural differences in facial expressions in a social situation: An experimental test of the concept of display rules. Unpublished doctoral dissertation, University of California, San Francisco.

Goldstein, A. G. (1983) Behavioral scientists' fascination with faces. *Journal of Nonverbal Behavior*, **7**, 223–55.

Goodenough, F. L. (1932) Expression of the emotions in a blind–deaf child. *Journal of Abnormal Social Psychology*, **27**, 328–33.

Grant, N. G. (1969) Human facial expression. *Man*, **4**, 525–36.

Heider, K. (1974) Affect display rules in the Dani. Paper presented at the Meeting of the American Anthropology Association, New Orleans.

Hunt, W. A. (1941) Recent developments in the field of emotion. *Psychological Bulletin*, **38**, 249–76.

Izard, C. E. (1971) *The Face of Emotion*. New York: Appleton-Centruy-Crofts.

Izard, C. E. (1977) *Human Emotions*. New York: Plenum Press.

Izard, C. E. (1979) The maximally discriminative facial movement coding system (MAX). Unpublished manuscript. Available from Instructional Resource Center, University of Delaware, Newark, Delaware.

Izard, C. E., and Haynes, O. M. (1988) On the form and universality of the contempt expression: a correction for Ekman and Friesen's claim of discovery. *Motivation and Emotion*, **12**, 1–16.

Klineberg, O. (1940) *Social Psychology*. New York: Henry Holt.

LaBarre, W. (1947) The cultural basis of emotions and gestures. *Journal of Personality*, **16**, 49–68.

Lersch, P. (1971) *Gesicht und seele*. Munich: Ernst Reinhardt Verlag. (First published 1932.)

Matsumoto, D. (1986) Cross-cultural communication of emotion. Doctoral dissertation, University of California, Berkeley.

Matsumoto, D., and Ekman, P. (1988, in press) American–Japanese cultural differences in rating the intensity of facial expressions of emotion. Manuscript submitted for publication.

McGrew, W. C. (1972) *An Ethological Study of Children's Behavior*. New York: Academic Press.

Mead, M. (1975) Review of *Darwin and Facial Expression*. *Journal of Communication*, **25**, 209–13.

Peiper, A. (1963) *Cerebral Function in Infancy and Childhood*. New York: Consultants Bureau.

Plutchik, R. (1962) *The Emotions: Facts, Theories and a New Model*. New York: Random House.

Redican, W. K. (1975) Facial expression in nonhuman primates. In L. A. Rosenblum (Ed.), *Primate Behavior*, Vol. 4, pp. 103–94. New York: Academic Press.

Redican, W. K. (1982) An evolutionary perspective on human facial displays. In P. Ekman (Ed.), *Emotion in the Human Face*, 2nd edn, pp. 212–80. Elmsford, NY: Pergamon Press.

Ruch, W. (1987) Personality aspects in the psychobiology of humour laughter. Paper presented at the Third Meeting of the ISSID, Toronto, June 1987.

Saha, G. B. (1973) Judgment of facial expression of emotion—a cross-cultural study. *Journal of Psychological Research*, **17**, 59–63.

Schlosberg, H. (1941) A scale for the judgment of facial expression. *Journal of Experimental Psychology*, **29**, 497–510.

Schlosberg, H. (1952) The description of facial expressions in terms of two dimensions. *Journal of Experimental Psychology*, **44**, 229–37.

Schlosberg, H. (1954) Three dimensions of emotion. *Psychological Review*, **61**, 81–8.

Schneider, K. (1987) Achievement-related emotions in preschoolers. In F. Hahseh and J. Kuhl (Eds), *Motivation, Intention and Volition*. Berlin: Springer.

Smith, W. J. (1985) Consistency and change in communication. In G. Zivin (Ed.), *The Development of Expressive Behavior*. pp. 51–75. Orlando: Academic Press.

Steiner, F. (1986) Differentiating smiles,. In E. Branniger-Huber and F. Steiner (Eds), *FACS in Psychotherapy Research*, pp. 139–48. Zurich: Department of Clinical Psychology, Universitat Zurich.

Tagiuri, R. (1968) Person perception. In G. Lindzey and E. Aronson (Eds), *Handbook of Social Psychology*, pp. 395–449. Reading, MA: Addisson-Wesley.

Tomkins, S. S. (1962) *Affect, Imagery, Consciousness*. Vol. 1. *The Positive Affects*. New York: Springer.

Tomkins, S. S. (1963) *Affect, Imagery, Consciousness*. Vol. 2. *The Negative Affects*. New York: Springer.

Tomkins, S. S., and McCarter, R. (1964) What and where are the primary affects? Some evidence for a theory. *Perception and Motor Skills*, **18**, 119–58.

Triandis, H. C., and Lambert, W. W. (1958) A restatement and test of Schlosberg's theory of emotion with two kinds of subjects from Greece. *Journal of Abnormal and Social Psychology*, **58**, 321–8.

Vinacke, W. E. (1949) The judgment of facial expressions by three national-racial groups in Hawaii. I. Caucasian faces. *Journal of Personality*, **17**, 407–29.

Vinacke, W. E., and Fong, R. W. (1955) The judgment of facial expressions by three national-racial groups in Hawaii. II. Oriental faces. *Journal of Social Psychology*, **41**, 184–95.

Weiss, F., Blum, G. S., and Gleberman, L. (1987) Anatomically based measurement of facial expressions in simulated versus hypnotically induced affect. *Motivation and Emotion*, **11**, 67–81.

Winklemeyer, R., Exline, R. V., Gottheil, E., and Paredes, A. (1971) Cross-cultural differences in judging emotions. Unpublished work.

Chapter 7

Vocal Correlates of Emotional Arousal and Affective Disturbance

Klaus R. Scherer

University of Geneva

ABSTRACT

Human vocalization simultaneously reflects digital features of the linguistic phonetic system and analog features of physiologically mediated emotional and motivational states. Consequently, acoustic parameters of voice and speech constitute reliable indicators of emotional arousal as well as of sociocommunicative behaviour. This chapter describes the physiological determinants of voice production and evaluates the acoustic parameters that yield useful indicators of emotional arousal states and of affective disturbance. A review of pertinent literature establishes the validity of vocal measurement as a diagnostic tool. In a final section of the chapter, theoretically based predictions of vocal correlates of different emotional states are proposed.

VOCAL PARAMETERS AS INDICATORS OF PSYCHOPHYSIOLOGICAL PROCESSES

Human speech is an extraordinary communication system in that it uses as its vehicle a phylogenetically much older vocal expression system, which functions in most mammals as well as in man as a physiologically mediated indicator of emotional arousal. Similar to the evolution of the brain, where newer neocortical

Handbook of Social Psychophysiology, Edited by H. Wagner and A. Manstead,
© 1989 John Wiley & Sons Ltd

structures with highly cognitive modes of functioning have been superimposed on older 'emotional' structures such as the limbic system, the evolution of human speech as a digital system of encoding information has been grafted upon, and makes use of, the analogue nonverbal system of affect vocalization.

It has long been accepted that, in most animals, vocalization primarily serves the function of signalling motivational and emotional states of the animal. This view has recently been attacked by Marler and his associates (Marler, 1984) who, on the basis of recent studies on alarm calls in monkeys (Seyfarth and Cheney, 1982), argue that animal calls may also have symbolic representational functions, for example in drawing attention to different types of predators via acoustically differentiated calls. However, it can be shown that even in these cases the calls are clearly linked to an evaluation of the antecedent situation which produces differentiated emotions (Scherer and Kappas, 1988) and that such calls are only produced in response to motivationally and emotionally relevant stimuli. The evolutionary basis of vocalization, then, seems to be very closely linked to motivational and emotional arousal. Consequently, vocalization can be considered to be one of the most direct correlates, and consequently one of the most powerful indicators, of motivational and emotional processes.

As we shall demonstrate below, voice production mechanisms are controlled by a large number of physiological processes, many of which are considered to be important psychophysiological variables (such as blood pressure, muscle tension, etc.). Given the nature of the production mechanism, we are able to infer variations in the underlying physiological processes from changes in the acoustic structure resulting from the respective vocalization patterns. To the extent that acoustically assessed vocalization reflects underlying physiological parameters, it is possible to use vocal parameters, which can be easily and unobtrusively registered and analyzed, in lieu of cumbersome and intrusive psychophysiological recording. Much of this chapter will be concerned with this approach, i.e. the attempt to use vocal analysis as a measure of motivational and emotional change.

However, an important caveat has to be introduced at this point. Contrary to physiological systems which mainly serve internal regulation functions for the organism, vocalization has developed as a social communicative signalling system. Consequently, the physiological factors determining the expression of the internal state of the organism [which is of fundamental importance for social interaction, see Scherer (1984, 1985)] have been supplemented by pressures exerted by the demands for certain patterns of impression in the receiver of the message. While a naive model of communication might hold that impression is totally determined by expression, it can be shown that in the course of the evolution of expressive communication systems, impression models have moulded the nature of expression [see Leyhausen (1967) for a thorough discussion of this point]. Scherer (Scherer, 1985; Scherer and Kappas, 1988) has introduced the distinction between push-effects and pull-effects to distinguish between the determining factors which operate on vocalization. Push-effects are produced by the physiological changes which accompany emotional arousal and which, consequently, change the voice production mechanism in predictable ways (e.g. increased tension of the laryngeal muscles producing higher fundamental frequency of the voice). Pull-effects, on the other hand, are independent of internal physiological processes in the organism. Their origin is found in factors external to the organism, such as ritualized or conventionalized acoustic signal patterns, which are required to ensure information transfer, constraints on the acoustic signal structure imposed by a communication channel or the environment, or the need for self-presentation (given the impression formation rules of the receivers).

In most cases, the acoustic structure of a vocalization, particularly in humans, is determined by both types of effects: the effects of emotion-related physiological changes internal to the organism, and effects of external constraints or social target patterns.

This dual determination of the acoustic structure of vocalization is the major difference between using vocal parameters of emotional arousal and using psychophysiological, particularly autonomic, indices. Whereas the latter are only marginally affected by the organism's regulation attempts, the former, given their important role in expression and communication, may, to a very large extent, be determined by factors that are independent of the underlying physiological state. One of the major tasks for researchers in the area of vocal expression of emotion, then, is to disentangle push-effects and pull-effects on the basis of the observable acoustic pattern. On the one hand, this is a very difficult chore and a problem far from being resolved—the use of vocal parameters to infer underlying emotional arousal is not a straightforward measurement operation. On the other hand, the assessment of pull-effects on emotional vocalization is of major importance in its own right. Since emotion is generally a highly social phenomenon, and since it is often difficult to distinguish emotional reaction from attempts to cope with this reaction and from consequent social regulation (see Scherer, Wallbott, and Summerfield, 1986), vocalization changes induced by such social regulation attempts may provide important information on the nature of the emotional episode as a whole.

In this chapter we shall deal mainly with push-effects on vocalization, in keeping with the general psychophysiological approach in this handbook. Using both theoretical arguments and empirical evidence, we shall attempt to show which acoustic parameters can be used as indicators of various types of emotional arousal and of affective disturbance. First, we shall briefly review the major production mechanisms of vocalization and the physiological and neurological systems that control these mechanisms. Figure 7.1 gives a general outline of the structures involved in voice production.

In the process of respiration, the lungs produce the energy required for vocalization in building up subglottal pressure in the trachea below the closed glottal folds. This subglottal air pressure, together with motor commands to the laryngeal musculature, brings about phonation—the regular vibration of the

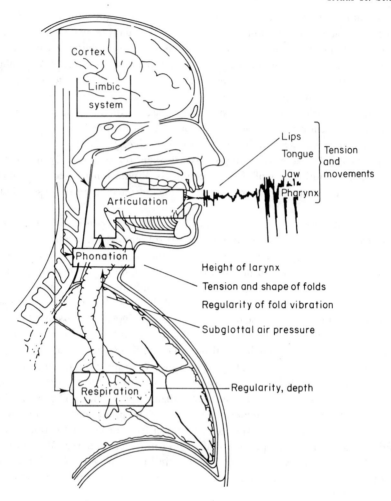

Figure 7.1. Overview of the voice production system and its major determinants.

vocal folds which releases air pulses into the supraglottal vocal tract. This rapid
series of pulses, which constitutes a primitive, triangular-shaped wave-form, is
then modified and filtered by the shape and the length of the supralaryngeal tract.
Changes in the shape and length of the tract are mostly produced by motor
commands to movable structures such as the tongue, the lips, and the jaw. These
variations in the shape of the vocal tract produce articulation, which is responsible
for the production of the basic linguistic units, the phonemes, and also for
emotionally relevant variations of the filter or transfer function. For detailed
surveys of the voice production process see Daniloff, Schuckers, and Feth (1980),
Fry (1979), Scherer (1982), and Zemlin (1968).

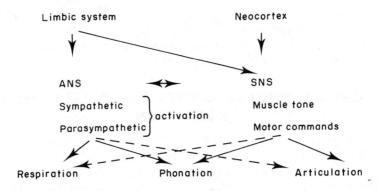

Figure 7.2. Effects of neurophysiological structures on voice production mechanisms.

Figure 7.2 shows, in a highly simplified manner, some of the main effects of the major neurophysiological structures on the voice production mechanisms shown in Figure 7.1. Speech production in the linguistic sense is obviously mostly controlled by the neocortex, a process that works mainly via specific motor commands which produce appropriate phonatory and articulatory movements for the desired sequence of speech sounds. However, some of the pull-effects discussed above, such as attempts at self-presentation using certain conventionalized patterns of vocalization, may also be produced in this manner. The intended vocal effects are mostly produced by phasic activation of the muscles serving phonation and articulation.

The effects of emotional arousal on the vocalization process that are primarily controlled by the limbic system (Jürgens, 1979; Robinson, 1972) are much more diffuse and complicated. They are mostly produced via tonic activation of the somatic nervous system (in particular the striated musculature), and sympathetic, as well as parasympathetic, activation of the autonomic nervous system. Given the predominance of the striated musculature in producing vocalization, many of these emotional effects are also likely to be mediated via the somatic nervous system. However, direct sympathetic or parasympathetic effects, such as respiration changes and the secretion of mucus, will also affect the nature of the vocal output.

Vocalization is a very sensitive output system—even slight changes in physiological regulation will produce very noticeable changes in the acoustic pattern. Even if a speaker attempts to reproduce a particular utterance in exactly the same way, in exactly the same state of arousal, some changes are likely to occur. The enormous sensitivity of the acoustic output to minor changes in voice production settings is both advantageous, since it provides a sensitive and rapidly responding system for monitoring emotional arousal, and disadvantageous, given the high degree of noise that is introduced by minor changes in respiration, phonation, and articulation, in addition to strong individual differences. A somewhat different, but equally serious, problem is the fact that a number of acoustic patterns can be produced by very different phonatory and articulatory settings. Consequently, it is very difficult to infer the exact nature of the underlying production process from a given acoustic pattern.

VOCALIZATION PARAMETERS IN MEASUREMENT OF EMOTION

The type of parameter to be used in assessing emotion from vocalization depends on the level of measurement chosen (see also Scherer, 1982). At the most basic level, one can directly measure some of the physiological determinants of the voice production process. An example would be EMG measurement of laryngeal muscles involved in phonation, or the amount of mucus secreted. In other words, one would use similar physiological variables to those used in psychophysiological research generally—with the constraint that the variables involved also play a role in the physiological process underlying vocalization. Since most of the neurophysiological structures involved in vocalization cannot be accessed readily, this approach is unlikely to be useful in most cases of emotion research. However, further research on the exact nature of the physiological processes involved in voice production would clearly advance our understanding of the details of the mechanism and would provide a better basis for inferring how emotion-related physiological change influences vocalization.

At the next level of analysis, one can assess a variety of variables related directly to the motor effects of the underlying physiological processes. For example, using appropriate apparatus, one can measure respiration rate, tongue movements, vocal fold vibration, etc. On this level, the actual movement patterns involved in voice production and filtering are investigated. While many of these parameters are highly valid indicators of emotional arousal, and can be measured very objectively and reliably, the process of measurement generally requires a rather sophisticated experimental set-up, in terms of apparatus and speaker-cooperation. Given the inconvenience involved in most of these measurement procedures, it is likely that the negative affect generated by the procedures will overwhelm any other emotion experienced by the speaker.

While the first two levels of measurement are based on direct observation of the voice production mechanisms, the remaining three levels, and their respective parameters, are all based on the acoustic waveform that is radiated from the mouth as a result of the voice production process. The speech sound-wave can be used in very different ways for the extraction of parameters.

At a level of analysis that is still close to voice production, one can try using experts to infer the nature of the voice production movements and settings that have yielded the acoustic output under study. An example of this approach is the attempt to establish a coding system for different voice qualities proposed by Laver (1980).

A different type of analysis is concerned with the detailed description of the acoustic waveform resulting from the vocalization. In general, electro-acoustic equipment or digital computers are used for the extraction of a large number of acoustic parameters that can serve to describe the sound-wave. We shall deal with these parameters in detail below. Another approach is to use judges in order to obtain ratings of acoustic features, generally using natural language categories for certain types of acoustic parameters. This approach is hampered by the fact that there are no precise natural language concepts for particular acoustic parameters. In addition, the nature of the human auditory sense organs, and in particular the tendency to integrate independent acoustic dimensions (e.g. the auditory impression of voice pitch is affected not only by the fundamental frequency of the vocal fold vibrations but also by energy distribution in the spectrum), renders this procedure problematic if physical acoustic description is desired.

However, if the communicative aspect of the vocalization is under study, the use of judges in order to assess the perceptually and communicatively relevant dimensions of the acoustic waveform may well be considered. This is particularly true for the final level of analysis, where the acoustic output of the speaker's vocalization is used as the basis for auditory judgements of the valence of the acoustic pattern, given a certain number of criteria of the listener, such as aesthetic preference or motivational relevance. At this level of analysis, it is not the nature of the acoustic sound-wave or the types of effects that produced it that are of interest, but rather the impression created by the particular vocalization on the receiver.

Which of these parameters should be used in a particular study depends on the questions asked and the constraints posed by the operationalization involved. However, the level of objective acoustical analysis of vocalization is of central importance for a number of empirical approaches. The acoustic waveform is the signal which is actually transferred in the communication process. It reflects both the production mechanism and its physiological determinants, and it is the basis for the various types of listener inferences (both expert and naive). Consequently, for many studies of the effects of emotion on vocalization, the acoustic analysis of speech patterns will be of major importance. Furthermore, the acoustic parameters can be obtained objectively, economically, and unobtrusively, from tape-recordings of the speaker's utterances. Given the central importance of acoustic measurement of the emotional vocalization, we shall devote most of our attention in this chapter to this type of analysis and the parameters that seem most useful in this connection. The emphasis on acoustic parameters also seems justified by the fact that whereas, until recently, the ability to extract the relevant parameters has been restricted to laboratories with access to sophisticated computer equipment, the appropriate techniques are now becoming available for use with standard microcomputers.

We shall now turn to a detailed description of the major acoustic parameters and a brief discussion of the appropriate measurement procedures and of the

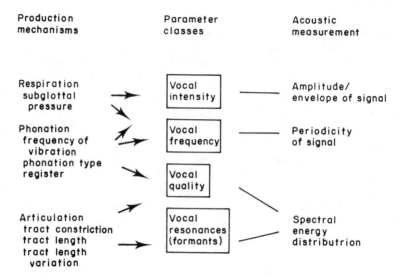

Figure 7.3. Effects of voice production mechanisms on acoustic parameters.

factors that are primarily responsible for variation in the respective parameter. Figure 7.3 shows the four major classes of vocal parameters, together with the production mechanisms that are responsible for changes in these parameters and the acoustic variables used in their measurement. We shall discuss each of these classes in turn. Figure 7.4 is provided to help to visualize the parameters discussed in terms of their measurement and graphic display based on acoustic analysis of the vocal signal [readers who are unfamiliar with acoustic phonetic material may find the following references useful: Daniloff *et al.* (1980), Fry (1979), Hollien (1981), Lieberman, (1977), Scherer (1982), and Zemlin (1968)].

Vocal intensity, subjectively heard as loudness of the voice, is jointly determined by respiratory and phonatory action. Higher intensity is generally due to increased subglottal pressure and greater laryngeal tension (see Daniloff *et al.*, 1980; Zemlin, 1968). The acoustic measurement of intensity is rather straightforward since it is directly related to the amplitude (or envelope) of the speech waveform. There are a large number of instruments available to measure amplitude of the acoustic waveform, either in voltage or in dB (see Hollien, 1981; Scherer, 1982). If recorded speech is being used, care has to be taken to allow for differential gain in recording and reproduction. Amplitude measurements can be reliably obtained for very short segments of the speech-wave, down to about 100 mseconds. The resulting amplitude values can be averaged over various portions of the speech utterance and a number of dispersion statistics, such as standard deviation and range, can be computed. The steepness of intensity rises (attack) and falls (decay) for voiced speech segments (see Figure 7.4b) can be obtained from the time signal or from the envelope. Graphically, amplitude can be plotted over time to yield the envelope or amplitude contour of the signal (see Figure 7.4e).

Vocal frequency, subjectively heard as pitch of the voice, is primarily determined by the frequency of vibration of the vocal folds, a process which is determined jointly by differential innervation of the laryngeal musculature and the extent of subglottal pressure. Acoustically, vocal frequency is measured by the fundamental frequency of the speech waveform, i.e. the lowest periodic cycle component of the complex waveform (that is, number of periods per second, see Figure 7.4c), and the harmonics (multiples of fundamental frequency). Fundamental frequency of a speech signal can be measured with a variety of devices now available (see Hollien, 1981). Of particular importance is the use of digital fundamental frequency extraction, for which a variety of different algorithms have been proposed (Hess, 1983). While fundamental frequency (F_0) extraction is theoretically straightforward, there are numerous practical difficulties that require particular caution in the extraction and interpretation of fundamental frequency. While, in principle, individual periods can be determined, most hardware F_0 detection devices and most automatic F_0 extraction algorithms require a period of about 100 mseconds for reliable F_0 extraction. As for amplitude, F_0 values can be averaged over different portions of the speech utterance, and the usual dispersion parameters can be computed. A graphical plot of the sequence of F_0 values across an utterance yields an intonation contour (see Figure 7.4d), which together with the envelope of the signal is one of the most important parameters for prosodic analysis. Of particular interest for studies of the vocal expression of emotion is F_0 perturbation, or pitch jitter, a variable that refers to the degree of variability in the length of adjoining periods (see Lieberman, 1961; Sorensen and Horii, 1984).

Since fundamental frequency is directly proportional to the length of the vocal folds, males, females and children have rather different modal fundamental frequencies [with a modal value of 128 Hz for males and 260 Hz for females, see Daniloff *et al.* (1980), p. 203]. Because of these important sex differences, great care has to be taken in comparing the F_0 measurements of males and females.

Vocal quality, subjectively heard as timbre, is determined by phonation type [see Daniloff *et al.* (1980), Ch. 6] and phonation register [pulse, modal, or falsetto registers, see Laver (1980)]. In addition, the general tension and the specific configuration produced by the articulatory setting has an impact on vocal quality. The acoustic measurement of vocal quality is still hotly debated in the literature. In general terms, the most direct effect of vocal quality is to produce changes in the energy distribution and the power spectrum (see Figure 7.4e). For example, shrill voices have a much higher proportion of energy in the upper frequency range (i.e. above 500 Hz.) whereas resonant voices in general have a greater proportion of energy in the lower frequency range. In general, researchers are still somewhat uncertain about which exact variable to use to capture differential energy distribution in the spectrum. Among some of the basic variables proposed are frequency range, i.e. the difference between F_0 and the highest point in the

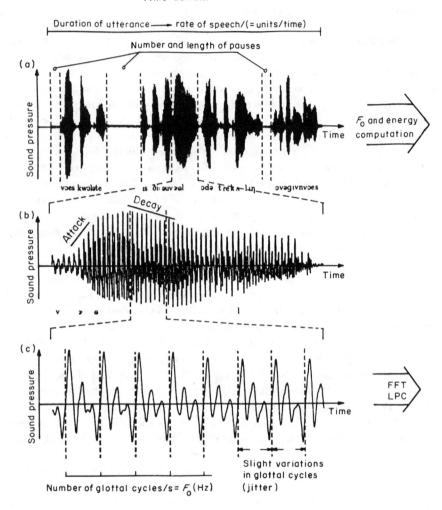

frequency spectrum where there is still measurable energy, and various propor-
tions of low versus high energy concentration (i.e. energy below 500 Hz in relation
to above 500 Hz, or below 1000 Hz in relation to above 1000 Hz; see Van
Bezooijen (1984), for review).

Of further interest is the so-called *spectral noise*, the aperiodic energy components
in the spectrum. While the definition and measurement of the specific variables

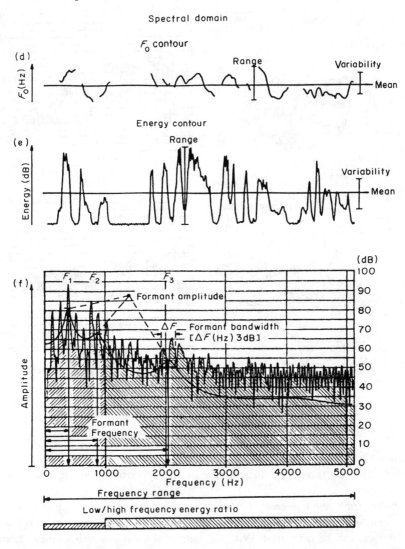

Figure 7.4. Major acoustic parameters and their measurement.

still present problems, it is rather straightforward to obtain power spectra for relatively short periods of speech (down to about 20 mseconds). The power spectrum can be displayed graphically either for a particular window (i.e. a sampling period of the speech-wave) or a sequence of these individual power spectra can be displayed in a 3D-perspective (see Figure 7.5). Another possibility is to use differential degree of shading to indicate the relative energy of different

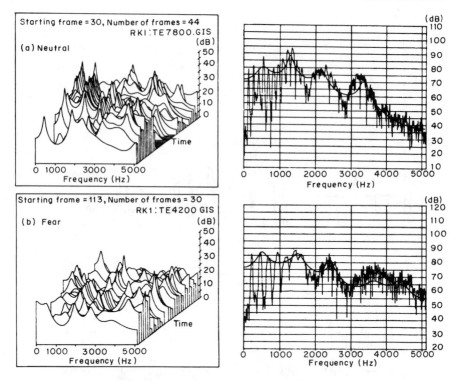

frequency components as is done in the spectrogram, the classic way of obtaining graphic displays of energy distribution in the spectrum (see the example in Figure 7.6).

Finally, the *vocal resonances*, or *formants*, which are used for the differential pronunciation of different sounds, particularly speech sounds such as vowels and diphthongs, can be measured. With the help of the various articulatory organs, such as the palate, the velum, the tongue, the lips, and the pharynx, the vocal tract can be constricted in several places and its length can be varied. As predicted by acoustic theory (see Fant, 1960) the site of constriction, the degree of constriction, and the relative degree of lip opening will determine the specific resonances of the acoustic tube formed by the vocal tract (see Figure 7.7).

Acoustically, the vocal resonances are measured as formants, i.e. specific energy peaks in the power spectrum, using methods similar to those used in the measurement of voice quality. A number of digital alogorithms are available for tracking formants in the spectrum. The parameters used are the frequency of a

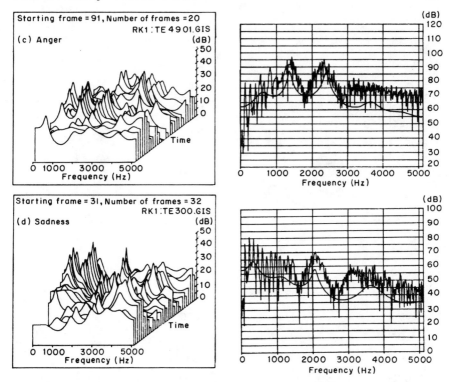

Figure 7.5. 3D-spectra (left) and power spectra with smoothed envelope showing the formants (right) for a logatome taken from a short standard utterance produced by an actor under four different emotional portrayal conditions.

formant (generally only the first three formants are used), its amplitude, and its bandwidth (which is defined as the area below the curve containing a specific proportion of energy) (see Figure 7.4e). Again, while in theory formant measurement is rather straightforward, in reality a large number of problems related to speaker, recording, and speech material may prevent accurate measurement. In terms of summary statistics, great care has to be taken to average only those formant values that are directly comparable, i.e. mean formants for particular vowels as well as the respective dispersion measures. The graphic display of formant contours is frequently used in psycholinguistic studies.

Table 1 provides a summary of the vocal parameters discussed so far, including the most important dispersion measures used. This overview lists those variables which have been used most frequently in research to date. It should be kept in mind, however, that most of these parameters have been developed in the context of research on speech transmission. It is quite possible that these measures need to be supplemented by others, yet to be developed, which are more specifically

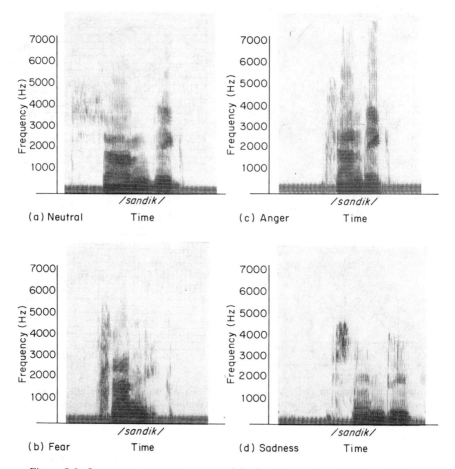

Figure 7.6. Sonagram, or spectrogram, of the logatomes shown in Figure 7.5.

oriented toward an assessment of the physiological substratum of voice production.

REVIEW OF THE EVIDENCE IN THE LITERATURE TO DATE

In the following section we shall review the results of the major studies that have been conducted with a view to determining the effect of emotion on vocal behavior. As mentioned in earlier reviews (Scherer, 1979, 1986a) the studies in this area are not very satisfactory since, in general, actor-portrayed emotional utterances have been studied, as opposed to naturally occurring emotional

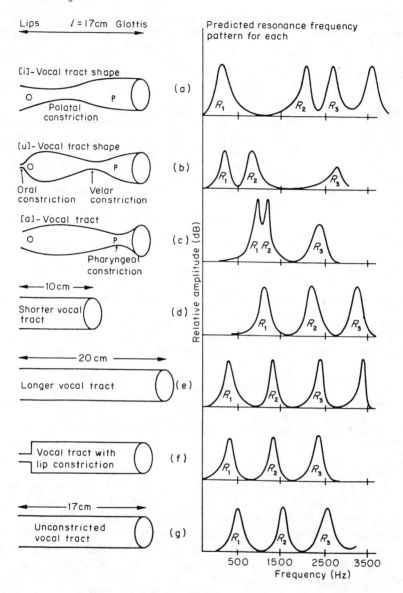

Figure 7.7. Resonance frequency patterns for vocal tracts of differing length, or constricted at differing places along the tract.
Note: all resonance patterns should be compared with that for (G), which is the resonance pattern for an unconstricted vocal tract.
(From Daniloff, Schuckers, and Feth (1980) *The Physiology of Speech and Hearing: An Introduction*, © 1980, pp. 17, 174, 203. Reprinted by permission of Prentice-Hall, Inc., Englewood Cliffs, NJ.)

Table 7.1. Overview of major acoustic parameters

Parameter	Description
F_0 perturbation	Slight variations in the duration of glottal cycles
F_0 mean	Fundamental frequency (vibration rate of vocal folds as averaged over a speech utterance)
F_0 range	Difference between highest and lowest F_0 in an utterance
F_0 variability	Measure of dispersion (e.g. standard deviation of F_0)
F_0 contour	Fundamental frequency values plotted over time (intonation)
F_1 mean	Frequency of the first (lowest) formant (significant energy concentration in the spectrum) averaged over an utterance
F_2 mean	Mean frequency of the second formant
Formant bandwidth	Width of the spectral band containing significant formant energy
Formant precision	Degree to which formant frequencies attain values prescribed by phonological system of a language
Intensity mean	Energy values for a speech sound wave averaged over an utterance
Intensity range	Difference between highest and lowest intensity values in an utterance
Intensity variability	Measure of dispersion of intensity values in an utterance (e.g. standard deviation)
Frequency range	Difference between F_0 and highest point in the frequency spectrum where there is still speech energy
High-frequency energy	Relative proportion of energy in the upper frequency region (e.g. > 1 kHz)
Spectral noise	Aperiodic energy components in the spectrum
Speech rate	Number of speech segments per time unit

Note: F_0 = fundamental frequency; F_1 = first formant; F_2 = second formant.
Source: Scherer (1986a), p. 149. (© 1986 by the American Psychological Association. Reprinted by permission of the publisher and author.)

vocalizations. Furthermore, in these encoding studies a number of variables have been only imperfectly controlled, such as the number of speakers, the type of emotions studied, the instructions for portrayal, the verbal material used, etc. (see Scherer, 1986a; Wallbott and Scherer, 1986). However, since there is a rather strong degree of convergence in most of these findings in spite of the methodological shortcomings, it seems useful to take stock of the results reported in the literature. This review will cover discrete emotions, emotional disorder (in particular depression), and stress.

VOCAL INDICATORS OF DISCRETE EMOTIONS

As has been argued elsewhere (Scherer, 1986a), one of the major problems in trying to reconcile some of the contradictions found in the literature is the fact that most researchers have used rather broad emotion categories—often including in the same category rather mild or passive forms of a particular emotion as well as strong and active forms. For example, this is true for anger; one must assume on the basis of the methods described in the relevant studies that sometimes cold anger, or irritation, (which can be rather subdued) has been studied, while at other times flaring rage has been studied. Although it is difficult on the basis of descriptions in the literature to separate these different emotional states, it seems important to do so in order to understand better the pattern in the data and to provide a broader basis for future work. Consequently, the following review will use fairly differentiated emotion categories (see also Scherer, 1986a). In the following, we shall restrict coverage of particular acoustic parameters and their relation to particular types of emotional arousal to those variables that have repeatedly been found to correlate with certain emotions (i.e. findings from a single study which have not been replicated are not reported).

Boredom/indifference

As one might expect on the basis of the assumption of lowered activation level, the results point to a decrease in mean F_0 (Davitz, 1964; Fairbanks and Pronovost, 1939) and mean intensity (Bortz, 1966; Davitz, 1964; Müller, 1960).

Displeasure/disgust

The results are not very consistent for this emotion, since three studies (Plaikner, 1970; Scherer, 1979; Scherer, Wallbott, Tolkmitt and Bergmann, 1985) find an increase in mean F_0 whereas two others (Kaiser, 1962; Van Bezooijen, 1984) find a lowering of mean F_0. It is possible that variation of the induction procedure used in these studies is partly responsible for this discrepancy. Studies finding an increase of F_0 induced displeasure/disgust with unpleasant films, whereas in the studies finding a decrease actors were asked to simulate disgust. This discrepancy raises the point that affect control or display strategies are likely to affect induction and portrayal studies in very different ways.

Contempt/scorn

This emotion has been included in the emotion sets studied in four of the relevant reports (Costanzo, Markel, and Costanzo, 1969; Fairbanks and Hoaglin, 1941; Fairbanks and Pronovost, 1939; Van Bezooijen, 1984). There is no consistent evidence for any one acoustic parameter; mainly due to the fact that each of the four studies has investigated different acoustic parameters.

Irritation/cold anger

The distinction made here between cold and hot anger has not been made in the literature. The following considerations are, therefore, based on a tentative classification of the research literature according to type of induction procedure or portrayal used. Cold anger seems to lead to an increase in mean F_0 (Eldred and Price, 1958; Roessler and Lester, 1976), mean intensity (Costanzo, Markel, and Costanzo, 1969; Eldred and Price, 1958), high frequency energy (Kaiser, 1962; Roessler and Lester, 1976) and a tendency for intonation contours F_0 contours to be directed downwards (Höffe, 1960; Kaiser, 1962).

Rage/hot anger

As for cold anger, one finds increases in mean F_0 (Davitz, 1964; Fairbanks and Pronovost, 1939; Fonagy, 1978; Höffe, 1960; Wallbott and Scherer, 1986; Williams and Stevens, 1969, 1972) and mean intensity (Bortz, 1966; Davitz, 1964; Höffe, 1960; Kotlyar and Morozov, 1976; Müller, 1960; Van Bezooijen, 1984; Williams and Stevans, 1969). However, by contrast with cold anger, what is particularly noticeable are increases in F_0 variability and total range over the utterances studied (Fairbanks and Pronovost, 1939; Havrdova and Moravek, 1979; Höffe, 1960; Williams and Stevens, 1969). Since there has been no study trying to compare cold anger and hot anger systematically, it is very difficult to try to use the existing evidence to discriminate these two varieties of anger. This problem is exacerbated by the fact that the state of measurement and reporting in this area does not permit one to make parametric comparisons in order to determine, for example, whether an F_0 change, is of small, medium, or great size.

Sadness/dejection

We find strong consensus on the acoustic correlates for this emotion. This may be due to the fact that there is less variability in the eliciting situations and the social strategies for display or control of this emotion (see Scherer, Wallbott, and Summerfield, 1986). Sadness seems generally to decrease mean F_0 (Coleman and Williams, 1979; Davitz, 1964; Eldred and Price, 1958; Fairbanks and Pronovost, 1939; Fonagy, 1978; Kaiser, 1962; Sedlacek and Sychra, 1963; Wallbott and Scherer, 1986; Williams and Stevens, 1969), F_0 range (Fairbanks and Pronovost, 1939; Fonagy, 1978; Sedlacek and Sychra, 1963; Van Bezooijen, 1984; Williams and Stevens, 1969; Zuberbier, 1957; Zwirner, 1930) and downward directed F_0 contours (Fairbanks and Pronovost, 1939; Kaiser, 1962; Sedlacek and Sychra, 1963; Zwirner, 1930). Similarly, mean intensity is lowered (Davitz, 1964; Eldred and Price, 1958; Hargreaves, Starkweather and Blacker, 1965; Huttar, 1968; Kaiser, 1962; Müller, 1960; Skinner, 1935; Zuberbier, 1957). Though based on very few studies, there is suggestive evidence for a decrease in high frequency energy (Hargreaves *et al.*, 1965; Kaiser, 1962; Skinner, 1935) and in the precision of articulation as indexed by formant precision (Zuberbier, 1957; Van Bezooijen, 1984).

Grief/desperation

As for anger, a differentiation between a passive reaction to loss, i.e. sadness and dejection, and a more active desperate grief reaction is rarely made in the emotion literature, and even more rarely studied. As will be shown below, one would, in theory, expect rather different acoustic correlates for grief/desperation from those found for sadness/dejection.

Worry/anxiety

As in the earlier distinctions between milder, more passive, and stronger, more active, forms of an emotion, we distinguish between worry/anxiety and fear/terror. Anxiety has been very frequently studied in relation to verbal and temporal measures (Siegman and Feldstein, 1987) but only rarely in terms of vocal parameters. A number of studies (Bonner, 1943; Hicks, 1979; Höffe, 1960; Plaikner, 1970) seem to suggest that mean F_0 increases.

Fear/terror

As for sadness, we find a strong consensus on acoustic correlates of fear. As one might expect on the basis of the very strong parasympathetic arousal, there is evidence for increase in mean F_0 (Coleman and Williams, 1979; Duncan, Laver and Jack, 1983; Fairbanks and Pronovost, 1939; Fonagy, 1978; Höffe, 1960; Kuroda, Fujiwara, Okamura, and Utsuki, 1976; Niwa, 1971; Roessler and Lester, 1976; Sulc, 1977; Utsuki and Okamura, 1976; Williams and Stevens, 1969), F_0 range (Fairbanks and Pronovost, 1939; Utsuki and Okamura, 1976; Williams and Stevens, 1969), F_0 variability (Fairbanks and Pronovost, 1939; Williams and Stevens, 1969), and high frequency energy (Roessler and Lester, 1976, 1979; Simonov and Frolov, 1973).

Enjoyment/happiness

Most studies have investigated active joy or elation rather than quiet enjoyment/happiness. Consequently, there is little or no empirical evidence relating to this state of peaceful enjoyment.

Joy/elation

Again, we find remarkably consistent increases in mean F_0 (Coleman and Williams, 1979; Davitz, 1964; Fonagy, 1978; Havrdova and Moravek, 1979; Höffe, 1960; Huttar, 1968; Kaiser, 1962; Sedlacek and Sychra, 1963; Skinner, 1935; Van Bezooijen, 1984), F_0 range (Fonagy, 1978; Havrdova and Moravek,

1979; Höffe, 1960; Huttar, 1968; Sedlacek and Sychra, 1963; Skinner, 1935), and F_0 variability (Havrdova and Moravek, 1979; Sedlacek and Sychra, 1963; Skinner, 1935). Mean intensity also seems to increase (Davitz, 1964; Höffe, 1960; Huttar, 1968; Kaiser, 1962; Kotlyar and Morosov, 1976; Müller, 1960; Skinner, 1935; Van Bezooijen, 1984).

In reviewing this pattern of findings, the reader will notice that, in general, emotion-induced voice changes seem to be determined by a single dimension formed by several of the parameters. Emotions with high arousal and activity are characterized by increased mean F_0, range, and variability, as well as intensity, whereas the opposite is true of more passive, withdrawn emotions. As noted previously (Scherer, 1981, 1986a) this dimension seems to reflect a general sympathetic response syndrome. This could be construed as evidence for the old argument that the major feature of emotional responding is sympathetic arousal and that it would be difficult to distinguish further the differentially labelled emotion states on the basis of physiological or vocal parameters.

However, it can be shown that judges asked to identify particular emotions on the basis of vocal speech samples attain a very high accuracy (mean accuracy across 45 studies equal 54.4%—or 46.7% if correction for guessing, taking the number of answer alternatives into account, is applied). This is the case even if the speech samples are masked with regard to both content and a large number of specific acoustic variables (Scherer, 1986a). Consequently, the acoustic correlates of the various emotions must be rather robust, quite redundant, and certainly highly differentiated. The reason why empirical research has so far been unable to pinpoint the differentiating acoustic variables may be related to the fact that some important vocal parameters, such as voice quality, which may be important for emotional dimensions such as pleasantness or control rather than straight activation, have so far not been systematically investigated (Scherer, 1986a, p. 145). An early study by Williams and Stevens (1972), in which these authors tried to measure a very large number of acoustic parameters, can still be regarded as justification for the hope that it will be possible to find very distinctive features for specific emotions in the voice. Below, we outline a series of theoretical predictions that might be useful for further research in this area.

VOCAL INDICATORS OF EMOTIONAL DISTURBANCE

So far, most work on emotional disturbance has been directed towards the study of depressive patients. Unfortunately, the general nosological difficulties in the field of psychiatry have had an impact on research in this area. One of the major problems is the lack of differentiation between different patient groups which, given the nature of their disorder, may exhibit very different vocal behaviour. This is true, for example, of the difference between endogenously depressed patients and biphasic, manic-depressive patients. Obviously, for a biphasic patient, one would expect very different vocal behaviour in a depressed phase as compared with a manic phase.

Disregarding these difficulties, we find that there is still a rather remarkable consistency in the findings reported in connection with the difference between normal and depressed speech and those pertaining to change after therapy. This is particularly true for intensity, where there is evidence that depressive patients speak with relatively low intensity (Eldred and Price, 1958; Moses, 1954; Whitman and Flicker, 1966; Zuberbier, 1957); similarly, intensity tends to increase after therapy (Hargreaves and Starkweather, 1964, 1965; Ostwald, 1961, 1963; Tolkmitt, Helfrich, Standke, and Scherer, 1982). Dynamic range, i.e. the range of intensity changes and variability, also seems to be very low in depression (Zuberbier, 1957).

As far as F_0 is concerned, there is much less convergence among the data. In several studies a rather low mean F_0 for depressives (Bannister, 1972; Eldred and Price, 1958; Moses, 1954; Roessler and Lester, 1976) is found, which is somewhat surprising given findings from our own laboratory (Tolkmitt et al., 1982; Klos, Ellgring, and Scherer, 1988) which show that F_0 seems to decrease after therapy. This latter finding has been linked to a decrease in general tension in the striated musculature (Scherer, 1979). It seems possible that depressive patients have lower F_0 in comparison with normal speakers, but that F_0 level is elevated during depressive phases. However, there is at least one study in which F_0 was found to increase with the severity of depression (Whitman and Flicker, 1966).

Most likely, however, the apparent discrepancy can be explained in terms of lack of homogeneity in patient groups, as mentioned above, and differences in measurement methodology. In summarizing the research findings we have referred to F_0 (which is an objective measure of vibration frequency of the vocal folds); however, a number of studies on both emotion and depression use subjective ratings of pitch, rather than objective analyses. Obviously, this is a procedure that does not necessarily yield a reliable estimate of F_0. As mentioned above, pitch judgement is often influenced by other acoustic variables, such as energy distribution in the spectrum and variability of pitch. Since several studies find a rather narrow range and restricted variability for F_0 pitch in depressive speech (Bannister, 1972; Hargreaves et al., 1965; Newman and Mather, 1938; Ostwald, 1964; Zuberbier, 1957), it is possible that judges are influenced by the reduced range and other acoustic factors in subjectively assessing pitch.

In many psychiatry textbooks one finds the observation that depressive speech sounds monotonous. Several studies (Moses, 1954; Newman and Mather, 1938; Zwirner, 1930) have found that patients tend to employ fairly stereotypic downward directed intonation contours that are frequently repeated. It is possible that the impression of monotonousness results from the lack of variability in the choice of intonation contours rather than the flatness of the contour.

Another interesting parameter is the precision of articulation, a factor which could be linked to general muscle tone. There is suggestive evidence that depressive speech is characterized by rather lax articulation (as reflected in formant precision) and that precision of articulation improves after therapy (Tolkmitt *et al.*, 1982; Zuberbier, 1957).

Most of the data in this area are still very preliminary and in need of replication. It would be particularly helpful to define more precisely the different nosological subgroups of emotional disturbance and to base further research on concrete hypotheses concerning the types of vocal changes expected for each subgroup. A series of theoretical predictions of this sort has been presented in Scherer (1987).

VOCAL INDICATORS OF STRESS

The possibility of measuring stress through vocal analysis has become very popular due to the notion of 'voice lie detection'. Unfortunately, the evidence lags far behind the bold claims that some of the commercial firms marketing 'voice lie detectors' (sic!) have made. So far there is no convincing empirical evidence that lying can be detected through simple electroacoustic devices (Hollien, 1981; Scherer, 1981). It is very important to distinguish between the detection of lying and the detection of stress. While lying could occur without any accompanying stress, and would therefore not be detectable in the voice, it is likely that stress does effect vocal parameters. Again, one of the major determinants of stress effects on the voice seems to be sympathetic arousal. As one might expect from the discussion above, this should primarily result in an increase in fundamental frequency and F_0 variability. This has been the typical finding in studies investigating this effect (cf. Ekman, Friesen, and Scherer, 1976; Scherer, 1981; Streeter, Krauss, Geller, Olson, and Apple, 1977; Williams and Stevens, 1969).

One of the major problems in the empirical assessment of stress effects is the powerful effect of individual differences. As is well known from studies of physiological correlates of stress, there seems to be an enormous degree of response specificity. In a series of experimental studies we were able to show that F_0 increase, as a consistent correlate of stress response, may be limited to persons using particular coping styles, as measured by personality scales. In a major experimental study we found that for both male and female subjects, only those with relatively elevated anxiety scores (regardless of whether they repressed or admitted their anxiety) showed F_0 increase (Scherer, Wallbott, Tolkmitt and Bergmann, 1985).

In these studies we were also able to show that the investigation of stress effects on the voice must take into account the type of *coping strategies* of the subject. In analysing the precision of formant values, our data indicated that a consistent effect for female anxiety-deniers (repressors) takes the form of a tendency to increase precision of articulation with increasing *cognitive* stress and to decrease this precision with mounting *emotional* stress. Thus, personality factors, coping style, and type of stress induction, all seem to determine the vocal response. It can be argued (Scherer, 1986b) that stress responses could profitably be analysed within the framework of a general theory of emotion, assuming that stress occurs in cases where a problem cannot be solved through normal emotional responding (with return to baseline within a standard time-frame).

A THEORETICAL MODEL OF EMOTION EFFECTS ON VOCAL PRODUCTION

One of the major problems in this area is that almost all of the studies that have been conducted are purely correlational in nature. In other words, researchers attempt to observe the covariation of particular vocal parameters with various types of affective state. In addition, many of these studies are based on work with actors' portrayals of emotion. Consequently, much of the definition of the emotional state that underlies the changed vocal performance rests on the verbal labelling of an emotional state, which, as we have seen, tends to be rather gross. Furthermore, this type of approach does not allow one to elucidate the type of physiological mechanism that underlies the observed correlation between emotional change and change in vocal production. In order to understand better the ways in which the psychophysiological processes accompanying emotional arousal

Table 7.2. Sequence of stimulus evaluation checks (SECs)

1. Novelty check. Evaluating whether there is a change in the pattern of external or internal stimulation, particularly whether a novel event has occurred or is to be expected.
2. Intrinsic pleasantness check. Evaluating whether a stimulus event is pleasant, inducing approach tendencies, or unpleasant, inducing avoidance tendencies; based on innate feature detectors or on learned associations.
3. Goal/need significance check. Evaluating whether a stimulus event is relevant to important goals or needs of the organism (relevance subcheck), whether the outcome is consistent with, or discrepant from, the state expected for this point in the goal/plan sequence (expectation subcheck), whether it is conducive or obstructive to reaching the respective goals or satisfying the relevant needs (conduciveness subcheck), and how urgently some kind of behavioural response is required (urgency subcheck).
4. Coping potential check. Evaluating the causation of a stimulus event (causation subcheck) and the coping potential available to the organism, particularly the degree of control over the event or its consequences (control subcheck), the relative power of the organism to change or avoid the outcome through fight or flight (power subcheck), and the potential for adjustment to the final outcome via internal restructuring (adjustment subcheck).
5. Norm/self compatibility check. Evaluating whether the event, particularly an action, conforms to social norms, cultural conventions, or expectations of significant others (external standards subcheck), and whether it is consistent with internalized norms or standards as part of the self-concept or ideal self (internal standards subcheck).

Source: Scherer (1986a) p. 147. (© 1986 by the American Psychological Association. Reprinted by permission of the publisher and author.)

affect voice production and the resulting acoustic output, it is necessary to develop specific hypotheses concerning the relationship between affect and vocalization.

Unfortunately, apart from Darwin's early speculations, there are very few attempts to predict specific physiological changes in the voice-producing organs as a result of specific emotions. This is also basically true for facial expression, where the patterns that have been observed for discrete emotions are generally linked to rather ill-defined neural programs (Izard, 1977a, b; Tomkins, 1962, 1963).

Recently, an attempt has been made to 'decompose' the classic emotional states into a number of components which may allow more specific predictions. Proposing a 'component process' theory, Scherer (1984, 1986a) has argued that emotional states are produced by the outcomes of a series of five stimulus evaluation checks. In other words, the organism is seen to scan the environment constantly and to evaluate information on the basis of the five criteria or checks listed in Table 7.2. As is shown in more detail elsewhere, most of the major emotions which are referenced by verbal labels can be conceived of as resulting from a specific constellation of outcomes of these five checks. Table 7.3 shows a theoretical prediction table, proposing an outcome profile as an explanatory construct for emotional states habitually labelled with the emotion word in question.

How does this approach generate specific predictions for emotional impact on voice production? The major difference from discrete emotion theories is that in the context of the component process model, a 'component patterning' theory (Scherer, 1984, 1986a) proposes specific changes in the various subsystems of the organism which are seen to subserve emotion (physiological responses, motor expression, motivational tendencies, subjective feeling states). Thus, the outcome of each check is seen to affect all the different emotion components in a 'value-added' function. Given that the organism constantly evaluates and reevaluates ongoing stimulation on the basis of these checks, one can expect constant modifications of the state of the various subsystems on the basis of the sequences of changes in the outcomes of the checks.

The changes expected for the various subsystems for each type of outcome are based on functional considerations with a strong phylogenetic bias. Table 7.4 shows the predictions made for the major components of emotion.

More specifically, on the basis of literature in acoustic phonetics and vocal physiology one can draw up a very detailed pattern of predictions for the voice production domain. This is shown in Table 7.5. Clearly, many of these predictions are rather gross and quite preliminary, given the state of our knowledge in this area. Doubtless, this type of table will have to be revised repeatedly as new evidence becomes available. On the other hand, it does present an initial basis for generating a number of hypotheses concerning vocal changes in emotion. Based on Tables 7.3 and 7.5 we can draw up a detailed prediction table for specific acoustic parameters, which can then be empirically investigated. This is shown in Table 7.6.

Table 7.3. Hypothetical outcomes of stimulus checks for selected emotional states

Emotional state	Novelty	Pleasantness	Goal/need significance				Coping potential			Norm compatibility	
			Relevance	Expectation	Conduciveness	Urgency	Control	Power	Adjust	External	Internal
Enjoyment/happiness	Low	High	Medium	Consistent	High	Very low	—	—	High	High	High
Elation/joy	High	High	High	Discrepant	High	Low	—	—	Medium	High	High
Displeasure/disgust	Open	Very low	Low	Discrepant	Low	Medium	Open	Open	High	Low	—
Contempt/scorn	Open	Low	Low	Discrepant	Low	Low	Open	High	High	Low	—
Sadness/dejection	Low	Low	High	Discrepant	Obstruct	Low	None	—	Medium	—	—
Grief/desperation	High	Low	High	Discrepant	Obstruct	High	Low	Low	Low	—	—
Anxiety/worry	Low	Open	Medium	Discrepant	Obstruct	Medium	Open	Low	Medium	—	—
Fear/terror	High	Low	High	Discrepant	Obstruct	Very high	Open	Very low	Medium	—	—
Irritation/cold anger	Low	Open	Medium	Discrepant	Obstruct	Medium	High	Medium	High	Low	Low
Rage/hot anger	High	Open	High	Discrepant	Obstruct	High	High	High	High	Low	Low
Boredom/indifference	Very low	Open	Low	Consistent	Obstruct	Low	Medium	Medium	High	—	—
Shame/guilt	Low	Open	High	Discrepant	Obstruct	Medium	High	Open	Medium	Very low	Very low

Source: Scherer (1986a) p. 147. (© 1986 by the American Psychological Association. Reprinted by permission of the publisher and author.)

Table 7.4. Component patterning theory predictions of SEC outcome effects on subsystems

SEC outcome	Organismic functions	Social functions	Support system	Action system					
				Muscle tone	Face	Voice	Instrumental	Posture	Locomotion
Novelty									
Novel	Orienting Focusing	Alerting	Orienting response	Local changes	Brows/lids up Open orifices	Interruption Inhalation	Interruption	Straightening Raising head	Interruption
Old	Homeostasis	Reassuring	No change	No change	No change	No change	No change	No change	No change
Intrinsic pleasantness									
Pleasant	Incorporation	Recommending	Sensitization of sensorium	Slight decrease	Expanding orifices 'sweet face'	Wide voice	Centripetal movement	Expanding Opening	Approach
Unpleasant	Expulsion Rejection	Warning Decommending	Defense response: desensitization	Increase	Closing orifices. 'sour face'	Narrow voice	Centrifugal movement	Shrinking Closing in	Avoidance Distancing
Goal/need significance									
Consistent	Relaxation	Announcing stability	Trophotropic shift	Decrease	Relaxed tone	Relaxed voice	Comfort position	Comfort position	Rest position
Discrepant	Activation	Announcing activity	Ergotropic dominance	Increase	Corrugator	Tense voice	Task-dependent	Task-dependent	Task-dependent
Coping potential									
No control	Readjustment	Indicating withdrawal	Trophotropic dominance Ergo–tropho balance Noradrenaline discharge Respiration volume up	Hypotonus	Lowered eyelids	Lax voice	No activity or slowing	Slump	No movement or slowing
High power control	Goal assertion	Dominance assertion		Slight decrease Tension in head and neck	Baring teeth Tensing mouth	Full voice	Agonistic movement	Anchoring body, lean forward	Approach
Low power control	Protection	Indicating submission	Ergotropic dominance Adrenaline discharge Peripheral vasoconstriction Respiration rate up	Hypertonus Tension in locomotor areas	Open mouth	Thin voice	Protective movement	Readiness for locomotion	Fast locomotion or freezing

Source: Scherer (1985), p. 216.

Table 7.5. Component patterning theory predictions of vocal changes after different SEC outcomes

	Novelty check	
Novel		**Old**
Interruption of phonation		No change
Sudden inhalation		
Silence		
Ingressive (fricative) sound with a glottal stop (noise-like spectrum)		

	Intrinsic pleasantness check	
Plesant		**Unpleasant**
Faucal and pharyngeal expansion, relaxation of tract walls		Faucal and pharyngeal constriction, tensing of tract walls
Vocal tract shortened by mouth, corners retracted upward		Vocal tract shortened by mouth corners retracted downward
More low-frequency energy, F_1 falling, slightly broader F_1 bandwidth, velopharyngeal nasality		More high-frequency energy, F_1 rising, F_2 and F_3 falling, narrow F_1 band-width, laryngopharyngeal nasality
Resonances raised		Resonances raised
Wide voice		*Narrow voice*

	Goal/need significance check	
Relevant and consistent		**Relevant and discrepant**
Shift toward trophotropic side: overall relaxation of vocal apparatus, increased salivation		Ergotropic dominance: overall tensing of vocal apparatus and respiratory system, decreased salivation
F_0 at lower end of range, low-to-moderate amplitude, balanced resonance with slight decrease in high-frequency energy		F_0 and amplitude increase, jitter and shimmer, increase in high-frequency energy, narrow F_1 bandwidth, pronounced formant frequency differences
Relaxed voice		*Tense voice*
If event conducive to goal: relaxed voice + wide voice		If event conducive to goal: tense voice + wide voice
If event obstructive to goal: relaxed voice + narrow voice		If event obstructive to goal: tense voice + narrow voice

Table 7.5 (Contd.)

Coping potential check	
Control	No control
Ergotropic dominance: (see tense voice)	Trophotropic dominance: hypotension of the musculature in the vocal apparatus and respiratory system
(see tense voice)	Low F_0 and restricted F_0 range, low amplitude, weak pulses, very low high-frequency energy, spectral noise, formant frequencies tending toward neutral setting, broad F_1 bandwidth
Tense voice	Lax voice
Power	No power
Deep, forceful respiration; chest register phonation	Rapid, shallow respiration; head register phonation
Low F_0 high amplitude, strong energy in entire frequency range	Raised F_0, widely spaced harmonics with relatively low energy
Full voice	Thin voice

Norm/self compatibility check	
Standards surpassed	Standards violated
Wide voice + full voice	Narrow voice + thin voice
+ Relaxed voice (if expected)	+ Lax voice (if no control)
+ Tense voice (if unexpected)	+ Tense voice (if control)

Source: Scherer (1986a), p. 156. (© 1986 by the American Psychological Association. Reprinted by permission of the publisher and author.)

Table 7.6. Changes predicted for selected acoustic parameters on the basis of the voice type predictions in Table 7.4

Parameters

Voice type	ENJ/ HAP	ELA/ JOY	DISP/ DISG	CON/ SCO	SAD/ DEJ	GRI/ DES	ANX/ WOR	FEAR/ TER	IRR/ COA	RAGE/ HOA	BOR/ IND	SHA/ GUI
F_0												
Perturbation	⋁∥	⋀						⋀⋀	⋀⋁	⋀⋁		⋀
Mean	⋁	⋀⋀	⋀	⋁	⋀⋁	⋀		⋀⋀	⋁	⋀⋁	⋁⋁	
Range	⋁∥	⋀⋀			⋁∥	⋀		⋀⋀	⋁	⋀⋀		⋀
Variability	⋁	⋀⋀			⋁∥	⋀	⋀	⋀⋀	⋁	⋀⋀		
Contour	⋁	⋀			⋁∥	⋀		⋀⋀	⋁	≫		⋀
Shift regularity	=	⋁						⋁	⋁	⋁		
F_1 mean	⋁	⋁	⋀	⋀	⋀	⋀	⋀	⋀	⋀	⋀	⋀	⋀
F_2 mean			⋁	⋁	⋁	⋁	⋁	⋁	⋁	⋁	⋁	⋁
F_1 bandwidth	⋀	⋁	≪	⋁	⋀⋁	≪	⋁	≪	≪	≪	⋀	⋁
Formant precision	⋀	⋀	⋀	⋀	⋁⋀	⋀	⋀	⋀	⋀	⋀		⋀
Intensity												
Mean	⋁	⋀⋀	⋀	≫	⋁⋁	⋀		⋀	⋀⋀	≫⋀	⋁	
Range	⋁∥	⋀	⋀		⋁			⋀	⋀	⋀	⟨⟩	
Variability	⋁	⋀			⋁			⋀		⋀		
Frequency range	⋀	⋀	⋀	≫	⋀	≫		≫	⋀	⋀	⋀	
High-frequency energy	⋁	⋁⋀	⋀	⋀	⋀	≫	⋀	≫⋀	≫	≫	⋀⋁	⋀
Spectral noise					⋀							
Speech rate	⋁	⋀⋀			⋁∥	⋀		⋀⋀		⋀⋀		
Transition time	⋀	⋁			⋀	⋁		⋁		⋁		

Note: ANX/WOR = anxiety/worry; BOR/IND = boredom/indifference; CON/SCO = contempt/scorn; DISP/DISG = displeasure/disgust; ELA/JOY = elation/joy; ENJ/HAP = enjoyment/happiness; FEAR/TER = fear/terror; GRI/DES = grief/desperation; IRR/COA = irritation/coldanger; RAGE/HOA = rage/hot anger; SAD/DEJ = sadness/dejection; SHA/GUI = shame/guilt; F_0 = fundamental frequency; F_1 = first formant; F_2 = second formant; > = increase; < = decrease; Double symbols indicate increased predicted strength of the change; two symbols pointing in opposite directions refer to cases in which antecedent voice types exert opposing influences.

Source: Scherer (1986a), p. 158. (© 1986 by the American Psychological Association. Reprinted by permission of the publisher and author.)

Much of the foregoing has been highly speculative in nature. However, it is argued that the approach taken here will help to establish closer links between theories of emotion, psychophysiological research, and the acoustic measurement of vocal behaviour. Should this approach prove feasible, it would help researchers to go beyond the fairly atheoretical correlational approach that presently characterizes the field, and would thereby provide a better understanding of the physiological mechanisms involved.

REFERENCES

Bannister, M. L. (1972) An instrumental and judgemental analysis of voice samples from psychiatrically hospitalized and nonhospitalized adolescents. Unpublished Ph.D thesis, University of Kansas.

Bonner, M. R. (1943) Changes in the speech pattern under emotional tension. *American Journal of Psychology*, **56**, 262–73.

Bortz, J. (1966) Physikalisch-akustische Korrelate der vokalen Kommunikation. *Arbeiten aus dem psychologischen Institut der Universität* Hamburg, **9**.

Coleman, R. F., and Williams, R. (1979) Identification of emotional states using perceptual and acoustic analyses. In V. Lawrence and B. Weinberg (Eds), *Transcript of the Eighth Symposium: Care of the Professional Voice*, Part I. New York: The Voice Foundation.

Costanzo, F. S., Markel, N. N., and Costanzo, P. R. (1969) Voice quality profile and perceived emotion. *Journal of Counseling Psychology*, **16**, 267–70.

Daniloff, R., Schuckers, G., and Feth, L. (1980) *The Physiology of Speech and Hearing: An Introduction*. Englewood Cliffs, NJ: Prentice-Hall.

Davitz, J. R. (1964) *The Communication of Emotional Meaning*. New York: McGraw-Hill.

Duncan, G., Laver, J., and Jack, M. A. (1983) A psycho-acoustic interpretation of variations in divers' voice fundamental frequency in a pressured helium-oxygen environment. *Work in Progress*, **16**, 9–16. Edinburgh: University of Edinburgh, Department of Linguistics.

Ekman, P., Friesen, W. V., and Scherer, K. R. (1976) Body movement and voice pitch in deceptive interaction. *Semiotica*, **16**, 23–7.

Eldred, S. H., and Price, D. B. (1958) A linguistic evaluation of feeling states in psychotherapy. *Psychiatry*, **21**, 11–121.

Fairbanks, G., and Hoaglin, L. W. (1941) An experimental study of the durational characteristics of the voice during the expression of emotion. *Speech Monographs*, **8**, 85–90.

Fairbanks, G., and Pronovost, W. (1939) An experimental study of the pitch characteristics of the voice during the expression of emotion. *Speech Monographs*, **6**, 87–104.

Fant, G. (1960) *Acoustic Theory of Speech Production*. The Hague: Mouton.

Fonagy, I. (1978) A new method of investigating the perception of prosodic features. *Language and Speech*, **21**, 34–49.

Fry, D. B. (1979) *The Physics of Speech*. Cambridge: Cambridge University Press.

Hargreaves, W. A., and Starkweather, J. A. (1964) Voice quality changes in depression. *Language and Speech*, **7**, 84–8.

Hargreaves, W. A., and Starkweather, J. A. (1965) Vocal and verbal indicators of depression. Unpublished manuscript, San Francisco.

Hargreaves, W. A., Starkweather, J. A., and Blacker, K. H. (1965) Voice quality in depression. *Journal of Abnormal Psychology*, **70**, 218–20.

Havrdova, Z., and Moravek, M. (1979) Changes of the voice expression during suggestively influenced states of experiencing. *Activitas Nervosa Superior*, **21**, 33–5.

Hess, W. (1983) *Pitch Determination of Speech Signals*. Berlin: Springer.

Hicks, J. W. (1979) An acoustical/temporal analysis of emotional stress in speech. *Dissertation Abstracts International*, **41** (4-A).

Hollien, H. (1981) Analog instrumentation for acoustic speech analysis. In J. Darby (Ed.), *Speech Evaluation in Psychiatry*, pp. 79–103. New York: Grune & Stratton.

Huttar, G. L. (1968) Relations between prosodic variables and emotions in normal American English utterances. *Journal of Speech and Hearing Research*, **11**, 481–7.

Höffe, W. L. (1960) Über Beziehungen von Sprachmelodie und Lautstärke. *Phonetica*, **5**, 129–59.

Izard, C. E. (1977a) The emergence of emotions and the development of consciousness in infancy. In J. M. Davidson, R. J. Davidson, and G. E. Schwartz (Eds), *Human Consciousness and its Transformations: A Psychobiological Perspective*. New York: Plenum Press.

Izard, C. E. (1977b) *Human Emotions*. New York: Plenum Press.

Jürgens, U. (1979) Vocalization as an emotional indicator. A neuroethological study in the squirrel monkey. *Behaviour*, **69**, 88–117.

Kaiser, L. (1962) Communication of affects by single vowels. *Synthese*, **14**m 300–19.

Klos, Th., Ellgring, H., and Scherer, K. R. (1988) Vocal changes in depression. Unpublished manuscript, University of Geneva.

Kotlyar, G. M., and Morozov, V. P. (1976) Acoustical correlates of the emotional content of vocalized speech. *Sov. Phys. Acoust.*, **22**, 208–11.

Kuroda, I., Fujiwara, O., Okamura, N., and Utsuki, N. (1976) Method for determining pilot stress through analysis of voice communication. *Aviation, Space, and Environmental Medicine*, **47**, 528–33.

Laver, J. (1980) *The Phonetic Description of Voice Quality*. Cambridge: Cambridge University Press.

Leyhausen, P. (1967) Biologie von Ausdruck und Eindruck, Teil 1. *Psychologische Forschung*, **31**, 113–76.

Lieberman, P. (1961) Perturbations in vocal pitch. *Journal of the Acoustical Society of America*, **33**, 597–603.

Lieberman, P. (1977) *Speech Physiology and Acoustic Phonetics: An Introduction*. New York: Macmillan.

Marler, P. (1984) Animal communication: affect or cognition? In K. R. Scherer and P. Ekman (Eds), *Approaches to Emotion*, pp. 345–68. Hillsdale, NJ: Erlbaum.

Moses, P. J. (1954) *The Voice of Neurosis*. New York: Grune & Stratton.

Müller A. L. (1960) Experimentelle Untersuchungen zur stimmlichen Darstellung von Gefühlen. Unpublished doctoral dissertation, Universität Göttingen.

Newman, S. S. and Mather, V. G. (1938) Analysis of spoken language of patients with affective disorders. *American Journal of Psychiatry*, **94**, 913–42.

Niwa, S. (1971) Changes of voice characteristics in urgent situations. (2) *Reports of the Aeromedical Laboratory, Japan Air Self Defense Force*, **11**, 246–51.

Ostwald, P. F. (1961) The sound of emotional disturbance. *Archives of General Psychiatry*, **5**, 587–92.

Ostwald, P. F. (1963) *Soundmaking: The Acoustic Communication of Emotion*. Springfield: C. C. Thomas.

Ostwald, P. F. (1964) Acoustic manifestations of emotional disturbance. *Disorders of Communication—Research Publications*, **42**, 450–65.

Plaikner, D. (1970) Die Veränderungen der menschlichen Stimme unter dem Einfluss psychischer Belastung. Unpublished doctoral dissertation, Universität Innsbruck.

Robinson, W. P. (1972) *Language and Social Behavior*. Harmondsworth: Penguin.

Roessler, R., and Lester, J. W. (1976) Voice predicts affect during psychotherapy. *Journal of Nervous and Mental Disease*, **163**, 166–176.

Roessler, R., and Lester, J. W. (1979) Vocal patterns in anxiety. In W. E. Fann, A. D. Pokorny, I. Koracau, and R. L. Williams (Eds), *Phenomenology and Treatment of Anxiety*. New York: Spectrum.

Scherer, K. R. (1979) Nonlinguistic vocal indicators of emotion and psychopathology. In C. E. Izard (Ed.), *Emotions in Personality and Psychopathology*, pp. 493–529. New York: Plenum Press.

Scherer, K. R. (1981) Vocal indicators of stress. In J. Darby (Ed.), *Speech Evaluation in Psychiatry*, pp. 171–87. New York: Grune & Stratton.

Scherer, K. R. (1982) Methods of research on vocal communication: paradigms and parameters. In K. R. Scherer and P. Ekman (Eds), *Handbook of Methods in Nonverbal Behaviour Research*, pp. 136–98. Cambridge: Cambridge University Press.

Scherer, K. R. (1984) On the nature and function of emotion: a component process approach. In K. R. Scherer and P. Ekman (Eds), *Approaches to Emotion*, pp. 293–318. Hillsdale, NJ: Erlbaum.

Scherer, K. R. (1985) Vocal affect signalling: a comparative approach. In J. Rosenblatt, C. Beer, M.-C. Busnel, and P. J. B. Slater (Eds), *Advances in the Study of Behavior*, Vol. 15, pp. 189–244. New York: Academic Press.

Scherer, K. R. (1986a) Vocal affect expression: a review and a model for future research. *Psychological Bulletin*, **99**, 143–65.

Scherer, K. R. (1986b) Voice, stress, and emotion. In M. H. Appley and R. Trumbull (Eds), *Dynamics of Stress*, pp. 159–81. New York: Plenum Press.

Scherer, K. R. (1987) Vocal assessment of affective disorders. In J. D. Maser, (Ed), *Depression and Expressive Behavior*, pp. 57–82. Hillsdale, NJ: Erlbaum.

Scherer, K. R. (1988, in press) Toward a dynamic theory of emotion: the component process model of affective states.

Scherer, K. R., and Kappas, A. (1988, in press) Vocal affect expression in primates. In D. Todt, P. Goedeking, and E. Newman, (Eds), *Primate vocal communication*, pp. 171–94. Heidelberg: Springer.

Scherer, K. R., Wallbott, H. G. and Summerfield, A. B. (Eds) (1986) *Experiencing Emotion: A Cross-Cultural Study*. Cambridge: Cambridge University Press.

Scherer, K. R., Wallbott, H. G., Tolkmitt, F., and Bergmann, G. (1985) *Die Stress reaktion: Physiologie und Verhalten*. Göttingen: Hogrefe.

Sedlacek, K., and Sychra, A. (1963) Die Melodie als Faktor des emotionellen Ausdrucks. *Folia Phoniatrica*, **15**, 89–98.

Seyfarth, R. M. and Cheney, D. L. (1982) How monkeys see the world: a review of recent research on East African vervet monkeys. In C. T. Snowdon, C. H. Brown, and M. R. Petersen (Eds), *Primate Communication*, pp. 239–52. Cambridge: Cambridge University Press.

Siegman, A. W., and Feldstein, S. (1987) *Nonverbal Behavior and Communication*, 2nd edn. Hillsdale, NJ: Erlbaum.

Simonov, P. V., and Frolov, M. V. (1973) Utilization of human voice for estimation of man's emotional stress and state attention. *Aerospace Medicine*, **44**, 256–8.

Skinner, E. R. (1935) A calibrated recording and analysis of the pitch, force and quality of vocal tones expressing happiness and sadness. *Speech Monographs*, **2**, 81–137.

Sorensen, D. and Horii, J. (1984) Directional perturbation factors for jitter and shimmer. *Journal of Communication Disorders*, **12**, 143–57.

Streeter, L. A., Krauss, R. M., Geller, V., Olson, C., and Apple, W. (1977) Pitch changes during attempted deception. *Journal of Personality and Social Psychology*, **35**, 345–50.

Sulc, J. (1977) To the problem of emotional changes in the human voice. *Activitas Nervosa Superior*, **19**, 215–16.

Tolkmitt, F. J., Helfrich, H., Standke, R., and Scherer, K. R. (1982) Vocal indicators of psychiatric treatment effects in depressives and schizophrenics. *Journal of Communication Disorders*, **15**, 209–22.

Tomkins, S. S. (1962) *Affect, Imagery, Consciousness. Vol. 1. The Positive Affects*. New York: Springer.

Tomkins, S. S. (1963) *Affect, Imagery, Consciousness. Vol. 2. The Negative Affects*. New York: Springer.

Utsuki, N., and Okamura, N. (1976) Relationship between emotional state and fundamental frequency of speech. *Reports of the Aeromedical Laboratory, Japan Air Self Defense Force*, **16**, 179–88.

Van Bezooijen, R. (1984) *The Characteristics and Recognizability of Vocal Expressions of Emotion*. Dordrecht: Foris.

Wallbott, H. G., and Scherer, K. R. (1986) Cues and channels in emotion recognition. *Journal of Personality and Social Psychology*, **51**, 690–9.

Whitman, E. N. and Flicker, D. J. (1966) A potential new measurement of emotional state: A preliminary report. *Newark Beth Israel Hospital*, **17**, 167–172.

Williams, C. E., and Stevens, K. N. (1969) On determining the emotional state of pilots during flight: An exploratory study. *Aerospace Medicine*, **40**, 1369–72.

Williams, C. E., and Stevens, K. N. (1972) Emotions and speech: Some acoustical correlates. *Journal of the Acoustical Society of America*, **52**, 1238–1250.

Zemlin, W. R. (1968) *Speech and Hearing Science* (2nd edn. 1981). Englewood Cliffs, NJ: Prentice-Hall.

Zuberbier, E. (1957) Zur Schreib- und Sprechmotorik der Depressiven. *Zeitschrift für Psychotherapie und Medizinische Psychologie*, **7**, 239–49.

Zwirner, E. (1930) Beitrag zur Sprache des Depressiven. *Phonometrie III, Spezielle Anwendungen I*, pp. 171–87. Basel: Karger.

Chapter 8

Subjective, Expressive, and Peripheral Bodily Components of Emotion

Ross Buck

University of Connecticut

ABSTRACT

A general view of motivation, emotion, and cognition is presented analyzing the peripheral, expressive, and subjective aspects of emotion. The stress–disease link is reviewed, suggesting that emotional expression and communication function in both self-regulation and social coordination. Subjective experience is discussed, considering both agnosia and appraisal process.

There appears to be general agreement that emotion has subjective, expressive, and peripheral bodily components (Kleinginna and Kleinginna, 1981). There has been much debate, however, on how these components are related to one another. At the same time, there has been increasing interest in the classic 'trilogy of mind' that has been central to the study of the nature of human beings since the time of the Greeks: motivation, emotion, and cognition. In this chapter I propose a general approach to both of these issues that places emotion in a central position in the process of adaptation that has characterized the evolution of life on this planet.

Handbook of Social Psychophysiology, Edited by H. Wagner and A. Manstead,
© 1989 John Wiley & Sons Ltd

EMOTION AND ADAPTATION

THE PROCESS OF ADAPTATION

Life has existed on the Earth for perhaps 3.5 billion years—the first fossil algae are thought to be 3.2 billion years old. During most of this period—the entire Precambrian period that ended less than 600 million years ago—life consisted primarily of microscopic organisms. These organisms had early solved the problem of carrying with them an 'internal environment' in which temperature, chemical, and energy balances approximated those in the primordial sea which supported the existence of the self-replicating DNA molecule. It is striking and humbling to recall that this primordial environment still exists within our bodies: that with the evolution of complex organisms there have evolved more and more complex ways of 'packaging' that original life-supporting environment. It is also undeniable, yet almost unbelievable, that every cell in the human body contains in its DNA the basic information necessary to construct the entire individual organism.

In this chapter I argue that the maintenance of this internal environment—the processes of adaptation and homeostasis—has always been, and continues to be, an essentially emotional process; and that, moreover, this process has always had, and continues to have, to equivalent of subjective, expressive, and peripheral bodily components. The reader may ask if I am suggesting that the equivalent of subjective, expressive, and peripheral bodily components of emotion exist in algae. The answer is yes.

The notion that basic adaptive and homeostatic responding exists in even the simplest organisms is perhaps not controversial. However, the notion that anything like emotional expression and subjective experience exists in such creatures may well raise a few eyebrows. My reasoning is as follows. First, I submit that sexual reproduction in animals requires that individuals be attracted to one another, recognize one another, and coordinate their behaviour so that reproduction occurs. This, in turn, requires mechanisms to both send information to, and receive information from, other organisms: mechanisms, in short, of emotional communication. Even some simple plants coordinate their reproductive activities by communication mechanisms. Maier and Müller (1986) describe how, in green and brown algae, cellular activities are timed and coordinated between individuals by means of sexual pheromones, and how this is necessary for the exchange and rearrangement of their genes. This is the essence of communication (Wilson, 1975).

Second, I submit that to the extent that a creature has knowledge of the external environment (external cognition), it simply makes sense that it must also have knowledge of its own internal environment (internal cognition) for purposes of comparison. It does no good for an organism to find food if it does not know whether or not it is hungry. Mechanisms for detecting information in the outside world *must* be accompanied by mechanisms for detecting information in the

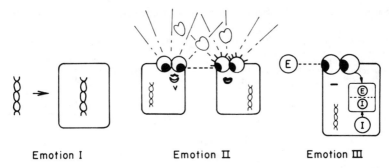

Figure 8.1. The three components of emotion. Emotion I involves the maintenance of the chemical, energy, and temperature balances necessary for the existence of the self-replicating DNA molecule, originally present in the primordial sea, within the organism. Emotion II involves the ability to attract, recognize, and coordinate behavior with other organisms which is necessary for sexual reproduction. Emotion III involves the ability to sense important information within the organism (I) so that it can be integrated with important information external to the organism (E). The eyes and mouths are, of course, metaphorical.

internal milieu. In complex animals, the latter are recognized to be feelings and desires—emotions and motives—but I suggest that they have an essential continuity with the mechanisms by which a simple animal or plant coordinates the presence of, for example, water in the external environment with the fluid balance within the organism.

The three components of emotion—adaptive/homeostatic, expressive, and subjective—are illustrated in Figure 8.1. I have suggested that they be labeled respectively Emotion I, II, and III (Buck, 1985).

The reader may object that, although these processes may indeed take place within simple organisms, it makes no sense to call them 'emotional;' that such a lebel may stretch the meaning of the term 'emotion' beyond all reasonable bounds. Many prefer to restrict the term 'emotion' to processes like happiness, sadness, fear, anger, surprise, disgust, and the like. I argue, in response, that such a view does not allow us to see the similarities and differences between these processes— which following Tomkins I prefer to label 'affects'—and processes like reflexes, instincts, and drives (see Buck, 1985). Moreover, I think that only a very broad view of emotion can take in all of those things that have been called 'emotional' over the years, and that it is possible to take such a broad view and still define 'emotion' in a meaningful way.

MOTIVATION AND EMOTION

Specifically, I suggest that emotion can be regarded as a process by which motivational potential built in to the organism is actualized when activated by a

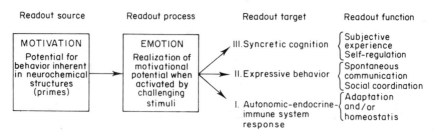

Figure 8.2. The readout process: source, targets, and functions served. From Figure 2 in Buck, R. (1985) Prime theory: an integrated view of motivation and emotion. *Psychological Review*, **92**, 389–413.

challenging stimulus. Emotion is thus a *readout* of motivational potential (Buck, 1985). There are three sorts of readout process that correspond to the three components of emotion: the Emotion I readout to peripheral bodily systems that serves functions of adaptation and homeostasis; the Emotion II readout to expressive behaviors that serves functions of social communication and organization; and the Emotion III readout to syncretic cognition (involving direct, immediate, experience or knowledge by acquaintance) that serves functions of self-regulation (see Figure 8.2).

This model suggests the relationship between motivation and emotion: motivation is the potential for behavior which is built in to the organism over the process of evolution; emotion is the readout of that potential when activated by a challenging stimulus. I suggest that there is a biologically based hierarchy of 'primary motivational–emotional systems,' or *primes*, which includes reflexes, instincts or fixed action patterns, drives, affects, and effectance motivation (see Buck, 1984, 1985). These are special-purpose processing systems that have been structured by phylogeny, e.g. over the course of evolution. The primes interact increasingly with general-purpose processing systems of learning and cognition as one goes up the hierarchy, so that their behavioral manifestations become increasingly flexible.

COGNITION

This, in turn, suggests the relationship of cognition to motivation and emotion. Cognition implies knowledge, and there are two sorts of knowledge that must be distinguished (see Buck, 1984). *Knowledge by acquaintance* involves immediate experience or awareness of, for example, the taste of a pear, or the color blue. We cannot put knowledge by acquaintance into words. As William James put it: 'I know the color blue when I see it, and the flavor of a pear when I taste it . . . . but *about* the inner nature of these facts or what makes them what they are I can say nothing at all. I cannot impart acquaintance with them to anyone who has not made it himself' (1890, p. 221). Knowledge by acquaintance is related to what Tucker (1981) has termed syncretic cognition.

In contrast, *knowledge by description* involves the *interpretation* of sense data, which requires process of transformation and analysis: e.g. analytic as opposed to syncretic cognition (see Tucker, 1981). Knowledge by description involves the knowledge that one has knowledge of something. My purely perceptual immediate experience of a table is knowledge by acquaintance; my knowledge that the table is a 'physical object' which if I touch it is hard and smooth and which does not disappear when I leave the room, is knowledge by description. The processes of cognitive development studied by Piaget involve, to a great extent, the increasing ability of the child to interpret its immediate knowledge of reality in terms of knowledge by description. I suggest that a good term for describing the interpretation of knowledge by acquaintance in terms of knowledge by description is *appraisal*, and shall return to it later in this chapter.

A GENERAL VIEW

The relationship of cognition, emotion, and motivation can now be suggested. Cognition is the result of an adaptive process by which organisms that were sensitive to certain events in the external and internal environments came to have an advantage over their fellows because they could respond more flexibility. Gradually, an ability to be sensitive and flexible was built in to the species. One aspect of this is the Emotion III process which gave the organism direct knowledge by acquaintance of certain information internal to the body, another is the process by which evolved the classic sensory and motor systems that deal with the external physical and social environment. In essence, then, cognition can be seen as an aspect of the operation of basic motivational–emotional systems involved in adaptation: the organism has a built-in potential to take in information—this is a motivational potential—and the process of taking in, storing, and otherwise appropriately dealing with such information, is an emotional process—a readout of the motivational potential.

Thus, the present view suggests that there exist basic cognitive motives and cognitive emotions that are analogous in structure to biological motives and emotions (in that emotion is a readout of motivational potential), but which deal with general information as opposed to specific biological functions (see Buck, 1984, 1985). The cognitive motives and emotions may be thought analogous to processes by which the organism develops its own software, while the biological motives and emotions are analogous to 'hard-wired' processes that run the hardware. Cognitive motives and emotions include basic exploratory motives and emotions, and with liguistic competence there also appear motives and emotions for understanding, cognitive consistency, distributive and retributive justice, and the like (Buck, 1988).

The remainder of this chapter will be devoted to a consideration of each of the three components of emotion in turn. It will then address the issue of how the three components are related to one another.

PERIPHERAL BODILY RESPONDING

Interest in peripheral bodily responding in emotion has traditionally been centered on two major issues: the role of peripheral events in the experience of emotion, and the bodily effects of emotional stress upon health and disease. There have been important and exciting developments in both of these areas.

PERIPHERAL CONTRIBUTIONS TO EMOTIONAL EXPERIENCE

Decades of research have demonstrated that feedback from peripheral visceral and somatic changes is not necessary for previously learned emotional behavior, although it may facilitate the acquistion of such behavior. Also, such feedback does not appear to be either necessary or sufficient for emotional experience, although it may contribute to some kinds of emotional experience (Buck, 1980).

There have been important recent developments in the understanding of the peripheral bodily concomitants of emotional experience. On one hand, one of the most widely cited studies dealing with the contribution of bodily sensation to emotional experience has been questioned, and on the other hand, a system by which the body may affect the brain has been newly identified and likened to a 'sixth sense.'

The study now under question is that of Hohmann (1966), who interviewed 25 patients about the effects of spinal damage upon emotional experience, and reported that spinal damage resulted in a lowering of reported emotional experience that was proportional to the amount of loss of bodily sensation. Two studies have failed to confirm Hohmann's result, finding instead no evidence that spinal-cord-injured patients report lessened emotional experience (Chwalisz, Diener, and Gallagher, 1988; Lowe and Carroll, 1985). The authors of both studies suggest that Hohmann's result may have reflected the grim outlook and long hospitalization that such patients faced during the late 1950s, when the data were gathered. They suggest that, today, advances in rehabilitation and aftercare have contributed to more positive outlooks among such patients.

The newly discovered feedback system to the brain involves the immune system, whose cells have been found to produce hormones including ACTH, endorphins, sex hormones, and growth hormone. Immunologist E. Blalock has suggested that 'it is as if the immune system is just a bunch of miniature, floating pituitary glands'. Through these hormones the immune system can, potentially, influence every system in the body, including the brain. In fact, it has been suggested that macrophage cells of the immune system actively transport substances through the blood–brain barrier (Pert, 1985). It may be that the response of the immune system to invading organisms can be regulated by the brain through this feedback system, since it apparently could provide up-to-date intelligence about the course of the battle, enabling bodily defenses to respond appropriately.

PERIPHERAL RESPONDING AND STRESS

The resulting brain–immune system interaction has important implications for the understanding of the bodily response to stress. The evidence that emotional factors are important in stress and disease has been mounting since the classic studies by Cannon, on the 'fight-or-flight response' associated with the autonomic nervous system, and by Selye, on the 'general adaptation response' associated particularly with the endocrine system. The rapidly growing understanding of the role of the immune system in these processes has both underscored the importance of emotion and provided more detailed and specific physiological models by which emotional factors might operate. Such models have been applied to the analysis of cardiovascular disease, cancer, and psychosomatic disorders.

Cardiovascular disease

Friedman and Rosenman (1974) have suggested that persons who manifest a Type-A behavior pattern (TABP) are engaged in a constant struggle with themselves and with others. This results in chronic sympathetic and endocrine system activation which has destructive effects on the arteries, due to increased levels of clotting substance in the blood and increased cholesterol, heart rate, and blood pressure. McClelland (1982) has found evidence that high levels of a need for power, which he relates to the TABP, are associated with high levels of sympathetic nervous system activity (assessed by urinary epinephrine) and low levels of immune system functioning (assessed by salivary immunoglobulin) as well as high levels of blood pressure and reported disease. Significantly, McClelland finds that a high level of affiliation motivation ameliorates the negative effects of the need for power: the need for power is associated with these potentially disruptive effects only among persons low in the need for affiliation.

Cancer

Stress may influence the genesis and course of cancer by triggering dormant malignant cells or by impairing the immune system so that it does not identify and attack such cells (Grossarth–Maticek, Kanazin, Schmidt, and Vetter, 1982). Both immunosuppression and increased autonomic/endocrine responding have been suggested as mediating the effects of emotional factors upon cancer (see Bammer and Newberry, 1982; Pettingale, 1985). These may, in turn, be exacerbated by emotional suppression. Prospective studies have suggested that a limited ability to express depression, anger and anxiety may be associated with a predisposition to cancer (see Grossarth-Maticek, Bastisams, and Kanazin, 1985; Shekelle *et al.*, 1981). In contrast to the impatient 'pent-up' aggressiveness of the TABP, the cancer-prone 'Type-C' personality pattern has been called 'pathologically nice' (see Greer and Watson, 1985; Renneker, 1981). Baltrusch and Waltz (1985) suggest that such persons are compliant, submissive, selfless, and anxious to please.

Psychosomatic disorders

The 'classic' psychosomatic illnesses are those in which emotional factors have long been implicated as a major factor in the etiology of the disorder. These include certain forms of ulcer, colitis, asthma, and headache. It has long been suggested that these disorders are associated with the physiological tension caused by a lack of emotional expression (Alexander, 1950), but it is not until recently that detailed physiological models of this process have been suggested. Sifneos (1967, 1973) coined the term *alexithymia* (literally 'no words for mood') to describe the inability of the psychosomatic patient to express his or her feelings. Reviews of this literature suggest that indeed an impairment in the expression of emotion is a necessary, if not sufficient, condition for the development of psychosomatic disorders (Anderson, 1981) and there have been interesting suggestions that alexithymia may involve a functional separation of the right and left cerebral hemispheres (TenHouten, Hoppe, Bogen, and Walter, 1985a, b, c, d).

It is noteworthy that the analysis of the emotional problems underlying cardiovascular disease, cancer, and psychosomatic disorder are alike in that all involve disturbed patterns of emotional expression (albeit of different sorts). In each case, it could be argued that these patterns could lead to disruptions in emotional communication: the Type A person may drive others away; the Type C person may never express negative emotions; the alexithymic person may not express emotion at all. In this regard it is very interesting that there is much evidence that close personal relationships have beneficial effects upon the response to stress and disease. Kiecolt-Glaser, Garner, Speicher, Penn, Holliday, and Glaser (1984) have demonstrated, for example, that examination stress, life change, and loneliness all have disruptive effects upon immune system functioning in medical school students; and as noted above McClelland (1982) found that the need for affiliation had a protective effect upon persons high in the need for power.

THE RELAXATION RESPONSE

Another recent development that is important for the understanding of peripheral bodily responses in emotion is the repeated demonstration of the utility of relaxation techniques in the alleviation of stress. During the 1960s there was much interest in biofeedback techniques which targeted a specific autonomically mediated response for control, such as heart rate, blood pressure, or vascular responses. For example, 'handwarming' was advocated as a treatment for migraine headache because, theoretically, it involves vasodilation in the hands which relieved vascular pressure in the head. However, studies found that hand *cooling* was as effective as hand warming in the alleviation of migraine (Gautier, Bois, Allaire, and Drolet, 1981). Also, studies using relaxation control groups have found little or no evidence that biofeedback is superior to relaxation alone in the alleviation of stress (see Ford, 1982).

These results suggest that the autonomic nervous system may indeed function in times of stress more or less as a unit, as Cannon (1915) suspected. Also, it suggests the reality of Hess's (1957) trophotropic response, which is the opposite of Cannon's emergency fight-or-flight response. The trophotropic response may be the physiological basis of the relaxation response, which Benson (1975) suggested is the common feature in relaxation, meditation, and biofeedback techniques.

EXPRESSIVE BEHAVIOR

As the foregoing suggests, there appear to be important relationships between the expression of emotion and its peripheral bodily effects. In general, it appears that expressive behavior is associated with lessened peripheral physiological upset (Buck, 1979). The reason for this may not reside solely within the individual, but rather may involve the emotionally regulatory effects of relationships with other individuals. Expressive behavior may be necessary for such regulatory effects to occur.

THE SOCIAL REGULATION OF EMOTION

Darwin's (1872) theory that the function of emotional expression involves social coordination has received much support, and contemporary studies of emotional communication assume its validity. However, expressive behaviors may have other functions as well. Specifically, there is evidence that emotional expression and communication have *self-regulatory* functions.

Studying infant rats, Hofer and his colleagues have demonstrated how the presence of the mother rat is associated with stimuli—warmth, activity, touching—that have specific regulatory functions for the infant. The mother's absence cause the constellation of symptons known as the maternal deprivation syndrome, but the artificial introduction of specific aspects of the mother's presence causes specific symptoms to disappear (see Hofer, 1984). Other studies have shown that infant rats eat the mother's feces during a period when they are eating solid food, but before their systems produce an acid necessary to fight the related increase in bacteria. At this time, the mother's feces contains particularly high levels of this acid (Moltz, reported in Cordes, 1985). In effect, the infant rat's homeostatic system requires the mother's presence to function properly.

Hofer (1984) argues that the homeostatic systems of humans are similarly open to social influence, and that in the context of a given personal relationship, the other person comes to function as a physiological regulator for the individual. He suggests that the disruption of physiological regulation that occurs with bereavement is due to the loss of this social regulation.

THE SOCIAL BIOFEEDBACK PROCESS

The social regulation of emotion can be conceptualized in terms of a process of *social biofeedback*, in which the expressive display of the individual is analogous to the measurement of a physiological function by a biofeedback device and the response of other persons to that display is analogous to the feedback signal (see Figure 8.3). It is by way of this feedback that the individual learns about the subjective experience of emotion.

In other words, I am arguing that—assuming that an emotional state is

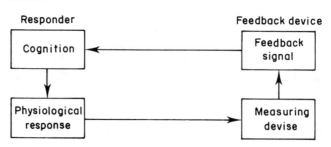

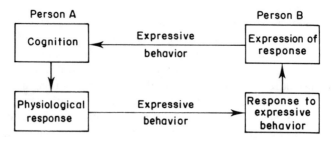

Figure 8.3. The social biofeedback process.
[From Figure 4.8 in Buck, R. (1988) Human Motivation and Emotion, 2nd edn. New York: John Wiley, Used by permission.]

associated with subjective, expressive, and peripheral physiological components—the expressive component leads to social biofeedback which informs the individual about the subjective components, with important implications for the peripheral physiological component. This is because these three components are differentially *accessible* to the responder and to others. The subjective component is accessible only to the responder, the expressive component is more accessible to others than it is to the responder, and the peripheral physiological component is not accessible at all without special equipment (Buck, 1971).

EMOTIONAL EDUCATION

The result of the social biofeedback process is *emotional education*, where the individual learns to understand his or her subjective feelings and desires, and to cope with them via goal-directed behavior. The specific 'lessons' learned in the emotional education process may vary widely in the United States from person to person. A young boy, for example, may learn to understand and express angry feelings with relative ease, because in American culture boys are expected to be aggressive and there are many male models available in the mass media who openly express angry feelings. The boy may have more difficulty, however, understanding feelings of sadness (since 'big boys don't cry'), or of fear, empathy, or caring. The emotional education of a young girl in American culture tends to be quite different. Others may tell her that she is 'bad' when she expresses angry feelings, so that she may have great difficulty understanding the subjective experience associated with anger. She may conceivably come to deny or repress such feelings, or feel anxious about them, or label them as 'bad' and feel guilty about them.

It is interesting in this regard that the personality patterns associated with cardiovascular disease, cancer, and psychosomatic illness have in common problems of emotional expression. These could lead to disruptions in the social biofeedback process, inadequate or incorrect emotional education, and consequent problems of self-regulation, that encourage different sorts of disease processes.

SUBJECTIVE EXPERIENCE

The foregoing arguments have assumed that emotion is associated with *direct* subjective experience that does not depend upon feedback from visceral processes or expressive behavior: it is a direct subjective readout that has evolved to inform the organism about the state of certain important internal systems. A number of drives and all of the affects have such direct readouts. These are always available to consciousness, although we pay attention to them only when they are strong. Thus, we always have available feelings of hunger and thirst, warmth or coldness, happiness and anger, etc., but like the feel of our shoes on our feet this information is typically weak and repetitive and therefore ignored.

APPROACHES TO SUBJECTIVE EXPERIENCE

Subjective experience continues to be a topic of experimental and philosophical debate. There are two major lines of theory in psychology in this regard. One, stemming from the James–Lange theory, has argued that subjective experience is based upon peripheral feedback from autonomic arousal and/or expressive behavior. Such theories include the notion that emotion involves cognitive attributions about arousal (Schachter and Singer, 1962), as well as the facial feedback hypothesis (see Buck, 1980). The other line of theory stems from the Cannon–Bard 'thalamic' theory of emotion, which argues that subjective experience is based upon subcortical and/or paleocortical brain systems independent of expressive behavior and peripheral bodily responding. These theories include those of Papez (1937) and MacLean (1973), as well as the views of contemporary neuroscientists including Panksepp and Tucker (this volume). It is important to note that the development of theories along the latter line has been *progressive*, with the different accounts building upon, clarifying, and in the end supporting, one another as more is learned about the nature of the subcortical and paleocortical systems in question.

We saw above that one of the most oft-quoted studies purporting to support the James–Lange theory—the Hohmann (1966) study—has been questioned by recent findings. Also, the evidence relating to the facial feedback hypothesis has remained unconvincing to me, despite arguments to the contrary (e.g. Laird, 1984). I argue that the facial feeback hypothesis is potentially misleading, for it takes facial expression out of the social context and views it as entirely within the individual. Although some feedback from facial expression may occur and have cuing effects for the responder, I believe that the 'readout' function of facial expression is more important, and that the most important 'facial feedback' is *interpersonal* feedback from others in reaction to the responder's expressions: e.g. social biofeedback (see Buck, 1984, pp. 46–67).

While the role of peripheral feedback in emotional experience remains questionable, theories emphasizing subcortical/paleocortical mechanisms have received strong support in recent years. Research on psychoactive drugs has demonstrated that many substances appear to have *direct* effects upon subjective experience in both humans and animals. Thus, via instrumental behavior, rats can accurately 'report' on the dosage they have received of such drugs as PCP (phencyclidine, or 'angel dust'). Research on the peptides has been particularly important in this regard. Peptides have been linked with the subjective experience of, at least, pain, pleasure, sexuality, and anxiety. As noted above, there is evidence that some of these substances may be produced in such 'peripheral' systems as the immune system as well as in the central nervous system.

PERCEPTION AND SUBJECTIVE EXPERIENCE

The ecological theory of direct perception provides a useful framework for approaching subjective experience. From the ecological point of view, perceiving is the act of noticing the potential uses of objects (the activities they afford) relative to the perceiver's capabilities and needs (Neisser, 1976; Gibson, 1966, 1979). This implies that organisms simultaneously and interactively gather information external and internal to the body.

The ecological position recognizes that organisms have evolved to be responsive to very specific aspects of the total information available in the environment: they perceive those aspects of the environment that carry biologically useful information. Perceptual mechanisms 'pick up' such information directly, without the need for mediation via higher-order cognitive processes. In the words of E. J. Gibson, the perceptual process 'is not one of *construction* but of *extraction* of structured information that is present in the light, in the air, on the skin, in short, in the world' (quoted by Gibbs, 1985, p. 114). This information must be present not only 'in the light, in the air, on the skin . . . ' but also *within* the skin. This constitutes the subjective Emotion III readout of emotion (Buck, 1984, 1988).

The individual becomes increasingly efficient at noticing potentially available affordances over the course of development (Goldfield, 1983). This is the *education of attention*, and in the case of subjective experience this involves the social biofeedback process and results in emotional education. The subjective experience of internal bodily information is known directly by acquaintance, but the emotional education process results in the organization of portions of this direct knowledge into knowledge by description. This process may be clarified by considering recent studies of prosopagnosia.

PROSOPAGNOSIA

Agnosias in general are modality-specific disorders of recognition that are not due to sensory dysfunction or unfamiliarity with the stimulus: the normal perceptual process is somehow 'stripped of meaning' (Bauer, 1984, p. 457). Damasio, Damasio, and Van Hoesen (1982) suggest that the primary defect in agnosia is a failure of the stimulus to evoke an appropriate acquired context of pertinent and previously stored information regarding that *particular* stimulus. Elementary perception is intact, and the patient has a store of contextually related memories that can be evoked, but that stimulus can no longer evoke those memories.

The nature of Prosopagnosia

In prosopagnosia the patient is unable to recognize faces. Such patients know that a face is a face. They can name it as such, and can name the parts of the face and point to them. Yet they cannot recognize a familiar face when asked to identify photographs of faces of family members and/or famous persons (see for example Etcoff, 1984). Damasio *et al.* (1982) note that patients become unable to identify familiar animals: thus a bird watcher became unable to identify birds, and a farmer could not identify his cows. Also, patients may be unable to recognize familiar cars. Patients have no difficulty recognizing birds, or cows, or cars in general: the defect involves the recognition of a familiar individual example. 'Recognition of the generic class to which the stimulus belongs presents no difficulty, but recognition of an individual member of that class, whose identity had previously been learned, is impaired' (Damasio *et al.*, 1982, p. 337).

There is evidence that the prosopagnosic patient may discriminate faces on an 'unconscious' level. Bauer (1984) showed a male prosopagnosic patient pictures of family members and famous personalities and gave him five names, one of which was correct. The patient was unable to recognize any of the pictures, and performed at a chance level when given multiple choices. However, the patient did show electrodermal responses to the correct names, suggesting that the facial identity was 'recognized' at some level.

Bauer's result was replicated on two female patients by Tranel and Damasio (1985), who related such 'covert' recognition to a model of face recognition and learning (Damasio *et al.*, 1982). This model suggests that conscious face recognition involves four steps: (1) perception; (2) the arousal by the perceptual event of a 'template' based on the elaboration of past visual perceptions of that face; (3) the activation of multimodal memories associated with the face; and (4) a conscious 'readout' including feelings of familiarity and an ability to give pertinent verbal accounts or to perform relevant nonverbal matching tasks. Tranel and Damasio (1985) suggest that prosopagnosia is associated with a defect in the template system: that prosopagnosia involves 'a complete or partial blocking of the activation that normally would be triggered by template matching' (p. 1454). They suggest further that the blocking of the associated memories does not block the autonomic response, resulting in a kind of 'unconscious perception.'

'Unconscious Perception'

There is other evidence of 'unconscious perception.' People can respond appropriately to stimuli presented at exposure levels below absolute threshold (Lazarus and McCleery, 1951), show preferences for stimuli not consciously recognized (Kunst–Wilson and Zajonc, 1980), recognize unattended material that cannot be verbally identified (Allport, Antonis, and Reynolds, 1972), become conditioned (i.e. conditioned taste aversion) while unconscious (Garcia and Rusiniak, 1980). There is recent evidence that the individual may respond to the emotional meaning of statements presented at duration levels below absolute threshold (i.e. in males the statement 'Mommy and I are one'). Such exposure may even create strong emotional reactions—possibly activating 'unconscious symboitic-like fantasies'—that are not activated by the same statement if presented normally (Silverman and Weinberger, 1985, p. 1296).

Prosopagnosia and the Nature of Knowledge

The shifts in processing at the different steps of the Damasio *et al.* (1982) model may represent a basic change in the way that the facial stimulus is 'known.' Specifically, I suggest that it represents a shift from knowledge by acquaintance to knowledge by description (see Buck, 1984, pp. 11–15, 1985).

This view of prosopagnosia has interesting implications when applied to the controversy between Lazarus and Zajonc regarding the 'primacy' of affect and cognition. I suggest that this controversy really involves a disagreement about the definition of 'cognition' which can be resolved if the distinction between knowledge by acquaintance and knowledge by description is accepted (see Buck, 1985, note 3).

This view of prosopagnosia is also relevant to the doubts of some philosophers about the reality of 'subjective experience.' Toward the end of *The Brown Book*, Ludwig Wittgenstein discussed 'the feeling of familiarity,' arguing that 'after abstracting all those experiences which we might call the experiences of expressing the feeling,' no essential feeling remains (1965, p. 184). 'I am inclined to suggest to you,' he continues, 'to put the expression of our experience in place of the experience.' However, it is clear that the loss in prosopagnosia cannot be regarded as a loss in expression. Instead, it appears to be a loss of a direct readout of information relevant to the recognition process that we in our culture have come to describe as 'a feeling of familiarity.' It will, of course, differ in quality depending upon the nature of the multimodal memories associated with the familiar object— thus the experience of seeing a dearly loved one will differ from the experience of seeing a pesky student coming to argue about a grade—but I submit that there *is* an essential feeling of recognition that is known by acquaintance, just as there are 'essential feelings' associated with certain drives, affects, and cognitive events. This is the Emotion III readout process (Buck, 1985).

THE AMYGDALAE AND APPRAISAL

Recent work on the amygdalae suggests that these structures contribute to the appraisal process. For example, LeDoux (1986) noted that bilateral amygdalectomy results in a dissociation between the sensory–perceptual and affective qualities of stimuli: 'objects are still perceived and emotional reactions are still expressed, but these functions are no longer coupled in the brain' (LeDoux, 1986, p. 341). An example is the Kluver–Bucy syndrome, where an amygdalectomized monkey might mouth a burning match or innately-feared snake.

LeDoux suggests that the amygdalae receive sensory input directly from the thalamus, and also from the neocortex, but that the thalamic pathway is several synapses shorter. The early input may 'prime the area to receive the better analyzed neocortical inputs, providing a crude picture of what is to come, narrowing the affective possibilities, and perhaps even organizing possible and actual responses' (LeDoux, 1986, pp. 345-6). If the system is disrupted, as in bilateral amygdalectomy, the sensory–perceptual qualities of stimuli are divorced from their emotional qualities in a kind of 'emotional agnosia.'

A MODEL OF APPRAISAL

The models of appraisal suggested by Damasio *et al.* (1982) and LeDoux (1986) stem from very different sorts of data—largely from clinical observations on humans in the former case and from animal experimentation in the latter. Nevertheless, it is possible that they can be combined into an integrated view of appraisal.

This model of appraisal is presented in Figure 8.4. Sensory stimuli act first on the reticular activating system, which is involved in the general cortical arousal to sudden and/or strong stimuli. Sensory pathways also project directly to the hypothalamus and also synapse in the thalamus, and information is passed to the amygdalae and other limbic system structures which are involved in the response to the conditioned or innate emotional qualities in the stimulus information. This impact of stimuli upon subcortical and paleocortical systems—including the reticular formation and amygdalae—may correspond to the initial steps in the Damasio *et al.* (1982) model: perception and template matching. The activation of these systems could in itself trigger autonomic responding.

The sensory pathways proceed to the primary sensory areas of the cortex, where they result in knowledge by acquaintance of the stimulus. Input from subcortical and paleocortical systems results in a simultaneous knowledge by acquaintance of the subjective emotional response to the stimulus. Together these lead to the arousal of appropriate templates, which in turn activate appropriate multimodal memories. The conscious readout of the memory activation, with associated feelings of familiarity and ability to give appropriate responses (i.e. verbal descriptions) constitutes the knowledge-by-description of the stimulus. This corresponds to the two subsequent steps of the Damasio *et al.* model: the activation of multimodal memories and the conscious 'readout' of feelings of familiarity that appear to be disrupted in cases of agnosia. There is also a knowledge-by-description of the nature of the emotional response to the stimulus, which is constrained by emotional education.

The term 'filter' may be appropriate in describing the earliest—subcortical and paleocortical—phases in this process (see Buck, 1986). There is evidence that sensory information is processed at the cortex only if it is accompanied by nonspecific influences from, for example, the reticular activating system (Lindsley, 1960). We are not aware of the feel of comfortable shoes because even though the

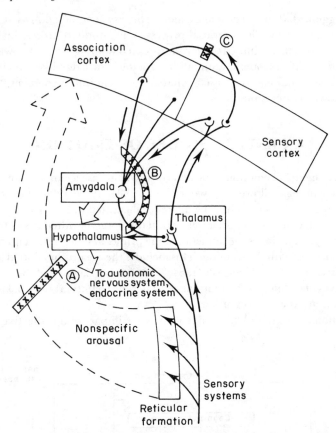

Figure 8.4. A general model of appraisal. Disconnection syndromes affect different aspects of the appraisal process. Cerveau isole (A) cuts the reticular formation from the rest of the brain, resulting in coma. Bilateral amydalectomy (B) results in the Kluver–Bucy syndrome, a kind of 'emotional agnosia.' The cutting of connections between a sensory area and relevant association areas results in modality-specific agnosia. Disconnection between the sensory cortex and the association cortex at (C) results in agnosia.
[From Figure 9.1 in Buck, R. (1988) *Human Motivation and Emotion*, 2nd edn. New York: John Wiley. Used by permission.]

sensory information about the feel of those shoes is available to the brain, it is usually ignored. The reticular system cannot *know* what the sensory stimuli are like; rather, certain decision rules are used to pass the information on or not. Thus, if the stimulation is weak or repetitive, it is ignored. Similar basic decision rules may be involved in attaching emotional relevance to incoming stimuli. Some stimuli have acquired importance during evolution: for example, expressive displays in the process of ritualization (Eibl–Eibesfeldt, 1970). Other stimuli acquire importance during individual development: i.e. a stimulus that evokes a conditioned emotional response (CER).

This suggests that subcortical and paleocortical systems function as 'filters' that determine the input to the appraisal process. The appraisal process involves the integration of this filtered information: combining the knowledge-by-acquaintance of the incoming stimulation with the knowledge-by-acquaintance of the subjective emotional response to that stimulation into a conscious 'readout' that is known by description.

A GENERAL MODEL OF EMOTION

The general model of emotion to be described will arouse feelings of familiarity in the reader who has followed my work (Buck, 1984, 1985, 1986), but it perhaps should be repeated once again. The model is illustrated in Figure 8.5. It assumes that internal or external stimuli impinge initially upon the 'filter' that I have been discussing, which includes the influence of the primes and of relevant learning (i.e. CERs) associated with the stimulus. This includes the area within dotted lines, and is a 'cognitive' process in Lazarus's (1984) sense but not Zajonc's (1984) sense: that is, it involves knowledge by acquaintance (syncretic cognition) but not knowledge by description (analytic cognition).

The action of this initial 'filter' determines the impact of the affective stimulus

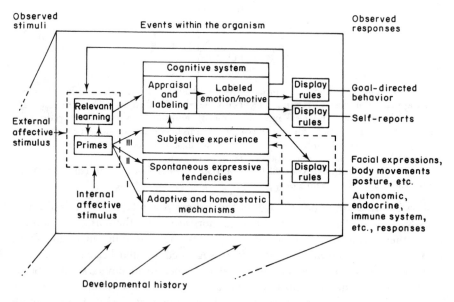

Figure 8.5. A general model of emotion. See text for description.
[From Figure 1.6 in R. Buck (1988) *Human Motivation and Emotion*, 2nd edn. New York: John Wiley. Used by permission.]

for that particular individual in that particular situation. That impact is registered by the primes in terms of peripheral physiological responses (Emotion I), expressive behavior tendencies (Emotion II), and direct subjective emotional experience (Emotion III). Subjective experience may also occur indirectly via feedback from the peripheral physiological systems and expressive behaviors, although I believe that the Emotion III readout is more important in most cases. The impact of the stimulus is also registered in analytic cognition, where the individual appraises the stimulus on the basis of the syncretic knowledge-by-acquaintance of the nature of the stimulus *and* the nature of the subjective experience associated with it. The result of the appraisal process is that the stimulus and the emotional reaction become known by description.

This gives the individual the basis for appropriate goal-directed coping responses and self-reports describing his or her response to the stimulus. These overt responses are, of course, subject to learned display rules that are appropriate in that situation. These may also affect expressive tendencies, although the individual's 'true feelings' may leak out in spontaneous expressive behaviors that are not consciously monitored. The 'true feelings' may also be manifest in peripheral physiological responses.

The interaction between the primes and the cognitive system presented in Figure 8.5 may be applied both to humans and to other animals. The critical distinguishing quality of human emotion is linguistic competence, which allows humans to organize our experience of both internal and external reality in ways fundamentally different from those of other animals (see Buck, 1984, 1985, 1986, 1988). It also frees human behavior from biological determinism and gives us the reality, not the illusion, of choice. Human behavior is free of the system of biological checks and balances that has characterized the evolution of life on the planet. The resulting human activities have altered the balance of nature, and threaten to overturn it in fundamental ways.

We are now at a point where we must choose the future course of the life process that began on this small planet perhaps 3.5 billion years ago. Thus far, many of these collective choices have been made with short-sighted and selfish ignorance. In a review of the state of the earth in the year 1987, Postel and Brown (1987) pointed out that human activities have brought about complex and pressing issues that must be addressed on a global scale. They argued that a sustainable future requires that humanity simultaneously must arrest the build-up of carbon dioxide in the atmosphere, protect the ozone layer, boost energy efficiency, develop renewable energy resources, and stop the growth of the human population. They note that no previous generation has faced such issues. 'Preceding generations have always been concerned about the future, but we are the first to be faced with decisions that will determine whether the earth our children will inherit will be habitable' (p. 48). It is indeed ironic that humanity's greatest achievement— linguistic competence and the freedom that it affords—may be the source of our destruction, if not in a bang, in a whimper.

In summary, this chapter presented a general view of motivation, emotion, and cognition, with particular reference to the peripheral, expressive, and subjective aspects of emotion. Recent evidence questioning traditional assumptions about the role of bodily feedback in emotional experience was presented, although there is new evidence that emotional experience may be affected by another peripheral system: the immune system. The effects of stress were reviewed, and the suggestion made that emotional expression and communication have functions of emotional self-regulation as well as social coordination. Specifically, it was argued that spontaneous communication is intimately involved with the exploration of the information present within the body: subjectively experienced motives and emotions. For this reason, spontaneous communication is directly involved in bioregulatory processes, and social biofeedback plays a major bioregulatory role. The nature of subjective experience was discussed with particular reference to the phenomenon of agnosia. A model of appraisal was presented in which the immediate experience of the object is combined with the immediate experience of the subjective emotional response to that object to produce knowledge-by-description of that object and the emotional response. It was suggested that prior to appraisal directly perceived information is 'filtered' by neurochemical systems that use relatively specific decision rules to pass on information to higher centres.

REFERENCES

Alexander, F. (1950) *Psychosomatic Medicine*. New York: Norton.

Allport, D. A., Antonis, B., and Reynolds, P. (1972) On the division of attention: a disproof of the single-channel hypothesis. *Quarterly Journal of Experimental Psychology*, **24**, 225–35.

Anderson, C. D. (1981) Expression of affect and physiological response in psychosomatic patients. *Journal of Psychosomatic Research*, **25**, 143–9.

Baltrusch, H. J., and Waltz, M. (1985) Cancer from a biobehavioral and social epidemiological perspective. *Social Science and Medicine*, **20**, 789–94.

Bammer, K., and Newberry, B. H. (1982) *Stress and Cancer*. Toronto: C. J. Hogrefe.

Bauer, R. M. (1984) Autonomic recognition of names and faces in prosopagnosia: a neuropsychological application of the guilty knowledge test. *Neuropsychologia*, **22**, 456–69.

Benson, H. (1975) *The Relaxation Response*. New York: William Morrow.

Buck, R. (1971) Differences in social learning underlying overt-behavioral, subjective, and physiological responses to emotion. Paper read at the Midwestern Psychological Association Convention, Detroit.

Buck, R. (1979) Individual differences in nonverbal sending accuracy and electrodermal responding: the externalizing–internalizing dimension. In R. Rosenthal (Ed.), *Skill in Nonverbal Communication: Individual Differences*. Cambridge, MA: Oelgeschlager, Gunn, & Hain.

Buck, R. (1980) Nonverbal behavior and the theory of emotion: the facial feedback hypothesis. *Journal of Personality and Social Psychology*, **38**, 811–24.

Buck, R. (1984) *The Communication of Emotion*. New York: Guildford Press.

Buck, R. (1985) Prime theory: an integrated view of motivation and emotion. *Psychological Review*, **92**, 389–413.

Buck, R. (1986) The psychology of emotion. In J. LeDoux and W. F. Hirst (Eds), *Mind and Brain: Dialogues between Cognitive Psychology and Neuroscience*. New York: Cambridge University Press.

Buck, R. (1988) *Human Motivation and Emotion*, 2nd Edn. New York: John Wiley.

Cannon, W. B. (1915) *Bodily Changes in Pain, Hunger, Fear, and Rage*. New York: Appleton.

Chwalisz, K., Drener, E., and Gallagher, D. (1988) Autonomic arousal feedback and emotional experience: evidence from the spinal cord injured. *Journal of Personality and Social Psychology*, **54**, 820–8.

Cordes, C. (1985) Research news from the BSA mini-convention: Early development. *ASA Monitor*. **16**(10), 10.

Damasio, A. R., Damasio, H., and Van Hoesen, G. W. (1982) Prosopagnosia: anatomic basis and behavioral mechanisms. *Neurology*, **32**, 331–41.

Darwin, C. (1872) *Expression of the Emotions in Man and Animals*. New York: Philosophical Library Edition published 1955.

Eibl–Eibesfeldt, I. (1970) *Ethology: The Biology of Behavior*. New York: Holt, Rinehart, & Winston.

Etcoff, N. L. (1984) Selective attention to facial identity and facial emotion. *Neuropsychologia*, **22**, 281–95.

Ford, M. R. (1982) Biofeedback training for headaches, Reynaud's disease, essential hypertension, and irritable bowel syndrome: a review of the long-term follow-up literature. *Biofeedback and Self-Regulation*, **7**, 521–35.

Friedman, M., and Rosenman, R. H. (1974). *Type-A Behavior and Your Heart*. New York: Knopf.

Garcia, J., and Rusiniak, K. W. (1980) What the nose learn from the mouth. In D. Muller–Schwarze and R. M. Silverstein (Eds), *Chemical Signals*. New York: Plenum Press.

Gautier, J., Bois, R., Allaire, D., and Drolet, M. (1981) Evaluation of skin temperature biofeedback training at two different sites for migraine. *Journal of Behavioral Medicine*, **4**, 407–49.

Gibbs, J. C. (1985) The problem of knowledge, still: A review of Liben's *Piaget and the Foundations of Knowledge Merrill–Palmer Quarterly*, **31**, 11–15.

Gibson, J. J. (1966) *The Senses Considered as Perceptual Systems*. Boston: Houghton–Mifflin.

Gibson, J. J. (1979) *An Ecological Approach to Visual Perception*. Boston: Houghton–Mifflin.

Goldfield, E. (1983) The ecological approach to perceiving as a foundation for understanding the development of knowing in infancy. *Developmental Review*, **3**, 371–404.

Greer, S., and Watson, M. (1985) Towards a psychobiological model of cancer: psychological considerations. *Social Science and Medicine*, **20**, 773–7.

Grossarth–Maticek, R., Kanazin, D. T., Schmidt, P., and Vetter, H. (1982) Psychosomatic factors in the process of cancerogenesis: theoretical models and empirical results. *Psychotherapy and Psychosomatics*, **38**, 284–302.

Grossarth–Maticek, R., Bastisams, J., and Kanazin, D. T. (1985) Psychosocial factors as strong predictors of mortality from cancer, ischaemic heart disease and stroke: the Yugoslav Prospective Study. *Journal of Psychosomatic Research*, **29**, 167–76.

Hess, W. R. (1957) *Functional Organization of the Diencephalon*. New York: Grune & Stratton.

Hofer, M. A. (1984) Relationships as regulators: a psychobiologic perspective on bereavement. *Psychosomatic Medicine*, **46**, 183–98.

Hohmann, G. W. (1966) Some effects of spinal cord lesions on experienced emotional feelings. *Psychophysiology*, **3**, 143–56.

James, W. (1980) *The Principles of Psychology*, Vol. 1. New York: Henry Holt.

Kiecolt–Glaser, J. K., Garner, W., Speicher, C., Penn, G., Holliday, J., and Glaser, R. (1984) Psychosocial modifiers of immunocompetence in medical students. *Psychosomatic Medicine*, **46**, 7–13.

Kleinginna, P. R., and Kleinginna, A. M. (1981) A categorized list of emotion definitions, with suggestions for a consensual definition. *Motivation and Emotion*, **5**, 348–379.

Kunst–Wilson, W. R., and Zajonc, R. B. (1980) Affective discrimination of stimuli that cannot be recognized. *Science*, **207**, 557–8.

Laird, J. D. (1984) The real role of facial response in the experience of emotion: a reply to Tourangeau and Ellsworth, and others. *Journal of Personality and Social Psychology*, **47**, 909–17.

Lazarus, R. S. (1984) On the primacy of cognition. *American Psychologist*, **39**, 124–9.

Lazarus, R. S., and McCleary, R. A. (1951) Autonomic discrimination without awareness: a study of subception. *Psychological Review*, **58**, 113–22.

LeDoux, J. (1986) A neurobiological view of the psychology of emotion. In J. LeDoux and W. Hirst (Eds), *Mind and Brain: Dialogues Between Cognitive Psychology and Neuroscience*. New York: Cambridge University Press.

Lindsley, D. B. (1960) Attention consciousness, sleep, and wakefulness. In J. Field, H. W. Magoun, and V. E. Hall (Eds), *Handbook of Physiology, Neurophysiolog, III*. Washington, DC: American Physiological Society.

Lowe, J., and Carroll, D. (1985) The effects of spinal injury on the intensity of emotional experience. *British Journal of Clinical Psychology*, **24**, 135–6.

MacLean, P. D. (1973) *A Triune Concept of the Brain and Behaviour*. Toronto: University of Toronto Press.

Maier, I., and Müller, D. G. (1986) Sexual pheromones in algae. *Biological Bulletin*, **170**, 145–76.

McCleiland, D. C. (1982) The need for power, sympathetic activation, and illness. *Motivation and Emotion*, **6**, 31–41.

Neisser, V. (1976) *Cognition and Reality*. San Francisco: W. H. Freeman.

Papez, J. W. (1937) A proposed mechanism of emotion. *Archives of Neurology and Psychiatry*, **38**, 725–43.

Pert, C. (1985) Neuropeptides and their receptors: substrates for the biochemistry of emotion. Keynote address at the inagural meeting of the International Society for Research on Emotions. Harvard University, 25, June 1985.

Pettingale, K. W. (1985) Towards a psychobiological model of cancer: biological considerations. *Social Science and Medicine*, **20**, 779–87.

Postel, S., and Brown, L. R. (1987) State f the earth 1987. *Natural History*, **96**(4), 41–8.

Renneker, R. (1981) Cancer and psychotherapy. In J. G. Goldberg (Ed.), *Psychotherapeutic Treatment of Cancer Patients*. New York: Free Press.

Schachter, S., and Singer, J. (1962) Cognitive, social and physiological determinants of emotional state. *Psychological Review*, **69**, 379–99.

Shekelle, R. B., Raynor, W. J., Ostfeld, A. M., Garron, D. C., Bieliauskas, L. A., Liu, S. C., Maliza, C., and Paul, O. (1981) Psychological depression and 17-year risk of death from cancer. *Psychosomatic Medicine*, **43**, 117–25.

Sifneos, P. E. (1967) Clinical observations on some patients suffering from a variety of psychosomatic diseases. *Acta Medicine Psychosomatic* **I**, 1–10.

Sifneos, P. E. (1973) The prevalence of 'alexithymic' characteristics in psychosomatic patients. *Psychotherapy and Psychosomatics*, **22**, 255–262.

Silverman, L. H., and Weinberger, J. (1985) Mommy and I are one: implications for psychotherapy. *American Psychologist*, **1985** 1296–1305.

TenHouten, W. D., Hoppe, K. D., Bogen, J. E., and Walter, D. O. (1985a) Alexithymia and the split brain, I. *Psychotherapy and Psychosomatics*, **43**, 202–8.

TenHouten, W. D., Hoppe, K. D., Bogen, J. E., and Walter, D. O. (1985b) Alexithymia and the split brain, II. *Psychotherapy and Psychosomatics*, **44**, 1–5.

TenHouten, W. D., Hoppe, K. D., Bogen, J. E., and Walter, D. O. (1985c) Alexithymia and the split brain, III. *Psychotherapy and Psychosomatics*, **44**, 89–94.

TenHouten, W. D., Hoppe, K. D., Bogen, J. E., and Walter, D. O. (1985d) Alexithymia and the split brain, IV. *Psychotherapy and Psychosomatics*, **44**, 113–21.

Tranel, D., and Damasio, A. R. (1985) Knowledge without awareness: an autonomic index of facial recognition by prosopagnosics. *Science*, **228**, 1453–54.

Tucker, D. M. (1981) Lateral brain function, emotion, and conceptualization. *Psychological Bulletin*. **89**, 19–46.

Wilson, E. O. (1975) *Sociobiology: The New Synthesis*. Cambridge, MA: Belknap.

Wittgenstein, L. (1958) *The Blue and the Brown Books*. New York: Philosophical Library Edition published 1965.

Zajonc, R. B. (1984) On the primacy of affect. *American Psychologist*, **39**, 117–23.

PART 4

AROUSAL AND SOCIAL PROCESSES

Introduction

As we move from a primarily biopsychological, intra-individual focus on the processes underpinning and accompanying emotion to a consideration of more interpersonal matters, one important intermediate issue concerns the role of arousal in behaviours that have some social content or social significance. The next three chapters all deal with the relationship between social processes and arousal.

   In the first of these chapters (Chapter 9, *Aggression and sex: independent and joint operations*) Zillmann first analyses aggressive and sexual behaviours separately, examining their functions and their psychophysiological manifestations, and then proceeds to an analysis of the degree to which such behaviours have related or joint functions and confounded psychophysiological manifestations. He presents theoretical and empirical grounds for believing that aggression can facilitate sexual behaviour and that sexual arousal can facilitate aggression. A consideration of the psychophysiological linkages between sex and aggression at each of several levels leads to the conclusion that sexual behaviour shares with the other 'emergency' reactions (fight and flight) sufficient sympathetic and parasympathetic linkages to warrant the motion of a fight–flight–coition trichotomy, within which arousal from one emotion will facilitate another later emotion, or arousal from one subsidiary emotion will facilitate another dominant emotion. Zillmann then reviews evidence on behavioural interdependencies between aggressive reactions and sex and concludes that while there is ample evidence that sexual arousal facilitates later agonistic behaviours there is, as yet, rather less support for the contention that agonistic reactions facilitate later sexual arousal. With regard to the important question of whether aggressive actions strengthen sexual excitement, Zillmann argues that progress in research on this complex issue has been hampered by the near-exclusive focus on genital measures of sexual excitement; greater attention to the sympathetic component of sexual excitedness should promote our understanding of the processes governing the interdependence of aggression and sex.

While Zillmann's chapter focuses on the arousal processes that influence behaviours directed at others, Geen and Bushman (Chapter 10, *The arousing effects of social presence*) address the effects of the presence of others on individual arousal. These effects are considered by means of reviewing the evidence from three lines of research: social facilitation, the psychology of affiliation, and the effects of population density and crowding. Various theoretical accounts of the facilitating or impairing effects of social presence on task performance accord in attributing a key role to elevated drive or arousal. However, Geen and Bushman's review of the pertinent evidence leads them to conclude that there is little by way of consistent empirical support for the view that the presence of others increases arousal. Research on the psychology of affiliation was stimulated by observations that the desire to affiliate with others is enhanced by fear manipulations. One type of explanation for such findings is that the presence of another person serves to reduce fear, and Geen and Bushman review the psychophysiological evidence relevant to this argument. They conclude that the presence of others can reduce arousal when the individual is exposed to threatening or fear-arousing conditions, but that social presence tends to result in *elevated* arousal when the individual is exposed to potentially embarrassing or humiliating circumstances. Research on the impact of crowding has tended to be reasonably consistent in showing that both social and spatial density can result in heightened arousal. Geen and Bushman conclude by noting the lack of integration across these three lines of research, and point to a number of convergent findings which suggest that attempts at such integration may prove to be profitable.

In the third chapter in this part of the book (Chapter 11, *Arousal theory and stress*) Weisse, Davidson, and Baum examine the role played by arousal in mediating the short-term and longer-term effects of stress. The authors begin by analysing definitions of arousal used by stress researchers, and note that stress is operationalized in widely varying ways by different researchers, with measurement techniques ranging from self-report to hormonal assays. The authors argue for a multidimensional conception of arousal and, therefore, for a multimethod approach to its measurement. They proceed to consider the relationship between arousal and stress, and note that different theorists are in broad agreement that arousal is a central component of the stress response: many would contend that it is a necessary but insufficient condition for stress. The impact of stress on illness has often been accounted for in terms of arousal; Weisse *et al.* review evidence relating to the possible impact of stress on cardiovascular disease, gastrointestinal disturbance, and immune system disorders. In each case there is evidence that physical disorders can be initiated or exacerbated by the sympathetic and/or pituitary–adrenocortical arousal that tends to occur under stressful circumstances—although the pathways by which these effects come about are not always known. Finally, Weisse *et al.* consider the consequences of chronic exposure to stressors, by reviewing research on post-traumatic stress disorder, on the residents living in the vicinity of Three Mile Island, and on living in a crowded neighbourhood. These chronically stressed groups have been found to differ from control groups on various psychophysiological indices. Heightened arousal characterizes the stressed groups, although this is sometimes evident in baseline or resting measures and in other cases only apparent in response to a new stressor. The functional significance of either elevated baseline arousal or increased reactivity to stressors remains unclear, but further study of the arousal changes associated with exposure to stress nevertheless provides a useful, and perhaps indispensable, approach to understanding the means by which stress adversely affects physical health.

Chapter 9

Aggression and Sex: Independent and Joint Operations

Dolf Zillmann
Indiana University

ABSTRACT

In this chapter, the functions of aggressive and sexual behaviors are at first analyzed independently. So are the psychophysiological manifestations of these behaviors. Thereafter, the analysis focuses on related and joint functions, and on confounded psychophysiological manifestations. A biopsychological framework for linkages between aggressive and sexual behaviors is developed. Commonalities in the psychophysiological control and mediation of these behaviors are then detailed. Central, autonomic, and endocrine mechanisms are considered. Commonalities are also traced in behavioral manifestations and in the functions they serve. Pertinent research findings are reviewed, and the mechanisms of independent and joint aggressive and sexual behaviors are evaluated in the light of the evidence. The discussion of findings highlights the conditions under which agonistic behaviors are facilitated by preceding or concurrent sexual behaviors, and the conditions under which sexual behaviors are facilitated by preceding or concurrent aggressive behaviors.

FUNCTIONS AND MANIFESTATIONS

AGGRESSIVE BEHAVIOR

It is commonplace to say that animals fight over food, mate, and shelter (e.g. Hinde, 1970; Johnson, 1972; Scott, 1973). The scarcity of resources within these

Handbook of Social Psychophysiology, Edited by H. Wagner and A. Manstead,
© 1989 John Wiley & Sons Ltd

domains assures competition and conflict; and if conflict cannot be resolved by nonaggressive means, intraspecific and, to a lesser degree, interspecific, aggression results. Predatory aggression must be considered the exception. It is activated by physical changes that result from food deprivation, and it does not generally result from social conflict over resources.

The common characteristic of aggressive behaviors is that they constitute efforts at taking from other organisms something that these organisms are not predisposed to surrender—be it life, food, mate, or shelter. This common characteristic is, in fact, the critical definitional criterion of aggression as pain- and injury-inflicting behavior (Zillmann, 1979). But notwithstanding the common element of coercion, aggression is obviously multifaceted in terms of both the conditions that are likely to evoke the behavior in question and the manifestations of that behavior.

Numerous typologies have been offered to distinguish between the many functions of aggression. We shall discuss only those that directly bear on psychophysiological considerations.

Moyer (1971) proposed a widely adopted classification in which eight types of aggression are separated: *predatory, intermale, fear-induced, irritable, territorial, maternal, instrumental*, and *sex-related*. Each and every type is thought to have its own, unique, autonomous, central representation. Such a conceptualization implies that for each type of aggressive behavior there exists a class of external stimuli and/or internal states (such as hormonal conditions) that activates a specific type of aggression that then dominates behavioral expression. Sexual behavior is presumed to be organized analogously. In this scheme of things, aggression of one type may rapidly follow aggression of another type, and sexual behavior may rapidly follow aggression, or vice versa. Admixtures of discretely elicited aggressive and sexual actions, fleeting as they may be, are thus conceivable. But because of the dominance of a particular type of behavior at any given time, aggression and sex are not expected to occur in fused form. Specifically, physiological processes by which the activation of one kind of behavior might coactivate another kind are not considered and are implicitly denied.

In the study of human aggression, Buss (1961, 1971) and Feshbach (1964, 1970) separated *instrumental* and *angry* acts on the basis of functional considerations. Although the physiological manifestations, or concomitants, of these different types of aggression were not specified, instrumental aggression was deemed to be executed in comparatively nonaroused states ('in cold blood'), and angry aggression was viewed as thriving on arousal ('in the heat of passion'). In this separation, instrumental aggression is akin to predation, and angry aggression amounts to defensive fighting that is triggered by threats to valued commodities (i.e. life, food, mate, shelter, and their extensions in human affairs, such as health, wealth, pride, and convenience). The distinction's utility may be questioned, however, as angry aggressive acts tend to be instrumental in one way or another. For example, angry acts may ward off attacks, insure continued control over resources, or prevent a decline of self-esteem.

An alternative distinction was offered by Zillmann (1979), who focused on motivational states and their likely physiological manifestations. He distinguished between *incentive-motivated* and *annoyance-motivated* aggressive behaviors. In incentive-motivated aggression, the organism is comparatively nonagitated (akin to predation) and seeks to gain control over valued commodities that others are unwilling to yield. The actions tend to be planned and rehearsed—in short, premeditated. In annoyance-motivated aggression, by contrast, the organism is notably agitated (as in defensive fighting and angry aggression) and seeks to reduce or terminate this noxious experience by attacking the agents and conditions that can be held responsible for causing the agitation. Such action is usually not premeditated and tends to occur spontaneously in response to circumstances.

Clearly, incentive-motivated aggression is not particularly interesting in psychophysiological terms. The mediating processes are primarily, if not purely, cognitive: anticipated gratification inspires plans of action directed at the attainment of the gratifying entities. Only the anticipation of opposing actions might foster apprehensions associated with appreciable physiological changes in noncentral structures. Annoyance-motivated aggression, on the other hand, is psychophysiologically of great interest. This is because its precipitating experiences, anxiety and/or anger, are connected with marked changes in noncentral structures, especially in the autonomic nervous system, as well as with associated changes in the skeletal musculature.

The experience of annoyance, together with the performance of the aggressive behavior motivated by it, have been subjected to considerable psychophysiological scrutiny (e.g. Averill, 1982; Delgado, 1968; Grings and Dawson, 1978; Zillmann, 1979, 1983a). Several basic conclusions can be drawn from the available research.

(1) Annoyance-motivated aggressive behavior is invariably associated with marked sympathetic dominance in the autonomic nervous system.
(2) The vigor of aggressive acts tends to be a function of prevailing levels of sympathetic excitation.
(3) The experience of annoyance is also invariably associated with sympathetic dominance in the autonomic nervous system.
(4) Furthermore, the intensity of the experience of annoyance is a function of prevailing levels of sympathetic excitation, presumably because interoception of this excitation reaches awareness and is appraised as a salient part of the experience (Schachter, 1964; Zillmann, 1983b).
(5) Intensely experienced annoyance that does not find immediate expression in aggressive behavior is likely to foster aggression at a later time; the intensity of aggressive actions that are eventually taken tends to be a function of the level of excitation that prevailed at the time of the initially experienced annoyance.
(6) Ideational stimuli have some degree of control over sympathetic activity that is linked with annoyance; they can both augment and diminish such excitation.

(7) Conversely, level of excitation exerts some degree of control over cognitive processes involved in the preparation and performance of aggressive behavior; with rising levels of excitation, cognition becomes increasingly subservient to annoyance-motivated aggressive actions.

The last generalization pertains to *impulsive* aggression. Such aggression has been construed as behavior devoid of commonly applied inhibitions, if not as reflexive (Berkowitz, 1974). Alternatively, it has been viewed as behavior whose cognitive, rational governance has been lost—owing to extreme levels of excitation that foster narrow attentional focus on consummatory responses (Easterbrook, 1959)—and that is being controlled by the more archaic, robust, mechanisms of learning as a default system (Zillmann, 1979).

SEXUAL BEHAVIOR

Compared with the many causes and manifestations of aggressive behaviors, sexual behavior is rather uniform. Granted that sexuality expresses itself in highly varied forms, the sexual process proper—namely, coition in all its conceivable make-ups—is remarkably stable. Coition can be said to serve *procreation* and *recreation*. Whatever its objective, it defines a behavior sequence that is composed of ordered stages, starting with the evocation of sexual interest and ending with relaxation after consummatory responses have been performed. There has been considerable disagreement and controversy, however, about exactly what is critical in between. Ellis (1906), for instance, proposed a tumescence–detumescence sequence in a simple two-stage model. Masters and Johnson (1966), probably the most influential contemporary scholars in this field, distinguished four stages instead: excitement, plateau, orgasm, and resolution. But Robinson (1976) alleged 'groundless differentiation' between excitement and plateau and argued for unification of these phases into one phase of continuously progressing excitement. An alternative triphasic model was proposed by Kaplan (1979), who emphasized the role of libido in a desire–excitement–orgasm sequence.

Notwithstanding the quibble over the number of critical stages, all accounts of the sexual behavior sequence agree on basic observations concerning the involvement of autonomic activity (e.g. Bancroft, 1983; Masters and Johnson, 1966; Rosen and Beck, 1986).

(1) Sexual arousal manifests itself in genital vasocongestion that is, for the main part, parasympathetically mediated.
(2) Sexual arousal is accompanied by strong sympathetic discharge in more or less all nongenital structures.
(3) Upon orgasm during the so-called resolution period, genital blood flow diminishes and returns to basal levels. Sympathetic hyperactivity dissipates alongside the normalization of genital blood flow.

Research on the sexual behavior sequence has left unclear the extent to which the subjective experience of sexual excitedness is based on interoception from genital vasocongestion or from nongenital sympathetic activity. It is generally assumed that individuals report themselves sexually aroused only if marked genital blood flooding is experienced. The intensity of the subjective experience is also presumed to derive from feedback of genital blood flooding (Zuckerman, 1971). However, proprioceptive feedback from the sympathetic accompaniment of genital vasocongestion has been implicated as well (Cantor, Zillmann, and Bryant, 1975); and it is conceivable that the experienced intensity of sexual excitedness relies more on sympathetic activity than on the genital response proper because proprioceptive differentiation of the former is superior to that of the latter. Interoception (and possibly exteroception) from genital vasocongestion thus might be a necessary condition for the experience of sexual excitedness, but it may be an insufficient determinant of the experienced intensity of such excitedness.

As with the experience of annoyance, ideational stimuli have some degree of control over sexual excitedness (Byrne, 1977). Both the parasympathetic genital and the sympathetic nongenital components of sexual excitedness can be activated, augmented, impaired, or terminated by appropriate stimuli. But sexual excitedness can also be produced, and reliably so, by tactile stimulation of the genitals. The parasympathetic outflow that controls genital vasocongestion is autonomously and robustly organized in reflex arcs in the sacral portion of the spinal cord (Weiss, 1972).

Finally, extreme levels of sexual excitedness may, analogous to extreme levels of annoyance, produce a so-called 'cognitive deficit' and urge sexual consummation. But whereas for impulsive aggressive behavior it has been experimentally demonstrated that the artificial elevation of sympathetic activity to extreme levels results in failure to execute and/or apply aggression-moderating cognitions (Zillmann, Bryant, Cantor, and Day, 1975), a similar deterioration of anti-consummatory, sexuality-curtailing cognitions at high levels of sexual excitedness has often been implied or suggested (e.g. Freud, 1905/1942) but never documented.

RELATIONS BETWEEN AGGRESSION AND SEX

Aggressive and sexual activities may be contiguous, with aggression following sex or sex following aggression, or they may occur simultaneously. If contiguous, both aggressive and sexual responses may be elicited by appropriate, unique stimuli; and the initially performed behavior may be without appreciable consequences for the subsequently performed behavior. This may also be the case in situations where aggressive and sexual activities appear to occur simultaneously. It could be assumed that, in such situations, elicited behavior oscillates rapidly between aggression and sex. Assumptions of this kind have become untenable, however, in light of recent theory and research in psychophysiology. The new theorizing and research findings have made the alternative premise acceptable. This premise states (a) that an initially instigated emotional behavior will occasion physiological changes that, as a rule, do not abruptly terminate; (b) that residues of these changes will enter into subsequent behavior; and (c) that these residues will influence both the expression and the experience of the subsequent behavior (Zillmann, 1983b).

Aggressive behavior often precedes sexual activities. Intermale fighting for sexual access is an obtrusive phenomenon in many species, especially nonprimate mammals. In humans, aggression and the threat of aggression are frequently used to force noncooperative sexual partners into compliance. Rape of women by men is a common phenomenon in more or less all cultures. But aggression, or its characteristic antecedent condition, acute conflict and annoyance, may also precede sexual engagements in a noninstrumental, incidental fashion. In fact, such engagements may be part of reconciliatory efforts by intimate partners (Berscheid and Walster, 1974; Kenrick and Cialdini, 1977). In all these cases, sexual behavior and its experience are potentially influenced by the antecedent aggressive action.

Sexual activities, or intentions toward such activities, may analogously influence aggressive actions that materialize in their wake. Much violence among intimates occurs in a sexual context; it is inspired by some form of sexual dissatisfaction that escalates into acute conflict and aggressive action (Faulk, 1977; Finkelhor and Yllo, 1982).

The joint, intertwined occurrence of elements of aggressive and sexual behavior is, of course, related to their contiguous occurrence. It is distinct, however, in that it tends to be deliberately created and planned in considerable detail. Speculations about the purpose served by this fusion of aggression and sex have ranged from enhancement of the sexual experience (e.g. von Krafft–Ebing, 1886) to violent degradation by means of sexual action (e.g. Brownmiller, 1975). Descriptively speaking, sex–aggression fusion appears to be a cultural universal (Ford and Beach, 1951), at least in its modest and moderate manifestation as scratching, biting, hitting, and choking during coition. In this form, it is rather spontaneous and noncoercive. In autoerotic ventures, usually involving choking, it is obviously deliberate; it is often planned in great detail and thoroughly rehearsed (Resnick, 1972). Sadomasochistic engagements are similarly deliberate and usually consented to by all parties involved (Luria and Rose, 1979). Rape is the conspicuous exception. It is deliberate on the part of the perpetrator, but obviously not on the part of the victim. About half of all rapes that are committed are construed as efforts, on the part of the perpetrator, to achieve some sort of sex–aggression fusion. Groth (1979), for example, estimated the proportion of violent, demeaning rape in the United States at 40% and that of sadistic rape at 5%. The remainder (55%) can be classified as rape in which aggression, or the threat thereof, serve the attainment of sexual access. This type of rape has been characterized as 'sexual theft' (Langevin, 1983) and may be thought of as precipitated by incentive-motivated aggression. Such classification does not mean, however, that the sex-precipitating and sex-accompanying aggressive actions are without consequence for the sexual behavior and its experience on the part of the rapist and the victim.

PSYCHOPHYSIOLOGICAL LINKAGES

THEORETICAL REORIENTATION

As insinuated earlier, theories about aggression and sexuality tended to focus on behavioral functions; and as these functions were conspicuously different, theories evolved in relative isolation, were disparate in kind, and seemed impossible to integrate. However, physiological and psychophysiological discoveries of commonalities between aggressive and sexual behaviors virtually forced a reorientation. Clearly, if the instigation of the one type of behavior liberates physical processes that influence this type and along with it, although probably to a lesser degree, another type of behavior, theory must address such interdependencies.

Regarding possible interdependencies between aggression and sex, a new, integrative conceptual framework for theory construction has been proposed by Zillmann (1984, 1986). Building on Cannon's (1929) fight-or-flight paradigm of the emergency emotions, coition is treated as a third emergency emotion and integrated in a fight–flight–coition paradigm. The behavior-precipitating emotions in this trichotomy—namely, anger, fear, and acute sexual arousal—are all characterized by substantial to extreme sympathetic hyperactivity (Averill, 1982; Izard, 1977; Marks, 1969). Sympathetic hyperactivity is generally less pronounced in other emotions—especially in the so-called positive emotions, such as delight or joy (Grings and Dawson, 1978). Cannon's explanation for the extraordinary intensity of the coping emotions was, of course, that only they had to furnish the energy for vigorous action in fight or flight. But sexual arousal also prepares the organism for vigorous action. Additionally, sexual activities are just as catabolic as Cannon's coping emotions. Fight, flight, and coition are all behaviors that rapidly deplete energy. The stimulus conditions for all these behaviors evoke reactions designed to provide the necessary energy. And all these behaviors are phasic or episodic, in that the energy provided characteristically fuels just one behavioral engagement.

In this context, it is most informative that psychophysiological efforts to differentiate sexual arousal and other hypersympathetic emotions, using conventional measures, have failed on all counts, except for primarily parasympathetically controlled genital vasocongestion. Penile blood-volume increases in men, and the analogous response of vaginal engorgement in women, are said to be the only distinguishing indicators of sexual excitedness (e.g. Rosen and Beck, 1986; Zuckerman, 1971). But even these reactions are less specific than initially thought. Observations on men suggest that some degree of erection may occur in all hypersympathetic emotions (Gajdusek, 1970) and in response to some nonsexual stimuli (Langevin, 1983). The fact remains that sexual arousal characteristically involves a strong parasympathetically controlled response component (i.e. genital vasocongestion) and other hypersympathetic states do not. This circumstance does not, however, jeopardize proposals that project interactions between aggressive and sexual behaviors on the basis of common elements. Each and every common response component potentially exerts some degree of influence that will make the behaviors interdependent.

COMMONALITIES IN CONTROL AND MEDIATION

Aggression and sex are linked in numerous ways that pertain to psychophysiology. The most fundamental linkages have been established in neurophysiology and endocrinology. We can only indicate them here and refer the reader who is interested in a more complete exposition to other sources (e.g. Brown and Wallace, 1980; Zillmann, 1984).

Central Linkages

Research on the central representation of sexual responses in relation to aggressive ones, including fear and flight reactions, has been pioneered by MacLean (1962, 1968a, b, 1973). In studies with male nonhuman primates (MacLean and Ploog, 1962) it was found that electrical brain stimulation of loci in extreme proximity to areas that control erection also produce fight- and flight-related responses; and that stimulation of loci in extreme proximity to areas controlling fight or flight reactions likewise produce erection. Furthermore, stimulation of fight–flight areas was found to produce sexual excitedness after some time, and that stimulation of sexual areas similarly co-instigates agonistic reactions after some delay. MacLean concluded that excitation in one region, owing to proximity and interconnectedness, tends to perfuse into the other, thereby producing the characteristically deferred co-elicitation effect. More specifically, he proposed that excitation of amygdaloid structures (those thought to control fight and flight) spills over into septal structures (those thought to control sexual behavior) and vice versa. Because both amygdaloid and septal structures are immediately linked to the anterior hypothalamus, MacLean assumed that excitation originating in the amygdala recruits septal excitation along the way; he further assumed that excitation originating in the septum likewise recruits amygdaloid excitation on its path.

MacLean's theory and research not only lay the foundation for a close association between fight, flight, and coition as primary emotions, but also emphasize their adaptive significance as a unit. As he considers that amygdaloid functioning is implicated with self-preservation (through fight and flight, among other things) and septal functioning with the sustentation of the species (through sexual action and reproductive activities in a broader sense), the neural-spillage hypothesis brings the two most basic, adaptive behavioral inclinations into joint operation.

The implications for human aggression, sex, and any admixture thereof, are less clear. On the one hand, MacLean's findings and interpretations shed light on the seemingly universal involvement of sucking, biting, scratching, and bruising in coital activities. On the other, his proposals might be drawn upon to characterize all sadomasochistic behaviors, even rape in all its forms, as biologically deep-rooted and neurophysiologically founded—and hence, as quite natural and appropriate. To put matters in perspective it should be recalled that most humans manage to separate violent and sexual urges most of the time. This would seem to temper sweeping interpretations. However, it could be argued that in some individuals, by natural variation or through injury, neural conditions might be created that facilitate spillage of excitation, and that make it difficult, if not impossible, for the individuals in question to separate aggressive and sexual impulsions.

The possibility that injury to the temporal lobe and limbic system may create the so-called *erotic violence syndrome* (Langevin, 1983) has received considerable attention. It is assumed that tissue damage fosters the sprouting of collateral afferent fibers that replace and strengthen old connections and that, on occasion, establish new ones (e.g. Finger and Stein, 1982; Stein, Rosen, and Butters, 1974). The fusion of aggressive and sexual impulsion may thus be facilitated, if not created.

Recent research by Langevin and his collaborators (Langevin *et al.*, 1985; Purins and Langevin, 1985) produced findings that are consistent with such considerations. Amongst sexual aggressives, sadists exhibited comparatively frequent and substantial temporal lobe abnormalities. Numerous related investigations show, however, that temporal lobe abnormalities, especially temporal lobe epilepsy, are also associated with a variety of nonviolent sexual anomalies (Blumer, 1970; Epstein, 1969; Kolarsky, Freund, Machek, and Polak, 1967).

The study of the central representation of aggression, sex, and its fusion in humans has confronted great obstacles. Partly as a result, eclectic research has produced inconsistent findings. This situation is likely to change drastically in the near future. New technological advances in measurement technique (such as positron emission tomography and nuclear magnetic resonance scanning) have made noninvasive assessments of tissue damage possible, and provide the means for superior research in this area of psychophysiology.

Autonomic Linkages

Within the autonomic nervous system, sympathetic dominance that characterizes Cannon's coping emotions is produced by thoracolumbar outflow (Crouch, 1978; Guyton, 1972). Particularly through the lesser and least splanchnic nerves from the lower thoracic plexus, impulses from higher brain centers impact the adrenal

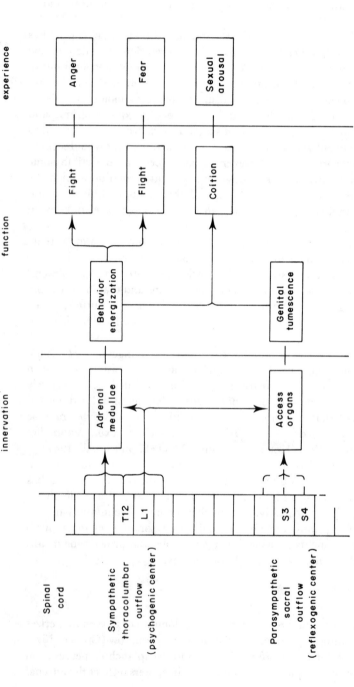

Figure 9.1. Scheme of spinal outflow in agonistic and sexual behaviors. The sexual access organs are innervated by parasympathetic fibers from the sacral nerves. The nerves constituting the reflexogenic sexual center are numbered S3 and S4 (S = sacral). The access organs are also innervated by sympathetic fibers from the thoracolumbar nerves. The nerves constituting the psychogenic sexual center are numbered T12 and L1 (T = thoracic, L = lumbar). The adrenal medullae are innervated by sympathetic fibers of the same origin: the lower thoracic nerves, especially the least splanchnic nerve from T12. Genital tumescence is thus linked to increased sympathetic excitation in the peripheral structures. Comparable sympathetic excitedness is characteristic of agonistic behaviors. Strong excitedness of this kind is capable of effecting sacral outflow that produces genital tumescence and related responses under sacral control. [Reproduced, with permission, from Zillmann, D. (1986) Coition as emotion, in D. Byrne and K. Kelley (Eds) *Alternative Approaches to the Study of Sexual Behavior*. Hillsdale, NJ: Lawrence Erlbaum Associates.]

medullae. Direct innervation by sympathetic fibers thus prompts the release of the catecholamines that mediate the general reaction of sympathetic excitedness.

Essentially the same sympathetic innervation serves sexual excitedness. Specifically, through the last thoracic and first lumbar nerves, impulses from higher centers reach the adrenal medullae, prompting catecholamine release. Most significantly, however, this outflow reaches the sexual organs as well (Crosby, Humphrey, and Lauer, 1962). The combined outflow function forms, in fact, what is called the 'psychogenic' sexual center (Weiss, 1972). Figure 9.1 shows its operation schematically. Psychogenic sexual stimulation—which translates to exposure to distal (i.e. visual and/or auditory) sexual stimuli—is therefore capable of producing both sympathetic excitedness and genital tumescence.

The obvious and confusing discrepancy between Cannon's coping emotions and sexual arousal concerns the alternative, yet primary, control of genital tumescence. Parasympathetic sacral outflow, known as the 'reflexogenic' sexual center, produces genital vasocongestion. This control, organized in spinal sexual reflexes (Bard, 1940; Beach, 1967), is also schematized in Figure 9.1. The parasympathetic innervation of the reflexogenic sexual center also exerts a degree of control over micturition and defecation (Bors and Comarr, 1971).

Mainly from research with men and women who have suffered spinal cord injuries (Weiss, 1972), the two autonomic systems controlling sexual arousal are known to be capable of rather autonomous functioning. The impairment or loss of either thoracolumbar or sacral outflow alone does not result in the loss of genital functioning. The capacity for genital tumescence is largely maintained. Intact sacral structures insure tumescence in response to appropriate tactile stimulation. Concomitant sympathetic arousal may suffer, however. Conversely, intact thoracolumbar structures mediate distal sexual stimulation and leave the sympathetic response component unimpaired, but tumescence may suffer somewhat. The functional autonomy is, of course, immaterial for individuals with unimpaired spinal and autonomic functioning. The systems simply operate in an interrelated fashion. Specifically, sympathetic outflow from the thoracolumbar cord acts *synergistically* with parasympathetic outflow from the sacral cord in producing both genital vasocongestion and sympathetic excitation in the peripheral structures.

Obviously, the joint operation of sympathetic and parasympathetic outflow differs for fight and flight, on the one hand, and sexual action, on the other. Whereas sympathetic activity seems equally involved in these behaviors, parasympathetic, sacral outflow tends to be specific to precoital and coital behaviors.

Endocrine Linkages

Adrenal functioning affects both aggressive and sexual behaviors in numerous ways. The adrenal cortex, for instance, secretes adrenal sex hormones that resemble the gonadal sex hormones, and these androgens have been found capable of potentiating both aggressive and sexual behaviors in either gender (Leshner, 1978). However, the influence of androgens is mostly *tonic* rather than phasic. It pertains to emergency situations mainly by creating favorable physical *precon*ditions for fight, flight, and coition as episodic behaviors. Whalen's (1966) concept of *arousability* relates to these preconditions. For agonistic behaviors, favorable preconditions are created through the virilization of the skeletal musculature at large (Ehrhardt, 1977). For sexual behavior, androgenization may create preconditions favorable to coital engagements by fostering penile or clitoral hypertrophy (Luttge, 1971), among other things (MacLusky and Naftolin, 1981). The adrenal cortex, furthermore, supplies glucocorticoids that provide energy for extended periods of time (Oken, 1967). The effect is again tonic and aids in furnishing the backdrop, so to speak, for behavioral emergencies such as fight, flight, or coition.

Androgens of gonadal and adrenal origin are known to have profound ontogenetic effects. The prenatal and neonatal administration of testosterone, in particular, strongly virilizes the organism (Goy, 1970; Whalen, 1971). It has remained controversial, however, whether such virilization facilitates both aggressive and sexual behaviors; and whether in the cases where it does, the facilitation is due to effects on motivation (Zillmann, 1984). Aggressiveness, for instance, might be facilitated by superior, muscular growth and by the resulting greater success in resolving aggressive encounters (Scott, 1973) rather than through greater eagerness to settle conflict by violent means.

The relationship between androgen levels and aggression is quite inconsistent. For example, Persky, Smith, and Basu (1971) reported a positive correlation between testosterone levels and aggressive personality traits in young men but not in older men. However, similar investigations by Meyer-Bahlburg, Boon, Sharma, and Edwards (1974) and by Monti, Brown, and Corriveau (1977) largely failed to show appreciable correlations. Doering, Brodie, Kraemer, Becker, and Hamburg (1974) also failed in their attempt to replicate the earlier positive findings. These investigators assessed the relationship in question both within (over a 2-month period) and across individuals. They noted some within-subject correlations but were unable to detect any other consistencies.

The elusive androgen–aggression linkage was also explored in criminal populations. Kreuz and Rose (1972), who studied this linkage in male prison inmates, were unable to demonstrate a correlation. Levels of testosterone were found to be essentially the same in aggressive and nonaggressive individuals. Ehrenkranz, Bliss, and Sheard (1974), on the other hand, did observe a reliable relationship between circulating testosterone and aggressiveness in such a population. Kreuz and Rose (1972), furthermore, classified their subjects on the basis of the extent to which the crimes that led to imprisonment entailed violence. Prisoners who had committed violent crimes proved to have higher testosterone levels than prisoners who had not employed violence during the commission of their crimes. Clearly, this finding is correlational and does not implicate a causal connection between testosterone level and the propensity for violent crime. It is conceivable that the relatively higher androgen levels resulted from the fact of earlier and longer incarceration, and from the special attention and corrective support that is usually afforded to prisoners with histories of violence.

Rada, Laws, and Kellner (1976) conducted an investigation on imprisoned rapists, in which subjects were similarly classified according to the degree of violence involved in their transgressions. The most violent men proved to have the highest levels of circulating testosterone. The correlation of androgen levels and violence employed was insignificant across rapists and nonrapists, however. The fact that especially violent rapists exhibited high androgen levels is again not conclusive, as it may result from special treatment during imprisonment; and the lack of reliable correlations further attests to the instability of the presumed correspondence between androgen and aggression. A similar investigation by Langevin *et al.* (1985) produced quite different results. Levels of both testosterone and androstenedione in sadists and normals did not appreciably differ, but tended to be high in nonsadistic sexual aggressives.

Studies on the short-term correspondence between androgen levels and aggressiveness appear to have yielded less conflicting results overall, but also fail to implicate a linkage between androgens, on the one hand, and aggression and sex, on the other. Scaramella and Brown (1978), for example, found testosterone levels to vary with aggressiveness in male hockey players. Mazur and Lamb (1980) observed that in young men, testosterone levels increased upon scoring decisive victories in tennis matches. No such increase occurred after matches that, although won, had been closely contested. Upon losing, testosterone levels declined. In a related study, Elias (1981) found that in winners of college wrestling matches testosterone levels did rise above the levels in losers. The Mazur–Lamb study contained an additional demonstration: success by chance (winning in a lottery) proved to be without appreciable effect on testosterone levels; effortful personal achievement (graduation from medical school), in contrast, elevated them markedly. Studies on stress experienced in demanding training programs, showing declining testosterone levels (Kreuz, Rose, and Jennings, 1972), appear to complement the observations concerning achievement and triumph.

Findings such as these have been interpreted as showing that a rise in social status that is accomplished through assertiveness and aggressive action occasions testosterone release; and it has been speculated (Kemper, 1986) that this release will carry with it an increase in libido and sexual activity. Such speculation may hold great intuitive appeal because the aggression–sex connection in question would provide an elegant explanation, in terms of behavioral economy, of the fighting for sexual access in many species—the loser in intermale skirmishes would be pacified by reduced sex drive; the victor benefits from the androgen rush that helps him to overcome exhaustion and pursue his reproductive calling. The biological analogue can also be used to project coital engagements as efforts in which dominance is to be established. The androgen rush triggered by sexual stimuli can be viewed as motivating aggression that finds expression in sexual domination.

But for better or worse, the linkage between androgen levels and sexual desire is far too frail to make such rationales compelling for human behavior. The fact is that little is known about the presumed linkage, and the few existing studies are inconclusive as far as the causal direction of effects is concerned.

Fox, Ismail, Love, Kirkham, and Loraine (1972) traced androgen fluctuations and changes in sexual behavior in men over periods of several months, and observed that testosterone levels consistently increased before and after coital activities. The findings leave it unclear, however, whether precoital testosterone increases precipitated sexual desire or resulted from it. An investigation by Pirke, Kockott, and Dittmar (1974) showed that exposure to an erotic film occasioned elevated testosterone levels. This finding would seem to suggest that the psychogenic induction of sexual arousal causes increased testosterone production, rather than increased testosterone levels fostering sexual interest and sexual arousal. Bancroft (1978) has reviewed the pertinent literature more fully and concluded that the relationship between androgen levels and libidinal urges is unreliable indeed. All this is not to say that androgens may not constitute a basis for a linkage between aggression and sex. Rather, it is to point to the fact that endocrinological work is marred by inconsistencies in correlational demonstrations as well as by a lack of experimental investigations in which critical variables are manipulated so as to allow causal determinations. Because of this, the linkages that have been pronounced must be considered highly tentative.

Returning to our concern with *phasic* behavior, we shall bypass the possible influence of gonadal and adrenocortical hormones, and concentrate on the action of the adrenal medullae. The medullae release the sympathomimetic catecholamines epinephrine and norepinephrine. Especially through the hyperglycemic effect of epinephrine, this release quasi-instantaneously provides the energy for vigorous action. The burst of energy to the skeletal muscles is comparatively short-lived, however. The extreme level of energy supply cannot be maintained for any length of time. The supply is readily exhausted by emergency action. If not, homeostatic regulation will normalize autonomic activity after some time (Adolph, 1968).

As the analysis of autonomic innervation suggests, catecholamine release should be equally involved in fight, flight, and coition, or in the precipitating emotions of these behaviors. Endocrinological research has firmly established that this is indeed the case (Leshner, 1978; Levi, 1965, 1969, 1972).

Behavioral Linkages

The strength of the sympathetic component of sexual arousal and of coital engagements has been assessed in peripheral manifestations. Masters and Johnson (1966) recorded heart rates ranging from 110 to more than 180 bpm for both males and females during coital activities. Hyperventilation was evident in both genders, with respiration rates above 40 per minute. Blood pressure underwent substantial changes, too. Compared with basal levels, systolic pressure increased between 40 and 100 mm Hg and males and between 30 and 80 mm Hg in females. Diastolic pressure also increased, but not as strongly: between 20 and 50 mm Hg in males and between 20 and 40 mm Hg in females. These and similar findings (Bartlett, 1956; Fox and Fox, 1969) are somewhat compromised, however, in that the skeletal-motor activity involved contributed to the excitatory reaction. This is obviously the case for data from coition, but it also applies to the automanipulative techniques that have been employed in the research. Nonetheless, the contention by Masters and Johnson (1966) that the physical exertion associated with coition is not sufficient to produce the observed cardiorespiratory concomitant of sexual activities seems well supported by findings concerning the impact of exposure to explicit portrayals of precoital and coital behaviors on sympathetic excitation. Exposure to graphic erotica is devoid of exertion, yet produces sympathetic reactions that are, though somewhat weaker overall, quite comparable to those during precoital and coital behaviors (Stern, Farr, and Ray, 1975; Zillmann, Bryant, Comisky, and Medoff, 1981). On systolic blood pressure, for example, exposure to erotica has been found to produce average increases as high as 20 mm Hg (Zillmann, 1971).

Anger and fear, not to mention fight and flight, are more difficult to produce in laboratory situations. Some of the procedures that could be used proved effective, however, in generating acute anger and acute fear. Although the created emotional states were probably far from extreme (compared with anger and fear outside the laboratory), their sympathetic component was pronounced and is generally comparable to that of sexual excitedness (Marks, 1969; Zillmann, 1979). During acute anger, for instance, systolic blood pressure was found to be elevated by about 20 mm Hg on average (Zillmann and Sapolsky, 1977); and during acute fear, it was found to be elevated by the very same amount (Ax, 1960).

In view of such sympathetic commonality amongst the emergency emotions, the parasympathetic discrepancy between agonistic reactions and sexual arousal is eye-catching. But as indicated earlier, this appearance is somewhat deceiving. First of all, the parasympathetic outflow that makes for the reflexogenic sexual center also reaches the detrusor muscle of the urinary bladder and the distal colon and rectum. This innervation not only plays a specific part in sexual functioning (Masters and Johnson, 1966), but is also linked to intense sympathetic excitedness and, presumably because of this, is involved in the nonsexual emergency emotions as well. It is common knowledge that extreme sympathetic excitation carries with it the parasympathetically controlled inclination to empty bladder and bowels. This inclination is so closely allied with fear (and with aggression to the extent that defensive fighting is characteristically precipitated by fear) that in the research with rodents and other mammals, nonhuman primates included, fear is measured through micturition and defecation (Nevin, 1973). The parasympathetic oddity attached to sympathetic dominance in the autonomic nervous system has even been granted survival value in that both fight and flight are facilitated by the prompt reduction of excess weight (Cannon, 1929).

But the fact that strong sympathetic reactions in emergency emotions tend to carry with them particular parasympathetic responses, all linked to sacral outflow, seems most obtrusively documented in anthropological research. Gajdusek (1970) reported that uncovered men exhibited some degree of erection during virtually all sympathetic emotions. Anger and fear, especially, seem to be associated with genital blood flooding. The utility of such reactions is not immediately apparent. It can only be speculated that the combination of thoracolumbar sympathetic outflow and sacral parasympathetic outflow (see Figure 9.1) forms a patterned response. Although this patterned response is appropriate only for sexual engagements, its interconnections are apparently so strong that the sexual component is drawn along in nonsexual emergencies.

THEORETICAL PROJECTIONS OF BEHAVIORAL INTERDEPENDENCIES

The described sympathetic and parasympathetic linkages between the emergency emotions allow projections of principal behavioral interdependencies. More specifically, on the basis of these linkages it can be expected that, within the fight–flight–coition trichotomy, arousal from a prior emotion will facilitate the subsequent emotion, and simultaneous arousal from a nondominant emotion will facilitate the dominant emotion.

Behavioral facilitation due to sympathetic commonality can be predicted from the excitation-transfer paradigm (Zillmann, 1978, 1983b). This paradigm is based on the following general assumptions:

(1) Owing to slack humoral mediation, sympathetic excitation dissipates slug-gishly, and excitatory residues are likely to enter into subsequent behaviors and experiences.
(2) Individuals generally do not partition confounded sympathetic excitation nor trace it to different contributing sources.
(3) Regardless of its specific sources, sympathetic excitation energizes the behavior enacted in response to prevailing stimuli.
(4) Arousal states tend to be attributed in toto to the most conspicuous inducers at hand.
(5) The perceived intensity of an arousal state tends to determine the intensity of an emotional experience.

Research evidence in support of these assumptions has been detailed elsewhere (Zillmann, 1983b).

For emotional behaviors in succession, the transfer paradigm predicts that residual sympathetic excitation from agonistic reactions will inseparably combine

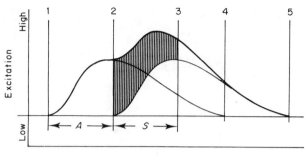

Figure 9.2. A model of excitation transfer in which residual excitation from a preceding excitatory reaction combines additively with the excitatory reaction to current stimulation. An antecedent stimulus condition (A), persisting from time 1 to time 2, is assumed to produce excitatory activity that has entirely decayed only at time 4. Similarly, a subsequent stimulus condition (S), persisting from time 2 to time 3, is assumed to produce excitatory activity that has entirely decayed only at time 5. Residual excitation from condition A and excitation specific to condition S combine from time 2 to time 4. The extent to which the transfer of residues from condition A increases the excitatory activity associated with condition S is shown in the shaded area.
[Reproduced, with permission, from Zillmann, D. (1979) *Hostility and Aggression*. Hillsdale, NJ: Lawrence Erlbaum Associates.]

with sympathetic excitation from sexual stimulation, and thereby facilitate subsequent sexual arousal and coital activities. Analogously, it predicts that residual excitation from sexual arousal will inseparably combine with excitation from the instigation of agonistic behaviors. Figure 9.2 presents a graph model of this facet of the theory.

For concurrently evoked emotional behaviors, the paradigm predicts that sympathetic excitation deriving from secondary sources will inseparably combine with excitation produced by the behavior- and/or experience-determining primary stimulation and facilitate that behavior and/or experience. If an agonistic reaction constitutes the primary emotion and sexual arousal is secondary, the portion of sympathetic excitation from sexual arousal will intensify the agonistic emotion. If an agonistic emotion is secondary and sexual arousal is primary, the portion of excitation from the agonistic emotion will facilitate sexual arousal and behavior. Figure 9.3 presents a graph model of this kind of behavior facilitation.

No particular paradigm exists from which the consequences of parasympathetic commonalities in the emergency emotions could be projected. Despite anatomical intertwinement, the pathways of sacral control are obviously not identical, and the involvement of some connections (e.g. from S2) has remained somewhat uncertain (Pick, 1970). As a result, specific predictions are not feasible. However, as sacral outflow is linked to extreme states of sympathetic excitedness, it is conceivable that

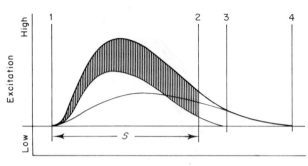

Time of activity

Figure 9.3. A model of excitation transfer in which excitation from a secondary excitatory reaction combines additively with the excitatory reaction to the primary, behavior-directing stimulation. The stimuli for the primary (PR) and secondary reaction (SR) concur from time 1 to time 2. It is assumed that the excitatory activity of PR has entirely decayed at time 3 and that decay of the activity of SR is complete at time 4. Behavior directed by the primary stimulation (S) is associated with the combined excitatory activity of PR and SR. The extent to which the transfer of secondary excitation increases excitation specific to the primary stimulation is shown in the shaded area.
[Reproduced, with permission, from Zillmann, D. (1984) *Connections Between Sex and Aggression*. Hillsdale, NJ: Lawrence Erlbaum Associates.]

this patterned autonomic reaction is favored in such states. This is to say that extreme sympathetic excitedness might produce a readiness for sacrally controlled responses and thereby facilitate their occurrence and, if they occur, their intensity. Such readiness is likely to be rather nonspecific. But response specificity might develop with continuing agonistic or sexual stimulation. If so, it could be expected that, when agonistic emotions come about in the wake of sexual excitedness, both micturition and defecation are facilitated. Analogously, it could be expected that genital vasocongestion is facilitated by preceding agonistic reactions.

EVIDENCE OF BEHAVIORAL INTERDEPENDENCIES

Psychophysiological research has firmly established some of the projected behavioral connections. Others, however, are supported by evidence that may be characterized as highly suggestive rather than as conclusive. Generally speaking, influences from sexual behaviors to aggressive behaviors have been more open to exploration than influences in the reverse direction or influences whose direction alternates and produces the intertwinement of sex–aggression fusion. The former influences are hence better understood than the latter. Since the coverage of the available research evidence here cannot possibly be exhaustive, we shall only indicate where connections are amply demonstrated and what principal form the research demonstrations have taken. We shall give comparatively more attention to the psychophysiological research that is less than compelling in establishing linkages between agonistic and sexual behaviors—partly in the hope of inspiring more definitive work.

FACILITATION OF AGONISTIC BEHAVIORS BY SEXUAL BEHAVIORS

It has been demonstrated in numerous investigations that the sympathetic component of sexual arousal is capable of facilitating agonistic behaviors. Specifically, it has been shown that feelings of irritation and annoyance, as well as hostile and aggressive actions, are readily intensified by sexual prearousal (cf. Zillmann, 1979, 1983a).

In the initial study exploring excitation transfer from sexual arousal to agonistic behavior (Zillmann, 1971), male subjects were aggressively instigated, sexually stimulated or not, and then provided with an opportunity to retaliate against their annoyer. Sexual arousal was accomplished by exposure to an erotic film featuring a heterosexual couple engaged in precoital behavior. In two nonsexual conditions, subjects were exposed to an aggressive film or to a film devoid of hostile action. The excitatory capacity of the neutral, aggressive, and sexual materials was determined by pretesting. Sympathetic reactions were assessed in peripheral manifestations. Systolic and diastolic blood pressures, as well as other indices, were ascertained before and after exposure. The analysis of such measures showed the excitatory potential of the sexual stimulus to be above that of the aggressive stimulus and, in turn, that of the aggressive stimulus to be above that of the neutral stimulus. On the basis of this information it was expected that residues of sympathetic excitation should be the strongest following exposure to the sexual film, intermediate after the aggressive film, and weakest after the neutral film. The intensity of aggressive actions taken during this period, owing to the combination of excitation in response to the renewed interaction with the annoyer and the residues from film exposure, should vary accordingly. The findings fully confirmed these expectations.

Subsequent studies that employed similar procedures confirmed these findings (Donnerstein and Hallam, 1978; Meyer, 1972; Zillmann, Hoyt, and Day, 1974). Additionally, the aggression-facilitating effect of sexual prearousal was observed under conceptually and procedurally very different conditions (Donnerstein, Donnerstein, and Evans, 1975; Ramirez, Bryant, and Zillmann, 1982). The findings were initially limited to males, but were eventually extended to females (Baron, 1979; Cantor, Zillmann, and Einsiedel, 1978).

Do these demonstrations compellingly implicate the sympathetic component of sexual arousal in the facilitation of agonistic experiences and actions? Could it not be argued, alternatively, that exposure to erotica is sexually frustrating, possibly repulsive, and that negative affect of this kind added to annoyance from the instigation to aggression? Plausible as it may sound, such an account is at variance with numerous observations. First, with few exceptions (Zillmann *et al.*, 1981b) erotica evoke hedonically positive reactions. Second, erotica that have only a negligible impact on sympathetic excitation either do not facilitate agonistic behaviors (Zillmann, Bryant, and Carveth, 1981a; Zillmann *et al.*, 1981b; Zillmann and Sapolsky, 1977) or, owing to their hedonic incompatibility with annoyance, actually diminish the intensity of these behaviors (Baron, 1974; Ramirez *et al.*, 1982). Third, when the strength of the sympathetic response of erotica and nonerotica (i.e. stimuli devoid of sexual denotations or connotations) is matched, both stimulus types, if sufficiently potent excitationally, facilitate agonistic behaviors to similar degrees (Zillmann *et al.*, 1981b). Equally damaging to any explanation based on sexual frustration, and further supportive of the proposal that the aggression-facilitating effect of sexual arousal is mediated by its sympathetic component, is evidence from research on physical exercise. When exertion is employed to produce excitation for transfer into agonistic behaviors, aggression facilitation is commensurate with that from comparable amounts of excitation deriving from sexual stimulation (Zillmann and Bryant, 1974; Zillmann, Katcher, and Milavsky, 1972).

FACILITATION OF SEXUAL BEHAVIORS BY AGONISTIC BEHAVIORS

The paucity of research on the facilitation of sexual experiences and behaviors, especially of experimental work, contrasts sharply with the preponderance of speculation in this area. Since Ovid's celebration of the joys of sex with partners scared out of their wits, in his famed *Artis amatoriae*, it has been suspected that male sexuality might benefit from agonistic accompaniments and female sexuality from the fear of such accompaniments (Freud, 1912/1943, 1940). Folklore has complemented conjectures of this kind with the truism that sex is never sweeter than 'right after a good fight.' In this vein, ethologists have provided uncounted illustrations of aggression-laden sexual behaviors in nonprimates and nonhuman primates. But all these illustrations are open to numerous interpretations and fail to prove anything about psychophysiological mechanisms. The same holds true, unfortunately, for a wealth of anthropological accounts of sex–aggression admixtures in a variety of human cultures (cf. Zillmann, 1984).

Much controlled research on nonprimate mammals, mainly rats, is more informative, but also fails to illuminate the mechanisms. It has been amply demonstrated (Barfield and Sachs, 1968; Caggiula and Eibergen, 1969; Crowley, Popolow, and Ward, 1973), for example, that the infliction of pain and the fear of such infliction inspire and enhance male sexual performances. In these demonstrations it is assumed that the agonistic treatment fosters sympathetic arousal that then sparks and invigorates sexual activities. But as sympathetic activity is assessed in the animals' general mobility only, conclusions about mediating events are rendered tentative. Related suggestive observations concerning sex–aggression linkages in primates (cf. DeVore, 1965) are similarly inconclusive.

Psychophysiological research on the facilitation of sexual behaviors by agonistic treatments in humans has been restricted to studying sexual arousal. Limited as the investigations in question may be, they have started to clear up the mechanisms involved in the presumed facilitation; and in aggregate, they are consistent with, and in this sense supportive of, the behavioral connections that have been projected from theoretical considerations.

One of the rare psychophysiological demonstrations of the enhancement of sexual arousal by agonistic reactions in humans was accomplished by Hoon, Wincze, and Hoon (1977). These investigators induced or did not induce fear-like distress in female subjects and immediately thereafter exposed them to sexually arousing distal stimuli. Vaginal blood-volume changes were monitored through-out these treatments; volume increases served as the measure of sexual excitedness. Under these conditions, the distressed females became more rapidly and more intensely sexually aroused than their nondistressed counterparts. A fear-like experience, then, produced conditions favorable to sacrally controlled parasympathetic responses as well as to sympathetic reactions.

The finding that distress can facilitate capillary engorgement in the vagina during subsequent sexual stimulation is of considerable importance. First, it would seem to confirm the popular beliefs about sexual enhancement after fright or fight. In fact, the findings might be interpreted as suggesting that rape creates superior physical conditions for coition and sexual experience. Furthermore, if it is assumed that the infliction of pain produces parasympathetic and sympathetic reactions characteristic of distressing experiences generally (Sternbach, 1968), the findings point to the possibility that presexual aversion (and conceivably aversion accompanying sexual actions) can be exploited for the enhancement of sexual pleasure. Second, the findings are consistent with the proposal that sympathetic excitation from agonistic treatments is capable of fostering parasympathetic sacral outflow. They thus shed light on the mechanics involved in the conversion of elements of aversion into pleasure, a conversion said to typify sadomasochistic sexual behaviors.

In view of the gravity of these findings, possible limitations of the investigation should be pointed out. As the distressing experience is of central importance, we shall focus on its manipulation. Distress was induced by exposure to films depicting tragic automobile accidents, including the occupants' death cries. The subjects, therefore, neither experienced pain themselves nor did they anticipate suffering pain; they witnessed the victimization of others instead. The type of emotional experience produced by such stimulation has been classified as 'empathetic distress' (Zillmann, 1980). Distress of this kind is usually less intense than distress from actual pain or fear of painful stimulation (Sternbach, 1968). It could be argued, therefore, that effects of empathetic distress are not representative of effects of distress from immediate threats to a person's own well-being or welfare. However, it also could be argued that generalizations are highly conservative because the distress manipulation employed by Hoon *et al.* was modest in comparison with treatments involving the infliction of pain or threats to that effect. The latter treatments are likely to foster more intense distress and, hence, might have produced a stronger facilitation of subsequently instigated sexual arousal. The fact remains that the findings cannot readily be generalized to effects of pain or apprehensions about aspects of physical assault upon self.

Generalizations about the distress facilitation of females' sexual arousal, as observed by Hoon *et al.*, are in further need of qualification. Wolchik, Beggs, Wincze, Sakheim, Barlow, and Mavissakalian (1980) attempted to extend the findings by Hoon *et al.* to males and succeeded only in part. The procedures employed were essentially those of the earlier study, except that penile tumescence was measured and a somewhat different type of distressing film was used in addition to the types of materials used previously. One prearousal film showed fatal and near fatal car accidents as in the earlier study. The other, additional prearousal film featured the anxieties of persons threatened with amputation of limbs. According to a pretest, the amputation film elicited stronger anxiety reactions than the accidents film.

Wolchik *et al.* observed that all three nonerotic films had negligible effects on erection. Subsequent exposure to erotic materials produced significantly different levels of penile tumescence, however. Preexposure to the most distressing (i.e. anxiety-inducing) film, presumably because it evoked the most intense sympathetic excitedness, resulted in greater tumescence than preexposure to the control film. The findings, up to this point, are supportive of the view that prearousal, especially noxious prearousal, is capable of facilitating sexual excitedness. Fearlike reactions thus appear to enhance sexual arousal in women and in men. Such an interpretation is challenged, however, by the related finding that preexposure to the accidents film produced less erection than preexposure to the presumably less arousing control film.

Pretesting had shown the accidents film to be depressing rather than anxiety-inducing. Because of this, Wolchik *et al.* considered the quality of the prior affect to be implicated in the mediation of the facilitation of sexual arousal. They thought anxiety capable of facilitating erection, but depression likely to inhibit it. This interpretation is consistent with the findings of their investigation. At the same time, however, it raises the question why, in the earlier study by Hoon *et al.*, women responded so differently to so similar a film. Why should men be depressed and women be scared by films depicting violent car accidents? Additionally, why should men be depressed by such depictions and respond with high anxiety to seeing others threatened with amputation of limbs?

If the pretest findings concerning anxiety versus depression are accepted at face value, it can be speculated that depression may have had a suppressing effect on subsequent erection because of especially low levels of sympathetic excitation commonly associated with that state. Only the direct assessment of excitatory activity during these stimulus transitions will eventually clarify the mechanisms involved. Until such clarification it would seem prudent to acknowledge that qualitatively different affective states may differently affect subsequent sexual arousal, and that only *distress that respondents construe as anxiety* has been shown to facilitate subsequent genital vasocongestion in both men and women.

The focus on penile erection and vaginal blood flow in the discussed studies may be viewed as overly narrow, if not as patently incomplete, as far as the facilitation of sexual *behavior* and/or sexual *experience* through noxious prearousal is concerned. Although pronounced genital vasocongestion is an essential part of sexual activity, especially for men, it does not, in and of itself, assure superior intensity or quality of sexual behavior and, in particular, of sexual experience. It can be argued that such behavior and experience will be enhanced only to the extent that genital vasocongestion is accompanied by strong sympathetic reactions. For reasons indicated earlier it may be expected that the sympathetic component of sexual excitedness influences sexual behavior and sexual experience more directly and more strongly than particular degrees of erection or vaginal blood flow. The more significant contribution of noxious prearousal to sexual excitedness may thus manifest itself through transfer in the sympathetic accompaniment. Such transfer is strongly suggested by various studies. Hare, Wood, Britain, and Frazelle (1971), for instance, exposed subjects to materials very similar to the accident films employed by Hoon *et al.* and by Wolchik *et al.* and observed distress responses associated with intense sympathetic reactions in both males and females. A similar investigation by Craig and Wood (1971) with male subjects corroborated these findings. It also showed that the peripheral manifestations of autonomic arousal associated with distress were virtually indistinguishable from those associated with sexual excitedness. It can be considered likely, then, that genital vasocongestion that is facilitated by distressing pretreatments will be accompanied by energizing excitatory responses that favor vigorous sexual action and that foster intense emotional experience.

Considered together, the studies by Hoon *et al.* (1977), Wolchik *et al.* (1980), Hare *et al.* (1971), and Craig and Wood (1971) are highly suggestive of the involvement of sympathetic residues from preceding states in the enhancement of sexual excitedness, but they do not establish this enhancement. An investigation by Cantor *et al.* (1975), however, demonstrated it directly.

Affectively neutral strenuous exercise was employed to produce sympathetic excitation for transfer into males' responses to sexual stimulation. Prearousal-enhancement of sexual excitedness was expected under conditions in which subjects were unlikely to recognize the source of prevailing residual excitation. Or alternatively, enhancement was not expected under conditions in which subjects either could correctly identify the source of residual excitation (as immediately after exertion, when heavy breathing and trembling hands were obtrusive reminders of the fact that they were still excited from exercise) or residues had become negligible. Three critical phases were determined by pretest: a first period in which subjects were still aroused from exercise (as measured in peripheral manifestations of sympathetic excitation) and perceived themselves as being still aroused from exertion; a second period in which subjects perceived themselves as having recovered but actually were still aroused from exertion; and a third period in which subjects perceived themselves as having recovered and actually had recovered. In the first phase, transfer is jeopardized by the person's inability to misconstrue residual excitation from exercise; the second phase constitutes the ideal transfer period; and the third phase serves as a control condition, as it is devoid of transferable residues.

Subjects in the main experiment again performed strenuous exercise and then were placed into one of the three predetermined phases for sexual stimulation. A film featuring coition served as the stimulus. It was halted at different times to allow subjects to record the degree to which they perceived themselves to be sexually excited. The findings were fully consistent with the predictions. Sexual excitedness, compared against the control, was significantly enhanced during the transfer period only. Despite higher levels of residual excitation, it was particularly low during the first phase.

The findings lend strong support to the excitation-transfer explanation of the facilitation of sexual excitedness. In so doing, they refocus attention on the implications of sympathetic commonality in the emergency emotions and on the significance of sympathetic excitedness for emotional experience.

Neglect of the sympathetic component of sexual excitedness has plagued another domain of psychophysiological research: the exploration of aggression–sex linkages in rapists and sexual sadists. On the premise that those who bring elements of aggression into sexual behavior might do so to complement inadequate excitatory responses or aggrandize adequate ones, it has been expected that sexual aggressives will respond more intensely to depictions of sexual activities that entail violence than to those that do not. As violent sexuality is the province of men, investigations focused on penile tumescence—unfortunately to the exclusion of concomitant facets of sexual excitedness. Abel and his collaborators (Abel, Barlow, Blanchard, and Guild, 1977) pioneered a procedure in which rapists and nonrapists were exposed to auditorily presented verbal accounts of a man's thoughts preceding and accompanying (a) intercourse with a consenting woman, (b) the rape of a woman, and (c) the nonsexual assault of a woman. Erection in response to fantasies accompanying consenting intercourse was strong and at comparable levels in rapists and nonrapists. It was poor and comparable in response to fantasies accompanying nonsexual assault. More importantly, however, rapists exhibited the same strength of erection to rape fantasies as to consenting-sex fantasies, whereas nonrapists responded less strongly to the rape fantasies. Nonrapists, then, responded with diminished tumescence when violent actions intruded into sexual activities. This differential penile response to 'rape depictions' gave rise to the construction of a rape index: the ratio of tumescence from coercive to consenting sex, with larger ratios identifying sexual aggressives.

This psychophysiological index fared well initially, but soon became problematic. Barbaree, Marshall, and Lanthier (1979), for instance, were able to differentiate rapists and nonrapists on the basis of the rape index. So were Quinsey, Chaplin, and Varney (1981). The latter study also showed what had been expected all along: that rapists tend to respond more strongly to rape fantasies than to fantasies about consenting sex. However, subsequent research produced different findings. Quinsey and Chaplin (1982), for instance, failed to find a significant correlation between the rape index and the amount of aggression used in the commission of rape. Instead, erection in response to nonsexual violence was related to the degree of force used in sexual offenses. In contrast to the findings reported by Quinsey *et al.* (1981), Baxter, Barbaree, and Marshall (1986) found that rapists, very much like nonrapists, may be more aroused by descriptions of consenting sex than by descriptions of rape. In fact, rapists responded minimally to particularly violent rape. Finally, Langevin *et al.* (1985) found penile reactions to fantasies of consenting sex, rape, and nonsexual assault in sexual aggressives and normals to be entirely parallel. Both groups were similarly aroused by sexual fantasies, regardless of the involvement of aggression. Additionally, both groups showed minimal reactions to fantasies of nonsexual assault. Even sadists failed to respond to depictions of nonsexual assault. Their penile reactions lacked intensity throughout and showed little variation across the stimulus conditions. In view of these and the earlier findings, the usefulness of the rape index has been called into question (Langevin, 1983; Langevin *et al.*, 1985).

Oddly enough, the initial investigations of penile tumescence in rapists and nonrapists contained information that should have urged the assessment of sympathetic activity alongside genital responses proper. Abel *et al.* (1977) had noted that rapists considered themselves less sexually aroused than nonrapists by fantasies of consenting and coercive sex—despite the fact that erection was at comparable levels. Kercher and Walker (1973) also had observed that rapists' and nonrapists' penile responses to a variety of graphic sexual portrayals were not appreciably different, but subjective reports of sexual excitedness were. Rapists again reported themselves less sexually aroused than nonrapists. Findings such as these point to the possibility that the difference in the sexual arousal of rapists and nonrapists might not so much lie in any penile response deficiency or response supplementation by aggressive stimulation on the part of rapists as in the hyposympathetic accompaniment of genital arousal in these men. Deficient sympathetic activity would explain their inability to consider themselves highly aroused sexually. Furthermore, on the basis of such deficiency it could be expected that some, knowingly or more likely unwittingly, may seek to complement sympathetic excitedness by involving exciting aggressive action.

In order to clarify and comprehend the processes that govern admixtures of aggressive and sexual behaviors, research cannot operationalize sexual arousal in terms of genital reactions alone. If future psychophysiological exploration in this highly sensitive area is to succeed, the sympathetic component of sexual excitedness, in both its objective and subjective or experiential manifestations, will have to be considered as well.

REFERENCES

Abel, G. G., Barlow, D. H., Blanchard, E. B., and Guild, D. (1977) The components of rapists' sexual arousal. *Archives of General Psychiatry*, **34**, 895–903.

Adolph, E. G. (1968) *Origins of Physiological Regulations*. New York: Academic Press.

Averill, J. R. (1982) *Anger and Aggression: An Essay on Emotion*. New York: Springer.

Ax, A. F. (1960) Psychophysiology of fear and anger. In L. J. West and M. Greenblatt (Eds), *Explorations in the Physiology of Emotions* (Psychiatric Research Reports No. 12, pp. 167–75). Washington, DC: American Psychiatric Association.

Bancroft, J. H. (1978) The relationship between hormones and sexual behavior in humans. In J. B. Hutchison (Ed.), *Biological Determinants of Sexual Behaviour*, pp. 493–515. Chichester: John Wiley.

Bancroft, J. H. (1983) *Human Sexuality and its Problems*. New York: Churchill Livingstone.

Barbaree, H. E., Marshall, W. L., and Lanthier, R. D. (1979) Deviant sexual arousal in rapists. *Behaviour Research and Therapy*, **17**, 215–22.

Bard, P. (1940) The hypothalamus and sexual behavior. *Research Publications of the Association for Research in Nervous and Mental Diseases*, **20**, 551–579.

Barfield, R. J., and Sachs, B. D. (1968) Sexual behavior: stimulation by painful electrical shock to skin in male rats. *Science*, **161**, 392–3.

Baron, R. A. (1974) The aggression-inhibiting influence of heightened sexual arousal. *Journal of Personality and Social Psychology*, **30**, 318–22.

Baron, R. A. (1979) Heightened sexual arousal and physical aggression: an extension to females. *Journal of Research in Personality*, **13**, 91–102.

Bartlett, R. G. (1956) Physiologic responses during coitus. *Journal of Applied Physiology*, **9**, 469–72.

Baxter, D. J., Barbaree, H. E., and Marshall, W. L. (1986) Sexual responses to consenting and forced sex in a large sample of rapists and nonrapists. *Behaviour Research and Therapy*, **24**, 513–20.

Beach, F. (1967) Cerebral and hormonal control of reflexive mechanisms involved in copulatory behavior. *Physiological Reviews*, **47**, 289–316.

Berkowitz, L. (1974) Some determinants of impulsive aggression: role of mediated associations with reinforcement for aggression. *Psychological Review*, **81**, 165–76.

Berscheid, E., and Walster, E. (1974) A little bit about love. In T. L. Huston (Ed.), *Foundations of Interpersonal Attraction*, pp. 355–81. New York: Academic Press.

Blumer, D. (1970) Changes of sexual behavior related to temporal lobe disorders in man. *Journal of Sex Research*, **6**, 173–80.

Bors, E., and Comarr, A. E. (1971) *Neurological Urology*. Baltimore: University Park Press.

Brown, T. S., and Wallace, P. M. (1980) *Physiological Psychology*. New York: Academic Press.

Brownmiller, S. (1975) *Against Our Will: Men, Women, and Rape*. New York: Simon & Schuster.

Buss, A. H. (1961) *The Psychology of Aggression*. New York: John Wiley.

Buss, A. H. (1971) Aggression pays. In J. L. Singer (Ed.), *The Control of Aggression and Violence: Cognitive and Physiological Factors*, pp. 7–18. New York: Academic Press.

Byrne, D. (1977) The imagery of sex. In J. Money and H. Musaph (Eds), *Handbook of Sexology*, pp. 327–50. Amsterdam: Elsevier/North-Holland Biomedical Press.

Caggiula, A. R., and Eibergen, R. (1969) Copulation of virgin male rats evoked by painful peripheral stimulation. *Journal of Comparative and Physiological Psychology*, **69**, 414–19.

Cannon, W. B. (1929) *Bodily Changes in Pain, Hunger, Fear and Rage: An Account of Researches into the Function of Emotional Excitement*, 2nd edn. New York: Appleton-Century-Crofts.

Cantor, J. R., Zillmann, D., and Bryant, J. (1975) Enhancement of experienced sexual arousal in response to erotic stimuli through misattribution of unrelated residual excitation. *Journal of Personality and Social Psychology*, **32**, 69–75.

Cantor, J. R., Zillmann, D., and Einsiedel, E. F. (1978) Female responses to provocation after exposure to aggressive and erotic films. *Communication Research*, **5**, 395–411.

Craig, K. D., and Wood, K. (1971) Autonomic components of observers' responses to pictures of homicide victims and nude females. *Journal of Experimental Research in Personality*, **5**, 304–9.

Crosby, E. C., Humphrey, T., and Lauer, E. W. (1962) *Correlative Anatomy of the Nervous System*. New York: Macmillan.

Crouch, J. E. (1978) *Functional Human Anatomy*, 3rd edn. Philadelphia: Lea & Febiger.

Crowley, W. R., Popolow, H. B., and Ward, O. B., Jr (1973) From dud to stud: copulatory behavior elicited through conditioned arousal in sexually inactive male rats. *Physiology and Behavior*, **10**, 391–4.

Delgado, J. M.R. (1968) Electrical stimulation of the limbic system. In *Proceedings of the XXIV International Congress of Physiological Sciences*, Vol. 6, pp. 222–3.

DeVore, I. (Ed.) (1965) *Primate Behavior: Field Studies of Monkeys and Apes*. New York: Holt, Rinehart & Winston.

Doering, C. H., Brodie, H. K. H., Kraemer, H., Becker, H., and Hamburg, D. A. (1974) Plasma testosterone levels and psychologic measures in men over a 2-month period. In R. C. Friedman, R. M. Richart, and R. L. vande Wiele (Eds), *Sex Differences in Behavior*, pp. 413–31. New York: John Wiley.

Donnerstein, E., Donnerstein, M., and Evans, R. (1975) Erotic stimuli and aggression: facilitation or inhibition. *Journal of Personality and Social Psychology*, **32**, 227–44.

Donnerstein, E., and Hallam, J. (1978) Facilitating effects of erotica on aggression against women. *Journal of Personality and Social Psychology*, **36**, 1270–77.

Easterbrook, J. A. (1959) The effect of emotion on cue utilization and the organization of behavior. *Psychological Review*, **66**, 183–201.

Ehrenkranz, J., Bliss, E., and Sheard, M. H. (1974) Plasma testosterone: correlation with aggressive behavior and social dominance in men. *Psychosomatic Medicine*, **36**, 469–75.

Ehrhardt, A. A. (1977) Prenatal androgenization and human psychosexual behavior. In J. Money and H. Musaph (Eds), *Handbook of Sexology*, Vol. 1, pp. 245–257. Amsterdam: Excerpta Medica.

Elias, M. (1981) Serum cortisol, testosterone, and testosterone-binding globulin responses to competitive fighting in human males. *Aggressive Behavior*, **7**, 215–24.

Ellis, H. (1906) *Studies in the Psychology of Sex*. New York: Random House.

Epstein, A. W. (1969) Fetishism: a comprehensive view. In J. Masserman (Ed.), *Dynamics of Deviant Sexuality*, pp. 81–7. New York: Grune & Stratton.

Faulk, M. (1977) Sexual factors in marital violence. *Medical Aspects of Human Sexuality*, **1977** (October), 30–38.

Feshbach, S. (1964) The function of aggression and the regulation of aggressive drive. *Psychological Review*, **71**, 257–72.

Feshbach, S. (1970) Aggression. In P. H. Mussen (Ed.), *Carmichael's Manual of Child Psychology*, Vol. 2, pp. 159–259. New York: John Wiley.

Finger, S., and Stein, D. G. (1982) *Brain Damage and Recovery*. New York: Academic Press.

Finkelhor, D., and Yllo, K. (1982) Forced sex in marriage: a preliminary research report. *Crime and Delinquency*, **28**, 459–78.

Ford, C. S., and Beach, F. A. (1951) *Patterns of Sexual Behavior*. New York: Harper.

Fox, C. A., and Fox, B. (1969) Blood pressure and respiratory patterns during human coitus. *Journal of Reproduction and Fertility*, **19**, 405–15.

Fox, C. A., Ismail, A. A., Love, D.N., Kirkham, K. E., and Loraine, J. A. (1972) Studies on the relationship between plasma testosterone levels and human sexual activity. *Journal of Endocrinology*, **52**, 51–8.

Freud, S. (1940) Das ökonomische Problem des Masochismus. In *Gesammelte Werke*, Vol. 13, pp. 369–83. London: Imago.

Freud, S. (1942) Drei Abhandlungen zur Sexualtheorie. In *Gesammelte Werke*, Vol. 5, pp. 27–145. London: Imago. (Original work published 1905.)

Freud, S. (1943) Beiträge zur Psychologie des Liebeslebens. In *Gesammelte Werke*, Vol. 8, pp. 65–91. London: Imago. (Original work published 1912.)

Gajdusek, D. C. (1970) Physiological and psychological characteristics of Stone Age man. In *Engineering and Science: Symposium on Biological Bases of Human Behavior*, pp. 26–33, 56–62. Pasadena: California Institute of Technology.

Goy, R. (1970) Early hormonal influences on the development of sexual and sex-related behavior. In F. O. Schmitt, G. C. Quarton, T. Melnechuck, and G. Adelman (Eds), *The Neurosciences: Second Study Program*, pp. 196–207. New York: Rockefeller University Press.

Grings, W. W., and Dawson, M. E. (1978) *Emotions and Bodily Responses: A Psychophysiological Approach*. New York: Academic Press.

Groth, A. N. (1979) *Men who Rape: The Psychology of the Offender*. New York: Plenum Press.

Guyton, A. C. (1972) *Structure and Function of the Nervous System*. Philadelphia: Saunders.

Hare, R., Wood, K., Britain, S., and Frazelle, J. (1971) Autonomic responses to affective visual stimulation: sex differences. *Journal of Experimental Research in Personality*, **5**, 14–22.

Hinde, R. A. (1970) *Animal Behaviour: A Synthesis of Ethology and Comparative Psychology*, 2nd edn. New York: McGraw-Hill.

Hoon, P. W., Wincze, J. P., and Hoon, E. F. (1977) A test of reciprocal inhibition: are anxiety and sexual arousal in women mutually inhibitory? *Journal of Abnormal Psychology*, **86**, 65–74.

Izard, C. E. (1977) *Human Emotions*. New York: Plenum Press.

Johnson, R. N. (1972) *Aggression in Man and Animals*. Philadelphia: Saunders.

Kaplan, H. S. (1979) *Disorders of Sexual Desire*. New York: Simon & Schuster.

Kemper, T. D. (1986) Personal communication.

Kenrick, D. T., and Cialdini, R. B. (1977) Romantic attraction: misattribution versus reinforcement explanations. *Journal of Personality and Social Psychology*, **35**, 381–91.

Kercher, G. A., and Walker, C. E. (1973) Reactions of convicted rapists to sexually explicit stimuli. *Journal of Abnormal Psychology*, **81**, 46–50.

Kolarsky, A., Freund, K., Machek, J., and Polak, O. (1967) Male sexual deviation: association with early temporal lobe damage. *Archives of General Psychiatry*, **17**, 735–43.

Kreuz, L. E., and Rose, R. M. (1972) Assessment of aggressive behavior and plasma testosterone in a young criminal population. *Psychosomatic Medicine*, **34**, 321–32.

Kreuz, L. E., Rose, R. M., and Jennings, J. R. (1972) Suppression of plasma testosterone levels and psychological stress. *Archives of General Psychiatry*, **26**, 479–82.

Langevin, R. (1983) *Sexual Strands: Understanding and Treating Sexual Anomalies in Men*. Hillsdale, NJ: Erlbaum.

Langevin, R., Ben–Aron, M. H., Coulthard, R., Heasman, G., Purins, J. E., Handy, L., Hucker, S. J., Russon, A. E., Day, D., Roper, V., Bain, J., Wortzman, G., and Webster, C. D. (1985) Sexual aggression: constructing a predictive equation: a controlled pilot study. In R. Langevin (Ed.), *Erotic Preference, Gender Identity and Aggression in Men: New Research Studies*, pp. 39–76: Hillsdale, NJ: Erlbaum.

Leshner, A. I. (1978) *An Introduction to Behavioral Endocrinology*. New York: Oxford University Press.

Levi, L. (1965) The urinary output of adrenalin and noradrenalin during pleasant and unpleasant emotional states: a preliminary report. *Psychosomatic Medicine*, **27**, 80–85.

Levi, L. (1969) Sympatho-adrenomedullary activity, diuresis, and emotional reactions during visual sexual stimulation in human females and males. *Psychosomatic Medicine*, **31**, 251–68.

Levi, L. (1972) Stress and distress in response to psychosocial stimuli: laboratory and real life studies on sympathoadrenomedullary and related reactions. *Acta Medica Scandinavica*, Suppl. 528.

Luttge, W. G. (1971) The role of gonadal hormones in the sexual behavior of the rhesus monkey and human: a literature survey. *Archives of Sexual Behavior*, **1**, 61–8.

Luria, Z., and Rose, M. D. (1979) *Psychology of Human Sexuality*. New York: John Wiley.

MacLean, P. D. (1962) New findings relevant to the evolution of psychosexual functions of the brain. *Journal of Nervous and Mental Disease*, **135**, 289–301.

MacLean, P. D. (1968a) Alternative neural pathways to violence. In L. Ng (Ed.), *Alternatives to Violence: A Stimulus to Dialogue*, pp. 24–34. New York: Time–Life Books.

MacLean, P. D. (1968b) Contrasting functions of limbic and neocortical systems of the brain and their relevance to psychophysiological aspects of medicine. In E. Gellhorn (Ed.), *Biological Foundations of Emotion*, pp. 73–106. Glenview, IL: Scott, Foresman.

MacLean, P. D. (1973) Special Award Lecture: New findings on brain function and sociosexual behavior. In J. Zubin and J. Money (Eds), *Contemporary Sexual Behavior: Critical Issues in the 1970s*, pp. 53–74. Baltimore: Johns Hopkins University Press.

MacLean, P. D., and Ploog, D. W. (1962) Cerebral representation of penile erection. *Journal of Neurophysiology*, **25**, 29–55.

MacLusky, N. J., and Naftolin, F. (1981) Sexual differentiation of the central nervous system. *Science*, **211**, 1294–1303.

Marks, I. M. (1969) *Fears and Phobias*. New York: Academic Press.

Masters, W., and Johnson, V. E. (1966) *Human Sexual Response*. Boston: Little, Brown.

Mazur, A., and Lamb, T. A. (1980) Testosterone, status, and mood in human males. *Hormones and Behavior*, **14**, 236–46.

Meyer, T. P. (1972) The effects of sexually arousing violent films on aggressive behavior. *Journal of Sex Research*, **8**, 324–33.

Meyer–Bahlburg, H. F. L., Boon, D. A., Sharma, M., and Edwards, J. A. (1974). Aggressiveness and testosterone measures in man. *Psychosomatic Medicine*, **36**, 269–74.

Monti, P. M., Brown, W. A., and Corriveau, D. P. (1977). Testosterone and components of aggressive and sexual behavior in men. *American Journal of Psychiatry*, **134**, 692–4.

Moyer, K. E. (1971) *The Physiology of Hostility*. Chicago: Markham.

Nevin, J. A. (Ed.) (1973) *The Study of Human Behavior: Learning, Motivation, Emotion, and Instinct*. Glenview, IL: Scott, Foresman.

Oken, D. (1967) The psychophysiology and psychoendocrinology of stress and emotion. In M. H. Appley and R. Trumbull (Eds), *Psychological Stress: Issues in Research*, pp. 43–76. New York: Appleton-Century-Crofts.

Persky, H., Smith, K. D., and Basu, G. K. (1971) Relation of psychologic measures of aggression and hostility to testosterone production in men. *Psychosomatic Medicine*, **33**, 265–77.

Pick, J. (1970) *The Autonomic Nervous System*. Philadelphia: Lippincott.

Pirke, K. M., Kockott, G., and Dittmar, F. (1974) Psychosexual stimulation and plasma testosterone in man. *Archives of Sexual Behavior*, **3**, 577–84.

Purins, J. E., and Langevin, R. (1985) Brain correlates of penile erection. In R. Langevin (Ed.), *Erotic Preference, Gender Identity, and Aggression in Men: New Research Studies*, pp. 113–33. Hillsdale, NJ: Erlbaum.

Quinsey, V. L., and Chaplin, T. C. (1982) Penile responses to nonsexual violence among rapists. *Criminal Justice and Behavior*, **9**, 372–81.

Quinsey, V. L., Chaplin, T. C., and Varney, G. (1981) A comparison of rapists' and non-sex offenders' sexual preferences for mutually consenting sex, rape, and physical abuse of women. *Behavioral Assessment*, **3**, 127–35.

Rada, R. T., Laws, D. R., and Kellner, R. (1976) Plasma testosterone levels in the rapist. *Psychosomatic Medicine*, **38**, 257–68.

Ramirez, J., Bryant, J., and Zillmann, D. (1982) Effects of erotica on retaliatory behavior as a function of level of prior provocation. *Journal of Personality and Social Psychology*, **43**, 971–8.

Resnick, H. (1972) Erotized repetitive hangings. *American Journal of Psychotherapy*, **26**, 4–21.

Robinson, P. (1976) *The Modernization of Sex*. New York: Harper & Row.

Rosen, C. R., and Beck, J. G. (1986) Models and measures of sexual response: psychophysiological assessment of male and female arousal. In D. Byrne and K. Kelley (Eds), *Alternative Approaches to the Study of Sexual Behavior*, pp. 43–86. Hillsdale, NJ: Erlbaum.

Scaramella, T. J., and Brown, W. A. (1978) Serum testosterone and aggressiveness in hockey players. *Psychosomatic Medicine*, **40**, 262–5.

Schachter, S. (1964) The interaction of cognitive and physiological determinants of emotional state. In L. Berkowitz (Ed.), *Advances in Experimental Social Psychology*, Vol. 1, pp. 49–80. New York: Academic Press.

Scott, J. P. (1973) Hostility and aggression. In B. Wolman (Ed.), *Handbook of General Psychology*, pp. 707–19. Englewood Cliffs, NJ: Prentice-Hall.

Stein, D. G., Rosen, J. J., and Butters, N. (Eds) (1974) *Plasticity and Recovery of Function in the Central Nervous System*. New York: Academic Press.

Stern, R. M., Farr, J. H., and Ray, W. J. (1975) Pleasure. In P. H. Venables and M. J. Christie (Eds), *Research in Psychophysiology*, pp. 208–33. London: John Wiley.

Sternbach, R. A. (1968) *Pain: A Psychophysiological Analysis*. New York: Academic Press.

von Krafft–Ebing, R. (1886) *Psychopathia sexualis: Eine klinischforensische Studie*. Stuttgart: Enke.

Weiss, H. D. (1972) The physiology of human penile erection. *Annals of Internal Medicine*, **76**, 793–9.

Whalen, R. E. (1966) Sexual motivation. *Psychological Review*, 73, 151–63.

Whalen, R. E. (1971) The ontogeny of sexuality. In H. Moltz (Ed.), *The Ontogeny of Vertebrate Behavior*, pp. 229–61. New York: Academic Press.

Wolchik, S. A., Beggs, V. E., Wincze, J. P., Sakheim, D. K., Barlow, D. H., and Mavissakalian, M. (1980) The effect of emotional arousal on subsequent sexual arousal in men. *Journal of Abnormal Psychology*, **89**, 595–8.

Zillmann, D. (1971) Excitation transfer in communication-mediated aggressive behavior. *Journal of Experimental Social Psychology*, **7**, 419–34.

Zillmann, D. (1978) Attribution and misattribution of excitatory reactions. In J. H. Harvey, W. J. Ickes, and R. F. Kidd (Eds), *New Directions in Attribution Research*, Vol. 2, pp. 335–68. Hillsdale, NJ: Erlbaum.

Zillmann, D. (1979) *Hostility and Aggression*. Hillsdale, NJ: Erlbaum.

Zillmann, D. (1980) Anatomy of suspense. In P. H. Tannenbaum (Ed.), *The Entertainment Functions of Television*, pp. 133–63. Hillsdale, NJ: Erlbaum.

Zillmann, D. (1983a) Arousal and aggression. In R. G. Geen and E. I. Donnerstein (Eds), *Aggression: Theoretical and Methodological Issues*, pp. 75–101. New York: Academic Press.

Zillmann, D. (1983b) Transfer of excitation in emotional behavior. In J. T. Cacioppo and R. E. Petty (Eds), *Social Psychophysiology: A Sourcebook*, pp. 215–40. New York: Guilford Press.

Zillmann, D. (1984) *Connections between Sex and Aggression*. Hillsdale, NJ: Erlbaum.

Zillmann, D. (1986) Coition as emotion. In D. Byrne and K. Kelley (Eds), *Alternative Approaches to the Study of Sexual Behavior*, pp. 173–99. Hillsdale, NJ: Erlbaum.

Zillmann, D., and Bryant, J. (1974) Effect of residual excitation on the emotional response to provocation and delayed aggressive behavior. *Journal of Personality and Social Psychology*, **30**, 782–91.

Zillmann, D., Bryant, J., Cantor, J. R., and Day, K. D. (1975) Irrelevance of mitigating circumstances in retaliatory behavior at high levels of excitation. *Journal of Research in Personality*, **9**, 282–93.

Zillmann, D., Bryant, J., and Carveth, R. A. (1981a) The effect of erotica featuring sadomasochism and bestiality on motivated intermale aggression. *Personality and Social Psychology Bulletin*, **7**, 153–9.

Zillmann, D., Bryant, J., Comisky, P. W., and Medoff, N. J. (1981b) Excitation and hedonic valence in the effect of erotica on motivated intermale aggression. *European Journal of Social Psychology*, **11**, 233–52.

Zillmann, D., Hoyt, J. L., and Day, K. D. (1974) Strength and duration of the effect of aggressive, violent, and erotic communications on subsequent aggressive behavior. *Communication Research*, **1**, 286–306.

Zillmann, D., Katcher, A. H., and Milavsky, B. (1972) Excitation transfer from physical exercise to subsequent aggressive behavior. *Journal of Experimental Social Psychology*, **8**, 247–59.

Zillmann, D., and Sapolsky, B. S. (1977) What mediates the effect of mild erotica on annoyance and hostile behavior in males? *Journal of Personality and Social Psychology*, **35**, 587–96.

Zuckerman, M. (1971) Physiological measures of sexual arousal in the human. *Psychological Bulletin*, **75**, 297–329.

Chapter 10

The Arousing Effects of Social Presence

Russell G. Geen and Brad J. Bushman
University of Missouri

ABSTRACT

Three bodies of literature on the arousing effects of social presence are reviewed. In each area of study—social facilitation, fear and affiliation, and population density—the data indicate that the presence of others may induce increased arousal. Theoretical viewpoints are discussed in each case.

The field of social psychology has always placed considerable emphasis on the influence of social settings on individual behavior. Frequently studied topics such as modeling, persuasion, conformity, and social reinforcement, for example, all represent instances of active social effects on individuals. In addition to these matters, social psychologists have, in recent years, been turning more and more to the study of the effects that the presence of *passive* others may have on individual performance. In such cases, it is the *presence* of others, rather than something that they may do, that helps to determine some aspects of the individual's behavior. Among the effects of the presence of passive others may be an increase in the individual's level of activation or arousal. This matter is addressed by three bodies of research evidence that will be reviewed in this paper. The first is the study of social facilitation, which, according to some theorists, involves a process whereby

Handbook of Social Psychophysiology, Edited by H. Wagner and A. Manstead,
© 1989 John Wiley & Sons Ltd

the presence of others, as either observers or coworkers, increases the arousal level of the individual during the commission of some task. The second has grown out of research initiated by Schachter (1959) on the psychology of affiliation. One hypothesis that has been central to this tradition is that the presence of others *reduces* the level of arousal of individuals who have been placed under stress. The third is the study of population density and crowding. A common finding in this research is that arousal is often elevated by conditions in which the individual has restricted personal space.

SOCIAL FACILITATION

In one of the earliest experimental investigations of social psychology, Triplett (1898) showed that performance of a simple motor task is enhanced by the company of another person doing the same task. The phenomenon thus became labelled *social facilitation* and the particular arrangement used by Triplett as the *coaction setting.* In the decade following Triplett's report, several studies of social facilitation in coaction settings were reported, but eventually attention shifted to a related situation in which a single performer is observed by one or more passive spectators. The *audience setting* soon became the primary paradigm for the study of the influence of others on performance.

In the first study involving an audience, a 1904 experiment by Meumann (Cottrell, 1972), performance on a simple motor task was found to be facilitated by the presence of a passive spectator. The first study of an audience effect reported in English (Moore, 1917) showed the opposite. The subjects with an audience produced poorer performances on complex multiplication tasks than did subjects working alone. These contradictory findings were characteristic of research on social facilitation for several decades. The literature on the subject reflects this fact in the term *social facilitation effect,* which is used in a general sense to include both social facilitation and inhibition of performance. We will follow custom by using this term in our review. Research reported over the period from 1900 to 1930 had certain characteristics (see Dashiell, 1935, for a review). First, it showed that audiences inhibited performance approximately as often as they facilitated it. Second, it revealed no single theoretical formulation that could account for both inhibition and facilitation with a single set of postulates. Third, it did not specify the precise conditions under which either facilitation or inhibition would occur, even though some studies suggested that the differential effects could be explained in terms of the nature of the task (Allport, 1924; Travis, 1925).

SOCIAL PRESENCE AND DRIVE

Research on the social facilitation effect languished after the 1930s until Zajonc (1965) rekindled interest in the problem with a paper in which he suggested an integrative theory that accounted for both facilitation and inhibition. Zajonc's proposition rested on two premises. The first is that the presence of coactors or spectators increases the individual's level of drive. The second is that drive multiplies with habit strength to energize dominant responses at the expense of subordinate ones. Because well-learned, familiar, or easy tasks are those in which dominant responses are likely to be correct, increased drive arising from the social setting will lead to facilitation of performance. Because the dominant responses in difficult or unfamiliar tasks are likely to be incorrect, socially engendered drive should lead to inhibition of performance. Social facilitation researchers have addressed both of these premises. Several studies have sought to discover whether social presence is arousing, and among these have been a number that involve the measurement of psychophysiological activity. These studies form the basis for the present review. Consideration of studies on the social facilitation effect in general is beyond the scope of this chapter. In addition, no attention is paid to theories of social facilitation which do not include arousal or drive as a mediating variable. Several more general reviews of research and viewpoints on the subject have been published (e.g. Bond and Titus, 1984; Cottrell, 1972; Geen, 1989; Geen and Bushman, 1987; Geen and Gange, 1977).

THEORIES OF SOCIALLY ENGENDERED DRIVE

In his original paper, Zajonc (1965) stated only that social presence increases drive, without speculating on any particular reason why such should be the case. Shortly afterwards, a controversy arose over whether audiences or coactors could produce increased drive simply by being present or whether they had to represent a potential threat to the person. Zajonc (1980) has used the term *mere presence* to characterize the former viewpoint, according to which no assumptions need be made about what other people are doing or what interpretations the individuals may place on their presence. This definition of the conditions for the social facilitation effect is a purely operational one. It is, therefore, the one most often criticized by those who seek intervening variables in the process. Three major explanations of the social facilitation effect have been offered as alternatives to the hypothesis of mere presence. These alternatives are based on the concepts of *evaluation apprehension, distraction,* and *uncertainty.*

The explanation of the social facilitation effect through evaluation apprehension expresses the idea that audiences and coactors create the conditions for anxiety over evaluation of the individual's performance. An audience elicits arousal only when it is regarded as a potential evaluator and dispenser of rewards and punishments (Cottrell, Wack, Sekerak, and Rittle, 1968). Coactors do so only when they are regarded as competitors for available rewards (Cottrell, 1972). The hypothesis that social presence causes increased arousal because it distracts individuals from their tasks has been advanced by Baron and his associates (e.g. Baron, 1986). Although distraction effects are often inseparable from those due to evaluation apprehension (Geen, 1981), the two have been disentangled operationally by Groff, Baron, and Moore (1983). Social arousal may also be the result of uncertainty about what the observers or coactors in a situation may do (Zajonc, 1980). The arousing effects of uncertainty are well documented in psychology (Glass and Singer, 1972). Guerin and Innes (1982) have extended Zajonc's views to a process that they call *social monitoring*. The purpose of social monitoring is reduction of uncertainty regarding the possible behavior of others. The presence of others should therefore elicit less arousal when those others can be monitored than when they cannot.

The three theories of social drive outlined here all agree that the presence of others produces a condition of elevated drive or arousal. The remainder of this section will consider the evidence for and against this assumption.

The first investigation into the relationship of an audience to physiological arousal was reported by Burtt (1921), who found that blood pressure and respiration rate among subjects who had been instructed to tell lies were higher in the presence of a large audience than in the presence of an audience of one. The study did not contain a condition in which subjects lied or told the truth while alone. For more than forty years after this study virtually no research on audience effects on arousal was conducted, so that Zajonc (1965) was forced to conclude that evidence for his social drive hypothesis was both scarce and indirect. More recent studies have sought evidence for social arousal in standard psychophysiological measures on human subjects who perform tasks either alone or in the company of others. These studies have involved measurement of palmar sweat, muscle tension, electrodermal activity, and heart rate.

SOCIAL PRESENCE AND PHYSIOLOGICAL AROUSAL

Palmar Sweat

The psychophysiological measure reported most often in studies of social facilitation is palmar sweat. Several methods of quantifying sweat gland activity have been reported. The most popular method (Dabbs, Johnson, and Leventhal, 1968) involves painting the subjects' fingertip with a moisture-repellant solution that dries to form a thin plastic film. Active sweat glands leave visually discernible traces on the film, and the number of such active glands in a given area (3–4 mm square) defines the Palmar Sweat Index (PSI). Another method (McNair, Droppleman, and Kussman, 1967) involves the impression of a fingerprint on a strip of chemically treated paper, with print density rated by judges on a 15-point scale. Print density is assumed to be a direct function of sweat gland activity. A method reported by Geen (1977) is similar to that of McNair *et al.* (1967), except that print density is operationally defined in terms of the amount of light that passes through the print to a photocell. Still another method is the sweat bottle technique developed Strahan, Todd, and Inglis (1974), in which a small container of distilled water is inverted and pressed against the fingertip. Ions from the sweat increase the electrical conductivity of the water; the more sweat collected, the greater the increase in conductivity.

Studies in which the PSI method has been used report mixed support for the hypothesis that social presence leads to increased arousal. In the context of a task requiring visual–motor coordination, Martens (1969a) took repeated measures of the PSI during both a preliminary session, in which subjects became familiar with the task, and a second session, in which their proficiency was tested. In each session some subjects worked before an audience of ten students and some worked without an audience. The experimenter was present in both sessions for all subjects. In both the preliminary and performance sessions, subjects who were observed by the audience showed higher PSI levels than those attended by the experimenter only. In addition, subjects who did the task before an audience during the preliminary phases and who later performed before an audience maintained high levels of PSI activity, whereas those who worked before an audience in the first phase but then shifted to the experimenter-only condition in the second phase showed a decrease in PSI level. A subsequent study by Martens (1969b) involving the same task and method of palmar sweat assessment also showed higher levels in the PSI among subjects who worked before an audience than among those who performed before the experimenter only.

Overall, Martens' studies have been taken as evidence for the hypothesis that social presence is arousing, even though neither experiment included a condition in which subjects were truly alone. They should, therefore, be more properly taken as evidence for a direct relationship between arousal level and audience size. A study by Geen (1977) did include a condition in which subjects worked alone on a difficult anagrams task, in addition to other conditions in which the subject worked with the experimenter present. In one of these conditions the experimenter passively observed the subject, whereas in another he both observed and clearly evaluated the subject's performance. Subjects had also been classified into high and low test-anxious groups according to their scores on the Sarason (1972) Test Anxiety Scale. Palmar sweat, quantified by the print-density method described above, was significantly higher in the observation and evaluation conditions than in the alone condition, but only for subjects high in test anxiety. Thus, individual differences in trait anxiety moderated the effects of social presence on palmar sweating, a finding that tends to support the evaluation apprehension hypothesis described above.

The findings of a study by Karst and Most (1973) can also be interpreted as showing that subjects' levels of trait anxiety interact with audience conditions to affect palmar sweating. Subjects in this study were required to deliver a short speech while being observed either by two experimenters who were present in the room, or by the two experimenters plus a small audience of students who were ostensibly watching through a one-way mirror. Palmar sweat prints were taken before and immediately after the subject made the speech, and then again during a post-speech interval. Print density was greater at the before speech and immediate post-speech measurement periods than at either the baseline or final measurements. The amount of palmar sweating just after the speech was *less* when an audience was said to be behind the mirror than when no such audience was said to be present. This finding is an obvious reversal of the more customary one relating audience size to arousal. It was accounted for, however, mostly by subjects who had, prior to the study, described themselves as highly confident about their public speaking ability. Speakers who expressed a low degree of self-confidence showed levels of palmar sweat in the audience condition as high as those shown in the experimenter-only condition. If we assume, as Karst and Most (1973) did, that high confidence represents a low level of speech anxiety, and low confidence a high level, these results seem to show that enlarging the audience (beyond the experimenters) was associated with reduced arousal in relatively nonanxious subjects. Possibly the confident and nonanxious speakers regarded the opportunity of speaking to an audience as a pleasant task, whereas anxious subjects did not. This suggestion is merely speculative, of course. As is the case in other studies reviewed here, the absence of a condition in which subjects performed alone makes interpretation of audience effects difficult.

Several other studies have shown that various measures of palmar sweating do not vary as a function of audience or observer conditions. Cohen and Davis (1973) administered a hidden-word task to subjects under several conditions of observation and/or evaluation by either peers or authority figures. Half the subjects were ostensibly being observed through a one-way mirror and half by closed-circuit television. No observers were physically present although the experimenter was in the laboratory. Palmar sweat, measured in terms of the PSI, varied only according to the means of observation used. Whereas subjects observed through a one-way mirror showed levels of palmar sweat during the task that were considerably below baseline levels, those observed by television revealed levels which, though lower than baseline, were closer to the latter. The differential effects of the mirror and the television camera appeared, therefore, to be related not to increases in arousal, but to the speed with which subjects habituated to the experimental setting. This study did not include a condition in which subjects could consider themselves alone and unobserved. Moreover, the one-way mirror and video camera were in evidence even in conditions when no observation was allegedly taking place. Interpretation of the findings in terms of their relevance for the drive theory of social facilitation is therefore difficult.

In four succeeding experiments, Cohen and his associates found no evidence of socially induced palmar sweating, even though in some of the studies other findings consistent with the drive theory of social facilitation were reported. Two of these experiments involved use of the PSI measure (Bargh and Cohen, 1978; Cohen, 1979) and two utilized the sweat-bottle technique (Cohen, 1980; Elliott and Cohen, 1981). The most significant psychophysiological finding from these studies was that subjects show higher levels of palmar sweat when they think that a permanent videotaped record of their performance is being made than when they do not.

After reviewing the evidence on palmar sweating in social facilitation experiments, Carver and Scheier (1981a, b) concluded that palmar sweat is an indicator not of arousal, but of attention to, and interaction with, one's environment (Dabbs, Johnson, and Leventhal, 1968). When attention is directed toward the environment, the level of palmar sweat may increase, whereas when attention is focused inward upon the self the direction of sweat gland activity may go in the other direction, i.e. there may occur a 'palmar drying.' The latter effect has, in fact, been shown in a situation involving heightened self-focusing (Paulus, Annis, and Risner, 1978). Carver and Scheier explain Martens' findings of increased sweating in audience settings by noting that Martens measured palmar sweat *between trials* of the subject's task, a time during which subjects' attention was usually directed away from the task and toward the immediate surroundings (Martens, 1969a). It should be noted that both Geen (1977) and Karst and Most (1973) used a technique by which sweat prints were obtained just after the task period. However, because the sheet on which the imprint was made had been attached to the subject's finger before the beginning of the task, it is possible that pre-task sweating could have been the major contributor to the outcome.

To test their hypothesis, Carver and Scheier (1981b) conducted an experiment in which subjects were given the task of copying German prose in two 5-minute sessions. In the first session the experimenter was in the room but out of sight of the subject. Moreover, he paid no attention to the subject. In the second session, the experimenter was again present. In one condition he ignored the subject and in another he watched as the subject worked. The PSI was assessed at four times: before the first task (baseline), during the first task, just prior to the second task, and during the second task. The results were consistent with Carver and Scheier's viewpoint. All subjects showed decreased PSI levels, relative to baseline levels, during the first task. Subjects in the audience condition (i.e. those who anticipated being observed by the experimenter) showed a large increase in palmar sweating just before the second task began, whereas subjects who expected to continue with an inattentive experimenter showed no change. Sweat levels then declined for subjects in both groups during the second task. Thus, increased palmar sweating in the audience condition was found prior to the learning trial, but a *decrease* occurred during the period of the task itself.

Electrodermal Measures

Studies in which arousal is inferred from electrodermal measures provide little support for the hypothesis that presence of others is arousing. A few experiments have involved measurement of tonic conductance levels in the presence of observers, but none has shown that conductance is responsive to audience conditions (Borden, Hendrick, and Walker, 1976; Geen, 1979; Henchy and Glass,

1968). Subjects in a study by McKinney, Gatchel, and Paulus (1983) were required to prepare a 3-minute speech and then to deliver it either to an empty room or to an audience of two or six people. The experimenter was in an adjoining room surreptitiously videotaping the session. Skin resistance and heart rate were continuously monitored during a baseline period, the preparation interval, and the speech itself. Subjects had been classified beforehand into groups that were respectively high and low in anxiety over public speaking on the basis of their responses to a questionnaire. Electrodermal activation increased from the baseline to the pre-speech measurement period, and increased even more during the speech itself. However, neither speech anxiety nor audience size had any differential effects on conductance. Subjects showed the same increase in conductance when giving the speech alone as they did when speaking to an audience. The finding that conductance increased as a function of preparation and delivery of the speech indicates only arousal in response to a stressful event, a finding that has been reported in similar contexts by others (e.g. Knight and Borden, 1979). It is unclear from the report of this experiment whether or not the subjects believed that the experimenter was observing them as they spoke. The experimenter was physically absent, communicating with subjects by means of an intercom. The authors state that the experiment did not contain a true no-audience condition, in part because physiological monitoring implies observation, however indirect.

One study which showed no audience effect on conductance levels did reveal that audiences affect the emission of skin conductance responses (SCRs). Geen (1979) measured the number of SCRs emitted during the first 2 minutes of a paired-associates task among subjects who worked either alone or in the presence of an observing experimenter. A SCR was defined as a change of at least 300 ohms resistance with a return to baseline in 3.5 seconds or less. Prior to the paired-associates task, the subject had undergone either a manipulated success or a failure on another task. Subjects who had just been through a failure showed a greater number of SCRs in the presence of the experimenter than when alone. Following success, subjects emitted relatively few SCRs whether alone or observed. Why subjects should show increased phasic activity, such as the SCR, but not change in tonic conductance, is not clear. Moore and Baron (1983) have suggested that the SCR may reflect a basic motivational process associated with stress or threat, whereas skin conductance level reflects cognitive processing. Given that Geen (1979) considered the audience to be a stimulus for evaluation apprehension, in which threat should be implicit, this reasoning is consistent with the general theory underlying the study.

Cardiovascular Measures

Some investigators have measured heart rate as an indicator of general arousal in studies of social facilitation. The evidence from these studies does not reveal a consistent relationship between the presence of others and increases in heart rate.

In two studies cited earlier (Borden *et al.*, 1976; Henchy and Glass, 1968) heart rate was not affected by audience conditions. Other investigators have shown increased heart rates in subjects who first prepared for, and then delivered, a speech (Knight and Borden, 1979; Singerman, Borkovec, and Baron, 1976), but these studies were not designed to test for audience effects, and their findings are only indirectly relevant to social facilitation. The investigation by McKinney *et al.* (1983), which was described earlier, did find an audience influence on heart rate in a public-speaking situation. Across the phases of the study (baseline, preparation, delivery), the heart rates of subjects in all conditions increased. Among subjects who were high in speech anxiety, the size of the audience influenced the increase in heart rate: subjects speaking to an audience of two showed a greater increase in heart rate than those speaking to no audience or to an audience of six. The finding that the small audience elicited a greater increase in heart rate than a larger one is puzzling. We should be aware that many contemporary psychophysiologists (e.g. Fowles, 1983) do not consider heart rate to be an indicator of general activation, but to reflect instead a state of preparation for the enactment of responses. Heart rate may, therefore, be linked to motivational processes involving the interaction of the person with the environment. Understanding its significance for the study of social facilitation must therefore await further development of theory on the motives of persons who perform before audiences.

Pulse rate and/or volume have been measured as concomitants of arousal in studies involving public speaking (Cotton, Baron, and Borkovec, 1980; Knight and Borden, 1979). One study of performance on a verbal task before an observer has involved these measures (Geen, 1979), but no effects of observation on pulse rate or pulse volume were found. Bell, Loomis, and Cervone (1982) have reported a study in which a coaction setting constituted one variable in a reaction time task, and have stated that coaction led to higher levels of blood pressure than were found in subjects performing individually. The data are presented in a regression analysis, however, so that inspection of the relevant group means is not possible. Finally, Bregman and McAllister (1983) examined the effects of the physical presence of the experimenter on performance in a biofeedack task. Subjects were instructed either to raise or to lower their skin temperatures. The presence of the experimenter in the room hindered acquisition of the thermal regulatory response in both the increase and decrease conditions, but more in the decrease than in the increase. A possible reason for the experimenter's hindering acquisition of an 'arousal down' response is that the normal consequence of that person's presence is to generate increased arousal.

Muscle Tension

Some evidence consistent with the drive theoretical approach comes from studies in which arousal is defined in terms of muscle tension. Chapman (1973, 1974) observed higher levels of muscle action potential in subjects who listened to a recording in the presence of the experimenter than in subjects who listened alone. Moreover, the effect was found whether the experimenter was visible or hidden behind a screen. However, Chapman's studies are susceptible to alternative explanations on methodological grounds (see Moore and Baron, 1983) and may not, therefore, represent strong support for drive theory.

Specific Effects of Distraction

Most of the studies reviewed in this section have been based on the general assumption that the presence of others should lead to an increase in physiological activation, as most theories of social facilitation would predict. An experiment by Moore, Logel, Weerts, Sanders, and Baron (1984) stands as an exception, in that it found *reduction* of activity in two psychophysiological systems under audience conditions. The study was carried out as a test of the distraction/conflict theory of social facilitation described earlier, and it involved a fixed-foreperiod reaction time task. In this task, which involves the presentation of a preliminary warning signal before the stimulus for the response, certain physiological reactions typically occur during the period between the two stimuli. As the subject prepares to respond, total somatic activity decreases, heart rate decelerates, and the amplitude of the skin conductance response increases. Because of these preparatory activities, the speed of reaction to the stimulus is facilitated. The interesting finding of the Moore *et al.* study was that the presence of an audience reduced the magnitude of the physiological activity that normally occurs during the foreperiod. Compared with subjects who performed alone, those who performed before an audience showed less cardiac deceleration and smaller increases in skin conductance, as well as longer reaction times. Virtually identical results were found among subjects who performed alone and were stimulated periodically by a flashing light. Overall, the results support the hypothesis of Baron (1986) and his associates that the principal effect of an audience is to distract the performer from the task at hand, much as a physical distractor would.

Conclusions

In general, psychophysiological evidence fails to provide much support for the hypothesis that the presence of others increases arousal. Most of the evidence that is usually adduced in suport of the hypothesis comes from investigations using the palmar sweat measure, and this evidence is hardly conclusive. Evidence from studies involving other measures is so scant as to be only suggestive at best. Few of the studies that do support the hypothesis have been adequately replicated, and little agreement exists as to the particular measurements to be used. As is well known, the various psychophysiological measures do not correlate highly with each other (Lacey, 1967), and even within a single system results arising from one technique may not be correlated highly with those from another. Palmar sweat is a case in point; four different techniques have been used (as described above), even though we have reason to doubt that they all measure the same components of the palmar sweat response (Strahan *et al.*, 1974). Finally, it should be noted that more recent models of the social facilitation effect (Baron, 1986; Geen, 1989; Geen and Bushman, 1987; Manstead and Semin, 1980; Moore and Baron, 1983) tend not to emphasize arousal as a necessary intervening variable. These models are designed along the lines of attentional and information processing variables, with the presence of others serving more to increase processing demands than to 'arouse' in the usual sense of that term.

EFFECTS OF A COMPANION ON ANXIETY AND FEAR

Another tradition of research and theory on the effects of social presence is somewhat at odds with the literature on social facilitation reviewed above. This tradition grew out of research by Schachter (1959), which showed that when people have been made afraid they have a desire to affiliate with other people. One explanation that Schachter suggested for this finding is that the presence of a companion at such times produces a reduction of fear (cf. Cottrell and Epley, 1977). Among the large number of experiments carried out in the aftermath of Schachter's work were some that put the fear-reduction hypothesis to the test with physiological measurement. The assumption behind these studies was that fear is manifested in physiological arousal, and that the presence of a companion should reduce arousal that had been elevated by the fear-inducing treatment. Other studies expanded upon this notion by linking affiliation to the reduction of arousal from aversive situations other than those involving fear. In this section we will review the most pertinent studies from this literature.

The overall conclusion that may be drawn from the several experiments is that arousal in such situations is mediated by two variables: the nature of the setting, and the relationship between the subject and the other person, or persons, present. In an early investigation, Kissel (1965) measured skin conductance as subjects worked at an insoluble and ostensibly frustrating task. Subjects who worked at the task in the presence of a friend showed lower conductance levels than those who worked either alone or with a stranger present. No conductance differences were found between the latter two conditions. Subjects in an experiment by Anger-meier, Phelps, and Reynolds (1967) were harassed by the experimenter as they performed a perceptual judgement task, either while alone or in the company of one or two others. With arousal defined in terms of increased heart rate, subjects who performed with two others present were less aroused than those who worked alone. The presence of a single companion, however, actually elicited a slightly *higher* heart rate than was found in subjects working by themselves. Angermeier *et al.* also reported that subjects who worked with one other person tended to consider that individual a possible competitor and to experience some embarrassment over making errors in that person's presence. This was not the case when two others worked with the subject.

Amoroso and Walters (1969) found some evidence of reduction of arousal through social presence in a fear-inducing situation. Subjects who anticipated electric shocks during a learning task while working alone showed higher heart rates than others who awaited the shocks in the presence of three other people. Among subjects who had not been led to expect shocks, the presence of the others had no effect on heart rate. These findings are generally consistent with Schachter's hypothesis that affiliation reduces fear. Different results were found in a study by Buck and Parke (1972) in which measures of physiological arousal were taken from male subjects as they awaited either electric shock or a painless, but potentially embarrassing, activity. The latter consisted of subjects' being required to suck on a baby's bottle and other infantile oral objects. As they awaited one of these two events, subjects were either alone or accompanied by a stranger. The latter either did not speak or made a minimally sympathetic and supportive statement to the subject. The electrodermal data showed that the presence of the other person had no effect on arousal among subjects who awaited shocks. The overall effect of the presence of the other person among subjects awaiting the possibly embarrassing oral behavior was an *increase* in arousal, especially when that person behaved in a friendly and supportive way.

The Buck and Parke (1972) findings indicate that the effects of social presence on arousal in a stressful situation depend on the nature of the stressor and, to some extent, on the behavior of the other person toward the subject. It would appear that subjects find the company of another person aversive when an embarrassing experience is impending, possibly because the other person will presumably be a witness to the embarrassment. The embarrassment may be more acute when the other person has been at least somewhat friendly than when he or she is aloof. A similar finding has been reported by Glass, Gordon, and Henchy (1970). Subjects in that study, who were all men, watched a film showing the ritual sexual mutilation of young males either alone, with a friend, or with a stranger. Subjects revealed higher levels of skin conductance with a friend in attendance than with a stranger. Glass and his colleagues concluded that the film may have stirred unconscious castration fears or latent homosexual feelings, and that subjects may have wished to be anonymous for that reason. The presence of a friend would probably have greater potential for embarrassment under such conditions than the presence of a stranger.

Comparison of the effects of social presence under conditions of fear and embarrassment was the subject of a large and detailed study by Friedman (1981). This experiment involved manipulation of fear and embarrassment, and of the amount of visual contact between the subject and another person. In one condition male subjects were told that they were awaiting electric shocks; in another they were informed that they would be shown pornographic photos as penile tumescence was measured. Subjects were either alone or in the presence of another man who displayed no outward signs of being fearful or aroused. This person sat on the other side of a one-way mirror from the subject; the mirror, moreover, could be altered in such a way that sometimes the two could see each other, sometimes the subject could see the other but not be seen by him, and sometimes neither could see the other.

In two experiments Friedman found consistent evidence indicating that (a) among men awaiting an embarrassing sexual experience, the 'mere presence' of the other man led to higher heart rates and a greater number of skin conductance responses than were shown among men waiting alone, and that (b) among men awaiting shock, the presence of the other man reduced arousal (both cardiac and electrodermal), but only when that person could be seen by the subject. These findings require some comment.

First, it is obvious that the mere presence of another person does not in itself reduce arousal in fearful subjects; the other person must be seen. Why is this? Friedman argues that the fearful subject imitated the calm and unexcited other person, and that this modeling reduced the subject's arousal. Why imitation and modeling should reduce autonomic activation is not clear. Invoking terms such as these explains nothing unless some connection can be shown between the behavior that results from the alleged process and underlying arousal. At least two alternative explanations of Friedman's findings for the fear condition may be considered. One is that subjects who could see the calm other felt constrained not to show fear and therefore inhibited the emotion. Kleck, Vaughan, Cartwright–Smith, Vaughan, Colby, and Lanzetta (1976) have shown that attenuation of the expression of expressive behavior in response to painful stimuli is accompanied by a general decrease in autonomic reactions to those stimuli. Another possibility is that the sight of another person elicits behavior and associated feelings that are incompatible with fear. Curiosity, sociability, and affiliation are possible reactions to another person that can interfere with fear responses. In this connection, we should note a study by Davidson and Kelley (1973), in which hospitalized patients showed smaller increases in skin conductance while watching a stressful film in the presence of a nurse than did other patients who watched the film alone. To argue that the patients used the nurse as a model is less convincing than to conclude that the nurse elicited behaviors and emotions incompatible with fear.

The second point to note in Friedman's findings is that among subjects who faced a potentially embarrassing situation the presence of the other person was associated with high arousal in all conditions. This finding is consistent with those of Buck and Parke (1972) and Glass *et al.* (1970) reported earlier. Friedman's subjects who expected to undergo penile measurement may have thought that the other man would know of their discomfort, and that thought may have greatly exacerbated their embarrassment.

In a sense, the fairly consistent finding that subjects who expect to be embarrassed feel aroused in the presence of others resembles the finding from the social facilitation literature that audiences are arousing only when the performer expects a negative outcome. In both cases the subject is apprehensive about making a bad impression on others, and as a result the others are stimuli for anxiety and arousal. Social presence may bring about decreased arousal when the person experiences an aversive condition (such as frustration, harassment, or impending shock) that may engender high levels of fear and general anxiety, but is not particularly likely to make the person socially anxious or worried about the impression being made on others. In this case the presence of others may elicit a positive affect that competes with, and thereby mitigates, feelings of fear.

SOCIAL/SPATIAL DENSITY AND PHYSIOLOGICAL AROUSAL

When Zajonc outlined his argument that the presence of conspecifics leads to increased arousal, his evidence consisted entirely of findings relating population density to neuroendocrine activity in lower animals (Zajonc, 1965; pp. 273–4). Although students of social facilitation since that time have largely ignored research on density and crowding, the findings of the latter tend to support the hypothesis that social presence often brings about arousal in the individual, and that people in groups, especially when concentrated into relatively small areas, are more highly aroused than people who are isolated or in less dense social environments.

SOCIAL AND SPATIAL DENSITY

Research on crowding reveals two antecedents: *social density*, which refers to the total number of people present, and *spatial density*, which refers to the amount of available space per person, independent of the number of people involved. Psychophysiological studies have shown that both contribute to arousal. Saegert (1974) showed that in laboratory settings containing either the subject alone or up to 12 other people, higher levels of palmar sweating were associated with larger groups. Similar findings were reported by Cox, Paulus, McCain, and Schkade (1979), who found a significant correlation between palmar sweating and the total number of others confined to various living arrangements in a prison. Aiello, Thompson, and Brodzinsky (1983) also found that skin conductance levels were higher among subjects who took part in an experiment in groups of six than among those who participated alone or with a single companion.

In a study carried out in three prisons, D'Atri and Ostfeld (1975) claimed to have found some evidence of higher blood pressure in settings of high spatial density than in those of lower density. In one prison, inmates who were housed in a seven-man dormitory showed higher levels of both systolic and diastolic blood pressure than those housed in either single occupancy cells or two-man cells. In two other prisons, blood pressure was generally higher in men confined to dormitories than in those housed in single occupancy cells. In all three settings, however, men in the dormitories were reported to have had approximately as much space per man as those in single cells. The findings do not, therefore, represent effects of spatial density but appear instead to be related more to social density. D'Atri and Ostfeld note in passing that men living in dormitories were at greater risk of harm from other inmates than were those living alone, and were therefore presumably under greater stress. This alone could have had a marked effect on hypertension. A subsequent investigation by D'Atri, Fitzgerald, Kasl, and Ostfeld (1981) showed that moving inmates from single cells to dormitories was accompanied by increased systolic pressure. Thus, a change from low to high social density appears to have the predicted effect of increasing inmates' arousal.

Several studies show that spatial density has effects on psychophysiological activation. Saegert (1974) found higher levels of palmar sweat among subjects who were allowed 6 square feet per person in the laboratory than among those given 24 square feet apiece. Evans (1979) ran adult subjects in groups of ten either in a room measuring 8 × 12 feet or one measuring 20 × 30 feet. Diastolic blood pressure and pulse rate were both significantly higher among subjects in the smaller room than among those in the larger one. A study by Hackworth (1976) found similar effects of relative room size on both systolic and diastolic blood pressure among boys aged 8–14 years. Aiello, Epstein, and Karlin (1975) conducted two experiments which, taken together, indicate that social and spatial density interact to influence arousal. In one experiment six-person groups were run in both large and small rooms in counterbalanced order. Skin conductance levels were higher when subjects were in the small room than when they were in the larger one. In the second experiment, subjects were run singly in each of the two rooms and no effects of room size on conductance were found. Thus, the presence of others and the size of the room acted jointly to determine conductance levels.

There is also some evidence that the arousal elicited by crowded conditions is relatively resistant to habituation. Epstein, Woolfolk, and Lehrer (1981) have studied the effects of repeated exposure to crowding. Twenty male subjects were tested on three separate occasions, a week apart, by being placed in a room for 20 minutes with three experimental confederates. One room was 16 × 12 feet and the other 4 × 2.67 feet. The latter led to such crowding of the four men that close physical contact was unavoidable. The pulse volume of subjects in the small room was significantly higher on all three occasions than that obtained in a pre-crowding baseline period. Pulse volume for uncrowded subjects showed a decline to baseline levels during the third and final session. Thus, being crowded into a tiny space with close contact prevented a habituation process that occurred in the noncrowded setting.

MODERATOR VARIABLES

Little has been reported concerning possible moderating variables in the relationship of crowding to arousal. Aiello, DeRisi, Epstein, and Karlin (1977) used settings similar to those in the study just described to test for moderating effects of individual differences in preferred interpersonal distance. The individual differences were measured both behaviorally and by using a self-report measure. The subjects, all women, were then placed in groups of four in either a 16 × 12 foot room or one measuring 4 × 2.5 feet. Higher levels of skin conductance were found in the small room than in the large one for women who preferred noncrowded situations. Among women who had a preference for closer interpersonal contact, the situation of high spatial density elicited no higher conductance levels than did the more spacious setting. Another variable that may play some role in the crowding–arousal relationship is the sex of the subject, although this variable has not been systematically studied. Nicosia, Hyman, Karlin, Epstein, and Aiello (1979) report that men and women reacted to crowding differently. Subjects were allocated to same-sex groups of four persons. These groups were assigned to either a small space (ca. 0.85 × 1.2 m) or a larger one (3 × 5 m). Crowded men showed a marked increase in conductance as the session went on, whereas crowded women did not. The authors suggested that this difference may have been due in part to the larger average size of men, which would presumably have made them feel more crowded in the small space than did the women. This conclusion is weakened, however, by the finding of Aiello, Nicosia, and Thompson (1979) that children and adolescents show generally higher levels of skin conductance in crowded than uncrowded conditions. One group in that study consisted of fourth graders, most of whom are probably smaller than most adult women. Our best conclusion is that more data are needed before sex differences in crowding effects can be explained.

DENSITY, AROUSAL, AND CONTROL

We can conclude that the arousing effects of spatial density have been clearly demonstrated in several studies. One question remains: why is population density associated with high levels of arousal? Two answers to this question have been suggested. One is that high density threatens the person with stimulus overload by producing stimulation at levels beyond the person's processing ability (Milgram, 1970). The other is that density creates constraints on behavior which lead to psychological reaction (Baum, Aiello, and Calesnick, 1978). These two ideas have one feature in common: both the behaviorally constrained person and the overloaded one have lost some degree of personal control over the environment, and this loss of control is postulated as the immediate cause of increased arousal (Schmidt and Keating, 1979).

This idea was implicit in two studies carried out in natural settings among

Swedish commuters by Lundberg and his associates (Lundberg, 1976; Singer, Lundberg, and Frankenhaueser, 1978). In both studies, excretion of the catecholamines epinephrine and norepinephrine was measured in persons after a train ride. Approximately half the riders got on the train at a station far from the destination; the remainder travelled about half that distance. Riders in the first group, therefore, were less crowded over the entire trip than were those who boarded later. Singer *et al.* (1978) showed that epinephrine excretion was smaller in those who rode the longer distance than in those who rode the shorter. Lundberg (1976) found similar results for both epinephrine and norepinephrine excretion. In addition, Lundberg found higher levels of the catecholamines in both groups of riders during a period of heavy use of the train (caused by a rationing of motor fuel) than it had been earlier when fewer people rode the train. In both studies, the lower catecholamine excretion was associated with a relative freedom and control over the situation. Persons boarding the train earlier had more control in choosing a seat than those who boarded later when the train was fuller. In addition, riding during periods of heavy use due to rationing allowed restricted freedom of choice of seats relative to that enjoyed during periods of less use.

One study has shown that the arousing effects of crowding may be mitigated to some extent by interventions designed to give the person more control over the situation. Karlin, Katz, Epstein, and Woolfolk (1979) placed groups of four male subjects in a small chamber in which close physical contact was maintained for 15 minutes. Half the subjects had been taught relaxation techniques which they were instructed to use during the session. The proportion of untrained subjects showing an increase in pulse rate over baseline levels was significantly greater than the proportion of trained subjects who showed a similar increase. Thus, the practice of systematic relaxation, which can be thought of as a coping device that restores some control to the person, reduces the physiological response to crowding.

CONCLUSION

In this paper we have reviewed studies relating the presence of others to physiological arousal. The overall conclusions that we draw from ths review are:

1. Evidence for the hypothesis that the presence of observers or coactors produces increased arousal in the social facilitation paradigm is weak. Most of the evidence comes from studies using palmar sweat as a dependent measure, and palmar sweat may not be an indicator of general activation. Experiments involving other common measures are few in number and require more replication before definite conclusions can be drawn.
2. The prediction from research on affiliation—that the presence of other people can reduce arousal in persons undergoing stressful experiences—is largely supported in cases where the stressor involves pain or some other treatment not

likely to humiliate the subject. When subjects are threatened with possibly embarrassing experiences, the presence of others is often associated with increased arousal.

3. Studies relating arousal to population density have shown that both social and spatial density can lead to elevated arousal. To date, few elaborations on this basic effect have been reported.

A few loose connections exist between these three areas of research. Audience size may be directly related to the amount of arousal elicited in the social facilitation experiment, for example (Latané and Nida, 1980), which is consistent with what we know about effects of social density. That embarrassment is an important mediator of arousal in studies of affiliation is consistent with the argument advanced elsewhere (e.g. Geen, 1989) that audiences and coactors produce increased arousal only if they are regarded as witnesses to the subject's failing on a task. These simple convergences in the data suggest that research designed to bring together the three literatures may be worth consideration.

REFERENCES

Aiello, J. R., DeRisi, D., Epstein, Y. M., and Karlin, R. A. (1977) Crowding and the role of interpersonal distance preference. *Sociometry*, **40**, 271–82.

Aiello, J. R., Epstein, Y. M., and Karlin, R. A. (1975) Effects of crowding on electrodermal activity. *Sociologial Symposium*, **14**, 43–57.

Aiello, J. R., Nicosia, G., and Thompson, D. E. (1979) Physiological, social, and behavioral consequences of crowding on children and adolescents. *Child Development*, **50**, 195–202.

Aiello, J. R., Thompson, D. E., and Brodzinsky, D. M. (1983) How funny is crowding, anyway? Effects of room size, group size, and the introduction of humor. *Basic and Applied Social Psychology*, **4**, 193–207.

Allport, F. H. (1924) *Social Psychology*. Boston: Houghton-Mifflin.

Amoroso, D. M., and Walters, R. H. (1969) Effects of anxiety and socially mediated anxiety reduction on paired-associate learning. *Journal of Personality and Social Psychology*, **11**, 388–96.

Angermeier, W. F., Phelps, J. B., and Reynolds, H. H. (1967) Verbal stress and heart rate in humans exposed in groups. *Psychonomic Science*, **8**, 515–16.

Bargh, J. A., and Cohen, J. L. (1978) Mediating factors in the arousal–performance relationship. *Motivation and Emotion*, **2**, 243–57.

Baron, R. S. (1986) Distraction–conflict theory: progress and problems. In L. Berkowitz (Ed), *Advances in Experimental Social Psychology*, Vol. 19. New York: Academic Press.

Baum, A., Aiello, J. R., and Calesnick, L. E. (1978) Crowding and personal control: social density and the development of learned helplessness. *Journal of Personality and Social Psychology*, **36**, 1000–11.

Bell, P. A., Loomis, R. J., and Cervone, J. C. (1982) Effects of heat, social facilitation, sex differences, and task difficulty on reaction time. *Human Factors*, **24**, 19–24.

Bond, C. F., and Titus, L. J. (1983) Social facilitation: a meta-analysis of 241 studies. *Psychological Bulletin*, **94**, 265–92.

Borden, R. J., Hendrick, C., and Walker, J. W. (1976) Affective, physiological, and attitudinal consequences of audience presence. *Bulletin of the Psychonomic Society*, **7**, 33–6.

Bregman, N. J., and McAllister, H. A. (1983) Voluntary control of skin temperature: role of experimenter presence versus absence. *Biofeedback and Self-Regulation*, **8**, 543–6.

Buck, R. W., and Parke, R. D. (1972) Behavioral and physiological response to the presence of a friendly or neutral person in two types of stressful situations. *Journal of Personality and Social Psychology*, **24**, 143–53.

Burtt, H. E. (1921) The inspiration–expiration ratio during truth and falsehood. *Journal of Experimental Psychology*, **4**, 1–23.

Carver, C. S., and Scheier, M. F. (1981a) *Attention and Self-Regulation: A Control-Theory Approach to Human Behavior*. New York: Springer.

Carver, C. S., and Scheier, M. F. (1981b) The self-attention-induced feedback loop and social facilitation. *Journal of Experimental Social Psychology*, **17**, 545–68.

Chapman, A. J. (1973) An electromyographic study of apprehension about evaluation. *Psychological Reports*, **33**, 811–14.

Chapman, A. J. (1974) An electromyographic study of social facilitation: a test of the 'mere presence' hypothesis. *British Journal of Psychology*, **65**, 123–8.

Cohen, J. L. (1979) Social facilitation increased evaluation apprehension through permanency of record. *Motivation and Emotion*, **3**, 19–33.

Cohen, J. L. (1980) Social facilitation: audience versus evaluation apprehension effects. *Motivation and Emotion*, **4**, 21–33.

Cohen, J. L., and Davis, J. H. (1973) Effects of audience status, evaluation, and time of action on performance with hidden-word problems. *Journal of Personality and Social Psychology*, **27**, 74–85.

Cotton, J. L., Baron, R. S., and Borkovec, T. D. (1980) Caffeine ingestion, misattribution therapy, and speech anxiety. *Journal of Research in Personality*, **14**, 196–206.

Cottrell, N. B. (1972) Social facilitation. In C. G. McClintock (Ed), *Experimental Social Psychology*. New York: Holt.

Cottrell, N. B., and Epley, S. W. (1977) Affiliation, social comparison, and socially mediated stress reduction. In J. M. Suls and R. L. Miller (Eds), *Social Comparison Processes: Theoretical and Empirical Perspectives*. Washington, DC: Hemisphere.

Cottrell, N. B., Wack, D. L., Sekerak, G. J., and Rittle, R. H. (1968) Social facilitation of dominant responses by the presence of an audience and the mere presence of others. *Journal of Personality and Social Psychology*, **9**, 245–50.

Cox, V. C., Paulus, P. B., McCain, G., and Schkade, J. K. (1979) Field research on the effects of crowding in prisons and on offshore drilling platforms. In J. R. Aiello and A. Baum (Eds), *Residential Crowding and Design*. New York: Plenum Press.

Dabbs, J. M., Johnson, J. E., and Leventhal, H. (1968) Palmar sweating: a quick and simple measure. *Journal of Experimental Psychology*, **78**, 347–350.

Dashiell, J. F. (1935) Experimental studies of the influence of social situations on the behavior of individual human adults. In C. Murchison (Ed), *Handbook of Social Psychology*. Worcester, MA: Clark University Press.

D'Atri, D. A., Fitzgerald, E. F., Kasl, S. V., and Ostfeld, A. M. (1981) Crowding in prison: the relationship between changes in housing mode and blood pressure. *Psychosomatic Medicine*, **43**, 95–105.

D'Atri, D. A., and Ostfeld, A. M. (1975) Crowding: its effect on the elevation of blood pressure in a prison setting. *Preventive Medicine*, **4**, 550–66.

Davidson, P. O., and Kelley, W. R. (1973) Social facilitation and coping with stress. *British Journal of Social and Clinical Psychology*, **12**, 130–6.

Elliott, E. S., and Cohen, J. L. (1981) Social facilitation effects via interpersonal distance. *Journal of Social Psychology*, **114**, 237–49.

Epstein, Y. M., Woolfolk, R. L., and Lehrer, P. M. (1981) Physiological, cognitive, and nonverbal responses to repeated exposure to crowding. *Journal of Applied Social Psychology*, **11**, 1–13.

Evans, G. W. (1979) Behavioral and physiological consequences of crowding in humans. *Journal of Applied Social Psychology*, **9**, 27–46.

Fowles, D. C. (1983) Motivational effects of heart rate and electrodermal activity: implications for research on personality and psychopathology. *Journal of Research in Personality*, **17**, 48–71.

Friedman, L. (1981) How affiliation affects stress in fear and anxiety situations. *Journal of Personality and Social Psychology*, **40**, 1102–17.

Geen, R. G. (1977) The effects of anticipation of positive and negative outcomes on audience anxiety. *Journal of Consulting and Clinical Psychology*, **45**, 715–16.

Geen, R. G. (1979) Effects of being observed on learning following success and failure experiences. *Motivation and Emotion*, **3**, 355–71.

Geen, R. G. (1981) Evaluation apprehension and social facilitation: a reply to Sanders. *Journal of Experimental Social Psycology*, **17**, 252–6.

Geen, R. G. (1989) Alternative conceptions of social facilitation. In P. Paulus (Ed), *Psychology of Group Influence*, 2nd edn. Hillsdale, NJ: Erlbaum.

Geen, R. G., and Bushman, B. J. (1987) Drive theory: the effects of socially engendered arousal. In B. Mullen and G. Goethals (Eds), *Theories of Group Behavior*. New York: Springer.

Geen, R. G., and Gange, J. J. (1977) Drive theory of social facilitation: twelve years of theory and research. *Psychological Bulletin*, **84**, 1267–88.

Glass, D. C., Gordon, A., and Henchy, T. (1970) The effects of social stimuli on psychophysiological reactivity to an aversive film. *Psychonomic Science*, **20**, 255–6.

Glass, D. C., and Singer, J. E. (1972) *Urban Stress*. New York: Academic Press.

Groff, B. D., Baron, R. S., and Moore, D. L. (1983) Distraction, attentional conflict, and drivelike behavior. *Journal of Experimental Social Psychology*, **19**, 359–80.

Guerin, B., and Innes, J. M. (1982) Social facilitation and social monitoring: a new look at Zajonc's mere presence hypothesis. *British Journal of Social Psychology*, **21**, 7–18.

Hackworth, J. R. (1976) Relationship between spatial density and sensory overload, personal space, and systolic and diastolic blood pressure. *Perceptual and Motor Skills*, **43**, 867–72.

Henchy, T., and Glass, D. C. (1968) Evaluation apprehension and the social facilitation of dominant and subordinate responses. *Journal of Personality and Social Psychology*, **10**, 446–54.

Karlin, R. A., Katz, S., Epstein, Y. M., and Woolfolk, R. L. (1979) The use of therapeutic interventions to reduce crowding-related arousal: a preliminary investigation. *Environmental Psychology and Nonverbal Behavior*, **3**, 219–27.

Karst, T. D., and Most, R. (1973) A comparison of stress measures in an experimental analogue of public speaking. *Journal of Consulting and Clinical Psychology*, **41**, 342–8.

Kissel, S. (1965) Stress-reducing properties of social stimuli. *Journal of Personality and Social Psychology*, **2**, 378–84.

Kleck, R. E., Vaughan, R. C., Cartwright-Smith, J., Vaughan, K. B., Colby, C. Z., and Lanzetta, J. T. (1976) Effects of being observed on expressive, subjective, and physiological responses to painful stimuli. *Journal of Personality and Social Psychology*, **34**, 1211–18.

Knight, M. L., and Borden, R. J. (1979) Autonomic and affective reactions of high and low socially anxious individuals awaiting public performance. *Psychophysiology*, **16**, 209–13.

Lacey, J. I. (1967) Somatic response patterning and stress: some revisions of activation theory. In M. Appley and R. Trumbull (Eds), *Psychological Stress*. New York: Appleton-Century-Crofts.

Latané, B., and Nida, S. (1980) Social impact theory and group influence: a social engineering perspective. In P. Paulus (Ed), *Psychology of Group Influence*, pp. 3–34. Hillsdale, NJ: Erlbaum.

Lundberg, U. (1976) Urban commuting: crowdedness and catecholamine excretion. *Journal of Human Stress*, **2** (3), 26–32.

Manstead, A. S. R., and Semin, G. R. (1980) Social facilitation effects: mere enhancement of dominant responses? *British Journal of Social and Clinical Psychology*, **19**, 119–36.

Martens, R. (1969a) Effects of an audience on learning and performance of a complex motor skill. *Journal of Personality and Social Psychology*, **12**, 252–60.

Martens, R. (1969b) Palmar sweating and the presence of an audience. *Journal of Experimental Social Psychology*, **5**, 371–4.

McKinney, M. E., Gatchel, R. J., and Paulus, P. B. (1983) The effects of audience size on high and low speech-anxious subjects during an actual speaking task. *Basic and Applied Social Psychology*, **4**, 73–87.

McNair, D. M., Droppleman, L. F., and Kussman, M. (1967) Finger sweat print tape bands. *Psychophysiology*, **3**, 280–4.

Milgram, S. (1970) The experience of living in cities. *Science*, **167**, 1461–8.

Moore, D. L., and Baron, R. S. (1983) Social facilitation: a psychophysiological analysis. In J. Cacioppo and R. Petty (Eds), *Social Psychophysiology: A Sourcebook*. New York: Guilford Press.

Moore, D. L., Logel, M. L., Weerts, T. C., Sanders, G. S., and Baron, R. S. (1984) Are audiences distracting? Behavioral and physiological data. Unpublished manuscript, University of Iowa.

Moore, H. T. (1917) Laboratory tests of anger, fear, and sex interests. *American Journal of Psychology*, **28**, 390–5.

Nicosia, G. J., Hyman, D., Karlin, R. A., Epstein, Y. M., and Aiello, J. R. (1979) Effects of bodily contact on reactions to crowding. *Journal of Applied Social Psychology*, **9**, 508–23.

Paulus, P. B., Annis, A. B., and Risner, H. T. (1978) An analysis of the mirror-induced objective self-awareness effect. *Bulletin of the Psychonomic Society*, **12**, 8–10.

Saegert, S. C. (1974) Effects of spatial and social density on arousal, mood and social orientation. Unpublished doctoral dissertation, University of Michigan.

Sarason, I. G. (1972) Experimental approaches to test anxiety: attention and the uses of information. In C. D. Spielberger (Ed), *Anxiety: Current Trends in Theory and Research*, Vol. 2. New York: Academic Press.

Schachter, S. (1959) *The Psychology of Affiliation*. Stanford, CA: Stanford University Press.

Schmidt, D. E., and Keating, J. P. (1979) Human crowding and personal control: an integration of the research. *Psychological Bulletin*, **86**, 680–700.

Singer, J. E., Lundberg, U., and Frankenhaueser, M. (1978) Stress of the train: a study of urban commuting. In A. Baum, J. E. Singer, and S. Valins (Eds), *Advances in Environmental Psychology*, Vol. 1. Hillsdale, NJ: Erlbaum.

Singerman, K. J., Borkovec, T. D., and Baron, R. S. (1976) Failure of 'misattribution therapy' manipulation with a clinically relevant target behavior. *Behavior Therapy*, **7**, 306–13.

Strahan, R. F., Todd, J. B., and Inglis, G. B. (1974) A palmar sweat measure particularly suited for naturalistic research. *Psychophysiology*, **11**, 715–20.

Travis, L. E. (1925) The effect of small audience upon hand–eye coordination. *Journal of Abnormal and Social Psychology*, **20**, 142–6.

Triplett, N. (1898) The dynamogenic factors in pacemaking and competition. *American Journal of Psychology*, **9**, 507–33.

Zajonc, R. B. (1965) Social facilitation. *Science*, **149**, 269–74.

Zajonc, R. B. (1980) Compresence. In P. Paulus (Ed), *Psychology of Group Influence*. Hillsdale, NJ: Erlbaum.

Chapter 11

Arousal Theory and Stress

Carol Silvia Weisse, Laura M. Davidson and Andrew Baum

Uniformed Services University of the Health Sciences

ABSTRACT

Arousal is a central construct in stress, emotion, and other important psychophysiological concepts. It is difficult to define, and is most often expressed as a change in some behaviour or measure of bodily function. However, arousal is the essense of response during stress and has several consequences for mood and behavior. In this chapter, several of these issues are considered, with some emphasis on the relationships between arousal and illness, the effects of chronic arousal, and the role of arousal in affective disorders and disturbances such as post-traumatic stress disorder (PTSD). The importance of broad-based, multi-level measurement of arousal is also discussed.

'Arousal' is a major theme in stress research. As a reliable characteristic of the stress response, arousal has become a valuable tool to stress researchers. Not only does arousal provide an important marker of stress, but factors known to mediate arousal are also moderators of the stress response. In addition, arousal offers mechanisms by which stress may contribute to illness processes. For this reason, knowledge about arousal, particularly its measurement and its effect on health,

Preparation of this chapter was supported by research grants from the Uniformed Services University of the Health Sciences (RO7265 and CO7205) and from the National Science Foundation (BNS). The opinions or assertions contained herein are the private ones of the authors and are not to be construed as official or reflecting the views of the Department of Defense or the Uniformed Services University of the Health Sciences.

Handbook of Social Psychophysiology, Edited by H. Wagner and A. Manstead,

affords an opportunity for closer examination and better understanding of the stress construct.

This chapter will review the role of arousal in stress research. An introduction to arousal theories and how researchers have interpreted the word arousal will serve as a beginning to the chapter. How arousal may offer an important link between stress and disease, and the implications of such a link will also be examined. Finally, we will discuss models of stress that have focused on arousal and describe current research investigating the complex relationship between environment and health.

WHAT IS AROUSAL?

Establishing a suitable definition for the arousal construct is not an easy task. In the past, arousal theories have faced considerable criticism, and currently there is no one, universally accepted definition. Heterogeneous views of arousal are in existence, generating confusion and incongruencies in research, particularly stress research, where the construct is often central. Casual use of the term confounds its meaning and threatens its utility in current stress studies. Clearly, a universal definition needs to be established. But first, we will address how arousal has been defined in the past and the methodologies that have set the framework for these definitions.

Historically, arousal has been an hypothesized drive state responsible for motivating behavior, and before the development of sophisticated psychophysiological recording apparatus, arousal was most easily, and hence most often, assessed from overt behavior. Task performance has been the prototypic behavioral framework used to assess arousal states. In a series of experiments conducted in the early 1900s, Yerkes and Dodson (1908) showed performance on a task to be a function of stimulus intensity and task complexity. From these studies came the Yerkes–Dodson law, proposing a curvilinear relationship between arousal and performance. According to this law, moderate levels of arousal were necessary for optimal performance (Kahneman, 1973). Since the Yerkes–Dodson law and the notion that arousal states could be reflected in performance, task performance deficits have served as markers of extreme arousal states.

Arousal has been analyzed in the context of behaviors other than performance. Aggression, open-field activity, defecation, and increased response rates are all behavioral representations of high arousal in animals. There are, however, behavioral models of arousal or anxiety characterized by a decline in responding, making a consistent behavioral model of arousal difficult. For example, conditioned suppression, originally referred to as conditioned emotional responding (Estes and Skinner, 1941), is a paradigm in which a decline in responding suggests fear or arousal in the organism. Therefore, behavioral models of arousal do not always necessarily concur. There are a wide array of behaviors accepted as representing arousal, making the construct a difficult one to define solely on the basis of behavioral techniques.

Studies of the brain had a major impact on arousal conceptualizations in that they provided a physiological correlate for the hypothesized drive state motivating behavior. Researchers transecting CNS regions were able to localize 'sleep' and 'waking' centers in the brainstem (Batini, Moruzzi, Palestini, Rossi, and Zanchetti, 1959; Bremer, 1937). Recordings made of electrical impulses in the brainstem, particularly within the ascending reticular activating system (ARAS), provided new and exciting data in support of arousal states, and arousal came to be viewed in terms of electrical brain activity. Techniques such as the electroencephalogram (EEG), contingent negative variation (CNV), and evoked potential (EP) were developed in the hope that they would provide researchers with the necessary tools for assessing covert cognitive processes which were not necessarily accompanied by overt behaviors. Since the development of these techniques, conditions typically associated with high arousal, such as anxiety and stress, have been related to changes in the electrical activity of the brain (Knott and Irwin, 1973; Leeuwen, vanKamp, Kok, Dequartel, and Tielen, 1967; Tecce, 1972). Recordings of brain activity are not, however, always simple or reliable means for studying specific cognitive events.

Because arousal has been viewed as a cognitive state, self-report techniques have been also used to assess arousal, yet the reliability and validity of such measures have been questioned. There appear to be individual differences and sex differences in the ability to perceive physiological arousal, and an increased ability to perceive visceral changes can occur with training (Blascovich and Katkin, 1983). Zillmann has reported instances of physiological arousal persistence even after the decay of psychological awareness (e.g. Zillmann, 1983). Hence, arousal states may not always be perceived, therefore may not always be reportable, making self-report measures of arousal less popular, at least as a sole measure.

With advances in technology, the field of psychophysiology has grown considerably over the years. Many new techniques have been developed to assess arousal, and the construct has expanded to include activity in a number of bodily systems. Arousal continues to be assessed from behaviours, from questionnaires, and from activity levels in the brain, but also from physiological activity occurring in the periphery. A variety of physiological measures of arousal have been established. These include a wide spectrum of events ranging from activity within the eyes, sweat glands, and muscles, to changes occurring within cardiovascular, respiratory, digestive, nervous, and endocrine systems. Physiological indicators of arousal have become, by far, the most popular and widely used of all techniques.

As one can see, arousal had been defined in as many ways as researchers have attempted to measure it. Today, self-report measures, behavioral measures like performance, and physiological measures such as heart rate, blood pressure, skin conductance, and levels of various hormones, are all popular indices. Important questions, however, still remain; for instance, do behavioral, cognitive, and physiological arousal states all reflect the same phenomenon? Furthermore, are certain assessment techniques more accurate measures of arousal than others? The classic view of arousal as activation (Duffy, 1934; Hebb, 1955; Lindsley, 1951; Malmo, 1959) has fostered the incorrect supposition that all psychophysiologic measures reflecting activation represent arousal and are, therefore, interchangeable variables. Activation is too simple to define arousal adequately, yet research still reflects the influence of these ideas popularized by activation theorists.

Lacey was one of the first to disagree with activation theorists who viewed arousal as a unitary dimension, that is, as autonomic changes occurring in much the same way in all systems of the body. Lacey (1967) argued that the existence of situational stereotypy, whereby different situations could evoke distinct patterns of somatic responses, would suggest arousal to be more multidimensional in nature than originally portrayed by activation theorists. He argued further that if dissociation could occur between behavioral and psychophysiologic arousal, a unitary approach was inadequate. Lacey described situations where one measure of autonomic arousal might indicate heightened activity while another measure could simultaneously suggest low arousal, and concluded that an arousal continuum from sleep to wakefulness or excitement (Berlyne, 1960) was a misleading representation of a more complex construct.

These findings have rightly encouraged many researchers to abandon the continuum conceptualization of arousal and, instead, to investigate the multidimensional nature of arousal. Arousal is not simple activation that is equally represented in all systems of the body. Therefore, measures cannot be regarded as interchangeable variables. Clearly, research designs that utilize multiple assessment techniques and examine the relationships between behavioral, cognitive, and physiological measures are needed. In addition, appropriate combination of measures should be established.

In conclusion, the word arousal is an overused term in the literature. At best, arousal can be defined as a psychophysiological change away from homeostasis which can occur in any number of bodily systems, cognitions, or behaviors. Because these changes may be recorded in different modalities, it is imperative to define and report clearly how changes are being assessed in research designs. It is hoped that the importance of arousal states in learning, memory, mood, health, and stress will provide the impetus for clearer definition, greater characterization, and more careful utilization of the arousal construct.

AROUSAL-BASED STRESS MODELS

Studies of stress grew out of arousal theory. In fact, stress and arousal were originally viewed synonymously. Cannon's (1914) early work incorporated the notion of arousal, referring to it as an emergency response. Cannon referred to the systemic physiological arousal that prepared an organism to cope with stressful or emergency conditions as the 'fight or flight' response. Mediated principally by adrenal medullary activity and sympathetic nervous system activity, this defining feature of arousal provided a template for nearly three-quarters of a century of research. Arousal, or increased activity of the sympathetic nervous system can be expressed in a number of ways, including an increase in heart rate, blood pressure, and respiration. Cannon suggested that stressful experiences could be characterized by this state, highlighting arousal as the major constituent of stress. By defining emotional stress in terms of sympathetic arousal, he emphasized the importance of its preparatory function for fight or flight against a stressful event.

Cannon's approach to stress laid the groundwork for further study. Major stress theories that followed portrayed stress as a standard physiological response in all emergency situations. This approach treats stress as a physiological response and its underlying assumption of nonspecificity is a prominent theme in the stress model developed by Selye. Selye (1956) argued that all noxious stimuli caused the same general stress response, but unlike Cannon, Selye focused on arousal of the pituitary–adrenocortical axis rather than the sympathetic nervous system. Selye found heightened secretion of glucocorticoids to be a common denominator in stressful events. He noted that a wide variety of negative stimuli (e.g. cold, pain, exercise, bacteria) caused organisms to respond with concomitant elevations of corticosteroids. From this, Selye proposed that stress was a specific syndrome that arose from all noxious events. This syndrome, referred to as the General Adaptation Syndrome (GAS), occurred in three stages.

According to Selye, all stressors trigger an initial alarm reaction, and, in this first phase of the GAS, the organism responds with a generalized arousal, preparing the organism for resistance, the second phase of the syndrome. During alarm, corticosteroids are released into circulation, but during resistance this secretory pattern ceases and adrenal activity focuses on replenishing stores of corticosteroids. Concurrently, steroids already released presumably 'do their work' and facilitate resistance to the stressor. Most stressors are thus overcome, activity within the pituitary–adrenocortical axis wanes, and the particular episode of stress is ended. However, if the stressor is persistent, intense, or otherwise difficult to overcome, a third stage is possible. Exhaustion reflects the depletion of stores of corticosteroids such that 'reloading' of steroids during resistance is no longer possible. During this third phase of the GAS, pathological consequences of the stressor become evident.

Both Cannon and Selye developed stress models illustrating the phenomenon whereby stressful stimuli or aversive conditions could nonspecifically induce physiological arousal. Cannon viewed physiological arousal as activation of the sympathetic nervous system, whereas Selye examined the role of the pituitary–adrenocortical system in the stress response. Both perceived arousal to be a key component of the stress response, but focused on different hormonal indices of arousal. Their work was also compatible with arousal models assuming unitary activation.

That arousal resulted from all stressors was generally accepted until Mason (e.g.

1975) challenged the nonspecific nature of the stress response. Mason argued that to assume that all stressful situations induced the same arousal or activation would be to ignore psychological determinants of stress, which he believed were ultimately responsible for determining the arousing nature of an event. According to Mason, perception and psychological relevance were necessary for the physiological arousal which occurred in response to stressful stimuli; objective characteristics of the event were not the sole determinants of stress or arousal. Mason showed that physical stressors did not arouse adrenal activity when psychological/perceptual factors were eliminated, and he described different arousal patterns associated with different psychological defenses. In a study of parents of children with leukemia, for example, it was found that not all parents responded similarly to this stressful situation (Friedman, Mason, and Hamburg, 1963). Parents exhibiting signs of denial showed decreases in adrenocortical arousal as indicated by decreases in circulating levels of corticosteroids, whereas parents 'suffering in silence' showed increases in corticosteroid production.

In other studies, Mason showed that by reducing the emotionally disturbing aspects of a stressful event, changes in adrenal activity could be minimized. He concluded that the stressfulness of an event was a function of the psychological state of the individual, and that generalizations concerning how individuals would respond could not be made without taking account of their psychological status. In addition, he noted the importance of psychosocial setting, as well as historical and developmental factors. Most importantly, Mason emphasized the need for research investigating patterns of secretory changes within the endocrine system, since not all noxious stimuli elicited comparable increases in epinephrine, norepinephrine, and cortisol. For a review of this work, see Mason (1975).

Frankenhauser (1971) attempted to delineate more carefully those psychological factors responsible for increasing sympathetic arousal. A series of studies suggested that sympathetic arousal could occur under a variety of psychological situations, including overstimulation, understimulation, anticipation, and conflict. Other studies have also shown increases in sympathetic arousal to both pleasant and unpleasant stimuli (Levi, 1965). However, in the main, the evidence suggests that negative events are associated with changes in sympathetic arousal. There is a paucity of studies showing increased sympathetic arousal in response to positive events or mental states such as hope, faith and love. Although there is evidence that all major life events, both positive and negative, are associated with health effects, the psychophysiological mechanisms underlying the relationship between life events and health are not well established (e.g. Rahe, 1975).

In the final analysis, arousal and stress remain inextricably linked. Whether a specific stress model has focused on sympathetic arousal, activity of the adrenal cortex, or changes in a variety of systems, arousal is portrayed as a central focus of stress responding. Recent work has made it clear that appraisal and the psychological relevance of an event are important aspects of stress, but arousal is still the most consistent outcome of stressful encounters. Can one occur without the other? At some level the close association of both physiological and behavioural arousal of one sort or another and stress has been responsible for the semantic nightmare often evoked by the term 'stress.' If arousal and stress are, in fact, the same, stress would include exercise, emotion, and all other conditions that cause or reflect deviation of some bodily system from its equilibrium point. This is an untenable position, and it is important to recognize that arousal is likely to be a necessary condition of stress but not, by itself, a sufficient one.

AROUSAL AND ILLNESS

Research examining stress and how stress may contribute to illness and an increased susceptibility to disease has relied heavily on the notion of physiological arousal. A wide range of illnesses and disorders have been proposed as being initiated, mediated, or exacerbated by increases in adrenal hormones that characteristically rise during stress. Both catecholamines and glucocorticoids, when elevated, have been linked to cardiovascular diseases, gastrointestinal disorders, immune disturbances, and cancer. This section will review mechanisms whereby arousal, as reflected by adrenal hormones, may contribute to these disease states.

CARDIOVASCULAR DISEASES

Among the major risk factors for coronary heart disease are cigarette smoking, hypertension, and elevated serum cholesterol. With the advent of the Type A behavior pattern and epidemiological evidence demonstrating an association between people exhibiting excessive competitiveness, impatience, and hostility, and the development of heart disease, researchers have sought to uncover psychophysiological mechanisms to account for this relationship. Because of the well-established relationship between stress and activation within both sympatho-adrenomedullary and pituitary–adrenocortical axes, one question has been how physiological arousal might contribute to coronary heart disease and hypertension.

Considerable evidence exists linking excess catecholamine release to cardio-vascular disorders. Studies supporting the role of sympathetic arousal in coronary heart disease and hypertension have been reviewed by Herd (1984) and Schneiderman (1983). In essence, studies reveal that surges of catecholamines may lead to damage of arterial walls directly or indirectly through a number of pathways. For example, by increasing heart rate and constricting blood vessels catecholamines can lead to increased blood pressure which may then in turn promote damage to the endothelium of coronary vessels. Injury to this inner lining of the blood vessels to the heart acts as an initiating event in atherosclerosis (Ross and Glomset, 1976).

When lipids enter damaged tissue, smooth muscle cell proliferation is stimulated, thus promoting the build-up of atherosclerotic plaque. Catecholamines mobilize lipids and may contribute to cardiovascular disease in this manner. Another way that catecholamines may indirectly foster the development of atherosclerotic plaque is by increasing platelet aggregation and enhancing blood clot formation. Finally, catecholamines can disturb the electrical activity of the heart and promote the development of arrhythmias or even ventricular fibrillation. Hence, a number of pathways have been proposed to describe how increased sympathetic nervous system activity may increase risk of cardiovascular disease.

There is also evidence that arousal within the pituitary–adrenocortical system can contribute to coronary heart disease. Glucocorticoids can act indirectly, as they have been shown to regulate catecholamine synthesis (Axelrod and Reisine, 1984). Cortisol also initiates lipolysis, increasing the chance that plasma lipids will enter damaged areas in the vessels and promote the development of atherosclerotic plaque. This notion is supported by results of a study showing that the severity of atherosclerosis was increased in monkeys receiving cortisol in conjunction with a diet high in saturated fat and cholesterol (Sprague, Troxler, Peterson, Schmidt, and Young, 1980). Thus, the role of glucocorticoids in coronary heart disease may be related to corticosteroid-induced alterations in lipid metabolism. There is less evidence for the role of corticosteroids in the development of cardiovascular diseases than there is for catecholamines, but both modes of physiological arousal initiate changes capable of facilitating disease states within the cardiovascular system.

GASTROINTESTINAL DISTURBANCES

Traditionally, ulcers have been described as disorders resulting from psychological stress and concomitant increases in gastric acid secretion (Wolf and Wolff, 1947). Ulcers have served as the prototype psychosomatic illness for years. Selye, in his early stress studies, noted that bleeding ulcers were among the classic disorders that developed in animals exposed to intense stressors. However, the actual psychophysiological mechanisms involved in this process are more complex than originally believed. With the advent of techniques enabling scientists to study the various linings within the gastrointestinal tract, mechanisms responsible for such stress-induced pathology have been more thoroughly investigated.

Among mechanisms suggested to be central to these disease processes are the stress hormones. Weiss (1984) has suggested that catecholamines released during sympathetic arousal may contribute to the development of ulcerations in the lining of the stomach by altering the motor activity of the organism; animals that showed greater ulceration were those that also exhibited greater movement. Evidence also exists relating increased release of catecholamines from neurons in the brain to an increased severity of gastric lesions (e.g. Djanhangurir, Taubin, and Landsberg,

1973; Osumi, Takaori, and Fujiwara, 1973). Thus, sympathetic arousal appears to be related to the development of ulcers, but the psychophysiological evidence concerning the mechanisms underlying this well-accepted relationship is still not well understood.

IMMUNITY

The recently established field of psychoneuroimmunology (Ader 1981) has provided extensive research supporting the notion that psychosocial factors, particularly stress, may contribute to illness. Reviews from both animal (Borysenko and Borysenko, 1982) and human (Jemmott and Locke, 1984) studies offer support for the role of stress in immune deregulation. Stress may also be involved in the etiology of cancer (Sklar and Anisman, 1979). For cancer, the chronicity of the stressor and the type of cancer appear to be major predictors of health outcome (Justice, 1985), but how stress is involved in the process of carcinogenesis is still unclear. Stressful situations appear to render organisms more susceptible to disease-causing agents. Sympathetic and pituitary–adrenocortical arousal may be one possible psychophysiological mechanism underlying this complex relationship.

Corticosteroids are well-known immunosuppressive agents, and in high concentrations, corticosteroids disrupt normal immune function (Basen, 1977). Corticosteroids can render an organism immunosuppressed by altering the distribution of circulating leukocytes, by inhibiting lymphocyte mitogenesis, or by suppressing the synthesis of cytokines necessary for the induction of effector cells. Hence, a widely proposed mediator between stress and an increased susceptibility to disease has been cortisol. Catecholamines have not been well characterized for their immunoregulatory properties, but recent evidence for the presence of adrenergic receptors on lymphocytes (Pochet, Delesperse, Gauseet, and Collet, 1979; Watanabe, La, and Yushida, 1981) and studies illustrating sympathetic innervation of lymphoid tissue (Williams, Peterson, Shea, Schmedtje, Bauer, and Felten, 1981) suggest that sympathetic arousal may, through the release of catecholamines, cause changes in the functional abilities of the immune system.

Changes in immunoresponsivity have been related to norepinephrine levels within lymphoid tissue (Del Rey, Besedovsky, Sorkin, Da Prada, and Arren-brecht, 1981), suggesting that the catecholamines may have a regulatory function within the immune system. More studies, however, are needed to establish the clinical relevance of sympathetically mediated changes within the immune system and to characterize further the nature of the relationship between catecholamines, glucocorticoids, and immunity. To date, the majority of studies examining stress and illness suggest that adrenal hormones do play an important role in immunity. In excess, both glucocorticoids and catecholamines may induce a state of immunosuppression, making an organism more susceptible to disease.

The hypothesis that arousal might moderate health by leading to change in immunity is a plausible one.

In this section we have considered a few examples of disease states that may be initiated or exacerbated by the physiological arousal which occurs under most stressful conditions. The focus has been on arousal within the pituitary–adrenocortical axis and the sympatho-adrenomedullary system; epinephrine, norepinephrine, and cortisol have been discussed in detail because they are well-characterized components of the stress response. Clearly, other hormonal and systemic changes occur throughout the body during stress, and these may play an equally important role in the development of certain disease states. However, space limitations do not permit a detailed review of these changes. Likewise, pathways by which behavioral and/or cognitive arousal may affect health are complex and require detailed study. One remaining aspect of the arousal–stress relationship that may provide insight into these processes is the effect of chronic arousal. Most accounts of arousal and stress explicitly consider acute episodes where arousal is brief or easily reduced. However, stressful conditions which elicit persistent physiological arousal may reflect more than a simple prolongation of acute stressor effects. Post-traumatic stress, for example, is a complex of psychophysiological responses reflecting chronic arousal.

ENVIRONMENTAL STRESS AND CHRONIC AROUSAL

Although stressors can produce a variety of consequences (e.g. depression, physical symptoms, behavioral changes), post-traumatic stress disorder (PTSD) represents one of the most profound complexes of symptoms associated with stress. Since PTSD has been hypothesized to be an exaggerated manifestation of the more typical stress response, understanding the etiology of this disorder should provide useful information about general stress responding (Davidson and Baum, 1986). In addition, because alterations in physiological arousal are a hallmark of the syndrome, and the disorder itself has been hypothesized to result from these changes, a discussion of PTSD may illustrate the importance of arousal to the stress construct.

Post-traumatic stress is a relatively new term (American Psychiatric Association, 1980) for a disorder which is as ancient as war and natural catastrophe. Although wars have been associated with the greatest numbers of known victims of PTSD, the disorder is not only a consequence of war. It may result from any stressor that is severe or traumatic enough to be considered outside the realm of normal human experience. Events that have been associated with the syndrome include natural disasters, such as floods, hurricanes, and earthquakes (especially when injury and death occur) and human-made events, such as war, imprisonment, and exposure to toxic substances.

Although a number of symptoms are associated with the disorder, two of its primary dimensions are intrusive thinking about the traumatic event and avoidance of stimuli associated with the event. Intrusive thinking about the traumatic event may take the form of recurrent recollections of the original trauma, dreams and nightmares, and perhaps even brief dissociative episodes during which the victim relives the initiating event. Avoiding stimuli associated with the trauma may result in decreasing involvement with the outside world, social problems, and a lack of interest in previously enjoyed activities. Anxiety and depression are also common. In addition, symptoms of autonomic changes occur, including hyperalertness, sleep disturbances, memory impairment, and difficulty in concentrating. Kolb, Burris, and Griffiths (1984) have suggested that many of the symptoms of PTSD may be related to abnormalities in the central adrenergic system 'either as a result of excessive secretion or enduring hypersensitivity at receptors consequent to a resetting of discharge potential' (p. 101).

Researchers have, in fact, noted physiological differences between people experiencing symptoms of PTSD and other groups of people. Blanchard, Kolb, Pallmeyer, and Gerardi (1982) exposed a group of PTSD combat veterans and a group of nonveteran controls to combat sounds and a challenging mental arithmetic task. They found that heart rate, systolic blood pressure, and EMG increased for both groups during the arithmetic task, but changed only for the PTSD group during exposure to combat sounds. Similarly, Malloy, Fairbank, and Keane (1983) examined physiological responses of Vietnam veterans with PTSD and compared their responses with those of a group of seemingly well-adjusted veterans and with those of a group with psychiatric diagnoses other than PTSD who had never been assigned to combat. Each subject's cardiovascular responses were measured under the neutral condition of watching pictures of a family and under the more upsetting conditions of combat scenes. The investigators found significant increases in heart rates relative to baseline during the combat scenes for the PTSD group only. There were no heart rate differences between the three groups during the neutral pictures.

In an effort to assess sympathetic nervous system activity more directly, Kosten, Mason, Giller, Ostroff, and Harkness (1987), measured catecholamine levels in a group of PTSD inpatients. They compared mean norepinephrine and epinephrine levels of patients with PTSD, major depressive disorder, mania, paranoid schizophrenia, or undifferentiated schizophrenia. Results indicated that norepinephrine and epinephrine were significantly elevated in the PTSD group and that these elevations were sustained throughout the course of hospitalization. These elevations were observed long after the initiating trauma had occurred and in the absence of any specific eliciting stimuli. To test the hypothesis that changes in the arousal systems were responsible for the symptoms associated with PTSD, Kolb *et al.* (1984) treated patients with two drugs, propranalol and clonidine, which block sympathetic output. Clonidine acts centrally in the brain, and propranalol acts centrally and peripherally at beta receptors. Preliminary work suggested that some of the symptoms of PTSD improved with each of these drugs, providing partial support for the hypothesized relationship between sympathetic arousal and symptom formation in PTSD.

The important question, however, is how changes in the sympathetic nervous system may produce the variety of symptoms associated with PTSD. Conditioned emotional responding may help to explain the intrusive and avoidance thinking which are hallmarks of PTSD (Keane, Fairbank, Caddell, Zimering, and Bender, 1985). Stimuli that are reminiscent of the initial trauma or stressor may evoke responses similar to those elicited in the original situation. This may occur as a result of classical conditioning; traumatic events elicit psychophysiological symptoms, and previously neutral stimuli, by virtue of their association with the original trauma, may come to evoke the same response.

Thus, classical and higher order conditioning may explain the intrusive nature of the initiating event. We know that veterans with PTSD are reactive to combat noise and scenes. They may be overly responsive to other reminders of the original trauma as well, and higher order conditioning may result in an ever-widening array of stimuli capable of producing physiological arousal in this group. Since so many stimuli may be capable of producing the conditioned response, it may become increasingly difficult to keep the trauma away from consciousness or attention. However, in an effort to prevent these episodes of intrusiveness, a person with PTSD may begin to avoid reminders of the event. Since so many stimuli may now be associated with the initiating event, persons with the disorder may withdraw almost entirely from their surroundings.

Schachter and Singer's (1962) two-factor theory of emotion may be used to explain further the initiation of symptoms in PTSD. Schachter and Singer found that the disguised injection of epinephrine could evoke different emotional responses as a function of the information available to the subject. When subjects were in a room with a confederate who appeared to be either euphoric or angry the subjects labeled their own felt arousal (which they were experiencing from the epinephrine) accordingly. Thus, the authors concluded that the importance of physiological arousal is in how it is labeled or interpreted. Subsequent research has not provided clear support for the notion that unexplained arousal is experienced as a function of cognitive circumstances, but has indicated that arousal is an important component of emotion and that emotional experience is labile in the presence of unexplained arousal (Manstead and Wagner, 1981). Through conditioned emotional responding and higher order conditioning, many situations may come to evoke changes in sympathetic arousal in PTSD groups. Because these changes are associated with combat experience, negative emotions accompany the arousal. Thus, anxiety and depression may become important components in the syndrome.

Generally, PTSD has been associated with intense or gruesome events such as natural disasters or war. Recent work among residents living near the Three Mile Island Nuclear Reactor (TMI) has suggested that PTSD may also be associated with less intense but persistent events. The nuclear accident at TMI provided a unique opportunity to study the relationship between a chronic environmental stressor, PTSD, and arousal. The accident at TMI occurred in March 1979, and involved the threat of radiation exposure. Following the initial accident, radioactive water, gas, and debris remained in the reactor's containment building; the radioactive gas continued to leak periodically and was finally released into the environment more than one year after the accident. More recently, the undamaged reactor at TMI began operating again. All of these events have provided continuing sources of stress for those living near the plant.

Several studies have used a multimodal research strategy to document stress responding associated with living in the TMI area (Davidson and Baum, 1986; Baum, Gatchel, and Schaeffer, 1983). Self-report, behavioral, and biological indices of stress have been used to compare the responses of people living near TMI with those of a control group of subjects living at least 80 miles from TMI. Results have demonstrated that residents of the TMI area reported more symptoms of distress, performed more poorly on tasks involving concentration and persistence, and showed greater evidence of sympathetic nervous system arousal after six years of experience with the TMI situation. Heightened arousal was indicated among TMI area residents by continued excretion of higher levels of norepinephrine and epinephrine in their urine, higher resting levels of systolic and diastolic blood pressure, and higher heart rates than controls. These changes in sympathetic arousal were also associated with nonclinical levels of PTSD symptomatology in the TMI group.

The physiological arousal experienced by the TMI area residents has been long-lasting. The questions raised by these continued elevations in catecholamines, heart rate, and blood pressure are many. However, one basic question is why arousal continues to be elevated so many years after the accident. The impression that one gets from the many studies of stress and associated psychophysiologic response is that responses to chronic stressors habituate, recover or otherwise return to 'normal.' That does not appear to be the case in this instance. Perhaps residents continue to be stressed because the reactors' cooling towers dominate the landscape and serve as a reminder of the original event and a symbol of the potential for a similar accident in the future.

Following a group of people who have moved from the TMI area would be one way to address this issue. If residents who have moved were no longer stressed, this would suggest that living in the TMI area was responsible for conditioned emotional responses similar to those described previously. Just as such a syndrome has been hypothesized to explain the etiology of PTSD symptomatology, it may also serve as an explanation for the symptoms in this group. Alternatively, if this relocated TMI group continued to show elevations in arousal, it may be because of the uncertainty generated by living in the TMI area at the time of the accident. Residents may fear that they were exposed to radiation and may wonder what the long-term consequences of that exposure will be. Another possible explanation is that exposure to stressors such as the one at TMI may permanently alter physiological equilibrium such that the set point of arousal systems are now elevated over the original baseline values. The answer to this basic 'why' question remains to be found.

Perhaps an even more interesting issue is what the implications of these findings are. Although it appears clear that norepinephrine and epinephrine have remained elevated, among some residents, the functional significance of these findings is unknown. Hormones such as epinephrine and norepinephrine produce their effects by interacting with their receptors to cause a functional change. Both the hormones and the receptors are subject to homeostatic regulation. The fact that norepinephrine and epinephrine continue to be elevated during chronic stress suggests that the homeostatic controls over the hormones have failed. However, receptors may provide a back-up regulatory system in case of chronic hormonal elevations. Continuous stimulation of receptors may lead to their desensitization. Desensitization may occur through a structural alteration in the receptor or by removal of the receptor from the cell membrane. However, this account is speculative and the functional significance of hormonal elevations remains unknown.

One study of the consequences of arousal accompanying chronic stress examined cardiovascular reactivity (Fleming, Baum, Davidson, Rectanus, and McArdle, 1987). The focus of the study was on how physiological changes during chronic stress may affect subsequent responses to new stressors. In this study, crowded urban residents served as the 'experimental' population and less-crowded residents as the control groups. Self-report and biochemical measures indicated that the crowded residents were indeed more chronically stressed than the less-crowded group. Chronic stress was once again associated with higher resting levels of epinephrine and norepinephrine. However, in this study baseline blood pressure measures did not differ between the two groups and, unexpectedly, the crowded group had lower baseline heart rates than the less-crowded group. Heart rate and blood pressure were also measured while subjects worked on a challenging task. During the task, residents of crowded streets showed greater increases in heart rate and blood pressure and took longer to return to baseline than did less-crowded residents. These findings illustrate one way in which a chronically stressed population may be more susceptible to subsequent stressors than an unstressed group. Although baseline cardiovascular measures did not differ between the two groups, the chronically stressed group was more affected by the acute challenge. Researchers have, in fact, suggested that reactivity in response to a threat may be independent of baseline elevations in physiological variables and may, in addition, be more indicative of pathogenic processes (Krantz, Baum, and Singer, 1983).

There are still a number of issues that remain to be resolved with regard to chronic stress and arousal. The consequences of prolonged arousal remain largely unknown; the mechanisms by which arousal is maintained and habituation pressures thwarted have not been identified; and the conditions or variables that support long-term heightened responding have not been studied. The nature of long-term physiological arousal may be different from the sequelae of lots of acute stress experiences strung together. Oppositional systemic changes, such as parasympathetic compensation for chronic arousal, may result in changes in resting levels of activity or changes in response to new challenges and/or threats to orderly bodily functioning. In accommodating to long-term physiological arousal, we may experience important changes in how we think, what we decide, and how we behave.

The studies described in this section provide useful information regarding environmental stress and chronic arousal. Studies of post-traumatic stress disorder, of the Three Mile Island situation, and of the stress associated with living in a crowded neighborhood represent unique approaches which have served to identify characteristic interactions that occur in stressful environments. These studies offer an important multimodal research strategy for investigating both the etiology and the effects of chronic stress. Baum, Grunberg, and Singer (1982) have outlined the importance of this multilevel approach in the study of stress. In a discussion of the use of self-report measures, performance tasks, and physiological indices used in research, they recommend that simultaneous assessment of behavioral, psychological, and physiological measures be used when examining the nature of the stress response.

SUMMARY AND CONCLUSIONS

We have discussed the role of arousal in stress, recognizing that arousal is a poorly defined construct. Lay definitions portray arousal as a stirring up, a mobilization to anger or to action, or as a state that impels action. Though we have not focused on the motivational aspects of arousal, many believe that the state of arousal accompanying stress drives individuals to seek to reduce the impact of the stressor. The definitions are compatible with the construct we have described. Most lay definitions concentrate on the emotional and visceral manifestations: to arouse is to excite. However, as we have pointed out, the object of this action (i.e. 'What is being stirred up?") is harder to specify. Emotional arousal reflects a provocation of emotions, be they cognitive, physiologic, or joint events (e.g. Schachter and Singer, 1962). Sympathetic arousal reflects excitement of the sympathetic nervous system and the organs it innervates. Cortical arousal suggests increased activity in the cortex, and its attendant effects. Arousal represents heightened activity in a variety of systems or products of systemic interactions, and serves as a motivational state, a cast of possible causes of organic dysfunction, and a determinant of behavior.

Clearly, not all conceptions of stress involve arousal, though most could. Those who research on, or theorize about, stress and life events, for example, do not typically measure or address arousal, viewing health changes as outcomes of stressors (e.g. Elliott and Eisdorfer, 1982). Models of life change or of stressful life events and their associated health changes typically consider environmental circumstances, psychological characteristics of people exposed to life events, external mediators such as social support, internal mediators such as coping skills, and/or appraisal (e.g. Dohrenwend, Krasnoff, Askenasy, and Dohrenwend, 1978). Mechanisms by which these components translate into health changes are less often specified. Some models suggest that psychophysiologic events associated with stress are among the major determinants of health in these cases, but this is often left as a 'black box' lacking elaboration or specification (e.g. Rahe and Arthur, 1978). While arousal is a likely element in this process, it is simply left unstated in many instances.

This suggests that arousal is one of many levels of analysis by which stress may be viewed. Mention of arousal is, therefore, more characteristic of models that are concerned with spelling out mechanisms by which stressors cause various outcomes. Analysis of stress effects on task performance, for example, yields a fairly consistent finding; task performance generally suffers during and/or after stressful experiences. However, depending on the level of this analysis, different predictions may be made and, possibly, different outcomes obtained. Consider the robust phenomenon of aftereffects. Following acute stressors, even if evidence suggests that subjects cope with and adapt to them, task performance deficits are observed (e.g. Cohen, 1980; Cohen, Evans, Stokols, and Krantz, 1986). Possible explanations for these effects, however, depend almost entirely on the primary level of analysis used.

If arousal during exposure to stress is the primary mechanism by which these effects occur, several explanations, involving such phenomena as lingering elevations in endogenous opioid peptides or other stress hormones, exist. If other mechanisms are considered, such as coping, then other explanations are likely. Thus, one might argue and predict, on the basis of arousal during stress, that certain types of biochemical responses determine task performance changes, or that different types of tasks might be differentially affected. Emphasis on coping, however, would not specify psychophysiologic determinants of task performance and might focus instead on the persistence of well-learned coping responses or on the effects of those coping behaviors beyond manipulation of accommodation to the stressor. While the arousal construct has proven useful in linking environmental events and health changes, task performance, and other outcomes, it is not the only way to view stress. We believe that it should be considered in conjunction with other elements involved in the commerce between organisms and their environments, as such joint determination can provide more powerful representations of behavior and health.

These issues aside, one important point remains certain—that multiple measures of various arousal states are preferable to the unitary measurement of one system. Because arousal can be conceptualized within behavioral, cognitive, and physiological systems, all three modalities need to be taken into consideration in stress research (Baum *et al.*, 1982). An even greater need exists for investigations into interrelationships that develop between different arousal systems. How, why, and when these measures are disconcordant when obtained simultaneously are important questions for future research.

REFERENCES

Ader, R. (Ed.) (1981) *Psychoneuroimmunology*. New York: Academic Press.

American Psychiatric Association (1980) *Diagnostic and Statistical Manual of Mental Disorders*, 3rd edn. Washington, DC: Author.

Axelrod, J., and Reisine, T. D. (1984) Stress hormones: their interaction and regulation. *Science*, **224**, 452–9.

Bassen, C. R. (1977) Immunosuppressive agents. In M. S. Thaler, R. D. Klausner, and H. J. Cohen (Eds), *Medical Immunology*, pp. 415–36. Philadelphia, PA: Lippincott.

Batini, C., Moruzzi, G., Palestini, M., Rossi, G. R., and Zanchetti, A. (1959) Effect of complete pointine transections on the sleep–wakefulness rhythm: the midpointine pretrigeminal preparation. *Archives Italiennes de Biologie*, **97**, 1–12.

Baum, A., Gatchel, R. J., and Schaeffer, M. A. (1983) Emotional, behavioral, and physiological effects of chronic stress at Three Mile Island. *Journal of Consulting and Clinical Psychology*, **51**, 565–72.

Baum, A., Grunberg, N. E., and Singer, J. E. (1982) The use of psychological and neuroendocrinological measurements in the study of stress. *Health Psychology*, **1**, 217–36.

Berlyne, D. E. (1960) *Conflict, Arousal and Curiosity*, New York: McGraw-Hill.

Blanchard, E. B., Kolb, L. C., Pallmeyer, T. P., and Gerardi, R. J. (1982) A psychophysiological study of post-traumatic stress disorder in Vietnam veterans. *Psychiatry Quarterly*, **54**, 220–7.

Blascovich, J., and Katkin, E. S. (1983) Visceral perception and social behavior. In J. T. Cacioppo and R. E. Petty (Eds), *Social Psychophysiology: A Sourcebook*, pp. 493–509. New York: Guilford Press.

Borysenko, M., and Borysenko, J. (1982) Stress, behavior and immunity: animal models and mediating mechanisms. *General Hospital Psychiatry*, **4**, 69–74.

Bremer, F. (1937) L'activite cerebrale au cours du sommeil et de la narcose. Contribution a l'etude du mechanisme du sommeil. *Bulletin de l'Academie Royale de Belgique*, **4**, 68–86.

Cannon, W. B. (1914) The emergency function of the adrenal medulla in pain and the major emotions. *American Journal of Psychology*, **33**, 356–72.

Cohen, S. (1980) Aftereffects of stress on human performance and social behavior: a review of research and theory. *Psychological Bulletin*, **88**, 82–108.

Cohen, S., Evans, G. W., Stokols, D., and Krantz, D. S. (1986) *Behavior, Health, and Environmental Stress*. New York: Plenum Press.

Davidson, L. M., and Baum, A. (1986) Chronic stress and posttraumatic stress disorders. *Journal of Consulting and Clinical Psychology*, **54**, 303–8.

Del Rey, A., Besedovsky, H. O., Sorkin, E., Da Prada, M., and Arrenbrecht, S. (1981) Immunoregulation mediated by the sympathetic nervous system. *Cellular Immunology*, **63**, 329–34.

Djanhanguiri, B., Taubin, H. L., and Landsberg, L. (1973) Increased sympathetic activity in the pathogenesis of restraint ulcer in the rat. *Journal of Pharmacology and Experimental Therapeutics*, **184**, 163–8.

Duffy, E. (1934) Emotion: an example of the need for reorientation in psychology. *Psychological Review*, **41**, 184–98.

Dohrenwend, B. S., Krasnoff, L., Askenasy, A. R., and Dohrenwend, B. P. (1978) Exemplification of a method for scaling life events: the PERI life events scale. *Journal of Health and Social Behavior*, **19**, 205–29.

Elliott, G. R., and Eisdorfer, C. (Eds) (1982) *Stress and Human Health*. New York: Springer.

Estes, W. K., and Skinner, B. F. (1941) Some quantitative properties of anxiety. *Journal of Experimental Psychology*, **29**, 390–400.

Fleming, I., Baum, A., Davidson, L. M., Rectanus, E., and McArdle, S. (1987), Chronic stress as a factor in physiologic reactivity to challenge. *Health Psychology*, **6**, 221–37.

Frankenhaeuser, M. (1971) Experimental approaches to the study of human behaviour as related to neuroendocrine functions. In L. Levi (Ed.), *Society, Stress and Disease*, Vol. 1, *The Psychological Environment and Psychosomatic Diseases*, pp. 22–35. New York: Oxford University Press.

Friedman, S. B., Mason, J. W., and Hamburg, D. A. (1963) Urinary 17-hydroxycort-icosteroid levels in parents of children with neoplastic disease. *Psychosomatic Medicine*, **35**, 364–76.

Hebb, D. O. (1955) Drives and the CNS (conceptual nervous system). *Psychological Review*, **63**, 143–254.

Herd, J. A. (1984) Cardivascular disease and hypertension. In W. D. Gentry (Ed.), *Handbook of Behavioral Medicine*, pp. 222–81. New York: Guilford Press.

Jemmott, J., and Locke, S. (1984) Psychosocial factors, immunologic mediation, and human susceptibility to infectious diseases: How much do we know? *Psychological Bulletin*, **95**, 78–108.

Justice, A. (1985) Review of the effects of stress on cancer in laboratory animals: importance of time of stress application and type of tumor. *Psychological Bulletin*, **98**(1), 108–38.

Kahneman, D. (1973) *Attention and Effort*. Englewood Cliffs, NJ: Prentice Hall.

Keane, T. M., Fairbank, J. A., Caddell, J. M., Zimering, R. T., and Bender, M. E. (1985) A behavioral approach to assessing and treating post-traumatic stress disorder in Vietnam veterans. In C. R. Figley (Ed.), *Trauma and its Wake*, pp. 257–94. New York: Brunner/Mazel.

Knott, J. R., and Irwin, D. A. (1973) Anxiety, stress, and the contingent negative variation. *Archives of General Psychiatry*, **29**, 29–39.

Kolb, L. C., Burris, B. C., and Griffiths, S. (1984) Propranolol and clonidine in treatment of the chronic post-traumatic stress disorders of war. In B. Van der Kolk (Ed.), *Post-Traumatic Stress Disorder: Psychological and Biological Sequelae*, pp. 97–107. Washington, DC: American Psychiatric Press.

Kosten, T. R., Mason, J. W. Giller, E. L., Ostroff, R. B., and Harkness, L. (1987) *Sustained Urinary Norepinephrine and Epinephrine Elevation in Post-Traumatic Stress Disorder*. *Psychoneu-roendocrinology*, **12**, 13–20.

Krantz, D S., Baum, A., and Singer, J. E. (1983) Behavior and cardiovascular disease: issues and overview. In D. S. Krantz, A. Baum, and J. E. Singer (Eds), *Handbook of Psychology and Health*, Vol. 3 *Cardiovascular Disorders and Behavior*, pp. 1–17. Hillsdale, NJ: Erlbaum.

Lacey, J. I. (1967) Somatic response patterning and stress: some revisions of activation theory. In M. H. Apley and R. Trumbull (Eds) *Psychological Stress*, pp. 14–42. New York: Appleton-Century-Crofts.

Leeuwen, W. S., vanKamp, A., Kok, M. L., Dequartel, F., and Tielan, A. (1967) EEG of unrestrained animals under stressful conditions. *Electroencephalogical Clinical Neurophysi-ology suppl.* **25**, 212–25.

Levi, L. (1965) The urinary output of adrenaline and noradrenaline during different experimentally induced pleasant and unpleasant emotional states. *Psychosomatic Medicine*, **27**, 80–5.

Lindsley, D. (1951) Emotion. In S. S. Stevens (Ed.), *Handbook of Experimental Psychology*, New York: John Wiley.

Malloy, P. F., Fairbank, J. A., and Keane, T. M. (1983) Validation of a multi-method assessment of posttraumatic stress disorder in Vietnam veterans. *Journal of Consulting and Clinical Psychology*, **51**, 488–94.

Malmo, R. B. (1959) Activation: a neuro-psychological dimension. *Psychological Review*, **66**, 367–86.

Manstead, A. S. R., and Wagner, H. L. (1981) Arousal, cognition, and emotion: an appraisal of two-factor theory. *Current Psychological Reviews*, **1**, 35–54.

Mason, J. W. (1975) Emotion as reflected in patterns of endocrine integration. In L. Levi (Ed.), *Emotions: Their Parameters and Measurement*, pp. 143–81. New York: Raven Press.

Osumi, Y., Takaori, S., and Fujiwara, M. (1973) Preventive effect of fusaric acid, a dopamine hydroxylase inhibitor, on the gastric ulceration induced by water-immersion in rats. *Japanese Journal of Pharmacology*, **23**, 904–906.

Pochet, R., Delesperse, G., Gauseet, P., and Collet, H. (1979) Distribution of beta adrenergic receptors on human lymphocyte subpopulations. *Clinical and Experimental Immunology*, **38**, 578–84.

Rahe, R. H. (1975) Life changes and near-future illness reports. In L. Levi (Ed.), *Emotions: Their Parameters and Measurement*, pp. 511–30. New York: Raven Press.

Rahe, R. H., and Arthur, R. J. (1978) Life change and illness studies. *Journal of Human Stress*, **4**, 15–23.

Ross, R., and Glomset, J. A. (1976) The pathogenesis of atherosclerosis. *New England Journal of Medicine*, **295**, 369–377.

Schachter, S., and Singer, J. E. (1962) Cognitive, social, and physiological determinants of emotional states. *Psychological Review*, **69**, 379–99.

Schneiderman, N. (1983) Animal behavior models of coronary heart disease. In D. S. Krantz, A. Baum, and J. E. Singer (Eds), *Handbook of Psychology and Health*, Vol. 3, *Cardiovascular Disorders and Behavior*, pp. 19–56. Hillsdale, NJ: Erlbaum.

Selye, H. (1956) *The Stress of Life*. New York: McGraw-Hill.

Sklar, L. S., and Anisman, H. (1979). Stress and cancer. *Psychological Bulletin*, **89**, 369–406.

Sprague, E. A., Troxler, G. G., Peterson, D. F., Schmidt, R. E., and Young, J. T. (1980) Effect of cortisol on the development of atherosclerosis in cynomolgus monkeys. In S. S. Kalter (Ed.), *The use of Nonhuman Primates in Cardiovascular Diseases*. Austin: University of Texas Press.

Tecce, J. J. (1972) Contingent negative variation and psychological processes in man. *Psychological Bulletin*, **77**, 73–108.

Watanabe, Y., La, R., and Yushida, H. (1981) The beta-adrenoreceptor in human lymphocytes. *Clinical and Experimental Physiology*, **8**(3), 273–6.

Weiss, J. (1984) Behavioral and psychological influences on gastrointestinal pathology: experimental techniques and findings. In W. D. Doyle (Ed.), *Handbook of Behavioral Medicine*, pp. 174–221. New York: Guilford Press.

Williams, J., Peterson, R., Shea, P., Schmedtje, J., Bauer, D., and Felten, D. (1981) Sympathetic innervation of murine thymus and spleen: evidence for functional link between the nervous and immune systems. *Brain Research Bulletin*, **61**, 83–94.

Wolf, S., and Wolff, H. G. (1947) *Human Gastric Function*. New York: Oxford University Press.

Yerkes, R. M., and Dodson, J. D. (1908) The relationship of strength of stimulus to rapidity of habit formation. *Journal of Comparative Neurology and Psychology*, **18**, 459–482.

Zillmann, D. (1983) Transfer of excitation in emotional behavior. In J. T. Cacioppo and R. E. Petty (Eds), *Social Psychophysiology: A Sourcebook*, pp. 215–40. New York: Guilford Press.

PART 5

PSYCHOPHYSIOLOGY AND INTERPERSONAL PROCESSES

Introduction

The final section of this volume contains four chapters that deal with mainstream social psychological topics—attitudes, social judgement, helping behaviour, and dyadic interaction—either from an explicitly psychophysiological perspective or in terms that are susceptible to a psychophysiological approach.

Cacioppo and Tassinary (Chapter 12, *The concept of attitudes: a psychophysiological analysis*) consider how a psychophysiological approach can advance the study of attitudes. For several decades attitude research has been a major enterprise for social psychologists, yet attitude researchers have generally been disinclined to exploit the potential afforded by psychophysiological concepts and methods. From the several possible reasons for this state of affairs, Cacioppo and Tassinary focus on one in particular, namely the epistemological status of physiological events and measures. What can one reasonably infer about psychological phenomena (such as attitudes) on the basis of physiological indices? This is a question that any psychologist employing physiological measures must consider at some level, but to our knowledge no one has previously examined this issue in such a thoroughgoing fashion as is provided here. The authors map out four possible types of relationship between psychological states and physiological events: invariant, concomitant, marker, and outcome. They argue that neither an invariant (isomorphic and cross-situational) nor a concomitant (cross-situational but non-isomorphic) relationship is required in order for psychophysiological analyses to contribute to our understanding of attitudes. A second issue considered by the authors concerns the impact of varying conceptualizations of attitudes on the selection of response measures. Four such conceptualizations are identified, and the contribution of psychophysiological research stimulated by each approach is reviewed within the fourfold classification of psychophysiological relationships already developed by the authors. Two striking points emerge from this review. First, the dominant view of attitudes as founded on knowledge about attitude-objects may be unduly 'rational', in much the same way that the models of the attribution process advanced by early attribution theorists are now thought to underestimate the role of cognitive heuristics in social judgement. The second, related, point is that the widespread assumption that self-reports serve as the 'standard of validity' in attitude research may need to be reconsidered, given that self-reports are very likely to underestimate spontaneous or impulsive responses to an attitude-object. There is, therefore, a pressing need for psychophysiological approaches to the study of attitudes.

The relationship between affect and psychological processes is an issue that is also addressed in the next chapter (Chapter 13, *Moods and social judgements*) by Clark and Williamson. The impact of moods on cognitive processes has become a major research topic in cognitive, social, and clinical psychology within the last decade. Clark and Williamson review the research assessing the impact of experimental manipulations of mood of social judgements made by subjects drawn from non-clinical populations. They conclude that positive mood manipulations have been shown to cause judgements to become congruent with mood state across a variety of judgements (of self, of others, of inanimate objects, of social situations) and across a variety of methods of manipulating mood state. The impact of negative mood manipulations on social judgements is less consistent. Sometimes such judgements become more negative, sometimes they are unaffected, and there is even evidence that judgements of others become more *positive*. The authors then review a series of possible mechanisms by which moods may influence social judgements. Moods may prime mood-congruent thoughts; moods may cue positive or negative response styles; moods may serve as information that is taken into account when making a judgement; subjects may misattribute mood-related arousal to the target of the judgement; moods may take up memory capacity, limiting the amount available for retrieval and thereby biasing judgements; finally, people may be motivated to maintain positive mood states and to curtail negative mood states by means of controlled strategies. Present research does not permit one to identify which process, or combination of processes, is responsible for the observed effects of mood on social judgement. Clark and Williamson therefore call for future research on this topic to be directed more carefully at three specific issues: the boundary conditions for mood effects on social judgement; the plausibility of the various candidates for mediating process; and the implications for social interaction.

The impact of mood on one aspect of social interaction, prosocial behaviour, is the focus of the next chapter (Chapter 14, *Mood states and prosocial behavior*), by Salovey and Rosenhan. They review research on the impact of moods on prosocial behaviour and conclude that there is ample evidence that pleasant moods in general and joy in particular facilitate subsequent helping behaviours. Just as with the research on mood and social judgement, however, the impact of negative mood states is less consistent. Whereas guilt and (to a lesser degree) shame generally lead to prosocial behaviour, sorrow is more likely to reduce helping than increase it. In accounting for these findings, Salovey and Rosenhan develop the notion that moods are especially likely to promote the accessibility of mood-congruent thoughts relating to the self, and that it is these self-related cognitions that are of particular importance in motivating subsequent behaviour. It is argued that whatever induces a mood state also changes the way in which the individual thinks about him- or herself; these temporary shifts in self-related cognitions promote or inhibit different social behaviours; and these behaviours, in turn, either maintain positive moods and self-cognitions or 'repair' negative moods and self-cognitions. This argument is supported by reference to research findings showing that self-focused attention mediates the impact of mood on helping, presumably by virtue of its effects on the relative salience of own versus others' needs and resources, and on the relative accessibility of different helping norms (e.g. charity versus reciprocity). Further support for the general argument comes from research examining the effects on helping of felt responsibility, self-concern, and perspective-taking. Although the emerging research focus on the mediating role played by self-related cognitions does not yet provide a general theory of the impact of mood on prosocial behaviour, the authors argue that this approach has the potential to yield such a theory.

In the final chapter of the book (Chapter 15, *The psychophysiology of dyadic interaction*) Notarius and Herrick consider the contribution that psychophysiological theory and research can make to our understanding of dyadic interaction. As they note, social psychophysiologists have been relatively slow to investigate ongoing social exchanges between persons, presumably because of the methodological difficulties involved in studying the physiological processes in two individuals as they freely interact with one another. Notarius and Herrick begin by reviewing research on physiological processes during interactions between (a) clients and therapists, and (b) married couples. It is noted that the presence of negative behaviours in the dyad (e.g. criticism, antagonism, dissatisfaction with the relationship) tends to have potent effects on the psychophysiological activity exhibited by each member of the dyad as they interact, and also on the degree to which such activity is correlated across the two persons. However, there is as yet insufficient research to permit generalizations to be made about the relationship between quality of exchange or relationship in the dyad and the type of physiological activity exhibited by the members of that dyad as they interact. Next, the authors consider methodological problems afflicting this line of research. Both the measurement of physiological activity and the assessment of social interaction present the researcher with challenging problems. Until the patterns of interaction that reliably distinguish between well- and poorly-functioning dyads are identified, any attempt to use psychophysiological measures as a way of examining the processes underlying effective or ineffective interaction will be severely hampered. Likewise, until researchers are able to specify in advance which physiological systems are most likely to be relevant to the type of dyadic exchange they are studying, it will be difficult to know whether the appropriate measures are being selected from the considerable array available. Notarius and Herrick note that we are closer to knowing what types of dyadic behaviour to study than to knowing which physiological responses should be measured. Finally, the authors argue that the associations between ongoing social exchange and physiological activity may have implications for long-term physical health and they conclude their chapter with a review of the pertinent evidence and a preliminary model of the relationships between interpersonal processes, intrapersonal physiological activity, and longer-term health outcomes.

Chapter 12

The Concept of Attitudes: A Psychophysiological Analysis

John T. Cacioppo and Louis G. Tassinary
Ohio State University   *University of Iowa*

ABSTRACT

A theory of psycho–physiological relationships is proposed, and the boundaries of logical induction based on each type of relationship are specified. This framework is then employed in a review of the extant conceptualizations of attitudes. The review reveals that implicit in most conceptualizations of attitudes is the principle that self-reports provide the standard of validity against which the results of other research on attitudes should be evaluated. Limitations to this strategy are noted, and alternatives to the reliance on self-reports as criterion measures are discussed.

THE CONCEPT OF ATTITUDE: A PSYCHOPHYSIOLOGICAL ANALYSIS

Attitude theorists have traditionally been reluctant to venture into the psycho-physiologists' bailiwick. A small number of early investigations can be identified in which physiological measures were recorded to study racial prejudice (e.g. Cooper, 1959; Rankin and Campbell, 1955), attitude conflict (e.g. Abel, 1930;

Preparation of this chapter was supported by National Science Foundation Grant No. BNS-8414853.

Handbook of Social Psychophysiology, Edited by H. Wagner and A. Manstead,

Smith, 1936), psychotherapeutic interviews (e.g. Boyd and DiMascio, 1954), interpersonal attraction (e.g. Kaplan, Burch, and Bloom, 1964), and empathy (e.g. Berger, 1962), but most of these investigations were conducted with the aim of finding objective physiological signatures corresponding to attitudes, or attitude components, which remained invariant up to and including the 'uncooperative subject' (Mueller, 1970; Webb, Campbell, Schwartz, and Sechrest, 1966). Traditions die hard: in the most recent *Handbook of Social Psychology*, the chapter on attitude measurement contains but a single page on physiological measures in a section entitled 'Responses over which subjects have no control' (Dawes and Smith, 1985), and physiological responses are dismissed as epiphenomena (McGuire, 1985, p. 240) or are referred to only in extra-attitudinal unidimensional energetic terms, i.e. as arousal.

Apparent reasons for this state of affairs, despite early and repeated references to the autonomic and somatic response patterning that emerges as a function of the stimulus, individual, and task demands (e.g. Cacioppo and Petty, 1981, 1983; Shapiro and Crider, 1969; Shapiro and Schwartz, 1970) and evidence pointing to the role of bodily responses in attitude change (e.g. Cacioppo, 1979; Wells and Petty, 1980), include: (a) the technical and physiological expertise required, (b) the abyss between the psychophysiologist's laboratory and the social settings to which attitude theorists wished to generalize, (c) the paucity of theoretic links or even analytic frameworks for linking physiological data and psychological constructs, (d) sociological factors stemming from the areas of inquiry judged 'appropriate' by the founding fathers of social psychology and of psychophysiology, (e) philosophical factors favoring the development of parsimonious and testable theories having the unintended effect of fostering a shift from a problem-oriented to a method-oriented approach to ensure falsifiability given readily available methods and procedures, and (f) epistemological factors regarding the status of physiological events and measures (see reviews by Cacioppo and Petty, 1986; Cacioppo, Petty, and Tassinary, 1989). We focus, in the present chapter, on the last of these obstacles, because it represents a continuing hinderance to attitude theory and research within psychophysiology, as well as within social psychology.

We advance three major positions in this chapter. First, a theory of psychophysiological relationships is proposed, and the boundaries of logical induction based on each category of relationship are specified. Evidence is reviewed showing that neither an invariant (i.e. isomorphic and cross situational) relationship nor a general (i.e. cross-situational) correlation between attitudes and peripheral physiological events is necessary for psychophysiological analyses to advance our understanding of psychological constructs such as attitudes.

Second, how one conceptualizes attitudes determines the measures one selects in studies of attitudes, the kinds of phenomena that are therefore brought to bear on behavior that is construed as representing an individual's attitudes, and the interpretation of the outcomes on these measures. Attention is given to various conceptualizations of attitudes, the psychophysiological research that resulted, and the logical implications and inference limitations of the physiological measurements.

Finally, most research on attitudes involves the manipulation of factors in the situation and asking people to report their attitudes. Implicit in this approach is the principle that self-reports provide the standard of validity against which the results of other research on attitudes should be evaluated. Discrepancies between self-reported attitudes and behaviors, for instance, are not typically conceptualized as impugning the validity of the self-reports, but rather as evidence that measurement error overwhelmed the assessment of the relevant attitude, and that alternative forces such as habits and social norms also influence individuals' behaviors (e.g. see review by McGuire, 1985). Such a conceptualization has emerged from methodological limitations rather than from theoretical conviction:

> in attitude studies we are primarily concerned with processes which are conscious and capable of verbalization and articulation. But at the same time we must recognize that other writers find it important to stress the extent to which attitudes are derivative from, and indirectly reductive of, unconscious conflicts and motivations. . . We do not see at present any clear-cut way of testing differential implications of these alternative formulations. (Hovland and Rosenberg, 1960, pp. 222–3)

With an appropriately designed logical trap, however, one can determine the extent to which the domain of attitudes and their consequences extend beyond what individuals are willing and, in some cases, are able to articulate. We begin by presenting a general taxonomy of relationships between psychological concepts and physiological observations, and we discuss the rules of evidence and inference implied by each. Readers interested in a more detailed discussion of how psychophysiology can provide a means of examining the influence of attitudes, or forces underlying attitudes, that people are unwilling or unable to report may also wish to consult Cacioppo and Petty (1982, 1986) and Cacioppo, Petty, and Losch (in press).

INDUCTIVE REASONING IN PSYCHOPHYSIOLOGY: STRONG INFERENCES DERIVED FROM PSYCHOPHYSIOLOGICAL RELATIONSHIPS

Psychophysiology is the scientific study of psychological phenomena (e.g. thought, emotion, attitudes) and behavior as related to, and revealed through, physiological principles and events in an intact human. By 'scientific study,' we mean that one selects one or more hypotheses about some phenomenon, devises a set of conditions with alternative possible outcomes which will exclude one or more of the hypotheses (or, minimally, will result in keeping or rejecting/revising a hypothesis), establishes the conditions and collects the observations while minimizing measurement error, and recyles through this sequence. But, as we shall see, adherence to this Baconian sequence is not sufficient to guarantee a positive yield. Verbal, behavioral, and physiological responses are acknowledged explicitly as being of interest, but the assumptions one makes about the relationship between psychological and physiological events determines the measures, paradigms (i.e. conditions), and interpretations one selects.

A useful way to construe the potential relationships between psychological events and physiological events is to consider these two groups of events as representing independent *sets*, where set is defined as a collection of elements which together are considered a whole. Psychological events could be conceived as one set, and physiological events could be conceived as another (see Figure 12.1). All elements in the set of psychological events are assumed to have some physiological referent, reflecting our adherence to the monistic identity theory (Smart, 1959). On the other hand, not all elements in the set of physiological events are conceived as having a connection to psychological elements. That is, there exists non-psychologically relevant physiological events (e.g. random physiological fluctuations; increased electrodermal activity due to minor variations in body temperature), which are not of great interest in psychophysiology except in terms of artifact detection. Such elements can, in effect, be ignored if non-psychological factors have been held constant, their influence on the physiological responses of interest has been identified and removed, or their influence does not extend to the physiological event of interest.

A key problem in psychophysiology, of course, is to specify the relationship between elements in the psychological set and those in the physiological set, and this problem is usually attacked by manipulating or blocking elements in the psychological set and measuring elements in the physiological set. It is surprising, therefore, that within the field of psychophysiology few if any attempts have been made either to provide a formal definition of the potential relations between these sets or to specify the necessary and sufficient conditions that underlie the inferences about elements in the psychological set given observations of elements in the physiological set. This is not difficult to do.

First, a one-to-one relation can exist, such that an element in the psychological set is associated with one, and only one, element in the physiological set [see Coombs, Dawes, and Tversky (1970) pp. 351–71, for the mathematics of the relations among sets described in this section]. Perhaps a more prevalent form of relation between the sets of psychological and physiological elements, however, is the one-to-many, meaning that an element in the psychological domain is associated with a subset of elements in the physiological domain. One-to-many relations between sets of psychological and physiological elements can be simplified greatly, reducing them to one-to-one relations, in the following fashion: define a second set of physiological elements, B', such that any subset of physiological elements associated with one (or more, see below) psychological elements is replaced by a single, unique, element in B' representing a physiological response pattern. Thus, one-to-one and one-to-many relations between the set of psychological elements A, and the set of physiological elements, B, both become one-to-one relations between the set of psychological elements, A, and the set of physiological elements (i.e. responses and response patterns), B' (Figure 12.1, panels a and b).

The third mathematical relation that can exist between the sets is many-to-one, meaning in our context that two or more psychological elements are associated with the same physiological element. Again, a complicating variant on this relation between the sets is the many-to-many, meaning that two or more psychological elements in A are associated with the same subset of elements (profile of responses) in B. As before, a new set of physiological elements, B', is defined such that any subset of physiological elements associated with one or more psychological elements is replaced by a new element representing a profile of physiological responses. Hence, each many-to-many relation between the sets of psychological and physiological elements again simplify to a many-to-one relation (see Figure 12.1, panel c). Further simplifications of these relationships can be achieved by specifying the temporal characteristics of the physiological events, but a discussion of these points is beyond the scope of the present chapter (but see Cacioppo & Tassinary, in press).

In addition, relations between the domain of psychological elements and the domain of physiological elements cannot be assumed to hold across situations and individuals—that is, such relationships may have limited ranges of validity (e.g. see Cacioppo, Petty, and Tassinary, 1989; Donchin, 1982). This implies that the relationship between psychological and physiological phenomena can be conceptualized in terms of a general 2 (One-to-one vs Many-to-one Relationship) × 2 (Situation Specific vs Cross-situational Relationship) taxonomy. The specific families (i.e. categories) of psychophysiological relationships that can be derived from this taxonomy are depicted in Figure 12.2. The criterial attributes for, and theoretical utility in, establishing each of these categories are contained completely in the two dimensions specified in Figure 12.2; causal attributes of the relation-

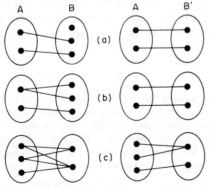

Figure 12.1. Depiction of logical relationships that exist between the domain of psychological constructs and the domain of physiological events.

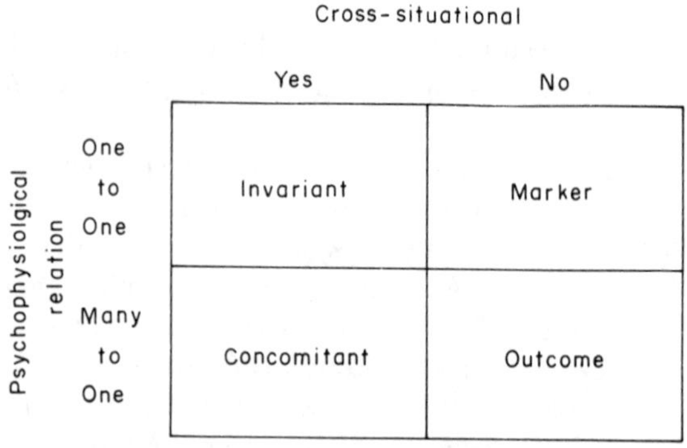

Cross-situational

Figure 12.2. Logical taxonomy of psychophysiological relationships. *Upper left panel*: An association wherein a psychological construct maps into a distinctive physiological event regardless of the context is termed an 'invariant.' *Lower left panel*: A relationship wherein a psychological construct translates into a multiply determined physiological event across situations is termed a 'concomitant.' *Upper right panel*: A relationship wherein a psychological construct translates into a distinctive physiological event in a specific assessment context is termed a 'marker.' *Lower right panel*: An association wherein a psychological construct maps into a multiply determined physiological event regardless of the context is termed an 'outcome.' A physiological event whose relationship to a psychological construct is defined as invariant, or marker, or concomitant can, within the range in which the psychophysiological relationships is valid, serve as an indicant of the psychological construct; a physiological event whose relationship to a psychological construct is defined as outcome or concomitant cannot serve logically as an indicant of any psychological construct.

ships, and whether the relationships are naturally occurring or artifically induced constitute yet other, orthogonal, dimensions and are explicitly excluded here for didactic purposes. For instance, the category in Figure 12.2 labeled 'psychophysiological concomitants' refers only to the conditions and implications of covariation and is *not* intended to discriminate between instances in which the psychological factor is causal in the physiological response, vice versa, or a third variable causes both. In the sections that follow, each type of psychophysiological relationship and the nature of the inferences that each suggests are outlined.

INVARIANTS

> The scientist is usually looking for invariance whether he knows it or not. Whenever he discovers a functional relation between two variables his next question follows naturally: under what conditions does it hold? In other words, under what transformation is the relation invariant? The quest for invariant relations is essentially the aspiration toward generality, and in psychology, as in physics, the principles that have wide application are those we prize. (Stevens, 1951, p. 20)

An invariant relationship between two variables refers to an isomorphic (one-to-one), context-independent (cross-situational) association (see Figures 12.1 and

12.2). To say that there is an invariant relationship means that: (1) a particular element in B' is present if, and only if, a specific element in A is present, (2) the specific element in A is present if, and only if, the corresponding element in B' is present, and (3) the relation between A and B' preserves all relevant arithmetical (algebraic) operations. The establishment of an invariant relationship between a pair of elements from the psychological and the physiological domains provides a strong basis for inference. The establishment of an invariant relationship between the psychological concept of arousal and EDA, for instance, would imply both that any increase in the psychological construct, arousal, leads to increases in EDA, and that any increase in EDA that results from the manipulation of 'psychological' factors is actually the result of corresponding changes in the overarching psychological construct, arousal.

Invariant relationships are usually assumed, rather than formally established, however, and such an assumption can be problematic because the inferences it allows are logically sound if, and only if, the assumption proves correct. The assumption of a cross-situational one-to-one relationship between psychological and physiological events is the most restrictive because the establishment of any dissociation between the physiological measure and psychological construct of interest invalidates the purported psychophysiological relationship. That is, the logical foundation and theoretical utility of the psychophysiological enterprise is undermined in studies of the psychological construct by such a finding if what the enterprise is assumed to offer are mappings of invariant psychophysiological relations. For instance, small increases in body temperature and the orienting responses both are associated with increased EDA, even though general bodily arousal may not increase (e.g. Graham and Clifton, 1966); observations such as these would invalidate any psychophysiological theory or hypothesis based on the assumption of an invariant relationship between arousal and EDA.

The psychophysiological enterprise need not be conceptualized as offering *only* mappings of context-independent, one-to-one relationships, however (cf. Cacioppo, Petty, and Tassinary, 1989; Donchin, 1982). That is, although theoretical parsimony may be served by aspirations of invariance, the requirement that physiological measures must map in a one-to-one manner on to a psychological construct across situations in order to be of use in studies of the psychological construct can result in the rejection of reliable, valid, and sensitive measures, and thereby blunt scientific advance. Indeed, revered self-report measures of attitudes, such as the Thurstone (1928), Likert (1932), and Osgood, Suci, and Tannenbaum (1957) semantic differential scales would need to be abandoned if they were held to the requirement of invariance.

CONCOMITANTS

A psychophysiological correlate or concomitant is defined as a many-to-one, cross-situational (context-independent) association between abstract events A and

B' (see Figures 12.1 and 12.2). That is, the search for psychophysiological concomitants assumes that there is a cross-situational covariation between the manipulated (or measured) psychological factors and a measured physiological response or pattern of responses. The assumption of a psychophysiological concomitant is less restrictive than the assumption of invariance, in that one-to-one correspondence is not required, although the stronger the correlation between psychological and physiological events, the more informative is the relationship.

Consider, for instance, the observation that pupillary responses varied as a function of individuals' attitudes toward visually presented stimuli—an observation which was followed by the conclusion that pupillary response was a 'correlate' or concomitant of people's attitudes (Hess, 1965; Metalis and Hess, 1982). This inference was not warranted logically by the evidence, however, since covariation of the target physiological response with a manipulated (or naturally varying) psychological event is necessary but insufficient evidence for the establishment of a psychophysiological concomitant. The reasons for this are straightforward.

First, the manipulation of the same psychological event (e.g. attitudes) in another context (e.g. using auditory rather than visual stimuli) may alter or eliminate the covariation between the psychological and physiological events because the target physiological response is evoked by a stimulus that had been fortuitously correlated with the psychological construct of interest in the initial measurement context. For instance, the attitude–pupil size hypothesis has not been supported using nonpictorial (e.g. auditory, tactile) stimuli, where it is possible to control the numerous light-reflex-related variables that can confound studies using pictorial stimuli (Goldwater, 1972). It is possible, in several of the studies showing a statistical covariation between attitudes and pupillary response, that the mean luminance of subjects' selected fixations varied inversely with their attitudes toward the visual stimulus (see Janisse and Peavler, 1974).

Second, the manipulation of the same psychological construct in another situation may alter or eliminate the covariation between the psychological and physiological events, because the physiological response of interest is evoked not only by variations in the psychological construct, but also by variations in one or more factors that were introduced in (or were a fundamental constituent of) the new measurement context. Tranel, Fowles, and Damasio (1985), for instance, demonstrated that the presentation of familiar faces (e.g. famous politicians, actors) evoked larger skin conductance responses (SCRs) than did the presentation of unfamiliar faces. This finding, and the procedure and set of stimuli employed, were subsequently used in a study of patients with prosopagnosia (an inability to recognize visually the faces of persons previously known) to demonstrate that the patients can discriminate autonomically between the familiar and unfamiliar faces despite the absence of any awareness of this knowledge. That is, the first study established a psychophysiological relationship in a specific measurement context, and the second study capitalized on this relationship. Assumptions that a psychophysiological concomitant had been established between familiarity and SCRs would imply that the same relationship would hold across situations and stimuli, which is what is meant by context-independent. Yet ample psychophysiological research has demonstrated that novel or unusual (i.e. unfamiliar) stimuli can evoke larger SCRs than familiar stimuli (e.g. see Landis, 1930; Lynn, 1966; Sternbach, 1966). Neither set of studies constitutes evidence for a psychophysiological concomitant, since the presence of evidence for diametrically opposed psychophysiological relationships (i.e. familiarity leads to more SCRs, unfamiliarity leads to more SCRs) indicates that these relationships are limited to the particular set of stimuli and subjects employed. For instance, if there were not many more unfamiliar than familiar faces in the set of experimental stimuli used by Tranel *et al.* (1985), had they employed 'unfamiliar' faces which were not drawn from a familiar university population, or if a different set of subjects were used for whom the unfamiliar faces were strikingly novel, then a completely different relationship between the 'familiar' faces and SCRs could have emerged.

There is no difficulty in finding evidence of faulty theoretical reasoning (i.e. induction) based on the premature assumption that one is dealing with a true psychophysiological correlate:

> I find in going through the literature that the psychogalvanic reflex has been elicited by the following varieties of stimuli...sensations and perceptions of any sense modality (sight, sounds, taste, etc.), associations (words, thoughts, etc.), mental work or effort, attentive movements or attitudes, imagination and ideas, tickling, painful or nocive stimuli, variations in respiratory movements or rate, suggestion and hyponosis, emotional behavior (fighting, crying, etc.), relating dreams, college examinations, and so forth...Forty investigators hold that it is specific to, or a measure of, emotion of the affective qualities; ten others state that it is not necessarily of an emotional or affective nature; twelve men hold that it is somehow to be identified with conation, volition, or attention, while five hold very definitely that it is nonvoluntary; twenty-one authorities state that it goes with one or another of the mental processes; eight state that it is the concomitant of all sensation and perception; five have called it an indicator of conflict and suppression; while four others have used it as an index of character, personality, or temperament. (Landis, 1930, p. 391)

The empirical establishment of a psychophysiological concomitant logically allows an investigator to make a probability statement about the absence or presence (if not the magnitude) of a particular psychological construct (e.g. attitude) when the target physiological response (e.g. pupillary response) has been observed. It is important to emphasize, however, that the estimate of the strength of the correlation used in such inferences should come from assessments of naturally occurring variations in the elements of A and B', sampled when either A or B' changes, rather than from evidence that manipulated or planned variations in A are associated with corresponding changes in B'. This is because knowledge that a statement is true (i.e. if A then B') does not imply that the converse is true (i.e. if B' then A). Hence, except in the rare circumstance in which one is dealing with an invariant relationship, establishing that the manipulation of an event or construct (construed abstractly as A) leads to a particular physiological response or profile of responses (construed as B') does *not* logically imply that if B' then A (i.e. B' predicts A). Measurements of the physiological response of interest each time the psychological construct changes—by whatever means—can lead to overestimates of predictions about the psychological construct based on the physiological response, especially when there are numerous changes in the physiological response not attributable to variations in the psychological construct of interest. For example, pupillary responses, like electrodermal responses, are evoked by a variety of factors, ranging from luminosity to mental effort to arousal to significant events. To infer that a person has a positive or negative attitude toward an object based simply on a pupillary response, therefore, is to commit the logical error of affirmation of the consequent.

MARKERS

A psychophysiological marker is defined as a one-to-one, situation-specific (i.e. context-dependent) relationship between abstract events A and B' (see Figures 12.1 and 12.2). That is, the psychophysiological marker relation assumes only that the occurrence of one (usually a physiological response, parameter of a response, or profile of responses) predicts the occurrence of the other (usually a psychological event) within a given context. Thus, markers are characterized by 'limited ranges of validity,' where by limited ranges of validity is meant that physiological events have a particular 'psychological meaning' only within conditions carefully prescribed theoretically and/or in a series of validation studies (cf. Cacioppo and Petty, 1985; Cacioppo, Martzke, Petty, and Tassinary, 1988; Coles, Gratton, and Gehring, 1987). Such a relationship may reflect a natural connection between psychological and physiological elements in a particular measurement situation or it may reflect an artificially induced (e.g. classically conditioned) association between these elements (e.g. see Cacioppo and Sandman, 1981; Petty and Cacioppo, 1986; Tursky and Jamner, 1983). It should also be noted that, although a context-dependent one-to-one relationship between psychological and physiological events represents the ideal, minimal violations of isomorphism between A and B' can nevertheless yield a useful (although imperfect) marker (e.g. as when viewed as a special case of a conditional probability).

Markers can vary in their *specificity* and *sensitivity*. The more distinctive the form of the physiological response and/or the pattern of associated physiological responses, the greater is the likelihood of achieving a one-to-one relationship between the physiological events and psychological construct, and the wider may be the range of validity of the relationship thereby achieved. At one extreme, carefully defined psychological constructs may be differentiated only by preceise topographical features of one or more physiological responses in the time, amplitude, or frequency domains. For instance, startle, orienting, and defense reactions all lead to increased electrodermal activity, but they differ with respect to the pattern of somatovisceral activity (e.g. heart rate response curve, pupillary response, postural adjustments) that unfolds over time. At the other extreme, global concepts (e.g. arousal) may be indexed more effectively by grosser, aggregate measures. Again, however, the relationship between these aggregate physiological responses and the theoretical construct may be strengthened if attention is given to defining the characteristics of the aggregate which make it a unique pattern of physiological events. Finally, although the assignment of psychological meaning to a physiological response does not depend logically on knowledge of the physiological mechanism underlying the response, the physiological basis of many physiological responses is well articulated (cf. Coles, Donchin, and Porges, 1986) and can inform expectations regarding the psychological significance of various combinations and/or forms of response (e.g. see Cacioppo and Tassinary, in press, Coles, Gratton, and Gehring, 1987).

In terms of sensitivity, a psychophysiological marker may simply signify the occurrence or nonoccurrence of a psychological process or event, possessing no information about the temporal or amplitude properties of the event in a specific assessment context. At the other extreme, a psychophysiological marker may be related in a prescribed assessment context to the psychological event by some well-defined temporal function, such that the measure can be used to delineate the onset and offset of the episode of interest, and it may vary in amplitude such that it mimics the intensity of the psychological event.

In sum, markers represent a fundamental relationship between psychological and physiological events which enables an inductive inference to be drawn about the nature of one, given the presence or absence of the other. The major requirements in establishing a response as a marker are: (1) to demonstrate that the presence of the target response reliably predicts the specific construct of interest, (2) to demonstrate that the presence of the target response is insensitive to (e.g. uncorrelated with) the presence or absence of other constructs, and (3) to specify the boundary conditions for the validity for the relationship. The term 'tracer' can be viewed as synonymous with marker, for each refers to a response or event so strictly associated with particular organismic–environmental conditions that its presence is indicative of the presence of these conditions. The term 'indicant' on the other hand, is more generic, including invariants and markers, since each allows the identification of A given B'.

OUTCOMES

Strictly speaking, an outcome is defined as a many-to-one, situation-specific (context-dependent) relationship between A and B' (see Figure 12.2). That is, a physiological response, or pattern of responses, that is affected by a variation (e.g. manipulation) of more than one psychological construct would be classified as an outcome. In practice, the first attribute of a psychophysiological relationship that *can* be established is that the variation (e.g. manipulation) of a psychological event is associated with a change in a physiological response (or profile of responses). Whether the response profile follows changes in the psychological event across situations (i.e. has the property of context independence), and whether the response profile follows only changes in the event (i.e. has the property of isomorphism) cannot be completely addressed initially. Hence, establishing that a physiological response (i.e. an element in B') varies as a function of a psychological change (i.e. an element in A) means one is dealing, at the very least, with an outcome relationship. A given psychophysiological relationship may appear to be an outcome relationship, but, as the question of isomorphism is examined, emerge as a marker; similarly, the question of generalizability can only be addressed following the establishment of an outcome relationship. Hence, a psychophysiological relationship which evidence suggests is an outcome may emerge as a concomitant once the range of validity is examined; and a relationship that appears to be a marker may emerge as an invariant upon studying the generalizability of the relationship. This progression is not problematic in terms of causing erroneous inferences, however, because any logical inference based on the assumption that one is dealing with an outcome relationship holds for marker, concomitant, or invariant psychophysiological relationships, as well. However, the outcome relationship provides the weakest basis for inference about psychological processes from physiological events of all psychophysiological relationships. For instance, the physiological events *cannot* serve logically as an indicant of a psychological construct; to make such an inference based on an outcome relationship is to commit the error of affirmation of the consequent.

Despite the outcome serving as the most elemental psychophysiological relationship, it can nevertheless provide a solid basis for strong inferences, albeit of a limited form. Specifically, a psychophysiological outcome enables systematic inferences to be drawn about psychological constructs and relationships *based on hypothetico-deductive logic*. That is, when two psychological models differ in predictions regarding one or more physiological outcome, then the logic of the experimental design allows theoretical inferences to be drawn based on psycho-physiological outcomes alone. Of course, no single operationalization of the constructs in a crucial experiment is likely to convince both theories' adherents. If multiple operationalizations of the theoretical constrcts result in the same physiological outcome, however, then strong theoretical inferences can be justified (Cacioppo and Petty, 1986; Cacioppo and Tassinary, in press).

SUMMARY

Although invariant psychophysiological relationships offer the greatest generality, physiological concomitants, markers, and outcomes also can provide important and sometimes otherwise unattainable information about psychological constructs and behavior. The initial step is to establish that variations in a psychological process or event lead to a physiological change, thereby establishing that the psychophysiological relationship is, at a minimum, an outcome. Knowledge that changes in a psychological state lead to a physiological response neither assures that the response will serve as a marker for the psychological state (since the converse of a statement does not follow logically from the statement), nor that the response is a concomitant or invariant of the psychological state (since the response may occur in only certain situations or individuals, or may occur for a large number of reasons besides changes in the particular psychological state).

The present analysis also makes it clear that the minimum assumption underlying the psychophysiological enterprise is that psychological and behavioral processes unfold as organismic–environmental transactions and, hence, have physiological manifestations, ramifications, or reflections, just as the explicit assumption in mental chronometry is that information processing unfolds over time (e.g. Posner, 1978). Even the least informative psychophysiological relationship (e.g. the outcome), therefore, can be a powerful theoretical and empirical tool when conceptualized in the same fashion as reaction time differences in the cognitive sciences (Cacioppo and Petty, 1986; Pylyshyn, 1980).

Finally, the theoretical specification of a psychophysiological relationship involves reaching into the unknown and, hence, requires intellectual invention and systematic efforts to minimize bias and error. Psychological theorizing based on known physiological and anatomical facts, exploratory research and pilot testing, and classic psychometric approaches, can each contribute in important ways here by their generation of testable hypotheses about a psychophysiological relationship. It should be equally clear, however, that the scientific effectiveness of psychophysiological analyses does not derive logically from physiologizing or from the measurement of organismic rather than verbal or chronometric responses. Its great value stems from its stimulation of interesting hypotheses and from the fact that when an experiment agrees with a prediction about orchestrated actions of the organism, a great many alternative hypotheses are usually excluded. The study of physiological mechanisms and techniques can sharpen our thinking and reduce the error of our measurements. They are means rather than ends in the psychophysiological enterprise, however; they offer little if by their use we lose sight of their utility in tests of theoretical predictions and causal inferences. To paraphrase Platt (1964), you can catch phenomena in a logical box or in a physiological box. The logical box is coarse but strong. The physiological box is fine-grained but flimsy. The physiological box is a beautiful way of wrapping up a problem, but it will not hold the phenomena unless they have been caught in a logical box to begin with. The logical requirements for inferring a psychophysiological relationship become more demanding, and this relationship becomes more informative in subsequent work, as one moves from outcomes to concomitants and markers to invariants.

We now turn to the major conceptualizations of attitudes that have been proposed, and we employ the psychophysiological theory proposed in this section to guide our discussions of these conceptualizations.

CONCEPTUALIZATIONS OF ATTITUDES

It has become customary in reviews of the attitude literature to bemoan the fact that there are many definitions of attitude and then dismiss any further discussion as logomachy (McGuire, 1969, 1985; Dawes and Smith, 1985). One's conceptualization of attitudes, however, strongly directs subsequent theorizing and experimentation through the selection of experimental paradigms, the methodological decisions regarding relevant independent and dependent variables, and the inferences drawn from violations of a theoretical expectancy (cf. Fodor, 1968).

THE CONCEPTUALIZATION OF ATTITUDES AS BODILY ORIENTATION

The term attitude appears to have come from the Italian term *attitudine*, which itself derived from the Latin *apto* when it refers to aptitude or fitness, and *acto* when it refers to postures of the body; the two roots *act* and *apt* both have their origin in the Sanskrit root *ag*, meaning to do or act (Bull, 1951). Its first modern use appeared at the turn of the eighteenth century, where it was used by artists to refer to the visible posture of a figure in statuary or in painting (Fleming, 1967). This meaning remains in use in the general language (it is the first definition in most dictionaries) and is also used in medical parlance to refer to bodily position or posture, especially with regard to the position of the limbs relative to each other and relative to the body (Reber, 1985).

Herbert Spencer (1862–1895) and Alexander Bain (1868) were among the first psychologists to use the term attitude and, given their decidedly mentalist perspective, introduced the concept into psychology as an internal state of preparation for action. This conceptualization can be viewed as an extension of, rather than an alternative to, the notion of attitude as a bodily orientation or posture:

> Attitude, like posture, takes two forms, the one static, the other dynamic. A static posture is a stabilized end-result of some action, and when a postural attitude is once attained this attitude in its turn becomes a determining factor in establishing the pattern of the next ensuing action. Our interest in attitude, accordingly, centers in its significance for action. (Herrick, 1951, p. ix)

This general conceptualization of attitudes was maintained through the early writings of Darwin (1965), Sherrington (1923), and Washburn (1916), and later in the writings of Bull (1951) and to some extent Zajonc and Markus (1982) and Wells and Petty (1980). For instance, in a number of places throughout his influential book, *The Expressions of the Emotions in Man and Animals*, Darwin (1965) uses the term attitude to illustrate how different attitudes result from the action of the principles of serviceable associated habits and antithesis:

> Now I have noticed scores of times that when two strange dogs meet on an open road, the one which first sees the other, though at a distance of one or two hundred yards, after the first glance always lowers its head, generally crouches a little, or even lies down; that is, he takes the proper attitude for concealing himself and for making a rush or spring, although the road is quite open and distance great. (p. 43)

Similarly, in his discussion of the functional aspects of the motor cortex, Sherrington (1906–1923) distinguished between two separate systems of motor control and coordination. The phasic reflex system was primarily concerned with reflexes of movement, whereas the tonic system was concerned with reflexes of attitude. The function of these latter reflexes was specifically to maintain static body positions through steady tonic innervation of the musculature as well as through reinforcing and compensatory movements.

By defining an attitude as an identifiable and behaviorally predisposing posture, and by assuming that a particular attitude is the result of the activation of a specific motor system, an invariant relationship is posited between the attitude concept and target physiological responses. Thus, an attitude could be reduced to physiological description (e.g. see Washburn, 1916, pp. 83–4). Bull (1951) modified this position slightly to posit a correlation rather than an invariance between 'motor attitudes' (postural orientation) and 'mental attitudes' (feeling state):

> A neuromuscular sequence is presented in which the 'expression' of emotion is considered as separable into the serial phases of preparatory motor attitude and consummatory action. Feeling is shown as belonging to an intermediary stage, being dependent on a delay occurring after the set-up of the preliminary motor attitude. It is actually the feeling or consciousness of the motor attitude, and indicates a holding up of the consummatory action.
> ... there can be motor attitude without mental attitude, but no mental attitude is possible without a motor attitude. (Bull, 1951, pp. 13, 21–2)

Physiological research such as that by Sherrington (1906–1923) and Papez (1937), and psychophysiological research such as that by Jacobson (1930a, b) and Landis and Hunt(1939) have been repeatedly cited in the psychophysiological literature as supporting the proposed link between somatic activity and thought, images, feelings, but the conceptualization of attitude as bodily position stimulated surprisingly little psychophysiological research on the concept or on attitude change. Two legacies from the attitude-as-posture model have had a profound influence on attitude theory, however. First, subsequent conceptualizations have included predispositions to respond as an attribute of attitudes (cf. Doob, 1947). Second, the assumption that attitudes have a cross-situational physiological signature can be found in subsequent empirical and theoretical work on attitudes. Two implications of the attitude-as-posture model which have not been pursued seriously until recently are the notion that some attitudes can be unreportable or have unreportable effects, and the notion that physiological responses may yield information about the attributes and consequences of attitudes.

We turn next to the conceptualization that led to major advances in the assessment of attitudes and that stimulated research on attitude change.

THE CONCEPTUALIZATION OF ATTITUDES AS AFFECT

The attitude scales developed by Thurstone (1928) in his seminal paper, 'Attitudes can be measured', were designed as measures of the individual's favorable or unfavorable potential action toward some object or issue of concern. Thurstone (1931) defined attitudes as 'the affect for or against a psychological object' (p. 261), and then defined affect as 'appetition or aversion' which varies in intensity. Similarly, Krech and Crutchfield (1948) emphasized feelings of being 'for or against' something and having 'positive or negative affect' in differentiating attitudes from opinions. Affective and evaluative responses were often used interchangeably by these early investigators (e.g. Green, 1954), although affect was distinguished from emotion by some (e.g. see Thurstone, 1931, p. 261).

The tendency by proponents of the conceptualization of 'attitudes as affect' to equate affect and evaluation has continued to the present:

> The terms 'affect' and 'evaluation' are used synonymously throughout this book. Although it might be argued that there is a difference between a person's judgment that an object makes him feel good and his evaluation that the object is good, there is little evidence to suggest that a reliable empirical distinction between these two variables can be made. (Fishbein and Ajzen, 1975, p. 11)

Although the distinctions between these two variables have been outlined elsewhere (e.g. see Cacioppo, Petty, Losch, and Kim, 1986; Zanna and Rempel, 1984), it is of interest to note that Fishbein (1980) was one of the first to demonstrate an empirical distinction between affect and evaluation in a study of attitude–behavior inconsistency when he found that smokers possessed negative evaluations of (attitudes towards) cigarettes (as measured by semantic differential scales such as harmful/beneficial, wise/foolish, positive/negative) but positive affective responses toward them (as measured by scales such as pleasant/unpleasant).

In addition, despite Thurstone's (1931) early admonishment that emotion may help explain how a particular attitudinal response toward an object developed but is not itself the attitude, affect in the attitude literature came to refer to the component of feeling (reportable) states that represented the valence and intensity dimensions of an emotional response. Rajecki (1982, p. 34) lists such terms as liking, loathing, angriness, happiness, sadness, pride, boredom, fearing, hating, and loving, and states that affect represents the evaluative aspect of these terms. Similarly, Mueller (1970) concluded that:

> In some characteristics attitude and emotion are identical: both have a cognitive basis, both can be placed along an evaluative or affective dimension, and both include an action tendency toward the stimulus object . . . very strong attitudes are, in fact, a special case of emotion. (p. 547)

Psychophysiological research regarding the autonomic differentiation of emotional states had as early as the 1930s yielded disappointing results, and the notion that specific autonomic responses could be paired with each emotion was abandoned by psychophysiologists and attitude theorists alike (e.g. see Abel, 1930; Cannon, 1927; Landis, 1930). This early psychophysiological research *did* reveal an outcome relationship such that strong emotional stimuli led to some evidence for sympathetic activation (e.g. increased EDA). Several subsequent studies examined the relevance of this psychophysiological outcome to attitudes. Smith (1936), for instance, studied social influence by monitoring the skin resistance responses (SRRs) of individuals as they were confronted by the information that their peers held attitudes that were discrepant from their own; Rankin and Campbell (1955) studied racial prejudice by monitoring the SRRs of individuals as they were exposed to white and black experimenters, as did Westie and DeFleur (1959) using slides of individuals; and Cooper (1959) studied prejudice generally by monitoring SRRs as individuals were exposed to complimentary comments about their most disliked ethnic group, derogatory comments about their most liked ethnic group, and complimentary or derogatory comments about ethnic groups toward which the individuals felt neutrally. The general consensus from this research was that intense attitudes evoked greater autonomic activation than weak attitudes, and this outcome, in combination with the failure to consider the logical limitations to inference of psychophysiological-outcome relationships and the conceptualization that affect was central to the concept of attitudes, led to the premature acceptance of the converse of the psychophysiological relationship that had been demonstrated—specifically, that autonomic responses serve as indicants of the 'emotional roots' or 'intensity' of an attitude (cf. Dawes and Smith, 1985; Lemon, 1973; McGuire, 1985; Mueller, 1970, 1986):

> Another possible behavioral specimen for attitude inference is autonomic response. There are two primary reasons for optimism. First, the respondent is unable to inhibit or alter the response voluntarily. Second, there presumably is a close relationship between such physiological responses and the emotional (or affective) states of the respondent. Thus, there is hope that autonomic responses to stimuli containing the attitude object may provide a *direct* and *measurable* reference to the emotional component of attitude. (Summers, 1970, p. 481, italics added)

> . . . it is assumed that the amount of the physiological reaction indicates the extent of the subject's arousal, the intensity of his feelings, and hence the extremity of his attitudes. (Oskamp, 1977, p. 46)

To summarize thus far, the attitudes-as-affect model led to the theory that physiological measures index the intensity but not the positive or negative nature of people's emotional reactions. This proposition was based on questionable reasoning rather than logical implications of the evidence for the conceptualization of attitudes as affect. Moreover, most prior psychophysiological analyses of attitudes have reflected the belief that affect and emotion are the province of students of the autonomic nervous system (cf. Coles, Gratton, and Fabiani, in press). Yet anyone who has ever seen the facial expression made by a person who tasted something they truly disliked, or who has just seen someone they truly love and have missed, might suspect that a person's physical actions and expressions may also harbor information, in limited contexts, about how he or she feels about an object or person. Ekman, Friesen, and Ancoli (1980), for instance, found they were able to gauge how much individuals liked particular segments of a videotape by monitoring the extent to which they smiled when viewing the segments.

Not all emotional processes are accompanied by visually or socially perceptible expressions or actions, however, and this fact has limited the utility of research on the expressions of emotions. For instance, Graham (1980) attempted to assess viewers' emotional responses to television advertisements using a comprehensive scoring procedure for measuring people's observable facial actions. Graham found that for most of his subjects there were too few observable facial expressions to the attitude stimuli to make further analyses worthwhile.

However, the neural activation of the striated (e.g. facial) muscles results in electrical impulses (muscle action potentials) that can be detected using the electromyogram (EMG), even when there are no perceptible muscle contractions. There is now evidence that suggests that emotional reactions which are too fleeting or subtle to evoke an overt expression can nevertheless be measured (Cacioppo and Petty, 1981; Cacioppo, Petty, Losch and Kim, 1986; Fridlund and Izard, 1983; Schwartz, 1975). For instance, Love (1972) videotaped people's facial expressions while they were exposed to a proattitudinal or counterattitudinal appeal; he reported finding no differences in overt facial expressions despite the fact that individuals reported more positive attitudes toward the proattitudinal than counterattitudinal communications. Cacioppo and Petty (1979a) subsequently replicated Love's (null) finding while also demonstrating that the level of EMG activity recorded over selected muscle regions of facial expression (e.g. brow, cheek) differentiated subjects who anticipated and were exposed to a proattitudinal appeal from those who anticipated and were exposed to a counterattitudinal appeal.

Cacioppo and Petty (1979a) also found that facial EMG patterning tended to be more pronounced during the pro- and counterattitudinal message presentations than during the period following the announcement of the topic and position of the message they were to hear but prior to the actual onset of the message presentation. This is consistent with the notion that EMG activity varies as a function of the intensity as well as the direction of transient and specific emotional reactions. Clearer evidence for this notion was provided, however, in studies by Cacioppo, Petty, Losch, and Kim (1986). Subjects were exposed to slides of moderately unpleasant, mildly unpleasant, mildly pleasant, and moderately pleasant scenes. Subjects viewed each slide for 5 seconds and rated how much they liked the scene that was depicted, how familiar the scene appeared, and how aroused it made them feel. Independent judges who were blind to experimental conditions rated videorecordings of subjects' facial actions during the 5-second stimulus presentations. The results indicated that the scenes were so mild that socially perceptible facial expressions were not evoked. That is, one could not tell from looking at the subjects whether they were viewing positive or negative photographs. Nevertheless, analyses of facial EMG revealed that the activity over muscles of facial expression varied as a function of the direction *and* intensity of the individuals' emotional reactions to the slides: the more subjects liked the scene, the lower the level of EMG activity over the corrugator supercilii muscle region; EMG activity over the zygomaticus major region tended to be greater for liked than disliked scenes; and EMG activity was higher over the periocular (lateral orbicularis oculi) region when moderately pleasant stimuli were presented than when mildly pleasant or unpleasant stimuli were presented.

In sum, recent studies suggest that positive and negative emotions can have effects on facial muscle patterns that are so subtle they may not be detectable to the naked eye. There is also some evidence to suggest that these subtle effects on the facial muscles, especially the muscles around the eyes and brow, are not easy for people to inhibit (Bush and Cacioppo, 1985). Hence, facial EMG may prove to be informative about people's emotional responses to attitude stimuli whether or not they are willing and able to articulate their underlying feelings. This does not mean that distinctive and naturally occurring EMG responses always, or even usually, reflect emotions, however. Facial expressions are clearly controllable, and facial expressions serve communicative, deceptive, and emotionally expressive functions with admirable facility. It would be an error based on these studies, therefore, to infer that the observation of increased EMG activity over the brow region meant the individual disliked something. An increase in EMG activity over the brow region, for instance, may simply mean the person is concentrating on, or perplexed by the attitude stimulus rather than disaffected with it.

Moreover, if the response did reflect disaffection, the emotional response might be transient, specific, and/or completely irrelevant to the psychological object of interest (cf. Dimberg, 1982; McHugo, Lanzetta, Sullivan, Masters, and Englis, 1985). For instance, in McHugo *et al.* (1985), students viewed videotaped excerpts of happiness/assurance, anger/threat, and fear/evasion expressive displays by President Reagan. Results revealed EMG activity was greater over the corrugator supercilii region and less over the zygomaticus major region during the negative than during the positive expressive displays by Reagan, especially during image-only presentations. Facial EMG activity did not vary as a function of the students' prior attitudes towards President Reagan, but then the most salient stimulus was a smiling or frowning Presidential image, not the President vis-à-vis their own attitudes. Dimberg (1982) found that subjects' facial EMGs can vary as a function of the facial expression presented to them—a result that could be attributable to facial mimicry and/or to affective reactions evoked by the expressive displays (Dimberg, 1986; Englis, Vaughan, and Lanzetta, 1982). Indeed, McHugo, Lanzetta, and Bush (1987) replicated portions of their earlier study but made the subjects' attitudes salient prior to their viewing the videotaped excerpts. Results revealed that facial EMG activity and reported emotions varied as a function of both President Reagan's expressive display *and* the subjects' initial attitude toward President Reagan. Even though the research reviewed in this section indicates that positive and negative emotions have predictable effects on facial EMG activity, and a recent study by Cacioppo, Martzke, Petty, and Tassinary (1988) supports the contention that facial EMG responses can mark emotions perhaps including settings such as those utilized by McHugo *et al.* (1985, 1987), these latter studies help underscore the fact that only through careful experimental control can one be confident that the psychological object of interest is serving as the evocative stimulus.

THE TRIPARTITE CONCEPTUALIZATION OF ATTITUDES

The trichotomy of feeling, knowing, and acting was first used by the early Greek philosophers as a way of conceptualizing not attitudes but human experience generally (McGuire, 1969, 1985). It was not until McDougall (1908–1961, supplementary Chapter 6) and, somewhat later and more explicitly by Smith (1947), that the trichotomy was applied to attitudes. The best-known and articulated tripartite conceptualization of attitudes, however, is that of Rosenberg and Hovland (1960):

> We here indicate that attitudes are predispositions to respond to some class of stimuli with certain classes of responses and designate the three major types of responses as cognitive, affective, and behavioral... To a large extent these response classes are themselves abstractions or constructs and are typically inferred... (p. 3)

Interestingly, physiological responses were an explicit part of their model, serving as a correlate. Specifically, responses reflecting the activation of the sympathetic nervous system were said to be informative regarding the affective (and only the affective) component of attitudes:

> Thus an individual's affective response toward another individual may be inferred from measures of such physiological variables as blood pressure or galvanic response, but is more typically inferred from verbal statements of how much he likes or dislikes him. (Hovland and Rosenberg, 1960, p. 3)

Based on coverage in contemporary introductory social psychology textbooks (e.g. Baron and Byrne, 1987; Forsyth, 1987; Michener, DeLamater, and Schwartz, 1986; Penrod, 1983; Shaver, 1987) and attitude texts (e.g. see Eiser, 1986; Mueller, 1986; Oskamp, 1977; Rajecki, 1982; Triandis, 1971; Zimbardo,

Ebbesen, and Maslach, 1977), the tripartite model of Rosenberg and Hovland (1960) is the most widely accepted conceptualization of attitudes (but see Cacioppo, Petty, and Geen, in press; Greenwald, in press). Moreover, there is evidence from early in the history of the tripartite model of attitudes that the relationship between sympathetic arousal and affective arousal (at least above some threshold) was assumed to be *invariant* despite the empirical research to date having shown only that sympathetic arousal was an *outcome* of an emotionally evocative event (e.g. see Rosenberg and Hovland, 1960, pp. 5–6). This logical leap was not without its critics over a half century ago (see, also, Landis, 1930):

> Several observers recording the GSR have more or less incidentally used in their observers' reports the following terms suggestive of attitudes; astonishment, surprise, satisfaction, relief, relaxation, consternation, bewilderment, confusion, strain, excitement, annoyance and amusement. These investigators were so intent upon translating the observers' protocols into the categories of conation, emotion and volition that they overlooked the possible significance, in terms of the organism, of the postural comments themselves regardless of their arbitrary categorical setting. (Abel, 1930, p. 49)

Still, the fact that verbal reports of affect were assigned the same status in the nomological net as more difficult-to-measure changes in sympathetic discharge justified the use of verbal reports in place of measures of bodily response; and the simple dismissal of whichever measure proved unfriendly to the investigator's hypotheses. For instance, most studies supporting the attitude tripartite have employed verbal rather than physiological measures of the affective component (e.g. Kothandapani, 1971; Ostrom, 1969). Furthermore, in perhaps the best study to date on the attitude tripartite conceptualization, Breckler (1984) argued that studies of the attitude tripartite should measure responses from a variety of domains—such as the verbal, nonverbal, and physiological response domains when operationalizing the components of Rosenberg and Hovland's (1960) model. Consequently, Breckler (1984) recorded heart rate in his first experiment to assess changes in sympathetic discharge as an index of the affective component of the target attitude. The results of this experiment failed to confirm his theoretical expectations, based on the Rosenberg and Hovland (1960) model, regarding the link between heart rate and the 'affective component' of attitudes.

As Experiment 2, Breckler (1984) conducted a 'verbal report anologue' (p. 1200) of his first experiment while deleting all physiological measures in the replication. The use of only verbal report measures produced a pattern of data more friendly to the tripartite conceptualization. Specifically, evidence was obtained for convergent validity across and discriminant validity within the self-report measures of cognitive, affective, and behavioral response to the attitude object. It was concluded the studies supported the Rosenberg and Hovland tripartite model of attitudes, and no explanation was offered for the failure of the model in terms of its physiological predictions.

Although one might extend the tripartite model by proposing CNS loci governing (and physiological markers reflecting) cognition, emotion, and con-ation, Rosenberg and Hovland's (1960) tripartite model posits only that sympathetic nervous responses serve as indices of affect. As reviewed in the preceding section: (1) emotional stimuli can lead to sympathetic activation, but the conditions under which the latter predicts (marks) the former are not yet well specified; (2) emotional stimuli can lead to incipient somatic changes in the muscles of mimicry as well as to sympathetic activation; and (3) sympathetic activation is associated with various antecedents besides emotion (e.g. mental effort; cf. Kahneman, 1973).

Second, Rosenberg and Hovland's model treated verbal measures as possessing all and more of the information than achievable through physiological assessments (cf. Hovland and Rosenberg, 1960, pp. 222–3). The anatomical architecture of visceral afferents, which minimizes the demands on the organism's limited cognitive resources, provides the basis for striking disparities between actual autonomic responses and verbal reports, as the peripheral physiological adjust-ments are designed to maintain homeostatic conditions in the organism and, thereby, provide the internal milieu required for sustaining thought, feeling, and coordinated behavior. The fractionation of verbal and physiological responses, therefore, can be viewed as a consequence of the body's eloquently orchestrated division of labor, an organization that provides the human organism with the capacity to adapt, aspire, and achieve more than other known species. Import-antly, this organization implies physiological responses can be used as outcomes or markers in contexts in which verbal reports are mute (e.g. Cacioppo, Tassinary, Stonebraker, and Petty, 1987; Cacioppo, Petty, and Losch, in press).

Third, physiological responses are not limited to the affective aspect of human experience but can be informative about, the cognitive and behavioral aspects as well. This suggestion is supported by a variety of studies, including long and independent lines of research on the electromyographic response-outcomes of cognition (e.g. silent language processing; see reviews by Cacioppo and Petty, 1981; Cacioppo, Petty, and Tassinary, 1989; Garrity, 1977; McGuigan, 1970, 1978), emotion (e.g. see reviews by Fridlund and Izard, 1983), and conation (e.g. Coles, Gratton, Bashore, Eriksen, and Donchin, 1985; Jacobsen, 1930a, b; Shaw, 1940). In a recent attitude study illustrating the physiological effects of all three forces, subjects were led to believe they were participating in research on involuntary neural responses during 'action and imagery' (Cacioppo, Petty, and Marshall–Goodell, 1984). Numerous dummy electrodes were placed on the subjects and a cover story was employed to deflect attention from the facial placements and the fact that the responses being monitored could be altered by the subject. Subjects on any given trial either: (a) lifted what was described as being a 'light' (16 gram) or 'heavy' (35 gram) weight (action); (b) imagined lifting the 'light' or 'heavy' weight (imagery); (c) silently read a neutral communication as if they agreed or disagreed with its thesis (action); or (d) imagined reading an editorial with which they agreed or disagreed (imagery). Based on the model of skeletomotor patterning (Cacioppo and Petty, 1981), we expected that perioral (orbicularis oris) EMG activity would be greater during the communicative attitudinal tasks than during the physical tasks; the affective processes invoked by the positive and negative attitudinal tasks would lead to distinguishable patterns of EMG activity over the brow (corrugator supercilii), cheek (zygomatic major), and possibly the nose (levator labii superioris—which is involved in expressions of disgust) regions; and the simple physical tasks would lead to distinguishable EMG activity over the superficial forearm flexors (whose actions control flexion about the wrist).

Imagining performing rather than actually performing the tasks was, of course, associated with lower mean levels of EMG activity. More interestingly, results provided support for the suggestion that somatic responses are influenced by, and therefore in well-conceived experimental designs can be informative about, cognition (e.g. the load on the articulatory loop), emotion (e.g. affective valence), and conation (e.g. imagined action). Specifically, results revealed that: (1) perioral EMG activity was higher during the silent language (attitudinal) than nonlanguage (physical) tasks; (2) EMG activity over the brow, cheek, and nasal muscle regions in the face (muscles of mimicry) varied as a function of whether subjects thought about the topic in an agreeable or disagreeable manner; and (3) EMG activity over the superficial forearm flexors was higher during the physical tasks than during the attitudinal tasks.

Yet another line of research has demonstrated consistently that the pupillary responses are influenced by cognitive processes such as attention (Libby, Lacey, and Lacey, 1973; Lynn, 1966) and cognitive effort (e.g. see review by Beatty, 1982). Beatty (1986), for instance, reviews evidence that the amplitude of pupillary dilations varies with the processing load or 'mental effort' required by a task, regardless of the sensory modality in which the task is presented, and that these pupillary responses are sensitive to within-task, between-task, and between-individual factors that control task-processing demands. In an illustrative study, three seven-digit strings were aurally presented at a rate of one per second (Kahneman and Beatty, 1966). After a brief pause, subjects repeated the digit string at the same rate. Results revealed that pupillary diameter increased with the presentation of each digit, reaching a maximum during the pause preceding the report:

> The task-evoked pupillary response ... provides a reliable and sensitive indication of within-task variations in processing load. It generates a reasonable and orderly index of between-task variations in processing load. It reflects differences in processing load between individuals who differ in psychometric ability when performing the same objective task. For these reasons, the task-evoked pupillary response provides a powerful analytic tool for the experimental study of processing load and the structure of processing resources. (Beatty, 1982, p. 291)

Beatty's conclusion clearly applies to studies utilizing pupillary responses as outcomes, but it does not apply to studies utilizing pupillary responses as markers, concomitants, or invariants—i.e. as indicants. This is due to the fact that no study to date has been conducted to determine the extent to which pupillary responses predict changes in processing load, or vary as a function of spontaneous changes in processing load. The extensive control of factors *known* to determine pupillary response in the processing load paradigms, however, suggests that pupillary responses are good candidates for markers of processing load in that specific assessment context (see Beatty, 1986). As this distinction illustrates, however, there is an important but fine line between strong inference and unwitting leaps of the logical gap between outcome and indicant.

In sum, cognitive and behavioral as well as affective determinants of visceral responding have been identified. It is hazardous at best, therefore, to assume that the affective substrates necessarily have been tapped given only that: (a) prior research has established that emotional arousal leads to autonomic activity (i.e. a psychophysiological outcome relationship); and (b) an attitude stimulus has evoked an autonomic reaction. On the positive side, these observations imply that autonomic [or what Rosenberg and Hovland, (1960) presumably meant by 'sympathetic nervous'] responses can be used within limited ranges of validity to investigate cognitive and behavioral aspects of the organismic–environmental transaction as well as affective aspects.

In addition, the Rosenberg and Hovland (1960) tripartite model implies that responses from the central and somatic nervous systems are irrelevant to the study of cognition, emotion, and behavior. Research on the evoked potential (e.g. Coles, Gratton, and Fabiani, in press; Donchin, Karis, Bashore, Coles, and Gratton, 1986) and on the messages carried by incipient (i.e. visually unobservable) facial actions illustrates the fallacy of this feature of the model. Recent psychophysiological research has indicated that negative emotional reactions influence the EMG activity over regions of the muscles of mimicry (e.g. the brow) and that silent language and numeric loads on working memory influenced the EMG activity over the perioral muscle region. The research further suggests that EMG discharges over the brow and over the perioral muscle region can be used in certain contexts to mark episodes of negative affect and silent language processing, respectively. Together, these studies have implications for the specificity and sensitivity of somatic markers when individuals cannot report, will not report, or do not know what to report about ongoing cognitive and emotional operations.

THE HOMEOSTASIS MODEL OF ATTITUDES

One possibly undesirable feature of the tripartite model is the nonparsimonious notion that affective, cognitive, and behavioral stimuli can influence affective, cognitive, and behavioral attitude components, *each* of which, in turn, can mediate affective, cognitive, and behavioral responses. There is agreement across conceptualizations that attitudes have cognitive, affective, and behavioral antecedents and consequences. Moreover, given that all human experience can be partitioned into categories of affect, cognition, and behavior (cf. McGuire, 1969,

1985), one can clearly and usefully conceptualize the knowledge structure underlying an attitude in terms of this age-old trichotomy as well.

The major theoretical arguments for the tripartite over any unidimensional conceptualization are: (1) the hypothetical construct, attitude, can be measured only by its presumed effects on response outcomes, and the trichotomy of cognition, emotion, and behavior represent response outcomes more completely than any single dimension; and (2) there are so many complex factors involved in a person's attitude toward a social issue that any single score cannot truly describe the person's attitude (Rosenberg and Hovland, 1960). While acknowledging that a single score does not represent completely a complex construct, Thurstone (1931) pointed out that this Procrustian consequence is intrinsic to the act of measurement:

> The measurement of any object or entity describes only one attribute of the object measured. This is a universal characteristic of all measurement. When the height of a table is measured, the whole table has not been described but only that attribute which was measured. (p. 259)

To say that an attitude toward a psychological object is complex, unique, and/or consists of multiple dimensions or features is to state the obvious, and giving each dimension or feature of the psychological object a name does nothing to explain the phenomena of interest (e.g. see Dewey and Bentley, 1949).

The logic underlying the former theoretical argument for the tripartite model is that an index of a construct is more reliable and valid if repeated and uncorrelated measures of the construct are made (Davis and Ostrom, 1987). There is nothing in this position that logically compels one to adopt the abstractions of cognition, emotion, or behavior, however—or a multidimensional rather than a unidimensional conceptualization of attitudes. For instance, Cacioppo, Petty, and Geen (in press) present evidence that the multitrait–multimethod pattern of data obtained in studies thought to support the tripartite model of attitudes can be mimicked by scaling independent *cognitive* representations (i.e. activity and potency) of the object along an evaluative dimension in the same manner as cognition, emotion, and behavior have been scaled along the evaluative dimension in studies of the attitude tripartite model (e.g. Breckler, 1984). Moreover, there is growing appreciation for the fact that one's verbal response system—the system tapped traditionally to assess cognition, emotion, and behavior in studies of the tripartite model of attitudes—may only partly overlap with somatic/expressive and autonomic response systems (Cacioppo, Petty, and Tassinary, 1989; Greenwald, 1982; Land, 1971). Hence, an argument could be made for replacing the traditional trichotomy of human experience (i.e. cognitive, emotional, behavioral) with a trichotomy of response channels (i.e. subjective, autonomic, somatic/expressive). Settling simply for verbal responses to assess a construct has strong implications, in that it endorses the use of what is readily measurable (a method-oriented approach) rather than the phenomena of interest (a problem-oriented approach) to justify a particular conceptualization of a psychological construct such as attitude.

As discussed previously in this chapter, early advocates of a unidimensional conceptualization of attitudes acknowledged the importance of the positive–negative dimension but equated attitudes with affect, or failed to distinguish affect from evaluation. This seems undesirable as well, as it blurs the fact that some attitudes, such as those serving a consummatory function, can be evocative of a great deal of affect, whereas others, such as those serving an instrumental function, may evoke little or no emotion. The stimulus category to which an attitude applies has a structure that includes beliefs about and attributes of the stimuli comprising the category; memories of prior behavioral, cognitive, and affective experiences; expectations and conations; and possibly one or more affect nodes through which affective responses can be activated. However, taking an evolutionary perspective, Cacioppo, Petty, and Geen (in press) have argued that a set of accurate summaries of the merits or demerits of the elements of stimulus categories (i.e. global evaluations, or attitudes, of psychological objects) represents an important conceptual structure by which environmental demands are simplified, analogous to the manner by which homeostasis represents an important physiological structure by which organismic demands are simplified. In this conceptualization, the attitude assessment is reduced to the measurement of the global and enduring evaluation of a psychological object, but the underpinnings of, interconnections among, and influence of, attitudes are not reducible to a single score on an evaluative dimension any more than is homeostasis reducible to a single state-measure or set-point.

Although homeostasis is used in part by physiologists to mean maintenance of constant conditions in the internal environment, it is a richer theoretical construct than this (Dempsey, 1951, pp. 229–34), with broader implications for the conceptualization of attitudes. Briefly, according to an evolutionary biological perspective, cell specialization and the isolation of interior cells from the external environment of the sea occurred as multicellular organisms developed and moved toward complexity. The former required that the organism somehow bring the same nurturant environment previously provided by the sea to the interior cells. Claude Bernard was the first to enunciate that extracellular fluid constitutes the immediate environment—the internalized sea—for complex multicellular organisms. Homeostasis represents the dynamic process by which constant conditions of life in the internal environment are achieved. It operates primarily through negative-feedback mechanisms, whose actions are initiated, or increased, as the discrepancy between the present state and the organismic set-point increases. Individuals do not have to 'do anything' to invoke homeostatic mechanisms, but rather they are said to be self-regulating. Individuals can, of course, engage in deliberate actions that alter homeostatic processes, as illustrated by dieting, but they need not do so for organismic processes to be invoked to maintain a constancy of the internal milieu in the face of environmental stimulation. This facet of homeostasis led Claude Bernard (1878) to conclude that: 'the constancy of the "milieu interieur" is the condition of a free and independent existence' (p. 879).

An individual's system of attitudes can be conceptualized as functioning homologously—that is, as providing a constancy of the 'milieu exterieur' to enable a free and independent existence. Individuals do not have the time, energy, or ability to access and review all of the contents of the relevant representational structure(s) each time they are confronted by a stimulus. An attitude toward the psychological object provides a rapid, cognitively inexpensive heuristic for deriving meaning from, imparting predictability to, and deriving behavioral guidelines for dealing with a complex, sometimes hostile world. Carrying this analogy further, one would expect the somatic response system and the cephalic and visceral systems supporting its actions (e.g. smooth muscles governing circulation and perfusion of vascular beds) to be involved.

Implicit here is that attitudes operate in part outside an individual's awareness. This does not imply that unreportable attitudes cannot be measured (cf. Cacioppo, Petty, and Losch, in press) or that the homeostasis model of attitudes is untestable. Long-term memories have subtle influences even when individuals cannot access them, and attitudes (global and enduring evaluative responses) should function similarly. For instance, although previous attitude research (e.g. see Fazio, in press) has shown that attitudes which come to mind quickly are more predictive of conations and short-term behaviors than those which do not, the present conceptualization suggests that attitudes which come to mind more slowly, or attitudes which have been repressed (e.g. through hypnotic suggestion), would, nevertheless, be predictive of behaviors (e.g. impulsive behaviors rather than intentions or intentional behaviors).

The homeostasis model of attitudes also provides an interesting reversal in how thought and attitudes have been conceptualized previously. A prominent position among attitude theorists is that attitudes are based on knowledge about the attitude objects (e.g. Fishbein and Ajzen, 1975; Lingle and Ostrom, 1981), and such a position implies that thought is primary—phylogenetically, ontogenetically, and derivatively. Attitudes might well function in the role of a summary statistic for people's beliefs about, and experiences with, an attitude object and be influenced by changes in beliefs and experiences. But—like the evolution of the physiological mechanisms underlying homeostasis—the need for more veridical, generalizable, and predictive evaluations of environmental events and challenges, through the forces of natural selection, can be viewed as having favored the development of the symbolic representation, manipulation, and organization of the external world. That is, not unlike the evolutionary pressures which shaped the physiological mechanisms underlying homeostasis, the hostile forces of nature (e.g. predators, parasites, food shortages, climate) coupled with the intense social interaction and manipulation (e.g. intergroup competition), which characterizes the human species, demands unprecedented speed, sensitivity, and accuracy in the development of approach/assurance and avoidance/threat response inclinations (i.e. attitudes), and these pressures may have favored the natural selection of human intelligence and reflective consciousness to improve species means of dealing adaptively with the forces of nature and with one another.

Consistent with this view, attitudes are formed even when unfamiliar stimuli are presented which evoke no conscious processing (Kunst-Wilson and Zajonc, 1980; Wilson, 1979). Moreover, as one ascends the phylogenetic scale there remains the need for organisms to approach/prefer certain stimuli and avoid/disdain others to foster the continuation of their genetic code, but one finds organisms' evaluative responses guided by increasingly malleable mechanisms ranging from deterministic reflexes to fixed action patterns to learned (e.g. conditioned) emotional responses to hedonically biased associative processes (e.g. wishful thinking) and relatively objective appraisals. The contribution of heredity toward these ends also moves from deterministic to propensities. One can find reflexes and fixed action patterns in humans, but the greater encephalization in humans places a greater emphasis on representational processes in the formation of global and enduring attitudes and systems of attitudes. For instance, research in ethology on the genetic determination of fixed action patterns to sign stimuli (e.g. see review by Kupfermann, 1985) and in classical conditioning regarding the increased likelihood of associations being formed between certain classes of stimuli and responses [including evaluative responses—e.g. see Ohman and Dimberg (1984), Lanzetta and Orr (1981), Seligman (1970)] suggest that biological predispositions exist in humans as well as in animals. Their influence, however, is limited greatly by symbolic representation (e.g. encoding), manipulation (e.g. cognitive responding), and organization (e.g. associative networks). In sum, the adaptive value of evaluative sensitivity and veracity within a generally stable and self-regulating system of attitudes can be conceptualized both as an emergent property of, and as a guiding force driving, representational processes and structures rather than simply as a hypothetical construct emerging subsequent to, and serving as a convenient summary statistic for, beliefs and knowledge about a stimulus.

Attitudes, like homeostasis, also tend to be maintained by the presence of negative-feedback mechanisms, whose actions are initiated, or increased, as the discrepancy between a set point (e.g. initial attitude) and an externally originated (e.g. recommended) position increases. The negative-feedback mechanisms governing an individual's attitude systems include pressures toward cognitive consistency (Rosenberg, 1960), biased information (e.g. top-down) processing which serves to preserve existing beliefs and attitudes (e.g. Cacioppo, Petty, and Sidera, 1982; Lord, Ross, & Lepper, 1979), counterargumentation of discrepant information (Petty and Cacioppo, 1986), source derogation (Aronson, Turner, and Carlsmith, 1963), reactions of incredulity (Osgood and Tannenbaum, 1955), a lighter scrutiny given to attitude-consistent than to attitude-inconsistent information (Cacioppo and Petty, 1979a, c), and the relative attractiveness of individuals with similar attitudes (Byrne, 1971). Moreover, as with homeostasis, individuals need not deliberately invoke these negative-feedback processes nor be capable of reporting their invocation for these processes to operate.

To summarize, according to the homeostasis conceptualization of attitudes, an individual's system of attitudes has expanded our ecological niche. Although one can deliberately retrieve one's attitudes and think about issue-relevant information, attitudes can also be accessed automatically by the presentation of an exemplar (see Fazio, in press). Furthermore, individuals need neither review the various elements that make up the stimulus category nor deliberately think through the implications of the various attributes of a stimulus upon the presentation of an exemplar from a class of stimuli for an evaluative response to emerge (Zajonc, 1980). Consequently, an individual's system of attitudes can provide a guide for reacting to new as well as to old exemplars from stimulus categories (e.g. environmental challenges) while minimizing the demands placed on one's limited processing resources. In this manner, an individual's system of attitudes contributes to a free and independent existence.

CONCLUSION

Attitudes have been conceptualized in a variety of ways, ranging from postural orientation to multidimensional representations of human experience. Not all psychological conceptualizations are equally useful or appropriate for the behavioral phenomena to which they are applied in contemporary scientific thought, however. The conceptualization of attitudes strongly directs subsequent theorizing and experimentation through the selection of experimental paradigms, the methodological decisions regarding relevant independent and dependent variables, and the inferences drawn from violations of a theoretical expectancy. Hence, serious consideration should be given to the testability, parsimony, provocativeness, and explanatory power for understanding the behavior of interest provided by these various conceptualizations.

Attitudes have historically been of interest in psychology, and the social sciences generally, because behavior is organized across time and situations such that a consistency is revealed toward psychological objects (i.e. categories and their elements) which cannot be explained in terms of the extant situational contingencies or in terms of other constructs, such as habits, social norms, or individual differences. The value of the abstraction, attitude, derives in large part from the reduction in the number of stimulus–response relationships that must be defined by adding an intervening ('psychological') variable (McGuire, 1985).

The attitude-as-posture hypothesis is insufficiently abstract to account adequately for the breadth of the behavioral organization of interest in contemporary attitude theory and research. Attitudes as a predisposition to respond—the second meaning to have emerged from the attitude-as-posture model—is a useful abstraction in that it places the behavioral organization within the organism, suggests that there is a stability in the guiding influence across time, and accommodates the view that the behavioral organization toward a psychological object involves behavior generally—not simply volitional or intentional behavior. The conceptualization of attitudes simply as a predisposition to respond is unsatisfactory, however, in that it begs the question; it provides a label for the behavioral organization while explaining nothing (consistency in responding exists because there is a predisposition to respond in that fashion). Thus, its strength is that it is descriptive; its weakness is that it is neither provocative nor predictive.

Attitudes as affect, where affect is a dimension of reportable emotion, has greater explanatory power and underscores the motivational aspects of the construct. Weaknesses in this conceptualization include: the underemphasis of the cognitive and behavioral contributions to, and consequences of, people's predisposition to respond in a particular manner toward a psychological object; discrepancies between people's cognitive evaluation of, and emotional response to, attitude objects; and differences in the stability, volatility, specificity, and simultaneity of people's emotions versus their predisposition to respond toward a psychological object (Cacioppo, Petty, Losch and Kim, 1986; Zanna and Rempel, 1984). Nevertheless, a determination of an individual's consistent affective responses toward prototypical objects or abstractions of a psychological object overcomes most of these concerns and, hence, has something to offer in studies of attitudes. Recent psychophysiological research suggests that, within limited assessment contexts, incipient facial EMG responses—responses so subtle that they are subject to little if any dissimulation—may also contribute to the assessment of a person's affective response. However, the equating of affective reactions and feeling states remains a limiting factor in the attitudes-as-affect model.

The concept of attitude as a tripartite of cognition, affect, and behavior has the value of underscoring the contributions and consequences of various domains of human experience to an individual's predisposition to respond toward a psychological object in a consistent manner, and psychophysiological research has revealed that factors from each domain of human experience influence somato-visceral activity. The major limitation of the tripartite conceptualization, however, is that it is cumbersome and provides no explanation for outcomes that could not be provided by simpler models (Cacioppo, Petty, and Geen, in press; Greenwald, in press).

The homeostasis model of attitudes is unique in offering an evolutionary account for the behavioral organization of interest, and in emphasizing the perspective that attitudes are *evaluative heuristics* for guiding organismic—environmental transactions. In agreement with previous conceptualizations, the central property of attitudes that reflects the behavioral organization of interest is the individual's stable and global positive/negative responses (evaluations) toward the psychological object. Contrary to previous conceptualizations of attitudes, the focus is on the forces (e.g. including negative-feedback mechanisms) underlying the development and maintenance of a global and stable evaluation and system of evaluations (ideologies); and on the freedom and independence for exploration and creative adaptation that results from the proper functioning of these forces.

Finally, an issue not yet addressed satisfactorily concerns the use of self-reports as the standard of validity in studies of attitude. Investigators have long recognized that verbal reports can introduce unintended and often unnoticed biases (e.g. Westie and DeFleur, 1959), and recent research suggests psychophysiological analyses can provide complementing information about the underlying attitude construct (e.g. Cacioppo and Petty, 1981). The potential limitations and biases introduced by relying on verbal reports as the standard of validity are illustrated strikingly in Gazzaniga and LeDoux's (1977) study of the young split-brain patient P.S. In one such investigation, an object-picture was presented simultaneously to each hemisphere. P.S. was then asked to choose from a series of object-pictures the ones which were the most closely related to the stimuli to which he had been exposed. Each hand was used to select from among several alternatives the object-picture closest to, or associated with, what P.S. believed he saw. Results revealed that P.S. was generally able to select the correct object-pictures. However, P.S.'s self-reports reflected confabulation guided largely by what had been presented to the left ('verbal') hemisphere, rather than a valid rendering of events and the consequent responses:

> For example, when a snow scene was presented to the right hemisphere and a chicken claw was presented to the left, P.S. quickly responded correctly by choosing a picture of a chicken from a series of four cards with his right hand, a picture of a shovel from a series of four cards with his left hand. The subject was then asked 'What did you see?' 'I saw a claw and I picked the chicken, and you have to clean out the chicken shed with a shovel.' (Gazzaniga, Steen, and Volpe, 1979, p. 350).

If attitudes have evolved as heuristics to free up limited processing resources and thereby foster creative adaptations to environmental challenges, then a well-established and stable attitude performing its function at maximum efficiency should attract little or no attention. That is, neither the attitude, nor the decision to act in a particular manner toward the attitude object should demand much in the way of the individual's limited cognitive resources. An individual's most readily reportable attitude toward a psychological object may be likely to reflect the individual's predispositions to analyze, articulate, and act *intentionally* in a positive or negative manner toward a stimulus, but underestimate the individual's *unintentional* (e.g. spontaneous, impulsive positive or negative responses toward the stimulus).

In sum, there are reasons to suspect the use of self-reports as the standard of validity in studies of attitude, but there is no definitive evidence regarding the theoretical consequences of equating attitudes with (reportable) feeling states or of restricting the domain to which the concept of attitudes applies to intentional behaviors (Fishbein, 1980). Providing empirical answers to these questions will require that alternative (e.g. psychophysiological) conceptualizations and measurement approaches be employed and contrasted with self-report assessments of felt attitudes. Although this endeavor should prove challenging, it may ultimately prove more edifying than surreptitiously narrowing the theoretical conceptualization and behavioral domain of interest to reflect readily available measures and previously confirmed outcomes.

REFERENCES

Abel, T. M. (1930) Attitudes and the galvanic skin reflex. *Journal of Experimental Psychology*, **13**, 47–60.

Allport, G. W. (1935) Attitudes. In C. Murchison (Ed.), *Handbook of Social Psychology*, Vol. 2. Worcester, MA: Clark University Press.

Aronson, E., Turner, J. A., and Carlsmith, J. M. (1963) Communicator credibility and communication discrepancy as determinants of opinion change. *Journal of Abnormal and Social Psychology*, **67**, 31–6.

Bain, A. (1868) *Mental Science: A Compendium of Psychology, and the History of Philosophy*. New York: Appleton-Century-Crofts.

Baron, R. A., and Byrne, D. (1987) *Social Psychology: Understanding Guman Interaction*, (5th edn. Boston, MA: Allyn and Bacon.

Beatty, J. (1982) Task-evoked pupillary responses, processing load, and the structure of processing resources. *Psychological Bulletin*, **91**, 276–92.

Beatty, J. (1986) The pupillary system. In M. G. H. Coles, E. Donchin, and S. W. Porges (Eds), *Psychophysiology: Systems, Processes, and Applications*. New York: Guilford Press.

Berger, S. M. (1962) Conditioning through vicarious instigation. *Psychological Review*, **69**, 450–66.

Bernard, C. (1878) *Lecons sur les phenomenes de la vie communs aux animaux et aux vegetaux*, Vol. 1. Paris: J. B. Bailiere.

Boyd, R. W., and DiMascio, A. (1954) Social behavior and autonomic physiology: a sociophysiologic study. *Journal of Nervous and Mental Disorders*, **120**, 207–12.

Breckler, S. J. (1984) Empirical validation of affect, behavior, and cognition as distinct components of attitude. *Journal of Personality and Social Psychology*, **47**, 1191–1205.

Bull, N. (1951) *The Attitude Theory of Emotion*. New York: Nervous and Mental Disease Monographs, No. 81.

Bush, L., and Cacioppo, J. T. (1985) The effects of voluntary control over facial expressions on facial EMG responses. *Psychophysiology*, **22**, 585–6 (Abstract).

Byrne, D. (1971) *The Attraction Paradigm*. New York: Academic Press.

Cacioppo, J. T. (1979) Effects of exogenous changes in heart rate on facilitation of thought and resistance to persuasion. *Journal of Personality and Social Psychology*, **37**, 489–98.

Cacioppo, J. T., Martzke, J., Petty, R., and Tassinary, L. (1988) Specific forms of facial EMG response index emotions during an interview: from Darwin to the continuous flow hypothesis of affect-laden information processing. *Journal of Personality and Social Psychology*, **54**, 592–604.

Cacioppo, J. T., and Petty, R. E. (1979a) Attitudes and cognitive response: an electrophysiological approach. *Journal of Personality and Social Psychology*, **37**, 2181–99.

Cacioppo, J. T., and Petty, R. E. (1979b) Effects of message repetition and position on cognitive response, recall, and persuasion. *Journal of Personality and Social Psychology,* **37**, 97–109.

Cacioppo, J. T., and Petty, R. E. (1979c) Lip and nonpreferred forearm EMG activity as a function of orienting task. *Journal of Biological Psychology,* **9**, 103–13.

Cacioppo, J. T., and Petty, R. E. (1981) Electromyograms as measures of extent affectivity of information processing. *American Psychologist,* **36**, 441–56.

Cacioppo, J. T., and Petty, R. E. (1982) A biosocial model of attitude change: signs, symptoms, and undetected physiological responses. In J. T. Cacioppo and R. E. Petty (Eds), *Perspectives in Cardiovascular Psychophysiology.* New York: Guilford Press.

Cacioppo, J. T., and Petty, R. E. (1983) *Social Psychophysiology: A Sourcebook.* New York: Guilford Press.

Cacioppo, J. T., and Petty, R. E. (1985) Physiological responses and advertising effects: is the cup half full or half empty? *Psychology and Marketing,* **2**, 115–26.

Cacioppo, J. T., and Petty, R. E. (1986) Social Processes. In: M. G. H. Coles, E. Donchin, and S. Porges (Eds), *Psychophysiology: Systems, Processes, and Applications,* pp. 646–79. New York: Guilford Press.

Cacioppo, J. T., Petty, R. E., and Geen, T. (in press) Attitude structure and function: from the tripartite to the homoestasis model of attitudes. In A. R. Pratkanis, S. J. Breckler, and A. G. Greenwald (Eds), *Attitude Structure and Function.* Hillsdale, NJ: Erlbaum.

Cacioppo, J. T., Petty, R. E., Kao, C. F., and Rodriguez, R. (1986) Central and peripheral routes to persuasion: an individual difference perspective. *Journal of Personality and Social Psychology,* **51**, 1032–43.

Cacioppo, J. T., Petty, R. E., and Losch, M. E. (in press) Psychophysiological approaches to attitudes: detecting opinions when people won't say, can't say, or don't even know. In T. C. Brock and S. Shavitt (Eds), *Psychology of Persuasion.* San Francisco: W. H. Freeman.

Cacioppo, J. T., Petty, R. E., Losch, M. E., and Kim, H. S. (1986) Electromyographic activity over facial muscle regions can differentiate the valence intensity of affective reactions. *Journal of Personality and Social Psychology,* **50**, 260–8.

Cacioppo, J. T., Petty, R. E., and Marshall-Goodell, B. (1984) Electromyographic specificity during simple physical and attitudinal tasks: location and topographical features of integrated EMG responses. *Biological Psychology,* **18**, 85–121.

Cacioppo, J. T., Petty, R. E., and Sidera, J. (1982) The effects of a salient self-schema on the evaluation of proattitudinal editorials: top-down versus bottom-up message processing. *Journal of Experimental Social Psychology,* **18**, 324–38.

Cacioppo, J. T., Petty, R. E., and Tassinary, L. (1989) Social psychophysiology: a new look. *Advances in Experimental Social Psychology,* **22**, 39–91.

Cacioppo, J. T., and Sandman, C. A. (1981) Psychophysiological functioning, cognitive responding, and attitudes. In: R. E. Petty, T. M. Ostrom, and T. C. Brock (Eds), *Cognitive Responses in Persuasion,* pp. 81–104. Hillsdale, NJ: Erlbaum.

Cacioppo, J. T., and Tassinary, L. G. (in press) Psychophysiology and psychophysiological inference. In: J. T. Cacioppo and L. G. Tassinary (Eds), *Principles of Psychophysiology: Physical, Social, and Inferential Elements.* New York: Cambridge University Press.

Cacioppo, J. T., Tassinary, L. G., Stonebraker, T. B., and Petty, R. E. (1987). Self-report and cardiovascular measures of arousal: Fractionation during residual arousal. *Biological Psychology,* **25**, 135–71.

Cannon, W. B. (1927) The James–Lange theory of emotions: a critical examination and an alternative theory. *American Journal of Psychology,* **36**, 106–24.

Coles, M. G. H., Donchin, E., and Porges, S. W. (1986) *Psychophysiology: Systems, Processes, and Applications.* New York: Guilford Press.

Coles, M. G. H., Gratton, G., Bashore, T. R., Ericksen, C. W., and Donchin, E. (1985) A psychophysiological investigation of the continuous flow model of human information processing. *Journal of Experimental Psychology: Human Perception and Performance*, **11**, 529–53.

Coles, M. G. H., Gratton, G., and Fabiani, M. (in press). Event-related potentials. In J. T. Cacioppo and L. G. Tassinary (Eds), *Principles of Psychophysiology: Physical, Social and Inferential Elements*. New York: Cambridge University Press.

Coles, M. G. H., Gratton, G., and Gehring, W. J. (1987) Theory in cognitive psychophysiology, *Journal of Psychophysiology*, **1**, 13–16.

Coombs, C. H., Dawes, R. M., and Tversky, A. (1970) *Mathematical Psychology: An Elementary Introduction*. Englewood Cliffs, NJ: Prentice Hall.

Cooper, J. B. (1959) Emotion and prejudice. *Science*, **130**, 314–18.

Darwin, C. (1965) *The Expression of the Emotions in Man and Animals*. Chicago: University of Chicago Press. (Originally published 1872.)

Davis, D. and Ostrom, T. (1987) Attitude measurement. In R. J. Corsini (Ed.), *Concise Encyclopedia of Psychology*, pp. 95–6. New York: John Wiley.

Dawes, R. M., and Smith, T. L. (1985) Attitude and opinion measurement. In G. Lindzey and E. Aronson (Eds), *Handbook of Social Psychology*, Vol. 1, *Theory and Method*, 3rd edn, pp. 509–66. New York: Random House.

Dempsey, E. W. (1951) Homeostasis. In S. S. Stevens (Ed.), *Handbook of Experimental Psychology*, pp. 209–36. New York: John Wiley.

Dewey, J., and Bentley, A. F. (1949) *Knowing and the Known*. Boston: Beacon Press.

Dimberg, U. (1982) Facial reactions to facial expressions. *Psychophysiology*, **19**, 643–47.

Dimberg, U. (1986) Facial reactions to fear-relevant and fear-irrelevant stimuli. *Biological Psychology*, **23**, 153–61.

Donchin, E. (1982) The relevance of dissociations and the irrelevance of dissociationism: a reply to Schwartz and Pritchard. *Psychophysiology*, **19**, 457–63.

Donchin, E., Karis, D., Bashore, T. R., Coles, M. G. H., and Gratton, G. (1986) Cognitive psychophysiology and human information processing. In M. G. H. Coles, E. Donchin, and S. W. Proges (Eds), *Psychophysiology: Systems, Processes, and Applications*, pp. 244–67. New York: Guilford Press.

Doob, L. W. (1947) The behavior of attitudes. *Psychological Review*, **54**, 135–56.

Eiser, J. R. (1986) *Social Psychology: Attitudes, Cognition, and Social Behavior*. Cambridge: Cambridge University Press.

Ekman, P., Friesen, W. V., and Ancoli, S. (1980) Facial signs of emotional experience. *Journal of Personality and Social Psychology*, **39**, 1125–34.

Englis, B. G., Vaughan, K. B., and Lanzetta, J. T. (1982) Conditioning of counter-empathic emotional responses. *Journal of Experimental Social Psychology*, **18**, 375–91.

Fazio, R. H. (in press). Attitude accessibility and behavior. In A. R. Pratkanis, S. J. Breckler, and A. G. Greenwald (Eds), *Attitude Structure and Function*. Hillsdale, NJ: Erlbaum.

Fishbein, M. (1980) A theory of reasoned action: some applications and implications. In H. Howe and M. Page (Eds), *Nebraska Symposium on Motivation*, Vol. 27. Lincoln: University of Nebraska Press.

Fishbein, M., and Ajzen, I. (1975) *Belief, Attitude, Intention, and Behavior: An Introduction to Theory and Research*. Reading, MA: Addison-Wesley.

Fleming, D. (1967) Attitude: a history of a concept. *Perspectives in American History*, **1**, 287–365.

Fodor, J. A. (1968) *Psychological Explanation: An Introduction to the Philosophy of Psychology*. New York: Random House.

Forsyth, D. R. (1987) *Social Psychology*. CA: Brooks/Cole.

Fridlund, A. J., and Izard, C. E. (1983) Electromyographic studies of facial expressions of emotions and patterns of emotion. In J. T. Cacioppo and R. E. Petty (Eds), *Social Psychophysiology: A Sourcebook*, pp. 243–86. New York: Guilford Press.

Garrity, L. I. (1977) Electromyography: a review of the current status of subvocal speech research. *Memory and Cognition*, **5**, 615–22.

Gazzaniga, M. S., and LeDoux, J. E. (1977) *The Integrated Mind*. New York: Plenum Press.

Gazzaniga, M. S., Steen, D., and Volpe, B. T. (1979) *Functional Neuroscience*. New York: Harper & Row.

Goldwater, B. C. (1972) Psychological significance of pupillary movements. *Psychological Bulletin*, **77**, 340–55.

Graham, F. K., and Clifton, R. K. (1966) Heart-rate change as a component of the orienting response. *Psychological Bulletin*, **65**, 305–20.

Graham, J. L. (1980) A new system for measuring nonverbal responses to marketing appeals. *1980 AMA Educator's Conference Proceedings*, **46**, 340–3.

Green, J. (1954) The use of an information test about the Nergo as an indirect technique for measuring attitudes, beliefs, and self-perceptions. Unpublished doctoral dissertation, Los Angeles: University of Southern California.

Greenwald, A. G. (1982) Is anyone in charge? Personanalysis versus the principle of personal unity. In J. Suls (Ed.), *Psychological Perspectives on the Self*, Vol. 1. Hillsdale, NJ: Erlbaum.

Greenwald, A. G. (in press) Defining attitude and attitude theory: 20 years later. In A. R. Pratkanis, S. J. Breckler, and A. G. Greenwald (Eds), *Attitude Structure and Function*. Hillsdale, NJ: Erlbaum.

Herrick, C. J. (1951) Introduction. In N. Bull, *The Attitude Theory of Emotion*, pp. ix–xiii. New York: Nervous and Mental Disease Monographs, No. 81.

Hess, E. H. (1965) Attitude and pupil size. *Scientific American*, **212**, 46–54.

Hovland, C. I., and Rosenberg, M. J. (1960) *Attitude Organization and Change*. New Haven: Yale University Press.

Jacobson, E. (1930a) Electrical measurements of neuromuscular states during mental activities. III. Visual imagination and recollection. *American Journal of Physiology*, **95**, 694–702.

Jacobson, E. (1930b) Electrical measurements of neuromuscular states during mental activities. IV. Evidence of contraction of specific muscles during imagination. *American Journal of Physiology*, **95**, 703–12.

Janisse, M. P., and Peavler, W. S. (1974) Pupillary research today: emotion in the eye. *Psychology Today*, **7**, 60–3.

Kahneman, D. (1973) *Attention and Effort*. Englewood Cliffs, NJ: Prentice-Hall.

Kahneman, D., and Beatty, J. (1966) Pupil diameter and load on memory. *Science*, **154**, 1583–5.

Kaplan, H. B., Burch, N. R., and Bloom, S. W. (1964) Psychophysiological covariation and sociometric relationships in small peer groups. In P. H. Leiderman and D. Shapiro (Eds), *Psychophysiological Approaches to Social Behavior*, pp. 92–109. Stanford: Stanford University Press.

Kothandapani, V. (1971) Validation of feeling, belief, and intention to act as three components of attitude and their contribution to prediction of contraceptive behavior. *Journal of Personality and Social Psychology*, **19**, 321–33.

Krech, D., and Crutchfield, R. S. (1948) *Theory and Problems of Social Psychology*. New York: McGraw-Hill.

Kunst-Wilson, W. R., and Zajonc, R. B. (1980) Affective discrimination of stimuli that cannot be recognized. *Science*, **207**, 557–8.

Kupfermann, I. (1985) Genetic determinants of behavior. In E. Kandel and J. Schwartz (Eds), *Principles of Neurological Science*, 2nd edn, pp. 795–804. NY: Elsevier.

Landis, C. (1930) Psychology and the psychogalvanic reflex. *Psychological Review*, **37**, 381–98.

Landis, C., and Hunt, W. A. (1939) *The Startle Pattern*. New York: Farrar.

Lang, P. J. (1971) The application of psychophysiological methods to the study of psychotherapy and behavior modification. In A. E. Bergin and S. L. Garfield (Eds), *Handbook of Psychotherapy and Behavior Change*. New York: John Wiley.

Lanzetta, J. T., and Orr, S. P. (1981) Stimulus properties of facial expressions and their influence on the classical conditioning of fear. *Motivation and Emotion*, **5**, 225–34.

Lemon, N. (1973) *Attitudes and Their Measurement*. New York: John Wiley.

Libby, W. L., Lacey, B. C., and Lacey, J. I. (1973) Pupillary and cardiac activity during visual attention. *Psychophysiology*, **10**, 270–94.

Likert, R. (1932) A technique for the measurement of attitudes. *Archives of Psychology*, **140**, 1–55.

Lingle, J. H., and Ostrom, T. M. (1981) Principles of memory and cognition in attitude formation. In R. E. Petty, T. M. Ostrom, and T. C. and Brock (Eds), *Cognitive Responses in Persuasion*. Hillsdale, NJ: Erlbaum.

Lord, C. G., Ross, L., and Lepper, M. R. (1979) Biased assimilation and attitude polarization: the effects of prior theories on subsequently considered evidence. *Journal of Personality and Social Psychology*, **37**, 2098–2109.

Love, R. E. (1972) Unobtrusive measurement of cognitive reactions to persuasive communications. Unpublished doctoral dissertation, Cleveland: Ohio State University.

Lynn, R. (1966) *Attention, Arousal, and the Orientation Reaction*. Oxford: Pergamon Press.

McDougall, W. (1961) *An Introduction to Social Psychology*. New York: Barnes & Noble. (Originally published 1908.)

McGuigan, F. J. (1970) Covert oral behavior during the silent performance of language tasks. *Psychological Bulletin*, **74**, 309–26.

McGuigan, F. J. (1978) *Cognitive Psychophysiology: Principles of Covert Behavior*. Englewood Cliffs, NJ: Prentice-Hall.

McGuire, W. J. (1969) The nature of attitudes and attitude change. In G. Lindzey and E. Aronson (Eds), *The Handbook of Social Psychology*, 2nd edn, Vol. 3. Reading, MA: Addison-Wesley.

McGuire, W. J. (1985) Attitudes and attitude change. In G. Lindzey and E. Aronson (Eds), *Handbook of Social Psychology*, 3rd edn, Vol. 2, pp. 233–346. New York: Random House.

McHugo, G. J., Lanzetta, J. T., and Bush, L. K. (1987) The effect of attitudes on emotional reactions to expressive displays of political leaders. Unpublished manuscript.

McHugo, G., Lanzatta, J. T., Sullivan, D. G., Masters, R. D., and Englis, B. (1985) Emotional reactions to a political leader's expressive displays. *Journal of Personality and Social Psychology*, **49**, 1513–29.

Metalis, S. A., and Hess, E. H. (1982) Pupillary response/semantic differential scale relationships. *Journal of Research in Personality*, **16**, 201–16.

Michener, H. A., DeLamater, J. D., and Schwartz, S. H. (1986) *Social Psychology*. Chicago, IL: Harcourt Brace Jovanovich.

Mueller, D. J. (1970) Physiological techniques of attitude measurement. In G. F. Summers (Ed.), *Attitude Measurement*, pp. 534–52. Chicago, IL: Rand McNally.

Mueller, D. J. (1986) *Measuring Social Attitudes: A Handbook for Researchers and Practitioners*. New York: Teachers College Press.

Ohman, A., and Dimberg, U. (1984) An evolutionary perspective on human social behavior. In W. Waid (Ed.), *Sociophysiology*, pp. 47–86. New York: Springer.

Osgood, C. E., Suci, G. J., and Tannenbaum, P. H. (1957) *The Measurement of Meaning*. Urbana, IL: University of Illinois Press.

Osgood, C. E., and Tannenbaum, P. H. (1955) The principle of congruity in the prediction of attitude change. *Psychological Review*, **62**, 42–55.

Oskamp, S. (1977) *Attitudes and Opinions*. Englewood Cliffs, NJ: Prentice-Hall.

Ostrom, T. M. (1969) The relationship between the affective, behavioral, and cognitive components of attitudes. *Journal of Experimental Social Psychology*, **5**, 12–30.

Papez, J. W. (1937) A proposed mechanism of emotion. *Archives of Neurology and Psychiatry*, **38**, 725–43.

Penrod, S. (1983) *Social Psychology*. Englewood Clifts, NJ: Prentice-Hall.

Petty, R. E., and Cacioppo, J. T. (1986) *Communication and Persuasion: Central and Peripheral to Persuasion*. NY: Springer.

Platt, J. R. (1964) Strong inference. *Science*, **146**, 347–53.

Posner, M. (1978) *Chronometric Explorations of Mind*. Hillsdale, NJ: Erlbaum.

Pylyshyn, Z. (1980) Computation and cognition: issues in the foundation of cognitive science. *The Behavioral and Brain Sciences*, **3**, 111–69.

Rajecki, D. W. (1982) *Attitudes: Themes and Advances*. Sunderland, MA: Sinauer Associates.

Rankin, R. E., and Campbell, D. T. (1955) Galvanic skin response to Negro and white experimenters. *Journal of Abnormal and Social Psychology*, **51**, 30–3.

Reber, A. S. (1985) *The Penguin Dictionary of Psychology*. New York: Viking Penguin.

Rosenberg, M. J. (1960) Cognitive reorganization in response to the hypnotic reversal of attitudinal affect. *Journal of Personality*, **28**, 39–63.

Rosenberg, M. J., and Hovland, C. I. (1960) Cognitive, affective, and behavioral components of attitude. In M. J. Rosenberg, C. I. Hovland, W. J. McGuire, R. P. Abelson, and J. W. Brehm (Eds), *Attitude Organization and Change: An Analysis of Consistency Among Attitude Components*, pp. 1–14. New Haven, CT.

Schwartz, G. E. (1975) Biofeedback, self-regulation, and the patterning of physiological processes. *American Scientist*, **63**, 314–24.

Seligman, M. (1970) On the generality of the laws of learning. *Psychological Review*, **77**, 406–18.

Shapiro, D., and Crider, A. (1969) Psychophysiological approaches to social psychology. In G. Lindzey and E. Aronson (Eds), *The Handbook of Social Psychology*, 2nd edn, Vol. 3. Reading, MA: Addison-Wesley.

Shapiro, D., and Schwartz, G. E. (1970) Psychophysiological contributions to social psychology. *Annual Review of Psychology*, **21**, 87–112.

Shaver, K. G. (1987) *Principles of Social Psychology*, 3rd edn. Hillsdale, NJ: Erlbaum.

Shaw, W. A. (1940) The relation of muscle action potentials to imaginal weight lifting. *Archives of Psychology*, **35**, 50.

Sherrington, C. S. (1923) *The Integrative Action of the Nervous System*. New Haven: Yale University Press. (Originally published 1906.)

Smart, J. J. C. (1959) Sensations and brain processes. *The Philosophical Review*, **68**, 141–56.

Smith, C. E. (1936) A study of the autonomic excitation resulting from the interaction of individual opinion and group opinion. *Journal of Abnormal and Social Psychology*, **30**, 138–64.

Smith, M. B. (1947) The personal setting of public opinions: A study of attitudes toward Russia. *Public Opinion Quarterly*, **11**, 507–23.

Spencer, H. (1895) *First Principles*. New York: Appleton. (Preface dated 1862).

Sternbach, R. A. (1966) *Principles of Psychophysiology*. New York: Academic Press.

Stevens, S. S. (1951) Mathematics, measurement, and psychophysics. In S. S. Stevens (Ed.), *Handbook of Experimental Psychology*, pp. 1–49. New York: John Wiley.

Summers, G. F. (1970) Overview. In G. F. Summers (Ed.), *Attitude Measurement*. Chicago: Rand McNally.

Thurstone, L. L. (1928) Attitudes can be measured. *American Journal of Sociology*, **33**, 529–44.

Thurstone, L. L. (1931) The measurement of social attitudes. *Journal of Abnormal and Social Psychology*, **26**, 249–69.

Tranel, D., Fowles, D. C., and Damasio, A. R. (1985) Electrodermal discrimination of familiar and unfamiliar faces: a methodology. *Psychophysiology*, **22**, 403–8.

Triandis, H. C. (1971) *Attitude and Attitude Change*. New York: John Wiley.

Tursky, B., and Jamner, L. D. (1983) Evaluation of social and political beliefs: A psychophysiological approach. In J. T. Cacioppo and R. E. Petty (Eds), *Social Psychophysiology: A Sourcebook*. New York: Guilford Press.

Washburn, M. F. (1916) *Movement and Mental Imagery: Outlines of a Motor Theory of the Complexer Mental Processes*. Boston: Houghton Mifflin.

Webb, E. J., Campbell, D. T., Schwartz, R. D., and Sechrest, L. (1966) *Unobtrusive Measures: Nonreactive Research in the Social Sciences*. Chicago: Rand McNally.

Wells, G. L., and Petty, R. E. (1980) The effects of overt headmovements on persuasion: compatibility and incompatibility of responses. *Basic and Applied Social Psychology*, **1**, 219–30.

Westie, F. R., and DeFleur, M. I. (1959) Autonomic responses and their relationship to race attitudes. *Journal of Abnormal and Social Psychology*, **58**, 340–7.

Wilson, W. R. (1979) Feeling more than we can know: exposure effects without learning. *Journal of Personality and Social Psychology*, **37**, 811–21.

Zajonc, R. B. (1980) Feeling and thinking: Preferences need no inferences. *American Psychologist*, **35**, 151–75.

Zajonc, R. B., and Markus, H. (1982) Affective and cognitive factors in preferences. *Journal of Consumer Research*, **9**, 123–31.

Zanna, M. P., and Rempel, J. K. (1984) A new look at an old concept. In D. Bar-Tal and A. Kruglanski (Eds), *The Social Psychology of Knowledge*. New York: Cambridge University Press.

Zimbardo, P. G., Ebbesen, E. B., and Maslach, C. (1977) *Influencing Attitudes and Changing Behavior*, 2nd edn. Reading, MA: Addison-Wesley.

Chapter 13

Moods and Social Judgements

Margaret S. Clark and Gail M. Williamson
Carnegie Mellon University

ABSTRACT

This chapter reviews literature suggesting that moods often bias judgements about ourselves, others, and objects in our environment. Biases typically, but not always, take the form of judgements becoming more congruent with the valence of one's mood. Such biases occur more consistently for positive than for negative moods. Six possible processes that may underlie these biases are discussed. It is concluded that several distinct processes or combinations of processes have undoubtedly contributed to the reported incidents of bias. More research is needed to answer the related questions of what boundary conditions for the mood effects exist, how common the various proposed mediating processes are, and under what circumstances each is most likely to operate.

This chapter deals with the effects of moods on social judgements. First, we review some of the many studies that have made it clear that everyday, transient moods, both positive and negative, influence a great variety of social judgements. In doing so, we have limited ourselves to studies in which mood has been experimentally manipulated, and in which subjects have been selected from non-clinical populations. Our reasons for this limitation are twofold. First, our interests lie in the effects of normal, everyday variations in mood. While these effects may have

Preparation of this chapter was supported by National Institute of Mental Health Grant 1R01 MH40390-02 to the first author. Correspondence regarding this paper should be addressed to Margaret S. Clark, Department of Psychology, Carnegie Mellon University, Pittsburgh, PA 15213.

Handbook of Social Psychophysiology, Edited by H. Wagner and A. Manstead,
© 1989 John Wiley & Sons Ltd

much in common with the effects of clinical depression, it has not been clearly established that this is the case. Second, it is easier to infer causality from the experimental studies we review than from the correlational work on depression.

After reviewing studies demonstrating the effects of mood on judgements, we turn to a discussion of mechanisms that might underlie these effects. This discussion will reveal that while the literature clearly establishes that moods do influence social judgements, and that while we have some evidence for a variety of processes that may underlie these effects, we still have a long way to go. We have yet to identify what processes most typically underlie the observed effects or under what conditions different processes are most likely to apply. Finally, we summarize progress in this area and discuss some prospects for future work.

EFFECTS OF POSITIVE AND NEGATIVE MOODS ON JUDGEMENTS

A search through the literature provides substantial evidence for the influence of affective states on judgements about the self, others, inanimate objects, and social situations. Generally, positive or happy moods are found to be associated with increased positivity of judgements. Sometimes negative, depressed, or sad moods are found to be associated with increased negativity of judgements. However, in the case of negative moods, many studies have not shown this effect.

Research investigating the effects of moods on judgements can be divided into three categories: (1) studies including a positive mood condition and a suitable control (neutral) condition, (2) studies including a negative mood condition and a suitable control (neutral) condition, and (3) studies including both positive and negative mood conditions but no suitable control (neutral) condition. (Of course, sometimes a single study falls into both the first and the second categories by virtue of including positive, neutral, and negative conditions.)

The first two types of studies demonstrate the effects that positive and negative states have on our social judgements. Unfortunately, the lack of a control group in the third type makes the interpretation of the results from studies of this type difficult. They can only reveal that moods have *some* impact on judgements. Specifically, if positive moods result in more positive judgements than negative moods, it may be because positive moods make judgements more positive and negative ones make them worse. However, three other interpretations are also plausible: (1) positive moods make judgements more positive and negative moods have no effect, (2) negative moods make judgements more negative and positive moods have no effect, or (3) both positive and negative moods make judgements more positive (perhaps through different processes), but the positive mood manipulation has a greater impact. This latter explanation could come about if, for instance, positive moods automatically increase accessibility of positive material in memory (making judgements more positive), negative moods increase motivation to intentionally think 'positively' (also making judgements more positive), and either the former process is more powerful than the latter process or the researchers have done a better job manipulating positive moods than manipulating negative moods.* Thus, while studies without neutral control groups will be briefly reviewed, they must be considered less informative than those in our first two categories.[†] We now review studies falling into each of our three categories.

STUDIES INCLUDING MANIPULATIONS OF POSITIVE MOOD AND A SUITABLE CONTROL CONDITION

Across a wide variety of mood manipulations and types of judgements, positive moods have been shown to cause judgements to become more congruent with the tone of the mood state.

Judgements about the self

Several studies have demonstrated that when we feel happy, we like ourselves and our lives more. For instance, Schwarz and Clore (1983) found that elation, produced by describing a recent happy event, was associated with reports of higher satisfaction with one's current life situation, relative to reports from subjects who have not been asked to describe a recent happy event, and Forgas and Moylan (1988) found that watching a happy movie increased subjects' optimism regarding their future personal fortunes, relative to subjects who had yet to watch the movie. Similarly, positive mood manipulations appear to cause us to feel stronger and better equipped to control our own and even others' lives. In one study, subjects who had successfully worked out a puzzle (and presumably felt good as a result) perceived another's success on an unrelated joint task to be more dependent on their efforts than did subjects who had not been asked to solve a puzzle (Berkowitz and Connor, 1966). In another study, being asked to remember

---

*A fourth, less plausible, logical possibility also exists. That is, such a pattern of results could come about if both positive and negative moods caused judgements to become less positive (again perhaps through different processes), but the negative mood manipulation has greater impact. However, we think this last possibility is unlikely since it is difficult to conceive of a process through which it might come about.

[†]Of course, these arguments also imply that we should carefully evaluate the nature of control conditions to determine the likelihood that subjects in those conditions truly felt neutral. Unfortunately, since many of the studies reviewed did not include manipulation checks on subjects' moods, this is a difficult judgement to make. In this review we assume that the neutral mood conditions described in connection with such studies *are* truly neutral while simultaneously acknowledging that there is some danger in doing so. We would note that in the absence of a mood manipulation, people report being in slightly positive moods (Bousfield, 1950; Clark, Ouellette, Powell, and Milberg, 1987). This may only be due to subjects wishing to present themselves in a socially desirable manner. However, if taken as a serious indication of 'average mood,' it suggests that observed differences between neutral and positive mood conditions can safely be attributed to increases in the positivity of moods, while some caution should be exercised in interpreting differences, or the lack thereof, between neutral and negative conditions.

a previous romantic success, relative to being asked to recall a neutral situation, produced improvements in reported self-efficacy, not only in the romantic domain, but also in interpersonal, athletic, and other domains (Kavanagh and Bower, 1985). In still other research, happy moods, caused by reading positive self-statements, have been shown to increase college students' feelings of internal rather than external locus of control [as measured on Rotter's (1966) scale] relative to feelings expressed by subjects who had not read any statements (Procidano and Heller, 1983). All these effects are consistent with the idea that positive mood increases the positivity of judgements.

However, not *every* relevant study has found induction of positive mood to lead to more favorable judgements about oneself. For instance, in a study by Masters and Furman (1976), preschool children were asked to think either happy or neutral thoughts. These manipulations had no effect on their beliefs about locus of control or on their anticipations of successful task performance. While the results of this study for the locus of control variable may seem to contradict the results of Procidano and Heller (1983) just described, the age differences in the two subject populations may account for the discrepancy. That is, it may be that seeing an internal locus of control and a high likelihood of succeeding on a future task as positive personal attributes comes with socialization and maturation, such that only older children and adults view these attributes as clearly positive (rather than neutral). If so, the results of both studies could still be viewed as consistent with the idea that being in a positive mood leads people to make more positive judgements about themselves.

Judgements about others, inanimate objects, and social situations

If being happy causes us to feel better about ourselves, one might also expect similar effects on how we evaluate the rest of the world. In fact, this is what the research to date reveals.

When we are in a good mood, we tend to see other people in a more favorable light. For example, subjects in elated moods, induced by the Velten method, rated others as being more altruistic, sociable, honest, creative, tolerant, and environmentally conscious than did subjects who had not read the Velten statements (Fiedler, Pampe and Scherf, 1986). Clark and Waddell (1983) found that subjects who had just succeeded on a task had more positive first associations when imagining a blind date or helping another than did subjects who had received no feedback about their performance. Schiffenbauer (1974) reported that listening to a comedy tape resulted in less frequent judgements that others' facial expressions were indicative of negative emotional states than did listening to an affectively neutral tape.* Also, Forgas and Moylan (1988) found that people who had just

---

*However, it should be noted that a manipulation check of the mood induction procedure indicated there were no statistically significant differences in reported affect between the subjects who had heard the comedy tape and those in the control group.

watched a happy film rated their political leaders more favorably than did subjects who had yet to watch the film (although they did not recommend more lenient sentences or see criminals as any less responsible for crimes such as drunken driving or heroin trafficking).

Finally, White, Fishbein, and Rutstein (1981, Study 2) reported still other results relevant to the effects of positive mood on liking for others. They found that after watching a comedy videotape, male subjects rated an attractive female as more romantically appealing than did subjects who had seen an affectively neutral videotape. However, in this same study, positive mood subjects also rated an *un*attractive female as significantly *less* appealing than did those in the neutral mood condition. White *et al.* explain this by arguing that the target must be at least a plausible source of one's positive feelings for induction of a positive emotional state to increase the positivity of our judgements of another person. If the target is not, the arousal that accompanies the affective state may be attributed to other feelings.* In general then, most of the evidence indicates that we tend to like other people more when we are happy, but there is also evidence indicating that positive mood manipulations may not always produce these effects if the target is not an appropriate source of one's positive feelings [i.e. the Forgas and Moylan (1988) results for drunken drivers and heroin traffickers and the White *et al.* (1981) results for unattractive opposite sex others].

If we generally like ourselves and other people more when we feel good, do we also feel more positively about objects in our environment? Research suggests that we do. Shoppers given free gifts rated their automobiles and television sets as performing better and requiring less service than shoppers who received no gift (Isen, Shalker, Clark, and Karp, 1978). Inducing a positive mood through either positive false meter feedback or finding a dime has been shown to lead subjects to judge the content of ambiguous slides as more pleasant than judgements made by people whose moods were not manipulated (Forest, Clark, Mills, and Isen, 1979; Isen and Shalker, 1982). Reading news reports of pleasant events produced a decline in estimates of how frequently risks and undesirable events occur (Johnson and Tversky, 1983), and seeing a happy movie, relative to seeing no movie, resulted in more positive judgements about political issues and the likelihood of future events (Forgas and Moylan, 1988). In still another study, preschool children instructed to think happy thoughts subsequently expressed more positive expectations for outcomes unrelated to their own behavior than did children instructed to think affectively neutral thoughts (Masters and Furman, 1976). Finally, subjects who had just exercised and were then told that they performed particularly well on a memory task subsequent reported more positive thoughts about their own university, as indicated by combined ratings of students, faculty, and facilities at that university, than did subjects who had exercised but had

---

*White *et al.* (1981) actually interpreted all of their results in terms of the effects of *arousal* rather than of moods on judgements of others. This interpretation is discussed in more detail later in our chapter.

received no such feedback (Clark, Milberg, and Ross, 1983, Study 3).*

To summarize, many studies have been reported that are consistent with the idea that positive mood increases the positivity of judgements. There are certainly alternative explanations for the results of some of these studies. For instance, successful subjects in the Berkowitz and Connor (1966) study may have perceived themselves as more generally competent than others and so felt their efforts would subsequently have more impact on others' success. Or, to give a more general example, as recent research by Rholes, Riskind, and Lane (1987) suggests, some of the observed effects may be due to a cognitive set created by some of the positive mood manipulations (possibly operating independent of mood) priming material from memory. Nonetheless, in our view, the literature to date provides enough converging evidence to conclude that positive moods often do tend to lead to mood congruent judgements. It also appears, however, that there are some limitations on this tendency. That is, the effect seems not to be obtained when the target has few positive attributes, such as when the target is physically unattractive (White *et al.*, 1981) or a criminal (Forgas and Moylan, 1988). There are also suggestions that the effect of positive moods on judgements may be weaker when the accompanying levels of autonomic arousal are particularly low (Clark *et al.*, 1983, Study 3).

STUDIES INCLUDING MANIPULATIONS OF NEGATIVE MOOD AND A SUITABLE CONTROL CONDITION

Next, we review research indicating that negative moods influence social judgements. In this case the findings are more mixed.

Judgements about the self

A review of the literature indicates that the effects of negative moods on judgements of the self are less straightforward than those of positive moods. Sometimes, negative moods have been shown to cause judgements of oneself to deteriorate. Sometimes, however, negative mood manipulations have produced no effects at all.

Two of the studies providing evidence that negative moods do cause judgements to become more negative are ones in which failure was shown to make subjects feel less powerful and less in control. In one, subjects susceptible to hypnosis first recalled a romantic failure and subsequently rated their self-efficacy as being lower than did subjects who had imagined an affectively neutral situation (Kavanagh

---

*Analogous effects of positive feedback on judgements were not obtained with subjects who had not exercised just prior to receipt of the feedback.

and Bower, 1985). In another, subjects who were unable to solve a puzzle felt that another's outcomes on a joint task were less dependent on how hard they (i.e. the subject making the judgement) worked than did members of a control group who were not given a puzzle (Berkowitz and Conner, 1966).

However, a study by Natale and Hantas (1982) did not as clearly show such biases. In that study, a depressed mood induced by hypnosis in female subjects led to decreases in reports of positive self-referent information and pleasant life experiences, but contrary to expectations, depressed subjects did not report significantly more unpleasant life experiences. In addition, Forgas and Moylan (1988) did not find significant differences in ratings of current life satisfaction between people who had just viewed either a sad or an aggressive movie and subjects who had yet to view these films.

Judgements about others, inanimate objects, and social situations

What about the effects of negative moods on our judgements of other people and the objects in our environment? Again the evidence is mixed. Some studies indicate that being in a bad mood prejudices judgements toward the pessimistic side, but other studies do not show this effect. Moreover, at least one study (White *et al.*, 1981, Study 2) provides evidence that induction of negative emotion can *increase* the positivity of judgements of another.

Considering the evidence for the effects of negative moods on judgements of others first, it should be noted that, in some studies, negative moods have led to more negative judgements. In one, the effect of ambient temperature on attraction (Griffitt, 1970) was examined. Subjects worked for 45 minutes in either an uncomfortably hot and humid room or for the same amount of time in a room with normal conditions. Subjects in the hot room rated their moods as being more negative and evaluated a stranger as being less attractive than did those in the more comfortable room. In other studies, students who listened to a tape designed to foster feelings of disgust more frequently judged slides of others as conveying expressions of disgust and fear than did students who heard an affectively neutral tape (Schiffenbauer, 1974).

Not only is there evidence that we do not like others as much when we are in a negative mood, but there is also evidence that we are less interested in interacting with them and that we feel others care less for us than would otherwise be the case. Specifically, subjects who failed to do well on an anagram task scored lower on a measure of social interest (defined as concern for others) than did those not asked to work on the task (Crandall, 1978, Study 2). Moreover, prior to a midterm exam, subjects reported less elation, more anxiety and, perhaps as a result, less social interest, than when tested during a regular class period (Crandall, 1978, Study 3). Finally, negative moods, induced by the Velten procedure, have been shown to result in lowered perceptions of the social support available from one's friends, when compared with the perceptions of subjects in a neutral affect group (Procidano and Heller, 1983, Study 2).*

However, negative moods do not always cause judgements of others to become more negative and, indeed, may sometimes cause them to become more positive. For example, although White *et al.* (1981, Study 2) found that male subjects who watched a videotape vividly depicting murder and mutilation (which had been previously shown to induce both negative mood and high arousal) judged an unattractive female as less appealing than did those in the neutral mood, low arousal condition, that was not the only effect they observed. They also found that subjects exposed to the same film judged an attractive female as *more* romantically appealing than did subjects in a neutral mood condition.†

Turning to judgements about one's own world as opposed to specific others in it, we can say that just as positive moods appear to make judgements about one's world rosy, there is *some* evidence that being in a bad mood makes one's world appear bleak and dreary. Subjects told that they have performed poorly on a test (Isen and Shalker, 1982) as well as those who have received negative feedback from a meter (Forest *et al.*, 1979) have been found to judge affectively ambiguous slides as less pleasant than do control subjects who have received either no feedback on the test or neutral feedback from the meter. Also, reading a brief newspaper account of a tragic event was sufficient to cause subjects to estimate that certain other risks and undesirable events were more likely to occur, when compared with estimates made by those reading a news account of neutral events (Johnson and Tversky, 1983). Finally, subjects failing at a puzzle task reported liking an experiment significantly less than did subjects who had not worked on a puzzle (Berkowitz and Connor, 1966).

However, once again, some studies have failed to show that negative moods cause judgements to become more negative. In the Forgas and Moylan (1988) study, moviegoers who had seen sad or aggressive movies—which had been previously shown to induce negative moods—did not make significantly different judgements about political matters, estimates of the likelihood of certain future events, nor did they assign different levels of responsibility, guilt, and punishment to drunken drivers or heroin traffickers than did those who had yet to see the movie. Also, in a study by Masters and Furman (1976), children who thought sad thoughts did not expect less serendipitous events than did children who thought neutral thoughts.

---

*The Procidano and Heller (1983) results must be interpreted with caution, however, since pretesting revealed that subjects who had been randomly assigned to read the negative mood statements were *initially* more depressed and anxious than others. Thus, it seems at least possible that they also had lower perceived social support from friends prior to the manipulation, and that the Velten procedure per se did not *cause* the observed decreases in perceived support.

†Again, the explanation given by White *et al.* (1981), Study 2 for these results was that the negative mood manipulation produced high arousal which subjects misattributed to feelings of attraction for the attractive target or to feelings of disgust for the unattractive target.

To summarize our second category of studies, a number have yielded results consistent with the idea that negative moods cause judgements of ourselves and our environment to become more negative. As was the case with the biasing effects of positive moods, some of the results we have reviewed can be explained in other ways. For example, in the Berkowitz and Connor (1966) study, failing on a task might have reduced general feelings of competence, and that (rather than negative mood *per se*) may have led subjects to feel that the effort they personally put into a joint task with another would have little impact on the other's outcome. And, again, some of the observed effects may be due to a cognitive set (possibly operating independently of mood) that some of the negative mood manipulations may have created (cf. Rholes *et al.*, 1987). However, our best guess is that negative moods really do sometimes bias judgements so that they become congruent with the negative state.

There are also a number of studies which have failed to obtain results consistent with the idea that negative moods bias judgements to be more negative. In the case of positive moods, we were able to pinpoint factors related to the nature of the targets that might explain why certain studies failed to show that positive moods cause judgements to become more positive. For negative moods, we are not able to point to such factors. All we can say is that the evidence to date suggests to us that negative biasing of judgements is a more fragile phenomenon than is positive biasing of judgements, but we do not know why. It is clear that additional work toward establishing the boundary conditions for negative mood effects is needed.

STUDIES INCLUDING MANIPULATIONS OF BOTH POSITIVE AND NEGATIVE MOODS WITH NO SUITABLE CONTROL CONDITION

A third set of studies is made up of those in which both positive and negative moods have been manipulated, but in which no neutral mood condition has been included. They are included in our review because they provide additional support for the idea that moods influence social judgements. However, as noted earlier, we cannot be sure whether the observed effects are due to positive moods, negative moods, or both.

Judgements about the self

To examine how changes in mood influence how we see ourselves and our social interactions, the effects of negative feelings produced by failure have often been contrasted with the effects of positive feelings produced by success. Researchers have found that, compared to successful subjects, those who were unsuccessful judged their chances of succeeding on future tasks as less likely (Feather, 1966) and reported feeling less egoistic (Weary, 1980).* Somewhat more indirect evidence comes from a study by Cialdini and his associates (Cialdini, Borden, Thorne, Walker, Freeman and Sloan, 1976, Study 2), in which subjects receiving positive feedback expressed less desire to associate themselves with a winning football team than did subjects given negative feedback. According to the authors, these results indicated a need to bolster lowered self-esteem among those receiving negative feedback but not among those receiving positive feedback.

Other means of inducing positive and negative moods have produced similar results. Using a musical mood induction procedure, Teasdale and Spencer (1984) found that elated subjects, when compared with experimentally depressed subjects, estimated that they had performed better on a previous task. Croyle and Uretsky (1987) found that after viewing negatively valenced film clips, students judged themselves to be less healthy than did those who had seen positive film clips. Forgas, Bower, and Krantz (1984) found that subjects asked to remember happy experiences from their past reported that they had been more socially adept in a recent interaction with another than did those asked to recall depressing events. In still another study, reading a story with a positive, rather than negative, ending caused subjects to describe themselves as more ambitious and less lonely (Diener and Iran–Nejad, 1986).

Taken together, these studies appear to demonstrate that negative moods lead to less favorable judgements about the self than do positive moods. However, as might be expected based on studies reviewed in the first two sections, results have not always been so clear cut. For example, in one study using the Velten technique to induce moods, negative mood subjects recalled more self-relevant items than did positive mood subjects, *regardless* of whether the items were positively or negatively oriented (Brown and Taylor, 1986). In addition, in this same study, while happy subjects remembered fewer negative traits than sad subjects, sad subjects remembered positive material as often as they did negative material.

Judgements about others and social situations

Literature falling into our third category also contains a number of studies in which the effects of positive and negative (but not neutral) moods on evaluations of others have been examined.

Four studies in which subjects were given either positive or negative feedback demonstrated effects of moods on feelings about others. Receiving positive, rather than negative, feedback resulted in higher ratings of a stimulus other's likeability and desirability as a work partner (Griffitt and Guay, 1969, Study 1), more favorable judgements of both a confederate and an experimenter (Griffitt

---

*Additionally, the failure group subjects, when in a highly public situation, demonstrated more egotism and fewer self-attributions for their failure than did subjects who had failed in a lower publicity condition.

and Guay, 1969, Study 2), and more positive evaluations of others' personality traits (Forgas and Bower, 1987). In addition, Salovey and Rodin (1984) found that students who had received negative self-relevant feedback were more likely to disparage the character of a similar, but successful, other than were those who had received positive feedback.

Other mood manipulation methods provide still more evidence for the idea that moods influence our perceptions of other people. After viewing a happy movie, subjects have been shown to evaluate an unknown other as more attractive (Gouaux, 1971) and to report slightly more liking for both a stranger and a dating partner (Friedman, Rubin, Jocobson, and Clore, 1978) than did subjects who had seen a depressing film. Recalling pleasant, as compared to unpleasant, past experiences under hypnosis resulted in more favorable perceptions of another's social behaviors (Forgas, Bower and Krantz, 1984).* Imagining scenarios in which their offers of help were accepted resulted in subjects' evaluating the intended recipient as more sociable than if they imagined their offer was rejected (Rosen, Mickler, and Spiers, 1986). Finally, Bower (1981) reports a study in which happy subjects wrote happy descriptions and angry subjects wrote angry descriptions when asked to give personality sketches of their family and friends.

In sum, the results of studies including manipulations of positive and negative moods (with no neutral mood control condition) generally support the idea that positive moods are associated with more positive judgements than are negative moods and thus, the more general conclusion that moods are important determinants of social perception. However, here again, it ought to be noted that there are other explanations for at least some of the results we have reviewed. For instance, while in the Rosen *et al.* (1986) study, imagining that one's offer of help was accepted/rejected may have caused moods to improve/deteriorate which in turn might have influenced judgements of the sociability of the other, it is also plausible (indeed, perhaps more plausible!) that this imagined acceptance/rejection directly influenced perceptions of the other's sociability. Moreover, at least one study including positive and negative mood conditions has *not* found patterns of judgements analogous to those reviewed above. Specifically, in a study by Forgas, Burnham, and Trimboli (1987), after viewing a happy/cheerful or a sad/depressing videotape, 8–10 year-old boys and girls gave their impressions of stimulus characters. In this study the children endorsed both extremely positive *and* extremely negative descriptions of target individuals when in a good mood. Conversely, children in a sad mood reported that both good and bad traits were less typical of the target person. These results, like some evidence

---

*This effect appeared to be due to the happy group recalling more positive than negative experiences while the negative group did not recall more negative than positive behavior. Further, in this study, happy people evaluated positive, informal interactions with others more favorably than difficult, formal episodes, but there were no differences in the ratings of these types of interactions by unhappy subjects.

reported earlier in this paper by Masters and Furman (1976), suggest caution in generalizing the effects of mood on judgements observed among adults to children.

POSSIBLE MECHANISMS UNDERLYING THE OBSERVED EFFECTS

Authors who have investigated the effects of moods on social judgements have each tended to suggest just one possible mediating process for the effects they have observed. In light of this, we would like to emphasize two things. First, contrary to the impression readers might take away from reading articles about any particular author's favorite interpretation of these findings, there are several possible mechanisms through which moods may influence judgements. Second, the results of most of the studies we have reviewed may be reasonably explained by more than one of these processes. To illustrate this, we now turn to a discussion of possible mechanisms that may underlie effects of moods on judgements.

MOOD-CUEING MOOD-CONGRUENT INFORMATION FROM MEMORY

One explanation for the often observed congruence between moods and social judgements has been that moods may increase the accessibility of mood-congruent thoughts stored in memory about the object to be judged (e.g. Isen, 1975; Isen *et al.*, 1978). The idea is that people have many thoughts about themselves, other people, and objects stored in their memories—some positive, some negative, some neutral. When making a judgement, they ordinarily do not attempt to recall every possible fact about the target. Rather, they consider only those thoughts that come most readily to mind. Mood may prime mood-congruent thoughts so that they come to mind more readily. Consequently, mood-congruent thoughts should be more likely than usual to be among the first recalled and, in turn, more likely to influence judgements, thus making those judgements more mood-congruent. For example, when making a judgement about whether one likes a male acquaintance, one may ordinarily recall some positive (he is intelligent), some negative (he is sloppy), and some neutral (his name is John) facts and then make a judgement based on those facts, say, a neutral judgement. If, however, moods make mood-congruent information come to mind more readily than usual, moods can bias the composition of the group of facts upon which the judgement is being made to be more mood-congruent. Thus, a person in a positive mood may not just recall that the target is intelligent, sloppy, and named John but also that he is sometimes very generous and nearly always cheerful. As a result, John may be rated more positively than usual.

How does mood-cueing mood-congruent material come about? Some have suggested that it results from state dependent mood effects (e.g. Bower, 1981).

Specifically, material learned when in a particular mood may be best recalled when in a similar state. This idea suggests, for example, that if we meet a new person at a party while we are having a good time and feeling happy, we will be able to recall information about that person best when we are once again feeling a similar state of happiness. This should occur *even* if that person was not responsible for our original happiness. However, often material we store when happy does have (or acquires) a positive valence itself (e.g. the person at the party was friendly; indeed, that may be why we were feeling good). Similarly, much material we store when distressed may have (or acquire) a negative valence itself. To the extent to which the evaluative valence of material we store *is* congruent with the mood at the time it is stored, mood state dependency can account for current moods increasing accessibility of mood-congruent material from memory which, in turn, may lead to mood-congruent judgements as suggested above.

A second, closely related, idea is that mood may selectively cue material that itself has a similarly toned affective meaning for the subject, *regardless* of the initial reason it acquired that meaning. It may have a similar meaning for the subject because it was originally stored at a time when the subject was experiencing a similar state and the subject attributed that affective state to the object (or person) about which (or whom) the information was stored. On the other hand, it may have acquired its affective meaning at some other point. For example, we may meet a person when we are not feeling any particular emotion and later find out something very positive about that person which makes us feel good about him or her. At a still later point in time, we may best be able to recall all sorts of information about him or her when we experience a positive mood state.

As already noted, the mood-cueing hypothesis can easily account for why moods lead to mood-congruent judgements. It can also account for why positive moods do not bias judgements of unambiguously negative targets [e.g. the physically unattractive women in White *et al.*'s (1981) study and the drunken drivers and heroin traffickers in the Forgas and Moylan (1988) study]. If the information about a target in memory is all negative, there simply is no positive material to be primed; if the information is predominantly negative, the few positive aspects that might be primed may not be sufficient to moderate the negative material that comes to mind easily. For similar reasons, this explanation would also suggest that negative moods should not be capable of biasing judgements of targets about which only (or predominantly) positive material is stored—a fact that *may* account for some of the failure to find negative mood effects on judgements. However, this is not clear from the literature currently available.

Is mood-cueing mood-congruent material *the* correct interpretation? What is the evidence for the existence of such processes? Some studies have found evidence for mood state dependence (e.g. Bartlett, Burleson, and Santrock, 1982; Bower, Monteiro, and Gilligar, 1978, Study 3), but there also have been reports of failures to find mood state dependent effects (e.g. Bower and Mayer, 1985; Isen *et al.* 1978, Study 2). Moreover, it has been pointed out that, while there is considerable evidence that *positive* moods facilitate recall of material from memory with a similar intrinsic meaning, there is far less evidence that negative moods produce the same effect (see Isen, 1985). This observation fits well with the asymmetry of the evidence for the effects of positive and negative moods on judgements, but does not fit well with those studies which have found effects of negative moods on judgements. In addition, although this type of process can account for some of the exceptions to mood-congruency effects, it cannot account for all the exceptions. For example, it cannot explain easily why negative moods often fail to have an impact on judgements about which most people should have stored relevant positive, negative, and neutral information [e.g. about one's current life satisfaction, (Forgas and Moylan, 1988)].

While mood-cueing mood-congruent information is a possible explanation for the results of some of the studies reviewed above, those in which moods have been shown to influence memory have most typically been conducted separately from those in which moods have been shown to bias judgements. Studies in which both types of dependent variables (i.e. recall of material from memory and judgements) are collected, and in which the relationship between the two can be examined, are needed. Should memory biases and biases in judgement be closely associated, important evidence would be provided for the process by which moods influence judgements.

To summarize, there is some evidence that moods cue mood-related material from memory. However, the evidence that this is *the* mediating process through which moods influence judgements is not particularly strong. Although considerable emphasis was placed on this potential mechanism in some early articles (e.g. Bower, 1981; Clark and Isen, 1982), it would be inappropriate to adopt this as the only explanation.

MOOD-CUEING GENERAL RESPONSE STYLES

An alternative possibility for how moods may influence judgements is that moods may cue broad, general styles of behaving. For instance, positive moods may make people generally more sociable, agreeable, and/or cheerful. Negative moods, in contrast, may make people generally less sociable, more disagreeable, and/or more gloomy (cf. Cunningham, 1988). Such general response styles could result in overall response tedencies to evaluate people and objects in a positive or negative manner without assuming that moods cue individual pieces of target-related, mood-congruent information from memory or mood state dependent memory effects.

However, is *this* the right explanation? It does explain moods leading to mood-congruent judgements as easily as does the mood-cueing idea. On the other hand, at least at first glance, there appears to be some evidence against this idea. After all, as Isen (1984) points out, positive moods do not make *all* judgements more positive, and negative moods do not make *all* judgements more negative. Nonetheless, it still seems possible that generalized mood-determined response biases or tendencies exist and *do* account for some of the effects of moods on judgements reported in the literature. To allow for this possibility, despite evidence that not all judgements are biased, it is simply necessary to assume that such biasing processes follow *or* are partially held in check after the fact by other processes. For instance, it may be that when making a judgement about a person or object, people first access prior evaluations about that person or object. If a single positive or negative evaluation is readily available, then it determines the judgement given. Through such a process most people may readily evaluate poison ivy or a drunken driver negatively and daffodils or kindness positively, regardless of their current mood. In contrast, when no single, unambiguous evaluation is readily available, mood-determined response biases may determine the nature of the judgement. Alternatively, the fact that moods do not bias all judgements might be explained by assuming that mood-elicited response biases produce an initial *urge* to respond in a particular way, but that this urge is followed by checking the reasonableness of one's response before the response actually takes place. If the biased response is judged to be reasonable, the response will be made; otherwise, it will not.

The idea that general response biases may underlie the impact of mood on judgements has not received much attention. It deserves more.

MOODS AS PIECES OF INFORMATION

Still another explanation for the effects of moods on judgements has been proposed by Schwarz and Clore (1983). It involves the assumption that one's mood can serve as a piece of information that may be taken into account when making a judgement. More specifically, a mood may be attributed (not necessarily correctly) as having been caused by objects and/or people present, or thought about, at the time the mood is experienced. Thus, when asked to make a judgement, people in a good mood may conclude that they must like the targets, and people in a bad mood may conclude that they must dislike the targets, given the way they are currently feeling. For instance, imagine one feels good when asked to make a judgement about one's brother who happens to be visiting at the time. One may misattribute one's current good mood as having been caused by the brother and thus, give him a favorable evaluation.

Consider how this explanation applies to one of the studies reviewed earlier (Forest *et al.*, 1979). In that study, subjects induced to feel good through false meter feedback subsequently judged neutral slides as more pleasant, and subjects induced to feel bad judged the slides as less pleasant, than did subjects who had received neutral feedback. All subjects may well have ceased focusing on the meter feedback (but continued to experience the mood) when given the slide judging task. Then, they may have used the way they felt as they looked at the slides as a cue to how they felt about the slides.

Clear evidence for the use of moods as pieces of information comes from two studies reported by Schwarz and Clore (1983). In the first study, positive or negative moods were induced by having subjects write out descriptions of a recent happy or sad life event. In the second study, subjects were interviewed on a sunny or a rainy day. In both studies, as predicted, subjects in the positive mood conditions reported being happier and more satisfied with their lives than did subjects in the negative mood conditions. Furthermore, in the first study, in which a neutral mood control condition was included, the mean happiness and satisfaction ratings from control subjects fell between the analogous ratings from subjects in the positive and negative mood conditions. Most importantly for the present point, the influence of negative mood was eliminated in the first study among subjects who had been led to believe that a soundproof room in which they were seated may have caused their negative mood. An analogous effect was obtained in the second study when subjects were reminded about the rain—also a reasonable cause of negative moods—by an experimenter's comments. That is, being reminded of the rain eliminated the effect of that rain on judgements. The removal of the negative effects by pointing to something negative in the environment cannot be explained by mood state dependency or by assuming the existence of a pervasive response bias caused by mood. However, the entire pattern of results can be explained by assuming that the subjects used their negative moods as pieces of information which were attributed to happiness and life satisfaction when no other cause was salient, but were explained as due to other causes when those other causes were more salient.

Interestingly, however, Schwarz and Clore obtained no evidence that their subjects misattributed their moods to the room when the experimenter told them it might make them feel good (in Study 1) or to a sunny day when the experimenter explicitly commented on the nice weather (in Study 2). The authors, therefore, suggested that people may be more motivated to explain negative than positive moods, perhaps because negative moods are seen as more unusual than positive moods (cf. Sommers, 1984). If positive moods had been more extreme and therefore unusual, the authors suggested, they too might have prompted a search for an explanation.

Like the mood-cueing mood-related material from memory and the response bias explanations, this explanation often can account for moods leading to mood-congruent judgements. Also like those explanations, it too can explain why positive moods do not bias judgements about clearly negative targets and why negative moods might not bias judgements about clearly positive targets. After all, it makes no sense to see an obviously mood-incongruent target as the cause of one's mood. Finally, like the response bias explanation, this one also does not depend upon there being clear evidence for mood state dependency.

But, is this process a common one? What are its boundaries? How much data does it actually account for? Available evidence does not allow us to answer these questions. We can, however, make some predictions on the basis of this proposed process which might be easily tested in future research. For instance, according to this process one would expect that the less salient the initial cause of a mood, the greater its impact on judgements ought to be. Also, moods obviously present prior to thinking about, or being in the presence of, a target ought to have less effect on judgements than moods whose onset appears to subjects to have occurred at the same time, or shortly after, a target appeared.

MISATTRIBUTION OF AROUSAL

Since many inductions of both positive and negative moods are likely simultaneously to lead to heightened autonomic system arousal [see Clark(1982) for a review of relevant evidence], still another route through which many moods may influence judgements is possible. Specifically, several researchers (Berscheid and Walster, 1974; Cantor, Bryant and Zillmann, 1974; Dutton and Aron, 1974; White *et al.*, 1981) have proposed that the arousal accompanying either a positive or a negative mood induction may be misattributed to a target in the environment, causing judgements of that target to become more extreme in the direction in which they already tended.

This type of explanation can explain *some* mood congruency effects. Specifically, it can account for why positive moods might make judgements about targets which were *already* perceived as positive more positive, and why negative moods might make judgements about targets which were *already* perceived as negative more negative. For example, it can explain some of the results obtained in the Clark and Waddell (1983) study. In that study, first associations when imagining helping someone else by picking up papers were positive, and they became significantly more positive if subjects had been induced to feel good by experiencing success. However, there are also many results that this idea cannot easily explain. For example, it cannot easily account for why judgements known to be neutral, or even negative, in the absence of a mood manipulation, became more positive in the presence of positive moods [e.g. Clark and Waddell (1983), in the case of first associations to an imagined blind date, Forest *et al.* (1979)]. Also, it cannot account for Johnson and Tversky's (1983) finding that a manipulation of positive mood produced a decline in estimates of how frequently undesirable events were likely to occur.

To be fair, advocates of this particular approach have not set it forth as a process that can explain the effects of moods, in general, on judgements. Moreover, there is some good evidence for such processes. Specifically, White *et al.* (1981) found that arousal induced through exercise, listening to a negative tape of a grisly mob killing (known to elicit arousal), *or* listening to a comedy tape (also known to elicit arousal) all increased attraction to a physically attractive, opposite sex confederate and all decreased attraction to a physically unattractive, opposite sex confederate. Further, Dutton and Aron (1974) found evidence that fear was associated with increased liking for an attractive, opposite sex confederate.* That negative moods caused judgements of an attractive other to *improve* in the White *et al.* and Dutton and Aron studies, and that positive moods caused judgements of an unattractive other to *deteriorate* in the White *et al.* study can easily be explained by this process, whereas they are *not* easily explained by any of the other processes we have proposed. These findings are not consistent with mood-cueing, response bias, or moods-as-pieces-of-information explanations.

MOODS AND MEMORY CAPACITY

Next, consider a fifth possibility for how moods might influence judgements. This one is capable of accounting for some of the effects of positive moods, but not for the effects of negative moods. We have included it here because, when *combined* with one of the processes already discussed, it may help to explain why the observed effects of positive moods appear to be more consistent and robust than the observed effects of negative moods.

This fifth possibility is based on the implications of combining three assumptions: (1) moods take up capacity in memory, thereby leaving less capacity for other tasks, such as retrieval of material from memory, (2) positively toned material comes to mind more readily than negative material, and (3) when people are asked to make a judgement, they ordinarily make a somewhat effortful search of memory to retrieve facts relevant to the judgement. Keeping these three processes in mind, consider what should happen to people in neutral, positive, and negative moods when they are asked to make a judgement. Those in a neutral mood may first think of positive material, but continuing with their search of memory are also likely to think of some negative material as well. The negative material should moderate their judgements. Those in positive or negative moods, however, since their information processing capacity is more restricted, may put less effort into the search. Consequently, they should be more likely to rely exclusively, or almost exclusively, on the more readily accessible, positive material than are people in neutral moods. The result should be more positive judgements.

Of course, while this explanation handles positive moods leading to more positive judgements, it cannot explain why negative moods lead to more negative judgements. Indeed, it would tend to suggest that negative moods, assuming that they too take up information processing capacity, should *also* lead to more positive judgements! Nonetheless, it seems worthwhile to include it here. If it is assumed that more than one of the processes we have discussed contribute to the influence of mood on judgements, this explanation may be *combined* with one or more of the other processes discussed previously to explain why positive mood seems to have stronger and more consistent effects on judgements than does negative mood.

---

*Kenrick and Cialdini (1977) and Kenrick, Cialdini, and Linder (1979) have provided an alternative explanation of Dutton and Aron's (1974) study in terms of negative reinforcement, but the alternative explanation cannot account for the White *et al.* (1981) results.

How plausible is this explanation? It is hard to judge, but we can at least say that there is some evidence for the three assumptions that underlie it. First, while, to our knowledge, the idea that positive moods, in particular, decrease capacity for processing information has not been straightforwardly tested, Ellis and his colleagues have provided some clear evidence that depressed moods take up attentional capacity and can, therefore, interfere with encoding and retrieval (see Ellis and Ashbrook, 1988; Ellis, Thomas, McFarland, and Lane, 1985; Ellis, Thomas, and Rodriguez, 1984). Second, a large number of studies have supported the idea that positive material comes to mind more readily than negative material [see Matlin and Stang (1978) for an extensive review of such studies, or Erber and Clark (1987) for a recent study also demonstrating this bias]. Finally, the idea that people are likely to base judgements on material that comes to mind most easily has received considerable support as well (e.g. Carroll, 1978; Tversky and Kahneman, 1974). If moods do influence judgements through the process described here, one would expect that the more difficult a judgement is to make (in terms of the cognitive capacity required), the greater the likelihood that moods will influence that judgement. Thus, like some of the explanations presented earlier, this one can also explain why positive moods have no effects on judgements of objects that are very clearly negative. These are undoubtably easy judgements to make, requiring little search of memory.

CONTROLLED, STRAGETIC PROCESSES

A sixth and final possibility for how moods may influence judgements can easily explain why positive moods may lead to mood-congruent judgements, and why negative moods may often fail to influence judgements, but it cannot easily account for why negative moods sometimes cause judgements to become more negative. Nonetheless, as with the fourth process discussed, the idea that this process operates in conjunction with other processes may account for the overall pattern of results observed in the literature.

This explanation assumes that people often make quite intentional efforts to maintain their positive mood states [see Clark and Isen (1982) for a discussion of controlled strategies]. Specifically, it may be that people in positive moods are especially likely to make positive judgements because they intentionally wish to focus on the positive aspects of themselves, others, and their environment, in order to maintain their positive state. Thus, a person in a good mood, when asked to evaluate his or her family may intentionally focus on retrieving positive (rather than neutral or negative) information about that family. Or, he or she may simply intentionally give a positive evaluation, without even searching memory for relevant information, in order to maintain the mood. Further, it is conceivable that, over time, such strategies may no longer be effortful but may instead become automatic. In either case, the end result may well be judgements that are congruent with one's mood state.

What about negative moods? Since people presumably do not ordinarily wish to maintain negative moods, this type of process suggests that people in negative moods may sometimes actively try *not* to make negative judgements so that their moods will not be prolonged. Perhaps, this accounts for why effects of negative moods are often *not* observed in the literature [e.g. Forgas and Moylan's (1988) observation that negative moods did not cause judgements of life satisfaction to deteriorate (relative to a neutral condition), but that positive moods caused such judgements to become more positive]. Indeed, one might predict, on the basis of this process, that negative moods might actually cause one to make more positive judgements, but available evidence does not suggest this.

It should also be noted that one need not view the fact that negative moods sometimes cause judgements to become more negative as evidence against this potential process. Such negative biasing could come about through some of the other processes suggested in this chapter and, may sometimes be counteracted by the types of intentional, effortful strategies suggested here *but* sometimes not. In particular, we would expect such effortful strategies to be less likely to be used if a person is tired, depressed, or under stress, than at other times (cf. Clark and Isen, 1982; Hasher and Zacks, 1979).

Finally, we would note that there ought to be some—presumably rare— occasions when, due to social constraints, one would not expect controlled strategies elicited by positive moods to lead to positive judgements and when one might expect controlled strategies elicited by negative moods to lead to controlled negative judgements. For instance, a person who has just received very positive feedback on a task might be asked to evaluate him- or herself and, in the interest of modesty, might intentionally evaluate him- or herself neutrally. Or, a person who is furious at another person may make all sorts of negative judgements about that other in order to retaliate against that person or, perhaps, so that he or she will not be the only one who feels bad. Although the general idea that people make efforts to control their moods has received empirical attention and support (e.g. Cialdini, Darby, and Vincent, 1973; Cialdini, Schaller, Houlihan, Arps, Fultz, and Beaman, 1987), the ideas that the effects of moods on judgements might be mediated by intentional efforts to maintain positive moods, alleviate negative moods, or accomplish other social purposes have not been tested directly.

CONCLUDING COMMENTS

The literature to date on the effects of moods on judgements leaves little room to doubt that moods very often *do* influence judgements. However, these effects are not always consistent and, although several plausible processes through which the effects might be mediated can be identified, it is not at all clear which processes or combination of processes are responsible for which effects.

At this point, there is little need for further studies demonstrating that moods can influence social judgements. Instead, it would seem potentially more fruitful to devote effort to more clearly delineating the boundary conditions for the mood effects that have been observed (especially for the mood-congruency effect) and to ascertaining the plausibility of various mediating processes. These two goals should be complementary. Identifying boundary conditions will provide important hints about the underlying processes, and developing theoretical ideas about possible underlying processes will suggest new boundary conditions. With regard to identifying the underlying mechanisms, it is our feeling that no single process is responsible for the observed effects. Rather, it seems likely that the observed pattern of results can best be explained by considering and investigating the possibility that several processes operate in conjunction.

Finally, as social psychologists who are ultimately concerned about patterns of interaction between two or more people, we would like to see the implications of this work for social interaction spelled out. For instance, positive moods appear to favorably color our impressions of ourselves, others, and the environment, but how does that influence our ongoing behavior? We do know that moods can influence certain behaviors. For instance, we know that positive moods can increase helping (Salovey and Rosenhan, 1989), self-disclosure (Cunningham, 1988) and willingness to comply with requests (Milberg and Clark, 1988) while negative moods can decrease helping [e.g. Moore, Underwood, and Rosenhan (1973) but see also Salovey and Rosenhan (1989)], and are associated with decreased compliance with another's request (Milberg and Clark, 1988). However, are these effects *due* to the effects of mood on our judgements about ourselves, others, and objects in our environment? We do not yet know. Answering questions such as this one will be important in the future. Doing so will help to integrate the research we have reviewed in this chapter with research on the effects of mood on social behavior such as that reviewed by Salovey and Rosenhan, in the following chapter of the present volume.

REFERENCES

Bartlett, J. C., Burleson, G., and Santrock, J. W. (1982) Emotional mood and memory in young children. *Journal of Experimental Child Psychology*, **34**, 59–76.

Berkowitz, L., and Connor, W. H. (1966) Success, failure, and social responsibility. *Journal of Personality and Social Psychology*, **4**, 664–9.

Berscheid, E., and Walster, E. (1974) A little bit about love. In T. Huston (Ed.), *Foundations of Interpersonal Attraction*. New York: Academic Press.

Bousfield, W. A. (1950) The relationship between mood and the production of affectively tones associates. *The Journal of General Psychology*, **42**, 67–85.

Bower, G. (1981) Mood and memory. *American Psychologist*, **36**, 129–48.

Bower, G. H. , and Mayer, J. D. (1985) Failure to replicate mood-dependent retrieval. *Bulletin of the Psychonomic Society*, **23**, 39–42.

Bower, G. H., Monteiro, K. P., and Gilligan, S. G. (1978) Emotional mood as a context for learning and recall. *Journal of Verbal Learning and Verbal Behavior*, **17**, 573–85.

Brown, J. D., and Taylor, S. E. (1986) Affect and the processing of personal information:

evidence for mood-activated self-schemata. *Journal of Experimental Social Psychology*, **22**, 436–52.

Cantor, J. R., Bryant, J., and Zillmann, D. (1974) The enhancement of humor appreciation by transferred excitation. *Journal of Personality and Social Psychology*, **30**, 812–21.

Carroll, J. S. (1978) The effect of imagining an event on expectations for the event: an interpretation in terms of the availability heuristic. *Journal of Experimental Social Psychology*, **14**, 88–96.

Cialdini, R. B., Borden, R. J., Thorne, A., Walker, M. R., Freeman, S., and Sloan, L. R. (1976) Basking in reflected glory: three (football) field studies, Study 2. *Journal of Personality and Social Psychology*, **34**, 366–75.

Cialdini, R. B., Darby, R. L., and Vincent, J. E. (1973) Transgression and altruism: a case for hedonism. *Journal of Experimental Social Psychology*, **9**, 502–16.

Cialdini, R. B., Schaller, M., Houlihan, D., Arps, K., Fultz, J., and Beaman, A. L. (1987) Empathy based helping: is it selflessly or selfishly motivated? *Journal of Personality and Social Psychology*, **52**, 749–58.

Clark, M. S. (1982) A role for arousal in the link between feeling states, judgments, and behavior. In M. S. Clark and S. T. Fiske (Eds), *Affect and Cognition: The Seventeenth Annual Carnegie Symposium on Cognition*, pp. 263–89. Hillsdale, NJ: Erlbaum.

Clark, M. S., and Isen, A. M. (1982) Toward understanding the relationship between feeling states and social behavior. In A. Hastorf and A. M. Isen (Eds) *Cognitive Social Psychology*, pp. 73–108. New York: Elsevier North-Holland.

Clark, M. S., Milberg, S., and Ross, J. (1983) Arousal cues arousal-related material from memory. *Journal of Verbal Learning and Verbal Behavior*, **22**, 633–49.

Clark, M. S., Ouellette, R., Powell, M., and Milberg, S. (1987) Recipient's mood, relationship type, and helping. *Journal of Personality and Social Psychology*, **53**, 94–108.

Clark, M. S., and Waddell, B. A. (1983) Effects of moods on thoughts about helping, attraction and information acquisition. *Social Psychology Quarterly*, **46**, 31–5.

Crandall, J. E. (1978) Effects of threat and failure on concern for others. *Journal of Research in Personality*, **12**, 350–60.

Coyle, R. T., and Uretsky, M. B. (1987) Effects of mood on the self-appraisal of health status. *Health Psychology*, **6**, 239–53.

Cunningham, M. (1988) Does happiness mean friendliness?: induced mood and hetero-sexual self-disclosure. *Personality and Social Psychology Bulletin*, **2**, 283–97.

Diener, E., and Iran-Nejad, A. (1986) The relationship in experience between various types of affect. *Journal of Personality and Social Psychology*, **50**, 1031–8.

Dutton, D., and Aron, A. (1974) Some evidence for heightened sexual attraction under conditions of high anxiety. *Journal of Personality and Social Psychology*, **30**, 510–17.

Ellis, H. C., and Ashbrook, P. W. (1988). Resource allocation model of the effects of depressed mood states on memory. In K. Fiedler and J. Forgas (Eds), *Affect, Cognition and Social Behavior*, pp. 25–43. Toronto: Hogrefe.

Ellis, H. C., Thomas, R. L., McFarland, A. D., and Lane, J. W. (1985) Emotional mood states and retrieval in episodic memory. *Journal of Experimental Psychology*, **11**, 363–70.

Ellis, H. C., Thomas, R. L., and Rodriguez, I. A. (1984) Emotional mood states and memory: elaborative encoding, semantic processing, and cognitive effort. *Journal of Experimental Psychology: Learning, Memory, and Cognition*, **10**, 470–82.

Erber, R., and Clark, M. S. (1987) The effects of arousal and mood on recall of one's own emotional experiences. Unpublished manuscript, Chestertown, MD: Washington College.

Feather, N. T. (1966) Effects of prior success or failure on expectations of success and subsequent performance. *Journal of Personality and Social Psychology*, **3**, 287–98.

Fiedler, K., Pampe, H., and Scherf, U. (1986) Mood and memory for tightly organized social information. *European Journal of Social Psychology*, **16**, 149–64.

Forest, D., Clark, M. S., Mills, J., and Isen, A. M. (1979) Helping as a function of feeling state and nature of the helping behavior. *Motivation and Emotion*, **3**, 161–9.

Forgas, J. P., Bower, G. H. (1987) Mood effects on person perception judgments. Unpublished manuscript.

Forgas, J. P., Bower, G. H., and Krantz, S. E. (1984) The influence of mood on perceptions of social interactions. *Journal of Experimental Social Psychology*, **20**, 497–513.

Forgas, J. P., Burnham, D. K., and Trimboli, C. (1987) Mood effects on memory and social judgments in children. Unpublished manuscript.

Forgas, J. P., and Moylan, S. (1988) After the movies: transient mood and social judgments. *Personality and Social Psychology Bulletin*, **4**, 478–89.

Friedman, H. S., Rubin, Z., Jacobson, J., and Clore, G. L. (1978) Induced affect and attraction toward dating partners and opposite-sex strangers. *Representative Research in Social Psychology*, **9**, 57–63.

Gouaux, C. (1971) Induced affective states and interpersonal attraction. *Journal of Personality and Social Psychology*, **20**, 37–43.

Griffitt, W., and Guay, P. (1969) 'Object' evaluation and conditioned affect. *Journal of Experimental Research in Personality*, **4**, 1–8.

Griffitt, W. (1970) Environmental effects on interpersonal affective behavior: ambient effective temperature and attraction. *Journal of Personality and Social Psychology*, **15**, 240–4.

Hasher, L., and Zacks, R. T. (1979) Automatic and effortful processes in memory. *Journal of Experimental Psychology: General*, **108**, 356–88.

Isen, A. M. (1975) Positive affect, accessibility of cognitions, and helping. Paper presented at a symposium, 'Directions in theory on helping behavior,' J. Piliavin, Chair, at the annual meeting of the Eastern Psychological Association, April 1975.

Isen, A. M. (1984) Toward understanding the role of affect in cognition. In R. Wyer and T. Srull (Eds) *Handbook of Social Cognition*, pp. 179–236. Hillsdale, NJ: Erlbaum.

Isen, A. M. (1985) Asymmetry of happiness and sadness in effects on memory in normal college students: comment on Hasher, Rose, Zacks, Sanft, and Doren. *Journal of Experimental Psychology: General*, **11**, 388–91.

Isen, A. M., and Shalker, T. E. (1982) The effect of feeling state on evaluation of positive, neutral, and negative stimuli: when you 'Accentuate the Positive,' do you 'Eliminate the Negative'?, *Social Psychology Quarterly*, **45**, 58–63.

Isen, A. M., Shalker, T. E., Clark, M., and Karp, L. (1978) Affect, accessibility of material in memory, and behavior: a cognitive loop? *Journal of Personality and Social Psychology*, **36**, 1–12.

Johnson, E. J., and Tversky, A. (1983) Affect, generalization, and the perception of risk. *Journal of Personality and Social Psychology*, **45**, 20–31.

Kavanagh, D. J., and Bower, G. H. (1985) Mood and self-efficacy: impact of joy and sadness on perceived capabilities. *Cognitive Therapy and Research*, **9**, 507–25.

Kenrick, D. T., and Cialdini, R. B., (1977) Romantic attraction: misattribution versus reinforcement explanations. *Journal of Personality and Social Psychology*, **35**, 381–91.

Kenrick, D. T., Cialdini, R. B., and Linder, D. E. (1979) Misattribution under fear-producing circumstances: four failures to replicate. *Personality and Social Psychology Bulletin*, **5**, 329–34.

Masters, J. C., and Furman, W. (1976) Effects of affective states on noncontingent outcome expactancies and beliefs in internal or external control. *Developmental Psychology*, **12**, 481–2.

Matlin, M., and Stang, D. (1978) *The Pollyanna Principle: Selectivity in Language, Memory, and Thought.* Cambridge, MA: Schenkman.

Milberg, S., and Clark, M. S. (1988) Moods and compliance. *British Journal of Social Psychology*, **27**, 79–90.

Moore, B. S., Underwood, B., and Rosenhan, D. L. (1973) Affect and altruism. *Developmental Psychology*, **8**, 99–194.

Natale, M., and Hantas, M. (1982) Effect of temporary mood states on selective memory about the self. *Journal of Personality and Social Psychology*, **42**, 927–34.

Procidano, M. E., and Heller, K. (1983) Measures of perceived social support from friends and from family: three validation studies. *American Journal of Community Psychology*, **11**, 1–24.

Rholes, W. S., Riskind, J. H., and Lane, J. W. (1987) Emotion states and memory biases: effects of cognitive priming and mood. *Journal of Personality and Social Psychology*, **52**, 91–9.

Rosen, S., Mickler, S., and Spiers, C. (1986) The spurned philanthropist. *Humboldt Journal of Social Relations*, **13**, 145–58.

Rotter, J. B. (1966) Generalized expectancies for internal versus external control of reinforcement. *Psychological Monographs*, **80**, (1, Whole No. 609).

Salovey, P., and Rodin, J. (1984) Some antecedents and consequences of social-comparison jealousy. *Journal of Personality and Social Psychology*, **47**, 780–92.

Salovey, P., and Rosenhan, D. L. (1989) Mood states and prosocial behavior. In: H. L. Wagner and A. S. R. Manstead (Eds), *Handbook of Social Psychophysiology*, pp. 369–89. Chichester: Wiley.

Schiffenbauer, A. (1974) Effect of observer's emotional state on judgements of the emotional state of others. *Journal of Personality and Social Psychology*, **30**, 31–5.

Schwartz, N., and Clore, G. L. (1983) Mood, misattribution, and judgments of well-being: informativ and directive functions of affective states. *Journal of Personality and Social Psychology*, **45**, 513–23.

Sommers, S. (1984) Reported emotions and conventions of emotionality among college students. *Journal of Personality and Social Psychology*, **46**, 207–15.

Teasdale, J. D., and Spencer, P. (1984) Induced mood and estimates of past success. *British Journal of Clinical Psychology*, **23**, 149–50.

Tversky, A., and Kahneman, D. (1974) Judgments under uncertainty: heuristics and biases. *Science*, **185**, 1124–31.

Weary, G. (1980) Examination of affect and egotism as mediators of bias in causal attributions. *Journal of Personality and Social Psychology*, **38**, 348–57.

White, G. L., Fishbein, S., and Rutstein, J. (1981) Passionate love and misattribution of arousal. *Journal of Personality and Social Psychology*, **41**, 56–62.

Chapter 14

Mood States and Prosocial Behavior

Peter Salovey and David L. Rosenhan
Yale University   *Stanford University*

ABSTRACT

The present chapter examines the impact of positive and negative moods on helping. Joy generally facilitates prosocial behavior, but the impact of negative moods such as guilt, shame, and sorrow is much more complex. These affect–action sequences may be made more understandable by examining the mood- and self-relevant cognitions that come to mind following the experience of affect in a context in which helping is a behavioral option.

Emotional reactions, even transient mood states, profoundly affect interpersonal behavior. Imagine yourself empathizing with a friend who describes (a) the joy he experienced upon learning of an unexpected promotion at work, and (b) how, on his way home at the end of that day, he stopped to help a disabled motorist change a flat tire. Does it occur to you that the altruistic act, (b), might be related to, if not motivated by, your friend's joyful reaction to his good fortune, (a)? Similarly,

Preparation of this chapter was supported in part by NIH Biomedical Research Support Grant SO7 RR07015, and by the Kenneth and Harle Montgomery Fund.

imagine a colleague whose paper, upon which she labored long and hard, was rejected (perhaps after an overly long wait) by the journal to which it was submitted. Minutes after receiving the news, she is harshly and insensitively critical of a colleague. Does it not seem reasonable to you that her regrettable behavior was provoked in part by her reaction to the bad news?

These affect–behavior sequences raise a significant question, which is: Is there anything that 'goes through one's head' once an affective reaction is excited but prior to initiating pro- or antisocial behavior? And if so, what might that be? Your joyful friend who received the big promotion might find that the thoughts that entered his mind when he encountered the disabled motorist included beliefs about being a generous person, about sharing resources with needy others, about being capable of actually helping someone change a flat tire. Similarly, in the sorrowful state induced by the fact that her effort was rejected by the journal, what comes to your colleague's mind might be memories of life's other failures, beliefs about personal flaws, and thoughts about having been cheated of her resources and entitlement.

That the behavior which ensues after an affective experience might be cognitively mediated seems plausible, perhaps even obvious, to some. However, when we reviewed the literature on affect and altruistic behavior at the beginning of this decade (Rosenhan, Karylowski, Salovey, and Hargis, 1981), we could only speculate about these processes, even though there were scores of mood-helping studies already in the literature. Indeed, in a paper that was highly critical of the entire mood-helping literature, Wispe (1980) reflected on this state of affairs, noting that 'after more than a decade of research... no strong rationale has emerged to explain why, or under what conditions, a happy person is supposed to help...this hypothesis, like its opposite [concerning negative moods]...is probably oversimplified...[and] untenable' (p. 9).

The last several years, however, have produced a variety of studies directly testing proposed cognitive explanations of the impact of moods on prosocial behavior. Hence, it is the purpose of this chapter, after briefly reviewing the historic mood-helping literature, to explore some of the cognitive mediators of affect–helping relationships. In particular, we focus on the self and especially thoughts about the self as important mediating variables.

AFFECT AND ALTRUISM

POSITIVE MOODS

Joyful moods have been linked to a variety of interpersonal and cognitive events. Happy individuals are more likely to initiate conversations with other people (Batson, Coke, Chard, Smith, and Taliaferro, 1979), and they express greater liking for individuals whom they have met for the first time (Gouaux, 1971; Griffitt, 1970; Veitch and Griffitt, 1976). People experiencing pleasant mood states are more likely to take risks, so long as these risks are not too great and do not endanger their pleasant mood state (Forest, Clark, Mills, and Isen, 1979; Isen, Means, Patrick, and Nowicki, 1982; Isen and Patrick, 1983; Isen and Simmonds, 1978). And they also appear to be more creative (Isen, Daubman, and Nowicki, 1987).

By far the most commonly researched and most stable result in the positive mood and social behavior arena, however, is that pleasant moods—joy most often—facilitate subsequent helping behaviors. Ever since Berkowitz and Connor (1966) first demonstrated the phenomenon, researchers have had relatively little trouble finding that induced or naturally occurring good moods lead to increased helpfulness. The stability of this finding—which has been variously labelled 'the glow of goodwill' (Berkowitz and Connor, 1966), the 'warm glow of success' (Isen, 1970), and 'feel good, do good' (Rosenhan, Salovey, and Hargis, 1981)—is illustrated in Table 14.1, adapted from Myers (1987). Whether mood is induced through success experiences (Isen, 1970), by manipulations of perceived competence (Kazdin and Bryan, 1971), via thinking happy thoughts (Moore, Underwood, and Rosenhan, 1973; Underwood, Froming, and Moore, 1977; Underwood, Moore, and Rosenhan, 1973), or simply by accidental good fortune such as receiving a cookie (Isen and Levin, 1972), finding a dime in a telephone booth (Cunningham, Steinberg, and Grev, 1980; Isen and Levin, 1972), or being given a free gift (Isen, Clark, and Schwartz, 1976), happiness promotes subsequent altruistic behavior.

NEGATIVE MOODS

Not surprisingly, the effects of negative moods on prosocial behavior are not nearly as consistent as positive moods. This lack of consistency in the consequences of negative states clearly parallels results in the mood and memory literature (Singer and Salovey, 1988), and seems to arise from a general motive on the part of subjects to relieve or disrupt negative mood states. (Not so of course, for positive states which individuals want to maintain.) Such a motive would likely disrupt the mood–cognition and mood–behavior relationships that would be expected if the negative mood were maintained. Researchers in the social cognition area have termed these meta-mood processes 'mood repair' (Isen, 1985; Mayer and Gaschke, 1987) and have suggested that 'people in bad moods may be more likely to switch from automatic to controlled processes . . . in order to escape the bad mood. Consequently, people often take charge of their minds' propensity to jump from gloomy thought to gloomy thought' (Fiske and Taylor, 1984, p. 328).

Guilt and Shame

As we noted in our earlier review (Rosenhan, Karylowski, Salovey, and Hargis, 1981), guilt, whether resulting from a person's own transgressions (e.g. being made

Table 14.1. Some representative studies illustrating the relationship between joy and helping

Citation	Mood induction procedure	Helping measure
Berkowitz and Connor (1966)	Success at a jigsaw puzzle	Working hard to help a peer
Isen (1970)	Success at perceptual judgements	Contributions; picking up a dropped book
Isen and Levin (1972)	Success at perceptual judgements; Receiving cookies; Finding 10 cents in a phone booth	Picking up a dropped book; Helping an experimenter; Picking up dropped papers
Aderman (1972)	Reading happy statements	Helping experimenters
Isen, Horn, and Rosenhan (1973)	Success at a game	Contributions for 'poor children'
Moore et al. (1973)	Thinking happy thoughts	Contributions for 'other kids'
Rosenhan et al. (1974)	Thinking happy thoughts	Contributions for 'other kids'
Isen et al. (1976)	Receiving a free sample	Relaying a wrong-number call
Sherrod et al. (1977)	Writing positive thoughts, viewing attractive slides	Helping another experimenter
Veitch, DeWood, and Bosko (1977)	Hearing a radio broadcast of good news	Helping look for a contact lens
Weyant (1978)	Success in solving anagrams	Contributions
Cunningham (1979)	Sunshine	Assisting an interviewer; Restaurant tips
Fried and Berkowitz (1979)	Soothing music	Helping an experimenter
Cunningham et al. (1980)	Finding 10 cents in a phone booth	Picking up dropped papers, contributions
Yinon and Bizman (1980)	Success on aptitude test	Tutoring a foreign student
Barden et al. (1981)	Thinking happy thoughts	Donating pennies
Rosenhan, Salovey, and Hargis (1981)	Imagining a Hawaiian vacation	Helping another experimenter
Wilson (1981)	Listening to a Steve Martin comedy	Lending money
Salovey and Rosenhan (1983)	Imagining a Hawaiian vacation	Helping another experimenter
O'Malley and Andrews (1983)	Listing happy experiences	Donating blood
Manucia et al. (1984)	Remembering happy times	Calling blood donors

Note: This table was adapted from Myers (1987) p. 471. Each of these articles reports a positive association between happiness and helping behavior.

to feel responsible for breaking a piece of laboratory equipment, causing harm to another person, or killing a laboratory animal) or witnessing harm being done to a third person, will generally lead to prosocial behavior directed toward either the victim of the harm-doing or to uninvolved others, even when such behavior is quite costly to the subject (e.g. donating blood). A sampling of these experiments is outlined in Table 14.2.

Psychoanalytic thinkers postulated that guilt is the motive for all altruistic behavior (Freud, 1937; Glover, 1925). Although this is clearly an overstatement, guilt does reliably promote altruism. But the mechanism underlying this relationship is unclear. Guilt could engender altruism because helping behavior relieves guilt, or because it restores self-esteem, or perhaps because it renews the guilty helper's faith in equity and a just world.

That altruistic behavior is motivated by a desire to relieve guilt is supported by studies of the effects of confessing transgressions. Confession, because it alleviates guilt, reduces altruistic behavior in transgressors—but not in observers (Carlsmith, Ellsworth, and Whiteside, cited in Freedman, 1970; Regan, 1971). Churchgoers, moreover, are more likely to donate money to charity on their way to confession than on their way home from it (Harris, Benson, and Hall, 1975).

The motivation to help among individuals who have witnessed, but not participated in, transgression may be somewhat more complex. Observers experience no guilt from 'having sinned,' because they have not. But they may feel guilty for silently endorsing the view that the world is not a fair or friendly place. Subsequent helping by transgression observers may thus be motivated by a combination of feelings of guilt and thoughts regarding fairness (Regan, 1971).

But witnesses may want to help for other reasons, for the emotion that is more likely aroused among witnesses of harmdoing is *sympathy for the victim*, rather than guilt. In fact, in studies where observers of harm-doing receive absolutely no feedback about the victim's feelings, thus engendering little sympathy, very little prosocial behavior on the part of the observer is elicited (Carlsmith and Gross, 1969; Freedman, Wallington, and Bless, 1967). However, when observers receive substantial and vivid feedback regarding the suffering of the victim, they offer help at a level higher than do actual transgressors (Konecni, 1972; Regan, 1971).

Transgressors whose harm-doing occurs publicly might be expected to feel emotions other than guilt: for example, shame or embarrassment. Generally, shame motivates prosocial behavior both because of mood-repair (the desire to reduce negative emotion) and image-repair (the desire to revise one's tarnished image). It is clear that repairing one's public image is not the sole motivator of altruism, since private embarrassment is as likely to generate helping behavior as public humiliation (Apsler, 1975). Indeed, image-repair as a motivator of altruism likely refers only to the privately held self-image. One helps in order to convince oneself that one really is decent and reasonable. The image one portrays to others seems less important than one's own view of oneself in generating prosocial behavior.

Table 14.2. Some representative studies illustrating the relationship between guilt and helping

Citation	Guilt manipulation	Helping measure	Result
Darlington and Macker (1966)	Ss belief that he had harmed confederate by failing to earn him points that would go toward psych grade	Agree to donate blood (request made by a third party)	Experimental group agreed more often than control group
Wallace and Sadalla (1966)	Short circuit a machine; S either caught (responsible) or not caught	Volunteer to participate in an aversive experiment	Caught Ss display higher compliance (no difference between not-caught Ss and control group)
Freedman *et al.* (1967)	Ss lie about not receiving information about test (which was supplied by confederate)	Agree to participate in another experiment	More compliance in the lie condition
Rawlings (1968)	S made responsible for partner's getting shocked or only witnesses	Accepting electric shock in order to prevent another person from receiving it	Ss in both conditions show higher altruism than non-shock control Ss (no difference between guilt and observation Ss)
Carlsmith and Gross (1969)	Ss belief that he had shocked the confederate	Help experimenter call people to sign a petition	Increased compliance from Ss in guilt condition
McMillan (1970)	Induce S to lie about information received which is either useful or irrelevant to a test (control group = no lie)	Help experimenter circulate petitions	Only those Ss who lied and for whom the information was useful helped more
McMillan (1971)	S lies about information received regarding upcoming test	Help in scoring tests	Ss with information much more likely to help than Ss in no-information group

Regan (1971)	S made to feel responsible for rat getting shocked *vs* witnessing (no fault)	Contribute money to a research project	Both witnesses and transgressors contributed more than controls
Konecni (1972)	Witnessing someone cause another person to drop a deck of computer cards	Help pick up the computer cards	Increased helping in this condition
Regan, Williams and Sparling (1972)	S made to believe he had broken experimenter's camera	Inform a confederate that her shopping bag was torn	Ss in guilt condition more likely to help
Cialdini *et al.* (1973)	Accidentally drop computer cards or witness experimenter drop the cards	Make calls for another experimenter	Increased helping from both transgressors and witnesses
Harris *et al.* (1975)	Behavior prior to or after church confession	Contribution to March of Dimes	More people donated prior to confession than afterwards
Harris and Samerotte (1976)	Failing to prevent theft of an object S was supposed to watch *vs* stopping the thief	Give money to confederate (victim of theft) to buy food	Guilt condition Ss more likely to give money
Cunningham, Steinberg, and Grev (1980)	Ss belief that he had broken experimenter's camera	Help confederate pick up dropped papers/charity request	Increased helping even though harm was unintentional

Although more work needs to be done, the present evidence suggests that guilt is a stronger motivator of helping behavior than shame. Dienstbier, Hillman, Hillman, Lehnhoff, and Valkenaar (1975) led children to believe that their emotional reactions to their own transgression arose either out of shame, because the transgression was public, or out of guilt, because they had in fact done something that they felt was wrong. Children who attributed their negative feelings to guilt subsequently behaved much more prosocially than those who experienced shame.

Sorrow

Unlike guilt, sympathy, and shame, which rather consistently promote prosocial behavior, sorrow, whether deriving from a sad experience or from failure, can, at times, increase helping (Cialdini, Darby, and Vincent, 1973), but it is more likely to reduce it (Carlson and Miller, 1987; Moore *et al.*, 1973; Underwood, Berenson, Berenson, Cheng, Wilson, Kulik, Moore and Wenzel, 1977; Underwood, Froming, and Moore, 1977), or to have no effect at all (Isen, 1970; Rosenhan, Underwood, and Moore, 1974). The findings, in short, are inconsistent.

Several investigators have attempted to understand these inconsistencies in different ways. For example, Morris and Kanfer (1983) believe that sadness reduces altruism because it enlarges preoccupation with self while narrowing concern for others. In fact, there is accumulating evidence that the kind of sadness associated with clinical depression produces self-concern and self-focused attention (Pyszczynski and Greenberg, 1985; Pyszczynski, Holt, and Greenberg, 1987; Smith and Greenberg, 1981), and self-focused attention reduces prosocial behavior (Gibbons and Wicklund, 1982). In a direct test of this idea, Thompson, Cowan, and Rosenhan (1980) induced sadness in ways that promoted attention to the subject's own thoughts and feelings or to the thoughts and feelings of another person. As predicted, self-focused sad subjects helped as little as neutral controls while other-focused sadness facilitated subsequent helping. Similar findings on the power of empathic sadness in promoting helpfulness have also been reported with children (Barnett, Howard, Melton, and Dino, 1982). We return to the role of self/other attentional focus in mood-helping relationships later in this chapter.

Cialdini and his colleagues (Baumann, Cialdini and Kenrick, 1981; Cialdini, Baumann, and Kenrick, 1981; Cialdini, Darby, and Vincent, 1973; Cialdini and Kenrick, 1976; Kenrick, Baumann, and Cialdini, 1979) have consistently argued that when prosocial behavior can be used as a way of relieving a negative state, sadness will lead to increased helping behavior. Those studies in which sorrow does not lead to helping, Cialdini *et al.* argue, are ones that utilize young children as subjects, and young hildren simply have not yet learned that altruism can be instrumental in mood repair. Consistent with this view, Shaffer and Graziano (1983) found that happy and sad subjects were likely to become helpful if, in both cases, the helping task has pleasant rather than unpleasant consequences.

There are, however, several studies that are simply inconsistent with the negative-state relief formulation (e.g. Barden, Garber, Leiman, Ford, and Masters, 1985; Isen, 1970; Thompson *et al.*, 1980; Underwood, Berenson, Berenson, Cheng, Wilson, Kulik, Moore and Wenzel, 1977). The model and supporting experiments have not held up well in meta-analytic studies (Carlson and Miller, 1987) and they have been criticized on theoretical and methodological grounds as well (e.g. Wispe, 1980).

SELF-RELEVANT THOUGHTS LINK FEELING STATES AND SOCIAL BEHAVIOR

For some time now, Isen's notion (Isen, 1975; Isen, Shalker, Clark, and Karp, 1978) that mood affects behavior by promoting the accessibility of similarly-toned material from memory has received rather consistent support (see Gilligan and Bower, 1984; Clark and Isen, 1982; Mayer and Salovey, 1988; Singer and Salovey, 1988, for reviews). For example, Clark and Waddell (1983) found that subjects who were in a pleasant mood state had significantly more positive first associations to situations in which helping was a possibility than did subjects in neutral or negative mood states. Recently, Salovey and Rodin (1985) suggested that the kinds of mood-congruent thoughts most likely to be rendered accessible by feeling states are thoughts regarding oneself. Such thoughts were proposed to be especially important in motivating subsequent behavior.

In this view, thoughts about oneself link mood states to subsequent changes in social behavior. Moods make salient aspects of the self in three phases that are depicted in Figure 14.1. In the first phase, a mood-evoking experience changes the way in which an individual organizes information about, and therefore evaluates, the self. As a result, certain aspects of the self become differentially available (cf. Clark and Isen, 1982; Isen, 1984; Isen, Shalker, Clark, and Karp, 1978). In the second phase, these temporary changes in the way in which one thinks about oneself promote or inhibit different social behaviors. And in the final phase, the

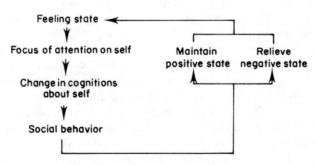

Figure 14.1. Model of how moods affect social behavior [From Salovey, 1986].

social behaviors serve either to maintain positive affect and positive self-cognitions, or to repair negative mood and negative self-cognitions.

At the center of this model of affect–cognition sequences is the suggestion that certain kinds of self-relevant thoughts are particularly likely to be influenced by mood. And changes in these thoughts would also be especially likely to motivate changes in subsequent behaviors. Salovey (1986) hypothesized that these thoughts would most likely include self-evaluation, self-efficacy expectations, self-complexity, and self-relevant dimensions of the self-concept. This view finds support in the recent work of Brown and Taylor (1986).

In fact, mood states, particularly joy, have profound effects on these kinds of self-relevant thoughts (Salovey, 1986). As compared with neutral mood subjects, people who were induced to experience happy moods were more likely to emphasize personal rather than social aspects of their self-concept, were more complex in their self-representations, and generally rated themselves higher on state (but not trait) measures of self-esteem (see also Amrhein, Salovey, and Rosenhan, 1981; Wright and Mischel, 1982). As will be discussed later, they also rated themselves as more capable of carrying out helping behaviors (i.e. helping self-efficacy).

SELF-RELEVANT MEDIATORS OF AFFECT-ALTRUISM SEQUENCES

SELF-FOCUSED ATTENTION

Some years ago, we found that attentional focus was a powerful mediator of the effects of happy and sad moods on subsequent helping behaviors. We had created several different sets of audiotapes that induced strong moods when subjects listened to them. Subjects were instructed to become completely absorbed in one of these evocative situations—a wonderful Hawaiian vacation to induce joy, and the death of a close friend from cancer to induce sorrow. We developed alternate versions of these tapes, some that encouraged subjects to focus attention on themselves during the evocative experience, and some that guided their attention away from themselves and on to the others who were depicted in the scenario. The two versions generated equal amounts of joy and sorrow in the subjects, but differed according to whether attention was focused on oneself or on another person. For example, for subjects experiencing sadness, the tape described either the worry, anxiety, and intense pain of the dying friend (external focus) or the subject's own pain and sorrow caused by the friend's death (self-focus).

Interestingly, when individuals felt joyful, they tended to offer help to others only when their joy was self-focused but not when they were experiencing empathic joy [i.e. focused on others (Rosenhan, Salovey, and Hargis, 1981)]. Conversely, when sadness was self-focused, helping was not very likely; yet, sadness

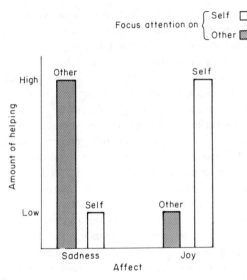

Figure 14.2. Amount of helping as a function of joy, sadness, and focus of attention [Joy data from Rosenhan *et al.* (1981); sadness data from Thompson *et al.* (1980)].

generated through focusing on the misfortune of another person promoted altruistic behavior [Thompson *et al.* (1980); see also Barnett, King, and Howard (1979) and Barnett *et al.* (1982) for replications of this effect in children]. The interaction between mood and attentional focus is depicted in Figure 14.2.

We believe that attentional focus helps to shape the first few thoughts that come to mind when one experiences a mood and is then provided with an opportunity to help others (Isen, Shalker, Clark, and Karp, 1978; Karylowski, 1977; Rosenhan, Karylowski, Salovey, and Hargis, 1981; Wegner and Guiliano, 1980). Individuals focusing attention on themselves are likely to think about their own needs and resources, while individuals focused externally may be primed to think about the needs and available resources of others. Mood and attentional focus seem to momentarily, but powerfully, alter one's tacit beliefs about one's relative resources or efficacy as compared with others. Helping occurs when there is a perceived imbalance of resources between the self and other, and when that imbalance favors the self. Thus, when one experiences pleasant states deriving from and focused on the self, one feels especially efficacious and resource-laden and thus more likely to offer help. Similarly, focusing on another's misfortune should also increase one's comparative sense of efficacy and also lead to helping. But experiencing positive feelings that are focused on another generates social comparison processes that may not wholly favor oneself, with the result that helping is reduced (cf. Salovey and Rodin, 1984).

A related hypothesis is that mood and attentional focus affect the relative accessibility of different helping norms (Salovey and Rosenhan, 1983). By the accessibility of helping norms, we mean the following: In thinking about oneself, what information is easiest to retrieve concerning oneself as a helper in social situations? Does one see oneself as an altruist, a helper who aids others with no expectation of extrinsic gain? Or is one a reciprocity-motivated helper, calculating how helping in a particular instance might lead to future gain for oneself in *quid pro quo* fashion (cf. Gouldner, 1960)? Or might one see oneself as a socially-responsible helper, helping because it is socially mandated in certain situations (cf. Berkowitz and Daniels, 1963; Schwartz, 1977)? These representations of the self-as-helper might shift depending on one's mood and attentional focus. When focused on the self, helping should be perceived as deriving from internal standards and beliefs rather than social expectations.

Salovey (1986) measured the effects of mood and attentional focus on these kinds of thoughts by using a helping self-efficacy questionnaire (modeled after Bandura, 1977) and by asking people to endorse norm-based, helping-related thoughts after reading various scenarios that described a helping opportunity. As compared with a neutral mood control group, people who felt joy thought themselves much more capable of carrying out a variety of helping behaviors. But the predicted interaction with attentional focus was not significant. Focus of attention however, played a subtle role in determining the nature of helping-relevant thoughts. Self-focused subjects were much more likely to perceive helping as deriving from two considerations: expectations of possible reciprocity and unalloyed charity, both motives originating in either a giving of the self, or in an expected return for the self. On the other hand, people whose attention was directed toward others tended to help for a more external reason: social responsibility, that is, a sense of civic duty or social obligation. As happiness intensified, thoughts about reciprocity declined, and thoughts about charity increased. Happiness does not trigger thoughts about social responsibility.

Thus, happiness, when focused on the self, seems to promote helping by increasing the availability of thoughts concerning oneself as a helper who is charitable rather than one who anticipates reciprocity. In our earlier studies (Rosenhan, Salovey, and Hargis, 1981; Thompson, *et al.*, 1980), the helping act was anonymous, rendering reciprocity unlikely. Hence, thoughts about charity were more likely to support helping than were thoughts about reciprocity. Remember, however, that externally focused happiness does not produce increased altruism. We believe this phenomenon can be explained by the fact that externally focused attention leads to thoughts about social responsibility or civic duty as the reason for helping others, and, as we have described, happy mood has very little impact on these kinds of thoughts.

Others who have investigated the interaction of mood and attentional focus, and their effects on helping, have obtained results compatible with this framework. For example, Kidd and Marshall (1982) induced happy, sad, and neutral moods in subjects by having them read sets of positive or negative sentences (Velten, 1968). Two different sets of sad sentences were prepared, one in which all of the items reflected on the self (the sentences began with first-person pronouns) and one in which the items related to someone else (third-person pronouns). Subjects who read the negative self-referent statements became self-preoccupied and introspective, and helped considerably less than subjects who read positive, neutral, or other-focused negative sentences. Sad moods that are associated with self-reflection (cf. Pyszczynski and Greenberg, 1985; Salovey and Rodin, 1985) decrease concern for the plight of others who might be in need of help by decreasing attention to the environment and to the welfare of others. Negative mood states, however, that are not rooted in the self actually increase helpfulness.

FELT RESPONSIBILITY

Although Wegner and Schaefer (1978) found that, overall, self-focused attention tends to promote the helping of others, most subsequent investigators have noted just the opposite: unless the helping request is made extremely salient, self-focused attention reduces helping behavior (Dovidio and MacKay, 1983; Gibbons and Wicklund, 1982; Rogers, Miller, Mayer, and Duval, 1982). In an attempt to resolve this discrepancy in reported findings, Mayer, Duval, Holtz, and Bowman (1985) conducted a study testing the idea that felt responsibility for others was the cognition that mediated the impact of self-focused attention on helping. They predicted that when self-focus was coupled with thoughts of being responsible for others, helping would result, and when it was not combined with these thoughts, helping would be inhibited. In fact, these researchers found that under conditions of high helping request salience, self-focus led to increased felt responsibility for the welfare of others and, thus, an increased willingness to help.

Although it has not yet been demonstrated directly, it seems perfectly reasonable that joyful moods could increase the availability of thoughts about one's responsibility for helping others as compared with sad moods. After all, happiness does increase thoughts about charity (Salovey, 1986). If so, we may have yet another explanation for why self-focused happiness is such a strong promoter of helping behavior, while self-focused sadness inhibits it. Similarly, self-focused sadness may actively decrease the likelihood that one will have thoughts concerning felt responsibility for others and hence, helping is not observed under these conditions.

This set of hypotheses seems consistent with research concerning the idea that, compared with the depressed, non-depressed individuals are much more likely to overestimate their perceived responsibility for a variety of external events (e.g. Alloy and Abramson, 1979). However, Rogers *et al.* (1982, Experiments 2 and 3) claim that feelings of personal responsibility for one's negative affect *increase* prosocial behavior, at least when the request for help is made very salient. They argue that making internal attributions of responsibility for events that have negative consequences causes increased self-awareness that leads to subsequent prosocial behavior. These observations contradict the data obtained in our laboratories and seem not to fit with contemporary views of depression which suggest that making internal attributions for events with negative consequences increases depressed affect and decreases the likelihood that the individual will initiate any behavior that could bring him or her pleasure (Abramson, Seligman, and Teasdale, 1978).

SELF-CONCERN

The observations of Rogers *et al.* (1982, Experiments 2 and 3) do not articulate with research conducted by Aderman and Berkowitz (1983) on people's unwillingness to be helpful after being given a task that increases self-concern. According to Aderman and Berkowitz (1983), self-concern really occurs when 'attention is directed primarily to uncertain and possibly even negative features of their self-concept' (p. 294). In this sense, self-concerned individuals are much more like the self-focused sad subjects who offered little help in the Thompson *et al.* (1980) study, than the self-focused joyful subjects of Rosenhan, Salovey, and Hargis (1981) who were quite helpful.

   In fact, Aderman and Berkowitz (1983) found that 'apprehensive self-attention' (their term) lessens the willingness to help others. They suggest that self-concerned individuals, because they are preoccupied with their own interests and worries, cannot easily place themselves in the shoes of the person needing help and do not vicariously experience this other person's feelings.

EMPATHY AND PERSPECTIVE-TAKING

Being able to 'place onself in another's shoes,' as mentioned above, is a reasonable operational definition of empathy, and a number of investigators have suggested that empathy and role-taking skills must be well-developed before mood states can have an impact on prosocial behavior (e.g. Froming, Allen, and Jensen, 1985; Hoffman, 1981; Krebs, 1975). More formally, empathy an be defined as either (a) the cognitive ability to recognize and understand the thoughts, feelings, or intentions of another person or (b) the vicarious experience of the emotional state of another individual (Barnett, 1982).*

   Underwood and Moore (1982) distinguish these two definitions by calling the first—which does not involve the arousal of a feeling state—'perspective-taking', and the second—in which the arousal of feelings is central—'empathy'. In their meta-analysis of the empathy, perspective-taking and altruism literature, they conclude that there are reliable and stable associations between altruism and

---

*There is a third definition of empathy, which is, the *generalized* emotional reaction that results from observing the plight of another. The implications of this definition are not examined here.

perceptual, social, and moral perspective-taking. Further, although the associations between empathy and altruism are relatively weak, Underwood and Moore believe them to be reliable, at least for adults.

For example, Toi and Batson (1982) exposed subjects to a person in distress and instructed them either to observe the victim's reactions (low empathy condition) or to imagine the victims' feelings (high empathy condition). High empathy subjects [who may resemble the other-focused sad subjects in Thompson *et al.*'s (1980) study], were more likely to offer the victim help, even when escape from the situation was easy. Barnett (1982) offers some suggestions about the conditions that vitiate the relationship between empathy and prosocial behavior. He notes that subjects who experience distress and concern when confronted by a needy other may not offer help if they perceive little personal responsibility, or if they feel incompetent to offer help, or if they fail to realize that helping might relieve them of their own distress. Subjects, particularly children, can become so overwhelmed by their own distress that concerns about their own well-being can overshadow concern for the other.

DIRECT EFFECTS VERSUS SIDE EFFECTS

One way to characterize mood's effects on helping is to discriminate between helping as a concomitant of the mood and helping as reflecting instrumental motives (Manucia, Baumann, and Cialdini, 1984). According to Manucia *et al.* (1984), if mood simply is conducive to the carrying out of helping acts, the concomitance model is correct. If, on the other hand, altruistic behavior produces gratification that relieves negative moods or prolongs positive moods, then an instrumental relationship between mood and prosocial behavior can be said to exist.

Manucia *et al.* (1984) suggest instrumental motives as the best explanation for helping in response to negative moods, but that concomitance is the most parsimonious view of the effects of good moods on helping. They conducted a study in which people were induced to experience happy, sad, and neutral moods under two different conditions. In one condition, people believed they had taken a drug that would 'lock in' their moods, fixing them at one level of intensity. In the other condition, they were led to believe that the drug would have no effects on their mood at all. In the latter condition, the experimenters presumed that subjects would simply be aware that their moods would fluctuate normally. Those who experienced a happy mood were more likely than controls to offer help, whether they believed their moods were 'fixed' or 'labile.' However, sad mood facilitated helping only when people believed that their moods could change. In the sad-fixed condition, helping remained at the level of the neutral mood controls.

Manucia *et al.* (1984) interpret these results as supporting an instrumental view of helping that follows negative mood induction. When sad subjects believe that helping cannot improve their mood, they are not especially helpful. On the other hand, helping by happy subjects is best explained by the concomitance model which suggests that helping arises from changes in thoughts and judgements (about liking of others, sense of control, general optimism, equity, or what have you) associated with happy moods.

Although Manucia *et al.*'s (1984) view, based on the work by Cialdini and his colleagues on the Negative State Relief Model of helping behavior (i.e. 'altruism as hedonism,' Baumann *et al.*, 1981; Cialdini *et al.*, 1973; Cialdini and Kenrick, 1976), accounts for some of the findings in the mood and helping literature, there are two sets of results that are incongruent with it. First, several studies find that sad subjects, who presumably are aware that helping might improve their moods, in fact do not always offer help (Thompson *et al.*, 1980; Underwood, Berenson, Berenson, Cheng, Wilson, Kulik, Moore and Wenzel, 1977). Second, there is a growing set of studies in which happy subjects actually help less than controls because they perceive the helping task as likely to spoil their pleasant affective states (Forest *et al.*, 1979; Isen and Simmonds, 1978; Shaffer and Graziano, 1983). The Negative State Relief Model explicitly does not assume a 'Positive State Maintenance' motive.

CONCLUSIONS

It has been the better part of a decade since we first reviewed this research area (Rosenhan, Karylowski, Salovey, and Hargis, 1981). At that time, we warned readers to 'expect the worst' because the research road was often 'dark and tortured' and relevant literatures 'foggy and conflicting' (p. 233). We felt that some aspects of this literature took 'Herculean' effort to organize (p. 237).

Now, some years later, we are pleasantly embarrassed (a contradiction in terms?). Not only do we find our earlier prose rather mauve, we find that it failed to predict the present situation accurately. For now it seems that the fog is lifting and that the intellectual landscape is clearer and more comprehensible. Why should that be?

The analysis of the impact of affect on behavior is intellectually barren for simple and obvious reasons. There is only a distant end to the number of possible affects, whether they be described as primary, secondary, or blended. Matching those affects to behavior *in the absence of a governing theory* is a trial-and-error matter that quite understandably generates 'foggy and conflicting' ideas and literatures. Thus, the examination of the cognitions that rise up separately from mood and helping, which has characterized the significant recent literature, is not merely an interesting way of doing research. *It promises to provide the intellectual connections between the affective and behavioral domains.* True, it does not yet provide governing theory. But it is a major step along the road to discovering such a theory. It now allows us to predict when certain moods will result in helping behavior and under what conditions those same moods will inhibit such behavior—and that is quite a step forward. Despite inconsistencies, especially in the sadness-helping area, the findings that have emerged recently promise to make the next decade of research on mood and helping interesting, not only for itself, but for the intellectual illumination they will provide for the entire affect/cognition/action sequence.

REFERENCES

Abramson, L. Y., Seligman, M. E. P., and Teasdale, J. D. (1978) Learned helplessness in humans: critique and reformulation. *Journal of Abnormal Psychology*, **87**, 49–74.

Aderman, D. (1972) Elation, depression, and helping behavior. *Journal of Personality and Social Psychology*, **24**, 91–101.

Aderman, D., and Berkowitz, L. (1983) Self-concern and the unwillingness to be helpful. *Social Psychology Quarterly*, **46**, 293–301.

Alloy, L. B., and Abramson, L. Y. (1979) Judgment of contingency in depressed and nondepressed students: sadder but wiser? *Journal of Experimental Psychology: General*, **108**, 441–85.

Amrhein, J., Salovey, P., and Rosenhan, D. L. (1981) Joy and sadness generate attributional vulnerability in men. Unpublished manuscript, Stanford University.

Apsler, R. (1975) Effects of embarrassment on behavior toward others. *Journal of Personality and Social Psychology*, **32**, 145–53.

Bandura, A. (1977) Self-efficacy: toward a unifying theory of behavioral change. *Psychological Review*, **84**, 191–215.

Barden, R. C., Garber, J., Duncan, S. W., and Masters, J. C. (1981) Cumulative effects of induced affective states in children: accentuation, inoculation, and remediation. *Journal of Personality and Social Psychology*, **40**, 750–760.

Barden, R. C., Garber, J., Leiman, B., Ford, M. E., and Masters, J. C. (1985) Factors governing the effective remediation of negative affect and its cognitive and behavioral consequences. *Journal of Personality and Social Psychology*, **49**, 1040–53.

Barnett, M. A. (1982) Empathy and prosocial behavior in children. In T. M. Field, A. Huston, H. C. Quay, L. Troll, and G. E. Finley (Eds), *Review of Human Development*, pp. 316–26. New York: John Wiley.

Barnett, M. A., Howard, J. A., Melton, E. M., and Dino, G. A. (1982) Effect of inducing sadness about self or other on helping behavior in high- and low-empathic children. *Child Development*, **53**, 920–3.

Barnett, M. A., King, L. M., and Howard, J. A. (1979) Inducing affect about self or other: effects on generosity in children. *Developmental Psychology*, **15**, 164–7.

Batson, C. D., Coke, J. S., Chard, F., Smith, D., and Taliaferro, A. (1979) Generality of the 'glow of goodwill': effects of mood on helping and information acquisition. *Social Psychology Quarterly*, **42**, 176–9.

Baumann, D. J., Cialdini, R. B., and Kenrick, D. T. (1981) Altruism as hedonism: helping and self-gratification as equivalent responses. *Journal of Personality and Social Psychology*, **40**, 1039–46.

Berkowitz, L., and Connor, W. H. (1966) Success, failure, and social responsibility. *Journal of Personality and Social Psychology*, **3**, 664–9.

Berkowitz, L., and Daniels, L. R. (1963) Responsibility and dependency. *Journal of Abnormal and Social Psychology*, **66**, 427–36.

Brown, J. D., and Taylor, S. E. (1986) Affect and the processing of personal information: evidence for mood-activated self-schemata. *Journal of Experimental Social Psychology*, **22**, 436–52.

Carlsmith, J. M., and Gross, A. E. (1969) Some effects of guilt on compliance. *Journal of Personality and Social Psychology*, **11**, 232–9.

Carlson, M., and Miller, N. (1987) Explanations of the relationship between negative mood and helping. *Psychological Bulletin*, **102**, 91–108.

Cialdini, R. B. Baumann, D. J., and Kenrick, D. T. (1981) Insights from sadness: a three step model of the development of altruism as hedonism. *Development Review*, **1**, 207–23.

Cialdini, R. B., Darby, B. L., and Vincent, J. E. (1973) Transgression and altruism: a case for hedonism. *Journal of Experimental Social Psychology*, **9**, 502–16.

Cialdini, R. B., and Kenrick, D. (1976) Altruism as hedonism: a social development perspective on the relationship of negative mood state and helping. *Journal of Personality and Social Psychology*, **34**, 907–14.

Clark, M. S., and Isen, A. M. (1982) Toward understanding the relationship between feeling states and social behavior. In A. Hastorf, and A. M. Isen (Eds), *Cognitive Social Psychology*, pp. 73–108. New York: Elsevier/North Holland.

Clark, M. S., and Waddell, B. A. (1983) Effects of moods on thoughts about helping, attraction and information acquisition. *Social Psychology Quarterly*, **46**, 31–5.

Cunningham, M. R. (1979) Weather, mood, and helping behavior: quasi-experiments with the sunshine Samaritan. *Journal of Personality and Social Psychology*, **37**, 1947–56.

Cunningham, M. R., Steinberg, J., and Grev, R. (1980) Wanting to and having to help: separate motivations for positive mood and guilt-induced helping. *Journal of Personality and Social Psychology*, **38**, 181–92.

Darlington, R. B., and Macker, C. E. (1966) Displacement of guilt-produced altruistic behavior. *Journal of Personality and Social Psychology*, **4**, 442–3.

Dienstbier, R. A., Hillman, D., Hillman, J., Lehnhoff, J., and Valkenaar, M. C. (1975) An emotional-attribution approach to moral behavior: interfacing cognitive and avoidance theories of moral development. *Psychology Review*, **82**, 299–315.

Dovidio, J. F., and Mackay, K. S. (1983) Helping behavior, attention, and mood. Presented at the annual convention of the American Psychological Association, Anaheim, CA, August 1983.

Fiske, S. T., and Taylor, S. E. (1984) *Social Cognition*. Reading, MA: Addison-Wesley.

Forest, D., Clark, M., Mills, J., and Isen, A. M. (1979) Helping as a function of feeling state and nature of the helping behavior. *Motivation and Emotion*, **3**, 161–9.

Freedman, J. L. (1970) Transgression, compliance, and guilt. In J. R. Macaulay and L. Berkowitz (Eds), *Altruism and Helping Behavior*. New York: Academic.

Freedman, J. L., Wallington, S. A., and Bless, E. (1967) Compliance without pressure: the effects of guilt. *Journal of Personality and Social Psychology*, **7**, 117–24.

Freud, A. (1937) *The Ego and the Mechanisms of Defense*. London: Hogarth Press.

Fried, R., and Berkowitz, L. (1979) Music hath charms . . . and can influence helpfulness. *Journal of Applied Social Psychology*, **9**, 199–208.

Froming, W. J., Allen, L, and Jensen, R. (1985) Altruism, role-taking, and self-awareness: the acquisition of norms governing altruistic behavior. *Child Development*, **56**, 1223–8.

Gibbons, F. X. and Wicklund, R. A. (1982) Self-focused attention and helping behavior. *Journal of Personality and Social Psychology*, **43**, 462–74.

Gilligan, S. G., and Bower, G. E. (1984) Cognitive consequences of emotional arousal. In C. Izard, J. Kagen, and R. Zajonc (Eds), *Emotions, Cognitions, and Behavior*, pp. 547–88. New York: Cambridge University Press.

Glover, E. (1925) Notes on oral character formation. *International Journal of Psychoanalysis*, **6**, 131–54.

Gouaux, C. (1971) Induced affective states and interpersonal attraction. *Journal of Personality and Social Psychology*, **20**, 37–43.

Gouldner, A. W. (1960) The norm of reciprocity: a preliminary statement. *American Sociological Review*, **25**, 161–78.

Griffitt, W. B. (1970) Environmental effects of interpersonal affective behavior: ambient effective temperature and attraction. *Journal of Personality and Social Psychology*, **15**, 240–4.

Harris, M. B., Benson, S. M., and Hall, C. (1975) The effects of confession on altruism. *Journal of Social Psychology*, **96**, 187–92.

Harris, M. B., and Samerotte, G. C. (1976) The effects of actual and attempted theft, need, and a previous favor on altruism. *Journal of Social Psychology*, **99**, 193–202.

Hoffman, M. (1981) Is altruism part of human nature? *Journal of Personality and Social Psychology*, **40**, 121–37.

Isen, A. M. (1970) Success, failure, attention and reaction to others: the warm glow of success. *Journal of Personality and Social Psychology*, **15**, 294–301.

Isen, A. M. (1975) Positive affect, accessibility of cognitions, and helping. Paper presented at a symposium, 'Directions in theory on helping behavior' J. Piliavin, Chair, at the annual meeting of the Eastern Psychological Association, April 1975.

Isen, A. M. (1984) Toward understanding the role of affection cognition. In R. S. Wyer, Jr and T. K. Srull (Eds), *Handbook of Social Cognition*, Vol. 3, pp. 179–236. Hillsdale, NJ: Erlbaum.

Isen, A. M. (1985) Asymmetry of happiness and sadness in effects on memory in normal college students: comments on Hasher, Rose, Zacks, Sanft, and Doren. *Journal of Experimental Psychology: General*, **114**, 388–91.

Isen, A. M., Clark, M., and Schwartz, M. F. (1976) Duration of the effect of good mood on helping: 'Footprints in the sands of time.' *Journal of Personality and Social Psychology*, **34**, 385–93.

Isen, A. M., Daubman, K. A., and Nowicki, G. P. (1987) Positive affect facilitates creative problem solving. *Journal of Personality and Social Psychology*, **52**, 1122–31.

Isen, A. M., Horn, N., and Rosenhan, D. L. (1973) Effect of success and failure on children's generosity. *Journal of Personality and Social Psychology*, **27**, 239–47.

Isen, A. M., and Levin, P. F. (1972) The effect of feeling good on helping: cookies and kindness. *Journal of Personality and Social Psychology*, **21**, 384–8.

Isen, A. M., Means, B., Patrick, R., and Nowicki, G. (1982) Some factors influencing decision-making and risk taking. In M. S. Clark and S. T. Fiske (Eds), *Affect and Cognition*, pp. 243–61. Hillsdale, NJ: Erlbaum.

Isen, A. M. and Patrick, R. (1983) The effects of positive feelings on risk-taking: when the chips are down. *Organizational Behavior and Human Performance*, **31**, 194–202.

Isen, A. M., Shalker, T. E., Clark, M., and Karp, L. (1978) Affect accessibility of material in memory and behavior: a cognitive loop? *Journal of Personality and Social Psychology*, **36**, 1–12.

Isen, A. M., and Simmonds, S. (1978) The effect of feeling good on a helping task that is incompatible with good mood. *Social Psychology*, **41**, 346–9.

Karylowski, J. (1977) Explaining altruistic behavior: a review. *Polish Psychological Bulletin*, **8**, 27–34.

Kazdin, A. E. and Bryan, J. H. (1971) Competence and volunteering. *Journal of Experimental Social Psychology*, **7**, 87–97.

Kenrick, D. T., Baumann, D. J., and Cialdini, R. B. (1979) A step in the socialization of altruism as hedonism: effects of negative mood on children's generosity under public and private conditions. *Journal of Personality and Social Psychology*, **37**, 747–55.

Kidd, R. F., and Marshall, L. (1982) Self-reflection, mood, and helpful behavior. *Journal of Research in Personality*, **16**, 319–34.

Konecni, V. J. (1972) Some effects of guilt on compliance: a field replication. *Journal of Personality and Social Psychology*, **23**, 30–2.

Krebs, D. (1975) Empathy and altruism. *Journal of Personality and Social Psychology*, **32**, 1134–46.

Manucia, G. K., Baumann, D. J., and Cialdini, R. B. (1984) Mood influences on helping: direct effects or side effects? *Journal of Personality and Social Psychology*, **46**, 357–64.

Mayer, F. S., Duval, S., Holtz, R., and Bowman, C. (1985) Self-focus, helping request salience, felt responsibility, and helping behavior. *Personality and Social Psychology Bulletin*, **11**, 133–44.

Mayer, J. D., and Gaschke, Y. N. (1988) The experience and meta-experience of mood. *Journal of Personality and Social Psychology*, **55**, 102–11.

Mayer, J. D., and Salovey, P. (1988, in press). Personality moderates the interaction of mood and cognition. In J. Forgas and K. Fieldler (Eds), *Affect, Cognition, and Social Behavior*, pp. 87–99. Toronto: Hogrefe.

McMillan, D. L. (1970) Transgression, Fate control and compliant behavior. *Psychonometric Science*, **21**, 103–4.

McMillan, D. L. (1971) Transgression, self-image and compliant behavior. *Journal of Personality and Social Psychology*, **20**, 176–9.

Moore, B., Underwood, B., and Rosenhan, D. L. (1973) Affect and altruism. *Developmental Psychology*, **8**, 99–104.

Morris, S. J., and Kanfer, F. H. (1983) Altruism and depression. *Personality and Social Psychology Bulletin*, **9**, 567–77.

Myers, D. G. (1987) *Social Psychology*, 2nd ed. New York: McGraw-Hill.

O'Malley, M. N., and Andrews, L. (1983) The effect of mood and incentives on helping: are there some things money can't buy? *Motivation and Emotion*, **7**, 179–89.

Pyszczynski, T., and Greenberg, J. (1985) Depression and preference for self-focusing stimuli following success and failure. *Journal of Personality and Social Psychology*, **49**, 1066–75.

Pyszczynski, T., Holt, K., and Greenberg, J. (1987) Depression, self-focused attention, and expectancies for positive and negative future life events for self and others. *Journal of Personality and Social Psychology*, **52**, 994–1001.

Rawlings, E. I. (1968) Witnessing harm to others: a reassessment of the role of guilt in altruistic behavior. *Journal of Personality and Social Psychology*, **10**, 337–80.

Regan, D. T., Williams, M., and Sparling, S. (1972) Voluntary expiation of guilt: a field replication. *Journal of Personality and Social Psychology*, **24**, 42.

Regan, J. W. (1971) Guilt, perceived injustice, and altruistic behavior. *Journal of Personality and Social Psychology*, **18**, 124–32.

Rogers, M., Miller, N., Mayer, F. S., and Duval, S. (1982) Personal responsibility and salience of the request for help: determinants of the relation between negative affect and helping behavior. *Journal of Personality and Social Psychology*, **43**, 956–70.

Rosenhan, D. L., Karylowski, J., Salovey, P., and Hargis, K. (1981) Emotion and altruism. In J. P. Rushton and R. M. Sorrentino (Eds), *Altruism and Helping Behavior*, pp. 233–48. Hillsdale, NJ: Erlbaum.

Rosenhan, D. L., Salovey, P., and Hargis, K. (1981) The joys of helping. *Journal of Personality and Social Psychology*, **40**, 899–905.

Rosenhan, D. L., Underwood, B., and Moore, B. S. (1974) Affect moderates self-gratification and altruism. *Journal of Personality and Social Psychology*, **30**, 546–52.

Salovey, P. (1986) The effects of mood and focus of attention on self-relevant thoughts and helping intention. Dissertation submitted to Yale University, December 1986.

Salovey, P., and Rodin, J. (1984) Some antecedents and consequences of social-comparison jealousy. *Journal of Personality and Social Psychology*, **47**, 780–92.

Salovey, P., and Rodin, J. (1985) Cognitions about the self: Connecting feeling states and social behavior. In P. Shaver (Ed), *Self, Situations, and Social Behavior: Review of Personality and Social Psychology*, Vol. 6, pp. 143–66. Beverly Hills: Sage.

Salovey, P., and Rosenhan, D. L. (1983) Effects of joy, attention, and recipient's status on helpfulness. Presented at the annual meeting of the American Psychological Association, Anaheim, CA.

Schwartz, S. (1977) Normative influences on altruism. In L. Berkowitz (Ed.), *Advances in Experimental Social Psychology*, Vol. 10, pp. 221–79. New York: Academic Press.

Shaffer, D. R., and Graziano, W. G. (1983) Effects of positive and negative moods on helping tasks having pleasant or unpleasant consequences. *Motivation and Emotion*, **7**, 269–78.

Sherrod, D. R., Armstrong, D., Hewitt, J., Madonia, B., Speno, S., and Teruya, D. (1977) Environmental attention, affect, and altruism. *Journal of Applied Social Psychology*, **7**, 359–71.

Singer, J. A., and Salovey, P. (1988) Mood and memory: evaluating the network theory of affect. *Clinical Psychology Review*, **8**, 211–51.

Smith, T. W., and Greenberg, J. (1981) Depression and self-focused attention. *Motivation and Emotion*, **5**, 323–31.

Thompson, W. C., Cowan, C. L., and Rosenhan, D. L. (1980) Focus of attention mediates the impact of negative affect on altruism. *Journal of Personality and Social Psychology*, **38**, 291–300.

Toi, M., and Batson, C. D. (1982) More evidence that empathy is a source of altruistic motivation. *Journal of Personality and Social Psychology*, **18**, 281–92.

Underwood, B., Berenson, J. F., Berenson, R. J., Cheng, K. K., Wilson, D., Kulik, J., Moore, B. S. and Wenzel, G. (1977) Attention, negative affect and altruism: an ecological validation. *Personality and Social Psychology Bulletin*, **3**, 54–8.

Underwood, B., Froming, W. J., and Moore, B. S. (1977) Mood, attention, and altruism: a search for mediating variables. *Developmental Psychology*, **13**, 541–2.

Underwood, B., and Moore, B. (1982) Perspective taking and altruism. *Psychological Bulletin*, **91**, 143–73.

Underwood, B., Moore, B., and Rosenhan, D. L. (1973) Affect and self-gratification. *Developmental Psychology*, **8**, 209–14.

Veitch, R., DeWood, R., and Bosko, K. (1977) Radio news broadcasts: their effects on interpersonal helping. *Soviometry*, **40**, 383–6.

Veitch, R., and Griffitt, W. (1976) Good news—bad news: affective and interpersonal effects. *Journal of Applied Social Psychology* **6**, 69–75.

Velten, E. A. (1968) A laboratory task for induction of mood states. *Behavior Research and Therapy*, **6**, 473–82.

Wallace, L., and Sadalla, E. (1966) Behavioral consequences of transgression. I. The effects of social recognition. *Journal of Experimental Research in Personality*, **1**, 187–94.

Wegner, D. M., and Guiliano, T. (1980) Arousal-induced attention to self. *Journal of Personality and Social Psychology*, **38**, 719–26.

Wegner, D. M., and Schaefer, D. (1978) The concentration of responsibility: an objective self-awareness analysis of group size effects in helping situations. *Journal of Personality and Social Psychology*, **36**, 147–55.

Weyant, J. M. (1978) Effects of mood states, costs, and benefits on helping. *Journal of Personality and Social Psychology*, **36**, 1169–76.

Wilson, D. W. (1981) Is helping a laughing matter? *Psychology Today*, **18**, 6–9.

Wispe, L. (1980) The role of moods in helping behavior. *Representative Research in Social Psychology*, **11**, 2–15.

Wright, J., and Mischel, W. (1982) Influence of affect on cognitive social learning person variables. *Journal of Personality and Social Psychology*, **43**, 901–14.

Yinon, Y. and Bizman, A. (1980) Noise, success, and failure as determinants of helping behavior. *Personality and Social Psychology Bulletin*, **6**, 125–30.

Chapter 15

The Psychophysiology of Dyadic Interaction

Clifford I. Notarius and Lisa R. Herrick
The Catholic University of America

ABSTRACT

The chapter (a) summarizes the literature on the psychophysiology of social interaction, (b) presents a commentary of the issues inherent in such study, and (c) explores three social psychophysiological mechanisms hypothesized to influence both the processes and the outcomes of each interpersonal encounter. A link between immediate social psychophysiological reactions and long-term health is discussed.

Jane Austin (1813), more than a century and a half ago, wrote clearly of the impact of social exchange upon her characters, Elizabeth and Darcy:

> They were within twenty yards of each other, and so abrupt was his appearance, that it was impossible to avoid his sight. Their eyes instantly met, and the cheeks of each were overspread with the deepest blush... it was plain that he was just that moment arrived ... she blushed again and again over the perverseness of the meeting. (*Pride and Prejudice*, pp. 272–3.)

We wish to thank Gerald Ginsberg, Howard Markman, and Martin Safer for their comments on a previous draft of the chapter and Jane Fishman for her tutorial on immune system functioning. Special thanks to John Cacioppo for his insightful comments on the chapter and the conversations that led to the final draft.

Handbook of Social Psychophysiology, Edited by H. Wagner and A. Manstead,

Each of us can, no doubt, recall times when we were confronted with a provocative interpersonal encounter and our hearts raced, our skin flushed, or our palms moistened with a cold sweat. We may be recalling our first kiss with a sweetheart— or being rebuked by a supervisor in front of colleagues at work. The mechanisms that bind these physiological responses to such different psychological events are complex, and this complexity is an integral part of the study of social exchange and physiology.

INTRODUCTION

In traditional research lines within social psychophysiology, the effects of others upon physiological response is often a static variable, such as the mere presence of another (e.g. Geen, 1976), the passive witnessing of another's distress (e.g. Krebs, 1975), or the receipt of information (e.g. VanEgeren, 1979), as opposed to the *process* of social interaction. While constructs such as attitude change (e.g. Petty and Cacioppo, 1983), cognitive dissonance (Fazio and Cooper, 1983), or social facilitation (Moore and Baron, 1983), have received much attention, researchers interested in the 'social' in social psychophysiology have investigated with less frequency the ongoing social exchange process between interactants. Although we have learned much from traditional approaches, we are perhaps approaching the capability to apply what we have learned from these studies to the exploration of the interrelations between psychophysiological processes and dynamic social exchange.

The experimental study of interdependencies among physiological response systems and social exchange poses a significant methodological challenge, and thus it is not surprising to find little systematic research. In traditional psychophysiological paradigms, the experimental situation is often structured to restrict external stimuli impinging upon the subject, save for the particular independent variable under study. Whereas complex social and environmental cues are often considered nuisance variables and are controlled in these studies, it is these very events that become the focus of interest in the emerging study of the psychophysiology of dyadic interaction.

It is our preference to view the existing literature on the psychophysiology of dyadic interaction as an hypothesis-generating database and a source of excitement for launching programmatic research in this important area of study. Accordingly, we will strive to advance some common themes running through the diverse group of studies that we review below. We will argue for a move towards specificity in research, in choosing both physiological measures and social contexts. Thus far, the literature reveals only a handful of studies that have justified the choice of physiological measures or interactional settings on a theoretical basis; most paradigms have been established with intuition, practicality, and convenience as the guiding force. This fact, along with methodological difficulties inherent in the study of psychophysiological responses during dyadic interaction, leaves many of the studies we review with questionable internal validity and with plausible alternative explanations for reported findings that cannot be ruled out. Although these studies are of limited use for confirmatory analyses, they are, nevertheless, of heuristic value.

Following a descriptive review of studies exploring the psychophysiology of client–therapist dyads and of married couples, we will turn to a more detailed discussion of methodological issues in the study of the psychophysiology of dyadic interaction. We will then discuss three social psychophysiological mechanisms that may contribute to a better understanding of the processes and outcomes of salient interpersonal encounters. Finally, we will offer a more speculative account of how physiological reactions to social interaction taking place in the here-and-now may affect our well-being over time.

THE PSYCHOPHYSIOLOGY OF SOCIAL EXCHANGE

CLIENT–THERAPIST DYADS

Stimulated by the prospects of enhancing understanding of the psychotherapy interview, the study of physiological processes during dyadic interaction had its start in the analysis of client–therapist pairs. In one of the first such studies, DiMascio, Boyd, and Greenblatt (1957) observed a single patient–therapist pair and categorized the social exchange process using Bales's (1950) Interaction Process Analysis (IPA). Their findings revealed strong correlations between the patient's expression of tension (e.g. impatience, nervous habits, anxious emotionality, demonstrations of shame or guilt, signs of frustration) and his own heart rate ($r = 0.69$) as well as the therapist's heart rate ($r = 0.52$). The patient's expression of antagonism (e.g. commands, attempts control, dominates the conversation, appears irritable) was associated with a decrease in the patient's heart rate ($r = -0.37$) but an increase in the therapist's ($r = 0.54$). The patient's expression of tension release (e.g. a show of cheerfulness, laughing, or joking) was also associated with a reduction in heart rate ($r = -0.58$). The magnitude of the r's is noteworthy since they are heteromethod correlations and thus are not high simply as a result of shared method variance. From this early study, we can begin to entertain the hypothesis that interactional receipt of messages characterized by negative emotions, such as anxiety or impatience (Bales's 'tension') or by angry attempts to influence or control the conversation (Bales's 'antagonism'), will lead to increased heart rate in the listener, and that at least some expressive behaviors (e.g. Bales's 'antagonism') appear to be associated with a decrease in heart rate in the speaker.

In another study of psychiatric patients, Malmo, Boag, and Smith (1957) monitored speech-muscle tension and heart rate while patients responded to a series of TAT cards under conditions of praise or criticism. As a group, those praised for their stories showed a drop in speech-muscle tension in the 15 seconds immediately following the examiner's praise, whereas those subjects who were criticized showed a slight increase in speech-muscle tension during the last 5 seconds. Malmo *et al.* also examined the degree of variation among patients in each of the two conditions, praise and criticism, and found a great deal of consistency in the responses of patients to criticism and intersubject variability among patients receiving praise. These authors concluded: '[T]here may be greater person-to-person uniformity in tensional reaction to criticism than in reaction to praise.... [*W*]*e may expect criticism to have a homogenizing effect on a group of individuals*' (pp. 117–18, italics added).

Therapists' criticism or confrontation of their clients was also found to be associated with higher skin resistance response (SRR) amplitude in both clients and therapists (McCarron and Appel, 1971). Therapists' reflections (e.g. 'Hm-mm') produced the lowest SRR amplitudes whereas therapists' interpretations (e.g. 'You wanted to be treated like a child') and interrogations (e.g. 'How do you feel about that?') were associated with moderate amplitude SRRs in clients and therapists. Thus, the receipt of criticism, conflict, or confrontations expressed in client–therapist dyads has been found to be associated with greater autonomic reactivity, whereas the sending of these messages has been found to be associated with both increases and decreases of autonomic activation (e.g. increased SSR amplitude in McCarron and Appel, 1971, and decreased heart rate in DiMascio *et al.*, 1957).

Lacey (1959) has provided an incisive review of the literature on the relation between somatic activity and interpersonal behavior in client–therapist dyads (e.g. Anderson, 1956; Auld, Dreyer, and Dollard, 1958; Dittes, 1957 a, b). In an elegant commentary on issues that must be considered in reaching correct interpretations of these data, he argues for a *transactional* study of the relation between somatic activity and behavior. A transactional approach recognizes that therapist's and client's thoughts, feelings, and behaviors are interactive and influenced by situational contexts. Therefore, we should be reasonably cautious in inferring the internal state of client or therapist or inferring underlying interactional processes from a single physiological indicator obtained in a single interactional context.

For example, Dittes (1957b) found an association between a client's electrodermal activity (frequency of skin conductance responses) and 'embarrassing sex statements.' This association was observed only when the therapist was independently rated as low in 'permissiveness and gentleness' and not when the therapist was rated high in permissiveness. It would thus be misleading to conclude that the client's electrodermal reactivity was a direct measure of the client's difficulty dealing with sexual themes; the relation was observed only within the confines of a specific interactional context.

These findings are also of interest because they suggest the importance of interpersonal tension/conflict (i.e. low permissiveness and low gentleness) in potentiating somatic response to emotionally significant stimuli. In fact, a different physiological pattern may emerge in response to the same stimulus as a function of the context in which the stimulus is embedded (cf. Gage and Safer, 1985). For example, a spouse presenting a relationship issue to a partner who is acting as a negative listener (e.g. a listener who is nonattentive) may exhibit a very different physiological response pattern than a spouse who presents a similar gripe to a partner who is listening attentively. We will return to this point and other details of Lacey's commentary in a later section of the chapter. First we consider another interpersonal context quite different from client–therapist dyads: interactions between marriage partners.

HUSBANDS AND WIVES

Marriage is certainly a potent interpersonal context and interaction between spouses can be expected to be accompanied by significant psychophysiological reactions. Marital interaction might be construed as an exemplary experimental situation for the analysis of human emotion as it involves naturally provocative interpersonal stimuli that are highly salient to participants. Pursuing this line of reasoning, Ewart, Taylor, Kraemer, and Agras (1984) were concerned with the effects of marital conflict on blood pressure control in a group of patients with diagnosed essential hypertension. Specifically, Ewart *et al.* investigated the extent to which communication skills training was associated with reduced blood pressure reactivity during discussion of a marital conflict. Twenty hypertensive patients (seven males and 13 females) and their partners were assigned randomly either to a communication skill training group or to an assessment-only control group. All couples were nondistressed. The intervention consisted of nine sessions over a six-week period. Blood pressure was measured pre- and post-intervention and the characteristics of, and changes in, marital communication were assessed by observers' coding of two 10-minute conflict discussions using the Marital Interaction Coding System (MICS), (Hops, Wills, Patterson, and Weiss, 1972; Weiss and Summers, 1983). On the basis of our review thus far, we might expect blood pressure decreases to be related to a decrease in the level of hostile, angry, negative exchanges.

Ewart *et al.* reported that couples exposed to the nine-session communication skills training intervention showed a significant decrease in the frequency of negative comments exchanged, whereas control couples exhibited an increase in negative comments. These communication changes were associated with significantly less systolic reactivity (a change of -8.8 mmHg) during problem-solving among hypertensive patients and their spouses; the control group displayed a smaller change in systolic reactivity (-3.5 mmHg). Note should be taken of the fact that systolic reactivity was less in both groups at post-test despite the fact that negative communication had increased among control group couples; thus, we must be cautious in inferring a causal relation between systolic reactivity and negative communication. It should also be carefully noted that the percentage of positive codes did not increase following the therapy. This suggests that the presence (or absence) of negative behaviors may be most influential in determining interactional outcomes.

In a technologically sophisticated series of studies, Levenson and Gottman (1983, 1985) studied 30 married couples. The couples came to the laboratory after having spent the day apart. The time apart was designed to increase the likelihood of conversation between the partners. On arrival the couples were provided with an overview of the procedure and introduced to recording devices to monitor heart rate (interbeat interval, IBI), the time interval between the R wave of the EKG and the arrival of the pulse pressure wave at the middle finger of the nondominant hand [pulse transit time (PTT) or what Obrist (1981) has called the R wave to pulse wave interval (RPI)], skin conductance level (SCL), and general somatic activity (ACT). This was the first interactional study to sample a broad range of physiological response systems; Levenson and Gottman noted that their intent was to sample functions of the heart, vasculature, sweat glands, and muscles.

Couples were led through the following series of tasks: a 5 minute quiet period that served as a preinteraction baseline, a 15-minute conversation in which spouses were 'to share the day as if they were home alone at day's end', a 20-minute period of questionnaires and discussion with the experimenter to identify a salient problem facing the couple, a second 5-minute quiet period, and another 15-minute conversation during which the couple attempted to reach a compromise or solution to the salient problem identified after the 'events of the day' discussion. Spouses returned individually to the laboratory within 2–3 days for a 'video-recall' session. During this session, husband or wife viewed a videotape of the couple's two 15-minute conversations and continually provided ratings of how positive or negative he or she felt by turning a dial labeled 'very negative' at 0° to 'neutral' at 90° to 'very positive' at 180°. The self-report affect ratings were sampled on-line every 5 mseconds and averaged into 10-second measurement epochs.

The physiological data were analyzed to assess the degree of coherence between husband and wife at each point in the paradigm. Physiological patterning between members of a group had been used previously as the primary dependent variable in a study of the relations between sociometric liking or disliking among group members, physiological responses of group members, and group process (Kaplan, Burch, and Bloom, 1964). Kaplan *et al.* found that pairs of students who did not like each other were more likely to display physiological covariation than were pairs of students who either liked each other or who felt neither liking nor disliking for each other. These results are somewhat limited in that the data analysis did not account for the influence of subjects' own physiological response pattern on the degree of covariation observed between pairs (i.e. the problem of autocorrelation was not addressed). Nevertheless, on the basis of these findings and the consistently observed tendency for distressed couples to display greater negative affect and negative affect reciprocity than nondistressed couples (Gottman, 1979; Gottman,

Markman, and Notarius, 1977; Margolin and Wampold, 1981; Notarius, Markman, and Gottman, 1983), Levenson and Gottman hypothesized a positive correlation between marital dissatisfaction and physiological covariation between spouses.

During the discussion of a relationship problem, but not during the events of the day discussion, the hypothesis was confirmed. Measures of covariation between husband and wife across the four response systems monitored (IBI, PTT, SCL, and ACT) assessed during the problem discussion, and controlled for autocorrelation, had a multiple r with the couple's average marital satisfaction score of 0.77. Levenson and Gottman concluded: '[M]easures of physiological linkage during the problem-area segment were able to account for 60% of the variance in marital satisfaction' (p. 593).

As Levenson and Gottman pointed out, the covariation between husband's and wife's physiological measures was independent of both self-reported affect and physiological measures in the individual partners. Thus, unique information was provided by the degree of physiological patterning present between husband and wife that was not related to the spouses' individual response patterns or to their ongoing affective evaluations of the interaction. It would be interesting to assess whether or not physiological covariation between spouses was related to observers' coding of the marital conversations. If such a relation were confirmed, it would suggest (a) that behavioral exchange, more than subjective perception of this exchange, was affecting the spouses and (b) that cognitive filters (Gottman, Notarius, Gonso, and Markman, 1976) were shaping the self-reported affect ratings and unlatching these from physiological covariation. In any event, the presence of negative behaviors appears to have the 'homogenizing' effect upon a couple that Malmo *et al.* (1957) speculated would befall a group when confronted with criticism.

PHYSIOLOGICAL PREDICTORS OF CHANGE IN MARITAL SATISFACTION

The role of physiological covariation as a marker of dyadic functioning must be carefully interpreted in the light of results from a second study reported by Levenson and Gottman (1985). Nineteen of the 30 couples who served as subjects in the earlier study were contacted 3 years later and indicated their current level of marital satisfaction. The objective of the study was to predict change in marital satisfaction over the 3-year period since the first study. Husbands' and wives' physiological indicators of arousal at time 1 were found to predict change in marital satisfaction over the 3 years, while degree of physiological covariation between spouses at time 1 failed at such prediction. In general, husband's heart rate, pulse transit time, and skin conductance; and wife's skin conductance monitored over the entire paradigm, were predictive of a change in the couple's level of marital satisfaction. For example, change in the couple's relationship satisfaction was correlated with the husband's heart rate at time 1 measured during the 5-minute resting period prior to beginning a conversation to resolve a relevant relationship issue $(r = 0.92)$. Change in the couple's relationship satisfaction also correlated with the husband's heart rate during the conversation that immediately followed $(r = 0.92$, the shorter the interval between heart beats, the greater was the decline in the couple's marital satisfaction over the 3-year period). Wife's skin conductance level (but not heart rate) showed a similar pattern. For example, change in the couple's relationship satisfaction was correlated with the wife's skin conductance level both prior to discussing a salient relationship issue $(r = -0.58$, the higher her SCL, the greater the decline in the couple's relationship satisfaction) and during the discussion of that issue $(r = -0.76)$.

Equally striking were the correlations between the two partners' affect ratings and change in the wife's (but not the husband's) material satisfaction over the 3-year period. For example, the likelihood of the wife reciprocating her husband's negative affect within 20 seconds at time 1 was strongly correlated $(r = -0.96)$ with a decline in her marital satisfaction from time 1 to time 2. Thus, self-ratings of affect and measures indicative of physiological arousal, but not of physiological covariation, were found to be related to an important relationship variable, change in marital satisfaction over a 3-year period.

It is not immediately apparent why physiological covariation would predict current marital satisfaction but not change in marital satisfaction during the next 3 years, and why measures associated with sympathetic arousal would predict change in marital satisfaction but be less related to current levels of satisfaction. At a minimum, this is a good example of the specificity of finding that will ultimately need to be accounted for if we are to build a theory able to account for the relations between an interactant's physiological reactivity and relevant interpersonal behavior or outcomes.

COMMENTARY

We have kept methodological and conceptual critique to a minimum in the above review so as to maintain a focus upon the relations among social exchange processes and psychophysiological reactivity. Our presentation strategy was not intended to minimize the considerable issues that confront the researcher. These issues will now be discussed. Reflecting on the complexities involved in researching the psychophysiology of psychotherapy interviews, Lang (1971) pessimistically concluded: '[T]he best context in which to study the physiology of emotional charge is *not* the relatively free-swinging, two person interaction, which is the format of classical psychotherapies . . . [F]or the time being, the interview is a bad testing ground, even for hypotheses relevant to interview behavior' (Lang, 1971, p. 112). The spirit of Lang's critique would apply equally to the study of dyads other than client–therapist pairs.

Is such pessimism still warranted? To answer this question we must consider some challenging issues inherent in the study of both physiological activity and interactional processes. First consider the measurement of somatic activity. We will not attempt a complete review of physiological principles relevant to the study of interactional process; reviews are available in Cacioppo and Petty (1983), Greenfield and Sternbach (1972), Grings and Dawson (1978), Hassett (1979), and Martin and Venables (1980). Instead we will highlight a critical issue: the validity of the arousal construct.

As previously mentioned, most researchers have appeared to base their choice of measures to index somatic reactivity upon convenience rather than a sound conceptual rationale. This state of affairs would be far less of an issue if various measures of physiological activity were correlated with each other. This is most definitely not the case (see, e.g. Lacey, 1967). Despite the widespread use of 'arousal' as a construct implying a uniform activation of the autonomic nervous system, the empirical data simply do not support such a conceptualization. Instead, several processes appear to interact and to produce quite specific individual response patterns.

These processes include *individual response stereotypy*—the tendency for individuals to show characteristic response patterns to various stressors; and *stimulus–response stereotypy*—the tendency for a given stimulus to evoke a common response pattern across subjects. Three types of stimulus–response stereotypy can be further specified: (1) directional fractionation—the tendency for two or more physiological systems to be inversely related; (2) orienting reactions—the body's physiological preparation to deal with a novel or unexpected stimulus; and (3) defensive reactions—the body's preparation to deal with an intense stimulus (Grings and Dawson, 1978; Hassett, 1978; Sternbach, 1966). These processes are not mutually exclusive and both individual and stimulus–response stereotypies may be operating simultaneously in certain situations (Engel, 1960).

On the basis of the empirical data we must reject the assumption of generalized arousal represented by correlated activity between and within indices of the central nervous system, the autonomic nervous system, the musculature or somatic system, and the self as accessed by self-report. It is more appropriate to consider specific activation patterns within particular response systems, to explore the relations between measures that are observed, and to devote our attention to valid interpretation of the observed pattern. Accepting this approach, a researcher would want to avoid *post-hoc* focus on one of three physiological measures (e.g. skin conductance response, heart rate, and systolic blood pressure) included in a study to measure 'arousal' and then claim that there were 'problems' with the other two measures. It would be most advantageous to predict, *a priori*, which physiological measure can be expected to show activation in a given paradigm, articulate the underlying mechanism responsible for such activation, and incorporate measures to demonstrate differential responding (i.e. to establish discriminant validity). Although this is an ideal goal, the current state of knowledge may not often allow these conditions to be met. In such cases, the researchers ought to be cautious about interpretations of the data and may wish to pursue replication of significant findings in order to enhance confidence in the reliability of findings that were not expected on an *a priori* basis.

The approach suggested above is of course compatible with the expectation of a more generalized arousal pattern in certain situations. When a potent stimulus elicits a 'fight or flight' response from a subject, we would expect to see a pattern of physiological activation orchestrated by the adrenergic system that includes, in part, shunting of the blood away from the skin surface and toward the muscles and organs, increased heart rate and contractile force, increased electrodermal activity, and dilation of the pupils. Under such circumstances, we could thus predict covariation among specific responses and we could point to the underlying mechanism responsible for the observed pattern of physiological reactivity. In analyzing data gathered in a situation expected to produce this level of response, the researcher might use a multivariate approach to capture and to assess appropriately the degree of relations that exist in the observed reactivity pattern among the measured responses.

The analysis of social interaction presents no less a challenge than does the measurement of phasic physiological responses. Just as researchers have appeared to choose a measure of physiological reactivity with little rationale, so too have they loosely chosen the interactional paradigm. Researchers have examined clients' reactions to TAT cards (e.g. Malmo *et al.*, 1957; Weiner, Singer, and Reiser, 1962), naturally occurring psychotherapy sessions (e.g. DiMascio, Boyd, Greenblatt, and Solomar 1955; DiMascio *et al.*, 1957), and stressful interviews (e.g. Davis and Malmo, 1951). Other paradigms have included group discussions with participants holding different degrees of liking toward other group members (Kaplan *et al.*, 1964), making perceptual judgements with structured feedback in the context of a group of friends or a group of strangers (Bogdonoff, Klein, Back, Nichols, Troyer, and Hood, 1964), and more ecologically valid, problem-solving conversations between marriage partners (Levenson and Gottman, 1983, 1985; Notarius and Johnson, 1982). Each situation is likely to place different demands upon participants and to elicit different response patterns. For example, social exchange between intimates who bring a relationship history with them into the laboratory can be expected to involve a different set of interactional behaviors [e.g. married partners relate differently to strangers than to their mate (Birchler, Weiss, and Vincent, 1975; Noller, 1984)], and to involve characteristic emotional and perceptual processes [e.g. causal attributions (Baucom, 1987)] than will interaction among strangers. Generalizing results from one situation to another when both physiological response and interactional setting are not comparable is problematic.

The variety of interactional settings studied can be attributed to a lack of knowledge concerning core interactional processes that characterize a dyad. Without systematic knowledge of conversational behaviors that distinguish between well-functioning, happy dyads and maladjusted, dissatisfied dyads, the investigator is left (a) to select behaviors of interest that may or may not have any relation to meaningful criteria, (b) to examine a broad array of behaviors, the breadth of which will create an enormous data analytic challenge, or (c) to risk analysis of behaviors that have little generalizability or are not comparable to other investigator's findings.

One reasonable solution to this issue might be to categorize dyadic interaction into dimensions proposed for the study of small groups. For example, Bales's (1950, 1970) *Interaction Process Analysis* codes social interaction into two major dimensions: instrumental and expressive. The instrumental dimension is further divided into questions and answers, and the expressive dimension is divided into positive and negative. Within each subcategory, three specific behaviors are coded. An alternative framework is provided by Kemper (1984) who hypothesized that social relationships can be placed into a two-dimensional space composed of *power*, having influence upon others when others are not compliant, and *status*, having influence upon others when others are compliant. Power refers to interactional behaviors that carry a negative valence and status to interactional events that are positively valenced. Markman and Notarius (1987) have reviewed the field of marital and family interaction and have noted that researchers have defined six primary dimensions of marital/family interaction: dominance or power, affect, communication clarity, information exchange, conflict, and support/validation. Each of these core interactional behaviors might be hypothesized to influence, and to be influenced by, the ongoing somatic reactions of the interactants.

The reliable categorization of behavior is an important first step to the extent that it results in an accurate descriptive account of the interaction *process*. However, early studies of functional and dysfunctional groups or families often did not result in clear group differences (see e.g. Jacob, 1975). Given such findings one could question the validity of the observational data or that of the theory arguing for the importance of interactional behavior. A third possibility is that the data analytic procedures were an inadequate and weak tool for detecting group differences. Until recently, interactional data were most frequently summarized as relative frequencies of code occurrences, thus ignoring the dimensions of time and sequence as essential characteristics of the communication process. Comparing the frequencies of happy and unhappy husbands' 'problem talk,' for example, may be informative but we would submit that it is not as meaningful as comparing the likelihood of a wife responding to her husband's 'problem talk' with an 'agreement' rather than a 'disagreement'. Or, to extend the process, frequency data are not likely to be as meaningful as comparing the husband's behavior following *both* his earlier 'problem talk' *and* his wife's subsequent 'disagreement.' Does he continue a cycle of negative exchange by offering another disagreement? Does he break the cycle of negative exchange by validating his wife's perspective? Or does he escalate the conflict by offering a harsh criticism of his mother-in-law?

Data analytic strategies that capture the sequential dependencies characterizing the structure of social exchange are now available (Allison and Liker, 1981; Gottman, 1979; Wampold and Margolin, 1982). Such an analysis revealed, for example, that distressed wives were approximately nine times as likely to respond negatively to their husbands' negative messages(i.e. to show negative reciprocity) than were nondistressed wives. No differences were observed among the responses of distressed and nondistressed husbands to their wives' negative messages (Notarius, Benson, Sloane, Vanzetti, and Hornyak, in press). Over the course of a conversation, these probabilistic differences will leave the interaction between distressed spouses in a state of negative exchange and will foster a break in reciprocal negative exchange between nondistressed spouses [see Raush (1972) for an extended illustration of this point]. We believe that these techniques greatly enhance our ability to discriminate functional interactional behaviors (e.g. those interactional processes characterizing a couple who report mutual satisfaction) from dysfunctional interactional behaviors (e.g. those processes characterizing a couple who are dissatisfied).

With the identification of critical interactional patterns that discriminate between functional and dysfunctional dyads the investigator can examine specific psychophysiological processes that might underlie or be associated with observed behavioral differences. One of the most consistent characteristics of interaction within distressed couples is the reciprocation of negative affect (Gottman *et al.*, 1977; Gottman, 1979; Hahlweg, Reisner, Kohli, Vollmer, Schindler, and Revenstorf, 1984; Morgolin and Wampold, 1981; Schaap, 1982). The presence of negative affect cycles appears to be more central to distress than does the presence or absence of positive affect exchange (Mettetal and Gottman, 1980; Gottman *et al.*, 1976). Assuming that negative affect reciprocity is the critical feature of distressed marital interaction, we wish to inquire about basic social psychophysiological processes that might contribute to a greater understanding of the behavioral manifestation of latched negative exchange between spouses. Since the negative exchange will contain high rates of disagreement and criticism, we can expect, on the basis of the data reviewed above, that these interpersonal messages will be associated with autonomic reactivity.

APPLYING SOCIAL PSYCHOPHYSIOLOGY TO THE STUDY OF SOCIAL INTERACTION

In this section of the chapter, we hope to illustrate the potential utility of studying dyadic interaction from a social psychophysiological perspective. We will consider three relevant relationship processes: (1) affective exchange, (2) relational efficacy, and (3) listener responses to a distressed other. We hope to demonstrate that social psychophysiological analyses can contribute to a better understanding of both the processes and the outcomes of specific interactional episodes that previous research has suggested to be important.

AFFECTIVE EXCHANGE AND EMOTIONAL DISCHARGE

A discharge model of emotion predicts an inverse relationship between overt emotional expression and somatic reactivity in the face of a stressor (see Buck, 1980). Support for this model has been based on laboratory studies in which a stressor is presented to subjects while some measure of facial expressivity is compared with some measure of autonomic activity. The stressors studied have included exposure to emotionally arousing 35 mm slides (Buck, Miller, and Caul, 1974), the threat of electric shock (Notarius and Levenson, 1979), and an interpersonal reprimand (Notarius, Wemple, Ingraham, Burns, and Kollar, 1982). Although support for the discharge model is mixed (Buck, 1984; Frijda, 1986), it appears most likely to operate in naturalistic situations wherein subjects have access to their natural expressive repertoires, have an incentive to control overt displays, and have not been exposed to a stimulus sufficiently powerful to align overt display and physiological response in most persons (e.g. the sudden appearance of a pedestrian while driving, requiring immediate action to avoid an accident). Thus, a discharge model of emotion may be most relevant in interpersonal situations that are engaging to all participants and in which each interactant has a personal investment; problem discussions with a spouse exemplify such a setting.

Notarius and Johnson (1982) studies the relation between skin potential responses and affective exchange in six couples while the spouses were engaged in a problem-solving discussion. They found that wives were more overtly expressive and had fewer skin potential responses than did husbands. Husbands also displayed more skin potential responses when stoically receiving their wives negative message than did wives in the same situation. The effect of this interpersonal process upon dyadic interaction might be quite significant. As a husband receives an emotionally provocative message from his wife, he appears to be more likely to experience greater physiological reactivity and more likely to inhibit emotional display. A wife is likely to read her husband's lack of overt emotional response as disinterest, nonattending, unresponsiveness, or all of these and is likely to escalate her affective display to solicit a response from him. Nonresponsiveness from an intimate appears to be an evocative interpersonal stimulus. As she escalates her emotional display, the husband's somatic response is likely to be enhanced and, in a nice illustration of a positive feeback loop, husband and wife systematically produce in each other the behaviors that they would most like to avoid (cf. Levenson and Gottman, 1983).

It is important to note the limitations of Notarius and Johnson's study. Only one measure of sympathetic activity was monitored and quantification procedures were crude. It would have been desirable to monitor several indices of physiological reactivity and to monitor gross body movement (to assess the extent to which physical movement was correlated with reactivity measures). With technological advances reducing the cost of monitoring and data processing equipment, and with greater conceptual understanding of the issues involved, the hypotheses generated by studies such as Notarius and Johnson's might be more appropriately evaluated.

RELATIONAL EFFICACY AND PHYSIOLOGICAL REACTIVITY

The second mechanism we wish to consider is relational efficacy (Doherty, 1981a, b; Notarius and Vanzetti, 1983; Weiss, 1981). Relational efficacy concerns the couple's expectancy that they will be able to resolve salient relationship problems. It has been operationalized by asking spouses to indicate 'Out of every 10 disagreements arising in each of the marital problem areas listed, how many do believe you and your spouse resolve to your mutual satisfaction' (the questionnaire lists ten areas such as money, communication, sex, in-laws; Notarius and Vanzetti, 1983). The relational efficacy construct is based on Bandura's (1977) self-efficacy theory. The theory predicts that efficacy expectancies are powerful predictors of coping behavior, determine how much effort people will expend to accomplish an objective, influence the subjective impact of negative outcomes, and contribute to the level of physiological arousal experienced in response to a stressor. The latter point is of obvious importance to the theme of this chapter. Bandura (1982) reported that individuals with low efficacy expectancies displayed higher heart rates when confronted with a feared stimulus than did individuals with high efficacy.

In an ongoing relationship, we would, therefore, expect that partners who have little belief in their ability to resolve a *particular* relationship disagreement (i.e. they have low relational efficacy is that particular area of their relationship), would begin the conversation with greater somatic reactivity than would spouses who believed themselves able to resolve their disagreement. Further, we would suggest that low relational efficacy would be associated with greater physiological reactivity during the conversation. Hence, low relational efficacy may contribute to an intrapersonal climate in which interactants are primed for somatic reactivity. To the extent that somatic reactivity is associated with dysfunctional interactional behaviors, this climate will contribute to interpersonal conflict.

The promise of this conceptualization is contained in the results reported by Levenson and Gottman (1983) and summarized above. After spouses spent 8 hours apart from each other, they met in a laboratory and were instructed that they would be having a conversation with their partner. They first sat quietly together without interacting so that 'baseline' physiological measures could be recorded from each spouse. We believe this to be a splendid paradigm for examining relational efficacy. Assuming that spouses differed in relational efficacy for the pending discussion, we would expect variability among spouses in their resting levels of somatic activity. Furthermore, we would predict that relational efficacy would be correlated with both somatic reactivity and social exchange. Levenson and Gottman (1985) reported that couples who were most physiologically aroused in this baseline period experienced that greatest decline in marital satisfaction over the ensuing 3 years. Although relational efficacy was not assessed in this study, the pattern of findings is consistent with predictions deriving from efficacy theory and suggests the potential utility of this cognitive construct in further study of the physiology of dyadic interaction.

EMPATHY AND THE MOTIVATION TO HELP A DISTRESSED OTHER

The third mechanism is admittedly more speculative. In accord with an interactional model of depression (Coyne, 1976a), conversation with a depressed individual is found to leave a listener more depressed than when he or she started the conversation and sufficiently irritated with the depressed person that the listener would not welcome further interaction with the distressed other (Coyne, 1976b; Strack and Coyne, 1983). Notarius and Herrick (1988) reasoned that the listener's reactions might in part be mediated by the response strategies he or she chooses for dealing with the dysphoric talker. A listener has a range of response strategies available including trying to cheer the person up, trying to solve current problem(s), trying to sustain the conversation with distracting chit-chat, sharing personal experiences related to the talker's concern, or attending to the talker's feelings and trying to provide affective validation. Studies on informal helping have found that people in distress tend to find listeners more 'helpful' when the listener allows the talker an 'opportunity to ventilate' than when advice is given (Lehman, Ellard, and Wortman, 1986). There is also evidence that help-seekers talk longer to listeners who respond with empathy than they do to those who offer suggestions (D'Augelli *et al.*, 1978; Ehrlich, D'Augelli, and Danish, 1979). We found that strategies aimed at affective validation and encouragement to ventilate feelings were associated with the best outcomes for listener (i.e. no feeling of depression or rejection for the talker) and, though not assessed in this study, we would expect these strategies to be associated with the best outcomes for the talker as well.

It is perhaps not surprising that affective validation is an effective strategy for listening to a troubled other (Gottman *et al.*, 1976). What is surprising is that this response tends to be rather low in the hierarchy of response alternatives many of us have in this interpersonal situation. Among couples, affective validation is characteristic of nondistressed couples (Gottman *et al.*, 1977) and in our study of female undergraduates it was characteristic of only 13 out of 30 subjects. A social psychophysiological analysis of empathic motivation of helping behavior suggests one possible reason for this state of affairs.

Batson and Coke (1983) have presented a two-stage model of empathic mediation of helping behaviors. An empathic response is defined as an emotional response that is congruent, cognitively, and physiologically, to the emotional response of another. The model predicts that taking a distressed other's perspective leads to an increase in one's own empathic response and subsequently to an increase in motivation to help another deal with the problem situation. Empirical support for the model comes primarily from observation of strangers in laboratory analogues of helping and not from study of people who know each other, even as acquaintances.

Consider now the task confronting an individual when he or she is confronted with a distressed friend. As a friend discusses his or her difficulties or concerns, empathic listeners are able to take the perspective of the other; to place themselves in the other's shoes. To the extent that they are able to see the world as the other does, these listeners will experience an emotional response (composed of motoric, physiologic, and cognitive elements) congruent with the friend's situation. And these empathic listeners will consequently be motivated to help reduce their friend's distress.

Some of these listeners will try to help by attempting to solve the friend's problem or by attempting to cheer up the friend. However, many personal concerns have no clear solutions, and individuals in distress often are not ready for, or desirous of, cheering. A study on social support encounters between friends that we are completing provides interesting anecdotal evidence on this point. For example, negative reactions of talkers paired with 'problem-solvers' suggest that the feelings of sadness and pain that come after a break-up with a lover cannot easily be dispelled with advice. Instead, concerns such as this one often require no more than repeated discussion and an opportunity to sort out one's thoughts and feelings.

In fact, we would argue that receipt of problem-solving suggestions when affective validation is sought will be experienced as disagreement and, as Gormly's research suggests (Baugher and Gormly, 1975; Gormly, 1974), the disagreement will be autonomically arousing for the distressed talker. Thus we hypothesize that the offering of solutions when affective validation would be most helpful is likely to leave the distressed person feeling unattended to and in a state of somatic arousal and also to leave the empathic listener aroused because their motivation to help has not had an adequate outlet or because their attempt to help has not met with success. Furthermore, the interrelation of somatic response and social exchange may serve to drive a negative affect cycle between helper and helpee.

Over time this interpersonal process, rooted in the empathic response of the listener, and his or her consequent desire to help the distressed other deal with a current concern, may leave both interactants feeling frustrated and somatically aroused. Predictions stemming from this scenario could easily be tested. A functional listener response requires the listener to deal with his or her own somatic activation (associated with an empathic response) and to attend to and validate the talker's affect. This model suggests that an empathic listener who is *effective* in communicating support to a distressed other may retire from a helping conversation with a residue of physiological activation (the specificity of which is unknown) stemming from the experience of an empathic response that has no convenient outlet. The specific topography of the physiological reactivity will most likely reflect person factors (e.g. cognitive expectancies, individual physiological response patterns), situational factors (e.g. the tendency for a given situation to produce similar physiological response patterns across individuals), or person-by-situation factors (e.g. a type-A individual confronted with what is perceived as an unreasonable request). We do not wish to push this discussion much futher, for it already greatly outsteps the data. Nevertheless, it does seem to illustrate the potential of carrying social psychophysiological methods and theories into the analysis of relevant relationship encounters in order to understand better both the process and the outcomes of specific interactional episodes.

IMPLICATIONS FOR WELL-BEING

Thus far, our discussion has been focused on specific interactional exchanges and their physiological concomitants during brief periods of time: during a marital problem-solving session, for example, or a psychotherapy interview. We now wish to expand our view and ask: 'Are there broader implications for interactants' well-being that may stem from the association between interactional behaviors and psychophysiological responses that occurs during specific encounters?' We believe the answer is 'yes'. If a *dysfunctional* pattern of interaction and associated physiological responses recur because of interactional deficits in a given individual, long-term effects on that individual's social life and physical health may become apparent.

Studies of the role of social support in health suggest that the lack of an intimate, confiding relationship, and the possessing of relationships that are low in empathy, reciprocity and closeness can (1) place one at risk for a variety of physical symptoms, (2) increase one's risk of mortality, and (3) slow the rate of one's recovery from illness and injury. For example, subjects who lack an intimate confident tend to report more physical symptoms like breathlessness and palpitations on a symptom checklist than do those who have such a relationship (Miller and Ingham, 1976). Relationships within one's family seem particularly important. For example, Edelstein and Linn (1985) found that, among a sample of diabetic men, those with better metabolic control of their disease perceived their families as lower in conflict than did those patients with poorer control. Focusing only on the marital relationship, Medalie and Goldbourt (1986) demonstrated that among highly anxious men, those who perceived their wives as supportive had a lower incidence of angina pectoris than did those men whose wives were viewed as less supportive. Greater intimacy with one's friends and family may lead to longer survival if one has cancer (Weisman and Worden, 1975), while among stroke victims, the rate of physical progress in rehabilitation may be improved if there is a higher level of empathy between the patient and a significant member of the patient's family (Robertson and Suinn, 1968). Presumably these associations reflect subtle psychophysiological processes occurring during the daily transactions that constitute family life.

Intimacy and empathic understanding seem to be two of the most important components of the kind of relationship that successfully provides a sense of support to the individuals involved. Having an opportunity to ventilate one's feelings and to confide in others may be one essential characteristic of interactions that leave individuals feeling supported. When friends provided bereaved subjects an opportunity to ventilate (or express openly) their feelings, the bereaved felt more strongly supported than when friends offered them other responses (e.g. advice) (Lehman *et al.*, 1986). Furthermore, confiding in others has been linked to lower rates of physical illness among the bereaved. Spouses of suicide and accidental-death victims who talked about the death with close friends reported significantly fewer health problems a year after the death than did spouses who did not confide in others (Pennebaker and O'Heeron, 1984).

Other studies (cited by Pennebaker and O'Heeron, 1984) have also suggested that people who deny or repress their thoughts and feelings have poorer health. 'Repressors (i.e. nonconfiders) demonstrate higher cancer rates (Kissen, 1966), mortality rates following breast cancer diagnosis (Derogatis, Abeloff, and Melisaratos, 1979), blood pressure (Davies, 1970) and physical disease rates in general (Blackburn, 1965)' (p. 473). In laboratory settings, repressors exhibited higher blood pressure, skin conductance, and forehead muscle tension when undergoing a psychologically stressful task than did non-repressors (Weinberger, Schwartz, and Davidson, 1979). In other laboratory settings (e.g. threat of shock, an interpersonal reprimand) nonexpressive subjects exhibited higher cardio-vascular responses (Notarius and Levenson, 1979; Notarius *et al.*, 1982) than did expressive subjects.

Recalling the empathic listening studies reviewed above, it appears that open and easy communication (e.g. the exchange of confidences) plays an essential role in keeping an individual physically, as well as emotionally, healthy. As Pennebaker and O'Heeron (1984) have noted: 'Over time, the physiological work of not confiding (i.e. behavioral inhibition) and of ruminating place cumulative stress on the body—thus increasing the long-term probability of stress-related disease' (p. 476). We suspect that not confiding is strongly associated with dysfunctional interactional encounters wherein individuals are themselves nonexpressive or have the misfortune of trying to elicit support from an unskilled, unhelpful listener. As the individual experiences repeated incidents of dysfunctional communication in interactions with others, the body may become increasingly vulnerable. Recently, a mechanism has been suggested to explain this process of evolving vulnerability.

PSYCHOSOCIAL FACTORS AND IMMUNOCOMPETENCE

Kiecolt–Glaser and her colleagues (Kiecolt–Glaser, Fisher, Ogrocki, Stout, Speicher, and Glaser, 1987) have reported that marital disruption (separation and divorce) and poorer marital quality were found to be associated with greater depression, and with poorer functioning of the spouses' immune systems. Marital distress was strongly and positively related to poorer cellular immune system control of virus latency. Among separated or divorced women, time since separation and feelings of attachment to the (ex)spouse were inversely related to depression, distress, and the competence of several immune functions. The more recent the separation and the stronger the woman's feelings of attachment (assessed via scores on the Attachment Scale; Kitson, 1982), the weaker was her defense against bacterial and viral infection. When the separated/divorced women were compared with a sample of married women, the latter were found to have significantly stronger immune functions assessed by a number of measures. Married women had higher percentages of helper T lymphocytes (which stimulate antibodies that ward off infection), while separated/divorced women had lower percentages of natural killer cells (which provide antiviral and antitumor defense) and weaker control of virus latency (specifically, antibody titers to latent Epstein–Barr virus).

Drawing a firm conclusion that marital distress or dissolution places spouses at risk for serious disease would be premature. Laudenslager and Reite (1984) point out that the immune system has numerous back-up mechanisms, so that a defect in any single measure of immunity does not necessarily mean that the organism is at risk. In this connection it is worth noting that the research conducted by Kiecolt–Glaser and her colleagues used a variety of methods to tap immune function and assessed a variety of immune responses. However, the findings on marital quality and separation included some inconsistencies (e.g. there were *no* significant differences between married and separated/divorced women in percentage of suppressor T lymphocytes or in the helper–suppressor ratio although differences in other functions—cited above—were found.) Until there is replication of this work using similar stressors and the same immunological measures, firm conclusions about which immune functions may be most susceptible to psychosocial influences such as marital distress and dissolution are unwarranted.

The psychophysiological paths by which an individual may advance toward health or illness may be varied and intertwined. Recalling the results of Levenson and Gottman (1985), and echoing the conclusions of Pennebaker and O'Heeron (1984), Kiecolt–Glaser and her colleagues point out that 'if there is consistent physiologic arousal associated with the presence of a spouse in a disturbed relationship, then it is quite possible that there are concurrent persistent alterations in endocrine function that mediate immunologic changes' (1987, p. 29). This supposition describes a relatively direct route from dyadic interaction to immunologic vulnerability.

Alternatively, immunocompetence may be indirectly, and more gradually affected by an individual's long-term mood state, which itself may be determined by repeated disturbances in an individual's significant relationships. Poor relationship quality and/or the absence of intimate relationships have been strongly linked with depression (e.g. Brown and Harris, 1978; Paykel, Emms, Fletcher, and Rassaby, 1980). Both depression (e.g. Kronfol, Silva, Greden Dembinski, Gardner, and Carroll, 1983) and loneliness (e.g. Kiecolt–Glaser, Ricker, George, Messick, Speicher, and Garner, 1984; Kiecolt–Glaser, Garner, Speicher, Penn, Holliday, and Glaser, 1984; Glaser, Kiecolt–Glaser, Speicher, and Holliday, 1985) have been associated with weaker immunity. Depression (based on MMPI scores) has also been linked to incidence of cancer in a 17-year follow-up study (Shekelle *et al.*, 1981).

Feeling depressed or lonely may be associated with feelings of helplessness (Seligman, 1975), which have also been linked to the incidence of cancer (Greene, 1966; LeShan, 1959). Endocrine products that mediate immunological responses (e.g. adrenal coticosteroids) may be affected by chronic psychological states like helplessness or hopelessness (Laudenslager and Reite, 1984), rather than, or in addition to, more immediate and specific behavioral events such as repeatedly arguing with one's spouse. (For a more detailed discussion of the links between endocrine functions and immunity, see Laudenslager and Reite, 1984).

TOWARD A MODEL ON THE PSYCHOPHYSIOLOGY OF DYADIC INTERACTION: PROXIMAL AND DISTAL EFFECTS

The research we have reviewed in this chapter illustrates a dynamic association between ongoing social interaction processes and somatic response and suggests that these associations may have long-term implications for our physical well-being. In Figure 15.1, we offer a rudimentary model in the hope that it will provide an overview of the domain of study and stimulate systematic research.

At the core of the model is the interdependent relation between interpersonal behavior and psychophysiological response. Both interpersonal behavior and somatic response are likely to be affected by individual differences that can arise from multiple sources including, for example, cognitive processes, social learning histories, conditioned emotional reactions, and biological/constitutional factors. These factors will contribute to any observed relation between somatic activity and interpersonal behavior.

As a result of the social interactional process characterizing a salient encounter, individuals will exit from the exchange feeling supported and comforted or feeling unsupported and distressed. Exiting with perceived support and without experiencing the psychophysiological concomitants of a dysfunctional encounter (e.g. an encounter without affective validation), an individual is likely to feel a

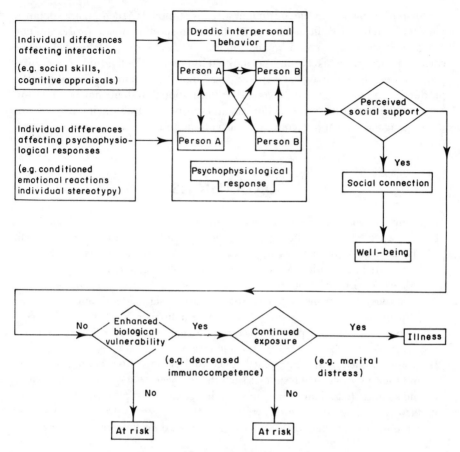

Figure 15.1. Toward a model of the psychophysiology of dyadic interaction.

sense of social connection and is hypothesized to have a greater probability of remaining healthy. Exiting with minimal perceived support and in the presence of somatic response associated with a troubling encounter, an individual is more likely to enter into an illness process. Whether or not there is actual illness will depend on many factors. We have noted two such factors in the model: enhanced biological vulnerability (e.g. decrease in immunocompetence, poor cardio-vascular conditioning, heart disease) and continued exposure to activating situations (e.g. marital distress). In the absence of enhanced vulnerability (e.g. a runner's cardiovascular conditioning may protect against high blood pressure) or continued exposure to activating situations, illness *per se* may not ensue, but we suggest that individuals are at risk for illness should their vulnerability status change or their exposure to activating situations increase.

Obviously, this is only the outline of a realistic model. Much greater detail is required to relate specific aspects of the model to specific disease processes. The model as it stands assumes a 'general illness process' and that is unlikely to be correct. It is far more likely that specific characteristics of individuals, interaction processes, psychophysiological responses, and biological factors are at play in the production of a given disease. Nevertheless, the notion that there may be a relation between characteristic social encounters and our physical well-being provides an exciting agenda awaiting continued attention and a systematic program of research.

CONCLUSIONS

In closing, we wish to emphasize two points:
(1) Advances in understanding the psychophysiology of dyadic interaction will be facilitated by a focus on specific aspects of social exchange that are associated with positive versus negative interactional outcomes (e.g. negative affect reciprocity) and by a focus on specific measures of physiological reactivity. Our review suggested that we are closer to identifying the specific aspects of dyadic interaction that warrant further study than we are to knowing the specific physiological responses that should be measured or are most likely to be affected by specific interactional exchanges.
(2) There exists a dynamic interplay between individuals' interactional behaviors and their physiological responses such that subjective (e.g. feeling supported) and somatic (e.g. demonstrating a rise in sysolic blood pressure) outcomes of each exchange are a direct result of this dynamic process. Long-term consequences of this process may have implications for our well-being.

REFERENCES

Allison, P. D., and Liker, J. K. (1982) Analyzing sequential categorical data on dyadic interaction: a comment on Gottman. *Pschological Bulletin*, **91**, 393–403.

Anderson, R. P. (1956) Physiological and verbal behavior during client-centered counseling. *Journal of Counseling Psychology*, **3**, 174–84.

Auld, F., Dreyer, H., and Dollard, J. (1958) Measurement of electrical skin resistance during interviews. *Psychological Reports*, **4**, 11–15.

Austen, Jane (1813) *Pride and Prejudice*. Baltimore, MD: Penguin.

Bales, R. F. (1950) *Interaction Process Analysis: A Method for the Study of Small Groups*. Chicago: University of Chicago Press.

Bales, R. (1970) *Personality and Interpersonal Behavior*. New York: Holt, Rinehart, & Winston.

Bandura, A. (1977) Self-efficacy: toward a unifying theory of behavior change. *Psychological Review*, **84**, 191–215.

Bandura, A. (1982) Self-efficacy mechanism in human agency. *American Psychologist*, **37**, 122–47.

Batson, C. D., and Coke, J. S. (1983) Empathic motivation of helping behavior. In J. T. Cacioppo and R. E. Petty (Eds), *Social Psychophysiology: A Source Book*. New York: Guilford Press.

Baucom, D. (1987) Attribution in distressed relations: how can we explain them? In D. Perlman and S. Duck (Eds), *Intimate Relationship*. Newbury Park, CA: Sage.

Baugher, D. M. and Gormly, J. (1975) Effects of personal competence on the significance of interpersonal agreement and disagreement: physiological activation and social evaluations. *Journal of Research in Personality*, **9**, 356–65.

Birchler, G. R., Weiss, R. L., and Vincent, J. P. (1975) Multimethod analysis of social reinforcement exchange between maritally distressed and nondistressed spouse and stranger dyads. *Journal of Personality and Social Psychology*, **31**, 349–60.

Blackburn, R. (1965) Emotionality, repression-sensitization, and maladjustment. *British Journal of Psychiatry*, **111**, 399–400.

Bogdonoff, M. D., Klein, R. K., Back, K. W., Nichols, C. R., Troyer, W. G., and Hood, T. C. (1964) Effect of group relationship and of the role of leadership upon lipid mobilization. *Psychosomatic Medicine*, **26**, 710–19.

Brown, G. W., and Harris, T. (1978) *Social Origins of Depression: A Study of Psychiatric Disorder in Women*. New York: Free Press.

Buck, R. W. (1980) Nonverbal behavior and the theory of emotion: the facial feedback hypothesis. *Journal of Personality and Social Psychology*, **38**, 811–24.

Buck, R. W. (1984) *The Communication of Emotion*. New York: Guilford Press.

Buck, R. W., Miller, R. E., and Caul, W. F. (1974) Sex, personality, and physiological variables in the communication of affect via facial expression. *Journal of Personality and Social Psychology*, **30**, 587–96.

Cacioppo, J. T., and Petty, R. E. (1983) *Social Psychophysiology: A Sourcebook*. New York: Guilford Press.

Coyne, J. C. (1976a) Towards an interactional description of depression. *Psychiatry*, **39**, 14–27.

Coyne, J. C. (1976b) Depression and the response of others. *Journal of Abnormal Psychology*, **85**, 186–93.

D'Augelli, A. R., Handis, M. H., Brumbaugh, L., Illig, V., Searer, R., Turner, D. W., and D'Augelli, J. D. (1978) The verbal helping behavior of experienced and novice telephone counselors. *Journal of Community Psychology*, **6**, 222–8.

Davies, M. (1970) Blood pressure and personality. *Journal of Psychosomatic Research*, **14**, 89–104.

Davis, F. H., and Malmo, R. B. (1951) Electromyographic recordings during interview. *American Journal of Psychiatry*, **107**, 908–16.

Derogatis, L. R., Abeloff, M. D., and Melisaratos, N. (1979) Psychological coping mechanisms and survival time in metastatic breast cancer. *Journal of the American Medical Association*, **242**, 1504–8.

DiMascio, A., Boyd, R. W., Greenblatt, M., and Solomon, H. C. (1955) The psychiatric interview: a sociophysiologic study. *Diseases of the Nervous System*, **16**, 4–9.

DiMascio, A., Boyd, R. W., and Greenblatt, M. (1957) Physiological correlates of tension and antagonism during psychotherapy: a study of interpersonal physiology. *Psychosomatic Medicine*, **19**, 99–104.

Dittes, J. E. (1957a) Extinction during psychotherapy of GSR accompanying 'embarrassing statements'. *Journal of Abnormal and Social Psychology*, **54**, 187–91.

Dittes, J. E. (1957b) Galvanic skin response as a measure of patient's reaction to therapist's permissiveness. *Journal of Abnormal and Social Psychology*, **55**, 295–303.

Doherty, W. J. (1981a) Cognitive processes in intimate conflict. I. Extending attribution theory. *American Journal of Family Therapy*, **9**, 3–13.

Doherty, W. J. (1981b) Cognitive processes in intimate conflict. II. Efficacy and learned helplessness. *American Journal of Family Therapy*, **9**, 35–44.

Edelstein, J., and Linn, M. (1985) The influence of the family on control of diabetes. *Social Science Medicine*, **21**, 541–544.

Ehrlich, R. P., D'Augelli, A. R., and Danish, S. J. (1979) Comparative effectiveness of six counselor verbal responses. *Journal of Counseling Psychology*, **26**, 390–8.

Engel, B. T. (1960) Stimulus-response and individual-response specificity. *Archives of General Psychiatry*, **2**, 305–13.

Ewart, C. K., Taylor, C. B., Kraemer, H. C., and Agras, W. S. (1984) Reducing blood pressure reactivity during interpersonal conflict: effects of marital communication training. *Behavior Therapy*, **15**, 473—84.

Fazio, R. H., and Cooper, J. (1983) Arousal in the dissonance process. In J. T. Cacioppo and R. E. Petty (Eds) *Social Psychophysiology: A Sourcebook*. New York: Guilford Press.

Frijda, N. H. (1986) *The Emotions*. Cambridge: Cambridge University Press.

Gage, D. F., and Safer, M. A. (1985) Hemisphere differences in the mood state-dependent effect for recognition of emotional faces. *Journal of Experimental Psychology: Learning, Memory, and Cognition*, **11**, 752–63.

Geen, R. G. (1976) The role of the social environment in the induction and reduction of anxiety. In C. D. Spielberger and I. G. Sarason (Eds), *Stress and Anxiety*, Vol. 3. Washington, DC: Hemisphere.

Glaser, R., Kiecolt-Glaser, J. K., Speicher, C. E., and Holliday, J. E. (1984) Stress, loneliness and changes in herpes virus latency. *Journal of Behavioral Medicine*, **8**, 249–60.

Gormly, J. (1974) A comparison of predictions from consistency and affect theories for arousal during interpersonal disagreement. *Journal of Personality and Social Psychology*, **30**, 658–63.

Gottman, J. (1979) *Marital Interaction: Experimental Investigations*. New York: Academic Press.

Gottman, J., Markman, H., and Notarius, C. (1977) The topography of marital conflict: a sequential analysis of verbal and nonverbal behavior. *Journal of Marriage and the Family*, **39**, 461–77.

Gottman, J., Notarius, C., Gonso, J., and Markman, H. (1976) *A Couple's Guide to Communication*. Champaign, IL: Research Press.

Greene, W. A. (1966) The psychosocial setting of the development of leukemia and lymphoma. *Annals of the New York Academy of Science*, **125**, 794–801.

Greenfield, N. S., and Sternbach, R. A. (1972) *Handbook of Psychophysiology*. New York: Holt, Rinehart, and Winston.

Grings, W. W., and Dawson, M. E. (1978) *Emotions and Bodily Responses*. New York: Academic Press.

Hahlweg, K., Reisner, L., Kohli, G., Vollmer, M., Schindler, L., and Revenstorf, D. (1984) Development and validity of a new system to analyze interpersonal communication: Kategoiriensystem fur partnerschaftliche Interaktion. In K. Hahlweg and N. Jacobson (Eds), *Marital Interaction: Analysis and Modification*. New York: Guilford Press.

Hassett, J. (1978) *A Primer of Psychophysiology*. San Franscisco: W. H. Freeman.

Hops, H., Wills, T., Patterson, G. R., and Weiss, R. (1972) Marital Interaction Coding System (MICS). Unpublished manuscript, University of Oregon.

Jacob, T. (1975) Family interaction in disturbedand normal families: methodological and substantive review. *Psychological Bulletin*, **82**, 33–65.

Kaplan, H., Burch, N. R., and Bloom, S. (1964) Physiological covariation and sociometric relationships in small peer groups. In P. H. Leiderman and D. Shapiro (Eds), *Psychobiological Approaches to Social Behavior*. Stanford: Standford University Press.

Kemper, T. D. (1984) Power, status and emotions: a sociological contribution to a psychophysiological domain. In K. R. Scherer and P. Ekman (Eds), *Approaches to Emotions*. Hillsdale, NJ: Erlbaum.

Kiecolt-Glaser, J. K., Garner, W., Speicher, C. E., Penn, G. M., Holliday, J., and Glaser, R. (1984) Psychosocial modifiers of immunocompetence in medical students. *Psychosomatic Medicine*, **46**, 7–14.

Kiecolt-Glaser, J. K., Ricker, D., George, J., Messick, G., Speicher, C. E., Garner, W., and Glaser, R. (1984) Urinary cortisol levels, cellular immunocompetency and loneliness in psychiatric inpatients. *Psychosomatic Medicine*, **46**, 15–23.

Kiecolt-Glaser, J. K., Fisher, L. D., Ogrocki, P., Stout, J., Speicher, C. E., and Glaser, R. (1987) Marital quality, marital disruption and immune function. *Psychosomatic Medicine*, **49**, 13–34.

Kissen, D. M. (1966) The significance of personality in lung cancer in men. *Annals of the New York Academy of Science*, **125**, 820–6.

Kitson, G. C. (1982) Attachment to the spouse in divorce: a scale and its application. *Journal of Marriage and the Family*, **44**, 379–93.

Krebs, D. C. (1975) Empathy and altruism. *Journal of Personality and Social Psychology*, **32**, 1134–46.

Kronfol, Z., Silva, J., Greden, J., Dembinski, S., Gardner, R., and Carroll, B. (1983) Impaired lymphocyte function in depressive illness. *Life Sciences*, **33**, 241–7.

Lacey, J. I. (1959) Psychophysiological approaches to the evaluation of psychotherapeutic process and outcome. In E. A. Rubenstein and M. B. Parloff (Eds), *Research in Psychotherapy*. Washington DC: American Psychological Association.

Lacey, J. I. (1967) Somatic response patterning and stress: some revisions of activation theory. In M. H. Appley and R. Trumbull (Eds), *Psychological Stress: Issues in Research*. New York: Appleton-Century-Crofts.

Lang, P. J. (1971) The application of psychophysiological methods to the study of psychotherapy and behavior modification. In A. E. Bergin and S. L. Garfield (Eds), *Handbook of Psychotherapy and Behavior Change: An Empirical Analysis*. New York: John Wiley.

Laudenslager, M. L., and Reite, M. L. (1984) Losses and separations: immunological consequences and health implications. In P. Shaver (Ed.), *Review of Personality and Social Psychology: Emotions, Relationships, and Health*. Beverly Hills, CA: Sage.

Lehman, D. R., Ellard, J. H., and Wortman, C. B. (1986) Social support for the bereaved. recipients' and providers' perspectives on what is helpful. *Journal of Consulting and Clinical Psychology*, **54**, 438–46.

LeShan, L. (1959) Psychological states as factors in the development of malignant disease: a critical review. *Journal of the National Cancer Institute*, **22**, 1–18.

Levenson, R. W. (1983) Personality research and psychophysiology: general considerations. *Journal of Research in Personality*, **17**, 1–21.

Levenson, R. W., and Gottman, J. M. (1983) Marital interaction: physiological linkage and affective exchange. *Journal of Personality and Social Psychology*, **45**, 587–97.

Levenson, R. W., and Gottman, J. M. (1985) Physiological and affective predictors of change in relationship satisfaction. *Journal of Personality and Social Psychology*, **49**, 85–94.

Malmo, R. B., Boag, T. J., and Smith, A. A. (1957) Physiological study of personal interaction. *Psychosomatic Medicine*, **19**, 105–19.

Margolin, G., and Wampold, B. (1981) Sequential analysis of conflict and accord in distressed and nondistressed marital partners. *Journal of Consulting and Clinical Psychology*, **49**, 554–67.

Markman, H., and Notarius, C. (1987) Coding marital and family interaction: current status. In T. Jacob (Ed.) *Family Interaction and Psychopathology: Theories, Methods and Findings*. New York: Plenum Press.

Martin, I., and Venables, P. H. (1980) *Techniques in Psychophysiology*. Chichester: John Wiley.

McCarron, L. T., and Appel, V. (1971) Categories of therapist verbalizations and patient–therapist autonomic response. *Journal of Consulting and Clinical Psychology*, **37**, 123–34.

Medalie, J. H., and Goldbourt, U. (1976). Angina pectoris among 10,000 men. II. Psychosocial and other risk factors as evidenced by a multivariate analysis of a five-year incidence study. *American Journal of Medicine*, **60**, 910–21.

Mettetal, G., and Gottman, J. (1980) Reciprocity and dominance in marital interaction. In J. Vincent (Ed.), *Advances in Family Intervention, Assessment and Theory*. Greenwich, CT: JAI Press.

Miller, P. M., and Ingham, J. G. (1976) Friends, confidants and symptoms. *Social Psychiatry*, **11**, 51–58.

Moore, D. L., and Baron, R. S. (1983) Social facilitation: a psychophysiological analysis. In J. T. Cacioppo and R. E. Petty (Eds), *Social psychophysiology: a sourcebook*. New York: Guilford Press.

Noller, P. (1984). *Nonverbal communication and marital interaction*. Oxford: Pergamon Press.

Notarius, C., Benson, P., Sloane, D., Vanzetti, N., and Hornyak, L. (in press). Exploring the interface between perception and behavior: An analysis of marital interaction in distressed and nondistressed couples. *Behavioral Assessment*.

Notarius, C., and Herrick, L. (1988) Listener response strategies to a distressed other. *Journal of Social and Personal Relationships*, **5**, 97–108.

Notarius, C., and Johnson, J. (1982) Emotional expression in husbands and wives. *Journal of Marriage and the Family*, **44**, 483–9.

Notarius, C., and Levenson, R. W. (1979) Expressive tendencies and physiological response to stress. *Journal of Personality and Social Psychology*, **37**, 1204–10.

Notarius, C., Markman, H., and Gottman, J. (1983) Couples Interaction Scoring System: clinical implications. In E. E. Filsinger (Ed.), *Marriage and Family Assessment: A Sourcebook for Family Therapy*. Beverly Hills, CA: Sage.

Notarius, C., and Vanzetti, N. (1983) Marital Agendas Protocol. In E. E. Filsinger (Ed.), *Marriage and Family Assessment: A Sourcebook for Family Therapy*. Beverly Hills, CA: Sage.

Notarius, C., Wemple, C., Ingraham, L., Burns, T., and Kollar, E. (1982) Multichannel responses to an interpersonal stressor: interrelationships among facial display, heart rate, self-report of emotion, and threat appraisal. *Journal of Personality and Social Psychology*, **43**, 400–8.

Obrist, P. A. (1981). *Cardiovascular Psychophysiology: A Perspective*. New York: Plenum Press.

Paykel, E. S., Emms, E. M., Fletcher, J., and Rassaby, E. S. (1980) Life events and social support in puerperal depression. *British Journal of Psychiatry*, **136**, 339–46.

Pennebaker, J. W., and O'Heeron, R. C. (1984) Confiding in others and illness rate among spouses of suicide and accidental-death victims. *Journal of Abnormal Psychology*, **93**, 473–6.

Petty, R. E., and Cacioppo, J. T. (1983) The role of bodily responses in attitude measurement and change. In J. T. Cacioppo, and R. E. Petty (Eds), *Social Psychophysiology: A Sourcebook*. New York: Guilford Press.

Raush, H. L. (1972) Process and change—a Markov model for interaction. *Family Process*, **13**, 275–298.

Robertson, E. K., and Suinn, R. M. (1968) The determination of rate of progress of stroke victims through empathy measures of patient and family. *Journal of Psychosomatic Research*, **12**, 189–91.

Schaap, C. (1982) *Communication and Adjustment in Marriage*. Amsterdam Swets and Zeitlinger B. U.

Seligman, M. E P (1975) *Helplessness: On Depression, Development, and Death*. San Francisco: W. H. Freeman.

Shekelle, R. B., Raynor, W. J., Ostfeld, A. M., Garron, D. C., Bieliavskas, L. A., Liv, S. C., Maliza, C., and Paul, O. (1981) Psychological depression and the 17-year risk of cancer. *Psychosomatic Medicine*, **43**, 117–125.

Sternbach, R. A. (1966) *Principles of Psychophysiology*. New York: Academic Press.

Strack, S., and Coyne, J. C. (1983) Social confirmation of dysphoria: shared and private reactions to depression. *Journal of Personality and Social Psychology*, **44**, 798–806.

VanEgeren, L. F. (1979) Social interactions, communications, and the coronary-prone behavior pattern: a psychophysiological study. *Psychosomatic Medicine*, **41**, 2–18.

Wampold, B., and Margolin, G. (1982) Nonparametric strategies to test the independence of behavioral states in sequential data. *Psychological Bulletin*, **92**, 755–65.

Weinberger, D. A., Schwartz, G. E., and Davidson, R. J. (1979) Low-anxious, high-anxious, and repressive coping styles: psychosomatic patterns and behavioral and physiological responses to stress. *Journal of Abnormal Psychology*, **88**, 369–80.

Weiner, H., Singer, M. T., and Reiser, M. F. (1962) Cardiovascular responses and their psychological correlates. I. A study in healthy young adults and patients with peptic ulcer and hypertension. *Psychosomatic Medicine*, **24**, 477–98.

Weisman, A. D., and Worden, J. W. (1975) Psychosocial analysis of cancer deaths. *Omega Journal of Death and Dying*, **6**, 61–75.

Weiss, R. L. (1981) The new kid on the block: behavioral systems approach. In E. E. Filsinger and R. A. Lewis, (Eds), *Assessing Marriage: New Behavioral Approaches*. Beverly Hills: Sage.

Weiss, R. L., and Summers, K. J. (1983) Marital Interaction Coding System. III. In E. E. Filsinger (Ed.), *Marriage and Family Assessment: A Sourcebook for Family Therapy*. Beverly Hills: Sage.

Author Index

Subject Index